Producing Power

Inside Technology Series
edited by Wiebe E. Bijker, W. Bernard Carlson, and Trevor Pinch

Sonja D. Schmid, *Producing Power: The Pre-Chernobyl History of the Soviet Nuclear Industry*

Casey O'Donnell, *Developer's Dilemma: The Secret World of Videogame Creators*

Christina Dunbar-Hester, *Low Power to the People: Pirates, Protest, and Politics in FM Radio Activism*

Eden Medina, Ivan da Costa Marques, and Christina Holmes, editors, *Beyond Imported Magic: Essays on Science, Technology, and Society in Latin America*

Anique Hommels, Jessica Mesman, and Wiebe E. Bijker, editors, *Vulnerability in Technological Cultures: New Directions in Research and Governance*

Amit Prasad, *Imperial Technoscience: Transnational Histories of MRI in the United States, Britain, and India*

Charis Thompson, *Good Science: The Ethical Choreography of Stem Cell Research*

Tarleton Gillespie, Pablo J. Boczkowski, and Kirsten A. Foot, editors, *Media Technologies: Essays on Communication, Materiality, and Society*

Catelijne Coopmans, Janet Vertesi, Michael Lynch, and Steve Woolgar, editors, *Representation in Scientific Practice Revisited*

Rebecca Slayton, *Arguments that Count: Physics, Computing, and Missile Defense, 1949–2012*

Stathis Arapostathis and Graeme Gooday, *Patently Contestable: Electrical Technologies and Inventor Identities on Trial in Britain*

Jens Lachmund, *Greening Berlin: The Co-Production of Science, Politics, and Urban Nature*

Chikako Takeshita, *The Global Biopolitics of the IUD: How Science Constructs Contraceptive Users and Women's Bodies*

Cyrus C. M. Mody, *Instrumental Community: Probe Microscopy and the Path to Nanotechnology*

Morana Alač, *Handling Digital Brains: A Laboratory Study of Multimodal Semiotic Interaction in the Age of Computers*

Gabrielle Hecht, editor, *Entangled Geographies: Empire and Technopolitics in the Global Cold War*

Michael E. Gorman, editor, *Trading Zones and Interactional Expertise: Creating New Kinds of Collaboration*

Matthias Gross, *Ignorance and Surprise: Science, Society, and Ecological Design*

Andrew Feenberg, *Between Reason and Experience: Essays in Technology and Modernity*

Wiebe E. Bijker, Roland Bal, and Ruud Hendricks, *The Paradox of Scientific Authority: The Role of Scientific Advice in Democracies*

Park Doing, *Velvet Revolution at the Synchrotron: Biology, Physics, and Change in Science*

Gabrielle Hecht, *The Radiance of France: Nuclear Power and National Identity after World War II*

Richard Rottenburg, *Far-Fetched Facts: A Parable of Development Aid*

Michel Callon, Pierre Lascoumes, and Yannick Barthe, *Acting in an Uncertain World: An Essay on Technical Democracy*

Ruth Oldenziel and Karin Zachmann, editors, *Cold War Kitchen: Americanization, Technology, and European Users*

Deborah G. Johnson and Jameson W. Wetmore, editors, *Technology and Society: Building Our Sociotechnical Future*

Trevor Pinch and Richard Swedberg, editors, *Living in a Material World: Economic Sociology Meets Science and Technology Studies*

Christopher R. Henke, *Cultivating Science, Harvesting Power: Science and Industrial Agriculture in California*

Helga Nowotny, *Insatiable Curiosity: Innovation in a Fragile Future*

Karin Bijsterveld, *Mechanical Sound: Technology, Culture, and Public Problems of Noise in the Twentieth Century*

Peter D. Norton, *Fighting Traffic: The Dawn of the Motor Age in the American City*

Joshua M. Greenberg, *From Betamax to Blockbuster: Video Stores tand the Invention of Movies on Video*

Mikael Hård and Thomas J. Misa, editors, *Urban Machinery: Inside Modern European Cities*

Christine Hine, *Systematics as Cyberscience: Computers, Change, and Continuity in Science*

Wesley Shrum, Joel Genuth, and Ivan Chompalov, editors, *Structures of Scientific Collaboration*

Shobita Parthasarathy, *Building Genetic Medicine: Breast Cancer, Technology, and the Comparative Politics of Health Care*

Kristen Haring, *Ham Radio's Technical Culture*

Atsushi Akera, *Calculating a Natural World: Scientists, Engineers and Computers during the Rise of U.S. Cold War Research*

Donald MacKenzie, *An Engine, Not a Camera: How Financial Models Shape Markets*

Geoffrey C. Bowker, *Memory Practices in the Sciences*

Christophe Lécuyer, *Making Silicon Valley: Innovation and the Growth of High Tech, 1930–1970*

Anique Hommels, *Unbuilding Cities: Obduracy in Urban Sociotechnical Change*

David Kaiser, editor, *Pedagogy and the Practice of Science: Historical and Contemporary Perspectives*

Charis Thompson, *Making Parents: The Ontological Choreography of Reproductive Technology*

Pablo J. Boczkowski, *Digitizing the News: Innovation in Online Newspapers*

Dominique Vinck, editor, *Everyday Engineering: An Ethnography of Design and Innovation*

Nelly Oudshoorn and Trevor Pinch, editors, *How Users Matter: The Co-Construction of Users and Technology*

Peter Keating and Alberto Cambrosio, *Biomedical Platforms: Realigning the Normal and the Pathological in Late-Twentieth-Century Medicine*

Paul Rosen, *Framing Production: Technology, Culture, and Change in the British Bicycle Industry*

Maggie Mort, *Building the Trident Network: A Study of the Enrollment of People, Knowledge, and Machines*

Donald MacKenzie, *Mechanizing Proof: Computing, Risk, and Trust*

Geoffrey C. Bowker and Susan Leigh Star, *Sorting Things Out: Classification and Its Consequences*

Charles Bazerman, *The Languages of Edison's Light*

Janet Abbate, *Inventing the Internet*

Herbert Gottweis, *Governing Molecules: The Discursive Politics of Genetic Engineering in Europe and the United States*

Kathryn Henderson, *On Line and On Paper: Visual Representation, Visual Culture, and Computer Graphics in Design Engineering*

Susanne K. Schmidt and Raymund Werle, *Coordinating Technology: Studies in the International Standardization of Telecommunications*

Marc Berg, *Rationalizing Medical Work: Decision Support Techniques and Medical Practices*

Eda Kranakis, *Constructing a Bridge: An Exploration of Engineering Culture, Design, and Research in Nineteenth-Century France and America*

Paul N. Edwards, *The Closed World: Computers and the Politics of Discourse in Cold War America*

Donald MacKenzie, *Knowing Machines: Essays on Technical Change*

Wiebe E. Bijker, *Of Bicycles, Bakelites, and Bulbs: Toward a Theory of Sociotechnical Change*

Louis L. Bucciarelli, *Designing Engineers*

Geoffrey C. Bowker, *Science on the Run: Information Management and Industrial Geophysics at Schlumberger, 1920-1940*

Wiebe E. Bijker and John Law, editors, *Shaping Technology / Building Society: Studies in Sociotechnical Change*

Stuart Blume, *Insight and Industry: On the Dynamics of Technological Change in Medicine*

Donald MacKenzie, *Inventing Accuracy: A Historical Sociology of Nuclear Missile Guidance*

Pamela E. Mack, *Viewing the Earth: The Social Construction of the Landsat Satellite System*

H. M. Collins, *Artificial Experts: Social Knowledge and Intelligent Machines*

http://mitpress.mit.edu/books/series/inside-technology

Producing Power

The Pre-Chernobyl History of the Soviet Nuclear Industry

Sonja D. Schmid

The MIT Press
Cambridge, Massachusetts
London, England

© 2015 Massachusetts Institute of Technology

All rights reserved. No part of this book may be reproduced in any form by any electronic or mechanical means (including photocopying, recording, or information storage and retrieval) without permission in writing from the publisher.

This book was set in ITC Stone Serif Std by Toppan Best-set Premedia Limited, Hong Kong.

Library of Congress Cataloging-in-Publication Data
Schmid, Sonja D., 1970-
Producing power : the pre-Chernobyl history of the Soviet nuclear industry / Sonja D. Schmid.
    pages cm. — (Inside technology)
Includes bibliographical references and index.
ISBN 978-0-262-02827-1 (hardcover : alk. paper), 978-0-262-53880-0 (pb.)
1. Nuclear engineering—Soviet Union—History—20th century. 2. Nuclear industry—Soviet Union—History—20th century. 3. Nuclear power plants—Soviet Union—History—20th century.
4. Nuclear energy—Research—Soviet Union—History—20th century. I. Title.
TK9085.S36 2015
333.792'4094709045—dc23

Meinen Eltern, Erika und Peter Schmid

Contents

Acknowledgments   ix
Note on Transliteration and Translation   xv
Acronyms and Abbreviations   xvii

Introduction   1
1 Envisioning a Nuclear-Powered State   17
2 Between Atomic Bombs and Power Plants: Sharing Organizational Responsibilities   41
3 Training Nuclear Experts: A Workforce for the Nuclear Industry   67
4 "May the Atom Be a Worker, Not a Soldier!": A New History of Soviet Reactor Design Choices   97
5 Chernobyl: From Accident to Sarcophagus   127
6 Conclusion   161
Epilogue: Writing about Chernobyl after Fukushima   171

Biographical Notes   177
Methodological Appendix   189
List of Interviews   199
Notes   203
Bibliography   313
Index   347

Acknowledgments

This book is partially based on research supported by the National Science Foundation under Grant No. SES-0240807 (Dissertation Improvement Grant). I also received generous support from Cornell University's Institute for European Studies, which awarded me a Luigi Einaudi Graduate Fellowship for my research in Russia. Cornell's University Committee on Human Subjects (UCHS) approved the human subjects protocol for this project (Protocol ID# 02–08–010). The Center for International Security and Cooperation at Stanford University supported me with multiple travel grants during my postdoctoral appointments, and with a very generous contribution to the final book editing. I am indebted to the Society for the History of Technology for awarding me the 2006 Brooke Hindle Postdoctoral Fellowship, to help turn the dissertation into a book. Finally, I am grateful to my colleagues in the Department of Science and Technology in Society at Virginia Tech for keeping teaching and service obligations in check, and especially to our chair, Ellsworth "Skip" Fuhrman, who decided to spend substantial amounts of money on my project in times of exceptionally tight budgets.

Apart from financial support, numerous people have contributed over many years to this book. Iouli Andreev and Wolfgang Kromp from the *Forum für Atomfragen* at the University of Vienna (now the Institute of Safety and Risk Sciences at the University of Natural Resources and Life Sciences, Vienna) nurtured initial ideas about this topic, and mastered the patience to explain the basics of nuclear physics and engineering to me—then a student in the humanities. I have benefited tremendously from the time I spent with Irina Andreeva and Iouli Andreev at their home over tea and Russian candy, discussing nuclear reactors, the Soviet system, and their experiences during the cleanup work at Chernobyl. Ulrike Felt, of the Department of Social Studies of Science at the University of Vienna, introduced me to the world of science and technology studies and provided a stimulating environment where I could discover theoretical and methodological approaches that would eventually frame my project. Cornell's Department of Science & Technology Studies supported my project from the minute I entered the graduate program and treated me to one of the most rewarding learning experiences of my life. My dissertation committee members, Bruce Lewenstein, Michael Dennis, Stephen Hilgartner, and Peter Holquist, were exceptionally helpful throughout the dissertation process and beyond, but I also benefited from discussions with Hélène Mialet, Christine Leuenberger, Ron Kline, Mike Lynch, and Trevor Pinch. Judith Reppy was my source for contemporary policy discussions that linked nuclear power to nuclear weapons, and generously supported me in ways I never expected. Last but not least, a number of friends and fellow graduate students provided continual inspiration, generous advice, and constructive criticism, especially Shobita Parthasarathy, Anna Maerker, John Downer, and Florian Charvolin. The department's staff, Judy Yonkin and Deborah Van Galder, kept me funded and helped me navigate Cornell's bureaucracy.

At Stanford's Center for International Security and Cooperation, I found a wonderful community to sharpen and expand the focus of the project. I want to thank in particular Lynn Eden and David Holloway for their mentoring and generous support over the years, Rebecca Slayton, Pavel Podvig, and Charles Perrow for reading and commenting on preliminary chapters, and Siegfried "Sig" Hecker for putting me in touch with phenomenal interviewees in Russia (and for the unexpected opportunity to reminisce about our Styrian homeland). The Hoover Institution, and particularly Anatol Shmelev, made one last round of relevant interviews possible and simultaneously laid the groundwork for an important oral history collection. I also thank Robert McGinn, former director of the Program for Science, Technology, and Society at Stanford, for giving me the time and space to think and write, and Bill Potter, as well as Elena Sokova and Nikolai Sokov, who helped me understand some of the broader security dimensions of nuclear energy while I was a postdoctoral fellow at the James Martin Center for Nonproliferation Studies in Monterey.

At Virginia Tech, I benefited from the valuable pretenure mentoring initiative offered by the College of Liberal Arts and Human Sciences. In my department, I thank especially Daniel Breslau, Matthew Wisnioski, Janet Abbate, and Barbara Allen, for providing mentoring, feedback, strategic advice, and practical support (from taking over teaching to babysitting). The faculty in the nuclear engineering program at Virginia Tech has warmly welcomed me and walked the walk by allowing me to get involved with teaching their students. The interaction with these students (in nuclear

Acknowledgments

engineering and STS) makes me realize how fortunate I am to work in a community of exceptional learners who continue to teach me how to look at the world in yet another way, and how to put my own views in perspective.

A significant part of the research for this project took place in Moscow. My starting point was the Institute of the History of Science and Technology (part of the Russian Academy of Sciences). I am indebted to the Institute's director at the time, Vladimir Orel, and to Aleksandr Pechenkin of the "Sector for Theoretical and Methodological Issues in the History of Science," for writing and signing countless letters to archives and other authorities for me. Larisa Belozerova and Lada Lekai in the International Office provided much-needed advice and practical help with everything from visas and registrations to fielding occasional inquiries about my scholarly integrity ("No, she is not a spy!"). Dmitrii Baiuk, managing editor of the quarterly *Studies in the History of Science and Technology* (*Voprosy istorii estestvoznanii i tekhniki*), Dmitrii Saprykin, and Elena Aronova supported me intellectually and morally, when key archives remained closed to me. Vladimir Vizgin and Igor Drovennikov from the "Sector for the History of Physics and Mechanics" welcomed me to the monthly seminar series on the history of the atomic project. At these seminars I met Mikhail Grabovskii, whose stories—both in person and in writing—were absolutely eye-opening, and Mikhail Gaidin from Obninsk, who subsequently introduced me to some of the most fascinating personalities involved in the Soviet nuclear program at his Museum Club in Obninsk.

I am indebted to the administrators of several archives, to the individuals handling documents in the stacks (which in my case often involved preparing files that had been requested for the very first time), and especially to the reading room staff: in Moscow, the Archive of the Russian Academy of Sciences (ARAN), the Russian State Archive for the Economy (RGAE), the Russian State Archive for Social and Political History (RGASPI, Komsomol branch), and the Russian State Archive for Contemporary History (RGANI); and in Samara, the Russian State Archive for Scientific and Technical Documentation (RGANTD, Samara branch).

While in Moscow, I kept up to date with publications on nuclear energy by visiting the Central Scientific and Research Institute "Atominform" (TsNIIAtominform) and the publishing houses "IzdAt" and "Energoatomizdat"; many thanks to their thoughtful staffs. Vladimir Iuzin from the journal *Atomic Energy* (*Atomnaia energiia*) helped me get in contact with some important interviewees and a couple of times even provided much-needed quiet space at the editorial office. I also wish to thank Viktor Sidorenko for making time to discuss my ideas and for referring me to his advisee Maria Vasilieva, who subsequently shared her work with me. I am grateful for Lenina Kaibysheva's help in locating her two volumes *Posle Chernobylia* ("After Chernobyl"), and to Vladimir Gubarev for sharing insightful stories about science, technology, and the mass media in the Soviet Union.

Paul Josephson's work has inspired me from the outset, and I owe him much for the success of this project. Mentioning his name has always opened doors in Russia, because he seems to be personal friends with every archivist, historian, and scientist even remotely connected to nuclear energy. I am particularly grateful to him for putting me in touch with Vladimir Iarovitsin, who arranged a number of interviews for me in Obninsk, and with Aleksandr Bolgarov, who showed me the Lithuanian nuclear power plant inside and out, and whose family hosted me during my visit to Visaginas.

Most of all, however, I am indebted to a number of nuclear experts who I promised to keep anonymous. No doubt many of them had some concerns that I worked for a foreign intelligence agency. And yet they not only eventually shared their personal accounts with me and agreed to be recorded, they often referred me to their friends and colleagues, or helped me find books otherwise unavailable. Many who I did not end up formally interviewing have nevertheless supported me in various ways (for example, by inviting me to exhibitions or conferences, or by trying to get permission for me to access archival collections). Without their interest in my work, and their trust in my sincerity as a researcher, this book would not have been feasible. Some of them have passed away since I talked to them, and while I regret that I won't be able to share the fruit of my labor with them, my hope is that I have accurately represented their points of view in my account.

Over the years this book was taking shape, I have benefited from interacting with individuals whose research areas overlap with mine, and who have stimulated my thinking in various ways, among them Slava Gerovich, Michael Gordin, Hugh Gusterson, David Kaiser, John Krige, Martha Lampland, and Verena Winiwarter. Asif Siddiqi not only invited me to participate in terrific conference panels, but offered encouragement and invaluable advice at exactly the right times. Gabrielle Hecht inspired me with her work on France's nuclear program, her determination to put the French story in a global context, and her approval of a fellow "nuclear nerd."

One person who joined this project late in 2013 deserves special thanks. The stars aligned mysteriously and fortuitously to connect this story with Kathleen Kearns. A master book editor, with no connection to nuclear energy matters or Soviet history, she expertly massaged what was still a

Acknowledgments

rough manuscript into a book that I started looking forward to reading. I am still amazed at how much her gentle and diligent approach transformed the manuscript, without ever misrepresenting my ideas or argument.

I am grateful to MIT Press, in particular Wiebe Bijker, Marguerite Avery, Katie Persons, and Marcy Ross, for their patience, encouragement, and diligence. Many thanks to Olga N. Orobei from the publishing house "Master" in Moscow, and Anna Korolevskaia from the National Chernobyl Museum in Kiev for providing invaluable support with image permissions, and to Dane Webster, who transformed my clumsy drawings into elegant graphs.

Finally, I need to thank my friends and family. Edward Biko Smith met me on the eve of my departure for Russia and has stuck with me through thick and thin since then. He moved with me multiple times, left jobs and found new ones, and always cooked delicious dinners. He kept me sane when the balance between teaching, writing, and having a life threatened to spiral out of control. Our son Konstantin, who arrived in 2008, has recentered my life in ways I never thought possible. I am deeply grateful to both of them for giving me the time to complete this project. My Austrian family and friends, both in Austria and in the United States, have helped me maintain my appreciation for homemade food, good company, and my native language. My parents have steadfastly supported me over the years, and although I know they would prefer for me to live a lot closer, they never questioned my choices. Growing up with their confidence in me has given me the courage to take on ambitious projects. For all the things they have done for me, big and small, I dedicate this book to them.

Note on Transliteration and Translation

I have used a modified version of the Library of Congress system, except for well-known names (Beria, not Beriia; Yeltsin, not El'tsyn, Gorky, not Gor'kii). For readability, in the main text I have dropped the apostrophe, which denotes a Cyrillic letter (e.g., Chernobyl, not Chernobyl'; Dollezhal, not Dollezhal'; Podolsk, not Podol'sk), or replaced it when appropriate (e.g., Emelyianov instead of Emel'ianov, Maryin instead of Mar'in, Petrosyiants instead of Petros'iants, Grigoryiants instead of Grigor'iants). I kept the apostrophe in the references and biographical notes, however. Note also that different versions of Russian names are sometimes used in English publications. In those cases, I have kept the published spelling and added the spelling I use in square brackets. All translations, unless otherwise noted, are mine.

Acronyms and Abbreviations

ABTU	Experimental high-temperature, gas-graphite reactor
ADE	Dual-use reactor; produces plutonium and electricity/heat
Agregat Sh	Graphite-helium reactor developed at the Institute for Physical Problems (*IFP*) in Moscow
Agregat VM	Graphite-water reactor developed by *Laboratory No. 2* and *NIKIET* in Moscow
Agregat VT	Beryllium-moderated reactor developed at *Laboratory V* in Obninsk
AM	The world's first nuclear reactor to deliver electricity to a national grid, Obninsk (AM, for "peaceful atom" (*atom mirnyi*), or "naval atom" (*atom morskoi*)
AMB	Graphite-moderated boiling-water reactor; two were built and operated at Beloiarsk, designed by *Laboratory V*, Obninsk. Often falsely referred to as "early versions" of the *RBMK*. "AMB" stands for "large peaceful atom" (*atom mirnyi bol'shoi*).
ARAN	Archive of the Russian Academy of Sciences (*Arkhiv Rossiiskoi akademii nauk*)
Arzamas-16	Code term for the town of Sarov, a closed city from 1946 to 1991; location of the All-Union Scientific Research Institute of Experimental Physics (VNIIEF), a nuclear weapons design facility

AST/ATETs	Dual-purpose nuclear power plants, producing electric power and heating (AST, *atomnye stantsii teplosnabzheniia*, or ATETs, *atomnye teploenergeticheskie tsentrali*)
Atomenergonaladka	Department within *Soiuzatomenergo* to repair nuclear power plant equipment
Atomenergoproekt	Group of three architect-engineering institutes for nuclear power plants (Moscow, Saint Petersburg, and Nizhnii Novgorod)
Atomenergoremont	Department within *Soiuzatomenergo* created in 1983 to provide maintenance and repair services to nuclear power plants
Atommash	Giant factory constructed to manufacture vessels for pressurized water reactors and other equipment for the nuclear power and related industries located in Volgodonsk
Atomnaia energiia	*Atomic Energy*, Soviet (now Russian) scholarly journal on nuclear energy
Atomshchiki	Engineers, typically with a background in nuclear physics or engineering, who worked for *Sredmash*
Brak	Defective products, the result of manufacturing errors
CANDU	Canada Deuterium Uranium reactor, Canadian-designed heavy-water reactor
CMEA	Council for Mutual Economic Assistance. Organization established in 1949 under Soviet leadership; assistance with civilian nuclear technology was the most successful initiative in the council's history.
CPSU	Communist Party of the Soviet Union
Den' atomshchika	Day of the Nuclear Engineer, celebrated in Russia on September 28
Den' energetika	Day of the Power Engineer, celebrated in Russia on December 22

Acronyms and Abbreviations

Derzhkomatom	Ukraine State Committee on Nuclear Power Plant Utilization. See *Ukratomenergoprom*.
DP	Additional graphite absorber rods retrofitted in *RBMK* reactors after the Chernobyl accident (*dopolnitel'nye poglotiteli*)
Dublirovanie	Literally "duplication." Refers to the Soviet practice of setting up duplicate independent teams or organizations to accomplish the same task.
EG	Graphite moderated, gas cooled reactor (*energeticheskii-gazovyi*)
EI-2	First dual-use reactor, nicknamed "Second Ivan," started up at "the Siberian nuclear power plant" (near Tomsk) in 1958. EI, *energeticheskii isotopnyi*, where the isotope referred to was plutonium.
Ekho Moskvy	Echo of Moscow, popular independent radio station broadcasting throughout Russia and other countries since 1990
Energeticheskii pusk	Phase when a new nuclear reactor is connected to the plant's electrical system and the transmission grid
Energetiki	Engineers, typically with a background in some non-nuclear engineering discipline, who worked for *Minenergo*
Federal'noe agenstvo po atomnoi energii	Federal Agency of Atomic Energy of the Russian Federation, created in 2004; successor organization of *Minatom*. See *Rosatom*.
FEI	Institute of Physics and Power Engineering (IPPE) (*Fiziko-energeticheskii institut*) at Obninsk, originally *Laboratory V*
FIAN	Institute of Physics, Soviet Academy of Sciences, Moscow
Fizicheskii pusk, or *fizpusk*	Phase when a new nuclear reactor is started up (goes critical) for the first time

General'nyi proektirovshchik	"Chief project manager," part of the nuclear industry's tripartite management structure. Typically, *Minenergo* performed this role.
GKNT	State Committee for Science and Technology (*Gosudarstvennyi komitet po nauke i tekhnike*), responsible for a unified national scientific and technical policy on nondefense projects
GKO	State Defense Committee (*Gosudarstvennyj komitet oborony*), created in 1941 in response to the German invasion of the Soviet Union. Managed the Soviet Atomic Bomb project from 1945 on.
Glasnost'	Literally "openness" or "transparency." Motto introduced by Mikhail Gorbachev to describe a new policy in the Soviet Union's government.
Glavatom	Chief Administration for the Utilization of Atomic Energy, formed from *Sredmash* in 1956
Glavatomenergo (*Minenergo*)	Chief Administration for the Construction of Atomic Power Plants, within *Minenergo*. Replaced in 1978 by the All-Union Industrial Association for Nuclear Power (*Soiuzatomenergo*).
Glavatomenergo (*Sredmash*)	Chief Administration for the Use of Atomic Energy within *Sredmash*, also referred to as GU-16. Created by the breakup of *GU IAE* in 1967.
Glavatompribor	Chief Administration of Atomic Instrument Making (GU-17), within *Sredmash*. Created by the breakup of *GU IAE* in 1967.
Glavlit	General Directorate for the Protection of State Secrets in the Press (*Glavnoe upravlenie po delam literatury i izdatel'stv*); Soviet censorship agency

Acronyms and Abbreviations

Glavnyi konstruktor	"Chief design engineer," part of the nuclear industry's tripartite management structure. Typically, engineering and construction bureaus reporting to *Sredmash* performed this role.
GOELRO	State Commission for the Electrification of Russia (*Gosudarstvennaia komissiia po elektrifikatsii Rossii*), the first state plan for national recovery and development focused on electrification of the Soviet Union under Lenin in 1920
Gosatomenergonadzor	State Oversight Committee for the Safe Conduct of Work in the Nuclear Power Industry. The supervisory agency for issues regarding the safety of nuclear power plants, research reactors, and commercial nuclear ships, established in 1983 as the Soviet Union's first independent safety oversight agency.
Gosatomnadzor	State Oversight Committee for Nuclear Safety, organized in 1972 under *Sredmash*; predecessor of *Gosatomenergonadzor*
Gosgorenergotekhnadzor	State Technical and Mining Oversight Committee for the Power Industry, created in 1966 within *Minenergo*
Gosgortekhnadzor	State Technical and Mining Oversight Committee, within *Minenergo*
Gosplan	State Committee for Planning (*Gosudarstvennyi komitet po planirovaniiu*), responsible for economic planning in the Soviet Union. The committee's scope of responsibilities varied from 1921 to 1991.
Gospromatomnadzor	Created in 1989 on the basis of *Gosatomenergonadzor* and *Gosgortekhnadzor*.
Gossannadzor	State Supervisor for Sanitation, within the Ministry of Health

Gossnab	State Committee for Material and Technical Supplies, responsible for allocating resources not handled by *Gosplan*, under the Council of Ministers
Gosstroi	State Committee for Construction, under the Council of Ministers
Gostekhnika	State Committee for Coordination of Scientific Research, under the Council of Ministers
Gruppa OPAS	Emergency response group within *Soiuzatomenergo* (*gruppa okazaniia pomoshchi atomnym stantsiiam pri avariiakh*)
GSPI-11	State Specialized Design Institute 11 (*Gosudarstvennyi spetsializirovannyi proektnyi institut*). Founded in 1939; based on a design and engineering enterprise in Leningrad that specialized in military contracts. Since September 1945 under the *PGU*, focusing on the creation of the Soviet nuclear weapons complex. Later also involved in the civilian nuclear industry, particularly the *RBMK* design. See *VNIPIET*.
GU IAE	Chief Administration for the Use of Atomic Energy (also referred to as p/ia 1024), within *Sredmash*
GULag	Main Administration of Corrective Labor Camps and Labor Settlements (*Glavnoe upravlenie ispravitel'no-trudovykh lagerei i kolonii*). The term is commonly used to describe the agency that ran the labor camps as well as the camps themselves.
IAE	Institute of Atomic Energy. Originated as *Laboratory No. 2* in 1943, home to the "father of the Soviet atomic bomb," Igor V. Kurchatov; renamed LIPAN (Laboratory for Measuring Instruments of the Academy of Sciences) in 1949, then renamed *IAE* (Institute of Atomic Energy) in 1956, and named in honor of Kurchatov in 1960.

Acronyms and Abbreviations

IAEA	International Atomic Energy Agency, founded in 1957, based at the United Nations headquarters in Vienna, Austria
IFP	Institute for Physical Problems in Moscow, founded in 1934, under the leadership of the physicist Petr L. Kapitsa
INES	International Nuclear and Radiological Events Scale, designed in 1989 by an international group of experts convened first by the *IAEA* and the Nuclear Energy Agency of the Organisation for Economic Co-operation and Development (OECD/NEA). The *IAEA* oversees its development in cooperation with the OECD/NEA.
INSAG	International Nuclear Safety Advisory Group; supports the *IAEA* director general. Published the *IAEA*'s first official Chernobyl accident report, INSAG-1, and its subsequent revision, INSAG-7.
Interatomenergo	International Economic Association within *CMEA* to coordinate delivery of nuclear power plant equipment, supervise plant start-ups, and train plant managers
Interatominstrument	International Economic Association within *CMEA* to supply equipment for nuclear power plants
IPPE	Institute of Physics and Power Engineering. See *FEI*.
ITAR-TASS	Information Telegraph Agency of Russia (1902 to present); Telegraph Agency of the Soviet Union (1925–1992). TASS was merged with ITAR in 1992; serves as a major news agency in Russia.
ITEF	Institute of Theoretical and Experimental Physics, previously known as *Laboratory No. 3*; founded in 1945, under the leadership of the physicist Abram I. Alikhanov

Izhora Works	Manufacturing company and complex of factories supplying equipment to the nuclear (reactor vessels) and other industries, located near Leningrad
KGB	Committee for State Security (*Komitet gosudarstvennoi bezopasnosti*)
Khar'kovskii turbinnyi zavod	Kharkov turbine factory; equipment manufacturer for the nuclear power industry in Kharkov, Ukraine
Kievenergo	Ukraine regional utility company coordinating electricity, heat, and hot-water delivery
Kollegiia	Collegium; governing board of an organization
Komsomol	Youth division of the Communist Party of the Soviet Union (*Kommunisticheskii soiuz molodezhi*)
Ksenovaia iama	Literally "xenon pit," referring to the period of time required for xenon to decay before a nuclear reactor can be restarted
Kurchatov Institute	See *IAE*.
kW	Kilowatt (1 kW = 1000 watts)
Laboratory No. 1	Code name for the Institute of Special Metals. Also referred to as *NII-9*.
Laboratory No. 2	Code name for the Institute of Atomic Energy. See *IAE*.
Laboratory No. 3	Code name for the Institute of Theoretical and Experimental Physics. See *ITEF*.
Laboratory V	Code name for the Institute for Physics and Power Engineering. See *FEI*.
LIPAN SSSR	See *IAE*.
Liquidators	Neologism derived from the Russian term *likvidatsiia*, commonly used to describe those involved with the Chernobyl accident cleanup
LOTEP	Leningrad Division of the All-Union State Design Institute (*Teploelektroproekt*)

Acronyms and Abbreviations

MEI	Moscow Power Engineering Institute (*Moskovskii Energeticheskii Institut*), a renowned college for higher technical and engineering education
MIFI	Moscow Engineering and Physics Institute (*Moskovskii inzhenerno-fizicheskii institut*). In 2009, it was rebranded as the National Nuclear Research University.
Minatomenergo	Ministry of Atomic Energy (*Ministerstvo atomnoi energetiki*), created in 1986 from the branch of *Minenergo* responsible for operating nuclear power plants; abolished in 1989
Minatomenergoprom	Ministry of Atomic Power and Industry (*Ministerstvo atomnoi energetiki i promyshlennosti*), created in 1989 through the merger of *Minatomenergo* and *Sredmash*; abolished in 1992
Minatom RF	Ministry of Atomic Energy of the Russian Federation (*Ministerstvo atomnoi energii Rossiiskoi Federatsii*), created in 1992 as the successor organization to the Ministry of Atomic Power and Industry (*Minatomenergoprom*). Reorganized in 2004 as the Federal Agency for Atomic Energy.
Minelektrotekhprom	Ministry of the Electrotechnical Industry (*Ministerstvo elektrotekhnicheskoi promyshlennosti*)
Minenergo	Ministry of Energy and Electrification (*Ministerstvo energetiki i elektrifikatsii*), in charge of building and operating all electric utility plants and the Soviet Union's network of transmission lines
Minenergomash	Ministry of Power Engineering (*Ministerstvo energeticheskogo mashinostroeniia*)
Minkhimmash	Ministry of Chemical Machine Building (*Ministerstvo khimicheskogo mashinostroeniia*)

Minoboronprom	Ministry of the Defense Industry (*Ministerstvo oboronnoi promyshlennosti*)
Minsredmash	See *Sredmash*.
Mintiazhmash	Ministry of Heavy Machine Building (*Ministerstvo tiazhelogo mashinostroeniia*)
Minzdrav	Ministry of Health (*Ministerstvo zdravookhraneniia*)
MVD	Ministry of Internal Affairs (*Ministerstvo vnutrennykh del*)
MVNTS	Interdepartmental Scientific-Technical Council (*Mezhvedomstevennyi nauchno-tekhnicheskii sovet*), under the aegis of GKNT. Created in 1986 as the successor organization to MVTS following the Chernobyl accident.
MVTS	Interdepartmental Technical Council on Nuclear Power Plants (*Mezhvedomstvennyi tekhnicheskii sovet po atomnym elektrostantsiiam pri Ministerstve srednego mashinostroeniia SSSR*), created in 1971 within *Sredmash* to coordinate all scientific and technical policies related to the nuclear power industry. Abolished in 1986 following the Chernobyl accident.
MW	Megawatt (1 MW = 1000 kilowatts or kW), one million watts. Standard unit of measurement of electrical power. MW*e* refers to the electrical power output; MW*t* (or MW*th*) refers to the thermal power output. Generally speaking, in nuclear reactors the thermal power is almost twice the electrical power output.
NAIIC	National Diet of Japan, Fukushima Nuclear Accident Independent Investigation Commission
NARA	National Archives and Records Administration, in College Park, Maryland

Acronyms and Abbreviations

Nauchnyi rukovoditel'	"Scientific director," part of the nuclear industry's tripartite management structure. Typically, the *IAE* performed this role.
NII	Scientific Research Institute (*Nauchno-issledovatel'skii institut*)
NII-8	Scientific Research Institute No. 8. See *NIKIET*.
NII-9	Institute of Special Metals. Also referred to as *Laboratory No. 1*.
NIIAR	Scientific Research Institute of Atomic Reactors, Melekess (Dmitrovgrad)
NIIKhimmash	See *NIKIET*.
NIKIET	Scientific Research and Design Institute of Energy Technologies (*Nauchno-issledovatel'skii i konstruktorskii institut energotekhniki*), originally created to support Nikolai Dollezhal's team during the construction of the first Soviet reactor, as a sector (*Gidrosektor*) of a chemical engineering institute (*NIIKhimmash*). Renamed *NIKIET* in 1952. The technical designs of military reactors, as well as the Obninsk power reactor, nuclear submarine reactors, and the *RBMK*, originated in NIKIET.
NKVD	People's Commissariat for Internal Affairs (*Narodnyi komissariat vnutrennikh del*), predecessor agency to the Ministry of Internal Affairs
Nomenklatura	Communist Party system to match influential positions with approved party members
NPP	Nuclear power plant
NTS	Scientific-Technical Council (*Nauchno-tekhnicheskii sovet*), an administrative unit within *Sredmash* to manage day-to-day affairs of the *MVTS*

OKB Gidropress	Experimental Design Bureau (*Opytnoe konstruktorskoe biuro*), located in Podolsk. Involved with design of the *VVER* as well as manufacturing parts for the *RBMK*.
OKBM	Experimental Design Bureau for Machine Building (*Opytnoe konstruktorskoe biuro mashinostroeniia*), Nizhnii Novgorod (the former Gorky)
Opytno-promyshlennaia operatsiia	A reactor's initial operating period before it is approved for industrial operations testing
PGU	First Chief Administration (*Pervoe glavnoe upravlenie*), established in 1946 to consolidate all (defense and civilian) nuclear research in a single organization
Pochtovye iashchiki	Literally "mailboxes"; code phrase used by *Sredmash* to conceal the names and locations of sensitive facilities
Pusko-naladochnye raboty	Period of start-up and testing work on a new nuclear reactor
RAN	Russian Academy of Sciences (*Rossiiskaia akademiia nauk*). Founded in 1724; from 1925 to 1991 known as the Academy of Sciences of the *USSR*, or Soviet Academy of Sciences (*Akademiia nauk SSSR*).
Raspredelenie	Literally "distribution"; phrase for the Communist Party system's assignment of university graduates to positions in industry or elsewhere
RBMK	Graphite-moderated, water-cooled, boiling-water reactor (*reaktor bol'shoi moshchnosti kanal'nyi/kipiashchii*). Developed from military uranium-graphite reactor designed to produce plutonium. Used as a standard power reactor only in the Soviet Union. Sometimes referred to as the "Chernobyl-type" reactor.

Acronyms and Abbreviations

RGAE	Russian State Archive for the Economy (*Rossiiskii gosudarstvennyi arkhiv ekonomiki*), Moscow
RGANI	Russian State Archive for Contemporary History (*Rossiiskii gosudarstvennyi arkhiv noveishchei istorii*), Moscow
RGANTD (Samara)	Russian State Archive for Scientific and Technical Documentation (*Rossiiskii gosudarstvennyi arkhiv nauchno-tekhnicheskoi dokumentatsii*), Samara branch
RGASPI (Komsomol)	Russian State Archive for Social and Political History (*Rossiiskii gosudarstvennyi arkhiv sotsial'noi i politicheskoi istorii*), *Komsomol* branch
Rosatom	Russian State Atomic Energy Corporation, created as the successor organization to the Federal Agency for Atomic Energy (*Federal'noe agenstvo po atomnoi energii*) in 2007. See *Minatom RF*.
Rosenergoatom	Russian nuclear power plant operations subsidiary of *Minatom* created in 1992
Sanitarnaia zona	Occupational health and safety zone around nuclear power plant
SAOR	The reactor emergency cooling system (*sistema avariinogo okhlazhdeniia reaktora*)
SM	High-power (*sverkh-moshchnyi*) reactor, name for a reactor at Melekess. Anecdotal evidence suggests "SM" may also stand for the initials of the reactor's primary designer's; Saveilii Moiseevich Feinberg.
Soiuzatomenergo	All-Union Industrial Association for Nuclear Power, created in 1978 to replace *Glavatomenergo* within *Minenergo*

Sredmash	Ministry of Medium Machine Building (*Ministerstvo srednego mashinostroeniia*), created in 1953 on the basis of the First Main Administration (*PGU*). Administered the Soviet military nuclear complex, as well as part of the civilian nuclear industry. Ceased to exist in 1989 when it was reorganized into *Minatomenergoprom*.
SSR	Soviet Socialist Republic
SSSR	See *USSR*.
STS	Science and Technology Studies, or Science and Technology in Society
SUZ	Control and Safety System (*sistema upravleniia i zashchity*)
TEPCO	Tokyo Electric Power Company
Ukratomenergoprom	Organization that consolidated all Ukrainian nuclear power plant facilities, created in 1991. Subsequently renamed *Derzhkomatom*.
Ukrytie	Concrete encasement covering Chernobyl unit 4, completed in November 1986; also known as "sarcophagus"
U.S. DOE	U.S. Department of Energy
USSR	Union of Soviet Socialist Republics; Soviet Union
VLKSM	All-Union Leninist Young Communist League, also known as *Komsomol* (*Vsesoiuznyi leninskii kommunisticheskii soiuz molodezhi*); youth division of the Communist Party of the Soviet Union.
VNIIAES	All-Union Scientific Research Institute for Nuclear Power Plant Operations (*Vsesoiuznyi nauchno-issledovatel'skii institut po ekspluatatsii atomnykh elektrostantsii*), created in 1979 to provide nuclear research support to *Soiuzatomenergo*

Acronyms and Abbreviations

VNIPIET	All-Union Scientific Research and Design Institute of Energy Technologies (*Vsesoiuznyi nauchno-issledovatel'skii i proektnyi institut energeticheskikh tekhnologii*). Successor to "p/ia 45," a Leningrad-based operation instrumental in building the Soviet nuclear weapons complex. See *GSPI-11*.
VPO Energiia	All-Union production association (which included the scientific institute *VNIIAES*)
VTI im. F.E. Dzerzhinskogo	All-Russia Thermal Engineering Institute (*Vsesoiuznyi teplotekhnicheskii institut*), named after F. E. Dzerzhinskii
VTUZy	Specialized technical colleges (*Vysshchie tekhnicheskie uchebnye zavedeniia*)
VVER	Water-moderated, water-cooled pressurized water reactor (*Vodo-vodianoi energeticheskii reaktor*). Standard reactor design for Russian domestic and export use.
Vydvizhenie	Literally "promotion"; Communist Party practice to train and promote individuals from working-class backgrounds
WANO	World Association of Nuclear Operators, founded in 1989 as a reaction to Chernobyl
Zanesenie v uchetnuiu kartochku	Literally "entry on the registration card"; phrase referring to a permanent entry on a Soviet citizen's Party registration card, analogous to a criminal record

Introduction

Expertise on Trial

On a warm Tuesday in July 1987, a bustling crowd of people swarmed around the nondescript "House of Culture" in the otherwise deserted city of Chernobyl. Inside, six men were being held accountable for the worst accident at a civilian nuclear facility in human history.[1] In the early morning on a fateful Saturday in April 1986, reactor number 4 of the Chernobyl nuclear power plant had exploded, spewing radioactive material all over the plant, its surroundings, and into the atmosphere, where wind and weather eventually distributed it across the globe.[2] News of the event gradually spread around the world as well, making the name of this Ukrainian city a household word. Now, some fourteen months later, the trial of those accused of having caused the accident would begin, less than ten miles from the destroyed reactor.

People all over the world were watching the proceedings closely. The Western media had reacted quizzically to the announcement that a trial would take place in the spring of 1987. After all, a high-ranking Soviet commission had already informed the International Atomic Energy Agency the previous August that human error had caused the accident.[3] Furthermore, Soviet newspapers had reported in July 1986 that the Communist Party's Central Committee had condemned and punished not only the director of the Chernobyl plant but also members of the institute where the reactor was designed, the nuclear oversight committee, and top representatives of the two ministries responsible for nuclear power plants.[4] And now these decisions were to be reenacted in a semipublic show trial. Calling the trial "a superfluous attempt to apportion blame," the *London Times* stated: "For those directly involved, knowledge of the aftermath is probably punishment enough. For the rest, the chain of responsibility extends far beyond the power station and far beyond Chernobyl."[5]

The trial was a strange anachronism in the context of Mikhail Gorbachev's wide-ranging reforms. The late 1980s had been a time of rapid social and political transformation in the Soviet Union, and public attitudes toward the accident, the culprits, and the management of the disaster mitigation were evolving in unpredictable ways. In the immediate aftermath of the disaster, Soviet authorities had granted international media unprecedented access to the accident site, the local communities, and knowledgeable professionals (doctors, for example), but they soon reversed course.[6] Touting Gorbachev's promise of *glasnost* (openness, or transparency), many hailed the trial as public. But authorities restricted access to the city of Chernobyl: it was, as Nikolai Karpan, a Chernobyl employee who attended the proceedings, put it, "an open trial in a closed city."[7] In a sense, the trial was an effort to reestablish control over the public display of political authority,[8] and in the weeks leading up to it, carefully worded press releases announced that those responsible for the accident would be prosecuted.[9]

The city was deemed clean enough for the trial to proceed even though it was within the zone—roughly 2,800 square kilometers or 1,100 square miles—that Soviet authorities had declared contaminated.[10] Before the trial began, workers had renovated the façade of the House of Culture and converted its main performance hall into a courtroom in which the judge and attorneys would literally be on stage. Although the authorities also set up a center for the press, the choice of location minimized attendance by journalists, one indicator that the trial would not be a typical show trial. One of the most important industrial show trials of the Stalinist period, the Shakhty trial, had been "arranged for maximum publicity … nearly one hundred reporters, Soviet and foreign, were present."[11] The proceedings at Chernobyl, by contrast, had "the atmosphere of a small village trial."[12] Only a handful of foreign journalists were allowed to attend, supposedly due to the confined space in the courtroom and limited accommodations in town.[13] These journalists were transported to Chernobyl by bus under police escort, the *New York Times* reported.[14]

On the trial's opening day, the journalists, relatives of the defendants, and workers from the nearby plant passed through an improvised admissions point, where they had to wipe their shoes on a piece of wet carpet and walk through a radiation detector. Apart from police cars, the streets were empty, houses stood deserted, and abandoned gardens were overflowing with fruit trees.[15]

Dressed in jackets and open-necked shirts, and sweating under the bright television lights, the defendants listened as the charges were presented (figure 0.1). Viktor Briukhanov, former director of the Chernobyl

Figure 0.1
At the Chernobyl trial. In July 1987, a Soviet judge tried six former employees of the Chernobyl nuclear power plant for criminal actions leading directly to the accident on April 26, 1986, the worst accident at a civilian nuclear facility. The director, Viktor Briukhanov (left), the chief engineer, Nikolai Fomin (right), and his deputy, Anatolii Diatlov (center), are shown here. They each received ten years in labor camps; the others received lesser sentences.
Source: Photograph by Volodymyr Repik, 1987. Courtesy of National Chernobyl Museum, Kiev, Ukraine.

nuclear power plant, was the chief defendant.[16] He had been put in charge of the plant during its first planning stages; now fifty-one, he had spent most of his career there.[17] A few months after the accident, the party had dismissed him from his post and revoked his party membership, and he had spent the previous year in a Kiev prison.[18] His wife still worked at the Chernobyl plant as an engineer.

The former chief engineer, Nikolai Fomin, was fifty years old at the time of the trial. He too had lost his post and his party membership after the accident and was arrested and imprisoned in the summer of 1986.[19] During the trial he would admit to feeling overwhelmed by his responsibilities at Chernobyl. Though Soviet authorities had not revealed it at the time, while Fomin was in a Kiev prison, he apparently suffered a nervous breakdown and attempted suicide. He was discovered in time and saved, and the authorities had postponed the trial until he recovered.[20]

Fomin's deputy, Anatolii Diatlov, was fifty-six at the time of the trial. He had been on duty in the control room of reactor number 4 when the accident occurred, and the dose of radiation he received had threatened his life. After undergoing treatment in a specialized hospital in Moscow, he too had been transferred to a prison in Kiev to await the trial.[21]

The other three defendants had been allowed to return to their jobs at the Chernobyl plant until the trial: Boris Rogozhkin, fifty-two at the time of the trial, had headed the early morning shift at the reactor; Aleksandr Kovalenko, forty-five, had been in charge of reactor number 4; and Yurii Laushkin, a fifty-year-old engineer, had been an inspector from the State Oversight Committee for the Safe Conduct of Work in the Nuclear Power Industry (*Gosatomenergonadzor*).

Presiding over the trial was judge Raimond Brize, deputy chairman of the Supreme Court and a senior member of the Soviet judicial system.[22] Judge Brize made it clear on the trial's first day that his court would limit itself to scrutinizing the errors made by the reactor operators and the officials in charge and not delve into the details of the reactor design.[23] At the time, the trial was intended as the first in a series of legal proceedings to examine the Chernobyl disaster, and therefore deliberately excluded all materials not pertaining to personnel errors.[24] The later hearings would address all other charges, though some journalists doubted that the additional trials would ever take place, especially given that the Central Committee had already expelled several high-ranking officials from the party.[25]

Before the Chernobyl trial began, common knowledge attributed the accident to multiple causes, among them unauthorized actions by plant workers, managerial shortcomings, defects in the reactor design, and poor site choice.[26] By the time the trial started, the Soviet nuclear industry had initiated reforms that addressed all these areas, implicitly acknowledging that human error was only one factor in a complex technological system. The industry had already taken steps to improve training programs, introduce performance incentives, and make more general management reforms and technical upgrades. Yet the state continued to seek to assign individualized blame for the disaster, and its persistence in doing so suggests that it intended the trial as nothing short of a chance to revisit the historical record and set it straight.

Some fifty witnesses would testify.[27] The clerk read the indictment, which took most of the four-hour opening session.[28] The prosecution charged the accused under article 220 of the Ukrainian Criminal Code, which covered violations of technical safety rules and other serious breaches of regulations at "explosion-prone plants."[29] Interestingly, this was the first time nuclear

Introduction

power plants were assigned to this legal category.[30] The defendants had been given time to study the allegations brought against them, charges that they had allowed "unsanctioned experiments to be performed by workers without adequate training."[31] The prosecution also charged Briukhanov, the former director, with having given false information about the scale of the disaster, a move that allegedly delayed the evacuation of the affected population.[32] As citizens of the Soviet Union, the six men may have known that those conducting the trial would require some admission of guilt, and perhaps even public repentance, from them. They probably also knew that the judge would not drop the charges, that he would sentence them no matter what they said, and that their convictions would be highly symbolic.

The Soviet state cared deeply about how the history books would portray Chernobyl and whether critics would blame the accident on industry mismanagement, human error, or reactor design flaws. Focusing on any one of these possible culprits implied adherence to a particular set of ideas about high-risk technologies, human-machine interactions, and technical and organizational methods for guaranteeing safety and reliability. Each view also implied a particular attitude about the legitimacy of the Soviet state and the Marxist doctrine that state was based on. Blaming the reactor designers, nuclear regulators, and top ministerial agents would question the foundation of the Soviet nuclear industry, its economic plans, its bureaucratic apparatus, and its internal controls. Worse yet, prosecuting the reactor designers and their organizations would cast doubt on Soviet science and engineering, the cornerstone of the entire communist project.[33] Mikhail Gorbachev could not afford to shatter the very foundations of what he was trying to save: the Soviet Union, a state built on scientific reason and technocratic ideals. Viewed in this light, putting six Chernobyl managers and operators on trial communicated the Soviets' willingness to clean house, symbolically as well as literally. Just as nuclear engineers installed a concrete sarcophagus in an attempt to control the destroyed reactor physically, the state attempted to use the trial of these six men to contain the disaster politically.

Soviet authorities allowed foreign journalists to report from the trial only on the opening day and during the announcement of the verdict.[34] And while many of these journalists complained that they witnessed only preapproved portions of the trial, Soviet reporters noted that just a couple of years earlier, any reporting at all on nuclear matters would have been unthinkable.[35] Many foreign observers assumed the Soviet media would cover the rest of the trial but, to their disappointment, the major Soviet newspapers reported very little on the proceedings, an omission that reinforced the impression of a cover-up.[36]

All six defendants denied the charges against them either completely or in part. In contrast to Briukhanov and Fomin, former deputy chief engineer Diatlov was very emotional on the first day of the trial. Reacting to the charges against him, he said: "With so many human deaths, I cannot say I am completely innocent."[37] However, he denied that he had violated safety rules, and instead blamed the reactor's design for the accident, an allegation echoed by other defendants.[38] As a United Press reporter observed, the defendants directed the court's attention to the state's failure to provide training, and—the judge's orders notwithstanding—to design issues, which put the Soviet nuclear industry itself on trial.[39]

From the perspective of Soviet information control, the fact that foreign journalists witnessed the defendants denying all or some of the charges on the very first day was a glitch. The Soviet media reported only that the three main defendants accepted professional responsibility—not the fact that they denied criminal liability for the accident.[40] Even though the official court transcript has not been released, alternative publications suggest that the defendants did have a chance to argue their case as the trial continued, although they spoke from the dock, as defendants.[41] Diatlov in particular rose to the occasion. He was clearly convinced of his innocence and while in prison had prepared exculpatory material, which he presented in great detail both throughout the trial and afterward.[42]

Though the defendants kept bringing up the reactor's design features, the prosecution categorically refused to address them, delegating the topic to one of the projected future trials. The defendants' testimony made clear that even experienced operators at the Chernobyl plant had not thoroughly understood either the specifics of the plant's reactor type (known as the RBMK[43]) or—more significantly—the risks of operating this reactor under certain conditions.

In addition, Soviet officials reportedly investigated the scientists and engineers responsible for the reactor design and the crews in charge of constructing the Chernobyl plant. The authorities also scrutinized those responsible for the evacuation of the plant's satellite town, Pripyat, and for the evacuees' medical care.[44]

Many of the nuclear scientists and reactor designers who testified at the trial were either directly or indirectly affiliated with the institute that had designed the RBMK. Though these expert witnesses did not themselves face criminal charges, they had a stake in deflecting blame from the reactor's specific features. It was therefore hardly surprising that they dismissed the interpretation that a design flaw had caused the accident.[45]

In addition to the possible causes identified before the trial, another, even more complex, explanation emerged (if only inadvertently) in the courtroom at Chernobyl, namely that the very nature of the Soviet economic system had caused the accident. Though its designers and supporters touted the centrally planned economy as rational, efficient, comprehensive, and superior to "capitalist anarchy," it had never lived up to this image. The race to fulfill plans by a centrally set date, typically the last day of the year or quarter, put enormous pressure on those trying to overcome problems caused by production bottlenecks, delivery delays, and an unstable, transient workforce. Nuclear power plants faced these problems too: administrators considered their operational plans fulfilled only if they spent every kopek in their budgets, regardless of whether the goods these funds were intended to buy had actually materialized. Planners expected new reactors to start delivering electricity to the grid on the target date and to conform to exacting specifications. Often, high-ranking party officials arrived on site for the start-up of a new reactor, adding to the haste in which work was completed. As one would expect under these circumstances, sometimes plant operators would postpone tests until after start-up, and the trial revealed that such delays occurred at Chernobyl. It is also safe to assume that in an attempt to oblige the authorities, Soviet plant managers had taken worse shortcuts in the past than rescheduling a nonessential test. Maintaining success within a centrally planned system involved a generous amount of improvisational talent, along with robust networks of patronage and an ability to focus on the ultimate goal, not to mention a good measure of personal assertiveness and patience. An able Soviet manager knew the consequences of complying or failing to comply with state-issued targets. He (far less often she) knew how to play the system with both legal and semilegal strategies: trading favors, putting pressure on subcontractors, and getting items even when they were officially unavailable.[46]

Although Soviet authorities tried to regulate the information that would reach the international press, the trial raised the question of whether the organizational structure underlying the centrally planned economic system in general, and the nuclear complex in particular, created unique problems for the management of the nuclear industry. The defendants' testimony also called attention to the competing pressures exerted by professionalism and Party politics on personnel recruitment and management in the Soviet economy. Finally, the testimony demonstrated that the decision to produce this particular reactor, the RBMK, on a massive scale and build it near large urban centers created other serious problems.

During the trial, prosecutors and some witnesses severely criticized the Chernobyl management team, but little-known aspects of their work also came to light, especially during Briukhanov's testimony. For example, the public learned that people with no specialized training in nuclear physics or nuclear engineering fulfilled very high-level, responsible tasks, often without expert supervision. Despite the director's repeated requests for accident simulators and the fact that they were a common best practice in most nations operating nuclear power plants, Chernobyl had none. In his testimony, Briukhanov also pointed out how difficult it had been to attract a thousand qualified workers for the launch of a new reactor and that only a recent decree had given him the financial authority to reserve budget funds to hire personnel well in advance so they could undergo training on site.[47]

The plant's former chief engineer, Fomin, was a case in point: originally trained as an electrician, he took short, intensive courses in nuclear reactor physics when he accepted the position at Chernobyl. But, according to his own statement, once his regular work schedule started at the plant, he no longer had time to study. He then relied on people like Diatlov, his deputy, who had expertise with nuclear reactors, albeit naval reactors with very different technical parameters.

The trial also brought up the issue of who was responsible for which aspects of operating a nuclear power plant. Those on the inside may have intuitively found their way through complex administrative channels and parallel hierarchies, but the bureaucratic maze made it hard to determine who had which duties. In particular, the trial underscored the tensions between the Ministry of Medium Machine Building (*Sredmash*) and the Ministry of Energy and Electrification (*Minenergo*), each of which had a role in administering the plant.[48]

Despite the testimony that identified alternative factors, on the final day of the trial Judge Brize convicted all six defendants of criminal negligence. In a ninety-minute summation, he found the men guilty of repeated violations of safety and operating regulations. In particular, he found Briukhanov guilty of having conveyed distorted information about the accident and of having been a poor plant manager.[49] He also blamed Briukhanov for the lax discipline among workers, who reportedly played cards or dominoes while on duty at the plant. He sentenced all the defendants to terms in labor camps: Briukhanov, Fomin, and Diatlov received ten years each, the other three defendants two, three, and five years respectively.[50] Brize gave Briukhanov an additional five years for abuse of power, to run concurrently with his ten-year sentence.[51] As a *Newsweek* correspondent poignantly observed,

The sentences, though harsh by American standards, were relatively mild compared with the punishment meted out in other Soviet cases involving white-collar violations. Stalin had people shot for "errors," and in Khrushchev's day at least two gold and currency dealers were executed for economic crimes. As recently as June [1987], the former party leader of Uzbekistan was condemned to death for corruption.[52]

The defendants showed no emotion during sentencing. They sat silent, with their heads bowed, while relatives in the courtroom wept.[53] In its official press release on the sentences, the Soviet news agency ITAR-TASS noted that the ten-year sentences were "the maximum penalty provided for in the penal code for the crime committed."[54] The agency singled out the former director, Briukhanov, as the main culprit in the accident:

Serving as a manager of a technologically complex enterprise, he failed to ensure its reliable and safe operation and the strict compliance of the personnel with the established regulations. Lack of control, low production and labor discipline existed at the plant before the accident. Not infrequently instances of breach of technological instructions were concealed with his knowledge and the causes of such breaches were not dealt with. ... [This] led to an "anything will do" attitude and an atmosphere of complacency and unconcern among the management of the nuclear power plant and some of its specialists. ... Having displayed confusion and cowardice, [Briukhanov] failed to take measures in order to limit the scope of the accident, did not put into operation the plan for protecting the personnel and the population from radiation, and in his reports deliberately understated data on the level of radiation—a factor which hindered the timely evacuation of people from the danger zone.[55]

According to TASS, Briukhanov knew the correct radiation levels, and his decision to deliberately misinform authorities was directly responsible for the delay in evacuating the satellite town.[56] TASS went on to say that Fomin and Diatlov had failed to provide adequate training for the operating personnel, that they had not enforced compliance with technological regulations, and that they had even breached instructions and directives themselves.[57] The former director of reactor number 4, Aleksandr Kovalenko, reportedly had not followed proper procedures when setting up the fateful test that set off the explosion, and Boris Rogozhkin, shift chief at reactor number 4 that morning, had failed to activate the emergency notification system to inform personnel of the danger.[58] Finally, the report maintained that the state inspector, Iurii Laushkin, had failed to enforce nuclear safety rules on several occasions. The press release concluded with the assertion that human error had led to the disaster, thus backing up not only the sentencing, but also the tenor of the Soviet government's earlier report to the International Atomic Energy Agency.[59] Both the report and the trial had considered the reactor's specific design features, at least to a limited extent, but both confined blame to the Chernobyl plant managers and reactor operators. The fact that the additional trials that had been planned never occurred made this version the only version: six individuals were solely to blame for the Chernobyl disaster.[60]

The Trial's Relevance

What was perhaps the last show trial of the Soviet era quite predictably ended with the sentencing of the Chernobyl plant's senior management, and yet the trial was not just about the guilt of six individuals who led or operated the plant when the accident occurred. That courtroom also saw other explanations for the nuclear disaster first appear in a semiofficial manner—if only to be postponed, delegated, or dismissed.

In fact, expertise itself was on trial. The proceedings raised questions about what circumstances justified, or even required, deviation from rules and regulations. Who made these decisions, and who should be making them? What counted as acceptable evidence that workers had followed or violated the rules? When did deviations from set rules become punishable in an economic context where improvisation was not only tolerated but often necessary, and how was one to know? In the case of the Chernobyl nuclear power plant, Judge Brize ruled that the practical expertise of the plant's director and reactor operators was inferior to that of the nuclear scientists and reactor designers at the Moscow-based research institutes and that the accident had occurred after operators deliberately violated regulations. His ruling thus reaffirmed a social and institutional hierarchy that had contributed, as I show in more detail later, to the deficiencies in knowledge transfer in the first place.

By its sheer magnitude, the Chernobyl disaster had put more at stake than the reliability of a team of workers, the managerial competence of the country's administrative organizations, or even the quality of a particular reactor design. The disaster threatened the authority of science and thus the very foundation of the Soviet state's principles. But political leaders and nuclear scientists would manage to integrate Chernobyl into a narrative of successful nuclear development and codify an official version of events. Thanks to Chernobyl, this version claims, the Soviet nuclear industry was now safer than ever.[61] For this statement to be credible, the judge had to assign responsibility solely to the operators. Undermining the legitimacy of the country's revered nuclear elite, and by extension that of the Soviet state, was unfathomable in a geopolitical universe in which the Soviet Union was a nuclear superpower on a par with the United States.

The Chernobyl trial exemplified how the Soviet leadership wanted the world at large to interpret and deal with the disaster. Not secrecy, but well-controlled information management was the order of the day.[62] This approach, and its uneasy transformation in the wake of the Chernobyl disaster, points to a problem intrinsic in the nuclear industry and its many sensitive, potentially dual-use aspects. Who knew how much, and who was supposed to know what? Who controlled what kind and what amount of information, how was it distributed to the various nonnuclear branches of the industry, and what remained classified even for operators of a nuclear reactor? For example, while designers had promoted the Chernobyl-type reactor to economic and military planners as a design that could easily be converted from electricity generation to plutonium production, to the public—and to the organizations operating these reactors!—they advertised it as a safe and economical machine, yet another grand achievement of Soviet science and technology.

Looked at another way, the trial illustrates how different versions of a story gain or lose legitimacy and how, ironically, a public trial can silence some aspects of a story. The following chapters unpack what this verdict sought to close once and for all. They bring to light conflicting stories and situate them in the broader historical, economic, and political context of the post–World War II Soviet Union and its nascent nuclear industry. More specifically, I show who told these stories, why some voices appeared more credible than others, and ultimately, how such accounts gave legitimacy to a distinct technopolitical system. By laying out the complex history of the Soviet nuclear industry, I identify the dimensions these different narratives could draw on for legitimacy.

In contrast to the Chernobyl trial, which gave legitimacy to one single explanation, my story emphasizes the multitude of legitimate accounts. I show how each of these versions makes sense, but also why some continue to enjoy more authority than others. Although Chernobyl serves as an illuminating framework for my story, this book is emphatically not another "definitive account" of how the Chernobyl accident "really" happened.[63] In fact, the existence of different, and at first glance incompatible, versions of what caused the accident is precisely what makes this story so compelling.

Explanations of the Chernobyl disaster, whether they originate within the former Soviet Union or abroad, typically emphasize one of the causes mentioned above: human error, design flaws, or mismanagement. At the time the trial ended, the plethora of contradictory reports from the government commission and from various ministries, groups, and individuals were only starting to appear in public, and representatives of different groups fought over who would, or would not, sign off on a particular statement. But for the first time, and thanks to Gorbachev's new policies, the omnipresent party control over industry and the involvement of the KGB in many of the accident investigation brigades became issues of debate, rather than unquestionable realities.

The design-flaw version gained traction when reports were leaked to the press that individual scientists had warned the director of the Kurchatov Institute, Anatolii Aleksandrov, about the reactor's potential to explode. The institute served as the scientific director for the RBMK, meaning it oversaw the development and construction of that reactor design as well as critical phases in its use. Aleksandrov further fueled speculation about the role of design when he stepped down as president of the Soviet Academy of Sciences after Chernobyl, reportedly to devote all his attention to improving the RBMK. As mentioned earlier, a Soviet delegation had officially informed the International Atomic Energy Agency in 1986 that human error caused the accident, yet internal responses to the disaster included design modifications, further evidence that the authorities considered design flaws a factor.

Reactor designers countered criticism directed at them with an analogy. When a driver hits a tree, they argued, you wouldn't blame the car's designer for the accident, but the bad driver. Likewise, when the operators at Chernobyl conducted unauthorized experiments, bypassed important safety systems, and violated numerous regulations, they effectively mistreated an otherwise perfectly safe and reliable reactor.[64] Designers also pointed to the dozen other reactors of the same design that were (and still are) operating all over the country. Aleksandrov was one of the most prominent advocates of this claim.

During the final years of the Soviet Union, some reactor specialists challenged the driver-error analogy. Their version went like this: When a driver hits the brakes and the car accelerates instead of stopping, this is fundamentally a design flaw and cannot be blamed on the driver. The driver in fact becomes a victim of bad design, or, worse yet, of bad information, because designers failed to disclose the potential consequences of operating a car with a known design flaw. Those who made this argument pointed out that the type of reactor at Chernobyl was difficult to operate and also notorious for its lack of redundant features that would protect against operator error. Moreover, one of the first reactors of this kind near Leningrad had suffered a similar but smaller-scale accident in 1975. Instead of alerting operators everywhere, however, authorities covered up the incident and restricted information about the problem it had revealed, even within the nuclear industry itself.

The third popular explanation for the Chernobyl disaster is mismanagement, a catchall term that incriminates the plant's executive staff, industry management, or the Soviet system in general. This explanation alleges that the work ethic at Soviet nuclear plants was generally poor, that operator training was insufficient or altogether lacking, and that managers sacrificed nuclear safety for the sake of meeting the production targets of the centrally planned economy. This explanation tends to miss the fact that despite the Chernobyl disaster, the Soviet nuclear industry as a whole neither failed nor developed in isolation from the West. Soviet nuclear specialists started to exchange ideas and experiences with their international peers as early as 1955, at the First United Nations Conference on Peaceful Uses of Atomic Energy in Geneva.[65] In the following decades, they continued to evaluate strategies, compare achievements, and even justify design choices with reference to international engineering preferences. The system explanation also tends to ignore the fact that a small but steadily growing segment of Soviet electricity production came as reliable base-load power from nuclear reactors, which often replaced polluting fossil fuel plants. Furthermore, the sector's growth and high-tech appeal, along with comparatively generous salaries and unparalleled social services (such as housing), attracted a well-educated, ambitious, and pragmatic workforce. In other words, the system worked, and continued to work, quite well, Chernobyl notwithstanding.

In the Soviet Union, the debate over these diverging explanations began immediately after the accident. It spread to the international arena and intensified in the years following the Chernobyl trial, even continuing after the collapse of the Soviet Union. Public outrage over mismanagement and reckless work habits at Chernobyl dominated the posttrial debate within the country and triggered unprecedented environmental activism.[66] Encouraged by the loosening of media censorship and diminishing Party control, newly formed public groups demanded that all nuclear power plants be shut down immediately. If human error was the single cause of the accident, these groups reasoned, this was the only rational action: after all, human error can never be avoided completely.

Like public groups, nuclear experts who disagreed with the official version of events took advantage of the new possibilities offered by Gorbachev's policies of glasnost. As I show in greater detail in chapter 5, in marked departure from their own practice, these nuclear experts started to speak out independently and publicly. In contrast to popular concerns about nuclear energy, which had been dismissed as "radiophobia," these experts' scientific authority afforded legitimacy to their dissenting perspectives. Even without additional trials, then, the management of the Soviet nuclear industry and especially the designers of the Chernobyl-type reactor became the target of harsh public criticism. But in the long run, even as the reactor technology was overhauled and a massive reorganization of the entire nuclear industry took place behind the scenes, the designers' version of events prevailed.

The designers' version continues to shape the common understanding of the Chernobyl disaster today. This book introduces alternative accounts, not to discredit one or the other, but to highlight what was at stake for the advocates of each version. It also investigates the underlying assumptions of these different versions: What notion of accountability motivated people to make these contradictory claims, during and after the Chernobyl trial? How do different versions of the disaster conceptualize safety and reliability?

Throughout the book, I emphasize the history leading up to the Chernobyl disaster. I argue that it would be a mistake to focus only on the accident and its immediate causes. Instead, the ensuing chapters illuminate the origins of the particular reactor design used at the Chernobyl plant in relation to the other designs chosen for mass implementation. I describe the considerations that drove specific developments in the Soviet nuclear power industry and demonstrate why this design made sense—economically, technically, and politically. Only a thorough examination of Chernobyl's prehistory will allow us to understand fully how and why the accident occurred, what it meant for the Soviet system and the Soviet nuclear industry, and ultimately how it matters to the international nuclear energy community today.

The Chapters Ahead

Chapter 1 provides a historical and functional overview of the Soviet economic system and shows how scientists and engineers persuaded planners to incorporate civilian nuclear power into the country's economic strategy. Because it traces how Soviet experts established nuclear power as a driving force of social, not just technical, progress, the chapter also offers a glimpse of the inner workings of the Soviet political and economic system. Understanding this broader context reveals not only some of the ideals underlying Soviet governance, but also how the pressure to make nuclear power competitive with fossil fuel plants contributed to what would happen at Chernobyl.

Chapter 2 examines in detail the nuclear industry's organizational framework and its dual origins in the countrywide electrification program on the one hand and the weapons program on the other. It shows that nuclear power plants held a contested position at the intersection of these two programs—with Minenergo running the former and Sredmash emerging from the latter—and it explains the role various institutions played in delineating spheres of influence and plant management responsibilities. In particular, the chapter highlights the ongoing rivalry between Sredmash and Minenergo and illustrates how organizational stresses fundamentally shaped the nuclear industry, its technical choices, personnel policy, and safety norms.

Chapter 3 traces how nuclear power plant operators emerged as a professional community, and explains how this community defined itself through the work it performed and through organizational alliances. The chapter covers what it meant to be a Soviet nuclear engineer, especially in terms of social mobility, prestige, and privileges. It looks at how the nuclear industry recruited and trained workers, what shaped those workers' professional identities, and how these identities evolved over time. The chapter contrasts the self-conception and ideals of nuclear experts working at elite research institutes with those of the professionals who handled the pressures of sometimes arbitrary economic plans at actual nuclear plants. It also identifies similarities that reached across these communities, such as a sincere sense of patriotic duty.

Chapter 4 presents a novel history of nuclear reactor design choices and shows how personalities and institutional and political wrangling played into those choices. The chapter argues that during the Cold War, achieving peaceful nuclear applications became yet another race, although the Soviet government went on to support a broad and multifaceted reactor research-and-development program much longer than many Western nations. Rather than condemning the RBMK as a flawed design and an altogether bad choice, this discussion shows that competing economic, technical, and diplomatic imperatives influenced Soviet nuclear industry leaders to choose the RBMK.

Chapter 5 returns to the Chernobyl accident. It briefly recapitulates how disaster mitigation progressed and then focuses on the extended period during which various bodies investigated the causes of the accident and assigned blame. The chapter recounts the fate of early whistleblowers and also lays out how Chernobyl fundamentally changed (and sometimes failed to change) the Soviet, and by extension global, nuclear industry.

In the conclusion, I debate whether the Chernobyl disaster was the predictable outcome of the plant's circumstances or an unexpected, improbable, catastrophe that nevertheless had underlying—and intertwining—long-term, systemic causes. I advocate taking a historical perspective and considering multiple complex causes because anything less will not help us avoid similar accidents. Ultimately, I argue that we cannot dismiss the Chernobyl disaster as an outcome specific to the Soviet system. The context could have been different—democratic and capitalist, for example—and still disaster could have struck.

Sadly, disaster did strike again, twenty-five years later, on March 11, 2011, at Japan's Fukushima Daiichi plant. In the epilogue, I grapple with the challenge of comparing nuclear disasters, despite significant differences, and with writing about one nuclear catastrophe while another is still unfolding. The accident investigation reports of Fukushima are already producing competing narratives, but if the aftermath of Chernobyl is any indication, the nuclear industry worldwide will soon resume normal operations.[67]

1 Envisioning a Nuclear-Powered State

The nuclear catastrophe at Chernobyl triggered public debate over the authority, credibility, and expertise of government officials, planners, and scientists. Given that some saw the disaster as a failure of the entire Soviet system, examining the political and economic contexts of Chernobyl's prehistory illuminates critical aspects of the accident and helps us understand both why it occurred and why it was significant for the Soviet system. Though hindsight colors how we view the decisions that led to the explosion, many of those decisions made sense at the time, not simply from a political standpoint but economically and technically as well. By examining how the inner workings of the Soviet system affected the development and operation of its nuclear industry, we can better understand these decisions.

The Soviet nuclear industry emerged in the unique context of a planned-administrative economy and an ideologically distinctive political system. Together, the state-party system and the planned character of the Soviet economy provided the framework within which the Soviet nuclear industry emerged. These structures offered certain options while constraining others. At the same time, the structures were themselves subject to modification. In this chapter, I explore how this larger political and economic context affected the development of the Soviet nuclear power industry. I cover the specifics of that development in the next chapter.

The decision to develop a nuclear power industry in the Soviet Union was not inevitable. In the late 1940s, the country faced no imminent energy crisis. Existing hydropower, coal, gas, and oil-fueled plants produced electricity, and the ample energy resources available didn't necessitate a shift to nuclear power. In the late 1950s, however, Soviet analysts predicted that energy demand was bound to rise drastically over the next few decades, partly due to the anticipated retrofitting of trains from coal to electricity, and partly because of a significant increase in the number of electric appliances in the home.¹ More electricity was needed, just when nuclear power generation was gaining visibility all over the world.

Soviet nuclear energy developed under political and economic circumstances radically different from those in other countries like the United States. The Soviet Union had no private industry and no free market competition.² Unlike Western economies that could draw on the rhetoric of free market forces to promote, and even subsidize, nuclear power, justifying the nuclear option in the Soviet Union took on unique forms.³ It was the Soviet state and its bureaucrats that made decisions, committed resources, and oversaw the implementation of economic plans.⁴ The specifics of the centrally planned economy set the parameters for the emerging nuclear power sector.

Economic concerns were paramount in the Soviet system, and the central planning apparatus required that state investments "pay off" both literally, in terms of economic growth, and figuratively, in terms of technological progress. The fact that prominent Soviet scientists backed nuclear power was tremendously important, as was nuclear energy's compatibility with Soviet ideals of electrifying the entire country and demonstrating Soviet scientific and technological prowess. As I will argue here, however, these programmatic arguments only accomplished so much: at some point, nuclear power generation had to demonstrate its cost-effectiveness—or at least establish that it had sufficient promise to become economically viable in the foreseeable future. Only by persuading decision makers of nuclear energy's economic potential could this emerging industry hope to be included in the country's long-term plans.

The idea of using controlled nuclear fission as a means of producing energy wasn't new. As early as 1922, Russian academician Vladimir Vernadskii, head of the then newly founded State Radium Institute in Leningrad, predicted: "We are approaching a tremendous revolution in human life with which nothing hitherto experienced can be compared. It will not be long before man will have atomic energy at his disposal as a source of energy that will make it possible for him to build his life as he pleases."⁵

In the immediate postwar period, many scientists and engineers who had contributed to the nuclear weapons program felt they could atone for their role in developing atomic and hydrogen bombs by directing their creative energy toward peaceful applications. They used the momentum and success of the military project, and the status they had gained from it, to promote civilian applications of nuclear energy and to expand the country's existing energy policy, which until then had relied on fossil fuels and hydropower. Their enthusiasm notwithstanding, these early promoters of nuclear power encountered significant resistance from economic planners: research and development takes considerable time before construction of a nuclear power plant can even begin, and construction itself takes many years.

The problems planners faced in simply choosing a plant location indicate how complex the issues were. Siting a new nuclear power plant required a number of prerequisites to be met: the site had to be compatible with environmental conditions, for example by possessing a sufficient water supply, having suitable seismic conditions, and being large enough so that the required occupational health and safety zone (*sanitarnaia zona*) could be established.[6] In addition, the region where a power plant site was planned needed to present a sufficiently high energy deficit. And although nuclear power plants could connect to the country's Unified Power System (*Edinaia energeticheskaia sistema*), a gigantic, Union-wide grid of transmission lines that distributed electricity and heat from generating plants to industry and households and that managed this distribution through an integrated dispatch system, the proximity of existing transmission lines to a new site was another determining factor.[7] Finally, the site needed to have access to a sufficiently developed industrial base nearby and to large numbers of construction workers.[8]

The emerging civilian nuclear industry faced additional hurdles as well. In contrast to the nuclear weapons program that began in earnest in 1945, the nuclear power industry would not be able to rely on virtually unlimited resources. Those who planned it could access some of the resources that had supported the atomic bomb project, but not enough to fulfill their ambitious goals.[9] For example, the existing steel-manufacturing industry could not produce sufficient quantities of the required parts on time. This supply issue was hardly an exception: industrial capacities in general remained a bottleneck for decades. When nuclear engineers started using zirconium for nuclear fuel cladding in the 1970s, the country's zirconium industry was not up to the task.[10] For several decades starting in the late 1940s, the challenge facing the scientists who favored nuclear power was to secure the government's support for an emerging technology that required long-term financial commitments and that had yet to prove its suitability for the country's energy mix.

Making Nuclear Relevant

The Soviet Union's—and the world's—first nuclear power plant started operation at Obninsk on June 27, 1954, and advocates argued that the little plant proved nuclear power's viability as part of the national power industry. Soviet nuclear physicists and engineers subsequently continued to experiment with a variety of different reactor designs that clearly demonstrated nuclear power's technical feasibility. But technical feasibility alone wasn't enough: in a national economy still exhausted by a world war and already entangled in a nuclear arms race, promoters had to make an argument that nuclear power would soon become competitive with conventional power generation. Well aware that the nuclear power program drew material resources from other sectors, scientists in the 1950s argued that nuclear power would provide an answer to many problems of scarcity by providing reliable, clean electricity and heat to all kinds of industries and to the general public. To establish the legitimacy of nuclear power, its promoters focused on three strategies. First, they invoked the international prestige of Soviet science; second, they conceptualized nuclear energy so as to make it consistent with the established ideological imagery of peace and progress; and finally, they created economic realities and leveraged political patronage to bolster their economic arguments. Let's look at each of these strategies in turn.

The Prestige of Soviet Science
Soviet scientists managed to explode nuclear weapons long before American intelligence expected them to; this success provided nuclear scientists with great authority, which they used to promote peaceful applications of nuclear energy to Soviet leaders. The power struggle following Stalin's death in 1953, however, made even the powerful nuclear elite realize that new political rulers would not automatically continue to support them.[11] To secure ongoing support, scientists invoked Soviet scientific prowess and international recognition, often with reference to Obninsk. For example, on June 27, 1955, Igor Kurchatov, the director of the Institute of Atomic Energy, and Anatolii Aleksandrov, his deputy and close collaborator, approached the minister of *Sredmash*, Avraamii Zaveniagin, and suggested building two nuclear power plants, each with a unique power reactor, as well as two other, experimental reactors.[12] These four reactor types, they argued, would allow them to choose the most promising direction for the development of a nuclear industry. They appealed to the high-tech character of nuclear energy and argued that its implementation in the country's economy would demonstrate Soviet mastery of this technology. This, in turn, would earn international recognition for Soviet science, the Soviet economy, and ultimately the country's political leadership. Nuclear power

plants, the physicists maintained, were more expensive than coal plants only because nuclear energy was still at an early stage of development.

Kurchatov's and Aleksandrov's arguments proved persuasive, and their vision was included in the country's ambitious sixth five-year plan (1956–1960), which foresaw 2–2.5 million kilowatts of power generated in nuclear reactors by the end of 1960.[13] Optimism prevailed that four more powerful nuclear reactors would be completed by that date.[14] This would demonstrate to the international community how advanced Soviet nuclear science and reactor engineering were and would also illustrate the virtues of a centrally planned economic administration. Soviet nuclear experts were so successful in persuading political decision makers of the benefits of nuclear energy—over the objections of planners who worried about economic viability—that some have described them as one of the most successful political lobbying groups that emerged in the Soviet Union.[15]

The Iconography of Nuclear Power

Another strategy to promote nuclear power drew on existing narratives of intellectual achievement, prosperity, and peace to create a new, nuclear, vision of the communist future.[16] As historian Paul Josephson has shown in his analysis of Soviet newspapers and journals from 1945 to 1975, Soviet nuclear physicists actively created a "culture" of atomic energy, a culture that became part of every Soviet citizen's dream of "the bright Communist future."[17]

Scientists also presented electrification as yet another "race" against the United States and its capitalist allies. The addition of nuclear energy would help the Soviet Union win this race while staying true to its civilizing mission of bringing electricity, and by extension progress and modernity, to provincial lands and remote areas. Prominent scientists thus positioned nuclear technology as a driving force of economic, and ultimately social, progress. At the same time, scientists tied into early Cold War rhetoric when they presented the Soviet Union as the country that first utilized the power of splitting atomic nuclei for peaceful purposes, while the United States was not only building nuclear weapons at breakneck speed, but had actually dropped atomic bombs on innocent civilians. A Soviet emphasis on peaceful applications of nuclear energy might even pressure the United States to deemphasize its nuclear weapons program in favor of civilian initiatives, and thus would positively affect national security.[18]

Promoting a vision of the enormous potential of nuclear power, establishing rhetorical legitimacy for nuclear power technologies, and ingraining the symbolic value of nuclear power in the popular imagination were important preconditions. But images and slogans were not enough to establish the economic legitimacy of nuclear power as an integral part of the country's future energy system. Only functioning nuclear power reactors could do that, and new technical and economic realities had to be created before those reactors could become operational. In the Soviet Union, this meant getting the capital investments necessary for building up a nuclear industry written into the country's plans.

Economic Arguments

In addition to convincing political leaders and the Soviet public that nuclear energy made ideological sense, nuclear promoters had to win the support of the planners, bureaucrats, and decision makers who managed the state's resources, both natural and financial. The strategy nuclear specialists adopted with these groups, the inner circle of Soviet industrial planners, was remarkably different from those discussed above. These planners didn't really care how prestigious Soviet science was, as long as it delivered tangible results: technologies to produce electricity faster, better, and more cheaply.

To appeal to this economic rationality, nuclear promoters stressed the asymmetrical distribution of the country's vast natural resources in relation to energy demand. Most fossil fuel deposits were located in Siberia, but energy was needed most in the European part of the Soviet Union. The options were either to transport raw materials from Siberia at significant cost, or to build high-voltage electricity transmission lines, which were also expensive and invariably involved significant inefficiencies. Hydropower, a major competitor for nuclear energy in the European part of the Soviet territory, required flooding vast areas, given that riverbeds were mostly flat. Such flooding, they argued, would reduce the land available for agriculture. Unlike a conventional plant, however, a nuclear power plant was independent of scarce natural resources, could be located near energy consumers, and therefore did not require long transmission lines. Despite their high initial cost, the promoters said, nuclear power plants would eventually turn out to be economically competitive.

Over time, as nuclear power gained traction, the ideological arguments in its favor faded and gave way to debates over its economic efficiency. Structural and organizational factors increasingly replaced the symbolic, ideological aspects that had been so critical for the early development of the Soviet nuclear industry. Integrating nuclear power into the national energy mix altered the country's economic planning in fundamental ways,

Envisioning a Nuclear-Powered State

affecting industrial sectors, regional planning, and university curricula. By the same token, the requirements of the plan pushed nuclear science and its associated technologies in new directions—affecting everything from reactor engineering to human resources to economic accounting. Before we move into these domains, we need to briefly explore the inner workings of the Soviet planned economy and examine how nuclear energy fit—or how its promoters made it fit—into these existing structures and processes.

The State as Chief Planner

In a centralized, tightly interconnected system like the Soviet one, every economic decision entailed a series of consequences and necessitated other decisions. The system was so complex that no single planner could orchestrate it.[19] In its complexity, it appeared tedious and slow to some, but awe-inspiring and near perfect to other observers.[20]

Some Cold War accounts depict the Soviet economy as a system where "everyone does what he is told, and ... everyone can be told exactly what to do," an explanation that economic historian Alec Nove has called "the totalitarian myth."[21] In fact, the goals of the centrally planned Soviet economic system were similar to the goals of Western market economies: growth, industrialization, and progress.[22]

State planning had been ubiquitous since the early twentieth century, because it allowed countries to concentrate their resources on certain centrally determined priorities.[23] Not unlike many of their contemporaries in the rest of Europe, early Soviet leaders saw a deliberate planning process as the superior mechanism to avoid inefficiencies—in the economy as well as in industry.[24] Lenin had envisioned a society "as if it were one giant enterprise, a single all-embracing factory or office."[25] A factory, to be sure, that avoided the profit-oriented, capitalist production of commodities, and instead manufactured what was actually needed in an efficient, rational, "scientific" manner.[26] Instead of trusting such abstract mechanisms as supply and demand, which were somehow embodied in "the market," Soviet economic theorists envisioned that expert planners would monitor and adjust the system centrally: only concentrating control and authority in one center would guarantee the smooth functioning of the gigantic Soviet economy and avoid the "anarchy" of free markets. These ideas, of course, were deeply rooted in scientific rationality, but to work they had to materialize in the form of institutions and become embodied in economic and industrial practice.

Planning, then, was seen as the practical implementation of scientific rules that would ensure the rational development of society. The Communist Party would take the leading role in shepherding the country toward a truly socialist economy and an ideal polity, and it would do this in part by developing a functioning administrative and planning apparatus.[27] Accordingly, the Communist Party determined not only what was to be produced, but how exactly this was to be accomplished.[28] Ultimately, it was the Communist Party that would decide whether nuclear power had demonstrated its economic efficiency and could, by its success, justify and legitimize an ideology of centrally orchestrated, scientifically informed, planning.

The Soviet nuclear power industry would thus develop in the context of this "extraordinary institutional penetration of the party-state," a uniquely Soviet feature and something that political scientist Valerie Bunce called "a *fusion* between politics and economics."[29] The nuclear industry also reflected the way the Soviet government and the Party structure duplicated each other. Small pockets of nuclear expertise existed under both the governing Council of Ministers and the Communist Party's Central Committee, but no formal mechanism brought experts in these separate entities together. Personal ties facilitated some informal coordination, but otherwise collaboration simply did not occur.[30] *De jure*, the highest executive organ was the Council of Ministers, which operated in parallel with the Central Committee. *De facto*, the supreme organ of government was the Politburo, a committee elected by the Central Committee.[31] The Politburo's chair, known as the General Secretary, also headed the Central Committee. The Council of Ministers and the Central Committee issued decisions and ordinances about the location, kind, and schedule of any new power plant, and the Politburo ultimately approved those decisions.

Economic Bureaucracy

The number and responsibilities of Soviet ministries varied greatly over time. In chapter 2, I go into more detail about the ministries that governed nuclear power; here I briefly review how such units were organized and how they fit into the larger political scheme. Chief administrations (*glavki*) managed the departments that made up Soviet ministries. A board (*kollegiia*) that included the minister and several deputies met regularly and issued decrees coordinating plans and arranging logistics for the enterprises under its tutelage.[32] A bundle of enterprises—factories, research institutes, design bureaus, universities, or power plants—belonged to the state, and one ministry controlled them all, at least in theory.[33] In reality, and specifically in the case of large-scale technologies like nuclear power, several

Envisioning a Nuclear-Powered State

ministries collaborated. Enterprises, the units at the bottom of the economic hierarchy, worked with contractors who could be under the jurisdiction of another ministry.[34]

Creating plans for the national economy followed a complex schedule. First, the Party and the government set the economic tasks for the upcoming period, determined the approximate growth in industrial production, and made preliminary decisions on the geographic siting of industrial facilities.[35] These directives then provided the basis for the various planning agencies (some responsible for annual plans, others for longer-term plans) to create more specific plans for the various branches of the national economy, including industry.[36] According to an idealized timeline for plan submission, coordination, and implementation, the planning agencies informed the ministries what they were expected to produce over the next year (for example, what percentage of any given power plant was to be completed) and the funds and material each ministry could expect to receive.[37] Individual ministries in turn passed the plans on to their affiliated regional enterprises, which used industry-specific analyses and predictions to modify the plans and resubmitted them to the ministries. Often, ministries and their enterprises applied for more inputs than they actually anticipated getting. They also stockpiled materials because they feared supply delays and workforce shortages.[38] The ministries coordinated and compiled their enterprises' requests and, in consultation with the planning agencies, crafted draft plans to be sent back to the government for approval.

Meanwhile, the central planning agency adjusted and amended the supply requirements from economic sectors and Soviet Socialist Republics according to the resources available Union-wide. The planners submitted a material supplies request to the Council of Ministers, which then informed the ministries and union republics of how it would allocate resources. The Council of Ministers, often in conjunction with the Central Committee, subsequently issued official decrees that confirmed the general plan for the country and also detailed tasks and deadlines for each ministry and each republic, sometimes introducing corrections on high-profile issues.[39] Typically, individual ministers or another member of the Council of Ministers would oversee and report on how these decrees were implemented. In effect, the complexity of this coordinating system led to delays: sometimes enterprises did not receive their production plans until well into the year the plan supposedly covered. Even after the Council of Ministers had approved a plan, modification was often standard practice.[40]

Thus, despite the fact that central planners were formally in command, the functioning of the Soviet economic system depended on the information and the proposals that the ministries, enterprises, and other economic units provided and received. For example, the directors of individual nuclear power plants (and other enterprises) could, and did, influence centralized plans by actively negotiating with representatives of the respective ministries.[41] In contrast to common ideas about "the country of the plan," where allegedly nothing was left to chance, the ability to work with unanticipated changes was in fact crucial—and widespread at every level of the system. As Alec Nove put it, "Inspired improvisation often enabled rough calculations to be somewhere near correct; the many grievous errors were 'cushioned' by the existence of non-priority sectors which took the brunt of shortage; and, thirdly, some centrally-held stocks could be used in *ad hoc* rescue operations."[42]

Centralized Planning

The promoters of nuclear energy had to convince planners nuclear power was necessary and beneficial, and they had to get their proposals included in the country's long-term plans. Since 1921, the "State General Planning Commission," usually referred to as *Gosplan*, had integrated output, supplies, and demand.[43] Gosplan and other planning agencies played a crucial role in resource allocation and in determining priorities. Gosplan's exact range of responsibilities continued to change, but the commission kept its key position at the heart of the planning process and could usually count on government and Party support for its decisions.[44] The Soviet style of government typically and consistently featured organizational rearrangements; in part, they reflected the government's attempts to help Gosplan facilitate cooperation among ministries as the economy grew and became more complex.[45]

Within Gosplan, nuclear power fell under the tutelage of Aleksei Pavlenko, head of the commission's Department of Energy and Electrification. This department prepared and coordinated plans for the hundreds of institutes, enterprises, and other organizations involved with the nuclear industry. Its plans included detailed production goals; during the construction period of a nuclear power plant, the plan determined (among many other things) the exact amount of money to be spent on various types of construction work (most prominently, the construction of industrial buildings and of apartment buildings in the satellite towns); the time frame, down to specific months, when work was supposed to be completed; the kind and amounts of construction materials and machinery, and which factories would deliver them.[46] Later in the construction process, the plan

Envisioning a Nuclear-Powered State

established the month (or at the very least, the quarter of the year) in which the reactor would start up, and after that, exactly how much electricity it would produce, as well as the dates for maintenance and repair shutdowns and even for announced inspections.[47]

Nuclear Power in a Planned Economy

Persistent imbalances and glaring inefficiencies repeatedly prompted reforms in the economic system as a whole.[48] Soviet leaders intended these reforms to optimize the country's administrative structures and accelerate socioeconomic transformation, while staying true to political ideals.[49] Over the decades during which the nuclear power industry developed, these leaders experimented with segmenting planning tasks along sectors of the economy (e.g., the nuclear sector), along functional lines (e.g., separating or merging supply, investment, and accounting), or along a territorial principle (planning in regional units).[50] Often, reforms aimed to perfect the planning process itself.[51] In fact, socialist regimes in the Soviet Union and Eastern Europe were "addicted to change."[52] As Valerie Bunce has argued, constant reforms, in combination with rapid economic growth, resulted in an unstable system and eventually undermined the very foundations of Soviet institutions.[53] Even though the nuclear sector survived many sweeping reforms relatively unscathed, the ongoing changes did affect the supply industry that the nuclear sector relied on.

Khrushchev: Temporary Decentralization

Nikita Khrushchev, who won the battle to succeed Stalin, launched a set of economic and political reforms in 1956 and 1957, just a few years after the Obninsk reactor started up.[54] In an effort to strengthen regional autonomy vis-à-vis the center, Khrushchev fundamentally altered the administration of the Soviet economy, and his first step was abolishing the all-Union ministries and transforming them into regional economic councils.[55]

Second, Khrushchev introduced a separation between industry and agriculture and assigned separate agricultural and industrial managers to every region, again to redistribute responsibilities between the center and the regions. Khrushchev also deprived enterprise directors of what he perceived as too much independence. Until World War II, these enterprise directors had to negotiate every decision with trade union representatives and local Party officials. Stalin abolished this "triangle" as too inefficient, and as a consequence, enterprise directors gained considerable influence, becoming "industrial czars." Khrushchev decided to reverse that trend by prescribing mandatory agreements with trade unions and by reinstating Party control over directors.[56]

And finally, Khrushchev changed the role of the Communist Party by merging the responsibilities of the Party and the government. Previously, the Party had been a small elite of thinkers, generalists, and visionaries, distinct from the larger crowd of economic planners and managers. Khrushchev brought Party cadres closer to the actual management of the economy and simultaneously made access to Party membership easier. This led to an increase in Party membership numbers but to a decrease in individual Party leaders' power.[57] Mikhail Pervukhin, one of the managers of the Soviet nuclear weapons program, was among Khrushchev's most outspoken critics. He opposed Khrushchev's attempt to weaken the central ministries' power, in part because he saw the centralized structure of industrial administration as the backbone of the Soviet nuclear sector. Khrushchev's reforms, in his view, put the nuclear industry at a disadvantage.[58]

In the late 1950s, Soviet planners realized that the scientists' initial predictions of how quickly and cheaply nuclear power would become competitive with conventional power generation had been overly optimistic, and there is evidence that at least some planners subsequently became quite skeptical toward nuclear power. Although Kurchatov and Aleksandrov had, in 1955, successfully persuaded the authorities to approve the construction of nuclear power plants, authorities delayed construction and deferred financial allocations, and some skeptics questioned the technical feasibility as well as the projected profitability of nuclear power.[59] Kurchatov decided to use his authority as a leading physicist, head of the Institute of Atomic Energy, and Party member to reach out to political decision makers to support civilian nuclear power. In 1957, together with his deputy, Aleksandrov, Kurchatov wrote a letter to Mikhail Pervukhin, then minister of Sredmash, and his first deputy, Efim Slavskii, asking for support to speed up the construction of the designated power reactors. In 1958, Kurchatov convened a meeting of Sredmash's Scientific and Technical Council at the Institute of Atomic Energy. Among the participants were representatives of the Council of Ministers; Iosif Kuzmin, the head of the State Planning Commission and deputy chairman of the Council of Ministers; Aleksei Pavlenko, then minister for power plants; and representatives of other relevant agencies. Though its conveners formally devoted the meeting to discussing the development of nuclear power, they clearly intended it to sell the idea of nuclear power to the country's top decision makers.

Kurchatov also lobbied for nuclear power by writing letters to local Party representatives, ministers, councils of the people's economy, and others; he invited Party representatives to his institute, explained what nuclear power could do, and asked for equipment to support further development. Often, these conversations ended with a cup of tea at Kurchatov's home. And yet, in 1958, the authorities cut back their ambitious plans for nuclear power development, and the plan for the year 1959 even lacked a list of equipment for the nuclear power plants then under construction at what came to be known as Beloiarsk and Novo-Voronezh. The revised plan also lacked deadlines for the delivery of turbines, steam generators, large-scale steel structures, and even stainless steel pipes.[60]

The seven-year plan that began in 1959 also reflected this cautious attitude: while planners had not completely abandoned the goal of developing a nuclear power industry, they curtailed what had initially been an ambitious program. During a visit to the United States in the summer of 1959, Deputy Premier Frol Kozlov remarked that "Soviet planners had been misled by their scientists on the economic aspects [of nuclear power]."[61] Costs for nuclear power plants were in fact ballooning.

In March 1959, Kurchatov wrote another letter to Kuzmin, the head of Gosplan, and urged him to secure supplies for the nuclear power plants: "The industrial nuclear power plants currently under construction in the Soviet Union are crucial for determining the most economical and reliable reactor types for future construction, for gaining operating experience with nuclear power plants, and for the preparation of operating personnel."[62] Kuzmin instead proposed to the government a drastic reduction in nuclear power plant construction, including a complete halt to construction at the Novo-Voronezh plant. Kuzmin's proposal won approval, an unexpected blow to the nuclear physicists whose ideas Kuzmin had previously supported.[63] Kurchatov was determined to block these plans; he and Aleksandrov again wrote letters to Party leaders and to Premier Kosygin promoting the continuation of the nuclear power program.

And yet Kuzmin's proposal could not have come as a complete surprise to Kurchatov and his fellow nuclear promoters: the nuclear industry suffered a chronic shortage of equipment and uranium supplies had been overestimated. Kurchatov agitated tirelessly for civilian nuclear power until his death in 1960, and his successors' continued efforts eventually yielded results. In 1962, construction work resumed and the nuclear power program was restarted, albeit with an amended trajectory.[64] Two reactors, at the Beloiarsk and Novo-Voronezh nuclear power plants, would start operating in 1964.

Once authorities restarted the nuclear power program, plans for the ensuing decades identified regions with scarce natural resources and high energy demands. The Russian and Ukrainian republics in particular were screened for suitable sites for nuclear power plants.[65] Planners also considered requests from other regions, like Armenia and the Baltic republics.[66]

As it would for decades, the nuclear power industry struggled in the late 1950s and early 1960s with the supply and quality of essential equipment. In addition, troubles with repair and maintenance as well as with the workforce turned out to be permanent rather than passing problems. Ongoing reforms aimed to address these problems, but by preventing any kind of meaningful stabilization or continuity, in many cases they aggravated them instead. Like other big technologies, nuclear power drew on a number of ministries and their respective enterprises, either directly or through subcontractors (*podriadchiki*). A specialized support industry for nuclear power plants had yet to be created, and contractors often lacked the experience and skills to complete assignments to the high quality standards required in the nuclear industry. Faced with such problems, nuclear power plant managers were supposed to amend plans, which involved cumbersome paperwork; when they decided instead to speed up construction by tweaking the plan without prior authorization from the central authorities, they risked prosecution.[67]

For example, in 1962, a group of inspectors found problems at the construction site of the Novo-Voronezh plant, and they reported their findings to Kosygin, then first deputy chairman of the Council of Ministers. The Kirov works in Leningrad had delivered defective circulation pumps to the site, and workers there had sent them back for repairs. Another factory significantly delayed delivery of the reactor vessel.[68] The Beloiarsk nuclear power plant site reported similar issues. Kosygin requested a joint examination of the situation by Gosplan, the Ministry of the Construction of Power Plants, the State Committee for the Utilization of Atomic Energy, and Sredmash. He also sought measures to improve the situation at the Novo-Voronezh site. In February 1962, Gosplan reported to Kosygin that the Central Committee had already requested a similar investigation of the situation at the nuclear power plants under construction.[69] Clearly, the Soviet government did not always act in a coordinated fashion, no matter how well Gosplan kept track of orders and problems and attempted to eliminate undesirable duplication.[70]

Post-Khrushchev: Return to Reforms-as-Usual

In October 1964, the Party reacted to the transformation of its cadres into administrative managers by ousting Khrushchev. It then almost immediately reversed his policies: the Party overturned the division between the agricultural and industrial sectors, reasserted its position as the elite ideological leadership, and once again clearly separated Party and government functions.[71] While Khrushchev had taken on the roles of general secretary and chairman of the Council of Ministers simultaneously, the new Party leader, Leonid Brezhnev, and the new chairman, Aleksei Kosygin, now split these tasks.[72] The Party reinstated ministries and stopped—even partly reversed—decentralization. New opportunities emerged for the fledgling nuclear sector, which relied heavily on a centralized support structure.

The following year, Kosygin implemented his own reforms, some of which profoundly affected the emerging nuclear power industry.[73] Kosygin had served in high government positions under Stalin and Khrushchev—for example, as minister of finance, first deputy chairman of *Gosekonomkomissiia*, first deputy chairman and chairman of Gosplan, and deputy chairman and chairman of the Council of Ministers.[74]

Both contemporary economic theory and past failures in the Soviet planning system inspired his reforms.[75] Many of Kosygin's changes marked a return to pre-Khrushchev principles, but he also retained some Krushchev-era reforms and introduced some entirely new features.[76] For example, he retained the 1957 separation of the supply organization (Gossnab) from the production planning agency (Gosplan).[77] Kosygin's reforms also marked a return to the industrial-sector principle, where each industrial sector was directly subordinated to a specific ministry.[78] The reforms abolished the industrial State Committees—among them the State Committee for the Peaceful Utilization of Nuclear Energy, which was reintegrated into the Ministry of Medium Machine Building (Sredmash). The "State Industrial Committee for Power and Electrification" became a ministry again, the Ministry of Energy and Electrification (Minenergo).[79] As I detail in the next chapter, rivalries and turf wars between these two ministries determined how the nuclear power industry would evolve. Both ministries were powerful. At the point when Kosygin was instituting his reforms, Sredmash had a monopoly on all things nuclear and it had great autonomy thanks to the national security relevance of much of its work. But in the grand scheme of Soviet economics, Minenergo was a giant with wide-ranging authority and long-standing support from political leaders who believed that electricity was the country's backbone. It was Minenergo's "steamroller" mentality (and minister) that would expand the nuclear industry rapidly.

Minenergo's long-standing minister, Petr Neporozhnii, was a talented hydropower engineer, loyal Party member, and industrial manager who was close to Kosygin and would become an ardent supporter of nuclear power. His opposite number, Efim Slavskii, minister of Sredmash, also had considerable clout, having been highly decorated during the atomic bomb project.[80] The shifting balance of power between the two ministries ultimately affected who would control—and who would ensure the safety of—the use of nuclear energy for both military and peaceful ends.

The tangible consequences of these reforms varied. At the very least, they seem to have provided opportunities for the redistribution of responsibilities: when ministries changed their name and scope of responsibilities, the individual factories and institutes associated with the previous ministry were not always automatically transferred to the new organization.[81] For example, when Minenergo regained ministry status, Neporozhnii immediately began to compile a list of enterprises, factories, and colleges that he argued should be subsumed under this new ministry, "in connection with the reorganization of the industry's management."[82]

Neporozhnii pursued an aggressive and remarkably successful strategy of negotiating with Gosplan for more money—a strategy that also benefited the struggling nuclear power industry.[83] In 1964, for example, he requested authorization to use flexible schemes for reimbursing contractors and autonomy in amending not just monthly plans, but three-month plans.[84] The Central Committee and Gosplan granted his request, which fundamentally altered the handling of the huge capital investments necessary in the nuclear industry.[85] Neporozhnii could now pay contractors after they completed intermediate goals, rather than withholding payment until the completion of one massive contract. This, in turn, enabled contractors to operate more efficiently, and thus quietly revolutionized nuclear power plant construction.

In February 1966, Neporozhnii wrote directly to Kosygin to suggest streamlining the planning and construction of power plants by uniting the management of tasks and investments under his ministry, essentially bypassing considerable state bureaucracy.[86] Neporozhnii also requested the flexible disposal of funds allocated specifically for industrial construction and for the construction of housing and communal infrastructure. He probably calculated that once Gosplan granted him the authority to allocate these funds, this decision could not easily be reversed. He attached draft decrees and even suggested deadlines for the decisions. On March 28,

1966, Gosplan responded positively to this request.[87] The fact that Neporozhnii's strategy worked illustrates not only how he used his extraordinary talent as an industrial manager to his sector's advantage, but also that the Soviet economic system had highly idiosyncratic and remarkably flexible aspects.

Still, only a year later, Neporozhnii complained to the Council of Ministers about the way Gosplan was handling investment funds earmarked for developing the power industry, including nuclear power, in 1968–1970.[88] He argued that Gosplan undervalued the development of the industry and persistently failed to allot capital investments that the Central Committee and the Council of Ministers had already approved. In the meantime, costs had increased, and further funding was needed to build new power lines that would help distribute the newly introduced power capacities.[89] He claimed that investments were insufficient to start the construction of the new power plants scheduled to be completed within the current five-year plan. In addition, Gosplan had decided to cut back on the construction of hydropower plants—a big mistake in Neporozhnii's eyes, since these plants were crucial for covering peaks in electricity demand.

Meanwhile, poor-quality parts also contributed to the continual delays in nuclear plant construction.[90] Pervukhin and Pavlenko from Gosplan's Department of Energy and Electrification took stock of work on the second reactor unit at the Novo-Voronezh site in a letter dated November 22, 1968. According to their assessment, just as had been the case in 1962, the start-up was behind schedule because of problems with the Kirov works in Leningrad. The Council of Ministers had approved the purchase of eight main circulation pumps on December 27, 1966, but the factory had not delivered all of them. Worse yet, the pump they had manufactured according to blueprints provided by Sredmash's central engineering bureau failed after just two days on the test stand. To save time, factory workers decided to patch up the new, already-mounted parts with older ones. Gosplan considered this unacceptable and urged leaders from the ministries involved to exert pressure on their enterprises to enforce extremely tight deadlines. Gosplan also enrolled additional factories and arranged for the surrounding electricity network to compensate for the lack of the planned, and therefore expected, productive capacities.[91] Clearly, nuclear energy had become a considerable factor in the national energy supply system by the late 1960s, and the failure to bring new reactors online as planned resulted in a need to rearrange available resources and allocate funds for additional energy costs.

Administrators continued to defer the deadlines for the completion of new nuclear power plants. In May 1969, minister Neporozhnii requested an extension for starting construction work on the Armenian and Chernobyl plants.[92] To accommodate this request, the Council of Ministers ordered the Construction Bank of the Soviet Union to finance these plants independently of the originally planned schedules.[93] Pushed to their limits, nuclear power managers sometimes even requested supplies imported from Western countries, arguing that Soviet industry could simply not keep up with demand. Although Soviet industry de facto bought and borrowed Western technologies on a regular basis, Soviet leaders criticized Western technologies on an ideological level.[94] The import option was therefore politically tricky, especially given the prestige and pride associated with the Soviet nuclear program. Suggestions to cooperate with allied countries within the framework of the Council of Mutual Economic Assistance (CMEA) were more acceptable, but the CMEA countries' nuclear industries were at the time even less developed than the Soviet industry was.[95] In 1969, too, Neporozhnii began to advocate for nuclear plants with increased power output (800 MW and more), arguing that this would improve their economic efficiency.[96] He called for the creation of additional facilities with 12,000 MW capacities by 1976—that is, over the next seven years. He made the case for this ambitious program by comparing it with programs in the United States, Great Britain, and West Germany, implying that the USSR needed to catch up to these countries.[97]

Kosygin's administrative reforms were later revoked, but the period when he was at the zenith of his power as chairman of the Council of Ministers (1964–1980) was a crucial time in the formation of the nuclear power industry. His organizational reforms, especially the reestablishment and empowerment of Minenergo and the continued separation of planning and supply agencies, may have supported the economic arguments in favor of the RBMK. This was the new 1000 MW reactor introduced in the late 1960s, which came online in the mid-1970s and was used at Chernobyl and other plants. In addition to the previously adopted plans for the ambitious expansion of nuclear-generated electricity, Kosygin's emphasis on economic accountability and profitability helped both nuclear reactor designers in Sredmash and nuclear industry promoters in Minenergo justify the construction of the huge new RBMK rather than incrementally improving and scaling up existing designs.

A Shift in Justification: Decoupling Economics from Ideology

The start-up of the Beloiarsk and Novo-Voronezh reactors in 1964 proved the technical feasibility of industrial-scale nuclear power plants. It took

Envisioning a Nuclear-Powered State

Figure 1.1
Map of Soviet Nuclear Power Plants. Nuclear power plants were sited according to a set of criteria that included proximity to a metropolitan area with high energy demand, great distance from fossil fuel resources, a significant reservoir of water for cooling, existing infrastructure (roads, transmission lines, etc.), and the availability of large contingents of construction workers. The map indicates the location and type of reactors installed at the nuclear power plants in the territory of the former Soviet Union (RBMK, VVER, others). Graphic design by Dane Webster.

until the early 1970s, however, when the first VVER-440 units started up at Novo-Voronezh, to substantiate the claim that nuclear power plants could compete economically with traditional power plants, and that nuclear plants could therefore be considered a legitimate part of the country's electricity system.

The period from 1966 to 1970 (the period covered by the eighth five-year plan) marked a turning point at which planners began to consider nuclear power seriously as an energy source (figure 1.1). This plan envisioned nuclear power plants producing a total of 3.5 million kW, and, with Neporozhnii's strong support, planners projected a steep rise thereafter (over 6 million kW in the ninth five-year plan, and over 12 million kW in the tenth).[98] In 1971 they planned on 26.8 million kW for the period 1971–1980, and in 1980 on 66.9 million kW for 1981–1990 and 100 million kW until 1993. In other words, in the period from 1956 to 1990, power generation at nuclear power plants would increase from zero to roughly 70 million kW (70,000 MW).[99]

Once the nuclear power industry had won a stable place within the country's long-term plan in the early 1970s and economic considerations had moved to center stage, new plants began coming online at an increasing pace. The successful start-up of the RBMK reactor in the mid-1970s renewed the optimism of both nuclear scientists and political decision makers regarding the potential of nuclear power and allowed a huge capacity to be added in a very short time. Under the banner of increasing nuclear power's economic efficiency, the industry scaled up nuclear reactors and streamlined the construction process. Increasingly, industry managers, and in particular minister Neporozhnii, aggressively pushed the construction of new nuclear power plants and presented planners with *faits accomplis*. Whenever a plant was under construction, Minenergo simultaneously contracted to build living quarters for the permanent workers at that particular plant. These living quarters included apartment buildings, healthcare facilities, and other basic social and cultural amenities. According to Viktor Riabko, head of one of the largest construction associations at the time (*Soiuzenergozhilstroi*), it had become "fashionable" in the 1980s to set up construction factories as well as the town for power plant employees itself in the immediate vicinity of a nuclear plant, within the required occupational health and safety zone. This was considered convenient, since it saved time for commuting workers and cut the cost for power and other communication lines.[100]

In the 1970s and 1980s, Neporozhnii persistently supported the idea of a production-line-like system of constructing nuclear power plants (*potochnoe stroitel'stvo*). He envisioned mobile teams of highly skilled workers serving at one nuclear power plant construction site after another; they would constitute the backbone of an extremely ambitious development plan for the nuclear power industry.[101] He also made the strategic decision to construct multiple reactors simultaneously. Almost all Soviet nuclear power plants would contain several reactors, and Neporozhnii saw the advantages of starting the construction of additional reactors before the first one was completed: given the chronic production bottlenecks, delays, and changes in plans, this parallel construction process offered latitude that a strictly consecutive construction process would not have allowed.[102]

As he continued to promote nuclear power, Neporozhnii justified his repeated requests for additional capital investments by pointing to the need to increase power capacity due to rising electricity demands.[103] He explicitly compared the new nuclear reactors with fossil fuel plants and concluded that their investment costs were approximately the same, while the electricity produced at nuclear plants was actually cheaper than that produced at conventional plants. Nuclear power plants, he argued, promised to free up laborers previously engaged in the mining and transportation industry.[104] According to Neporozhnii, farming out the manufacturing of equipment for the nuclear power industry to a variety of nonspecialized factories and experimental production facilities was problematic because their output was often lacking in quality. Sredmash had guaranteed it would supply nuclear power plants with nuclear fuel, so he needed the financial means to support the expansion of the supply industry for these plants.[105]

At Gosplan, the staff of the Department of Energy and Electrification responded that Neporozhnii's suggestions were not new; on the contrary, his plan actually lagged behind what the Council of Ministers' Presidium had already agreed on in August 1969. They stressed that Minenergo and Gosplan needed to determine jointly how much advance financing future nuclear power plants would require. They also argued that Minenergo was responsible for choosing sites for new nuclear power plants in the central regions, Ukraine, and the northwestern territory of the country, where energy demands were highest and coal, oil, or gas insufficient and expensive. Minenergo also needed to choose the type and capacity for each new nuclear power plant, in cooperation with "interested ministries."[106]

Neporozhnii's conflict with Gosplan escalated in 1971, when the agency's deputy chairman, Vasilii Isaev, fiercely rejected Neporozhnii's latest funding request, this time for additional workers' pay and housing, to meet the intended plan goals.[107] Isaev wrote, referring to the minister's discretionary funds: "It is unacceptable that every year, the funds allocated to Minenergo specifically for nonindustrial construction work turn out to be insufficient specifically for nuclear power plants."[108] Undeterred, Neporozhnii continued his quest and approached the deputy chairman of the Council of Ministers, Veniamin Dymshits, directly. Neporozhnii justified his financial requests by citing the unique needs of nuclear power plants, including a very large number of workers, who needed housing, which in turn required construction workers.[109] The Council of Ministers forwarded this proposal to Gosplan, whose agents agreed to meet Neporozhnii's request, with the explanation that "in February 1972, Minenergo had decided to reduce the estimated cost of [a number of] nuclear power plants." Also, the requested amount was smaller than that estimated reduction.[110]

In 1973, Pavlenko of Gosplan's Department of Energy and Electrification reported that the plans for nuclear power plants for the years 1974–1980 had been overly ambitious. He pointed out problems with the supply of specialized materials and equipment and mentioned that construction work at nuclear power plant sites was falling behind schedule. He argued that not even importing equipment for the nuclear power industry could remedy this situation fully. His letter ended with no recommendation, but with a telling comparison: power plants running on natural gas were cheaper, in terms of both capital investment and annual investments.[111]

In response, Gosplan's leadership appointed an expert commission, consisting of economists and engineers, to conduct an authoritative assessment of whether gas or nuclear power plants were likely to be more profitable in the European part of the Soviet Union.[112] The commission confirmed Pavlenko's original assessment and concluded that until 1980, natural gas power plants would have 20 to 25 percent better economic indicators than nuclear power plants. Additional start-ups of nuclear power plants until 1980 were unrealistic due to significant delays in construction work and problems with the supply of specialized equipment.[113] The Volgodonsk reactor vessel plant (*Atommash*), which would relieve the Izhora works by mass-producing reactor pressure vessels, was already behind schedule, and the anticipated production period for a reactor vessel there was 2.5 years.[114] The experts expressed optimism, however, that after 1980, "technical progress in the development of the nuclear power industry" would make nuclear power plants competitive with gas power plants. The expert commission also concluded that in order to boost the gas industry, natural gas might be exported to capitalist countries, if the profit would be directed to developing the national gas industry, and to importing equipment the Soviet Union lacked.[115]

In 1974, the State Committee for Science and Technology (GKNT), Gosplan, and Minenergo discussed the optimal capacity of future power plants and that of the overall power engineering industry.[116] They reported to the Council of Ministers that by late 1974, the first RBMK-1000 at the Leningrad site had reached its intended output level of 1000 MW and compared this to the general trend of scaling up the power output of industrial plants. Their report anticipated reactors (both pressurized water and graphite-water) with 2000 MW output after 1980. But the experts recommended that for the European part of the Soviet Union, standardized 800 MW reactors, grouped in ensembles of six (for a combined output of 4800 MW), would be the ideal size.[117]

A year later, in 1975, a similar group (GKNT, Gosplan, and several ministries) wrote a seventeen-page report on the development of the power industry for the Council of Ministers to discuss at their next session.[118] In contrast to earlier strategic plans, nuclear power had now become an important player in the country's energy mix. The current five-year plan foresaw 59,000 MW in power generation, with nuclear power plants providing almost 9 percent of this new capacity. In 1971–1975, the VVER-440 was the most common new reactor, but in 1976–1980, planners projected a shift toward the more powerful *"tysiachniki,"* 1000 MW reactors (both VVER and RBMK), followed by the launch of the RBMK-1500 and an improved version of the VVER-1000 in 1981–1985.[119] The rationale for this continuous scaling up was, not surprisingly, economies of scale, which would allow decreased capital investments in construction work, labor costs, and fuel prices, as well as reductions of up to 50 percent in operating personnel.[120] The report further identified transmission lines and automated operating systems as major fields of activity within the power engineering industry.

By the late 1960s, the change in how proponents justified nuclear energy was complete. The industry's fundamentally altered institutional status allowed a rhetoric of economic efficiency to dominate arguments over nuclear energy's role in the country's development.

Conclusion

By the early 1980s, nuclear power had overcome its initial setbacks. Its proponents had convinced Soviet strategic planners it was the way to produce the electricity that economic progress required.[121] Promoters had successfully integrated into Soviet iconography visions about how nuclear power would help achieve the bright communist future.[122] Perhaps surprisingly, the rhetoric of economic efficiency had more success than earlier efforts to portray nuclear power as a driving force facilitating technical and societal progress.

In the long run, the key to the industry's advancement was its integration into the bureaucratic prose of long-term state plans. This is not to say that nuclear power lost its propagandistic value; in fact, in the former Soviet Union, it remains to this day one of the most widely promoted forms of energy production. Even after official plans were written and approved, proponents had to continue to argue that nuclear power plants were both necessary and feasible; after all, plans could be changed. But as the Soviet nuclear industry matured, the significance of the ideological rhetoric diminished, while economic and technical criteria moved to the forefront of decision makers' agendas.[123]

Although promoters of nuclear energy argued early on for the scientific merit of a variety of different reactors (a topic I discuss in detail in chapter 4), they increasingly bolstered their political and economic arguments by stressing the international context and the country's future energy needs.

Scaling up power capacities would meet the system's hunger for growth and progress, they argued, and the nuclear sector could contribute a rapidly increasing share of the country's energy mix.

By starting construction work at multiple sites at once, minister Neporozhnii did everything in his power to prevent plans for new nuclear power plants from being curtailed. Despite continuing supply problems, the successful start-up of the new RBMK power reactor in the mid-1970s renewed the optimism of both nuclear scientists and political decision makers regarding nuclear power's potential. Faith in scientific and technological progress was strong, and nuclear power had become both ideologically convincing and technically feasible. It also promised to be economically profitable, especially in the European part of the Soviet Union.

The state played a crucial role in nuclear power programs all over the world, and the Soviet Union was no exception. The nuclear industry could not have expanded so rapidly if Soviet decision makers had not made massive investments and long-term commitments.[124] Only the full incorporation of the civilian nuclear industry into the economic planning process allowed industry managers to justify nuclear power in terms of rational development and economic efficiency.[125] Once they had done so, the high-level commitment to peaceful uses of nuclear energy refashioned both economic planning and ideology in the Soviet state.

2 Between Atomic Bombs and Power Plants: Sharing Organizational Responsibilities

The Soviet civilian nuclear industry has its roots in two grand projects of the twentieth century: the state electrification plan that Lenin championed beginning in 1920 and the nuclear weapons program that Stalin launched in 1943.[1] As the nuclear energy industry grew, the bureaucracy that ran the electrification effort and the one that ran the nuclear weapons program would both undergo frequent changes, and precise responsibilities would shift repeatedly between them. By tracing in more detail how the organizational structures that controlled nuclear energy evolved, we can understand more clearly the difficult position nuclear power held, poised as it was between the nuclear weapons complex and the conventional power industry.

As is true of any large technological system, nuclear power's organizational context had a profound effect on how it grew. Once in place, any bureaucracy becomes a technology in and of itself: it steers and controls decision-making processes.[2] In addition, the process of rationalization or bureaucratization can itself be understood as a mode of control.[3] As Max Weber has argued, "The bureaucratic form routinizes the process of administration exactly as the machine routinizes production."[4] Because administrative structures do not always develop at the same pace as the technologies they are supposed to govern, those structures often represent the Achilles heel of otherwise mature technological systems.[5] As I have mentioned, responsibility for Soviet nuclear power was split between two entities: the electrification bureaucracy, which would become the Ministry of Energy and Electrification, or *Minenergo*; and the nuclear weapons bureaucracy, which would become the Ministry of Medium Machine Building, or *Sredmash*. These competing bureaucracies created a volatile organizational environment and triggered ongoing tussles over authority and accountability; in addition, institutional inertia would sometimes affect the pace of the industry's progress. The shifting relationship between Sredmash and Minenergo also affected how Soviet scientists and planners understood risks, capabilities, and requirements. Not only did this relationship have an impact on purely technical decisions, but it also significantly shaped decision makers' views about what was important, desirable, and safe, or, by contrast, what was risky, unacceptable, or simply irrelevant.[6] Consequently, examining the two ministries and their interactions helps illuminate why the Soviet nuclear industry developed the way it did.[7] The previous chapter outlined the political and economic context within which the management structures that controlled the Soviet nuclear power industry functioned. This chapter focuses on the historical development of the management structures themselves.

During the 1920s and 1930s, state leaders around the world sought tools of governance that would help raise efficiency and profitability. Regardless of political affiliation, many looked to the Soviet Union as a leader in setting up and operating an expert bureaucracy explicitly founded in scientific rationality.[8] As the nuclear power industry continued to coalesce in the late 1940s and early 1950s, the organizations that ran it endorsed ideals of scientific management, just as the Soviet Union's leadership did. Exactly how to administer nuclear power plants was a question that scientists, economists, and politicians actively debated for a long time; ultimately, the country's technical elite drove continuous and determined attempts to find the most rational form of managerial organization.[9]

When Soviet leaders began to organize the nascent nuclear power industry in the late 1940s, they envisioned the cooperation of more than 400 engineering and scientific research institutes, construction bureaus, and other organizations.[10] From the perspective of a centralized planning authority, the key to organizing the civilian nuclear sector was to craft an effective bureaucracy to deal with uncertainty, crisis, and the allocation of responsibility.[11] Interestingly, as I showed in chapter 1, this rigorous bureaucratization would go hand in hand with a need to improvise in response to the adversities of a planned, centrally administered economy. Those who advocated nuclear power during this period followed a dual strategy: on the one hand, they promoted the creation of new administrative management structures (a nuclear infrastructure), and on the other, they relied on individual nuclear experts who had been molded during the early years of the military nuclear program. In doing so, they both demonstrated their belief that bureaucratization would guarantee the most rational form of organization and assured the success of this new bureaucracy by appointing to key positions individuals who not only possessed technical expertise but also came with substantial managerial experience and firmly established personal networks.[12]

Given that the organization that would become Sredmash was already running the Soviet Union's military nuclear program, it is not surprising that the civilian nuclear industry inherited features from the nuclear arms race. The early civilian program preserved organizational traditions established in the weapons program: a heightened sense of responsibility, a clear system for executing decisions, the diligent selection and training of cadres, and a system of information exchange under conditions of secrecy.

At the same time, the demands of industrial production—practicality, reliability, and economies of scale—affected the civilian nuclear industry. As in other branches of Soviet industry, nuclear managers strove to standardize materials, equipment, construction processes, and work practices. The idea of implementing standardized reactors would even prompt the mass production of turbines, pumps, and pipes before these parts could prove their worth in actual nuclear power plants.[13] However, the ideal of a completely standardized reactor or its standardized production would never become a reality—in the Soviet Union or elsewhere.[14]

Because reactors and the rest of the nuclear plant were kept under different ministries' jurisdictions, the attempts by one ministry to standardize while the other tried continuously to change and improve created an ambiguous process that almost by definition could not reach stabilization. Furthermore, Sredmash and Minenergo competed over how to best manage expertise, share experience, and transfer knowledge.[15] Although the official division of nuclear energy responsibilities between Minenergo and Sredmash did not occur until 1966, the two bureaucracies' priorities diverged much earlier.

Dual Origins

In 1920, in the belief that only a reliable electricity supply would facilitate the growth of industry and the progress of the Soviet economy, about 200 scientists and engineers planned and implemented what became known as the State Plan for the Electrification of Russia, or the GOELRO plan.[16] These experts were all bourgeois specialists—that is, scientists and engineers trained in pre-Soviet times.[17] Their plan anticipated the construction of thirty massive new power plants and a substantial network of transmission lines over ten to fifteen years. The young Soviet government, a regime that "believed in the promise of machines to liberate," approved the plan in December 1920.[18] Elevated to mythical status, GOELRO would remain a driving force within the power engineering community and an important part of Soviet ideology and popular imagination.[19] The plan relied on ideas of scientific management that had reached the Russian electrical engineering community even before the October Revolution of 1917. These ideas may well have convinced the commission's bourgeois specialists that the new government was "removing the restraints of tsarism and supporting their modernizing mission."[20]

With his famous slogan "Communism equals Soviet power plus the electrification of the entire country," Lenin explicitly linked technological progress with social transformation.[21] He saw the GOELRO plan as supporting the communist state's overall effort to industrialize, modernize, and "civilize" Russia's vast rural areas. As a result of the electrification plan, the total output of Soviet power plants more than tripled by 1932.[22]

Meanwhile, Russian scientists had started research on radioactive materials in the early 1910s. When the State Radium Institute in what was then Petrograd opened in 1922, that research gained momentum. In Moscow, the physicist Sergei Vavilov founded the Physics Institute of the Soviet Academy of Sciences (FIAN) in 1934. A year after the discovery of fission in 1938, the Academy created a Commission on Isotopes under the leadership of geochemist Vladimir Vernadskii. In 1940, the Academy's Presidium established a Special Committee for the Problem of Uranium, which conducted and coordinated research in the area of isotope separation and nuclear fission, and started systematic exploration of uranium deposits.[23] During World War II, most nuclear scientists abandoned their research and joined the war effort.[24]

The nuclear weapons program started very modestly in 1943, when Georgii Flerov, a nuclear physicist, noticed that U.S. publications on anything nuclear had virtually disappeared from the open scholarly press. Flerov alerted the authorities, and after intelligence confirmed Flerov's suspicion, Stalin created a research institute, Laboratory No. 2, that was to become the top-secret heart of the Soviet nuclear weapons project.[25]

Nominally under the Soviet Academy of Sciences, the institute opened in 1943 as a scientific base for physicist Igor V. Kurchatov, the mastermind behind the Soviet nuclear weapons project. Laboratory No. 2 had one task: to produce a Soviet atomic bomb. After the United States tested an atomic bomb on July 16, 1945, Stalin significantly increased funding for Kurchatov's group. Following the bombing of Hiroshima, the Soviet State Defense Committee (GKO) launched a fully funded crash program, thereby laying the ground work for a nuclear arms race that would soon escalate.[26]

Shrouded in secrecy, the Soviet state set up organizations and facilities to support an army of scientists and engineers who developed and mastered fission and fusion devices soon after their American counterparts. In 1945, Stalin appointed Lavrentii Beria chair of a Special Committee on the Atomic Bomb. This committee consisted of specialists from science and industry, as well as representatives from party, state, and the secret police, but no military men.[27]

That changed in the spring of 1946, at the beginning of the first postwar five-year plan, when Stalin named General Boris L. Vannikov, previously director of the secret Ministry of Agricultural Machine Building (the cover name for the munitions industry), as the administrative director of the Soviet nuclear program. From then on, the First Chief Administration (*Pervoe Glavnoe Upravlenie* or PGU) carried out all research related to nuclear energy, both military and civilian. The PGU was accountable personally to Beria and received direct support from the highest executive authority, the Council of Ministers.[28]

On December 25, 1946, in Kurchatov's Laboratory No. 2 in Moscow, physicists set in motion a controlled nuclear chain reaction in F-1, the Soviet Union's first experimental nuclear reactor. "Annushka," the first Soviet reactor to produce weapons-grade plutonium, started up in June 1948 at Cheliabinsk-40. On August 29, 1949, the Soviets tested their first plutonium bomb. On July 1, 1953, in the midst of the power struggle following Stalin's death, the Council of Ministers elevated the PGU to the Ministry of Medium Machine Building (Sredmash) and put it in charge of supervising all work connected to atomic energy.[29] A month later, on August 12, 1953, the first Soviet hydrogen bomb detonated—less than a year after the first American H-bomb test.

The gigantic national effort to create nuclear weapons came to be known as the atomic project (*atomnyi proekt*).[30] The nuclear weapons program required tremendous sacrifices from the individuals who worked within it. The atomic project's leadership style was brutal, but employees experienced extraordinary solidarity and displayed a willingness to take significant risks. These characteristics shaped an entire generation of scientists, engineers, and administrators by forming their professional ethos, determining their overall priorities, and even fashioning their personal attitudes.[31]

The civilian nuclear program developed immediately following, and partly parallel to, the nuclear weapons program.[32] Even before the first successful nuclear detonation, however, Kurchatov had turned his ambitions to peaceful applications of nuclear energy. As I have mentioned, once he had delivered the first Soviet fission and fusion bombs, he became a tireless advocate of nuclear power plants, using his access to the highest political councils and his substantial clout to influence national policies on nuclear energy.[33]

As early as 1946, Kurchatov ordered tests to check whether graphite-water reactors could be used to generate electric power as well as to produce plutonium.[34] A 5 MW graphite-water reactor began operation on June 27, 1954, at Obninsk, near Moscow, the first nuclear reactor to deliver electricity to a national grid.

Its small size notwithstanding, Obninsk became known as the world's first nuclear power plant and the first genuinely peaceful application of nuclear energy.[35] However, it actually served military purposes, and the reactor's acronym—"AM," allegedly for *atom mirnyi* or "peaceful atom"—originally referred to naval applications ("naval atom" or *atom morskoi*).[36] The double meaning made sense given that researchers were accelerating their work on nuclear naval propulsion at the time, and the Obninsk reactor served as a test stand for reactor designs suitable for submarine deployment. Only when project leaders determined that they could not reduce the graphite-water design sufficiently in weight and size to deploy it on naval vessels, especially submarines, did the Obninsk reactor morph into the poster child for the peaceful atom.[37]

In the years following Obninsk's start-up, it became clear that a nuclear power plant not only posed a series of unique challenges—for instance, the safety of reactor operations and the secure handling of nuclear fuel—but also occupied a precarious position at the boundary of electricity generation and nuclear weapons. A nuclear power plant, then, required the active cooperation of ministries and other entities that were not used to collaborating. It comes as no surprise that in the Soviet Union (as in the rest of the world), governing the growing nuclear power sector posed unprecedented organizational challenges.

A Tale of Two Ministries

Minenergo: Power for the People's Economy

The Ministry of Energy and Electrification (Minenergo) began in 1939 as the "People's Commissariat of Power Plants and Electrical Industry," one of six new organizations that replaced the "People's Commissariat of Machine Building."[38] Over the next twenty-three years, this agency underwent no fewer than seven reorganizations in which power plants were separated from and rejoined with the electrical industry in various configurations, only to emerge in 1962 with a set of responsibilities very similar to those it had in its 1939 incarnation. The ministry that ultimately resulted from these continuous reforms was in charge of the country's power plants—their construction and operation, as well as the infrastructure for transmitting electricity.[39]

Glavatomenergo: Preparing the Power Industry for Nuclear Energy
In 1956, in anticipation of an increased demand for new nuclear power plants, Minenergo formed a suborganization to address the specific needs of those plants, including the training of future nuclear power plant personnel. This "Chief Administration for the Construction of Atomic Power Plants," *Glavatomenergo*, became the major nuclear engineering organization in the civilian power engineering sector. Konstantin Lavrenenko, an engineer who was prominently involved in the management of the postwar electric power industry, became the new organization's first director.[40]

Glavatomenergo's first assignment was to take over from regional construction enterprises the financing, assembly, and overall supervision for the Beloiarsk and Novo-Voronezh nuclear plants, which were both intended as experimental stations and were both still at very early stages of construction at the time.[41] One year later, in 1957, Glavatomenergo's plans already comprised four "industrial-scale" nuclear power plants, including the Beloiarsk and Novo-Voronezh plants.[42] The highly optimistic dates of completion for these plants were 1960 and 1961, respectively.[43]

Petr Neporozhnii was appointed head of Minenergo in 1962 (figure 2.1).[44] Initially indifferent to nuclear energy, he became a dedicated advocate for nuclear power plants, as I discussed in chapter 1. He also promoted a conveyer-belt-like system to maximize the speed and efficiency of constructing new plants.[45]

Neporozhnii was born in 1910 near Kiev, in a rural family. In 1933, he graduated from the Leningrad Institute of Maritime Transportation Engineering (*Leningradskii institut inzhenerov vodnogo transporta*) as a hydropower engineer. After serving in the Soviet Navy from 1933 to 1935, he became involved in managing the construction of large hydropower plants. From 1940 to 1954, he was chief engineer and director of a planning institute in Tashkent (Uzbekistan), and chief engineer for hydropower plants near Leningrad and in Ukraine. In 1954, he started his political career in Ukraine as deputy chairman of the Ukrainian Council of Ministers, and he later became chairman of the Ukrainian State Committee for Construction (*Gosstroi*). After a few years he moved from the regional to the central level: from 1959 to 1962, he was first deputy minister of the All-Union Ministry of the Construction of Power Plants. He would serve twenty-three years as

Figure 2.1
The minister of Energy and Electrification (Minenergo), Petr S. Neporozhnii, who managed the Soviet Union's conventional power industry from the early 1960s on, also became responsible for constructing and operating nuclear power plants beginning in 1966. Initially skeptical of nuclear power, he eventually became an avid promoter. The image shows Neporozhnii in the 1970s.
Source: Courtesy of the publishing house "Master," Moscow. Originally published in A. I. Vol'skii and A. B. Chubais, eds., *Elektroenergetika*, series *Stroiteli Rossii: XX vek* (Moscow: "Master," 2003), 96. Reprinted with permission.

minister of Minenergo and retired in 1985, at age seventy-five. His ministry oversaw and coordinated every type of conventional power plant designed, built, and operated in the territory of the Soviet Union, the entire Soviet electricity grid, as well as the centralized heat supply for industry and households.[46]

For the first four years of Neporozhnii's tenure, Minenergo considered the contribution of nuclear plants to the country's energy supply negligible. Even the plans for 1966–1970 forecast that nuclear power would contribute less than 1.5 percent of overall electricity production.[47] Such low expectations would change only in 1966, when Minenergo took on more comprehensive responsibilities for the construction and operation of nuclear power plants.

The efficient construction, operation, and management of both conventional and nuclear power plants increased Minenergo's political clout and gave its minister unusual leeway in developing and pursuing his own agenda. And yet, even though Neporozhnii's ministry enjoyed the patronage of influential authorities, the nuclear power industry was not as protected as the nuclear weapons community, and Neporozhnii could not provide his employees with privileges comparable to those enjoyed by technical specialists in the other ministry responsible for nuclear power plants, the Ministry of Medium Machine Building, or Sredmash.[48]

Sredmash: The Secret Nuclear Ministry

Before 1986, very little was known in the Soviet Union or the West about the inner workings of Sredmash, the ministry formed in 1953 around the Soviet nuclear weapons program. Secrecy effectively shielded the work, staff, and organizations of this ministry, even vis-à-vis its collaborators. After this top-secret Soviet ministry ceased to exist in 1986, scholarly works, as well as autobiographical accounts, began to shed light on its origins and operations.[49]

Sredmash's first four years were turbulent. In July 1953, two of the principal managers of the atomic weapons project, Viacheslav Malyshev and Boris Vannikov, became Sredmash's first minister and first deputy minister, respectively. Vannikov's career had been truly astounding: a former people's commissioner for armament, he had repeatedly fallen out of Stalin's favor and was in prison when he received his appointment, in 1941, as deputy chairman of the People's Commissariat of Defense, a position he held until 1942. The reasons for his arrests remain obscure, but according to Grabovskii's plausible (although anecdotal) account, Vannikov had been arrested for publicly disagreeing with Stalin.[50]

Just a year and a half after becoming Sredmash's first minister, on February 28, 1955, Malyshev was promoted to chairman of *Gostekhnika*, the Council of Ministers' revived committee for new technologies. Avraamii Zaveniagin, once a close collaborator of Beria's, succeeded Malyshev at Sredmash. Zaveniagin had proved himself an exceptional industrial manager at the steel town of Magnitogorsk, and as deputy chairman of the Council of Ministers gave Sredmash direct access to the highest level of government.[51] But Zaveniagin died the following year and Vannikov temporarily replaced him.[52] In April 1957, Mikhail Pervukhin became minister. An experienced manager and top-level functionary (at the time of his appointment, he was deputy chairman of the Council of Ministers), Pervukhin also brought significant technical and economic expertise to the job. But his involvement with the "antiparty group" cost him his ministerial position after only a few months.[53]

The way was now clear for Efim Slavskii. Born in 1898 into a rural Ukrainian family, Slavskii joined the party when he was twenty, served in the Red Army for ten years (1918–1928), and after completing his studies at the Moscow Mining Academy, worked in the nonferrous metals industry. In 1940, he became director of the Dnepropetrovsk Aluminum Factory, and later director of the Urals Aluminum Factory. His political career started in 1945, when he became deputy people's commissar, and later deputy minister of nonferrous metals. In April 1946, he joined the atomic project as deputy director of the First Chief Administration (PGU). From 1947 to 1949, he was director of "Kombinat No. 817," the secret reprocessing facility at Cheliabinsk-40, before rising to deputy, and then first deputy director of the PGU.[54]

At Sredmash's inception in 1953, Slavskii became deputy minister. He directed its *Glavatom* subdivision from 1956 until 1957, when he became minister of the whole agency, an office he held for almost thirty years. He masterfully used the political authority his ministry inherited from the atomic bomb project to secure scarce resources and to strengthen his ministry's standing.[55] As a member of the Council of Ministers, Slavskii had access to the highest levels of decision making, and he exercised significant control over the planning and budgeting processes affecting his ministry's activities. Under his aegis, Sredmash retained its centralized, closed character and became a largely autonomous organization.[56]

Glavatom: Administering Peaceful Uses of Atomic Energy

Over time, several different suborganizations took on specific tasks in the administration of nuclear power plants. The aforementioned Glavatom, the Chief Administration—later the State Committee—for the Use of Atomic Energy, was one of them. Sredmash created this agency in the spring of 1956 to deal exclusively with peaceful applications of atomic energy, and—in contrast to the rest of Sredmash—to engage in international cooperation.[57] It was the only declassified part of Sredmash.[58] In the parlance of the time, peaceful applications encompassed a wide variety of fields and disciplines, including mechanical engineering, transportation, the food industry, biology, medicine, and power engineering.[59] Glavatom's second director was Vasilii Emelyianov, who was well known in the West as a member of the program committee for the first United Nations Conference on Peaceful Uses of Atomic Energy in 1955, the head of the Soviet delegation to that conference, and, from 1957 to 1959, a Soviet delegate to the International Atomic Energy Agency (IAEA).⁶⁰

On August 26, 1960, Khrushchev's government attempted to detach from Sredmash the management of reactors operated exclusively for civilian uses by elevating Glavatom from a Chief Administration under the ministry's control into a State Committee under the Council of Ministers.⁶¹ Emelyianov remained chairman of this Committee for the Use of Atomic Energy until February 1962, when Andranik Petrosyiants (previously Sredmash's deputy minister) assumed office. Petrosyiants would remain in this position until Sredmash ceased to exist in 1986; he represented the ministry in all international contacts and became a key public figure in international nuclear cooperation, especially in the Council for Mutual Economic Assistance (CMEA).⁶²

The new State Committee had an enormous apparatus: it comprised nine administrations and nine sections.⁶³ When it began reporting directly to the Council of Ministers, its members gained immediate access to decision makers but discovered that these decision makers also controlled the committee's activities more directly.⁶⁴

The Institute of Atomic Energy: Scientific Leadership for All Things Nuclear
In 1949, Kurchatov's Laboratory No. 2 became the Laboratory for Measuring Instruments of the Soviet Academy of Sciences (LIPAN SSSR) and, in 1956, the Institute of Atomic Energy (IAE), a name change that indicated its new, broader set of responsibilities.⁶⁵ From its founding until his death in 1960, Kurchatov served as director, and the institute has been known since his death as the Kurchatov Institute.⁶⁶

According to David Holloway's well-documented portrayal, Kurchatov's personality and the shock he experienced on the detonation of the first Soviet hydrogen bomb were driving forces in the transition to the civilian use of nuclear energy and crucial for the declassification (or, more precisely, the lack of classification in the first place) of fusion research.⁶⁷ The personal clout Kurchatov gained from the nuclear weapons program allowed him liberties unheard of in the Stalinist and post-Stalinist Soviet Union. Although a committed communist, he was able to create and maintain an atmosphere in his institute that provided a refuge for science and scientists largely shielded from the practical consequences of political ideology.⁶⁸ On January 15, 1960, in his last public speech at the meeting of the Supreme Soviet, the Soviet Union's highest legislative body, Kurchatov said: "I am happy that I was born in Russia and dedicated my abilities to the atomic science of the great country of the Soviets."⁶⁹

Dividing Responsibilities for Nuclear Power Plants

Both Sredmash and Minenergo would later establish additional suborganizations to administer aspects of the nuclear power program. Meanwhile, at the ministry level, the tensions between them continued. In the late 1950s and early 1960s, Sredmash operated reactors that produced weapons-grade nuclear materials and, starting in the late 1950s, outfitted nuclear-powered submarines and icebreakers. Minenergo, on the other hand, operated hydropower and fossil fuel plants, provided municipal heating, and continued to expand the country's electricity grid, while trying to establish a unified system to coordinate it all.[70] As I have mentioned, Sredmash and Minenergo disagreed over professional expertise, competed for political patronage, and questioned each other's trustworthiness in nuclear matters. Both ministries were extraordinarily powerful. Slavskii headed an industrial empire protected by skillfully deployed rhetoric of military heroism and well-maintained connections to top-level decision makers. Minenergo was a giant empire in its own right, with a long institutional tradition and high-level political patronage. Neither Slavskii nor Neporozhnii needed nuclear power to legitimize their importance, and yet, starting in the early 1960s, both ministers decided to promote nuclear power over the skepticism of planners.[71]

One question Soviet nuclear policymakers struggled with was whether nuclear power plants should be managed on a par with conventional power plants.[72] Were they novel, essentially different, and uniquely risky technologies, or were they just another technology used to turn water into steam?[73] In August 1966, the Council of Ministers implicitly answered that question when it transferred responsibilities for nuclear power plants, both operating and under construction, from Sredmash to Minenergo.[74] The move seemed all too logical: Sredmash was busy with military assignments and ultimately had little interest in handling the day-to-day business of operating, maintaining, and repairing civilian reactors. Minenergo, by contrast, was eager to integrate such powerful modern facilities into its existing fleet of power plants.

The Council made Minenergo responsible for planning, management, construction, assembly, and operation of nuclear power plants, while Sredmash would continue to conduct scientific research, design and develop reactors, and provide documentation containing technical specifications and component drawings for specialized equipment to the respective factories. Sredmash would also keep supplying fuel assemblies for the reactors.[75] The State Planning Commission (Gosplan) would serve as the coordinating agency.[76]

With the transfer of the nuclear power plants, Minenergo took control of a number of engineering colleges, planning and construction institutes, and experimental facilities.[77] It also took responsibility for recruiting the nuclear industry's workforce, and Minenergo's leadership set up specialized training centers for operating personnel.[78] As part of a conscious strategy to preserve expertise and tacit knowledge, the ministry "imported" countless individuals from Sredmash to serve in key positions. Minenergo clearly intended to bring their personal experience, as well as their home institution's institutional expertise and professional culture, to the new organizations it was establishing, but as we will see in chapter 3, the two ministries' organizational cultures would not always blend well.

Soiuzatomenergo: Reviving Minenergo's Nuclear Competencies
One of Minenergo's deputy ministers took on responsibility specifically for nuclear plants.[79] The ministry's Chief Administration Glavatomenergo was reinstated, and Artem Grigoriants, former chief engineer at Obninsk and veteran of Sredmash's State Committee for the Use of Atomic Energy, became its director.[80] At the time of the transfer, the Beloiarsk and Novo-Voronezh nuclear power reactors were operating; several more were under construction and in the planning stage.[81]

Over the years following the transfer, Minenergo would create additional organizations to support the increasing number of nuclear power plants. The Council of Ministers decreed on May 23, 1978, that Glavatomenergo would cease to exist and the newly created All-Union Industrial Association for Nuclear Power (*Soiuzatomenergo*) would become the sole specialized industrial-economic nuclear energy organization within Minenergo. The proto-organization for today's "Rosenergoatom," Soiuzatomenergo encompassed nuclear power plants as well as scientific research institutes and specialized support organizations.[82] It was responsible for realizing a cohesive scientific-technical nuclear power policy, and for the timely start-up and safe operation of nuclear power plants.[83] *Atomenergonaladka*, an industrial enterprise responsible for the maintenance of nuclear power plants, and *Atomenergoremont*, in charge of repairing nuclear power plant equipment, supported Soiuzatomenergo's work.[84] In 1979, Minenergo would set up the All-Union Research Institute for the Operation of Nuclear Power Plants (VNIIAES) to provide research support to Soiuzatomenergo.

Meanwhile, Sredmash was still operating military nuclear reactors and nuclear power reactor prototypes. That ministry too tried to ensure adequate training of the reactor operators, as well as mechanisms to ensure the reliability of difficult transitions in nuclear reactors. One of these mechanisms was the deployment of so-called start-up commissions (*puskovye komissii*), which consisted of representatives of the design institutes, the engineering bureaus, and the organizations in charge of the reactor's future operation as well as specialists from other plants and senior colleagues. The commission supervised the start-up of every new reactor, a particularly difficult phase, and turned it over to the operators only once it reached a stable level of operation.[85] Other mechanisms to ease transitions included a quality control service (the so-called *avtorskii nadzor*) provided by the designer as well as a system of operational inspections.[86]

Despite having delegated the reactors' routine, efficient, and safe operation to Minenergo, Sredmash remained in charge of the "hearts" of the nuclear power plants, the reactors themselves. Its research and engineering institutes continued to design the reactors, produce and deliver the fuel elements, and provide general advice and technical supervision for the plants.[87] Sredmash also kept the authority to decide whether a particular nuclear power plant or research institute would be transferred to Minenergo in the first place.

Even after Minenergo took over many responsibilities connected with nuclear power in 1966, idiosyncrasies in the organizational framework governing the industry remained. For example, consider the story of the Leningrad nuclear power plant. Back in the late 1950s, Minenergo had planned this plant and its experts had picked the site for what was to become a powerful generating station for the nearby metropolis. Apparently, Kurchatov himself had proposed installing a pressurized water reactor based on pioneering prototypes then being completed in Southern Russia, at the Novo-Voronezh nuclear site.[88]

In March 1958, Minenergo was managing the construction of the Leningrad plant, but problems with the delivery of equipment for the pressurized water reactor type continued.[89] By December of the same year, a report from Minenergo to the Central Committee mentioned, for the first time, another reactor design. Accordingly, the Scientific Research Institute No. 8 (NII-8, the future NIKIET) was conducting work "on the design of an improved reactor of the type AMB"—an abbreviation used for the graphite-water design under construction at the Beloiarsk site.[90] This "improved design" would be approved for the "Leningrad nuclear power plant" a decade later, in 1967,[91] at which point the site changed and Sredmash took over construction work.[92] From then on, the Leningrad nuclear power plant remained under Sredmash's control.[93] In addition to Leningrad, Sredmash would also retain control of the breeder reactor at Shevchenko (which went operational in 1973), and the Lithuanian nuclear power reactors (the first of which started operation in 1982).[94]

Sredmash's Glavatomenergo (GU-16): Controlling Nuclear Design
Like Minenergo's, Sredmash's internal structure continued to evolve. In 1967, Sredmash put nuclear power engineering under its newly established Chief Administration 16 (GU-16), also known as Glavatomenergo (which confusingly shares a name with Minenergo's nuclear administration).[95] The leading scientific-technical institutes, construction bureaus, and experimental centers dealing with nuclear power, as well as new nuclear power plants, reported directly to GU-16.[96] The specialists there not only administered the construction of nuclear reactors; they were also in charge of scientific and technical support. While relying on the expertise of specialists from chief scientific research institutes and design and construction organizations, the experts in GU-16 were in charge of making all final technical decisions.[97] The GU-16 was thus a crucial link in the chain from design to implementation in the Soviet nuclear power industry.

Kurchatov's Legacy at the Institute of Atomic Energy
In 1975, the Institute of Atomic Energy strengthened its ties with the Soviet Academy of Sciences (of which the institute remained a part) when Anatolii Aleksandrov, Kurchatov's successor as the institute's director, became president of the Academy. Aleksandrov was a unique figure in the Soviet nuclear industry. He first stepped into the spotlight when he temporarily took over Petr Kapitsa's position as the director of the Institute of Physical Problems in 1946. Kapitsa, who Stalin had appointed to the Special Committee on August 20, 1945, overtly refused to cooperate with Beria on the atomic bomb project and wrote to Stalin complaining about Beria's management style. He lost his position, but not his freedom.[98]

After Kapitsa was reinstated in 1955, Aleksandrov became Kurchatov's deputy at the Institute of Atomic Energy. He was personally involved in the development and design of pressurized water reactors and very publicly presented the implementation of such reactors for propulsion in nuclear icebreakers.[99] Aleksandrov also advocated for other designs, including graphite-water reactors developed in cooperation with Nikolai Dollezhal's institute, which had built the country's plutonium-producing reactors (see chapter 4). Despite the fact that large parts of his publication record remain classified, Aleksandrov became the poster scientist for advertising the enormous progress achieved in the field of nuclear power engineering.[100]

The Interdepartmental Technical Council (MVTS): Making Nuclear Policy
Only insiders know about Aleksandrov's role as chairman of the Interdepartmental Technical Council on Nuclear Power Plants (MVTS), the single most influential nuclear policymaking agency, established by government decree in September 1971.[101] This council coordinated all scientific and technical policies and activities relating to the growth of the nuclear power industry and ensured that these policies were actually realized during the design, construction, and operational phases. The council's decisions were binding for all ministries and their enterprises. Council members included the top representatives of all leading ministries, experts from Gosplan's Department for Energy and Electrification, and members of the Academy of Sciences, along with representatives of scientific research institutes, design bureaus, various industrial organizations, and other specialists in nuclear power and closely related fields of science, technology, and production (figure 2.2).[102] Despite this broad definition of the country's nuclear elite, one minister was conspicuously absent from the council for its first five years: although his ministry had built and operated most nuclear power plants since 1966, Petr Neporozhnii of Minenergo became a member of this influential board only on May 28, 1976.[103]

The Interdepartmental Technical Council met three or four times a year, for several days at a time. Unfortunately, only the overall meeting topics, not the content of the detailed technical discussions, have been published.[104] The day-to-day functioning of this huge apparatus was facilitated by Sredmash's Scientific-Technical Council (NTS), an internal, strictly classified council responsible for technical nuclear policies—among them nuclear safety. The Scientific-Technical Council prepared, and pre-approved, all nuclear policies before they reached interdepartmental agencies, or executive and legislative organs.[105] For example, the Scientific-Technical Council approved a set of safety regulations (OPB-73) on January 11, 1972,[106] before the Interdepartmental Technical Council endorsed them on February 19, 1973, after three months of deliberation. Another example of this procedure was the modernization of pressurized water reactors (VVERs). After extensive discussions in Sredmash's Scientific-Technical Council about whether steel containments for VVER reactors would increase their safety, the Interdepartmental Technical Council decided on January 19, 1976, to adopt the containment as a standard feature of all future VVERs.[107] The Interdepartmental Technical Council therefore relied on Sredmash's internal Scientific-Technical Council not only for scientific expertise and technical recommendations, but also for established organizational routines.

Figure 2.2
Nuclear decision makers: The minister of Medium Machine Building (Sredmash), Efim P. Slavskii (left), and the president of the Soviet Academy of Sciences and director of the Kurchatov Institute of Atomic Energy, Anatolii P. Aleksandrov, were the two most powerful men in the Soviet nuclear industry. Their approval effectively decided where new nuclear power plants would be built, what reactor design would be chosen, and which engineering bureau would be awarded a contract.
Source: Courtesy of Petr A. Aleksandrov and the publishing house "Master," Moscow. Originally published in A. I. Vol'skii and A. B. Chubais, eds., *Elektroenergetika*, series *Stroiteli Rossii: XX vek* (Moscow: "Master," 2003), 108. Reprinted with permission.

Governing Nuclear Power at the All-Union Level

While Sredmash and Minenergo refined their internal structures, changes were also underway in the larger, Union-level entities that governed the two ministries. Often miniscule pockets of nuclear expertise in the central bureaucracies—the Council of Ministers, the Party's Central Committee, Gosplan, and others—rarely seem to have worked together to ensure a coordinated nuclear energy policy. Rather, they seem to have existed mainly to give their respective bosses justification for participating in nuclear policymaking. In the following section, I discuss only those bodies that directly and meaningfully contributed to the choice of nuclear reactor designs: as critics, enablers, or supervisors.[108]

The Central Committee's Sector for Nuclear Energy

In 1969, Vladimir Maryin, an experienced power engineer who participated in the construction of the Novo-Voronezh nuclear power plant, joined the Central Committee's Department of Heavy Industry and Energy as an expert advisor *(instruktor)* on nuclear energy. According to Grigorii Medvedev, who during the late 1970s worked for Soiuzatomenergo, Maryin was a hands-on, pragmatic administrator who provided direct and personal assistance to managers at nuclear construction sites, sometimes bypassing Minenergo's languid process. In the early 1980s, the Central Committee finally created a Sector for Nuclear Energy in its Department of Heavy Industry and Energy and added staff support to Maryin's one-man enterprise.[109] One of the new staff members was Gennadii Shasharin, a power engineer–turned–nuclear expert, who would later become Minenergo's deputy minister for nuclear power plants. Another was Georgii Kopchinskii, a nuclear engineer who was director of the Smolensk nuclear power plant before accepting an administrative position in Moscow.[110] Working for this sector, at least for a limited amount of time, was not necessarily a logical career step for enthusiastic nuclear power engineers, but the Central Committee gave the sector's staff significant authority in supervising the nuclear industry, including the otherwise "untouchable" reactor designers and engineers. As we will see in chapter 5, this led to some conflict over the RBMK reactor, even prior to Chernobyl. Most importantly, the industry-minded staff of the Central Committee's sector challenged the designers' implied assumption that civilian operators would be just as capable as operators of military reactors at working around a reactor's erratic performance.[111]

Gosplan's Department of Energy and Electrification

The Department of Energy and Electrification within Gosplan long predates the nuclear industry, but once the government started allocating funds to nuclear power plants, the department took on responsibility for those plants.[112] Aleksei Pavlenko, the former minister for power plants, ran the department from 1959 until his retirement in 1974. He was in charge of site selection, orchestrated the site-development process, and took part in the consideration and confirmation of designs and cost estimates. His department drew up one-year and five-year plans, analyzed the experience gained from already-operating nuclear plants, developed long-term perspectives for nuclear power development, and oversaw the execution of all these plans. Pavlenko's department also monitored factories handling production orders for the nuclear industry, including on-site visits by specialists.[113]

Nuclear Oversight Authorities

Attempts to secure and regulate the safety of industrial work under Soviet rule go back to the mining industry of the early 1920s. Soviet nuclear regulation originated in the "State Service for Radiation Safety Control" established in 1946 at Laboratory No. 2 (*Gosudarstvennaia sluzhba kontrolia radiatsionnoi bezopasnosti*). From 1958 to 1970, Sredmash, with assistance from the Ministry of Health and Laboratory V at Obninsk, performed nuclear safety oversight for all nuclear facilities. Glavatomenergo, meanwhile, drafted their first version of nuclear safety rules in 1957, long before nuclear power plants officially came under Minenergo's authority, and modeled them on the safety rules already in force for conventional power plants.[114] In 1966, the year Minenergo took responsibility for nuclear power plants, the ministry set up an organization called "State Technical and Mining Oversight Committee for the Power Industry" (*Gosgorenergotekhnadzor*).[115] This new inspectorate operated in addition to the already-existing "State Technical and Mining Inspectorate" (*Gosgortekhnadzor*), an organization responsible for the safety of mining operations and industrial safety, and had to ensure the safety of industrial work specifically at power plant construction sites.

The first documents spelling out nuclear safety regulations as such were written in 1963 and 1964 and approved in 1968.[116] On October 22, 1970, the Council of Ministers divided nuclear safety oversight over the construction and operation of nuclear power plants and research reactors among the Ministry of Health, Sredmash, and Gosgortekhnadzor. Gosgortekhnadzor subsequently oversaw the safety of the construction and operation of nuclear plants, while Sredmash was to guarantee the supervision of nuclear safety. In March 1971, the Soviet Academy of Sciences raised the issue of nuclear power plant safety in a communication with Gosplan and specifically suggested harmonizing domestic safety regulations with international practice.[117] That same year, Gosgortekhnadzor, the Ministry of Health, Sredmash, and Minenergo developed and temporarily adopted a set of rules and regulations on nuclear power plant safety, and a few years later, in 1974, a declassified version of the document (*Obshchie polozheniia obespecheniia bezopasnosti pri proektirovanii, stroitel'stve i ekspluatatsii AES*, OPB-73) would become the first legally binding nuclear safety legislation.[118]

In 1972, Sredmash created a specialized State Oversight Committee for Nuclear Safety (*Gosatomnadzor*) that replaced the nuclear safety supervision at nuclear power plants that the institute of the scientific director provided. (At the time, the Institute of Physics and Power Engineering supervised the

Beloiarsk plant, and the Kurchatov Institute of Atomic Energy supervised the Novo-Voronezh plant.)[119] However, this new agency remained under the control of Sredmash, whose leadership questioned the necessity of strict nuclear safety rules.[120] A new nuclear safety division within Gosgortekhnadzor and within the Ministry of Health complemented Gosatomnadzor's work.[121]

It was not until 1983 that the Soviet government created the independent State Oversight Committee for the Safe Conduct of Work in the Nuclear Power Industry (*Gosatomenergonadzor*), which replaced the earlier oversight agency under Sredmash.[122] Evgenii Kulov, previously deputy minister of Sredmash, became Gosatomenergonadzor's first chairman, a role equivalent in rank to a minister.[123] Gosatomenergonadzor supervised three areas: nuclear power plant safety, design work, and the production of equipment for nuclear power plants.[124] The nuclear fuel cycle and other, non-civilian nuclear applications remained under Sredmash's exclusive control.[125]

It is worth emphasizing that this agency handled oversight, control, and inspection—not regulation. The difference was more than merely semantic because it reflected the fact that the Soviet committee and its Western cousins took on different tasks. It was only in 1992 that the now Russian agency became a regulatory agency, which, in addition to having safety oversight, also developed normative documents and issued licenses.[126]

One possible explanation for the extraordinarily slowness with which the Soviet Union established an independent supervisory agency for its nuclear industry may be that the state owned all assets. That prevented the separation of operating and regulating accountability that the United States, for example, imposed by giving license provider and licensee equal but separate responsibilities for nuclear safety. In the Soviet Union, by contrast, different tiers and levels in a hierarchical management system traditionally had different safety responsibilities.[127] The authors of Soviet nuclear safety regulations faced the enduring problem that the state was in charge of all nuclear safety functions. When leaders eventually subsumed the management of all nuclear power plants under one roof, this problem not only remained, it in fact intensified. In 1982, partly as a reaction to the Three Mile Island accident in the United States, Soviet officials revised the original nuclear safety regulations (OPB-73) and approved an updated version, OPB-82.[128]

As this short chronology of organizational design in the Soviet nuclear sector has shown, the bureaucracies in charge of managing the Soviet nuclear industry and their changing degrees of autonomy significantly shaped decisions that were supposedly purely technical. The emerging map of responsibilities in the nuclear sector determined how decision makers assessed the role of nuclear power for the country's energy mix, the industry's growth potential, and the technical designs best suited to achieving these goals.

The Transfer Revisited

Authorities intended for the 1966 transfer of responsibilities for nuclear power plants from Sredmash to Minenergo to create a rational, effective framework for managing the civilian nuclear sector, but the complicated division of labor that ensued did not provide a definitive answer to the question of how best to manage nuclear power plants. As we have seen, the state planners' intention of creating an organizational framework that would rationally balance nuclear energy's military heritage with the conventional power industry's requirements ran up against considerable obstacles. Struggles over organizing a workable division of labor between Sredmash and Minenergo involved the implicit (and after Chernobyl explicit) question about which values—secrecy and military discipline on the one hand, or plan-oriented efficiency on the other—should govern the construction, operation, and regulation of nuclear power plants. This interministerial rivalry not only threatened to jeopardize indispensable cooperation between the two sectors; it in fact prevented the proactive design of an organization to manage the civilian nuclear industry and instead forced planners to incrementally expand existing infrastructures. This ultimately obscured professional accountability, while reinforcing existing institutional boundaries.[129]

In entrusting Minenergo with operating nuclear power plants, Soviet authorities assumed that nuclear specialists had learned to contain the risks of controlled nuclear fission, that the available reactor designs and already-working reactors demonstrated this accomplishment, that appropriate organizational structures were in place, and that reliable technical professionals would guarantee the safe operation of nuclear power plants. The transfer of nuclear power plants to Minenergo thus signified that the Soviet Union had mastered nuclear technology and normalized nuclear fission. Those in charge deemed that civilian engineers whose work ethic no longer reflected the institutional culture of the nuclear weapons program, but instead that of industry and production, were fit to operate nuclear power reactors.

Ostensibly, Sredmash tried to meet the unique requirements of nuclear power plants, particularly those with novel reactor designs, after the transfer.[130] The division of responsibilities, however, implied a hierarchy of expertise in which the Sredmash leadership considered Minenergo's nuclear capabilities inferior to their own. This attitude, in turn, deepened existing rivalries and blurred responsibilities. More fundamentally, it led to asymmetries in the degree of agency, level of experience, and access to and distribution of knowledge.

With the benefit of hindsight, nuclear specialists sometimes call the transfer of nuclear power plants from Sredmash to Minenergo a big mistake, invoking Minenergo's supposed lack of military discipline and qualified specialists. Some nuclear experts claim that Minenergo was not ready organizationally for its new responsibilities at the time of the transfer.[131] Such critics emphasize that the positive attributes of a semimilitary organization were lost, while new civilian forms were developing very slowly.[132] Some even claim that the Chernobyl disaster was a direct result of immature managerial reorganizations and that comparable violations of operating instructions would not have happened under a stricter management. But hindsight is not always perfect, and this judgment is in fact too categorical. The maturity, reliability, and "safety culture" of any given organization, or system of interconnected organizations, only becomes fully evident after an accident. As the leading Soviet nuclear safety authority, Viktor Sidorenko, cautioned, the judgment that Minenergo was "not ready" organizationally

can be easily challenged by recollecting events that happened during the development of the military atomic project (suffice it to remember the Kyshtym accident, where a nuclear waste storage facility exploded), as well as by recalling the accidents at the Leningrad [nuclear power plant], which was under the control of [Sredmash] (not with the same catastrophic consequences as at Chernobyl's unit 4, but clearly a "harbinger" of the Chernobyl accident that did not receive due attention).[133]

And yet at the same time, Sidorenko insists that the military-style organization of nuclear power plant management under Sredmash did compensate for and balance out a general lack of "safety culture" in the Soviet Union.[134] According to him, Sredmash's paramilitary management style was characterized by a keen sense of personal accountability, efficient decision-making processes, careful recruitment practices, and the possibility of exchanging information even under conditions of intense secrecy.[135] Perhaps this was because "we were personally accountable; we answered with our 'skin' for operational safety," as Boris Dubovskii, a late veteran of the Soviet nuclear weapons program, recalled. Such accountability, efficiency, and care were critical because, as one of my interviewees put it, "You can't put a soldier with an automatic rifle behind each power plant operator."[136]

In contrast to Sredmash, Minenergo was an unambiguously civilian agency that confidently dismissed secrecy and elitism in favor of competent pragmatism and economic rationality.[137] Power engineers, not always trained nuclear experts, were responsible for Minenergo's nuclear power plant management, and one thing these managers lacked was Sredmash's extensive system of research support. Minenergo's priority was to push an ambitious construction schedule of new plants, and over time, the specifics of nuclear technologies became diluted as leaders increasingly subordinated them to the demands of generating competitively priced electricity for the national grid.

Although authorities tried to preserve the knowledge of Sredmash's semimilitary organization and provided the new nuclear power workforce with training at the best institutions in the country, the transfer entailed unanticipated changes in work routines and priorities.[138] As I detail in chapter 3, only after Chernobyl did nuclear experts reconsider the significance of on-the-job training, which had been Sredmash's dominant practice. The normalization of nuclear technology, these experts recognized, had not clarified the accountability of the organizations involved.

Conclusion: Organizational Changes and Institutional Cultures

The institutional framework for managing the nuclear power industry in the Soviet Union emerged only gradually, over several decades, despite continuing efforts to develop the best organizational form.[139] Rapid expansion and struggles for control among the ministries involved characterized the industry's development. The ongoing reorganizations and reassignments of tasks—which ultimately also assigned or denied expertise, responsibility, and accountability—reflected these struggles. Organizational shifts were attempts at reflecting the new technology's requirements, which only gradually revealed themselves as the numbers of nuclear power plants grew. These organizational changes were also devices to establish social, political, and legal order. The resulting bureaucracies provided clear hierarchies, a division of labor and power, and a system of accountability.[140] The positions Sredmash and Minenergo held in the Soviet state's bureaucracy determined what they perceived as the greatest risk (the risk of technical failure or the risk of economic loss) and how these differing risk perceptions affected not only attitudes, but the division of tasks and responsibilities. The ongoing reorganization of the civilian nuclear sector, the debates over the special (or not-so-special) status of nuclear power plants, and the consequent intervention of bureaucratic organizations contradict prevailing assumptions about how a centralized, planned economy worked.

As we saw in the previous chapter, the constant reforms affecting the Soviet economy in general also affected Minenergo, and, to a lesser extent, Sredmash, but the fact that their respective leaders stayed in power for such long periods of time balanced out some of these instabilities. Both Slavskii and Neporozhnii had worked their way up the social ladder through engineering careers and service in party organizations.[141] The fact that their ministries were cornerstones of Soviet foreign policy and the economy, respectively, protected them from ongoing, and often drastic, economic reforms.[142] Only the combination of Chernobyl with the imminent collapse of Soviet institutions during *perestroika* provided the final blows to Minenergo's obsession with growth and to Sredmash's aspirations to secrecy-clad autarchy within the state.

Finally, the goal of standardization motivated the transfer of nuclear reactor technology from Sredmash's secret, semimilitary organization to Minenergo's highly visible civilian organization.[143] In their efforts to improve the economic efficiency of nuclear power plants vis-à-vis other power plants, Soviet leaders and industry managers viewed standardization as the most promising strategy, both technically and managerially. They aimed to bring the price of nuclear power down by scaling up to reach greater power capacities, by reducing the complexity of auxiliary systems and fuel construction, and by using nuclear fuel more intensely.[144] But in a young industry that essentially consisted of prototypes, these planners struggled with determining which technology was mature enough for standardization and ultimately mass implementation.

Not only did the Soviet nuclear power industry have a dual origin, it also performed until 1966 a dual and somewhat paradoxical function: as part of a highly secret industry shielded from the outside world and as valuable propaganda for Soviet science and technology.[145] The 1966 transfer of tasks and responsibilities, of artifacts and cadres both made nuclear power routine and established the norm that this was how nuclear plants *should* be managed. What made this normalization possible was the nuclear industry's emerging organizational infrastructure. This infrastructure helped bridge the major boundary between civilian and military nuclear applications. At the same time, the new organizational infrastructure justified a specific division of tasks and responsibilities, reaffirmed distinct institutional cultures, and reinforced discrete professional identities. Responsibilities in this emerging nuclear bureaucracy determined how scientists and engineers, political decision makers, economic planners, and the rank-and-file nuclear workforce thought about nuclear energy's relevance. In other words, the organizations that managed the emerging nuclear industry not only reflected the specific character of a centralized state bureaucracy or the goals of a planned economy. They also actively defined technical features of the reactors ultimately chosen for mass implementation and delineated tasks for the country's nuclear workforce: their required level of expertise, their understanding of risk, and their commitment to safety.

3 Training Nuclear Experts: A Workforce for the Nuclear Industry

To train qualified cadres for the Soviet civilian nuclear power industry, its architects engaged in an ongoing discussion about the kind and amount of knowledge these workers required. How much did a plant operator need to know to safely operate a reactor and prevent an accident? Asked another way, should trainers hold back certain technical knowledge from plant operators to save training time or preserve security? When *Sredmash* outsourced nuclear power plants to *Minenergo* in August 1966, these were far from academic questions.[1]

In this chapter, I examine how the transfer precipitated the loss of crucial experiential skills, of implicit knowledge, and of practices, routines, and unspoken protocols. Formal accounts of nuclear personnel training seldom acknowledge this kind of unspoken knowledge, except occasionally in the wake of an accident.[2] But Soviet managers at the time of the transfer were deeply concerned about the loss of knowledge and experience and tried to correct it.

The allocation of all nuclear design and engineering tasks to Sredmash and all nonnuclear construction and planning tasks to Minenergo affected not only which workers knew what. It also reinforced clearly delineated and bounded professional identities among the various strata of nuclear industry personnel. The most prominent distinction was between the specialists working for Sredmash, the so-called *atomshchiki,* and those working for Minenergo, the so-called *energetiki*. In the wake of the Chernobyl disaster, those who sought to assign blame emphasized the distinction between engineers with nuclear credentials and power engineers with nonnuclear backgrounds.[3] Official press reports depicted technical specialists who happened to work for Minenergo at the time of the accident as mere operators and put Sredmash employees in the role of heroic scientists and patriotic engineers whose only mistake had been to entrust civilian operators with a task beyond their level of expertise.

However, such a clearcut distinction between the skills, roles, and expertise of atomshchiki and energetiki is difficult to maintain. In this chapter, I present a more nuanced picture of Soviet nuclear power workers, examining their recruitment, training, roles, and professional identities. I trace how this workforce defined itself through both its work and its organizational alliances, and I contrast the self-concept of nuclear experts working in research, development, and teaching with that of the power industry professionals, who worked at actual nuclear plants, and under the pressures of economic planning.

To fully appreciate these distinctions, it helps to look first at a nuclear power plant as a complex, entangled sociotechnical system that combines human agency and technical operations.[4] Actual operating experience and specific political, economic, and cultural contexts determine how much weight the different parts of this system have and the interactions among those parts. For example, when the U.S. nuclear power program began, recurring incidents of human error in nuclear plants led to increased automation.[5] In the Soviet Union, by contrast, encounters with highly unreliable instrumentation at the first nuclear installations led industry leaders to drastically improve training and deliberately increase their reliance on human expertise, experience, and intuition in the control room.[6] In part because Soviet planners considered their operators so highly skilled, they built their nuclear power plants without some of the redundant safety features most Western plants required. Viewed as sociotechnical systems, Soviet nuclear power plants relied on technical specialists and their efficient performance *as* redundancy features.

The sociotechnical system didn't consist solely of individuals, technologies, and organizations, but of underlying historical, economic, and geopolitical contexts that actively shaped what designers considered functional, profitable, and safe technologies, what educators deemed certifiable qualifications, and how industrial managers orchestrated complex workplace labor processes. Finally, the Soviet system counted on each individual's contribution to the country's economic productivity and pursued a policy of full employment: the state had a vested interest in employing specialists who had received tuition-free higher education at a level appropriate to their training. While reassignments were quite common, especially in new industries such as the nuclear sector, reassignments to lower posts and layoffs were rare and typically indicated a demotion. These contexts influenced which expert was selected for which position, what knowledge was codified, who received access to which information, and how these different ways of knowing in turn shaped professional (and sometimes very personal) identities.

Most of the scientists and engineers who organized the Soviet nuclear industry were part of Stalin's new intelligentsia of "white-collar technocrats." Especially in the context of the Chernobyl disaster, their pragmatic attitude and the fact that they cooperated with the Soviet regime—and the Stalinist regime for that matter—raise the question of whether this association corrupted and discredited science. The post-Chernobyl debate allows unique insights into earlier, and more general, attitudes in the nuclear energy community. The intensity that for decades has characterized debates about Chernobyl suggests that rather than cynicism, deep commitment and an often personal conviction of the necessity and rationality of nuclear energy permeated this heterogeneous community of experts.[7]

Soviet scientists and engineers had helped create the industrial base the nuclear weapons project needed. The detonation of the first Soviet atomic bomb in 1949 earned them high honors, and they subsequently enjoyed unprecedented liberties in an otherwise heavily regulated society.[8] Some of these experts moved into administrative positions, but even those who stayed in research and development enjoyed privileged standing among top decision-making bodies in the state-party system. Recent Russian publications celebrate them as ingenious creators who altruistically devoted their lives and talents to their fatherland.[9] This spirit of duty and inevitability persisted within the nuclear sector for decades to come. But celebrating an accomplished elite obscures the fact that even during the atomic bomb project, when leaders could quote the motto *"nado"* (it's necessary) and send anyone with some technical training to a military facility, the military-industrial complex experienced an enduring shortage of qualified cadres.

This may seem surprising, because Soviet leaders had begun early on to train an army of engineers to facilitate rapid industrialization and economic progress, and by the end of the 1960s, the Soviet Union had achieved an internationally acclaimed level in engineering education.[10] Not only was technical training among the most prestigious kinds of higher education, it also provided major opportunities for professional and social advancement. The growing nuclear industry promised aspiring scientists and engineers particularly compelling careers.

As I showed in chapter 1, civilian nuclear power needed an enormous industrial base that barely existed when planners charted the program's rapid growth. In addition to bottlenecks in the supply industry, planners faced a significant shortage of qualified personnel to operate the growing number of nuclear power plants. The scale and complexity of the staffing problem in the nuclear industry can hardly be overestimated. The shortage of qualified nuclear specialists began to subside only slowly, as institutions of higher education put together specialized curricula tailored explicitly to the future nuclear power workforce and graduated the first cohorts of students in the early 1960s.

A Career in the Nuclear Industry

As in the United States and elsewhere, the entire first generation of cadres for the Soviet nuclear program was not formally trained in nuclear physics or engineering because such programs did not yet exist.[11] A prominent example is Nikolai Dollezhal, a mechanical engineer from a very modest background who advanced from working in the chemical industry to designing the reactors that produced plutonium for Soviet nuclear bombs. Dollezhal subsequently became the director of one of the country's most important, and most secret, research and development institutes for nuclear reactors.[12] His institute, later called Scientific Research and Design Institute of Energy Technologies (NIKIET), built, among many other nuclear things, the RBMK, the Chernobyl-type reactor.

During the weapons program, recruiters hired young specialists with general technical education straight out of college. These young people entered a highly secretive environment and received specialized training on the job. The military, national security, and scientific elements of their new work situation not only shaped the young organization's initial mission, but also determined its qualities once it became a ministry.[13] Sredmash never answered to the military; rather, it could rely on its own paramilitary units for construction purposes (and, incidentally, for accident mitigation).

Working for Sredmash was not just a job that involved special permits and secured workplaces: working for Sredmash was a way of life. Some of its characteristic features were readiness to abandon work routines at short notice and to sacrifice personal commitments for duties significant to state security. In return for such sacrifice, Sredmash employees usually received good salaries, and, as compensation for a certain degree of social isolation, had access to superior food, exceptional healthcare, free public transportation, and adequate housing.[14] This was true not only for those who lived in secret cities behind barbed wire, but also for those who lived what by Soviet standards were regular lives.[15] Nuclear employees often married other nuclear employees, and it was not unusual for their children to pursue careers in the nuclear industry as well.

Three Communist Party practices affected which individuals ended up in nuclear professions. First, the party had long relied on the practice of *vydvizhenie*, the promotion of individuals from working-class backgrounds, for recruitment. Arguably, an education in engineering played a similar role in the Soviet Union of the 1920s.[16] Training in engineering allowed ambitious individuals from modest backgrounds not only to establish themselves as members of a revered profession, but to advance quickly into the political elites.[17] Engineering graduates thus benefited disproportionately from the Soviet system, which in turn considered them politically reliable.[18]

Specialized programs in nuclear physics and engineering initially appeared within existing engineering departments.[19] Universities formed new curricula that combined theoretical instruction at the country's leading technical colleges with practical training at select research and design institutes, at the nuclear power plant in Obninsk, and at secret nuclear facilities.[20] These programs were initially highly restricted, with even lecture notes subject to classification.[21] Depending on their grades, graduates could often choose among several offers, ranging from jobs at the first industrial-scale nuclear power plants to positions at secret nuclear installations.[22] This flexibility in choosing positions was somewhat unusual, given the highly regulated nature of the Soviet labor market.

In return for receiving higher education free of charge, graduates of Soviet universities and polytechnic institutes had to serve for a certain amount of time (usually three years) in a position assigned to them. This system of selecting, training, and assigning recent college graduates was known as *raspredelenie*. Raspredelenie literally means "distribution," and refers to the mechanism that matched the least experienced part of the country's workforce with the requirements of the country's economy. The raspredelenie system encountered problems common to the entire Soviet economy: enterprises had to request specialists so far in advance that their needs had usually changed by the time these graduates actually arrived. *Gosplan*, the agency administering the process, usually assigned fewer graduates than enterprises asked for, which led those enterprises to request more than necessary just in case. On average only half of the young specialists arrived at positions that matched their training (*po spetsial'nosti*). The others ended up with less suitable work and even janitorial jobs, which understandably prompted many to leave their assignments early. Another problem was that graduates did not always go where they were sent, causing enterprises to increase their requests even more the next time.[23]

These problems seem to have affected the nuclear industry less than some others. Many saw the nuclear industry as a prestigious sector, an exciting new area of specialization, and a kind of work highly relevant for society as a whole. Furthermore, the country's need for nuclear experts was so great that those who had successfully completed a college program had very little chance of an inadequate assignment.[24]

Higher positions in the Soviet nuclear industry generally required Party membership, but most nuclear specialists seem to have considered joining more a ritual than a meaningful procedure. In those experts' belief system, duty, honor, and patriotism were more important than the Party, and their shared loyalty to these ideals increased cohesion within their field.[25] Still, the Party controlled appointments to key positions throughout the Soviet economy through a system called *nomenklatura*.[26]

Party functionaries cross-checked a list of appointments with a list of individuals they considered loyal, and, more often than not, qualified.[27] For example, the Party had to approve ministers, various top managers in the unions and the army, as well as enterprise directors. In the civilian nuclear industry, the nomenklatura system initially played a negligible role because the cohort of nuclear specialists was small. They were all needed, regardless of how strong their ideological convictions were.[28] When the industry grew, however, and especially once Minenergo appointed top-level staff at nuclear plants, an appropriate Party commission had to confirm nominations for plant director, chief engineer, and their supporting deputies.

Sometimes this practice led to considerable conflict and maneuvering—for example, when a Party commission opposed a candidate. Furthermore, the Party controlled the design of all institutions, the allocation of resources, and even the specification of administrative tasks.[29] Once the nuclear industry was established, the Party's Central Committee had to confirm, and in some cases even nominate, candidates for top positions. These positions included posts with mostly managerial duties, such as deputy minister, director or deputy director of a Chief Administration, and nuclear power plant director, but they also included technical posts such as chief engineer.

This process may have encouraged the transfer of individual specialists among institutions—after the Party had approved them in one position, chances were high it would approve them in another. Once the nuclear power industry was well underway, the nomenklatura system, although somewhat negotiable, generally required top-level appointees to demonstrate high political reliability in addition to their technical expertise.[30]

Professionalization: Training, Recruitment, Retention

Nuclear power specialists represented a new profession with its own organizations, institutional culture, and work ethic, and over time they developed a distinct professional identity as civilian nuclear power experts.[31] Initially, the industry drafted scientists and engineers from many backgrounds and trained them on the job. This practice compensated both for the shortage of highly qualified nuclear physicists and engineers and for the legacy of fear, secrecy, and discipline the nuclear weapons project acquired in the Stalin era. Later, when the emphasis on peaceful applications grew and economic efficiency became nuclear power's main priority, scientific and technical cadres increasingly trained in much more narrow, specialized areas in response to actual needs.

More and more, university-taught skills combined with practical training at relevant facilities became the norm. As training programs for nuclear power specialists expanded and became more standardized, the kind of experiential knowledge early nuclear specialists had been raised with gradually became less prevalent. On-the-job training for each specialist was no longer possible, and students had no way to acquire tacit knowledge without direct, personal guidance.

Educators who required students to do part of their thesis research on site at an actual nuclear plant clearly valued tacit knowledge, or knowledge that cannot be verbalized. This type of knowledge reaches beyond written instructions and codified rules. It's based on experience, on learning by doing, and often more on intuition than formal training.[32] For a long time, industry leaders underestimated the significance of these skills and conducted no research into how to preserve and teach them.[33] When Sredmash and Minenergo worked out the details of the civilian nuclear industry, they did not yet understand what tacit skills workers would need. Hence administrators conducted the frantic reorganizations I discussed in chapter 2 and the almost compulsive division of tasks I discuss below. As I have mentioned, when they redistributed tasks, these leaders typically transferred individual specialists and hoped they would bring along their tacit knowledge. Sometimes this worked, and sometimes it didn't. The loss of tacit knowledge during the transfer of nuclear power plants to Minenergo represented one of the fundamental challenges for the emerging Soviet nuclear industry, and I devote much of this chapter to the efforts by Soviet scientists, engineers, and planners to identify and preserve tacit skills.

A personnel initiative that dates to 1956, a decade before the transfer, illustrates the speed with which industry leaders had to train new workers—and how that speed further threatened access to tacit knowledge. Anticipating a series of new nuclear power plants, Konstantin Lavrenenko, director of Minenergo's Chief Administration for the Construction of Atomic Power Plants (*Glavatomenergo*), launched several personnel initiatives. He was clearly starting from scratch. According to the original schedule, the start-up of the Beloiarsk and Novo-Voronezh nuclear power plants was imminent, but Glavatomenergo had not yet figured out how to staff them: in its 1957 annual report, Lavrenenko's team considered various "management schemes of nuclear power plants, the structure of work shifts and departments, [and] the distribution of personnel within shift teams, which is very different from common power plants."[34]

The team needed to work quickly to ensure the plants would have properly trained personnel. One of the Soviet Union's leading technical universities, the Moscow Power Engineering Institute (*Moskovskii Energeticheskii Institut, MEI*), had opened the country's first Department of Nuclear Power Plants, along with its own, full-fledged nuclear engineering curriculum, in 1956. The department's creator and first chair was Tereza Margulova, a leading nuclear power expert whose textbook, *Nuclear Power Plants*, not only later earned her the State Prize, but in five editions would educate several generations of Soviet nuclear power experts.[35]

Following a decree the Council of Ministers issued on April 4, 1957, Glavatomenergo arranged courses in the design, assembly, and operation of nuclear power plants at MEI.[36] Apparently, the students attending these courses were experienced industry specialists: all had higher education degrees; most were mechanical or electrical engineers; and some were physicists and chemists.[37] Glavatomenergo handpicked them for their future tasks: according to Lavrenenko's annual report for 1957, "Taking into account the high requirements that a future nuclear power plant employee will be faced with, Glavatomenergo, together with the personnel department of the ministry, conducted a search for qualified power engineers/industrialists and planners at the ministry's enterprises."[38]

Over the course of one or two years, teachers from leading scientific-technical institutes and specialized laboratories gave the students a broad introduction to nuclear technologies. In addition, many students went to Obninsk for more practical training.[39] This process often took the form of an apprenticeship, where incoming personnel "shadowed" more experienced colleagues for extended periods of time and slowly accumulated knowledge about "how things were being done." Future plant division leaders—and in particular, future chief engineers—served in any and all positions at Obninsk before going on to their designated roles at the new plants.[40]

Many freshly minted engineers found immediate employment in the civilian nuclear industry.[41] When the first reactors at Beloiarsk and Novo-Voronezh started operating, the people in the control room came from three realms: plutonium production reactors (Sredmash), the regular power industry (Minenergo), and nuclear submarines.[42] And while these communities typically mingled on site, personnel from the power industry dominated at the Beloiarsk site, while most specialists at Novo-Voronezh happened to come from Sredmash.[43] These specialists continued their training on site, complemented by visits to research and design institutes, as well as other plants.

In addition to the technical schools in Moscow (the aforementioned *MEI* and the Moscow Engineering and Physics Institute, *MIFI*), specialized technical colleges (so-called *VTUZy, Vysshchie tekhnicheskie uchebnye zavedeniia*) in Obninsk, Tomsk, and Sverdlovsk started preparing students from more traditional technical disciplines—such as power engineering, communication engineering, and materials science—for the nuclear industry's specific requirements.[44] But this formalized education provided little more than basic training that often did not prepare these young specialists for actual conditions at one of the country's new nuclear plants. This training did, however, normalize the path into the nuclear industry, by offering standardized professional expertise. Replacing experiential knowledge with standardized training for aspiring nuclear specialists, then, left a critical gap in the process of producing new nuclear knowledge.

Transfer and Normalization

At the time of the transfer in 1966, both ministers, Slavskii at Sredmash and Neporozhnii at Minenergo, shared technocratic visions of progress, despite their deep suspicion of each other's work and expertise.[45] Although the civilian nuclear sector had a growing number of qualified specialists, Slavskii's experts were ambivalent about the transfer. For example, they frequently complained about Minenergo's inadequate construction practices; Neporozhnii's engineers, in turn, expressed frustration about how Sredmash's design and engineering institutes would impose delays and last-minute changes to the construction plans. The dual legacy of secrecy on the one hand and the demands of industrial production and electrification on the other informed a highly selective transfer of responsibilities for nuclear power plants and ultimately facilitated in Sredmash's experts a condescending attitude toward Minenergo's engineers. Sredmash's military-influenced work ethic relied on quick decision making and a relentless focus on prioritizing and accomplishing a task at hand—a "shock-style" (*akkordnyi stil'*) approach Minenergo's workers were unfamiliar with.[46]

The differences between the two bureaucracies had even more impact during difficult transition regimens (such as start-up and shutdown) and crisis situations. When Sredmash transferred responsibilities for nuclear power plants to Minenergo, representatives from Sredmash's design, research, regulatory, and engineering institutes still staffed the start-up commissions discussed in chapter 2. Future control room operators took part in the start-up process, and they received theoretical and practical training either at other units of the same plant or at a different plant with similar reactors. But although the Soviet nuclear navy used simulator training by the 1960s, training centers for nuclear power plant operators did not have simulators until the late 1970s.[47]

However, the Sredmash leadership did implicitly acknowledge the need for continuity and the significance of tacit knowledge by transferring individual specialists to civilian organizations. But empirical knowledge (for example, how to deal with a specific emergency situation that operators had previously encountered) is not always attached to a single individual; more typically, it involves the expertise, skills, and memories of a group of people.[48]

As the industry's organizational and legal framework took shape, workplace safety regulations grew more specific. To refine workers' skills and competence, planners established certification and recertification procedures for nuclear personnel. And yet, experts in the field knew that the best training and the most diligent compliance with regulations needed to be complemented at times by professional judgment and improvisation. Just as a good Soviet manager would find unorthodox ways to tinker with his accounting system so he could report he had fulfilled the plan, so would a nuclear reactor operator balance written rules and ad hoc occurrences. Especially in the industry's early years, Soviet civilian nuclear experts from the managerial level to the reactor control room navigated this tension between following bureaucratic prescriptions and using their professional judgment, between written rules and on-site improvisation.

Planners hoped that by creating bureaucratic structures—routine, efficient, reliable processes and a clear, hierarchical division of tasks—they would make improvisation skills less crucial and eventually superfluous. But since these structures never reached stabilization, improvisation remained imperative, and individual nuclear experts acted as a balancing factor in the face of changing, and overly bureaucratic, administrative structures.

This was especially true for the cadres molded by the early years of the nuclear program. Administrators expected these cadres to improvise where and when bureaucratic structures proved inadequate.[49]

In practice, then, the idea that bureaucratization would guarantee a rational form of organization went hand in hand with the use of individuals capable of improvising. Administrators appointed such individuals, usually experienced engineers and managers, to key positions because they had access to relevant networks. They were expected to circumvent the very bureaucratic structures whose efficiency they were supposed to guarantee. This implicit expectation, and often necessity, of decision making in the face of uncertainty and of standing by those decisions nurtured a sense of autonomy and responsibility among the nuclear industry's leadership.[50] By the same token, however, it emboldened workers—again, from the management level down to the rank and file—to take action in response to unexpected situations without initially attempting to seek approval.

Increasingly, the tacit knowledge that the industry had been so careful to pass on to the people working at nuclear facilities was becoming formalized, and where that seemed insufficient, it was compartmentalized and strategically added on to normal operations. This resulted in a rigid and contradictory structure of accountability that still envisioned expert judgment as the ultimate redundancy feature, while simultaneously restricting operators in their actions and undermining their preparedness to exercise their judgment.

International Comparisons

In the late 1960s, the broad scope of the United Nations conferences on Peaceful Uses of Atomic Energy, which had so successfully reunited the international scientific community after the hiatus of World War II, gradually gave way to more specialized meetings. Some of them discussed the training of an effective workforce for the emerging nuclear power industry.[51]

In 1968, Minenergo systematically compared Soviet power plants with foreign ones, specifically those in France and the United States, according to a document it sent Gosplan that year. The report's main insight was that the number of technical and engineering personnel was several times smaller abroad, "but a direct comparison cannot be made due to the completely different structure of management and the limited functions of the personnel operating foreign power plants."[52] For example, France and the United States usually outsourced repair work to specialized contractors, whereas these tasks fell to power plant employees in the Soviet Union. Furthermore, French and U.S. equipment was higher quality, which allowed better performance with less personnel involvement. Whereas Soviet managers typically had to make do with whatever material or equipment was in store at the plants or risk exceedingly long wait times, the supply for French and U.S. plants was centralized and could deliver requested items within a few days. Moreover, most of the fuel inventory and supply was mechanized and the majority of equipment automated, in stark contrast to Soviet plants.[53] Minenergo justified the higher Soviet numbers with the imminent transition to larger-power reactors, which would require large reservoirs of highly trained cadres.

International comparison was just one more indication of the industry's increasing professionalization. Along with assessments like these came detailed plans on how the Soviets could emulate achievements in foreign nuclear industries. The initial shortage of qualified cadres seems to have ended by the late 1960s, even to the extent of having overstaffed plants. By 1970, increased power capacities per reactor unit required fewer control room operators per kilowatt hour, and Minenergo started reducing personnel in an effort to lower overall construction costs: fewer people meant fewer housing units and a smaller social infrastructure in a plant's satellite town.[54] Neporozhnii reported in a 1970 letter to the deputy chairman of the Council of Ministers, Mikhail Efremov, that Minenergo had reduced the operating personnel at the Smolensk nuclear plant from 1,240 to 1,025 individuals and intended to make similar changes at all plants with RBMKs.[55] Only three years later, the Smolensk nuclear power plant noted problems hiring and retaining workers. Among the reasons the writer of the plant's 1973 annual report gave were the small salary and the lack of bonuses, the unavailability of housing, the lack of consumer goods, and other aspects of the social infrastructure.[56]

Cynical Career Choices?

Who pursued careers in the nuclear industry? In addition to the highly visible scientists and engineers introduced above, many appeared in the ministries' reports as numbers and percentages, as the nameless, faceless workers and employees that the state needed to train, house, and pay. What drove young Soviet men and women to study nuclear physics or power engineering, or, if they had received another kind of training, what motivated them to move into the nuclear industry? Nuclear engineering programs at the country's top schools were by no means open to everyone, but the practice of vydvizhenie allowed talented and ambitious students from the provinces opportunities all but unheard of within the constraints of Soviet society.[57]

The utopia of a nuclear-powered communist future did not directly inspire educational choices.[58] Like any other technical education, a university program in nuclear engineering appealed to individuals inclined to do applied work.[59] Most technical specialists entered the nuclear power industry with pragmatic expectations it would be an interesting area to apply their skills, and a branch of industry that would likely ensure stable salaries and generous social programs.

In contrast, duty and patriotism motivated those who had joined the nuclear weapons project during or immediately after World War II. Once Soviet nuclear weapons were a reality, some of the older, highly decorated generation of nuclear specialists moved up into important political or managerial functions in the Soviet polity; others used their clout to influence decision making in the country's highest political circles.[60] Still others ended up creating college curricula and training the specialists who would eventually join research and design institutes or become leading nuclear power experts. Throughout, Sredmash's workforce continued to believe in their organizational mission, the protection of the homeland, even as they slowly added nuclear power technologies to their portfolio.

Even later, in the 1960s and 1970s, planning a career after having received a technical education in the Soviet Union became difficult not only due to the state's authority to assign and reassign people to different positions (raspredelenie) and the sometimes unpredictable whims of Party politics. It was also challenging because the training Soviet engineers received often served as little more than a starting point, especially in the nuclear industry.[61] Few of them anticipated—nor could they have anticipated—what awaited them in the emerging industry. On-the-job training could vary greatly because different work assignments required different kinds of workers.

But did this limited control over their career trajectories turn bright, eager young engineers into cynics, eventually leading to the "pervasive apathy of the Brezhnev era"?[62] In his analysis of the Soviet Youth League, the *Komsomol*, Steven Solnick found rampant cynicism among active members of leading Soviet institutions:

Komsomol secretaries who were supposedly in charge of indoctrination were actively squelching any members' expressions of zeal that might require special attention on their part. VUZ [colleges] and labor ministry officials were criticizing university graduates for shunning job assignments in their chosen field even as these same officials inflated labor demand figures and wasted those specialists who did show up. Military officers in charge of conscription similarly castigated youth who sought to evade service even as they dispatched ill or lame young men to work alongside hardened criminals in brutal conditions.[63]

Contrary to what we might expect, Solnick showed that this cynicism and apathy did not threaten the stability of the regime. Komsomol activists, rather than promoting the regime's political rhetoric, nurtured an attitude of indifference to it.[64] Solnick's conclusion that cynicism was a pervasive reality of Soviet life by the early 1970s led him to dismiss ideological decay as a reason for the collapse of Soviet institutions in the late 1980s: ideology, in his analysis, was dead long before then. In a similar vein, Stephen Kotkin pointed out Gorbachev's curious "socialist romanticism" that made him hold on to the October revolution's ideals, "a world of abundance, social justice, and people's power"—values that in the mid-1980s no longer resonated with most Soviet people.[65]

Such views led many Western analysts to expect that any intellectual would eventually turn against the Communist Party. But Soviet nuclear specialists do not quite fit this picture: they were part of the Soviet Union's technical intelligentsia, which produced more leaders than dissidents.[66] Soviet nuclear scientists and engineers may have held cynical views of some aspects of Soviet life, but by and large, they considered themselves privileged participants in the construction of a rational society and able contributors to the industrialization and progress of their country.[67] Confident in their technical expertise and technocratic legitimacy, most of them saw opportunities to contribute constructively to state policies. They acknowledged the significance of nuclear power for the country's, and ultimately the world's, energy supply and saw their task as helping to realize the vision of a large-scale nuclear industry.[68]

Many nuclear specialists, and technical experts in general, were critical of managerial decisions within the nuclear industry and bewildered by the intricacies of the planning process, particularly the blatant contrast between how managers defined plan fulfillment as an executive ideal yet practiced it merely as a rhetorical ritual.[69] And yet, even university graduates who ended up in the nuclear industry by chance usually treated their work with respect and a high sense of responsibility. They saw themselves as an integral part of a state that embodied their very own professional ethos. Had they turned cynical about the state, they would have turned cynical about their own work, their own values.[70]

Their faith in technology as the rational answer to society's problems aligned with the state's ideological goals, but most of the nuclear specialists saw science and technology as something clearly distinct from politics. In this culturally specific definition, "political" and "ideological" both referred to the goals and rules Communist Party ideologues set and the public rhetoric used to disseminate them. Nuclear specialists dismissed as unsound and irrational such "political" decisions as for example the moratorium on new nuclear power plant construction in the wake of Chernobyl (and later, the decommissioning of the Lithuanian reactors as part of the European Union accession process).[71] But they did not see progress itself as a political concept: rather, the logical, rational outcome of scientific research was technical, and ultimately societal, progress. Nuclear specialists, then, shared the Soviet state's technocratic views of societal development—that is, practical, applied versions of scientific development for industrial and foreign policy under the direction of scientific experts.[72] This deep trust in scientific rationality made nuclear experts less vulnerable to apathy and cynicism than other groups and institutions (figure 3.1).

The nuclear sector, both military and civilian, produced very few dissidents—although those that did emerge were formidable opponents for the Soviet leadership and suffered the state's merciless response.[73] If there was disagreement among nuclear specialists, it remained limited to very narrow technical circles—a practice sustained by the nuclear specialists themselves, not just imposed on them through pressure from above.[74] Apparently, these technical intellectuals found the ideals of a liberal polity far less appealing than the vision of progress driven by scientific rationality and the relative intellectual freedom within their own scientific community.

Historian David Holloway has pointed out that "Russian intellectuals before and after the October Revolution regarded science as a force for rationality and democracy. They believed that it had a cultural value in and of itself, above and beyond the knowledge that was accumulated."[75] Perhaps more than other groups, nuclear scientists and engineers subscribed to a regime of discipline and to a system of accountability ultimately based on a deep sense of duty and responsibility. Their goal was to fit in seamlessly, to function elegantly as part of a large machine.[76]

Professional Communities: Tacit Knowledge and Improvisation

In his comparative study of the nuclear specialists behind the wartime reactors in the United Kingdom, the United States, and Canada, and the development of nuclear power industries since then, Sean Johnston has shown how professional identities emerged, stabilized, and reconfigured over several decades.[77] He argues that the specific needs of the emerging field of

Figure 3.1
Operating an RBMK was no easy job: notoriously unreliable instrumentation made operations difficult even under the best of circumstances. Control room teams typically consisted of highly trained, experienced nuclear specialists necessary to operate the reactor safely. While the architects of the Soviet nuclear industry relied on their reactor operators' expertise to handle unexpected situations, they paradoxically also expected them to obey ever-changing rules and operating procedures. Shown is a control room operator at the Kursk nuclear power plant.
Source: Courtesy of the Publishing House "Master," Moscow. Originally published in *Elektroenergetika* (ed. A. I. Vol'skii and A. B. Chubais, series *Stroiteli Rossii: XX vek* (Moscow: "Master," 2003), 239). Reprinted with permission.

nuclear energy cut across established categories of occupations, disciplines, and professions. Nuclear energy "required the skills of nuclear engineers, technologists, and technicians, 'atomic scientists,' radiochemists, and health physicists, before they bore those names."[78] The new specialists came from backgrounds that were both familiar and new: some had professional skills that translated easily, others needed to thoroughly transform their skill sets to perform in the nuclear industry, and finally some—for example reactor engineers—had utterly new skills. In addition, these nuclear professions developed in the context of national security and Cold War secrecy. Johnston notes that although the expertise for both reactors and bombs originated in secret terrain, distinct goals led to an early division of labor between reactor designers and bomb designers.[79] In each country, these distinct goals, along with changing career constraints and institutional contexts, concerted government management, secrecy, and other factors led heterogeneous configurations of nuclear specialists to form.[80]

Johnston's analysis consciously eclipses the Soviet experience, in part because it remained "invisible to Western practitioners until the mid-1950s, and so played little part in constructing early nuclear know-how in the Anglo-Saxon countries."[81] However, he finds that the state's role in "creating technical alliances, controlling the circulation of knowledge, and mediating professional roles" revealed broad similarities between English-speaking democracies and the Soviet state—a provocative claim that nevertheless resonates with this book's argument.[82]

Soviet professional identities developed together with the nascent organizational framework of the nuclear power industry. Diverse communities of technical specialists collaborated in this new branch of industry, producing its own community of cadres, who shared ideas, goals, training, success, and setbacks. The cooperation among nuclear energy cadres proved rhetorically and organizationally flexible and involved constant boundary work between the atomshchiki of Sredmash and the energetiki of Minenergo.[83]

As an example shows, the distinction between these two categories remains alive and well. On May 29, 2003, in a live interview on the radio station *Ekho Moskvy* (Echo of Moscow), Aleksandr Rumiantsev, then minister of Atomic Energy of the Russian Federation, was asked about the danger of sensitive nuclear knowledge finding its way to Iran:

Rumiantsev: We are training nuclear power plant operators ... just like operators of conventional power plants ... it's the same ... you won't notice any difference between the control panels of ... a nuclear power plant and a gas power plant. None of the operating regulations are in any way connected with nuclear physics ... The person who designs and builds the nuclear power plant, who supplies its fuel and then extracts and reprocesses it afterwards, that's the [one who actually has the] nuclear technology.

Interviewer [in audible disbelief]: So in other words ... these people don't know what's going on ... in the nuclear reactor?

Rumiantsev: ... *the operators are allowed not to know.* I think the majority of people don't know what ... an internal combustion engine is, and yet they drive. ... They drive just fine.[84]

Rumiantsev's words illustrate the persistent idea that nuclear reactor operators should be highly qualified and capable of making the correct decisions under difficult conditions but at the same time should be subject to rather arbitrary constraints.[85] The boundary is tricky to draw between protecting sensitive technical know-how on the one hand and educating as many specialists, as thoroughly as possible, on the other. When the goal is safety and security, when should administrators "black box" technological processes and when should they provide general transparency?

The work of nuclear power plant operators can be dull and routine—not exactly the challenging environment a highly qualified specialist would be looking for. But rather than merely observing the rules and passively adjusting to the technology the designers developed, operators actively interact with the reactors on a daily basis and by doing so, they constantly generate new, experiential knowledge and develop skills to efficiently maneuver around design deficiencies.[86]

The operators of Soviet nuclear power plants, perhaps not unlike nuclear reactor operators elsewhere in the world, were thus expected to perform an almost schizophrenic task: as highly trained, competent experts, they were qualified to make correct decisions under difficult conditions, but at the same time they were required to limit their decisions to the options designers put in writing.

Written instructions and rules can capture certain experiential knowledge, but tacit knowledge can also entail knowing how to deal with rules and instructions, which ones are "hard rules," under what circumstances an action counts as following a rule, and what deviations are acceptable in any given context. For example, in his autobiographically inspired novel *Ivan II: Top Secret*, Mikhail Grabovskii described an accident at the EI-2, the Siberian dual-use reactor and predecessor of the RBMK. The young operators on duty struggled with handling an unfamiliar situation and finally turned to an experienced senior engineer, whose quick reaction prevented the accident from getting out of control.[87] Even if there had been written guidelines, consulting them would have taken too much time.

Training Nuclear Experts

Tacit knowledge is fundamentally at odds with the idea of standardization—the holy grail of modern industry.[88] Despite attempts to standardize reactors, simplify production of technical components, and streamline operator training, each reactor is different and unique, even when several reactors are of the same kind. A veteran of the Soviet nuclear complex put it this way: "Reactors are like children ... you get to know their peculiarities while spending time with them; you've got to feel how the reactor breathes."[89]

Tripartite Structure of Nuclear Power Plant Management

The transfer of nuclear power plants to civilian authorities led to a new standard division of labor that relied on scientific, administrative, and economic best practices that had proven successful in other industries. Specifically, this process entailed a tripartite organization of labor, and a distinction between scientific director (*nauchnyi rukovoditel'*), chief design engineer (*glavnyi konstruktor*), and chief project manager (*generalnyi proektirovshchik*).[90] Originally, Sredmash had performed all of these tasks, and as I have noted previously, it remained in charge of the actual nuclear reactors even after the decision to transfer nuclear power plants to Minenergo.

The Scientific Director

The Institute of Atomic Energy, under Kurchatov and then Aleksandrov, served as scientific director for most Soviet nuclear power plants.[91] Kurchatov and Aleksandrov developed the VVER, and after 1966 the institute served as scientific director of the RBMK.[92] In 1971, Aleksandrov was appointed chairman of the Interdepartmental Technical Council (MVTS), and he remained in that post until the MVTS was abolished in 1986.[93] In addition, Aleksandrov was single-handedly responsible for research and design conducted at the Institute of Atomic Energy and for presiding over the Soviet Academy of Sciences. Some interpreted this situation as a de facto absence of scientific leadership for nuclear power reactors because Aleksandrov had to attend committee meetings and handle other bureaucratic tasks instead of visiting plants and consulting with engineers, designers, operators, and the like.[94] Of course, a number of deputies supported Aleksandrov, but it is still noteworthy that he chose to hold on to all these positions: each was crucial to the nuclear industry and each provided enormous power and access to the highest-level decision makers. Aleksandrov closely collaborated with Efim Slavskii, the influential leader of Sredmash, and any suggestion, any proposal, in the area of nuclear energy had to pass this powerful duo's review. Making a decision without their consent was literally impossible.[95]

One other research institute performed well as scientific director in nuclear power engineering: Laboratory V in Obninsk. Laboratory V took on the scientific directorship for the reactors at the Beloiarsk, Bilibino, and Shevchenko nuclear power plants—all innovative prototypes that ultimately did not manage to reach the critical threshold of standardized production. Following Kurchatov's death, Laboratory V (renamed the Institute of Physics and Power Engineering, FEI) gradually lost its leading role in designing thermal reactors. It did, however, consolidate its status as the country's unmatched leader in developing fast neutron (breeder) reactor technology.

The Chief Design Engineer

Research and engineering institutes and construction bureaus usually performed the role of chief design engineer (*glavnyi konstruktor*). In close cooperation with the scientific director, the chief design engineer was responsible for reactor core computations, for coordinating the production of all components pertaining to the nuclear part of the plant (most importantly, the fuel elements), for subjecting all components to rigorous quality control tests, and for supervising the implementation of their technologies (both material and processes) on site. The latter task was also referred to as *avtorskii nadzor*, a kind of ongoing quality control: inspectors from the chief design engineer's institute would spend months on the construction site of a new nuclear power plant, supervising every step of the construction and assembly process, and signing off on required certificates.[96] When these inspectors did not sign a certificate, the construction process had to be halted and a meeting with the scientific director called.[97]

The engineering and construction bureaus that performed the role of chief design engineer in the civilian nuclear industry reported to Sredmash. One of the leading institutes was Dollezhal's Scientific Research and Design Institute of Energy Technologies, NIKIET.[98] Another institute, the construction bureau OKB Gidropress in Podolsk near Moscow, became chief design engineer for pressurized water reactors, the other major design for the Soviet civilian nuclear industry.[99]

The General Project Manager

The general project manager's task was to plan, supervise, and administer the construction and assembly of the nonnuclear parts of a nuclear power plant. In particular, the project manager was in charge of the planning and logistics regarding construction materials for a plant and for designing an occupational health and safety zone (*sanitarnaia zona*) around the plant's territory. The general project manager also coordinated human resources and oversaw the construction of the plant's entire infrastructure (roads connecting the plant with other industrial sites and nearby cities, transmission lines linking the new town and plant to existing grids, a sewage system, specialized cleaning and decontamination services, and so on). Last but not least, the general project manager was responsible for building the plant's satellite town, including childcare facilities, schools, shops, canteens, basic medical infrastructure, clubs and movie theaters, and public transportation. The general project manager coordinated contractors and was accountable for the overall progress on site. Usually, Minenergo oversaw the organization taking on general project management.[100]

As I have mentioned, official reports after Chernobyl alleged a distinction between atomshchiki, the nuclear experts who worked for Sredmash and designed reactors, and energetiki, the nonnuclear power engineers who worked for Minenergo and operated those reactors day to day. These reports characterized the former as highly qualified, diligent, and disciplined, and the latter as less diligent, somewhat less qualified, and less disciplined.

Atomshchiki

Atomshchiki belonged to an elite that sometimes worked on both military and civilian applications, on cutting-edge research and mundane operations, in secret Sredmash facilities and public electrical power plants. Many of them built, operated, and experimented with research reactors, developing and testing novel paths in reactor engineering. Unless they worked in one of the secret cities or one of the research centers elsewhere in the country, their research and design institutions tended to be concentrated in Moscow.[101]

Atomshchiki often worked at reactor design engineering bureaus—that is, the institutes assigned to computations and the experimental testing of nuclear reactors. Among the most prominent of these institutes were NIKIET, Gidropress (in Podolsk), and the Experimental Design Bureau for Machine Building (OKBM) in the city of Gorky (now Nizhnii Novgorod), which also developed naval reactors and specialized in fast neutron reactors.[102]

Characteristically, the specialists at nuclear research and design institutes and engineering bureaus worked closely with the operating authorities at any given plant during construction. But unless the operating personnel reported problems that required the designers' attention, once a reactor reached the target power output level (a process that could take several years), the atomshchiki retreated and turned operation over to the plant's personnel, typically energetiki.

When nuclear power plants were transferred to Minenergo, atomshchiki who moved into top administrative positions in the civilian nuclear industry felt obliged to pass on their sense of duty, responsibility, and patriotism to the enthusiastic, hard-working energetiki. This was Sredmash's attempt to preserve some of its professional culture within the changed organizational framework and to maintain the connection between nuclear power plants and their front- and back-end infrastructure (uranium enrichment facilities, fuel manufacturing, and spent fuel and waste management), a connection that the transfer had weakened.[103]

The numerous reorganizations of responsibility that followed the transfer show clearly that initial plans did not accomplish the desired goals. Concepts of safety and reliability as well as specific organizational structures kept changing, and that fact made the division of labor outlined above even more tenuous.

Energetiki

After 1966, most nuclear power plant operators were Minenergo power engineers.[104] Those working shifts in the reactor's control room were only a small segment of a plant's operating personnel. Plant operators also coordinated and controlled the reactor's connection with the nonnuclear part of the plant, the steam generators and turbines. Furthermore, plant personnel included maintenance and repair engineering teams, scientists and technicians in chemical laboratories, physicians and other medical professionals, radiation control specialists, and many more.

Planners envisioned that a cadre of civilian engineers—young technical specialists, sometimes with but more often without specialized training in nuclear engineering—would operate nuclear power plants on a day-to-day basis. As a rule, energetiki did not enjoy the same privileges as their peers in Sredmash. Nevertheless, constructing, managing, and operating nuclear as well as conventional power plants gave Neporozhnii unusual leeway in developing and pursuing his own agenda.[105]

Differences and Commonalities

Even though these two professional groups, atomshchiki and energetiki, exhibited clear differences, they were also intertwined in many ways, and

Training Nuclear Experts

Figure 3.2
Inside a reactor hall of the Leningrad nuclear power plant in Sosnovy Bor, Russia. Nuclear power plant staff performed a variety of duties that often involved individuals with different levels of training. In the image, a team is shown standing next to the reactor's biological shield. During refueling, a tall, remotely controlled machine would move on top of one of the gray squares, pull out the spent fuel element, and insert a fresh one.
Source: Photograph by Alexey Danichev, 2008. Provided to Wikimedia Commons by the Russian International News Agency (RIA Novosti) as part of a cooperation project. RIA Novosti archive, image #305011/Alexey Danichev/CC-BY-SA 3.0.

their cooperation seems to have worked. The civilian nuclear industry profoundly relied on the sound judgment of these engineer-operators (figure 3.2). Precision instrumentation was still scarce, and automation of reactor operation remained an elusive goal.[106] Operators' judgment was a key element built into a complex sociotechnical system of technologies, practices, and rules. Numerous devices served to train operators and to ensure they performed reliably—for example, voluminous instruction manuals and regulations that required strict adherence to these instructions and all other written rules and procedures.[107] In addition, annual exams tested operators' technical proficiency and familiarity with rules and regulatory changes. A detailed system of rewards and reprimands tied test scores and performance on the job to bonuses and even to a considerable part of an operator's base salary. In case of a mishap or a violation of work discipline, managers could pull rewards and issue formal reprimands.[108]

The most striking difference between the two groups appears to have been that only atomshchiki tended to understand the consequences a severe accident at a nuclear power plant might have; several of them witnessed, managed, and mitigated nuclear accidents at military installations prior to the Chernobyl accident. In fact, Sredmash had handled some serious accidents at military as well as civilian installations: an explosion at a radioactive waste storage facility near Kyshtym in 1957, and the partial core meltdown at the Leningrad nuclear power plant in 1975, to name but two.[109]

By contrast, energetiki generally assumed that Soviet nuclear power plants were safe.[110] These engineers no doubt knew that they were dealing with a high-risk technology, but their instructions on how to respond if something went wrong only covered design-basis accidents. Minenergo inspectors regularly reviewed nuclear power plants starting in the early 1970s. These inspectors listed the overall number of accidents, calculated the resulting loss of electricity generation, and identified which accidents operator error had caused.[111] Interestingly, their reports always attributed manufacturing errors (*brak*) to the personnel, not to the technology or compressed production schedules.[112] Inspectors emphasized the short-term loss of energy supply rather than any flaws in the plant's safety system that an accident might have revealed.[113]

Minister Neporozhnii clearly understood that nuclear power plants were special—if nothing else, his ministry was required to establish safety zones around them, though not around conventional plants. From the outset, nuclear industry planners had clearly seen that the nuclear workforce had distinctive education requirements: "The execution of their assigned functions, however, requires from the ... senior operator[s] intricate knowledge of physics, thermodynamics, electrical engineering, that is, theoretical knowledge that [only] persons with a specialized higher education from a technical school or a college possess."[114] Despite having once compared nuclear reactors to ordinary boilers at conventional power plants, Neporozhnii treated nuclear power plants differently from conventional plants; reportedly, he started his day by calling each nuclear plant to check their operational status.[115]

An episode from one of the first industrial-scale nuclear power plants illustrates how administrators channeled, sanitized, and ultimately buried knowledge about problems and failures in modified operating regulations. In February 1968, the operators at the "Beloiarka," as they fondly referred to the Beloiarsk nuclear power plant, confronted an unanticipated problem:

after repair work, cooling malfunctioned in one channel and it melted when power was rising.[116] In response, a Glavatomenergo commission inspected the plant and its labor organization. In March 1968, Ivan Emelyianov, NIKIET's deputy director, signed a document that admitted critical mistakes in calculating the power distribution to individual channels.[117] The commission decided that in the future, two experts would conduct independent computations and a computer would repeat the computations twice; only if all results agreed would designers trust the numbers and use them for further computations.[118] In September 1968, the chief design engineer decided to introduce new control rods every year to balance out any potential computing mistakes.[119] No one attempted to record and disseminate this experience-based, case-specific learning process. Instead, NIKIET implemented new guidelines for conducting these computations, altered some technical parameters, and updated the operating regulations.[120]

Another unanticipated problem confronted teams of operators at the Novo-Voronezh nuclear power plant. In September 1971, Minenergo reported to the Council of Ministers that accidents at reactors 1 and 2 there prompted significant changes in the technical design of unit 3. They hoped that these changes would make maintenance and repair work at unit 3 easier.[121] They did not, however, utilize the accident experience systematically to help operators better understand the technologies they were running.

As in Beloiarsk, resolving unanticipated problems required a combination of subject expertise, experience, and improvisation. Nuclear industry managers attempted to incorporate early experiences with problematic and even dangerous situations into rules and instructions, but neither the authorities nor the operators themselves cataloged, analyzed, or tried to integrate any of the lessons they had learned into future operator training. Once the management changed (and reassignments were frequent), the experiential base of this formal knowledge was lost. Every new generation of nuclear power plant operators had similar experiences with accidents because they got rules rather than stories and abstract rather than concrete knowledge.[122]

And when in the 1970s problems with the RBMK control rods first came to light, a topic I return to in chapters 4 and 5, the designers reacted by modifying operating instructions for control room staff—that is, they revised regulations and insisted that operators follow instructions to the letter. They never explained why this was important or what might happen if operators ignored or bent these rules. They also did not modify the control rods' physical design until after Chernobyl.[123] In other words, they tried to fix a sociotechnical system by addressing neither the social factors (operator expertise) nor the technical specifications (the control rod design). Instead, they focused on the organizational mechanisms that governed the interaction between humans and machines.[124] And while this was not an incorrect response per se, it reflected norms and routines rooted in the specific institutional traditions of the secret nuclear weapons complex.[125]

With hindsight, it seems obvious that if human operators were the key to the safe operation of the RBMK, they needed access to all information, including that pertaining to problems and accidents. Also, it is hard to comprehend why no one fixed a critical piece of equipment after problems with it arose. And yet, postponing major redesign until the next planned maintenance shutdown was an accepted industry practice—not only in the nuclear sector. Furthermore, the Cold War made tight information control seem not only necessary but also reasonable, especially with nuclear materials. Fear of espionage and sabotage influenced the decisions about how much knowledge, and what kind of knowledge, reactor designers were willing to share with reactor operators.

Only in reaction to the Three Mile Island accident in 1979 did researchers begin to consider that design flaws might cause accidents at civilian nuclear facilities. In the Soviet Union, Sidorenko reports, nuclear physicists at the Sector for Nuclear Reactors at the Institute of Atomic Energy began to analyze the possibility of severe accidents at nuclear power plants in the late 1970s.[126] It is unclear whether the physicists shared this emerging information—particularly information about the potentially catastrophic scale of an accident at a nuclear plant—with Minenergo and the operators, and if so, in what form.[127]

Official reports after the Chernobyl disaster contended that if Sredmash had been in charge, the accident would not have happened. As I have mentioned, the Soviet delegation that reported to the International Atomic Energy Agency in the summer of 1986 also concluded that the operators, not the designers, were to blame for the disaster.[128]

Maybe Sredmash's personnel were better trained, reacted faster, and made better decisions, but maybe they were just lucky or better able to cover up mishaps. Be that as it may, atomshchiki tended to see potential human error as the main risk to reactor safety, while energetiki tended to perceive the capricious technology the designers created as the main risk and as an obstacle to meeting Minenergo's production goals.

Secrecy

Nuclear power's technical sophistication, the secrecy surrounding it, and the utopian promises associated with nuclear energy's future sometimes evoked a certain romantic idealism about the industry. Sredmash maintained the bomb project's secrecy by classifying much of the information its employees worked with and so preventing them from taking that information out of an office or talking about it with outsiders. Often, Sredmash classified even the name of a work site, and employees would refer to it only by a number. Such so-called post office boxes (*pochtovye iashchiki*) included not only facilities located in "secret cities" but also institutes in Moscow and Leningrad.

This secrecy was a handy mechanism to regulate access to knowledge, and—at least in theory—to manage risk perception in the light of rumors about accidents and safety problems in the nuclear industry. Organizational constraints also determined the role of trust in the relationship between Sredmash and Minenergo. In important ways, Minenergo had no choice but to trust Sredmash; questioning decorated military heroes was decidedly not an option. The reverse was also true. Sredmash had to trust Minenergo to manage sensitive nuclear materials.[129]

In one way or another, the secrecy established during the atomic bomb project affected all internal technical communication in the civilian nuclear industry, even in areas of knowledge that many technical specialists considered unproblematic. When in the early 1980s the newly established State Oversight Committee for the Safe Conduct of Work in the Nuclear Power Industry (*Gosatomenergonadzor*) attempted to create a database of incidents and accidents at nuclear power plants to help operators learn from mistakes and avoid them in the future, NIKIET categorically rejected the initiative. Its representatives argued that even though Minenergo was already operating these very reactors, such information was confidential and should be kept within Sredmash.[130]

But Soviet nuclear experts did revisit the problem of information sharing on a regular basis, and the constant administrative changes in the nuclear industry affirm their efforts to improve and refine the existing division of labor and the resulting principles of information control. Ultimately, they retained a conservative model, giving a "need to know" approach preference over a "need to tell" attitude, which privileged those with better access to information. Only after the collapse of the Soviet system did multiple specialists, including Sidorenko, openly identify secrecy as one major stumbling block for the creation of a professional culture that included awareness that both humans and machines were fallible.[131]

But was secrecy justified in some cases and not others? Was Sredmash's restrictive information control based on legitimate differences in technical expertise between it and Minenergo, or simply on bureaucratic protectionism? Should only specialists experienced at handling radioactive materials—that is, specialists trained in the nuclear weapons program—manage specific processes?[132] Among Soviet nuclear energy experts, secrecy was both the glue that bonded a heterogeneous group of technical specialists together and a divisive element that introduced doubt and suspicion. Ironically, secrecy may have reinforced such values as diligence, responsibility, and faith in scientific rationality.

Nuclear specialists understood the secrecy attached to any and all Sredmash projects, even civilian ones, in the context of a Cold War political, technical, and economic showdown between competing doctrines. Secrecy seemed necessary, even if their work would ultimately benefit the public good, and nuclear specialists considered disagreement with official policies justified only when it would serve this overarching national interest. In other words, secrecy protected specialists and their work from public scrutiny, and simultaneously protected their work for the common good.[133] By the same token, it helped mask the significance of tacit knowledge and prevented learning across organizational boundaries.

Conclusion

Atomshchiki brought dutiful, authoritarian, and patriotic attitudes to their work in the civilian nuclear power industry, while energetiki brought technological enthusiasm, openness, and utopian fervor. Eventually, the two groups came to share a set of values, even emotions, relating to nuclear energy. Both groups acknowledged nuclear power's importance for the country's, and ultimately the world's, energy supply. They saw their task as helping to realize the vision of a large-scale nuclear power industry that would, by virtue of its beneficent applications in medicine, science, industry, and transport, contribute to and even drive social progress toward a modern and just society. The centralized, priority-driven economy in which they worked created an atmosphere of rigid accountability and encouraged both groups to nurture such values as diligence, responsibility, and duty. Nuclear specialists from both backgrounds experienced the sudden, fierce public opposition to nuclear energy that followed the Chernobyl tragedy as a personal attack.

A nuclear specialist could achieve excellence and develop a strong commitment to the nuclear energy sector whether his or her original training or initial work assignment was with Sredmash or Minenergo. No doubt some energetiki viewed a nuclear reactor as little more than another way of boiling water. But for others, nuclear energy was the fulcrum of the power industry, the ultimate driver of progress, and the pinnacle of scientific and technical prowess. Likewise, the atomshchiki were anything but a homogeneous group. Nuclear specialists developed competing reactor types that reflected, perhaps inadvertently, these specialists' ideological priorities. Depending on the design they promoted, these specialists chose specific rhetorical strategies that tapped into different repertoires of justification—invoking national security, scientific novelty, or technoeconomic prowess. Despite the many differences, atomshchiki and energetiki ultimately shared expertise, risks, and rewards. The problem of creating, advancing, and sharing nuclear knowledge affected them all, as did the loss of tacit, experiential knowledge and its consequences.

4 "May the Atom Be a Worker, Not a Soldier!": A New History of Soviet Reactor Design Choices

When the international scientific community convened in Geneva in the summer of 1955 to attend the first United Nations Conference on the Peaceful Uses of Atomic Energy, the Soviet contributions created quite a stir. Soviet scientists announced what they had achieved the previous year—connecting a small nuclear reactor near Moscow to the public grid and thus creating the world's first nuclear power plant. With a control room that resembled a toyshop, the little graphite-water reactor near the Obninskoe train station would turn out to be the cradle of Soviet nuclear power technology and expertise. Although its 5 MW generating capacity was barely enough to power a locomotive, it established the Soviets as the first to make fission energy available for civilian use. The UN conference confirmed that Stalin's nuclear physicists and engineers were among the international leaders in this cutting-edge area of science and technology.

The Obninsk reactor would serve as an experimental base for all subsequent graphite-water power reactors and as a training site for generations of nuclear specialists. It also served as a public showcase, a demonstration of Soviet scientific and technical prowess that would jump-start yet another Cold War race, this one for peaceful nuclear applications.

The Obninsk plant was the first civilian outcome of the Soviet military atomic project. Though it was much smaller than military reactors, it was based on the same materials, and its history began even before the detonation of the first Soviet atomic bomb. In 1948, nuclear scientists and engineers put forth several design proposals for experimental reactors, and on May 16, 1949, the government issued a decree to start planning an experimental nuclear plant.[1] A year later, on July 29, 1950, Stalin signed another decree ordering construction of installation V-10 (*ustanovka V-10*) at Laboratory V in Obninsk. Originally, planners intended the plant to have a combined power output of 500 kW from three different types of compact reactors, one from each of three different nuclear research institutes.[2] In the end, the Obninsk plant had only the graphite-water type. Its selection was the first in what would become a prolonged and complex series of decisions about reactor design in the Soviet nuclear industry.

In this chapter, I introduce the reactor designs that planners considered for power plants in the Soviet Union during the 1950s and 1960s, the reactor types they chose to build experimentally, and the ones they ultimately chose to implement on an industrial scale. By reconstructing which research institutes promoted which design and who lobbied for which type, we can better understand why the Soviet government, despite tight resources, agreed to financially support a protracted, expensive research-and-development process that led to the construction of numerous prototypes. We can also trace why the Soviet Union chose two major reactor designs for their civilian nuclear power program and implemented them in parallel, rather than consolidating scarce resources behind one design.

In 1955, the architects of the Soviet nuclear power program chose an initial design to standardize and implement all across the country. They picked the VVER, whose initials stood for *vodo-vodianoi energeticheskii reaktor* or water-water power reactor. A light water cooled and moderated, pressurized water reactor, the VVER was similar but not identical in design to Western pressurized water reactors.[3]

Over a decade later, planners decided to also implement the RBMK, a graphite-moderated, light water cooled, boiling-water reactor. Since 1986, some have referred to the RBMK as the "Chernobyl-type" reactor, and many nuclear physicists and engineers both in the former Soviet Union and abroad have condemned it as inherently unsafe. As we will see, the RBMK was in fact a puzzling choice for standardization and widespread implementation, in part because well before Soviet planners decided to use it, nuclear power programs all over the world had already adopted pressurized water designs.

In the history of Soviet nuclear reactors that follows, I focus on power-generating designs and their immediate predecessors, and I devote the most space and attention to the pool of designs that economic planners and political decision makers actually considered for mass implementation. Because the choice of the RBMK raises numerous questions, I spend more time on that design and less on the VVER. I also analyze the series of contingencies (historical and otherwise) that affected Soviet reactor design choices. I argue that choosing certain reactor designs and abandoning others were not steps along a strictly logical path. Instead, the selections resulted from a long, twisted process that involved technological artifacts, many decision makers, trial and error, innumerable personal interventions, international cooperation and delimitation, rivalry between military and civilian interests, as well as economic considerations. The decision turned in part on the reputation of certain design institutes, on the clout of individual scientists, and on political patronage.

A Multidirectional Approach

The first Soviet nuclear reactors produced plutonium for nuclear weapons. As I have mentioned, Kurchatov ordered tests on graphite-water reactors in 1946 to determine their suitability for power production, and by 1948, scientists were also scrutinizing several other reactor designs for civilian applications.[4] These reactors' dual military/civilian features were not always perceived as a negative: it was, after all, the Cold War, and producing isotopes for nuclear weapons was at least as legitimate as supplying electricity and heat for public consumption.

Unlike other nations that settled on their reactor types during the 1950s, Soviet scientists kept experimenting for another decade with a variety of different reactor designs, apparently with the backing of the Soviet government. Deliberately or not, by repeatedly halting and modifying the nuclear power program, the Soviet government effectively supported an expensive research-and-development process that led to several operational power reactor prototypes. Once planners decided to restart the nuclear power program and, more importantly, committed to funding it in the 1960s, scientists presented them with the luxury of options—something most other nations did not have at the time.

Plans for the development of the civilian nuclear industry often closely reflected international trends rather than solid economic indicators. As a consequence, though the Soviet program was repeatedly amended and at times curtailed, it maintained an ambitious trend toward growth and expansion. After Obninsk came online, the next five-year plan (1956–1960) laid out optimistic intentions to create more and more powerful plants, but government officials repeatedly changed those plans and cut back the financial allocations for them. The planning elite continued to hotly contest the projected profitability of nuclear power and even the technical feasibility of large nuclear power plants, as we have seen in chapter one.

Ultimately, Soviet leaders streamlined their nuclear program considerably later than the leaders of many democratic market economies did—a somewhat paradoxical phenomenon in the "country of the plan."[5] Simultaneously pursuing the development of multiple reactor types has sometimes been justified as a "multiple research options approach."[6] At least in the 1950s, Soviet planners considered permanent stabilization of reactor designs not only not a priority, but outright undesirable.

In 1956, Kurchatov reported that the Soviet Union was constructing up to ten different reactor types.[7] In addition, a massive supply industry, especially heavy industry and fuel manufacturing, grew alongside these reactors. Scientists argued that only by developing in many directions and experimenting with a variety of design options, coolants, and cooling schemes could they produce a rich and diverse scientific and technical knowledge base for the nuclear industry.[8] In other words, what from today's perspective might look like an irrational, chaotic diversity of approaches made good sense at the time.

Furthermore, a multidirectional strategy had proven reliable during the military nuclear program, so economic planners in fact considered a diversified approach to civilian reactors preferable to choosing one design too early.[9] Funding a series of competing designs minimized the risk of failure and increased the probability of overcoming technical problems. The idea of "duplication" (*dublirovanie*) can be traced back to Stalin, who, instead of trusting one person or group, tended to assign responsibilities for the same task to at least two independently operating teams. According to an apocryphal (but probable) story, Stalin had in fact duplicated the entire group set up to develop the atomic bomb.[10]

But the power of tradition notwithstanding, supporting researchers' creativity and the development of multiple reactor designs to the stage of functioning prototypes put enormous strain on the country's financial, material, and labor resources. Such a strategy distributed scarce funding widely and risked insufficient support for the development of a few designs. It was also at least potentially more expensive. These massive resource allocations increasingly required justification.

The pursuit of this multidirectional model of technological development also meant that reactor designers enjoyed a significantly extended period of funded research and development for different reactor options, before having to choose a limited number of designs for mass implementation. At the time, it was still unclear which problems would prove most significant. Reactor designers competed fiercely, and negotiations over design selection reached relative stabilization only by the late 1960s, some ten years after the United States had settled on its commercial reactor models. The specific features of the Soviet state did not let tensions over the choice escalate into public controversy; the state's decisions had to be indisputably rational—or at least had to be perceived as such.[11]

Obninsk proved the technical feasibility of nuclear power plants, but proving their economic viability remained a challenge. In a 1956 speech at Harwell in the United Kingdom, Kurchatov stressed the significance of civilian reactors' operational safety, but within the Soviet Union, the ability of nuclear power plants to produce electricity at prices competitive with conventional power plants was of paramount concern.[12]

This balancing act between domestic priorities and the aspiration to impress international audiences also shaped the arguments Soviet reactor designers made for or against a specific reactor type. At different times they invoked similarities with and differences from Western reactor designs and stressed how a given design either fit with international trends and preferences in nuclear engineering or, by contrast, established the Soviet Union's national uniqueness.

From "Laboratory V" to the Institute of Physics and Power Engineering

Like many other nuclear institutes, including Kurchatov's Laboratory No. 2 in Moscow, Laboratory V executed both open contracts for the civilian nuclear industry and secret research and development for the weapons program.[13] As I detailed in chapter three, Soviet nuclear research centers did not simply develop a reactor design and then turn it over to industry but instead took on the role of scientific director.

Laboratory V was created in December 1945 as part of the national nuclear crash program.[14] Initially, a total of 40 scientists and 200 staff members ran three scientific divisions for theoretical physics, radiochemistry, and reactor materials. Almost immediately after the first successful nuclear weapons tests, Aleksandr Leipunskii, an accomplished nuclear physicist, was appointed scientific director of Laboratory V. Leipunskii's career is extraordinary by any standard: born in the Russian Empire, he studied under Ioffe in Leningrad and under Rutherford in Cambridge; in the 1930s, he convinced famous German physicists to join the scientific staff at the Ukrainian Physical-Technical Institute in Kiev, of which he was the director. But before Leipunskii started to develop Soviet nuclear weapons and later nuclear reactors, Stalin had him locked up for allegedly assisting "enemies of the people" and similar charges.[15] Leipunskii survived, the Party renewed his membership in 1946, and his career soared: he not only directed the Institute of Physics at the Ukrainian Academy of Sciences, but also served as scientific consultant for Laboratory No. 2, as a member of the Scientific-Technical Council of the Council of Ministers' PGU, and as dean of the Moscow Mechanical Institute (the later MIFI).[16] Leipunskii came to Obninsk straight from the Semipalatinsk test site, and his institute was tasked with preparing a pilot nuclear power plant to test compact reactor types for submarine propulsion.[17]

In 1960, after Kurchatov's death, Laboratory V would be renamed the Institute of Physics and Power Engineering (Fiziko-energeticheskii institut, FEI). Over the years and under Leipunskii's capable leadership, it established itself as the leading research-and-development center for breeder reactors, submarine propulsion reactors, and reactors for space.

Obninsk

The three reactor types Obninsk was supposed to test in the mid-1950s included one from the Institute of Physical Problems in Moscow with a graphite moderator and helium coolant (*"agregat Sh"*) and one with a beryllium moderator (*"agregat VT"*) from Laboratory V. The third type, the only one actually built, was a graphite-water reactor (*"agregat VM"*) that Laboratory No. 2 and Dollezhal's design and construction institute *NIIKhimmash* developed jointly (figure 4.1).[18]

In mid-1951, Kurchatov became scientific director of the Obninsk project and Nikolai Dollezhal and his institute became chief design engineer. The construction bureau OKB Gidropress took responsibility for constructing the steam generator, and the State Specialized Design Institute GSPI (later called NIPIET) for constructing the plant.[19] This long list of participants illustrates that building even a modestly sized reactor involved a small army of leading scientific, industrial, and managerial experts and their institutions. It also shows that the specific collaboration and division of labor first set up for Obninsk represented a fusion of the arrangements characteristic of the weapons program and those typical of the conventional power industries.

Minister Zaveniagin invoked the shortage of enriched uranium to justify why only the graphite-water reactor was actually built.[20] The wartime experiences of Soviet physicists may in fact have affected the choice of reactor design for Obninsk, as several researchers have suggested.[21] But although enriched uranium was certainly a scarce resource, choosing already-proven design features allowed the Soviets to avoid losing time by experimenting with new reactors and to establish a lead in the new race for nuclear power.[22]

The idea for the active zone of this graphite-water reactor came from Igor Kurchatov and Savelii Feinberg.[23] While Kurchatov was one of the country's most visible nuclear scientists—he spoke at Party congresses and appeared as an author in the pages of *Pravda* and *Izvestiia*—Feinberg was hardly known outside the nuclear physics community.[24] In later years, he would

Figure 4.1
The world's first nuclear power plant in Obninsk started up in the summer of 1954. Generations of future nuclear specialists first learned their trade at the plant's small 5 MW graphite reactor. The picture shows the control room in 2009, seven years after the reactor had been shut down. The reactor control panel resembles a toyshop, compared to later, industrial-scale plants.
Source: Photograph by Ilya Varlamov, http://zyalt.livejournal.com. Reprinted with permission.

spearhead the development of the SM-2 at Melekess, a research reactor that started up in 1961, and would be among the brains behind the RBMK.[25]

Beloiarsk
Laboratory V nuclear physicists who worked on the Obninsk plant subsequently designed two larger graphite reactors for one of the first commercial-scale nuclear power plants, the Beloiarsk plant near the city of Sverdlovsk (today Ekaterinburg).[26] But their designs remained prototypes, never standardized.

The Beloiarsk plant used graphite-water channel type reactors but included innovative design modifications aimed at improving the steam parameters and thus the efficiency and profitability of the plant. Nuclear superheating of steam generated indices comparable to conventional power plants.[27] The Beloiarsk reactors were modeled on the Obninsk reactor, but their electrical power was much greater: 100 MW and 200 MW respectively. The first reactor at Beloiarsk operated from 1964 to 1983, and the second from 1967 to 1990. Allegedly, designers soon recognized that the Beloiarsk design was a dead end: "Based on the experience of operating the two ... units at the Beloiarsk site, it became clear that this direction was not promising in economic terms. At the same time, experience with military reactors had been accumulated, and these reactors looked promising, regarding their construction and their economic indicators."[28]

But the development of the RBMK, a different type of graphite-water reactor based on military designs, began in 1964, the same year the first Beloiarsk reactor started operating.[29] Clearly industry officials decided to develop the RBMK design before the Beloiarsk reactors could have proven economically inefficient. The early prototypes at Beloiarsk struggled with a multitude of problems related to technical calculations, industrial capacity, manufacturing know-how and expertise, economic efficiency, safety and reliability of operation, and the availability of qualified cadres, to name but a few. An argument that their economic parameters disqualified them early on, then, reflects the tendency of many histories of technology to flatten and streamline a turbulent, volatile past and to transform the challenges posed by unruly technologies into a linear narrative of logical development.[30] Also, the military reactors' design, which ultimately won out over the Beloiarsk design, had not yet been adjusted to produce electricity: the military reactors' task was to produce plutonium. It was far from easy—and it took a long time—to learn to operate them in a way that used the surplus heat they produced as a by-product.[31]

Ultimately, the economic argument would, of course, become important. According to Vladimir Goncharov, a leading nuclear physicist at the Institute of Atomic Energy, operating the Beloiarsk reactor types revealed a series of technical flaws—for example, problems caused by the utilization of stainless steel in the active zone. (Later, zirconium would replace the steel.) These ongoing technical difficulties also resulted in unsatisfactory economic indicators. Nevertheless, the operation of the Beloiarsk reactors, perhaps precisely because of their design quirks and the insights that resulted from having to cope with challenging problems on a daily basis, helped nuclear specialists accumulate tremendous experience, which was later used to design reactors with 1000 MW power output.[32]

Bilibino, Breeders, and Beyond

Scientists in Obninsk also developed other designs. In 1963, nuclear physicists started working on small reactors for a combined heat and electricity nuclear plant in the remote Chukotka region. The Bilibino Station (BATETs) was the first nuclear plant north of the Arctic Circle.[33] The parallel construction of its four reactors and the plant's quick start-up within three years exemplified the idea that nuclear reactors would eventually be built in a conveyer-belt fashion. Bilibino's identical heterogeneous graphite-water reactors, called EGP-6 for their six loops, featured an innovative scheme for natural coolant circulation through the reactor channels.[34] However, like the Beloiarsk reactors, the Bilibino design was never built at any other location.[35] Instead, nuclear power planners switched to a different design that the nuclear weapons complex had used extensively, that promised economies of scale more quickly, and that was supported by a different set of scientists and engineers.

Laboratory V also developed fast neutron reactors. This reactor type accomplished fission by relying on fast neutrons as opposed to slow, or moderated, neutrons. The cores of these reactors could be configured to produce more fissile material than was needed to start up—hence their nickname "breeders." Breeders also needed significantly less enriched uranium than the VVERs or RBMKs to operate, and if properly configured they could produce customizable amounts of start-up fuel. Ultimately, the Soviets saw fast neutron reactors as the pillars of a closed fuel cycle based on a "plutonium economy," and therefore as the logical next step in the development of nuclear power.[36]

Theoretical research on breeder reactors began in 1947 and practical research in 1949, under Leipunskii's leadership.[37] From modest beginnings in 1955, when the first breeder reactor (BR-1) started up in Obninsk, Leipunskii's team developed multiple experimental prototypes.[38] But even before Chernobyl and despite predictions to the contrary, breeder reactors in the Soviet Union never reached the stage of mass diffusion. Explanations range from the high cost of fast reactors to the significant risk of fires to proliferation concerns.[39] This picture may have changed somewhat in the post-Chernobyl era, where costly equipment updates and safety retrofits have made traditional thermal reactors more expensive and breeders in turn more competitive. One could speculate that abandoning Laboratory V's designs also had to do with the growing rivalry between the Institute of Atomic Energy and Obninsk over the power to influence the development of a large-scale nuclear power industry.

Kurchatov's Laboratory No. 2

Laboratory No. 2, the Mosow-based research facility created for Kurchatov's group of nuclear weapons developers, was nominally under the Soviet

Academy of Sciences. Its later incarnations were called the Laboratory for Measuring Instruments, the Institute of Atomic Energy, and the Kurchatov Institute.[40]

The "Second Ivan" (EI-2)

In close collaboration with the Institute of Atomic Energy, the design institute that had built Soviet production reactors proposed a reactor that would both produce plutonium and generate electricity. For this purpose, the Scientific Research and Design Institute of Energy Technologies (NIKIET) modified a graphite-water reactor for dual use and promoted it as the "Siberian nuclear power plant."[41] The EI-2 ("E" stands for power (*energeticheskii*), "I" for isotope, i.e., plutonium production) was a graphite-moderated, channel type, boiling water reactor, sometimes referred to as "Second Ivan" (the "First Ivan" being a production reactor of similar design at the same site).[42]

Construction of the EI-2 commenced in 1954, and it started operation in 1958.[43] In the summer of 1958, during the Second United Nations Conference on Peaceful Uses of Atomic Energy in Geneva, Soviet media announced that the Siberian nuclear power plant had been launched successfully. Meanwhile, the commission on site was unable to get the reactor to start up. In the presence of high government officials, the reactor specialists agonized over how to accomplish the launch. A representative of the Institute of Atomic Energy apparently suggested replacing part of the nuclear fuel, an option rejected due to the scarcity of enriched uranium. Another member of the start-up commission, relying on his experience with the plant at Obninsk, ventured that the reactor's graphite had absorbed too much humidity during the lengthy start-up process and proposed a solution that involved "drying" the graphite. Powered by an outside source, engineers reversed the process of heat supply: the coolant (water) was heated and used to warm up and eventually "dry" the graphite moderator. After an extended period, the graphite returned to its design parameters, and the reactor start-up succeeded.[44]

Not unlike the plutonium production facility at Hanford, Washington, these first Soviet plutonium reactors used water from the adjacent river to cool the core and afterward released the water back into the river.[45] They were called *priamotochnye*, which referred to the continuous flow of coolant. Today, they are recognized as a main source of radioactive contamination at their formerly secret military sites. In the late 1960s, *Sredmash* completed several more dual-use graphite-water reactors based on the EI-2 design to produce weapons-grade plutonium as well as heat and hot water for the nearby towns.[46] These dual-use reactors were located at sites long kept secret. The EI-2, and the subsequent ADE reactors, all dual-use designs with graphite moderator and water coolant, were immediate predecessors of the RBMK.[47]

In early 1968, Slavskii and Neporozhnii approached the chairman of the Council of Ministers, Kosygin, with a proposal to use the heat generated as a by-product at the plutonium production reactors for district heating in the nearby city of Tomsk.[48] Although it was typically Minenergo that administered power and heating plants, in this case Sredmash was appointed the project manager, and the capital investments were allocated to its budget under "electrical power engineering." Despite the fact that the project's cost more than doubled by 1970, *Gosplan* eventually increased the annual capital investments to make the project possible.[49]

Starting with the "Second Ivan," it became clear that dual-use reactors created all kinds of management problems: it proved tricky to run facilities that contained secret parts and processes related to military applications and were at the same time supposed to connect with the civilian power industry. Planners realized that it would be easier to separate nuclear power plants from military production reactors—the former could not only be optimized for electricity generation but also built at sites near large, energy-hungry urban centers. As part of the power industry, nuclear plants could connect to the country's Unified Power System, the gigantic, Union-wide grid of transmission lines that distributed electricity and heat from generating plants to industry and households, and that managed this distribution through an integrated dispatch system. But to connect to this system, a power plant site not only had to meet the siting considerations I mentioned earlier—sufficient water supply, suitable seismic conditions, and adequate space for an occupational health and safety zone—but also demonstrate sufficiently high energy demand, existing transmission lines, and easy access to both a developed industrial base and large numbers of construction workers.[50]

The VVER

Simultaneously with the first Beloiarsk reactor, Soviet scientists from Laboratory No. 2 began to supervise the construction of a second industrial-scale reactor of a different design. In 1956, the government newspaper *Izvestiia* published an interview with Slavskii, then chairman of the Chief Administration for the Use of Atomic Energy but soon to become minister of Sredmash.[51] Slavskii mentioned that Kurchatov and Aleksandrov were spearheading a project involving a reactor of elegantly simple construction, compact size, and efficient fuel use.[52] In fact, two years earlier,

Kurchatov had instructed the construction bureau OKB Gidropress to draw up plans, and later a technical design, for a pressurized water reactor with thermal power of 760 MW.[53] At first, planners discussed several potential sites, including a plant near Moscow that would provide electricity and heat.[54] Ultimately, they chose a site 500 km south of Moscow, at the river Don and near the city of Voronezh, and workers built a series of five unique reactors, each larger than the one before. But construction did not proceed smoothly. In a letter to Sredmash on June 6, 1957, Kurchatov and Aleksandrov lamented implementation delays and called for a return to previously approved schedules.[55]

Kurchatov took great interest in the construction of the Novo-Voronezh nuclear power plant. He never hesitated to intervene on behalf of the plant and to use his political clout vis-à-vis the government and the Party to request that already-approved plans be fulfilled. He sometimes asked local Party committees to help the factories that were running late manufacture equipment for the nuclear industry. He often succeeded, but despite his efforts, the sixth five-year plan (1956–1960) was not a good one for nuclear power and remained unfulfilled.[56] Only in 1962, two years after his death, would construction at Novo-Voronezh resume full force and the nuclear industry finally acquire momentum.

In 1964, the first VVER, a 210 MW prototype, went operational at the Novo-Voronezh site; it operated until 1984.[57] Unit 2 (a 365 MW prototype) came online in 1969 and operated until 1990, and units 3 and 4 (440 MW each) started operation in 1971 and 1972, respectively. The VVER-440 became the first standardized Soviet pressurized water reactor and the reactor model for export. In parallel with the construction of units 3 and 4 at Novo-Voronezh, Soviet specialists started construction of two reactors in Finland. This joint Soviet-Finnish venture prompted the Soviet nuclear industry to develop nuclear power plant safety requirements that met international standards.[58] The VVERs at Loviisa started operation in 1977 and 1980, respectively.

In 1969, design work for unit 5 at Novo-Voronezh began. This would become the first VVER with a power increase to 1000 MW. Designers achieved this increase by improving the reactor's fuel burn-up while only marginally enlarging the reactor vessel's diameter. Still, several more design changes became necessary: designers intensified the coolant flow rate through the core and increased the length and surface of the fuel elements, which also made the core higher.[59] The vessel walls had to be thinner—and so be made from different materials—to accommodate the reactor core. In contrast to the early VVER models, which were vulnerable to gradual weakening (embrittlement), the later VVER models would feature a stainless steel cladding on the inside of the reactor pressure vessel. Unit 5 at Novo-Voronezh went critical in 1980, eleven years after construction had begun and two years after construction of these reactors for other sites had already started. Between 1984 and 1993, fourteen reactors of the VVER-1000 type went online.[60]

Like the RBMK, the VVER design had its roots in military applications: developers created it for nuclear submarine propulsion.[61] In contrast to the graphite-water design, which was too large and heavy for submarines, the pressurized water design allowed high uranium burn-ups (and thus efficiency) from a comparatively small core.[62] The United States also used pressurized water reactors for their nuclear submarines, and just as in the Soviet Union, early use—together with reliability—ultimately gave this reactor type an advantage over other designs that had less or no operational track record.[63] The submarine reactor was smaller than the pressurized water reactors later used in power plants, and it had much higher fuel enrichment.[64] Pressurized water reactors were also used for the first civilian transport applications, starting with the nuclear icebreaker *Lenin*, which was launched in 1957 and started full operation in 1959.[65]

The VVER design features two circuits or loops. Powerful pumps circulate pressurized water through the reactor core; the water serves simultaneously as moderator and coolant. The heat from the first loop is passed on to the second loop, and the fact that only the water in this second loop reaches the turbines once it has turned to steam diminishes radioactive emissions. VVER reactors also featured horizontal steam generators that provided more lag time under accident conditions than typical Western pressurized water designs, which relied on vertical steam generators.[66] The pressure vessel, by far the most complicated piece of equipment, was the Achilles heel of the entire VVER line: it was forged of solid shells without longitudinal welds, which meant it required extraordinary factory equipment and welders' skills.[67]

The thickness of the reactor vessel's walls and its diameter limit the maximum pressure coolant can attain inside the reactor.[68] The Izhora factory in Leningrad, the only factory in the country capable of guaranteeing the high quality standards required, manufactured the VVER vessels, which had to meet strength requirements and show good resistance to radiation.[69] The reactor vessel also had to fit the load standards of Soviet trains, so it could be transported from the factory to the nuclear power plant across bridges and through tunnels.[70] In other words, the Soviet transportation system's capacity for oversized cargo determined the maximum size of the reactor, which at least initially limited its power output.[71]

The VVER design was thermally more efficient than its competitors at the time and therefore—at least in theory—cost less to operate.[72] All VVERs have to be shut down for refueling.[73] Typically, plant operators completed that process during the annual shutdown for maintenance and repair, but some saw this aspect of the VVER design as a disadvantage compared with the RBMK's online refueling option.[74] Finally, designers equipped all VVERs after the first-generation 440 with a steel and concrete containment structure.[75]

Planners also expected to use the pressurized water design in nuclear district heating plants.[76] The five-year plan for 1956–1960 specified construction of such a combined electricity and heating plant in Khovrino, near Moscow. Planners later abandoned that site in favor of the Novo-Voronezh nuclear power plant, but in 1981 construction began on two nuclear district heating plants, one near Gorky (now Nizhnii Novgorod), the other near Voronezh. Other projected sites included Leningrad, Odessa, and the Kola Peninsula region. To be profitable, nuclear heating plants had to be located near densely populated areas, and for that reason, designers incorporated additional safety features in these reactors.[77]

Public opposition following the Chernobyl disaster prevented both the Gorky and Voronezh plants from going operational.[78] Although Sidorenko, an early advocate of nuclear district heating plants, believed that the industry could convince the public of the plants' safety and foresaw that the first such plant would operate by the year 2000, neither prediction has come true.[79]

The RBMK

In 1965, Sredmash's first deputy minister, Aleksandr Churin, and academician Aleksandrov convened a meeting at the Bolshevik factory in Leningrad. The topic of the discussion was a proposal the Institute of Atomic Energy put forward to develop a 1000 MW graphite-water reactor that would help meet the plan target of electricity generation at nuclear power plants. This venerable steel factory, whose tradition reaches back to Czar Alexander II, had produced heavy machinery for Soviet industry, including tractors and tanks. Bolshevik's construction bureau was the top candidate for the task of chief design engineer for the B-190 reactor (as it was then referred to). But when Sredmash's Scientific-Technical Council received Bolshevik's first design draft a year later, the council found it technically unsound.[80]

Time was of the essence. The government had issued a decree on September 29, 1966, ordering that the first two units at the Leningrad and Kursk nuclear power plants use these new reactors. After the disappointing evaluations received for the Bolshevik design, planners resorted to familiar players: Savelii Feinberg and Nikolai Dollezhal set out to revise Bolshevik's initial design proposal. Dollezhal's home institute, code-named Scientific Research Institute No. 8 (NII-8), already possessed significant experience with military and dual-use reactors. NII-8 engineers had designed and built the country's production reactors and the Second Ivan. But now they had to drastically improve the new reactor's physical and thermal efficiency so it would work exclusively for generating electrical power.[81] Dollezhal's institute was appointed chief design engineer and the Kurchatov Institute of Atomic Energy was designated the scientific director.[82] Dollezhal made the design and construction of what his institute called the RBMK-1000s their first priority.[83] NII-8 presented a new design, which included significant modifications, to Sredmash's first deputy minister Churin in February 1967. In June 1967, Churin approved these suggestions and the RBMK design was commissioned in 1968.[84] In other words, the government authorized the construction of four massive, 1000 MW nuclear power reactors before the reactor design was developed, let alone approved. This course of action makes sense only in the context of a planned economy and in light of an established tradition of duplicating critical research-and-development phases.[85]

At this point, we need to review a few basic specifications of the RBMK, because they are integral to the rest of this story. The RBMK-1000 consists of a large graphite block structure (about seven meters high, and about twelve meters in diameter) that serves as the moderator for slowing down neutrons. The fuel, slightly enriched uranium dioxide, is encased in pellets and is assembled in the form of a rod.[86] Eighteen such fuel rods, each with a diameter of 13.6 mm, are cylindrically arranged to form 3.5-meter-long fuel assemblies. These fuel assemblies are suspended into the 1,661 vertical tubes mounted throughout the reactor core, and the channel head is sealed.[87] Of those tubes, 211 are reserved for control rods that can be moved up and down to regulate the reactor's reactivity. Each fuel channel, a fuel assembly inserted into a tube, is individually cooled by pressurized water that enters at the bottom of the tube and passes the fuel from below; the water boils by the time it reaches the upper part of the tube. A nitrogen-helium gas mixture that slowly circulates in the space between the graphite and the channels is used to control the integrity of the channels.[88] The coolant has a temperature of 290°C when it reaches the steam drum, where steam is separated from water and passes on to the turbine.[89] There is only one circuit, which increases the reactor's efficiency but allows slightly radioactive steam to reach the turbines.

The RBMK can be refueled online, using a remote-controlled refueling crane; consequently the reactor is almost constantly available, and operators control the level of fuel burn-up, and, correspondingly, plutonium production.[90] In contrast to the Second Ivan, the RBMK's fuel elements stayed in the core longer and were exchanged less frequently.[91] At least initially, when plutonium was still scarce, the possibility of customizing the production of weapons-grade plutonium was seen as an attractive asset of this reactor type.[92] The RBMK's designers were well aware of the potential for plutonium production—one indication being that the RBMK was never exported beyond the borders of the Soviet Union.[93]

The RBMK can also be assembled largely on site, since many parts do not require sophisticated factory manufacturing. Once the designers had accumulated experience with the RBMK, they managed to expand the reactor's output without significantly modifying the size of the active zone: the two RBMKs built in Lithuania had a 1500 MW output with the same reactor core size as the standard 1000 MW RBMKs. The RBMK design was considered particularly safe because of its modular structure: accidents were likely to affect only individual channels, never all of them.[94] But the RBMK was also massive, and the channel design involved complicated internal plumbing.[95]

Its disadvantages (which nuclear specialists at the time considered either irrelevant or controllable) include the relatively slow emergency shutdown systems, the lack of a containment structure (which would have doubled the cost and presented an engineering challenge due to the enormous size of this reactor), and most importantly, a positive void coefficient, a feature that was involved in the Chernobyl accident. "Void coefficient" refers to the interaction of coolant and moderator. A positive void coefficient means that when cooling water is lost in the RBMK (water converts to steam, which reduces its cooling capacities), the speed of the chain reaction in the reactor core *increases* instead of decreasing, because the graphite moderator still facilitates nuclear fission. (By contrast, the void coefficient in a VVER is negative: when water is lost, reactivity decreases, because water serves as both the coolant and the moderator.)[96]

The first RBMK-1000 was built at Sosnovyi Bor, a dedicated Sredmash site on the Bay of Finland near the city of Leningrad (figure 4.2). On September 10, 1973, at 10:35 p.m., the physical launch of the reactor started

Figure 4.2
Construction and assembly of the Leningrad nuclear power plant, where the country's first RBMKs would start operating in the early 1970s. The first reactor started up seven years from groundbreaking; two years later, unit 2 came online, with units 3 and 4 starting up in 1979 and 1981, respectively. These relatively short construction periods (by contemporary standards) are all the more remarkable given difficult weather conditions, manufacturing delays, and rapid labor turnover. Nuclear construction sites all over the country would continue to face similar challenges. The image shows the assembly of the reactor pit at Leningrad's unit 4. The banner reads: "It is our socialist obligation to deliver the reactor pit by the October anniversary—we will fulfill it!" This promise is then crossed out and replaced by: "We fulfilled it!"
Source: Courtesy of the Publishing House "Master," Moscow. Originally published in *Elektroenergetika* (ed. A. I. Vol'skii and A. B. Chubais, series *Stroiteli Rossii: XX vek* (Moscow: "Master," 2003), 234–235). Reprinted with permission.

with the insertion of the first fuel assembly.[97] Savelii Feinberg headed the start-up commission, which consisted of over sixty representatives from the Institute of Atomic Energy.[98] On September 12, at 6:35 p.m., the reactor reached criticality. After the festivities came the power start-up—that is, the connection of the nuclear reactor to the electrical part of the plant.[99] On November 15, 1973, the reactor was brought to a level of 150 MW, and the official start-up took place on the evening of December 21, 1973, the day before the "Day of the Power Engineer."[100] Both Aleksandrov and Dollezhal, representatives of the scientific director and the chief design engineer, respectively, were present for that event. After the reactor had been working at 160 MW power for three days, the commission approved the reactor for experimental industrial operation.[101] Engineers had to compensate for less than optimal design decisions, especially with the fuel assemblies that kept wedging in their channels.[102] Several of these fuel assemblies had to be sent back to Moscow for repeated testing. Finally, on November 1, 1974, the reactor reached its designated power level.[103]

The second reactor at Sosnovyi Bor came online in 1975, and the first RBMK at the Kursk nuclear power plant a year later. Over the next ten years, a total of fourteen RBMK-1000 reactors (at sites near Leningrad, Smolensk, Kursk, and Chernobyl) went operational, in addition to one RBMK-1500 at the Ignalina nuclear power plant in Lithuania. Their capacity would eventually constitute half of all Soviet nuclear power plants, and in 1985, they produced 60 percent of the Soviet Union's nuclear electricity.[104] After Chernobyl, but before the collapse of the Soviet Union, a second 1500 MW RBMK in Lithuania as well as a third 1000 MW unit at the Smolensk site started up.

In contrast to the Beloiarsk reactors, which used steel in the core, RBMKs from the outset relied on zirconium—a material whose characteristics designers considered superior for use in the reactor core.[105] Overall, the RBMK underwent no fewer than seven distinct modifications. Former Minenergo deputy minister Gennadii Shasharin grouped them into three generations, which differ with regard to their emergency cooling and their accident localization (containment) systems.[106]

The first generation of RBMKs comprises the first two units at Leningrad and the first two units at Kursk and Chernobyl, all of which went critical between 1973 and 1979. Even within that first generation, there are differences, for example in plant layout: at Kursk and Chernobyl, the two reactors that share auxiliary systems are closer together.[107] Construction of the first-generation RBMKs began before the first edition of the "General Regulations for Nuclear Power Plant Safety" took effect.[108] These reactors did not have a backup system in place should cooling pipes break. They effectively had no emergency core cooling system, nor an accident localization system.[109]

Units 3 and 4 at Leningrad (commissioned in 1979 and 1981 respectively) do have an emergency cooling system, an accident localization system, as well as an improved emergency power supply. They represent the first units of the second-generation RBMK, the generation that comprises the largest number of reactors in operation. It includes units 3 and 4 at Kursk, units 3 and 4 at Chernobyl, and units 1 and 2 at Smolensk. These six units were commissioned between 1978 and 1983. Some design features were further improved, and these reactors boast even more safety features. Unit 3 at Smolensk featured improved techniques for maintenance and control. And finally, the two RBMKs at the Ignalina nuclear power plant in Lithuania achieved a significantly increased thermal capacity, and thus electrical output, without increasing the size of the reactors. The increase was achieved instead by better heat removal and by increasing the flow rate in the pipes' steam sections. Control, protection, and safety systems were modernized, and some automated control system processes changed.

Finally, the fifth unit at the Kursk nuclear power plant, whose construction was halted after the Chernobyl disaster and has proceeded in starts and fits ever since, embodies the third generation of RBMKs. The most significant design change realized there was reducing the graphite volume and the shape of the graphite columns and so the steam coefficient of reactivity.[110] This reactor constituted an important showcase for the Soviet nuclear community: scientists hoped it would prove that RBMKs were not inherently dangerous reactors, as some claimed after Chernobyl. This reactor would demonstrate that RBMKs *could* be made safe. For several years in the early 2000s, nuclear officials considered a new reactor design, the multiloop reactor MKR, for the country's nuclear future. Based on the RBMK design and the experience accumulated by operating these reactors, in theory it would retain these reactors' "positive features, [eliminate] the negative ones and [absorb] all the favourable potential features of inherent UGR [uranium graphite reactor] safety."[111]

Soviets often touted the RBMK as the "national feature of domestic nuclear power," because this particular design was unique to the Soviet Union.[112] The RBMK allowed the nuclear industry to expand based on an existing supply industry and experience with production reactors while it avoided the problems associated with the manufacture of unique pressure vessels and steam generators.[113]

Gas-Cooled Reactors

The pressurized water reactor emerged as the most common design internationally, which allowed various countries to exchange operating experience. Still, Laboratory No. 2 (and later LIPAN) developed two other functional reactor designs that to some degree competed with the VVER and the RBMK. Between 1947 and 1955, with an eye on the United Kingdom, which chose gas-cooled reactors for its civilian program, Kurchatov's reactor designers worked on gas-cooled reactors with helium as the primary coolant. Aleksandrov himself proposed a reactor called *Sharik* that combined a graphite moderator, uranium dioxide fuel elements, and helium coolant.[114] His lab originally scheduled tests at Obninsk, but in 1955 that work lost its funding to the VVER. Only in 1957 did designers resume work on gas-cooled reactors, this time focusing on high-temperature reactors with carbon dioxide coolant as the British were doing. Goncharov notes that the sixth five-year plan (1956–1960) contained the development of gas-cooled reactors with an electrical power output of 50–100 MW for commercial nuclear power plants. Construction of a gas-cooled third reactor at the Beloiarsk site started in 1955 but was halted in 1963 in favor of a fast neutron design (the BN-600).[115] A group of scientists under Nikolai Ponomarev-Stepnoi experimented with spherical fuel elements for high-temperature gas-graphite reactors, and in 1968 planners considered gas-cooled designs along with the VVER and the RBMK for the Kursk and Chernobyl sites.[116]

The erratic development of gas-cooled reactors continued into the late 1970s, when designers drew on experiments with spherical fuel elements for another graphite-helium design idea, the ABTU reactor. In May 1974, the government decided to build such a high-temperature, gas-graphite reactor with an electrical power output of 50 MW near Obninsk. But ultimately, the Soviet Union never built any gas-cooled design except as a research reactor.[117]

Heavy-Water Reactors

Research on heavy-water reactors started at Laboratory No. 2 during the atomic bomb project, with the goal of producing plutonium.[118] Heavy water (deuterium) works particularly well as moderator because it slows neutrons down without absorbing many, and it can be combined with natural (not enriched) uranium. But heavy water was a scarce resource in most of Europe, and expensive to produce. In 1949, a heavy-water research reactor began operation at Laboratory No. 3, which was subsequently renamed the Institute of Theoretical and Experimental Physics (ITEF).[119] In 1957, together with Czechoslovakian engineers, Soviet nuclear specialists started building the first heavy-water moderated power reactor, the model KS-150, at a site near Bohunice (which today is in Slovakia).[120] This joint project was part of the Council of Mutual Economic Assistance (CMEA) nuclear program, and the reactor went critical in December 1972. Notably, this was the first and only time the Soviets built a reactor type outside the borders of the USSR before first building and operating it within the country.[121] The Bohunice reactor (A-1) suffered a major accident in 1979, and neither Czechoslovakia nor the Soviet Union pursued the heavy-water design for future nuclear power plans.[122] Instead, Soviet nuclear planners decided to focus on developing the VVER and researching breeder reactors.

Competition and Standardization: Selecting "Soviet" Reactors

Given that Soviet decision makers and planners had a panoply of choices in the mid-1960s, why did they finally choose the VVER and the RBMK as the standard Soviet designs for the emerging nuclear industry?

The remainder of this chapter presents a more nuanced view of the period from the early 1960s to the mid-1970s, when the decision to produce electricity on a large scale in nuclear reactors provoked significant organizational restructuring in both the nuclear weapons sector and the power industry. Administrators selected the VVER and RBMK as major political and economic reforms brewed domestically. In addition, renewed international scientific exchange that offered insights into, and allowed comparisons with, trends in reactor engineering elsewhere in the world informed their choices.

Beginning in the early 1970s, the nuclear power industry finally acquired momentum all over the Soviet Union, as well as in allied socialist countries.[123] Between 1975 and 1986, thirty-three reactors started up in the USSR (among them sixteen VVERs and fourteen RBMKs, for a total capacity of 27,764 MW), compared to only thirteen reactors (among them six VVERs and one RBMK, for a total capacity of 4,014 MW) during the twenty years from 1954 to 1974 (figure 4.3).[124] In the face of this tremendous growth, why didn't Soviet economists and policymakers push just one reactor design? Or—conversely—why did they not choose more than two? After all, in 1962, the authorities had approved four designs for industrial-scale construction.[125]

As we have seen, Soviet planners often avoided putting their eggs in one basket and instead supported multiple parallel research directions.[126] Then too, designing reactors for power generation in the 1950s and 1960s was a surprisingly uncoordinated effort, despite the planned character of

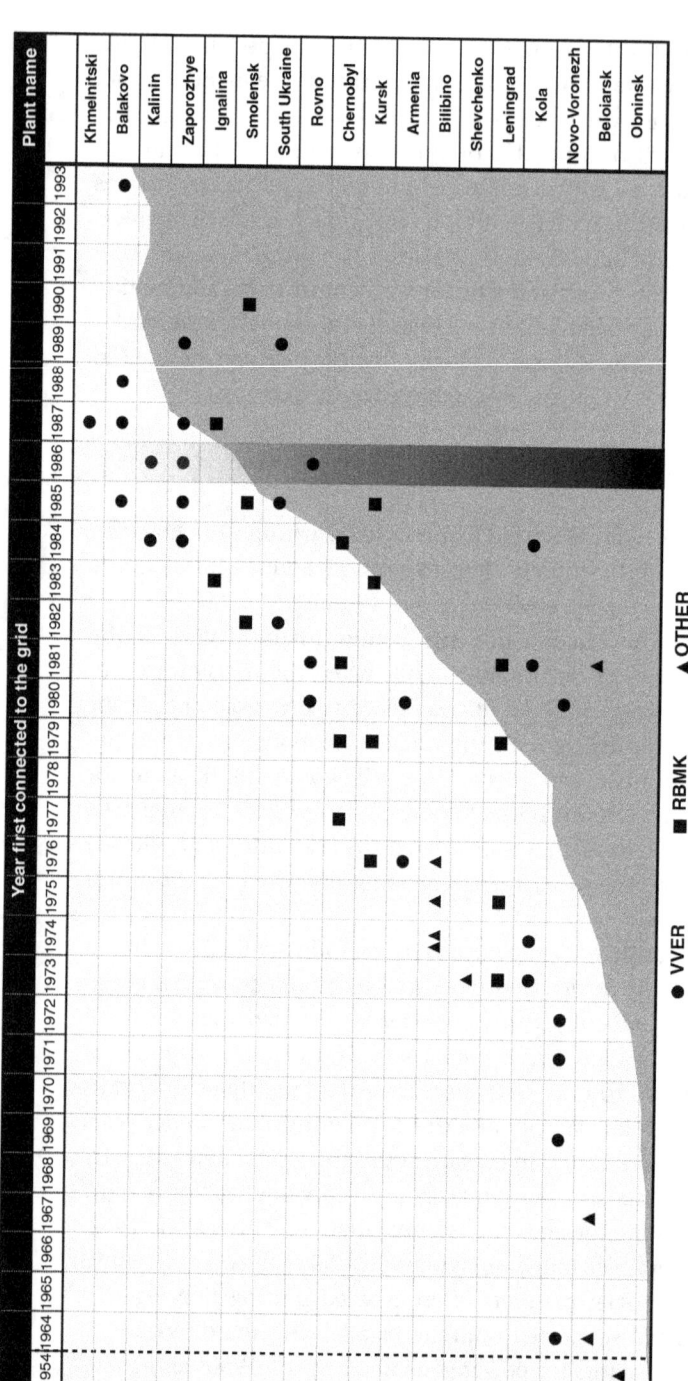

Figure 4.3

Between 1954 and 1993, fifty-five nuclear power reactors were started up in the former Soviet Union: twenty-nine VVERs, seventeen RBMKs, and nine others. Until the early 1980s, the RBMK made major contributions to nuclear electricity, while the VVER caught up only by 1987. Shown are the types of reactors that started delivering electricity to the grid each year, and the growth in nuclear power generation (in GW) overall. The figure takes into account the shutdown of units 1 and 2 at Beloiarsk in 1981 and 1989 (100 and 200 MW, respectively), the shutdown of units 1 and 2 at Novo-Voronezh in 1984 and 1990 (210 and 365 MW, respectively), the shutdown of the two 440 MW units at the Armenian nuclear power plant in 1989 as well as the subsequent restarting of the second unit in 1993, and finally, the loss of Chernobyl's unit 4 in 1986 and the shutdown of unit 2 in 1991 (1000 MW each).

Source: Graphic design by Dana Webster

the economy and the tight economic constraints at the time. Although existing infrastructure and comparatively long experience operating military graphite-water reactors no doubt contributed to the decision to adopt the RBMK as one of the two standard reactors in the Soviet Union, what counted as rational in the 1960s Soviet Union may not appear rational to us in hindsight. It is important to remember that this decision could have been made differently. While economic, technical, and diplomatic imperatives certainly mattered, these imperatives also competed with each other—consequently no single factor can on its own explain the specific trajectory the Soviet nuclear industry took. By documenting in detail the technical, economic, and institutional histories of these decisions, as well as the historical contingencies, constraints, and experiences that shaped these decisions, we can begin to acknowledge that Soviet scientists, engineers, and planners did not take decisions of such magnitude lightly. The extended negotiations I chronicle here ultimately formed the collective judgment of a community of experts. In light of Chernobyl's dramatic failure, domestic and international parties turned their scrutiny on this judgment. To more fully understand why Soviet nuclear experts made the choices they did, it is pivotal to draw together the topics we have touched on in previous chapters: the context of a planned, command-administrative economic system, the historical setting of the Cold War, and the emerging institutional structures—domestically and internationally—that governed nuclear energy.

Justifying the Choice

Soviet decision makers' 1965 decision to select the RBMK as one of the civilian program's reactors depended on several assumptions. They assumed, first, that they could convert a reactor designed to produce plutonium into a power reactor; second, that this reactor would technologically and economically surpass the graphite-water reactors already operating; and third, that the design and construction bureau that had built the military reactors could quickly produce enough new civilian reactors that they would—in combination with the pressurized water reactor—actually fulfill the plan to rapidly expand the nuclear industry. In other words, instead of choosing technically outstanding designs from the available prototypes or waiting until operating reactor types could prove or disprove their economic merit, Soviet planners chose designs they thought would meet ambitious plan targets for nuclear power generation. By 1980, seven RBMK-1000s were producing electricity, which gave their designers cause for pride, and a little poetry:

Говорят что в СССР	They say that in the USSR
Будут только ВВЭР	there will be only the VVER
Но энергию пока	but until now, as we can see,
Нам дают РБМК.	the RBMK supplies our energy.[127]

Logistical Challenges and Eager Allies

In 1964, the VVER looked like a winner. Not only was it already operating successfully, with a larger version under construction, but it was also the design other countries preferred. And yet, by 1965, nuclear energy officials realized that mass production of VVERs would take longer than anticipated. The one factory in the entire Soviet Union that could manufacture the VVER's pressure vessels, the Izhora works in Leningrad, was already inundated with other assignments.[128] A new, gigantic factory to produce these vessels was under construction but plagued by construction glitches, delays, and insufficient funding. The VVER, it turned out, would not be able to carry the nuclear industry's rapid expansion alone (figure 4.4).[129]

The industry needed a second reactor type, one that different branches of industry could supply with materials and equipment.[130] The RBMK promised just that.[131] It required graphite, cement, and pipe suppliers, while VVERs depended on high-quality, factory-based steel forging. The supply industry for the graphite-water line already existed, because military reactors relied on the same ingredients. By contrast, the industry supplying the VVER equipment was still in its early stages.

Officials thought parallel development of the VVER line and a second reactor line that drew on an already-established industry would let nuclear power expand rapidly. A quick review of Leningrad's history with regard to nuclear power illustrates how that decision turned out. The government first decreed a nuclear power plant near this city on March 16, 1956. It envisioned a nuclear heating plant with a VVER, a 200 MW pressurized water reactor. But a year later, on April 4, 1957, leaders dropped these plans. When the nuclear industry reemerged in the 1960s, they changed the site, the type of reactor, and the ministry in charge of construction. As mentioned above, it was ultimately Sredmash that would build the country's first set of RBMKs 50 miles from Leningrad at Sosnovyi Bor.[132]

Another argument often made in favor of the RBMK was its relative ease of assembly. Its parts could be installed on site, the concrete produced locally, and even the nuclear core of the plant could be largely assembled on site.[133] When engineers scaled up the VVER from 440 to 1000 MW, they had hardly any leeway to enlarge the vessel. Instead, they had to rely on different materials to increase the core's performance.[134] The RBMK's modular

Figure 4.4
Builders of *Atommash* in Volgodonsk, a city in Southern Russia. The giant factory, which dwarfs the city built next to it, was intended to mass-produce nuclear reactor equipment. The picture shows workers who participated in the construction of the factory.
Source: Photograph by L. Nosov, 1977. Provided to Wikimedia Commons by the Russian International News Agency (RIA Novosti) as part of a cooperation project. RIA Novosti archive, image #587071/L. Nosov/CC-BY-SA 3.0.

design, by contrast, allowed engineers to start out with a large 1000 MW reactor and to scale it up later without the constraints of a factory schedule or railroad specifications.

Finally, reactor selection had an international dimension as well. Several of the Soviet Union's Eastern European neighbors were pressuring the USSR to provide them with nuclear assistance. In the wake of Eisenhower's "Atoms for Peace" speech at the United Nations General Assembly in December 1953, the Soviet Union—reluctantly—signed agreements that obligated the country to start delivering nuclear power reactors (in addition to research reactors) to the German Democratic Republic, Czechoslovakia, Hungary, and Bulgaria.[135] And even though the Soviets heavily delegated manufacturing tasks to individual factories in Eastern Europe, obligations beyond their own borders put additional strains on the domestic supply line for the VVER. The limitations in industrial capacity, the logistical challenges, and the international obligations may explain why the VVER could not carry the expansion of the Soviet nuclear industry alone, but they do not explain why the RBMK was chosen as the second type. Another graphite-water design was already in operation at Beloiarsk, and a technologically innovative, scaled-up version was under construction.[136] Other existing reactor prototypes, such as the heavy-water and gas-cooled designs discussed earlier, relied on different branches of industry just as the RBMK did. The width of train bridges seems a strangely tame obstacle for a state that aspired to nothing less than world revolution.[137] On-site assembly, while likely cheaper than factory manufacturing, had its obvious downside: less control over the purity of materials and over how well workers put the parts together. Overall, historical accounts that use economic justifications to explain Soviet reactor design choices seem to be missing significant pieces of the puzzle.

The Expertise Factor

When nuclear experts and planners vetted reactor designs, they also considered the availability of experienced personnel. They selected reactor types with military origins because they saw the military-style discipline enforced at plutonium production facilities and during naval reactor operations as a distinctive asset. They expected that members of that workforce would now help a growing number of civilian engineers master nuclear power reactor operations.

And yet, as I have mentioned, even the engineers who worked at naval or military production reactors had often trained in general engineering programs and learned about nuclear facilities only on the job. These engineers' experience would not translate seamlessly, and they would not automatically find themselves in a position of authority vis-à-vis ambitious civilian engineers.

Actually, few people anywhere in the country had much experience with nuclear reactors for electricity production. Despite its tremendous symbolic value, the reactor at Obninsk was little more than a test and training plant, and only the operating personnel at Beloiarsk and Novo-Voronezh had some limited experience with operating power reactors. Many of the early managers and operators from these two initial plants went on to outstanding careers in the nuclear power industry.[138] But while decision makers argued for the VVER in part by pointing out that Novo-Voronezh personnel had experience operating a pressurized water reactor, they did not acknowledge that Beloiarsk personnel (mostly energetiki) had similarly accumulated experience with graphite-water reactors, experience that compared favorably with that of the technical experts familiar with military reactors.

As I showed in chapter 3, when Minenergo began to develop curricula that prepared engineering students and credentialed engineers for careers in the nuclear industry in the late 1950s, the emerging cooperation gradually began to produce a new cadre of nuclear power experts.

Designers' Dilemmas and the Global Stage

Converting graphite-water reactors designed for producing weapons-grade plutonium to machines optimized for electricity generation involved immense technical challenges—and so did modifying naval propulsion reactors to power reactors of entirely different size, purpose, and core physics. Aleksandrov cooperated closely with Dollezhal and Slavskii to promote the VVER and RBMK designs. The three men provided the RBMK in particular with the patronage it needed to become an unexpected front runner.

Soviet scientists and reactor engineers eagerly advertised their early advances in nuclear technology—for example, by taking Western visitors on tours of select facilities.[139] They closely observed the design choices France, Britain, and the United States made for civilian reactors.[140] Recognition abroad always brought prestige for Soviet science at home, and Soviet nuclear specialists utilized international contacts to promote their ideas with domestic decision makers. But different groups leveraged such international connections in different ways. For instance, VVER advocates invoked international scientific consensus about the pressurized water design being a safe, economical, and deservedly popular option. They emphasized international harmonization in reactor engineering, and they argued that choosing pressurized water reactors would facilitate cooperation and accelerate learning among countries operating similar nuclear reactors.[141]

Supporters of the RBMK, by contrast, insisted that their design was uniquely Soviet and condescendingly referred to the VVER as "the American reactor." They stressed that Soviet scientists and engineers had developed graphite-water reactors without any assistance from abroad.[142] As in other nations, however, exactly what was Soviet about the Soviet program was tricky to identify in the context of international exchange (both licit and illicit).[143] Nevertheless, the alleged indigenous purity of the RBMK design was a powerful argument in the struggle for legitimacy within the Soviet nuclear power program. Like their French counterparts, Soviet reactor designers used similarities with, and differences from, other countries' reactor designs as rhetorical resources to promote and contest specific proposals.[144] But unlike in France, where different institutions developed competing designs, both Soviet designs originated in the same design institute, Kurchatov's Institute of Atomic Energy.

Technology Triumphs

Decision makers made technical superiority the ultimate justification for the two reactor types they chose. The argument that both the RBMK and VVER were technologically advanced has even survived the Chernobyl disaster.[145] Those who promoted this view defined technical excellence in terms of imaginative solutions appropriate for the specific context of the Soviet nuclear industry, but also in terms of universal criteria such as demonstrated operation (prototypes) and safety features.

But the argument that the VVER and RBMK were the most advanced reactor technologies at the time, and in particular, that the adoption of the RBMK was a natural development, the normal outcome of a logical process, does not hold. As I pointed out above, when the Soviet government decided to equip future nuclear power plants with RBMKs, Sredmash had not even approved the technical design. Modifying the design of plutonium production reactors turned out to be a complex task that took much longer than planners anticipated. In addition, international observers in Geneva were unenthusiastic about the "Siberian" reactor, a direct predecessor of the RBMK.[146] Nuclear experts elsewhere considered the RBMK design neither technologically novel nor particularly worrisome by international standards—overall, they saw it as a functioning but dull machine. In the Soviet Union, however, planners saw its potential both as an official propaganda tool to advertise Soviet technical prowess and uniqueness, and, less publicly, as a backup option to satisfy national security interests.

Conclusion

The dominant historiography of the Soviet nuclear power program needs revision. In contrast to accounts that foreground the economic or technical advantages of certain reactor designs, I argue that those who chose the RBMK and VVER did not know at the time which of the many reactor types available would offer economic advantages or technical superiority. The RBMK was neither the cheapest nor the technologically most sophisticated design available, nor did it have the most substantial track record. Soviet nuclear experts (and experts in other nations) chose reactor designs not because they were the best or most functional ones available. The designs they picked worked, and they probably worked at least as well as others, but factors such as the material constraints of Soviet industry, familiarity with operating similar designs, and the organizational status of different research institutes better explain why some technical configurations acquired momentum and eventually succeeded, while others faltered.

Critics of the RBMK attribute the design's selection to dysfunctional organizations, individual career ambitions, and deliberate recklessness; they argue, with a dash of nationalist rhetoric, that this choice set the world on a direct course toward the Chernobyl disaster. I disagree. We don't need to accept (or reject!) all the details of official Soviet historiography on the nuclear power industry to acknowledge that all technological development involves ambitious engineers, political alliances, and, yes, risk taking. The degree to which strong, independent regulatory agencies, incentives for competition, or public debate keep such factors in check will vary by country, industry, and historical period. A line of reasoning that triumphantly identifies in retrospect where things went wrong obscures the fact that what we consider good and safe always depends on context. The RBMK was a design that only made sense in the specific context outlined above. In this specific context, however, selecting the RBMK made very good sense.

5 Chernobyl: From Accident to Sarcophagus

In many ways, Chernobyl was an accident waiting to happen, and some readers may interpret the following account as entirely in line with this view. What I will demonstrate in this chapter is more complicated, however. While there were warning signs that all was not well with the RBMK, the Chernobyl plant crew, and the Soviet nuclear industry in general, and while it is true that some ignored or minimized many of these warning signs, other people and organizations worked tirelessly to address them. Many people in the industry had to make difficult decisions under great uncertainty, and when they knew they couldn't achieve the optimum solution, zero risk, they tried to at least reduce the risk they saw. These decision makers did not have the clarity hindsight conveniently provides. When they couldn't get fire-resistant roof tiles in time, they had to decide whether to risk delaying a reactor's start-up, a delay that could cost them funds for salaries and workers' bonuses in years to come. They had to decide whether to stop operating all reactors until every system had been upgraded, a decision that would have left many households dark, schools cold, and industrial facilities idle. And they had to decide whether to treat nuclear power plants as special or ordinary, with all the consequences this categorization entailed. Nobody made such decisions alone: teams, committees, councils, sectors, divisions, and other forums all debated these decisions, weighed options, disagreed, and compromised. Sometimes they got it right, sometimes they got lucky, and sometimes things went really badly. Catastrophically badly, as they did in the early hours of April 26, 1986, at Chernobyl's reactor number 4 (figure 5.1).

In this chapter, I recapitulate the main stages of the accident itself—the explosion and immediate response, including the evacuation of the plant's satellite town. Next, I analyze the phase when a more specific emergency response strategy took shape and culminated in the completion of the reactor entombment (the sarcophagus). I scrutinize the protracted period of accident investigations, when reports were written, revised, and refuted. This period started during the extended emergency response phase, when the Soviet and international authorities assigned blame, and it continued after the sarcophagus was built. During this period, organizations operating nuclear power plants introduced safety improvements at their reactors, not always in a synchronized fashion. To fully examine the design issue, I reconsider the concerns that nuclear scientists raised about the RBMK before Chernobyl. Finally, I look at how the accident changed the nuclear power industry in the former Soviet Union.

The Accident

On April 25, 1986, the operators on duty in the control room of unit 4 at the Chernobyl nuclear power plant conducted a scheduled test.[1] They wanted to see whether, with their energy supply cut, the turbines would have enough momentum to supply electricity to the plant's systems for more than the 20 to 30 seconds the emergency diesel generators needed to start up.[2] To do the test, they had to switch off one of the safety subsystems.[3] They planned to do the test just before the next regular maintenance shutdown.[4] Their instructions stipulated a thermal power level of 700–1000 MW. If the power dropped below this margin, they were supposed to terminate the test and shut down the reactor immediately.

When the head of unit 4's control room staff, Aleksandr Akimov, started his shift in the afternoon of April 25, the reactor was in transition, a state that occurred whenever operators were either shutting it down or starting it up. In those situations, a reactor is typically less stable than during regular operation. In addition, during shift change, the incoming operators had to catch up with the logbook, assess the current state of the reactor, and prepare for the tasks allocated to their shift.[5] Observers in Russia and the United States have noted that these moments in the control room are always challenging and often push the reactor operators' skills to the limit.[6]

The operators at Chernobyl's unit 4 had begun to decrease the power level when the regional grid operator, *Kievenergo*, prohibited the reactor's shutdown due to high energy demand.[7] Kievenergo did allow the operators to resume the scheduled test at 11:25 p.m., once the period of peak demand had passed.[8] The operators then tried to raise the power level again, not realizing that the reactor had already entered the period of xenon poisoning, during which raising the power level is difficult if not impossible.[9]

To understand what happened next, we need a few additional technical details about the RBMK.[10] The control rods that sit in water-filled, vertical

Chernobyl

Figure 5.1
Destroyed reactor number 4 at Chernobyl. On April 26, 1986, an explosion completely destroyed reactor number 4 and ejected large amounts of highly radioactive debris into the plant's surroundings and high into the atmosphere, where wind and rain carried the fallout to regions near and far. Remediation work commenced immediately, despite the unprecedented levels of radiation.
Source: Photograph by Anatol Rasskazov, 1986. Courtesy of National Chernobyl Museum, Kiev, Ukraine.

channels in its graphite core are made of a neutron-absorbing material and serve to regulate the reactor's power level. When completely inserted into the core, as for example at start-up and shutdown (position D in figure 5.2), the control rods absorb all the neutrons emitted by the uranium fuel, and no nuclear fission can take place.[11] Reactor operators adjust the level of the control rods to increase, stabilize, or decrease the reactor's power level.[12] When operators raise them—that is, pull them partially out of the core—neutrons emitted by the fuel are free to interact with the moderator (the graphite). The moderator slows the neutrons down to a speed at which they are likely to split other nuclei, a process that eventually facilitates a nuclear chain reaction. Automatic controls regulate some control rods, others can be operated manually, and some are emergency rods programmed to react to signals indicating an accident.[13]

The control rods in the RBMK consist of two parts, one boron-iron alloy part that absorbs neutrons, and another part (the so-called displacer, usually made of graphite or zirconium) that does not. When a control rod is pulled completely out of the core, only the part that facilitates the chain reaction remains in the core (position C in figure 5.2). This control rod design makes the reactor economically more efficient, because it prevents the control rod channel from filling up with water, which is a neutron absorber and would therefore slow down the chain reaction. If a control rod is pulled out too far, however (position A in figure 5.2), water floods the lower part of the empty channel and, due to its neutron-absorbing properties, reduces the reactivity in the core. When the control rod is subsequently reinserted (position B in figure 5.2), its nonabsorbing portion replaces the water and thus introduces additional reactivity to the core.

The operators at Chernobyl unit 4 completed the last part of the scheduled test, and at 1:23:40 a.m., one of them pushed the emergency shutdown button.[14] The workers didn't think there was an emergency: while it may not be the most elegant way to shut down the reactor, RBMK operators habitually used the "scram" button under nonemergency circumstances to activate the reactor's automated shutdown, presumably as a shortcut to shutting it down manually. That night, the operators had pulled most of the rods almost all the way out as they tried to raise the reactor's power level. The control rods that remained partially inserted into the core added up to the equivalent of only eight or nine full control rods. This violated the instructions, which required the equivalent of fifteen control rods in the core at any given time.[15] Once the operators activated the automated shutdown, more than 200 control rods started inexorably lowering, and the first part of each rod to enter the core was not the neutron-absorbing part

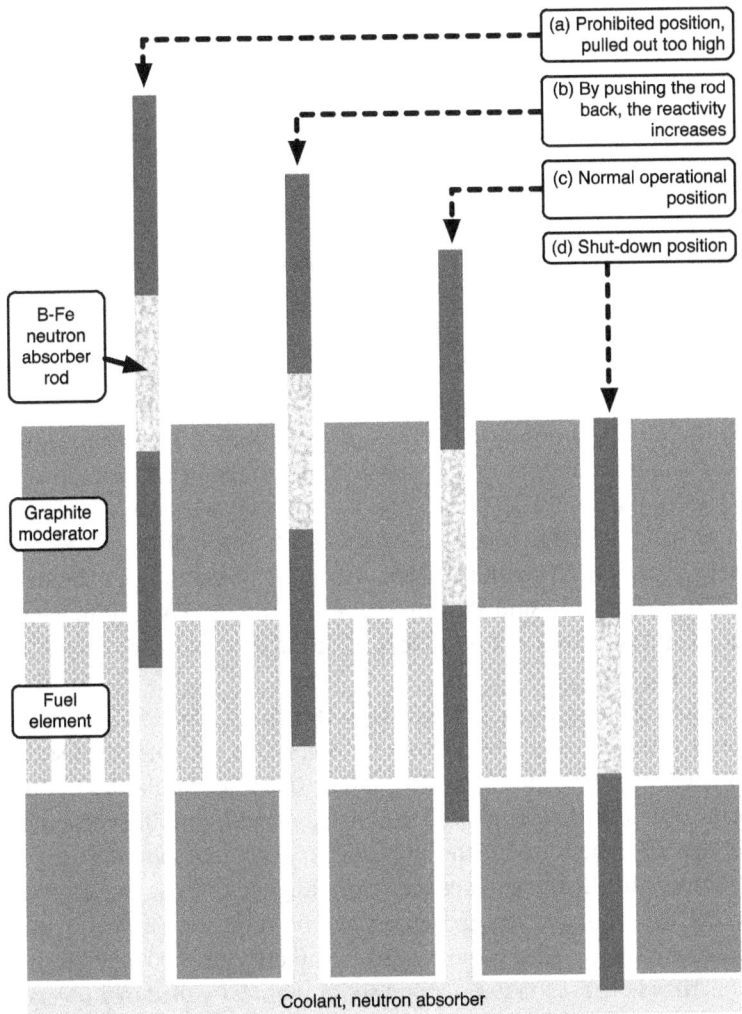

Figure 5.2
The chart shows the design and various possible positions of the RBMK's control rods. In an effort to raise the reactor's power level, operators at Chernobyl's reactor number 4 had pulled most of the control rods out very high, to a position labeled "prohibited" on the chart. When the operators initiated the automatic reactor shutdown (SCRAM), the control rods started moving down into the reactor core. Since they had been pulled out too far, their insertion did not shut down the nuclear reaction as intended, but instead introduced additional reactivity into the core. This led to the destruction of the reactor.
Source: Graphic design by Dane Webster.

but the graphite part. Replacing the neutron-absorbing water columns, the rods thus introduced additional reactivity into the core. In other words, the control rods that were supposed to terminate the chain reaction did just the opposite—they pushed it into an uncontrollable state. The operators could do nothing but watch: the system was automated and they could no longer intervene.

The introduction of additional reactivity to the core led to a rapid, uncontrollable power increase, prompting reactivity to rise exponentially.[16] As the deputy minister of Energy and Electrification, Gennadii Shasharin, put it: "One thing is clear: the reactor bolted."[17] The control rods made it only about halfway down their path. An immediate tenfold rise in power triggered the first warning signal, the second—which indicated a 100-fold rise in power—followed within three seconds.[18] The latter signal (excess pressure) usually comes on when a coolant pipe in the reactor ruptures or suffers a major leak. The fact that these alarms went off is evidence that not all safety systems had been switched off, as initial reports would claim.[19] Then the staff on duty heard a rumble "resembling a human moan."[20] This first explosion destroyed the reactor.[21] According to Aleksandr Iadrikhinskii's authoritative report, a second explosion destroyed the reactor building.[22]

The explosion ejected much of the graphite from the core of unit 4 into the plant's surroundings and set the rest on fire.[23] This fire not only distributed radioactive particles into the atmosphere but it jeopardized the electric communications that the plant's unit 4 shared with unit 3. Firefighters were the first to come to the plant after the explosion. Despite their inadequate equipment (the fire engines were not designed to fight fires at great heights and distances, and the firefighters had no protection against radiation), they managed to extinguish the fire completely by 5:00 a.m. Twelve received perilous doses of radiation, and six of them later died in a specialized clinic in Moscow.[24] Their work was crucial, since the consequences might have been far worse had the fire reached the adjacent reactor, unit 3, or reactors 1 and 2, neither of which was protected by fire-resistant construction materials.[25]

The shift on duty gathered to drink an iodine-alcohol mixture, a stopgap measure to counteract the thyroid gland's uptake of radioactive iodine: "Diatlov [the plant's deputy chief engineer] prepared the solution with difficulty, because his hands were shaking, and drank."[26] The authorities didn't decide to distribute potassium-iodide tablets to the general population in the area affected by the disaster until May 6, when the greatest danger was already over.[27]

The radiation-measuring instruments on hand continuously indicated the maximum on their scales; they were not calibrated to measure such high radiation levels. Other instruments with larger-scope gauges were kept in an area between units 3 and 4, and the explosion had made it impossible to reach them.[28] Eventually, other nuclear power plants would supply the required instruments, but too late to help those on duty that day.[29]

The plant's director, Viktor Briukhanov, who rushed to the plant from his apartment in Pripyat, called Moscow to report the accident. However, at the time of his call, he did not—could not—give conclusive information on the gravity of the situation.[30]

The very day the accident occurred, the Council of Ministers established a government commission at the Chernobyl site and appointed Boris Shcherbina its chairman.[31] Shcherbina, a former minister for Construction in the Oil and Gas Industries, was deputy chairman of the Council of Ministers at the time of the accident and also headed the Council of Ministers' powerful Bureau for the Fuel and Energy Complex. Shcherbina's commission included the minister of Minenergo, deputy ministers of Health, Internal Affairs, and Sredmash, Ukrainian leaders, a deputy attorney general, representatives from the Power Industry Workers' Union and the KGB, and of course nuclear specialists. Clearly Moscow understood the extraordinary character of the situation.[32]

Shcherbina's commission created several working groups and allocated responsibilities for specific tasks. Aleksandr Semenov, for example, at the time deputy minister of Minenergo, was put in charge of implementing a program to shut down Chernobyl's reactor number 4 and was given detailed deadlines for each step.[33] The government commission, Semenov's group, and other specialists serving on site were receiving high doses of radiation and consequently their membership had to be exchanged frequently.[34] The first fifteen airplanes transporting people to Chernobyl and flying the route Moscow-Kiev-Moscow had to clean their contaminated seats and discard some of them.[35]

Minenergo set up its own working groups. Gennadii Veretennikov, the director of *Soiuzatomenergo*, headed a coordinating group in Moscow. Soiuzatomenergo already had a preapproved action plan in case an accident occurred at a nuclear power plant. Never implemented before, this action plan called for a team of experts to be dispatched to the accident site, and provided for around-the-clock support from Moscow.[36] Following this plan, on the morning of April 26, 1986, Boris Prushinskii, the chief engineer of Soiuzatomenergo, Armen Abagian, the director of Minenergo's nuclear research institute (VNIIAES), and Konstantin Polushkin, a leading representative of the RBMK's chief engineering institute (NIKIET), flew from Moscow to Kiev. Gennadii Shasharin, then first deputy minister of Minenergo, headed another working group directly at the Chernobyl site. Shasharin's group was responsible for analyzing the accident and for keeping the plant's remaining three reactors safe.

In immediate response to the accident, the Communist Party's Politburo established the Strategic Group under Nikolai Ryzhkov, then chairman of the Council of Ministers.[37] This group had the highest authority of all; it consisted of several Politburo members, ministers, and the president of the Academy of Sciences, Anatolii Aleksandrov.[38] It established a direct phone line to connect its members in Moscow and the government commission at the Chernobyl site. Members of the government commission also reported regularly in person to the Strategic Group in Moscow, in secret meetings, whose minutes have been to this day only partially declassified.[39]

When nuclear specialists arrived at the Chernobyl site from Moscow, their first concern was whether the reactor could reach criticality again.[40] The explosion had destroyed both the control rods, which would have kept the chain reaction under control, and the core cooling system, which would have ensured the removal of decay heat. On the evening of April 26, the government commission ordered the shutdown of reactors 1 and 2. By the morning of April 27, all remaining reactors at Chernobyl were off line.[41]

On the day of the accident, almost 50,000 people were living in the town of Pripyat, in the immediate vicinity of the Chernobyl nuclear plant; almost 30 percent of them were children.[42] Apparently, Chernobyl's director Briukhanov requested an evacuation when he first notified Moscow officials of the accident, and several other individuals also suggested an evacuation very early on.[43] According to the emergency response plan, the Ministry of Internal Affairs should have told the people of Pripyat to stay inside and shelter in place, but this did not happen.[44] Even if it had, those in the metropolis may not have listened: Kiev residents were holding May Day parades, celebrating outdoor weddings, and taking schoolchildren on field trips. The authorities had a heated and prolonged debate over evacuating the plant's satellite town, and on April 27 at 11:00 a.m., some 33 hours after the reactor exploded, they announced they would evacuate Pripyat and establish a 30-kilometer exclusion zone around the destroyed reactor.[45] Buses started leaving the town at 2:00 p.m. that day, and the evacuation was complete by 5:00 p.m.[46] Overall, more than 135,000 people left Pripyat and the surrounding areas.[47] By the evening of April 27 various working groups had arranged the delivery of 3,000 tons of lead and other necessary material to the site and the setup of two improvised concrete factories. Multiple medical centers provided support to the mitigation workers.[48]

Initial Disaster Response

In the days that followed, additional groups at the local, regional, and republican level, as well as civil defense organizations and party commissions, all got involved in mitigating the disaster. The effort would continue until 1988, and about 30,000 people would take part.[49]

The operation proceeded by trial and error rather than with a scientific approach, and a coherent strategy developed only slowly.[50] Specialists from other nuclear power plants, especially from Kursk and Smolensk, and some who had worked previously at the Chernobyl plant came to support or replace those at the accident site. Many recruits and nonspecialized hired workers were not familiar with radiologically dangerous environments.[51] This was even more the case for the volunteers who started to pour in at the same time. The influx of willing but unorganized individuals posed new challenges for the accident mitigation management.[52] One problem, for example, was the quantity of contaminated clothing, which overwhelmed the plant's specialized cleaners. Early on, no safe disposal sites existed for contaminated clothes and equipment.

Army helicopters dropped heavy sacks filled with a neutron-absorbing material on the destroyed reactor to secure it.[53] During 1,800 flights, these helicopters dropped more than 5,000 tons of material on the ruins of unit 4, in a desperate attempt to prevent the reactor from reaching criticality again.[54] The helicopters had no shielding against radiation; the pilots eventually started putting lead plates under their seats.[55]

High radiation made robots, both Soviet and foreign, "go crazy" and malfunction; they had to be supplemented, and in some cases replaced by, so-called biorobots, soldiers donning protective lead outfits.[56] Photographs of these soldiers became some of the most notorious images of the Chernobyl cleanup efforts. Under extremely dangerous conditions, these "volunteers" shoveled graphite from the rooftop back into the ruins of reactor number 4, working for only a minute or two before they accumulated a lifetime dose of radiation and left the site.

On the fifth day after the accident, radioactive emissions from the reactor started to increase anew. One explanation for this phenomenon was that the material dropped on the reactor prevented adequate heat removal. Another was that when the heavy loads landed on the reactor's biological shield, which the explosion had lifted and which had landed back on its base at an angle, they made the shield shift slightly, possibly allowing the release of more radioactive material.[57] The Soviet delegation later told the IAEA that about 25 percent of the postaccident radioactive emissions occurred during the first day. Emissions then decreased over the next five days, only to rise again on days six to nine to 70 percent of the first day's release and then finally decrease to about 1 percent of the initial level.[58]

Another threat was radioactive contamination of groundwater, which half of Ukraine's population depended on for drinking water.[59] A separate working group took on building an underground barrier under the entire plant, only to have its work later limited to the most dangerous areas.[60]

The realization that the reactor, possibly the entire plant, and perhaps the entire area would have to be abandoned for good, only gradually sank in. For weeks after the initial explosion, top officials in Ukraine and at the central ministerial level still called for a rapid return to "normal operations."[61]

International media reports contributed to the confusion over how bad things really were: Scandinavian reindeer were mass-slaughtered, British sheep quarantined, and Greek agricultural products taken out of circulation (and swooped up by U.S. armed forces); German regions fought over the proper way to decontaminate lettuce.[62] When the radioactive dust settled, the world had a new set of realities to live with: significant portions of Europe had been contaminated, so much so that authorities recommend limiting the consumption of wild mushrooms and berries to this day. The alarm over exposure to radiation was not misplaced. To mention just one of the accident's long-term health impacts, the rate of thyroid cancer in children exposed to radioactive iodine, especially in Belorus, Ukraine, and Russia, would increase significantly.[63]

Constructing the Sarcophagus: Longer-Term Mitigation

To contain radiation within unit 4's remains, officials decided in May 1986 to build a concrete encasement (*ukrytie*). But construction of this so-called sarcophagus didn't begin immediately, apparently because the president of the Academy of Sciences, Anatolii Aleksandrov, and his deputy, Evgenii Velikhov, disagreed about whether building it was dangerous.[64] Nikolai Ryzhkov, chairman of the Council of Ministers, ordered them to sort out their differences by the following day (May 20), and only then did construction start. Having witnessed this controversy, the deputy minister of Minenergo, Aleksandr Semenov, concluded: "Back then I, and I think other participants in this meeting, found it strange that two academicians and nuclear specialists could not give an unambiguous answer to a given task; it occurred [to me] that maybe not everything was well with nuclear science."[65] Sredmash took responsibility for the design and construction of the sarcophagus. Already in charge of most accident mitigation work, Sredmash had the full support of the military, which meant that it had battalions of soldiers at its disposal.[66] The Leningrad design and construction institute VNIPIET took on the role of project manager for the encasement.[67] Together, these entities completed the sarcophagus that November (figure 5.3).[68]

Construction workers built temporary housing in radiologically safe areas outside Pripyat. In July, they built the town Zelenyi Mys (Green Cape) on the banks of the Kiev reservoir to accommodate both the workforce that would maintain the remaining reactors and continue the cleanup around reactor number 4 and the nuclear specialists who flew in from Moscow and other nuclear power plants.[69] Simultaneously, construction began on new permanent living quarters for the nuclear plant workforce and their families.[70]

Placing Blame for Chernobyl: Conflicting Reports

The Chernobyl disaster and the subsequent arguments about blame, accountability, and acceptable risk bear striking analogies to the *Challenger* accident Diane Vaughan has analyzed.[71] As with the *Challenger* incident, which preceded Chernobyl by only a few months, Chernobyl prompted a heated discussion about whom to blame (engineers or managers in the *Challenger* case, operators or designers in the Chernobyl case) and about the legitimacy of earlier decisions regarding acceptable degrees of safety and redundancy. In retrospect, it may seem obvious where fault lies. But by considering each of the various accounts of the accident seriously, we can tease out sharply divergent scenarios, each of which has different implications for the nuclear power industry.

If human error alone caused the accident, as one of the influential accounts would have it, this exonerates the reactor designers to some extent: had the reactor operators followed procedure, everything would have been fine. But as the young Soviet antinuclear movement figured out pretty quickly, this argument can backfire once we acknowledge that human beings never follow all the rules all the time, not even in a nuclear reactor control room. If the design of a reactor lets rule violations, or even simple mistakes, escalate into a nuclear catastrophe, that reactor probably should not be operating.

Conversely, if a design flaw caused the accident, then the question arises why nobody fixed this flaw, especially if designers knew about it, as some

Figure 5.3
The Chernobyl "Sarcophagus." Facing the extreme conditions of a nuclear disaster, the Ministry of Medium Machine Building (*Sredmash*) led the national effort to cover the ruins of Chernobyl's reactor number 4 with a concrete entombment. By November 1986, armies of professionals, soldiers, and volunteers managed to complete the construction of the so-called Sarcophagus.
Source: Photograph by Volodymir Repik, 1986. Courtesy of National Chernobyl Museum, Kiev, Ukraine.

evidence suggests. But the argument that the designers were irresponsible for not immediately fixing the problem doesn't withstand scrutiny either. Complex technological systems usually have innumerable problems, and even a modern probabilistic risk assessment expert will prioritize these problems by urgency, rather than suggest eliminating them all. We all operate and use imperfect systems on a daily basis. We know about flaws and know how to work around them (think of a quirky car, a buggy computer program, or annoying security protocols). In other words, a faulty control rod design does not mean a nuclear reactor cannot work, but it does require knowledgeable, skilled operators who understand how to compensate for the flaw, know their limitations, and are committed to safety above everything else, including plan targets, bonuses, and, yes, orders.

The contradictory reports on Chernobyl also raise the question of who had access to what information. Many serious critics have charged that the Soviet nuclear industry maintained undue secrecy, which implies that access to everything by anyone, full transparency, could have prevented Chernobyl. From there, it is a small step to more general statements about the advantages of transparent democratic systems and the inherent disadvantages of the secretive Soviet system. But the dichotomy is wrong: complete secrecy, like full transparency, does not exist. There will always be leaks and leakers, and there will always be restricted knowledge, in any political system, in any industry, and especially in the nuclear industry with its many sensitive, potentially dual-use areas of expertise. Our collective attention is better focused on who makes the rules that guard sensitive expertise and what processes we set in motion to administer these rules. As the reports and especially the whistleblowers' accounts show, the Soviet nuclear power community was full of critical, outspoken, confrontational individuals who took considerable personal and professional risks to pinpoint problems and report them. But in a system without a free press or an independent regulator, they had to report them to their peers and their higher-ups. Chernobyl happened at a point in time when that restrictive system was starting to crack, even though it was still going strong. The accident investigation reports illustrate the contradictory dynamics affecting that system.

The Government Commission's Report
The report the government commission ultimately submitted to the Strategic Group was not its first. Shortly after the accident, Gennadii Shasharin, Boris Prushinskii, and Armen Abagian—all leading Minenergo experts—refused to sign the report the commission had prepared at the Chernobyl site.[72] They argued it was impossible to arrive at a final conclusion after just one week. Their refusal to sign caused a scandal, and on May 13, Shcherbina, the chairman of the government commission, ordered Shasharin, Viktor Sidorenko (from the oversight committee *Gosatomenergonadzor*), and Valerii Legasov (from the Institute of Atomic Energy) to report to him in person in Moscow. He was putting together the final report, and he wanted these experts to sort out their differences so he could finish it.[73] Shasharin, who as first deputy minister of Minenergo was in charge of nuclear power plants, continued to see things differently from Sidorenko and Legasov, both members of the government commission.

Despite his inability to achieve unanimity, Shcherbina submitted his group's report to the Central Committee's Strategic Group in June 1986. Written in accessible, nontechnical language, it covered the development of nuclear power in the Soviet Union and described the Chernobyl plant before getting into the accident and mitigation measures.[74] The report concluded that the reactor operators, Leonid Toptunov and Aleksandr Akimov (both of whom died soon thereafter from acute radiation sickness), had directly caused the accident. It also made some general recommendations for increasing the safety of nuclear power plants.

Those who attended two meetings of the Interdepartmental Technical Council in June 1986 confirmed the government commission's version of events.[75] The actual scientific and technical reports on the accident were initially classified and were only declassified when foreign specialists started publishing their own analyses based on IAEA reports and material published in the Soviet Union prior to the accident.[76]

Minenergo's Assessment

Shasharin considered the government commission's account of the accident premature, crafted when experts knew too little to draw definite conclusions or attribute blame. In particular, he took issue with the conclusion that the reactor operators on duty that night had directly caused the accident.[77] Analyzing the course of events with the help of reactor parameters recorded just before the accident, Shasharin concluded that there were no warning signals at the time the operator pushed the emergency shutdown button:[78]

> The operator activated ... the reactor emergency shutdown system, he activated it before the warning and accident signals indicating a rise in power appeared, signals that would have triggered the emergency shutdown system automatically (it was not turned off). ... But the emergency shutdown button ... thrust [the reactor] into a prompt-critical state. ... One publication stated that the operator confused the buttons. No, the operator pushed the right button. The situation was paradoxical ... had the operator not pushed the emergency shutdown button, the reactor would have "extinguished" itself on its own, because the remaining reactivity was close to zero.[79]

Well aware that many would perceive his critique of the government commission's conclusions as defending the ministry he represented, Shasharin was nevertheless determined to challenge the assessment that operators' actions had led directly to the catastrophe. Human error, he acknowledged, could never be fully eliminated, even among highly qualified specialists. If one operator's mistake could lead to a reactor explosion, as the government commission's version claimed, then the antinuclear opposition was right and nuclear power should indeed be abandoned.[80] Shasharin's analysis highlighted deficiencies in the reactor design.[81] He made that case several times in person to the government commission and in writing to both the Council of Ministers and Ryzhkov, the council's chairman.

Shcherbina had a copy of Minenergo's report, and he no doubt realized that it differed significantly from the one the members of his own commission had written.[82] In the end, however, rather than presenting both versions in his own report, let alone trying to reconcile their incompatibilities, he chose to trust the authority of "big science."[83]

The Central Committee's Decree

By the time the government commission reported to the Politburo's Strategic Group in early June 1986, the members of the latter already had alternative explanations at their disposal, and concluded that the efforts of Minenergo, Sredmash, and Gosatomenergonadzor to increase the safety of nuclear power plants were insufficient.[84] In particular, the Strategic Group lamented that plants had insufficient fire protection, outdated equipment, no simulator training for plant personnel, and a tense atmosphere. The Strategic Group's assessment marked the beginning of a protracted process of assigning blame and debating ultimately irreconcilable differences.

In a top-secret decree issued July 14, 1986, the Central Committee blamed the accident on organizational culture, a lack of a rigorous attitude toward personnel performance, and a lack of discipline in all organizations involved—a remarkable departure from the government commission's report.[85] A *Pravda* article that appeared on July 20, 1986 named those dismissed in the wake of the disaster but did not give all the decree's details.[86]

Like the government commission, the Central Committee criticized Minenergo's leadership (specifically minister Maiorets and his first deputy Shasharin) and pointed out severe problems within the operating organization Soiuzatomenergo (specifically mentioning its director, Veretennikov). But the Central Committee also said the chief design engineer (NIKIET) and the scientific director (the Institute of Atomic Energy) had made serious mistakes and criticized Sredmash (specifically minister Slavskii and his first deputy Meshkov) for not having reacted to suggestions about improving the reactor's safety, despite being fully aware of the design's flaws.[87] The Central Committee attributed this passivity to Sredmash's lack of self-criticism and its narrow-minded, compartmentalized approach. It also identified an overly conciliatory attitude within Gosatomenergonadzor and singled out the agency's top managers Evgenii Kulov and Viktor Sidorenko. The decree argued that all of the aforementioned leaders knew about the problems but consciously decided not to address them. It also mentioned that the Central Committee had raised concerns about RBMK design deficiencies back in 1983 and that the Interdepartmental Technical Council had sent a mollifying response: "The assertion of the leaders of Sredmash and the Soviet

Academy of Sciences that the reactors operating at nuclear power plants were absolutely reliable led to [an attitude of] underestimating the importance of developing accident response measures."[88] More self-critical than the agencies it criticized had been, the Central Committee charged some of its own departments with excessive leniency in controlling the activities of the ministries and agencies under their supervision. The Central Committee instructed the government commission, together with the State Committee for Science and Technology, Minenergo, Sredmash, the Academy of Sciences, and Gosatomenergonadzor, to work out and implement practical measures to modify operating RBMKs and to modernize those under construction. The committee made clear that it considered these design modifications a necessary complement to measures aimed at improving operator performance.[89]

The Central Committee's decree not only distributed blame across the entire nuclear sector, identifying individuals and technical artifacts at fault; it also had manifest consequences for the careers of high-ranking industry managers. The Central Committee expelled the director of the Chernobyl plant from the Party for major mistakes and severe negligence in his work. It severely reprimanded Shasharin, for a lack of organization and poor personnel management, and it dismissed him from his position.[90] Shasharin's superior, minister Maiorets, who had only served in his position for about a year, got away with a strict reprimand on his record.[91]

Sredmash's deputy minister Aleksandr Meshkov lost his position. The committee reprimanded and dismissed the deputy director of Sredmash's chief design institute, NIKIET, Ivan Emelyianov, for underestimating the significance of nuclear safety concerns during the RBMK's design stage and for not reacting to critical comments and suggestions on how to improve the design, which, the decree said, "was one of the reasons for the accident at the Chernobyl nuclear power plant."[92] For unsatisfactory supervision of safety in the nuclear power industry and a lenient attitude toward violations of norms and rules, the chairman of the oversight committee Gosatomenergonadzor, Evegenii Kulov, also received a severe reprimand and dismissal from his position.[93]

The decree instructed both Sredmash's board (*kollegiia*) and Slavskii personally to pay due attention to scientific research and practical design work in order to increase reactor safety. It informed Aleksandrov, the director of the Institute of Atomic Energy, and president of the Soviet Academy of Sciences, and chairman of the Interdepartmental Technical Council, that he needed to eliminate all significant safety defects to guarantee that nuclear power plants would be completely safe.

Chernobyl also marked the end of Slavskii's reign: after almost thirty years in office, he resigned from his position as minister of Medium Machine Building in November 1986. I am unable to judge whether his resignation was forced or voluntary. Most likely, the Central Committee allowed this legendary manager of the Soviet nuclear complex to step down on his own initiative.[94]

Containing International Consequences

As details about the disaster came to light, several European countries stopped imports from the Soviet Union and tourism plummeted. On May 6, 1986, the government set up a press conference for foreign journalists in Moscow and invited other countries' ambassadors to visit Chernobyl. On May 14, Mikhail Gorbachev appeared on Soviet television—a measure intended to strongly influence public opinion.[95] Vladimir Dolgikh, secretary of the Central Committee, directed Minenergo's information service, *Informenergo*, to document the cleanup work, and the service sent its journalists and filmmakers to Chernobyl, where they meticulously recorded the remediation efforts.[96]

In late August 1986, at an International Atomic Energy Agency conference in Vienna, a Soviet delegation presented the officially approved assessment of the accident, as well as a detailed account of potential medical and environmental consequences, to an international audience.[97] Valerii Legasov, deputy director of the Institute of Atomic Energy, led the Soviet delegation to the IAEA.[98] None of Minenergo's staff was invited to participate.[99] The journal *Atomnaia energiia* published the delegation's report the same year.[100] This report did not reflect the conflicting analyses of the accident discussed above. Instead, it clearly blamed the operators and charged them with violating operating instructions and with conducting unauthorized experiments. The report's greatest flaw is probably its date: when the Soviet delegation reported their conclusions to the IAEA, hundreds of experts were still on the Chernobyl site, trying to figure out what had actually happened.

Just before the first anniversary of Chernobyl, the Central Committee's Department for Heavy Industry and Energy began what it called counterpropagandistic activities (*kontrpropagandistskie aktsii*). The approaching anniversary had prompted increased press coverage abroad, most of which the party perceived as overly negative. It was concerned that the "demoralizing centers of imperialism" might use the occasion to launch yet another anti-Soviet campaign.[101] The Central Committee supported the production of a series of movies, popular-scientific brochures on the promising future of nuclear power, and exhibitions in several pavilions at the All-Union Exhibition of the Achievements of the People's Economy (VDNKh), a prominent exhibition space in Moscow.[102]

To confirm the official verdict of operator error one last time, the state began the trial of Chernobyl's top management in July 1987. As we saw in the introduction to the book, the court convicted the plant's operators and top managers but never tried the reactor designers, possibly because the Soviet Union did not want to risk losing its international prestige in the area of nuclear science and possibly for fear of lawsuits.[103]

Unheeded Whistleblowers: The Long Controversy over the RBMK

The postaccident loosening and eventual elimination of censorship prompted several nuclear specialists to use new avenues for voicing their concerns, which in turn allows us to consider narratives that countered the official explanations.[104] It is safe to assume that these published accounts were only the tip of the iceberg and that most who put together reports on the Chernobyl disaster submitted them internally.[105] Many who later published their accounts first tried and failed to use official channels, which in part explains the accounts' emotional, often accusatory tone.[106]

During the years following Chernobyl, a number of nuclear specialists came forward with testimony about a controversy that predated the accident. They had warned about significant problems with the RBMK before Chernobyl and were not heard—or not heeded. To understand why, we need to take into account the closed nature of Soviet society and the symbiotic relationship between technical experts and the state. These factors, along with the gradual realization that what everyone had thought was forever—Party control, rational planning, and technical progress—was starting to crumble, explain a delay that would have been unfathomable in the media-obsessed Western world.[107]

Anatolii Diatlov

One of the catalysts for this altered perception was Anatolii Diatlov, Chernobyl's deputy chief engineer, who published a letter from prison that reached the international community. In it, he gave a detailed description of the reactor construction and argued that construction flaws, not operators' mistakes, had led to the explosion at Chernobyl.[108] Diatlov argued that the operators did not commit any mistakes; in pushing the emergency shutdown button, which was supposed to reliably cut off the nuclear chain reaction under any and all circumstances, they were following instructions. The operators, he wrote, were unaware of the RBMK's positive steam coefficient.[109] Some have dismissed Diatlov's account as self-interested; after all, he was one of the operators his explanation seeks to exonerate. His publications also contain a strong emotional component, but still, several independent nuclear experts familiar with the RBMK design have since confirmed Diatlov's assessment of its technical problems.

Vladimir Volkov
When nuclear specialists first proposed the RBMK design in 1965, reviews were none too encouraging.[110] Among others, Ivan Zhezherun, Vladimir Volkov, and V. Ivanov, all physicists from the scientific director (the Institute of Atomic Energy), pointed out the design's dangers. Volkov in particular warned reactor designers in an internal report that experimental data for the RBMK was insufficient; he cautioned against operating it.[111]

At first, the designers ignored Volkov's concerns and went ahead with the RBMK reactor at the Leningrad nuclear power plant, the country's first. In 1975, right after this reactor started up, it shut down automatically, which led a fuel channel to rupture and a small part of the core to melt.[112] The incident did not have catastrophic consequences, but operators observed a brief flash of reactivity when they inserted the control rods into the core.[113] A commission consisting of representatives of the Institute of Atomic Energy and NIKIET analyzed the causes of the Leningrad accident and in 1976 issued a set of recommendations to improve the reactor's design.[114] First and foremost, the commission recommended reducing the RBMK's steam coefficient by increasing fuel enrichment, reducing the quantity of graphite in the core, and introducing additional absorber rods. These experts also suggested design changes for the control rods and the creation of a fast emergency shutdown system.[115] Sredmash did not pursue these recommendations at that time; it did so only as part of the post-Chernobyl modernization of RBMKs. As I have mentioned, Minenergo, the organization that would operate future RBMKs, had no access to the documentation on the Leningrad accident.

In 1983, during the physical launch of Chernobyl's unit 4, the start-up commission observed that when the control rods were lowered into the core to shut the reactor down, they initially contributed additional reactivity. The inspector from *Gosatomnadzor* (then still under Sredmash) acknowledged this fact and still approved the reactor for full operation.[116] Designers updated the operators' manual to specify how many control rods should be inserted at all times for safety, but they made no technical changes. In other words, operators could still pull out more than the prescribed number of control rods. Operators worked under the paradoxical expectation that they could competently operate a less-than-ideal reactor (that is, rely on their professional judgment and expertise) and at the same time obediently follow the rules.

After the Chernobyl accident, Volkov sent the report he had written to Aleksandrov back in the 1970s to the prosecutor's office. Almost instantaneously, by the first of May 1986, he was banned from entering his workplace, the Institute of Atomic Energy.[117] Volkov promptly wrote letters to Mikhail Gorbachev, to the chairman of the Council of Ministers, Nikolai Ryzhkov, and to the attorney general, A. Rekunkov. In the letters, he argued: "The accident at the Chernobyl nuclear power plant was caused not by the actions of the operating personnel, but by the construction of the active zone and the lack of understanding of the processes taking place in it. ... A loss of coolant in the active zone led to an increase of reactivity ... which ... led to the destruction of the reactor."[118]

Although some interpret Volkov's initiative as an attempt to prove the nuclear power plant operators' innocence, he was also very critical of Minenergo. He argued that "Minenergo has operated nuclear power plants with RBMKs with an unstable core in terms of neutron physics, for quite some time, but [Minenergo] did not attribute due importance to the repeated warning signals [of dangerous, and dangerously fast, power increases] every time the emergency shutdown system was activated, and it did not demand a diligent examination of accidents."[119]

Nikolai Shteinberg

While possibly the first to blow the whistle on the RBMK's design and operation, Volkov was not alone. In 1989, Aleksandr Iadrikhinskii, a nuclear safety inspector from the Kursk nuclear power plant, submitted a report on the Chernobyl accident and the safety of RBMK reactors to the nuclear supervisory committee Gosatomenergonadzor.[120] This internal report prompted heated discussions in the nuclear expert community, and on February 27, 1990, in response to Gorbachev's initiative, Gosatomenergonadzor created a commission under Nikolai Shteinberg to reinvestigate the Chernobyl accident in light of Volkov's and Iadrikhinskii's reports.[121] Shteinberg, former chief engineer at Chernobyl, would lead this prominent and authoritative commission in thoroughly reinvestigating the Chernobyl disaster.[122] In January 1991, the group presented their conclusions, which clearly shifted the emphasis from blaming the personnel for operating mistakes to criticizing the designers for having allowed this reactor type to be built and operated in the first place.[123] What came to be known as the "Shteinberg report" had far-reaching effects. The report stated officially that Aleksandrov and Dollezhal had neglected to pursue the recommendations Volkov and his colleagues had made after the 1975 accident at the Leningrad plant and had effectively ignored the Interdepartmental Technical Council decision on reducing the positive steam coefficient.[124]

As a direct result of the Shteinberg report's findings, the International Atomic Energy Agency revised its original accident analysis, the widely read and cited INSAG-1, which the agency had based mostly on the official Soviet report. The IAEA experts published a new document (INSAG-7) that included as appendixes both the Shteinberg report and another revisionist expert report from VNIIAES.[125] Nuclear experts understood the more nuanced findings of these revised reports and updated many publicly accessible Chernobyl accounts accordingly, but INSAG-7 never generated the same news storm as the initial reports from 1986 had.

However, within the Soviet, and later post-Soviet, nuclear community, the significance of Diatlov's writings, Volkov's efforts, and the Shteinberg report can hardly be emphasized enough. Apart from their specific findings, they created a blueprint for expert disagreement in public, and in the public media, that had simply not existed under Soviet rule—or that had entailed political consequences that few technical specialists were willing to risk.[126] Following Volkov's, Diatlov's, and Shteinberg's lead, several widely cited experts now voiced their disagreement with the official explanation of the Chernobyl accident. Let's turn to some of them next.

Boris Dubovskii

Boris Dubovskii was an experienced nuclear physicist who had cooperated with Kurchatov to start up the first Soviet experimental reactor in Moscow. Dubovskii served as the head of Sredmash's Nuclear Safety Inspection from 1958 to 1973, and he subsequently directed the Sector for Nuclear Safety at the Institute of Physics and Power Engineering (FEI) in Obninsk.[127] In an interview published in October 1994 in the popular Saint Petersburg weekly *Smena*, Dubovskii mentioned two predecessors of the Chernobyl accident that he said should have alerted the designers to problems.[128] One was the 1975 accident at the first RBMK in Leningrad, the other a similar accident in 1982 at the Chernobyl plant.[129]

Sredmash leaders did not grant Dubovskii, even in his function as a nuclear safety official, access to investigation records for either accident. Based on his own analyses, he concluded that under certain circumstances the lower part of the RBMK core turned into a separate, explosive reactor.[130]

At Leningrad in 1975 and at Chernobyl in 1982, according to Dubovskii, the reactor design prevented the proper release of excess steam.[131] He also viewed the slow speed of the emergency shutdown mechanism as a problem that was especially dangerous for the lower part of the core. In his analysis of these earlier accidents, Dubovskii had suggested adding absorber rods in the lower core, but this proposal, like many others, was only realized after Chernobyl.[132]

When Dubovskii stated publicly that he considered flaws in the reactor design, not the operators' actions, responsible for the Chernobyl disaster, he was pushed into retirement.[133] His conclusion that until 1986, all RBMKs had operated without a regular safety system, let alone an effective emergency shutdown system, proved too heretical.[134]

Undeterred, Dubovskii wrote a letter to Mikhail Gorbachev on November 27, 1989, in which he argued that it was "impossible to eliminate mistakes by the operators in the future," and urged the General Secretary to look at "the real causes" of the Chernobyl accident.[135] In addition to the technical issues, for which he blamed the designers, however, Dubovskii also criticized the nuclear power industry's management system, which he said had lost an acute sense of responsibility and abandoned the rigid system of accountability the nuclear weapons project had had.

Viktor Sidorenko

Viktor Sidorenko had joined the Institute of Atomic Energy in 1952, right after graduating from the Moscow Power Engineering Institute (MEI). In 1983, he was head of the Institute's Sector for Nuclear Reactors, when his colleagues approached him with disconcerting news. Their computations showed that the graphite-water reactor being implemented at nuclear plants all over the country had a real, if improbable, potential to suffer a severe accident due to a design flaw in the control rods.[136] Sidorenko took this alarming report to the institute's leaders, who met it with conspicuous indifference. The reactor's design engineers at NIKIET declared that the problem was well known but highly unlikely to trigger an accident. Therefore, the institute leadership postponed mitigation until it was time for all control rods to undergo refurbishment.[137] Sredmash's top authorities, who also received the report, did not react either. Instead of requiring design changes, they held that more detailed operating instructions would ensure that this scenario would not occur.

When the Chernobyl reactor exploded, one of Sidorenko's colleagues reportedly told him, "That very thing happened."[138] By then Sidorenko was deputy director of Gosatomenergonadzor, and he recounts sarcastically what this evidence meant in the early glasnost era: the Communist Party did not interpret the existence of his earlier report as a demonstration that he had accurately diagnosed and reported a dangerous situation to the appropriate authorities. Rather, it charged him with unscrupulousness (*besprintsipnost'*): he knew and yet did not act on his knowledge.[139]

The Central Committee's Sector for Nuclear Energy

At the time of the Chernobyl accident, Vladimir Maryin had been working in the Party's Central Committee apparatus for seventeen years. Representing the Sector for Nuclear Energy, he repeatedly confronted complaints about operating problems in RBMK reactors in the early 1980s. Simple factory defects often caused these problems, but they kept reactors from getting automated safety systems. Instead, operators had to work around nonstandard, partly defective equipment.[140]

In May 1983, the Central Committee's secretary, Vladimir Dolgikh, invited Anatolii Aleksandrov, director of the Institute of Atomic Energy (IAE), and Evgenii Riazantsev, who had succeeded Sidorenko as director of the Sector for Nuclear Reactors at the IAE, to discuss the concerns that RBMK operating personnel had reported to the Central Committee's Sector for Nuclear Energy.[141] Maryin and his close collaborator Georgii Kopchinskii prepared a list of questions for this meeting.[142] They knew that Sredmash and the IAE were well aware of these problems, but the organizations' indifferent response alarmed them.[143] When Maryin and Kopchinskii complained that the RBMK "conformed neither to international nor to national nuclear and radiation safety requirements," Arkadii Volskii, the deputy director of the Central Committee's Department of Mechanical Engineering, dismissed their concerns by stating that "these deficiencies are well known and why worry people yet another time."[144] The Interdepartmental Technical Council convened on June 13, 1983, to discuss "The deficiencies in the operation of nuclear power plants with RBMK-1000 and the increase of these nuclear power plants' reliability."[145] After that meeting, a frustrated Maryin concluded: "It should be noted that the administration of the Interdepartmental Scientific-Technical Council under the Ministry of Medium Machine Building [sic] did not consider the materials sent to them with the appropriate sincerity. Some questions were not even assigned to anyone for examination."[146]

On August 16, 1986, the Central Committee and the Council of Ministers abolished the MVTS for its disastrous mishandling of these concerns.[147] In its place, the authorities created an Interdepartmental Scientific-Technical Council (MVNTS) as part of the State Committee for Science and

Technology.[148] On February 8, 1988, the MVNTS came under the authority of the Council of Ministers' Bureau for the Fuel and Energy Complex, and operated under *Gospromatomnadzor's* wings.[149]

Chernobyl's Consequences

Chernobyl left a deep impact on every imaginable aspect of nuclear power. The disaster immediately affected the Soviet Union's economic development, personnel training, industry management, reactor designs, and, most importantly, the organizational structure of its entire nuclear sector. It profoundly affected political activism as well.

In contrast to the 1979 accident at the Three Mile Island nuclear power plant in the United States, the Soviet system controlled the mass media and for quite some time managed to suppress critical public discussion within its borders.[150] However, in 1986 and 1987, new Soviet citizen movements started to form as a direct reaction to the accident.[151] Beginning around 1989, these environmentalists of a new generation gained access to the Soviet press, eventually forcing out censorship, and mobilized to oppose new nuclear power plant projects violently. In the period following the Chernobyl disaster, this activism radically tore open many previously stable elements of the nuclear industry.

The emergent antinuclear groups challenged the nuclear industry's culture of secrecy, the lack of information on and discussion about site selection, the methods used to determine and predict energy demand, the choice of reactors, the lack of support for alternative energy, state control of the media (including patronizing experts), as well as local authorities' powerlessness and the complete lack of public participation in decision-making processes. By questioning the legitimacy of earlier technological choices, these groups also challenged the official historical narrative about the smooth and rational development of nuclear power in the Soviet Union. Chernobyl united people in fear and resistance, and mobilized them to oppose nuclear power.

The initial success of the antinuclear movement followed from a combination of changes in political strategy, most notably, Gorbachev's policy of transparency (glasnost). With the support of local politicians, Soviet society—in large part driven by the new environmentalist rhetoric—achieved a halt of construction of many nuclear power plants, even those near completion. Many regional authorities, most prominently the newly emboldened Ukrainian government, supported these movements by declaring a moratorium in 1990 on all nuclear power plants then under construction.[152]

Planning and construction work were dropped for the Rostov, Bashkir, Tatar, Kostroma, Crimean, and Krasnodar nuclear power plants, for units 5 and 6 at Balakovo, unit 4 at the South-Ukrainian and Khmelnitskii nuclear plants, the nuclear heating plants at Voronezh, Gorky (Nizhnii Novgorod), and Arkhangelsk, as well as siting work for new nuclear power plants with a total capacity of 109,000 MW. The Central Committee decided to abandon the RBMK design and asked the Council of Ministers to submit an amended energy program.[153] Authorities changed siting policies for nuclear power plants, too: in addition to sufficient water supply and sufficient energy demand, post-Chernobyl policies required additional seismic tests, greater distance from urban centers, and ecological compatibility (environmental impact) studies for new nuclear plant sites.[154] At the same time, requirements that authorities considered preeminent in the past, such as the proximity of high-voltage power lines or large contingents of construction workers ready to deploy, lost importance. The Central Committee's July 14, 1986, decree also required that the Council of Ministers approve all future design and siting decisions.[155]

As the entire Soviet industry collapsed in the late 1980s and early 1990s, energy consumption stagnated or decreased significantly, which rendered new nuclear power plants unnecessary. While some regions abandoned their nuclear ambitions after Chernobyl or tried to switch to alternative energy sources, other areas continued to depend heavily on nuclear power. In these areas, the energy supply situation soon forced politicians once again to resort to nuclear energy. Armenia, for example, closed its nuclear power plant after a severe earthquake in 1988, concerned about the facility's safety.[156] To keep warm, people cut down the national forests during the first winter without nuclear power, and the authorities subsequently restarted unit 2.[157]

When the Soviet Union officially ended in December 1991, its successor states inherited a nuclear industry in disarray.[158] For instance, Lithuania, a small state that after independence temporarily generated a higher percentage of nuclear electricity than France, agreed to shut down its two RBMK-1500 reactors at Ignalina in exchange for accession to the European Union. They did so despite the fact that Sweden and Finland had already invested significant amounts of money and expertise in upgrading the reactors.

The first post-Soviet Russian government under Boris Yeltsin, while sympathetic to concerns over nuclear safety, in the end opted for a stable, long-term energy supply that included nuclear power.[159]

Reforming Recruitment

The Chernobyl disaster also deeply affected discussions about training for the nuclear workforce: what responsibilities workers should have, whether their training was adequate, and to whom they were ultimately accountable. The post-Chernobyl era saw a marked increase in the number of accident simulators at nuclear power plants, and simulator training became mandatory for reactor operators.[160] This latter measure implicitly acknowledged that operator training had not been as good as it should have been before Chernobyl. When the nuclear safety law was rewritten after the accident, operator error featured prominently in it, and post-Chernobyl reactor operators found themselves in another paradoxical situation: on the one hand, they were now being trained to make better decisions in accident-like situations—that is, they were learning to better assess potentially dangerous situations and to react appropriately. On the other, instructors told them not to interfere with the automated systems because their actions could threaten the otherwise smoothly functioning technology. It is therefore unclear if the new system, with this contradictory conception of its human elements, was safer than the one it replaced.

In the wake of the disaster, authorities also thoroughly scrutinized recruitment policies for the nuclear power industry. In part this was a response to Minenergo's often criticized decision to appoint Nikolai Fomin, who was not a nuclear physicist or engineer, as chief engineer at Chernobyl. Fomin, who became chief engineer one and a half years before the accident, had not been Minenergo's first choice, however. The deputy minister of Energy and Electrification, Shasharin, and the head of the operating organization Soiuzatomenergo, Veretennikov, had both favored Vladimir Bronnikov, who had previously worked as deputy chief engineer at Chernobyl. He was an experienced operator and a highly qualified nuclear specialist who later became director of the Zaporozhye nuclear power plant.[161] Minenergo had suggested Fomin, a good administrator, for a post as director of one of the Ukrainian nuclear power plants under construction.[162] But the Ukrainian Communist Party objected to these plans, and as a result, Fomin became Chernobyl's chief engineer, with the prospect of replacing the director, Briukhanov, once he left for another position in Moscow.[163] Minenergo's managers agreed to the compromise because they expected the entire plant leadership to cooperate closely as a team.[164] In Minenergo's experience, a nuclear power plant's administration worked best if the top management, consisting of the director, the chief engineer, and their deputies, had training in different, mutually complementary areas. At the Chernobyl plant, the distribution of expertise was not ideal, but it was acceptable, Shasharin argued, because two of the deputy chief engineers were nuclear physicists and engineers. Unfortunately, Fomin did not consult his deputies before approving the test in unit 4.

In the end, however, the nuclear industry continued to rely on nonspecialists in addition to nuclear experts: there simply were not enough qualified specialists available. Chernobyl only exacerbated the problem, and the nuclear workforce not only in the Soviet Union, but worldwide, continues to experience a significant generation gap.

Reconsidering the RBMK

When evidence came to the fore that nuclear experts had had concerns about specific design features of the RBMK all along, most notably the positive steam coefficient, these revelations cast doubt on designers, and more broadly, on Soviet science. The Soviet Union was the only state that developed the graphite-water design into a power reactor—specialists elsewhere favored a light-water design at the time.[165] Aside from the problems mentioned above, the RBMK lacks a containment structure. Such a structure would have been costly and immensely complicated due to the enormous size of the core. What's more, it might not have prevented the disaster anyway.[166]

Nuclear scientists questioned past choices, but shutting down all operating RBMKs as unsafe and eliminating a total of 14,000 MW of base-load electricity was simply not an option. Instead, scientists and engineers had to find ways to improve the safety of operating RBMKs.[167] The design modifications they implemented in the years following Chernobyl (for instance, modifying the construction of RBMK control rods and increasing fuel enrichment) provide a convincing argument in favor of the design-flaw story.[168]

Reactor designers also introduced 70 to 100 additional absorber rods to decrease the positive steam coefficient, another modification prompted by Chernobyl but based on early experiences with the RBMK.[169] They also significantly increased the speed with which the emergency rods would fall into the core and improved the Control and Safety System (*SUZ—sistema upravleniia i zashchity*). If the underlying problems were well understood and these technical modifications were possible, why did it take so long to implement them? It is hardly surprising that organizational issues (turf wars and inertia, among others) constituted the nuclear industry's fundamental quandary.

Restructuring the Nuclear Power Industry

The USSR's first response to Chernobyl—before modifying the reactors or providing better training to their operators—was to restructure yet again the management of nuclear power. While it took about five years to implement technical modifications, and emergency training for RBMK operators only gradually improved after the accident, in the immediate aftermath of the disaster the authorities emphasized organizational modifications (figure 5.4).[170] As I have mentioned, deep mistrust toward established nuclear

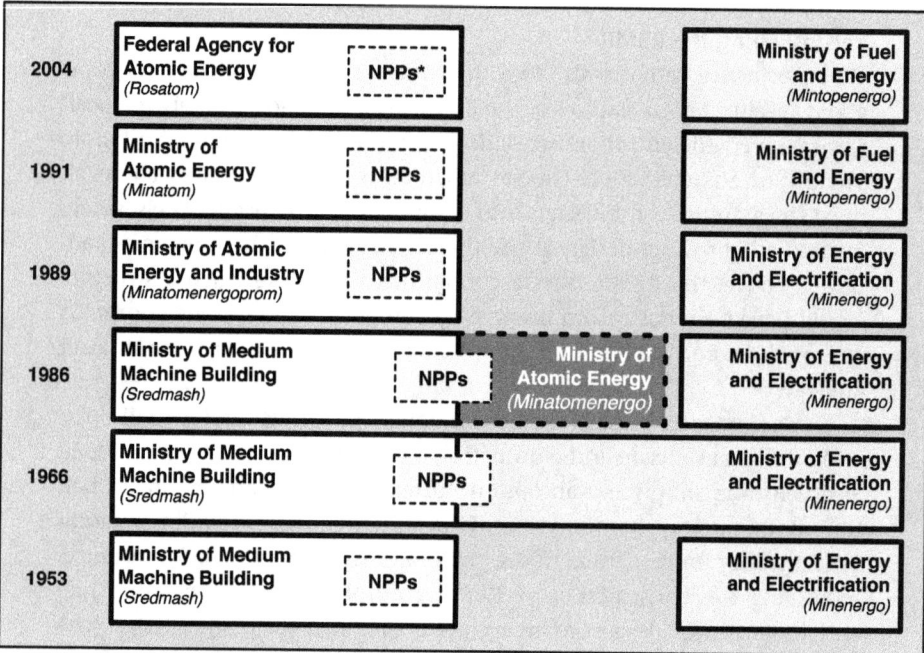

*Nuclear power plants

Figure 5.4
In the 1950s, the Ministry of Medium Machine Building (*Sredmash*), which was in charge of Soviet nuclear weapons, managed the design and construction of nuclear power reactors. Once the Soviet leadership made a commitment to expanding the generation of electricity at nuclear power plants, in 1966, the Ministry of Energy and Electrification (*Minenergo*) took over responsibility for their construction and operation. After two decades of successful growth, the Chernobyl disaster threw the industry into crisis. One of the first reactions to the disaster was administrative reform: initially, a new ministry (*Minatomenergo*) was put in charge of managing nuclear power plants only. After three years, this ministry merged with the former Sredmash to form a new ministry for all things nuclear, which in slightly modified form and under changing names exists today. *Source*: Graphic design by Dane Webster.

science and design engineering institutes ultimately led to the elimination of the influential Interdepartmental Technical Council. But the disaster profoundly affected every last organization involved with nuclear power.

Immediately following the accident, the new Ministry of Atomic Energy (*Minatomenergo*) began coordinating and managing all nuclear power plants, including the Leningrad and Ignalina plants and the Rovno nuclear plant (transferred from the Ukrainian Ministry of Power Engineering).[171] Minatomenergo's infrastructure mirrored that of Soiuzatomenergo, the organization within Minenergo that had managed nuclear power plants. The new body also took over Minenergo's design, support, and other organizations relating to nuclear power, as well as some Sredmash design organizations.

Nikolai Lukonin, former director of the Leningrad and Ignalina nuclear power plants, became minister of atomic energy at the inception of the new ministry in 1986. Lukonin came from the Sredmash apparatus; his appointment reflected yet another attempt to transfer Sredmash's expertise and to ensure the new ministry's work would be of high quality.

In creating the new ministry, the Soviet government intended to concentrate all stages of design, construction, and operation under one roof.[172] And yet, Sredmash continued to control the research and engineering organizations designing and developing nuclear reactors, the scientific research organizations in charge of determining the scientific direction, and all research and industrial structures connected with the manufacturing of the nuclear fuel for nuclear power plants. The fundamental division of labor thus remained unresolved. Minatomenergo and Sredmash both existed until June 1989, when the government decided to merge the two ministries into one Ministry of Atomic Energy and Industry (*Minatomenergoprom*). The creation of Minatomenergoprom was essentially a return to an all-powerful Sredmash—under a new name.[173] Vitalii Konovalov, a decorated industrial manager who had worked in the Sredmash apparatus since 1986, was appointed minister.[174] Viktor Sidorenko, who transferred from the oversight committee, became first deputy minister in charge of nuclear power engineering.[175]

Minatomenergoprom organized and coordinated scientific research, design and engineering work, as well as construction work in the area of nuclear science, technology, and industry, including military objects. The ministry managed all organizations and enterprises within the nuclear energy branch, thus uniting all the scientific and production aspects of nuclear technology: uranium mining, enrichment processes, production of weapons-grade materials, production of nuclear fuel for power plants, construction and operation of nuclear power plants, and the reprocessing and storage of radioactive waste.[176]

This ministry's primary concern was maintaining the country's nuclear complex as a unified whole. For that purpose, its leadership suggested creating the state corporation *Atom*, which would eventually turn into a joint-stock company. They argued that this corporation would correspond better with an emerging market economy, but ultimately it was an attempt to keep nuclear facilities beyond the territory of the Russian Federal SSR (namely, facilities in Ukraine, Lithuania, Kazakhstan, and other Soviet republics) united in one organization and under a single command.[177] After the Soviet Union disintegrated, Minatomenergoprom was dissolved without having implemented any of the structural changes it had suggested.[178] The new Ministry of Atomic Energy of the Russian Federation (*Ministerstvo atomnoi energii Rossiiskoi Federatsii*), also known as *Minatom*, took Minatomenergoprom's place.[179]

Viktor Mikhailov, who had previously worked for the nuclear weapons complex, became minister of Minatom.[180] In November 1992, ministry authorities established a Commission for Nuclear Energy to coordinate its relevant subdivisions. Deputy minister Viktor Sidorenko chaired this commission and led its efforts to create a uniform technological policy, decide management issues, and prepare strategic plans for the nuclear industry.[181] The commission worked until September 23, 1993, when Lev Riabev, who had succeeded Slavskii as Sredmash's leader in 1986, became first deputy minister and started coordinating all questions relating to the civilian nuclear industry.[182] Minatom passed several important policies, including strategic plans for the development of the Russian nuclear power industry.[183]

In March 1992, Russian President Boris Yeltsin established the agency *Rosenergoatom* within Minatom. The plan was to eventually turn Rosenergoatom into the operating organization for all Russian nuclear power plants, providing one general management for these plants, while they remained independent economic units.[184] Rosenergoatom managed and coordinated all nuclear power plants in operation, under construction, and in the planning stage, as well as all enterprises and organizations facilitating the operation of nuclear power plants.[185]

During the initial period of its existence, Rosenergoatom had to focus on the safe operation of the nuclear power plants under its management, and particularly on modernizing several plants and improving their safety features.[186] By the end of the 1990s, subdivisions of Rosenergoatom had emerged—for example, for construction work, investments, long-term planning, design, and technological subsidiaries.[187] However, Rosenergoatom's mandate vis-à-vis the nuclear power plants did not stabilize until 2000; until then, Rosenergoatom remained a purely managerial organization.[188]

Ukrainian Nuclear Institutions

It is beyond the scope of this book to explore the administration of nuclear energy in the Newly Independent States, but since Chernobyl happened in Ukraine, a short summary of the development of a Ukrainian nuclear power infrastructure is appropriate. In 1990, after imposing its moratorium, the Ukrainian SSR integrated organizations involved with nuclear power plants under a company called *Ukratomenergoprom*, which later took the Ukrainian name *Derzhkomatom*. After becoming an independent state in 1991, Ukraine lifted the moratorium in October 1993 and construction resumed at three sites.[189] Since then, the government has commissioned six new reactors with a power capacity of 1000 MW each, bringing the number of Ukraine's nuclear power reactors to fifteen.[190] In 2004, Ukraine generated more than 53 percent of its electrical power at nuclear plants.

In October 1996, the Ukrainian government created the state-owned National Atomic Energy Generating Company of Ukraine (*Energoatom*) to introduce a "uniform technical and economic policy in the field," and alleviate the industry's grim economic situation.[191] This organization managed all five Ukrainian nuclear power plants under the aegis of the Ukrainian Ministry of Fuel and Energy. This ministry, in turn, set the priorities for nuclear power within the national energy policy. It was the operating agency responsible for raising the power output at nuclear power plants, while guaranteeing the safe operation of all Ukrainian nuclear plants. Specifically, the Ministry of Fuel and Energy was in charge of assembling new nuclear power plants, reconstructing operating ones, buying nuclear fuel and disposing of radioactive waste, and training specialists for the nuclear power industry. In 2004, Energoatom employed about 38,000 people.

Energoatom closely collaborates with the International Atomic Energy Agency (IAEA), the European Union, the U.S. Department of Energy, the World Association of Nuclear Operators (WANO), and Russian nuclear organizations. The Russian Federation until recently provided all the nuclear fuel for the Ukrainian reactors and took back the spent fuel. It also supplied equipment and participated in the construction of unit 2 at the Khmelnitskii and unit 4 at the Rovno (Rivne) nuclear plants. For many years, a Russian-Ukrainian committee that included Russia's Rosenergoatom met twice a year and conducted joint inspections at Ukrainian nuclear plants. Starting in 1995, representatives of British Energy advised Energoatom on how to become a privatized corporation. Interestingly, this entity includes a broad spectrum of social services for Energoatom's employees, such as housing, cultural programs, and other services, which the Ukrainian Academy of Sciences' Institute of Sociology helped develop.[192] The corporation intended these measures to attract and retain a highly qualified workforce, but it found it challenging to continue them given the new economic realities of the post-Soviet era.

When the last reactor at Chernobyl shut down, a newly created suborganization of Energoatom, *Atomremontservis,* absorbed the plant's former employees. In 2001, the Ukrainian government decided to create a new "State Specialized Enterprise" that separated out all operations involving Chernobyl.[193] Subsequently, Energoatom stopped administering the closed plant. While this division nominally created a separate organization in charge of maintenance, safe decommissioning, nuclear fuel and radioactive waste management, monitoring, and the massively delayed Shelter project, this organizational split may cause the loss of valuable skills, experience, and postdisaster best practices not only for the Ukrainian nuclear sector, but for the nuclear industry worldwide.[194]

Conclusion

The scope of the nuclear emergency at Chernobyl was unprecedented, and emergency response, accident mitigation, and decontamination work all proved extremely challenging—even chaotic—despite international support. Even though it was completely unprepared for a disaster of this magnitude, the centralized Soviet system worked surprisingly well. The state could draw on resources, supplies, and mitigation personnel that might not have been available, and would likely have been much more difficult to mobilize, in a less centralized system. Beginning on the day of the accident, this centralized system set up a coordinating structure with multiple task forces on site that regularly reported back to the center. The state drew on an army of conscripts and recruited, or "volunteered," thousands of "liquidators" to help mitigate the disaster. Most importantly, however, Chernobyl constituted a watershed moment for the global nuclear power industry. A severe accident at a civilian nuclear facility was no longer a remote, hypothetical, and infinitesimally small probability. It had turned into a realistic possibility.

At different times after the accident, various and often contradictory assessments of the Chernobyl disaster enjoyed very different authority, and I have tried to give these assessments even-handed consideration. Taking a detailed look at the controversy that broke out over the technical design of the RBMK after Chernobyl has allowed me to trace the historical roots not only of the design choice, but also of this debate. The post-Chernobyl controversy also illustrates that while unified on the surface, the Soviet nuclear sector, and by extension the Soviet system in general, was anything but monolithic. The fact that after the accident, both antinuclear groups and nuclear specialists criticized the earlier decision to build RBMKs all over the country can help us understand how political power, distributed as it was, influenced design decisions in the Soviet nuclear power industry. This debate also marks a fundamental change in the ways technical experts related to the state and in how they interpreted their role vis-à-vis their own organizations, the broader public, and the country's rulers.

The Chernobyl disaster prompted massive changes in the Soviet and post-Soviet nuclear industry. It did not, unfortunately, have the same effect on the international nuclear industry. In part because the initial assessment that operator error was the main cause of the accident was so widely circulated, many Western nations, including the United States, concluded "this could never happen here." Although the accident did prompt changes outside the Soviet Union, it was easy, and tempting, to interpret the disaster as the logical outcome of a corrupt political apparatus, a dysfunctional economic system, an outdated reactor design with insufficient, or insufficiently automated, safety features, and, most importantly, inept operators—both in the control room and at the management level. While Chernobyl was Soviet through and through—its reactor design, its reactor operators, and its institutional context—it was also a warning sign for nuclear industries elsewhere, a warning sign that those of us outside the former Soviet Union have ignored, perhaps arrogantly, certain that our own safety updates can wait until the next planned shutdown for maintenance.

6 Conclusion

This book has used the Chernobyl disaster as a historical and conceptual window into the Soviet nuclear power industry because only by thoroughly analyzing Chernobyl's prehistory will we gain a deeper, more nuanced understanding of the accident's systemic causes. Everything about Chernobyl was Soviet—the reactor design, the operators, the bureaucracy. The disaster shook a system that designers intended to be safe, a system that, according to its own standards and norms, was perfectly functional. But while we need to look seriously at how the Soviet economic system, its bureaucracy, and ideology affected the industry's history and organization, we also need to avoid the Cold War fallacy of interpreting this context only as problematic. The Soviet state may have forced its nuclear managers to improvise in the face of inefficiency, red tape, and chronic supply shortages, but it also granted nuclear experts much more financial, regulatory, and political leeway than their peers in Western democracies enjoyed. Once we allow ourselves to recognize the many ways that Soviet ideology and economic planning supported the large sociotechnical system that the nuclear power industry became, we can acknowledge that that system achieved remarkable success—in spite of, but also because of, the political environment in which it developed.

But acknowledging this leads to a troubling conclusion. Although the disaster involved Soviet organizations, people, and technologies, we can't point to a singular, inherently Soviet aspect of operating nuclear power reactors as the root cause of the catastrophe. Chernobyl was the end point of a long history of decisions, processes, and practices, all of which had worked well for quite some time. Rather than retroactively condemning these practices and decisions—or communist ideology—as leading inevitably to worst-case scenarios, we need to fully understand what counted as normal, acceptable, and sufficient before hell broke loose, before the elements of a complex sociotechnical system lined up in an extraordinarily unfortunate way. Any industrialized society that utilizes sensitive, high-risk, and potentially dual-use technologies relies on some form of the processes I have described in this book. Sadly, Fukushima has demonstrated that we cannot dismiss the Chernobyl disaster as an outcome specific to the Soviet system.

I have argued that in order to appreciate Chernobyl's prehistory, we need to appreciate that Soviet nuclear reactors were simultaneously sensitive, potentially dual-use industrial facilities and the objects of considerable scientific and technological pride.[1] The Soviet organizations that managed the nascent nuclear industry significantly shaped not only technical decisions but also prevailing ideas about what was important, desirable, or safe—and what, by contrast, was irrelevant, unacceptable, or risky. Although the 1966 transfer of responsibilities for nuclear power plants from the secret ministry in charge of nuclear weapons to the civilian ministry responsible for electricity production fundamentally normalized nuclear power generation, bureaucratic control continued to shift. The ongoing regrouping and reassigning of responsibilities for nuclear power plants not only contradicts many conventional assumptions about how a centralized, planned economy functions, but also illustrates the immense challenges involved in managing expertise, sharing experience, and transferring knowledge at a crucial intersection of authority and accountability.[2] Organizational shifts, then, both reflected technology's requirements and served to establish and reconfigure the social, political, and legal order: they provided clear hierarchies, labor and power structures, and a system for attributing blame.

I have chronicled how scientists and engineers skillfully drew on specific political and economic aspects of the Soviet system to establish nuclear power as a legitimate technology that required long-term commitment and massive capital investments. These nuclear power specialists believed and argued that this technology would improve the economic foundations of Soviet society. They also understood that getting nuclear power included in long-term economic plans would let them push the technology in new directions, opening up some paths while closing others. The propagandistic rhetoric that early nuclear program advocates used shaped the emerging industry's organizational structure but gave way as the system matured to a focus on economic efficiency, rational development, and "nuclear normalcy."[3]

By tracing the division of labor between those who plan and those who operate nuclear reactors, I have shown how the corresponding organizational delineation of responsibilities shaped and reinforced the Soviet nuclear industry's professional identities and organizational culture, most

Conclusion

notably emphasizing a distinction between *atomshchiki* and *energetiki*. I have also argued that the values of the civilian nuclear workforce—diligence, responsibility, and a deep faith in scientific rationality—made them less vulnerable to apathy and cynicism than other groups and institutions.

Because Soviet planners thought reliable human operators made redundant safety features unnecessary, they built nuclear power plants without some of the features most Western plants required. This fact made thorough operator training tremendously important, and I have argued that some facets of the Soviet system led to a significant gap in that training. While the architects of the Soviet civilian nuclear industry certainly knew the value of—and worked to preserve—experiential and tacit knowledge, that knowledge increasingly became formalized, compartmentalized, or appended to normal operations. This resulted in a rigid and contradictory structure of accountability in which managers saw human reactor operators as redundancy features and yet restricted their actions and undermined their preparedness to override the system when problems arose. Furthermore, the ongoing reorganizations within the civilian nuclear industry—although aimed at finding the ideal governance structure—ultimately prevented any stable set of institutional routines and practices from developing.

In reconstructing the history of Soviet reactor design choices, I have shown that it did not unfold in a logical sequence.[4] Instead, an expensive, multidirectional research-and-development program, a series of contingencies, and an extraordinarily convoluted process led the Soviets to select their reactor designs. The whole effort to design reactors for power generation was surprisingly uncoordinated, despite the planned character and tight financial constraints of the Soviet economy. As I have shown, leaders made the Chernobyl-type RBMK reactor one of their two choices because they assumed that Soviet experts could convert a military reactor design to one optimized for civilian use, that the RBMK would technologically and economically surpass the already-operational graphite-water reactors, and that the country could produce these reactors quickly enough to help fulfill its ambitious plans for nuclear power generation.

I argued that Soviet nuclear power experts selected the reactors they did in part because their designs had military origins. But major political and economic reforms domestically and nuclear power engineering trends abroad also had a significant impact on the decision. In my view, all the preceding factors are more significant than dysfunctional organizations, individual career ambitions, and a certain recklessness. These latter factors certainly had a role, but in and of themselves they did not set the world on a direct course to disaster.

All technological development everywhere involves ambitious engineers, political alliances, and risk taking to some degree, and any retrospective account must acknowledge that what we consider good and safe always depends on context. With this in mind, I have emphasized that Soviet scientists, engineers, and planners chose the RBMK after extended negotiations—in other words, their choice represents the collective judgment of a community of experts.

While it certainly included dedicated, sophisticated experts, I have shown that the Soviet political apparatus was not uniform. The economic system was not monolithic either. While deficient in many ways, for the most part it worked in favor of the nuclear industry. The RBMK reactor design was not unproblematic, but those working in the industry understood it well, and industry leaders ensured that designers improved it continuously. Soviet operators, both at the Chernobyl site and at the central managerial level, were highly qualified, skilled, and loyal specialists. Neither the operators nor the scientists and engineers who designed and developed the RBMK were reckless, careless ignoramuses, though many accounts of the accident portrayed them that way. Finally, and perhaps most importantly, I have emphasized that we need to study further the organizational structures that bind together the politics, economics, technologies, and people in the civilian nuclear industry.[5] Too often, scholars and practitioners alike focus on only one area—such as industry, economics, or universities—and disregard the complex interactions between these systems, the ways they shape, modify, and constrain each other. What Chernobyl has demonstrated (and Fukushima has only confirmed) is that organizing a civilian nuclear industry remains at best a high-stakes process of trial and error.

The Chernobyl disaster had complex causes that reached far back into the history of Soviet science, engineering, and economic management. The early Soviet nuclear program, although visionary, creative, and diverse, had to mature quickly if it was to survive economically. Leaders chose certain reactor designs as much because the supply industry could meet their requirements as because of their technical or economic merits and their international popularity. Training and recruiting specialists for the burgeoning nuclear industry was a challenge, and preserving and transferring the military nuclear program's experience and work ethos while quickly expanding the nuclear industry under civilian control was another (figure 6.1).

Organizations held together the different facets of the emerging nuclear industry: its economic objectives, technical specifics, and personnel strategies. Soviet scientists, planners, and industrial managers continued to

Conclusion

Figure 6.1
Nuclear reactor operators in the control room at the Smolensk nuclear power plant in 2009. Nothing epitomizes the challenges associated with the safe operation of nuclear power plants as clearly as the "human factor." Technological advances notwithstanding, expertise, experience, and other skills will invariably remain significant elements of any nuclear future—in the former Soviet Union and elsewhere.
Source: Photograph by Ilya Varlamov, http://zyalt.livejournal.com. Reprinted with permission.

modify and tinker with these organizational structures in an attempt to improve the industry's management as well as its profitability, reliability, and safety. High-level administrators and on-site reactor operators alike had both a personal and a professional stake in making the nuclear industry succeed; the Chernobyl disaster hit them on both levels.

The controversy that emerged in the years following the disaster sheds new light on the technical, organizational, economic, political, and personal complexity of events that may seem to have obvious causes. Why did Chernobyl happen in the Soviet Union? Was it because the confident technological enthusiasm exemplified by the motto "We are able to do it, and we can do it all" guided the mass production of nuclear power plants and turned yesterday's fossil fuel plant managers into nuclear specialists overnight?[6] Was the Soviet industry's backwardness—for example, the absence of reliable supporting technology, especially computers—to blame?[7] Did the loss of fundamental expertise during the transfer of nuclear power plants from the secret nuclear ministry to a general power ministry create the preconditions for the Chernobyl accident?[8] Did Soviet leaders organize the Soviet nuclear regulatory agency too late, and did Sredmash's and NIKIET's leadership hamper its proper functioning?[9] Or was the centralized management structure, with its acute attention to social standing and its disrespect for people of lower rank, in the way of an effective safety culture?[10] Should Soviet industry leaders have retired earlier, rather than remaining in office for several decades?

Each of these questions has some validity. And yet, the Soviet Union is not the only place such problems have occurred: we find expert hubris, conflict between military and civilian organizations, supply problems in frontier science, mismanagement, and ambitious individuals in other politico-economic contexts as well. Processes and practices that are common in any society and any economy created the preconditions for this disaster. What is unique about the Chernobyl case is that it happened just as unprecedented political and economic changes made possible a debate about its causes that could not have occurred sooner.

That debate eventually led to the uncovering of an earlier controversy, a process enabled by the concurrent opening of the media under Gorbachev's policy of glasnost. As it became clear that powerful groups had ignored, or even silenced, cautious and critical voices, leaders reassessed the late 1960s decision to implement the RBMK as a standard Soviet design. The post-Chernobyl debates suggest that the RBMK had not been the best proposal technically. Rather, economic considerations and the designers' rhetorical skills in invoking national security interests swayed the decision makers.

Chernobyl also affected how politicians portrayed nuclear power in the Soviet Union. Before the accident, they presented nuclear power as yet another Soviet science success story, one more technological achievement that served enlightened progress toward peace and communism. The disaster prompted the public to once again associate nuclear power with the horrors of nuclear war—an association that promoters of the "peaceful atom" had worked long and hard to annul. The accident thus reopened the question of the industry's political legitimacy, but in a changed political climate where government officials, planners, and scientists had to reestablish their authority, credibility, influence, and expertise in the face of a nuclear catastrophe.

Chernobyl also forced state planners to reconsider safety issues. The disaster revealed serious flaws in the complex and often duplicated management structure of Soviet science, industry, and government. Officials

Conclusion

had two difficult and somewhat conflicting jobs to do: assigning blame and accountability in their own country and controlling political damage in the international arena. The international public had only recently warmed up to their (domestically contested) general secretary Mikhail Gorbachev; now, that public charged the Soviet Union with having put the entire population of Europe, and potentially the world, in harm's way.

In addition, the Chernobyl disaster added momentum to the emancipation of the Soviet people, although that process continued to be controversial and heterogeneous. It involved coping with the complexity of the post-Soviet media and the power struggles between state and private interests; learning how to evaluate new institutions and their contacts with or independence from the state, international organizations, or private capital; and developing skills to assess the credibility of political actors in a confusing young democracy. The media controversy over Chernobyl that raged in the late 1980s and early 1990s was something established scientists like Aleksandrov and dissenting experts like Shasharin, Volkov, and Dubovskii had never experienced. Then again, neither had anyone else who had grown up in Soviet times. Soviet citizens who were used to reading between the lines of ideological discourse struggled to orient themselves in an increasingly diverse, barely regulated universe where the mass media was unleashed. When science and technology became subject to critical scrutiny and when multiple experts presented plausible (but incompatible) arguments, Soviet citizens had to learn new ways of assigning credibility.

In the context of this fundamentally new phenomenon—public disagreement between experts—and of the gradual opening of Soviet society, any reference to Chernobyl threatened to become a state-breaking device. Given the close connection between nuclear power and the state, every criticism of Chernobyl turned into a criticism of the state. The emerging environmentalist, and especially antinuclear, movement deployed Chernobyl as a rhetorical resource to attack the long-established authority of the state and its scientists.[11] At the same time, advocates of nuclear power eventually managed to turn Chernobyl into a state-making device by portraying the accident as a lesson that had to be learned, a crisis that was successfully overcome.[12] By pointing fingers at the operators, these advocates could hold on to the image of heroic designers and stress continuity with the country's historical achievements. But they simultaneously revamped training programs for reactor operators, in effect admitting that such programs could be significantly improved. Similarly, when nuclear scientists modified design aspects of the RBMK to restore public faith that nuclear power was safe, they acknowledged that something had been wrong with the RBMK design all along. By reforming the management of the nuclear industry, planners and top managers followed the same strategy of continuous organizational change they had earlier condemned as yielding unsatisfactory results.[13]

Political transitions like the collapse of the Soviet Union tend to remind us how fragile a political system's organizations can be. The institutions that ensure the safety of a high-risk technology like nuclear power are crucial, particularly in times of crisis. The post-Soviet nuclear industry faced a difficult conversion: a sharp drop in military production, an abrupt decline in the commissioning of new nuclear power plants, the phasing-out of some reactor units, and a significant decrease in uranium mining and reprocessing.

When the disintegration of the Soviet system became imminent, and the country was preparing to transition to a market economy, Minatomenergoprom's leadership wanted to make sure the nuclear industry would remain one united complex and maintain its established infrastructure and economic connections. By suggesting a state corporation that would become a joint-stock company, they engaged in classic social engineering—that is, they designed social change as if it were a technical problem with exactly one correct solution.[14] Political leaders resisted the plans as an undesirable legitimization of other Soviet republics' desire for independence and turned down the scientists' proposal. As a consequence, when the Soviet Union did fall apart, the nuclear energy enterprises outside of what emerged as the Russian Federation (about 30 percent of the former Soviet nuclear sector) were cut off from the previously centralized management, with no structure in place that would coordinate cooperation. Among the enterprises lost were all uranium mining organizations and about half of the previously Soviet nuclear power plants.[15]

The fact that nuclear scientists planned a stock company while most politicians were still resisting the imminent collapse of Soviet political and economic structures is telling: these scientists were experienced social engineers who expertly sailed troubled political waters.[16] The solution they offered was a political plan for nuclear energy policy and industry governance that reached well beyond their narrow technical expertise. It was a proposal that anticipated political, economic, and institutional changes that many politicians at that time were still unable to see, or were at the very least unwilling to accept.[17] This episode also reflects the confidence of nuclear experts that their word would be heard and respected in the highest councils of political power, a confidence they had acquired with

Conclusion

the successful detonation of the atomic bomb and maintained for years as they built the civilian nuclear industry. But Chernobyl had forced the relationship between nuclear experts and political decision makers to take a sharp turn. Nuclear experts saw their political clout declining and instead of attributing that fact to the political upheaval in the Soviet system, they experienced it as a challenge to scientific rationality. They considered their prognoses and suggestions rational and therefore objectively best for society and the common good. For a short while after Chernobyl, the Soviet leadership seemed ready to favor public opinion over expert advice, even if that would risk jeopardizing a reliable energy supply for the country.[18]

Outlook

Since that time, the pendulum has swung back: leaders take public opinion and opinion research into account, but decision making is firmly in experts' hands. And yet, there has not been a full return to technocratic rule: nuclear power managers in today's Russia have to work very hard for policymakers' support. In a long, difficult process, large parts of the nuclear industry have shifted to a market-economic model that includes several separate corporations.

Under this model, the argument that top managers in the nuclear industry must have training in nuclear physics or engineering no longer applies. Where collaboration and consultation among managers with complementary skill sets is critical, there is in principle nothing wrong with, for example, a leader of a state's nuclear energy program whose training is in water transport engineering and economics. Sergei Kirienko, who fits this description, was appointed head of the Federal Agency for Atomic Energy (now Rosatom) in 2005, and after a difficult period of transition he has made the concern a profitable enterprise. Rosatom today is one of the few companies worldwide that supports every stage of the fuel cycle—from uranium mining, to enrichment, to power generation, to reprocessing, and waste storage.[19] One of Rosatom's more attention-grabbing projects was the "floating nuclear power plant." Construction of a prototype, the "Academician Lomonosov," began in 2007; it would combine two small reactors (starting at 35 MW) on a mobile base that could be deployed to remote areas in the Far East and Far North.[20]

In 2008, the Russian Federation government authorized the construction of four new VVER-type reactors near Saint Petersburg, to replace the aging RBMK reactors currently operating there. Construction of units 1 and 2 is in full swing, and test-phase operation is scheduled to start in 2016.[21]

Site preparation began in 2010 for a new Baltic nuclear plant in the Russian enclave of Kaliningrad, but the project has since stalled.[22] In November 2013, Putin's government approved a plan to build an additional twenty-one new nuclear power reactors by 2030. Planners designated ten reactors for entirely new plants, near Kostroma (350 km northeast of Moscow), near Nizhnii Novgorod (the former Gorky), in the Republic of Tatarstan (Western Russia), in Seversk (near Tomsk, Siberia), and in the Southern Urals (200 km south of Ekaterinburg). The Southern Urals plant will be the only new one equipped with fast neutron reactors—all other plants will feature latest-generation VVERs. In addition, ten more brand-new VVER-1200s will replace the aging reactors at the Kola nuclear power plant and the operating RBMKs at the Kursk and Smolensk nuclear plants.

The Southern Urals plant's sodium-cooled fast reactor, the BN-1200, is apparently still a technical design project at the Afrikantov Experimental Design Bureau for Mechanical Engineering, with a construction start scheduled for 2015. Plans call for its prototype to be built at the Beloiarsk site, which already hosts the operational BN-600 as well as the BN-800, where the physical start-up is underway. Planners urged the construction of these reactors to reduce the plutonium stockpiles that reprocessing spent nuclear fuel from other plants has created.

From 2011 to 2012, Rosatom increased its export orders by 30 percent, including orders to build new nuclear power plants in Turkey, Jordan, and Bangladesh, and the company plans to solicit orders to construct some thirty reactors abroad by 2030.[23] Many of the design institutes, engineering bureaus, and large machine-building factories born under the Soviet civilian nuclear program have come back to life under Rosatom's new and all-encompassing expansion strategy. The former Moscow Engineering and Physics Institute (MIFI) in 2008 rebranded itself as the National Nuclear Research University and focuses on preparing specialists for the nuclear industry.[24] The civilian nuclear sector in today's Russia is a highly successful enterprise. Under Kirienko's leadership, nuclear energy has become normalized again.

Epilogue: Writing about Chernobyl after Fukushima

Before March 11, 2011, classifying Chernobyl as the worst disaster at a civilian nuclear plant in history was a no-brainer. But as politicians, journalists, and scholars were gearing up to commemorate Chernobyl's twenty-fifth anniversary in April 2011, a massive earthquake off the eastern coast of Japan's Honshu Island triggered a tsunami that would devastate the Tohoku area. The tsunami killed almost 16,000 people, destroyed or severely damaged hundreds of thousands of buildings, and caused a total station blackout at the Fukushima Daiichi nuclear power plant. Because the tsunami devastated the surrounding infrastructure and massive aftershocks aggravated the damage, plant personnel could not address the station blackout for days, and as a result three reactors suffered core meltdowns and three explosions each destroyed a reactor building. According to the Red Cross, some 78,000 people were evacuated.[1] Since then, the plant has continued to release significant amounts of radioactivity, particularly contaminated water, into the environment.

Comparing disasters is always tricky, even two nuclear disasters both of which international experts ranked at 7 (a major accident) on the 7-level International Nuclear and Radiological Events Scale.[2] The Chernobyl and Fukushima disasters were very different, starting with the technology: while Chernobyl involved one Soviet-designed graphite-water reactor, Fukushima involved three U.S.-designed boiling-water reactors. Chernobyl happened roughly 70 miles from Kiev, Fukushima about 150 miles from Tokyo, the nearest major population centers. When the tsunami struck, and before the nuclear crisis unfolded, authorities in Japan evacuated parts of the population preemptively and advised others to shelter in place. The evacuation of Chernobyl's satellite town did not start until some 30 hours after the onset of the emergency, and authorities didn't evacuate other nearby villages until days later. Chernobyl occurred in a country that was struggling economically and undergoing unprecedented political changes, and international experts did not rate Soviet technology very highly, especially in the commercial sector. Fukushima, by contrast, occurred in a country whose engineering expertise and sophistication were legendary. Japanese engineers led the world in earthquake-resistant building methods, and nobody doubted that if anyone could build a nuclear reactor on top of an active fault line, it was the Japanese. If an earthquake occurred, the reactor would simply shut itself down safely, sway gently, and restart in due time. Fukushima's reactors had containments, multiple redundant safety systems, and current emergency plans—none of which were in place at Chernobyl.

And yet, all those meticulous plans failed, one after another, as the station blackout at Fukushima dragged on for day after excruciating day. As the Fukushima nuclear emergency unfolded, another set of differences appeared. Fukushima's crew had a big handicap compared to Chernobyl's: they could not count on an all-powerful, centralized government that could rouse top scientists, engineers, and managers to figure out, once and for all, what needed to be done, and then move heaven and earth to make it happen. A private utility company, Tokyo Electric (or TEPCO), operated the Fukushima plant, and given the gravity of the situation, at times they had trouble rounding up a hundred workers to hold the line. At one point, TEPCO even contemplated abandoning the plant because of the life-threatening radiation levels.[3] The thought of abandoning the Chernobyl plant never crossed anyone's mind in 1986; quite the contrary, the pressure was on to return the plant to normal operations as quickly as possible. Recruits and volunteers labored jointly to complete the sarcophagus seven months after the explosion, marking the official end of the immediate disaster mitigation phase. In Fukushima, two years after the tsunami, the nuclear disaster is still ongoing. Nobody knows exactly how severe the damage to the reactors is. Spent fuel—hot, radioactive, dangerous spent fuel—remains in each of the wrecked buildings. Radioactive water continues to leak into the Pacific Ocean, despite desperate efforts to catch and store it in hastily built tanks. And we know with certainty that the next earthquake is only a few months, or maybe weeks, away.

Such important differences notwithstanding, we can already see emerge in the interpretation of Fukushima dynamics of simplification and blame similar to those (and as disturbing as those) this book has documented with Chernobyl. It did not take long before international critics started accusing the plant personnel of not acting quickly and decisively enough. The Fukushima version of the operator-error narrative did not charge personnel with conducting unauthorized experiments, as Soviet operators allegedly had in 1986. Ironically, critics charged Fukushima's workers instead with spending too much time coordinating with the utility's headquarters, the prime minister's office, and other superiors. Implicitly, these critics suggested the Japanese were better at rule-following, while their Soviet counterparts had been better at improvising. But there is evidence to the contrary, evidence that Fukushima's staff came up with extremely creative ideas, which unfortunately failed.[4] What's more, there is evidence that they also eventually defied orders when the process of getting authorization threatened the plant's safety.[5] Extraordinary situations by their very nature require improvisation, but different contexts produce different improvisations.

As readers of this book may have suspected, the design argument soon emerged as well. Fukushima's so-called Mark-1 containment design was originally from General Electric, and it has some twenty "sisters" on U.S. soil. After the accident, an aghast international public learned that in the mid-1970s, three top GE engineers had criticized the design as seriously flawed and resigned from their positions in protest.[6] Reactor construction in the United States nevertheless continued, and the industry dismissed the dissident engineers' concerns as overblown. In the case of Fukushima's reactors, the industry argued, TEPCO had modified the reactor design to suit specific Japanese needs. In other words, the industry implied that the American original had somehow become "tainted" in the process, and that only American plants of this design were "pure" and therefore safe.

And of course, the organizational argument joined the Kabuki dance soon thereafter: critics saw TEPCO, which also operated a number of other Japanese nuclear and nonnuclear power plants, as the embodiment of corporate greed. The utility's leaders maintained a "cozy" relationship with the regulator and even had some serious cases of corruption on their record. And TEPCO had clearly cut corners: against the advice of scientists, they had built their tsunami wall lower than the historically recorded maximum waterline, they had built several reactors on one site, and they had built close to the water—the general public and nuclear experts alike were outraged. Based on some reports, one could have concluded that the Japanese nuclear industry had been concocted by maniacs who deliberately risked the safety of millions, including their own families.

Again, hindsight seemed to make the causes obvious, a contextualized understanding unnecessary. But such an understanding would take into account that combining multiple reactors at one site was (and still is) common practice around the globe; like economies of scale elsewhere, it helps defray the substantial cost of sophisticated infrastructure and expertise. Building a nuclear plant close to a body of water is a simple technical necessity because unimaginable amounts of water are needed for cooling;

this often puts a plant on or near a fault line simply because that's where riverbeds tend to form. And finally, economic common sense dictated the need to find a compromise between planning for the absolute worst-case scenario and the probability of that worst case. Only then could a utility determine how much to invest in, for example, tsunami protection walls.

As after Chernobyl, multiple commissions, from government bodies to independent foundations, created accident investigation reports that reached at times contradictory conclusions. The international media and expert community (notably, the IAEA) took note of one assessment that appeared only in the English-language foreword to the Japanese parliament's (the Diet's) report and possibly does not even reflect the entire commission's point of view, because it was authored only by the commission's chairman, namely that this accident was "made in Japan."[7] In other words, it could never happen here (wherever "here" is). This cultural interpretation of Fukushima will no doubt stand in the way of learning from this disaster, no matter how many commissions and working groups are set up to identify lessons to be learned.[8]

Under tremendous public pressure, Japan shut down all its nuclear power plants after the triple disaster of March 2011—a step Soviet leaders would not even have considered in 1986. To maintain Japan's modern lifestyle, the country has for the time being switched to expensive, polluting fossil fuels, and will (literally) burn through its CO_2 emission reduction targets. Public opinion appears to support a nuclear phaseout. To restart a nuclear reactor, a utility now has to meet additional, exceedingly stringent safety requirements, and even if they do, the governor of the local prefecture still has the authority to veto the start-up.

But the postdisaster restructuring of Japan's nuclear industry also bears similarities to Chernobyl's aftermath. After TEPCO decided (or perhaps realized) that Fukushima Daiichi would never operate again, the company's managers—again in striking similarity to the Ukrainian agencies—singled out the plant from their other operations, most likely to limit future liability claims. As with Chernobyl, this singling out of "the troublemaker" inevitably leads to a loss of expertise in disaster response, safe maintenance of a damaged nuclear facility, and decommissioning. And as with Chernobyl, we will most likely lose the unique knowledge that participants in these operations will accumulate.

The repercussions from Fukushima are thus no less dramatic than Chernobyl's: we are witnessing, yet again, a massive overhaul of technical safety protocols at nuclear power plants, a thorough reevaluation of operating procedures, especially in emergency situations, and a fundamental review of the safety oversight and regulatory apparatus. Fukushima, in contrast to Chernobyl, may have global implications: not only have some countries decided to phase out their nuclear programs, but the process of harmonizing safety norms and measures that the European Union's "Stress Tests" initiated have no precedent in history.[9] Nuclear safety after Fukushima has become "the world's business."[10]

We have not even begun to comprehend Fukushima's full impact—on the environment, human health, or the national and international economy, let alone on Japan's national psyche. Let me venture to predict that along with one powerful narrative that views Fukushima as the end of Japan's nuclear exceptionalism, there will be another competing narrative that integrates nuclear energy back into the fabric of Japanese modernity. This latter narrative will portray Fukushima as a hard lesson that had to be learned and nuclear power as a normal industry that, although it suffered a bad accident, is inevitable for the nation's economic, technological, and even environmental survival. Only time will tell which narrative will prevail. But if Chernobyl is a guide, twenty-five years from now Japan's nuclear power program will have again returned to normalcy.

Biographical Notes

Abagian, Armen Artavazdovich (1933–2005). Director of the All-Union Scientific Research Institute for Nuclear Power Plant Operations (VNIIAES) from 1984 to 2005. Under his leadership, VNIIAES became the leading source of scientific and technical support for the civilian nuclear industry. Trained as a physicist, he worked at the Obninsk Institute for Nuclear Power Engineering for twenty years, specializing in the problems of radiation protection and the design of special-purpose nuclear power plants. Abagian was a member of the coordinating group, under G. A. Veretennikov, that investigated the Chernobyl accident for Minenergo and a coauthor of the report to the International Atomic Energy Agency (IAEA) on the causes of the Chernobyl accident.

Aleksandrov, Anatolii Petrovich (1903–1994). Director of the Institute of Atomic Energy (Kurchatov Institute) from 1960, following I. V. Kurchatov's death. Trained as a nuclear physicist, he was a protégée of Abram F. Ioffe and worked under him at the Radium Institute and Ioffe's Physical-Technical Institute. He and Kurchatov both moved to the Institute of Atomic Energy in 1943 to work on the Soviet atomic bomb project. During his years at the institute Aleksandrov was instrumental in developing reactors for the Soviet naval fleet, both commercial and military. He also served as the scientific director for the development of the RBMK reactor. In 1975, Aleksandrov became president of the Academy of Sciences, retiring after the Chernobyl accident.

Beria, Lavrentii Pavlovich (1899–1953). In 1942, while serving as deputy prime minister, controlling the Soviet Union's internal security system as well as strategic raw materials production using slave labor in the GULag camps, Beria was appointed administrative leader of atomic research. He chaired the Special Committee on the Atomic Bomb from 1945 to 1953. After Stalin's death, he was tried and executed for crimes against the state.

Briukhanov, Viktor Petrovich (b. 1936). Director of the Chernobyl nuclear power plant from 1970 to 1986. He worked at a fossil fuel and a hydropower plant before being promoted to his position at Chernobyl. Following the Chernobyl accident, he received ten years in prison. Briukhanov was released in 1991 and worked as a consultant for Ukrinterenergo, a Ukrainian energy company, until his retirement. He has been interviewed during many a Chernobyl anniversary and always steadfastly denied the charges that sent him to prison.

Diatlov, Anatolii Stepanovich (1931–1995). Deputy chief engineer at the Chernobyl nuclear power plant from 1973 to 1986. Trained as a physicist, he worked at a shipyard installing reactors on submarines for thirteen years before coming to Chernobyl. Diatlov was the test supervisor on duty at the time of the Chernobyl accident. He received ten years in prison but was released in 1991 due to illness.

Dolgikh, Vladimir Ivanovich (b. 1924). Secretary of the Central Committee from 1972 to 1988. Trained as a metallurgical mining engineer, he was a member of the Central Committee from 1971 to 1989, and a candidate for the Politburo from 1982 to 1988. From 1976 to 1984, he headed the Central Committee's Department of Heavy Industry and Energy. In this role, he was responsible for overseeing the Soviet Union's energy production, including nuclear energy. Officially retired since 1988, he currently serves as the senator from Moscow to the Federation Council.

Dollezhal', Nikolai Antonovich (1899–2000). Trained as a mechanical engineer; academician since 1962; director of the Scientific Research and Design Institute of Energy Technologies (NIKIET). His institute designed the nuclear power plant for the first Soviet nuclear submarine, the world's first nuclear power plant in Obninsk, the first dual-purpose (civilian energy and weapons-grade plutonium) power reactor for Siberia, the first purely industrial reactor for Beloiarsk, and the RBMK.

Dubovskii, Boris Grigor'evich (1919–2008). Physicist who worked under I. V. Kurchatov at Laboratory No. 2. In 1944, he produced the first micrograms of plutonium transmuted outside the United States. In 1946, while working on the first experimental reactor, he designed and manufactured the first professional dosimetry service. He worked at military facilities before coming to Obninsk, where he spent the rest of his career. He supervised the start-up of the Obninsk plant, and subsequently two industrial-scale reactors at the Beloiarsk site. He organized and headed the All-Union Nuclear Safety Service (1958–1973) and actively participated in the creation of norms for nuclear safety. Following the Chernobyl accident, he publically criticized the failure of NIKIET to make design improvements he had recommended many years before.

Dymshits, Veniamin Emmanuelovich (1910–1993). Deputy chairman of the Council of Ministers from 1962 to 1985, and first chairman of the State Committee for Material and Technical Supplies, Gossnab, from 1965 to 1976. Originally a miner from the Donbass, Dymshits worked his way up through the Party and eventually completed a technical college degree in Moscow while working at numerous industrial construction sites. Not supportive of perestroika, he retired in 1985.

Emel'ianov, Ivan Iakovlevich (1913–1991). First deputy director (for science) at the Scientific Research and Design Institute of Energy Technologies (NIKIET) since 1954, but had worked at what would eventually become known as NIKIET since 1946. Trained as an engineer, he worked in the aviation industry until World War II. Emel'ianov developed the control and safety systems for the RBMK reactors, noting early on the possibility for instability in the control rods. Following Chernobyl, he lost his leadership position but still led the redesign efforts to automate the RBMK control and safety systems.

Emel'ianov, Vasilii Semenovich (1901–1988). Director of the Chief Administration for the Utilization of Atomic Energy from 1957 to 1962, replacing Efim Slavskii. Trained as a metallurgist, he began working in the nuclear industry after World War II. Emel'ianov was well known in the international nuclear energy community due to his membership on the program committee for the First UN International Conference on the Peaceful Uses of Atomic Energy in 1955, and also because he served as a member of the Scientific Advisory Committee to the IAEA's Director General from 1958 to 1965. He was President of the Third Geneva Conference on the Peaceful Uses of Atomic Energy in 1964.

Feinberg, Savelii Moiseevich (1910–1973). Headed the nuclear reactor theory section at the Institute of Atomic Energy; credited with the invention of the RBMK's core design. Originally a construction engineer with a strong interest in mathematics, he started working for I. V. Kurchatov in 1946. He contributed to the research and design of many Soviet reactors, including the research reactor SM-2 at Melekess (Dmitrovgrad).

Flerov, Georgii Nikolaevich (1913–1990). While working as a junior nuclear physicist supporting the war effort, in 1942 Flerov first noticed the conspicuous silence surrounding nuclear fission in publications from the

United States, Britain, and Germany. From this, he concluded that all three countries must be working on an atomic bomb and urged his superiors to "build the uranium bomb without delay." From 1942 until the end of the war, Flerov worked with I. V. Kurchatov on the Soviet atomic bomb project. After the war, he continued his research in theoretical nuclear physics, and served as the director of the Joint Institute for Nuclear Research in Dubna for over thirty years (the institute now bears his name).

Fomin, Nikolai Maksimovich (b. 1935). Chief engineer at the Chernobyl nuclear power plant in 1985–1986. An electrician by training, he began work at Chernobyl in 1972 under V. P. Briukhanov. Following the Chernobyl accident, he received ten years in prison. Fomin was transferred from prison to a neuropsychiatric hospital in 1988. Two years later he was declared sane and released early. He went to work at the Kalinin nuclear power plant in 1990, remaining for five years until his retirement.

Grigor'iants, Artem Nikolaevich (1916–2002). Chief engineer of Sredmash's Chief Administration for the Use of Atomic Energy in 1958–1959. From 1959 to 1967 he worked at Sredmash and from 1967 to 1978 he was director of Minenergo's Glavatomenergo. He was part of a team that developed the Beloiarsk nuclear power plant. Trained as an electrical engineer, he worked at the Obninsk nuclear power plant from 1953 on and from 1956 to 1958 served as the plant's chief engineer. From 1978 to 1985, Grigor'iants was head of the Soviet construction crew in what was then Czechoslovakia.

Iadrikhinskii, Aleksandr A. (no dates). Nuclear specialist and safety inspector at the Kursk nuclear power plant. He had expressed concern to Gosatomenergonadzor about the design of the control and safety rods in the RBMK even before the Chernobyl accident. In 1989, he authored a report that became the basis for a reexamination of the Chernobyl disaster by Gosatomenergonadzor and that resulted in the "Shteinberg report" of 1991.

Isaev, Vasillii Iakovlevich (1917–2008). First deputy chairman of the State Committee for Planning (Gosplan) from 1966 until his retirement in 1984. Isaev worked in the construction industry throughout his career. While first deputy chairman he oversaw the construction industry and allocation of capital investments. He is credited with managing a significant increase in construction and labor productivity in the early 1970s.

Kapitsa, Petr Leonidovich (1894–1984). Founder of the Institute of Physical Problems in Moscow and director from 1934 to 1946, when he was removed by Stalin for quarreling with Beria. He was reinstated in 1955. A physicist by training, Kapitsa began his institute in Moscow with equipment he brought with him from the Cavendish Lab at Oxford, where he worked for over ten years before returning home. Kapitsa served as a member of the presidium of the Academy of Sciences from 1957 until his death. He was awarded the 1978 Nobel Prize in Physics.

Kopchinskii, Georgii Alekseevich (b. 1939). Deputy chief engineer at the Chernobyl nuclear power plant from 1973 on and later director of the Smolensk nuclear power plant. Starting in 1983, he worked in the Central Committee's Sector for Nuclear Energy; as of 1989, he headed the Council of Ministers' Department of Nuclear Energy (in the Bureau for the Fuel and Energy Complex). A graduate of MEI's department of Nuclear Power Plants, he is a leading nuclear safety expert in Ukrainian state agencies.

Kozlov, Frol Romanovich (1908–1965). First deputy chairman of the Council of Ministers from 1958 to 1960 and second secretary of the Communist Party from 1960 to 1963. Kozlov began his career as a factory laborer and worked his way up through the Party system. In 1957, he backed his mentor, N. S. Krushchev, against the Antiparty Group and for many years was considered Krushchev's likely replacement.

Kulov, Evgenii Vladimirovich (1929–1996). Chairman of the State Oversight Committee for the Safe Conduct of Work in the Nuclear Power Industry, Gosatomenergonadzor, from its inception in 1983 until 1986. Trained as a mechanical engineer, he began working for Sredmash in 1953 and by 1982 had worked his way up to deputy minister. He was dismissed from his position in 1986 following the Chernobyl accident.

Kurchatov, Igor' Vasil'evich (1903–1960). Known as the "Father of the Soviet Atomic Bomb," Kurchatov was trained as a physicist and naval engineer and worked at the State Radium Institute prior to World War II. In 1942, he was appointed scientific director of atomic research under Stalin. His "Laboratory No. 2" (the later Institute of Atomic Energy) would become the center of the Soviet nuclear weapons program. Under his leadership, the Soviet Union tested its first nuclear bomb in 1949 and its first hydrogen bomb in 1953. Although he continued to lead the Soviet Union's nuclear weapons program until his death, from the mid-1950s onward he also devoted himself to the development of commercial nuclear energy. He oversaw development and start-up of the Obninsk nuclear power plant in 1954, the first civilian nuclear power plant in the world.

Kuz'min, Iosif Iosifovich (1910–1996). First deputy chairman of the Council of Ministers from 1957 to 1958 and director of Gosplan from 1957 to 1959. Kuz'min opposed the development of a civilian nuclear program. He was succeeded on the Council of Ministers by F. R. Kozlov.

Lavrenenko, Konstantin Dmitrievich (1908–unknown). The first director of Minenergo's Glavatomenergo from 1956 to 1958. Subsequently, he worked at Gosplan and later the State Committee for Science and Technology (GKNT).

Legasov, Valerii Alekseevich (1936–1988). First deputy director of the Institute of Atomic Energy from 1983 to 1988. He was a professor of physics at Moscow State University from 1978 to 1983 and chairman of the Radiochemistry and Chemical Technology Department there from 1983 until his death. Legasov served under B. E. Shcherbina as a member of the government commission investigating the Chernobyl accident. He was also head of the Soviet delegation and presented the official accident report to the International Atomic Energy Agency in 1986. He committed suicide on the second anniversary of the Chernobyl accident, reportedly distraught over the secrecy in the Soviet nuclear industry and the suppression of transparency about the accident.

Leipunskii, Aleksandr Il'ich (1903–1972). Nuclear physicist, director of the fast neutron reactor program at Laboratory V in Obninsk from 1949–1972. Leipunskii studied under A. F. Ioffe in Leningrad and under E. Rutherford in Cambridge. In 1928, he transferred from Ioffe's Institute in Leningrad to the newly founded Ukrainian Physical-Technical Institute in Kharkov, where he became deputy director in 1930, and director 1933. In 1938, he was arrested for allegedly assisting "enemies of the people," but the following year, Stalin assigned him to the Soviet nuclear weapons project. From 1941 until 1949, he directed two different institutes at the Ukrainian Academy of Sciences, before he came to Obninsk in 1949.

Maiorets, Anatolii Ivanovich (b. 1929). Minister of Energy and Electrification (Minenergo) from 1985 to 1989, replacing P. S. Neporozhnii. He began his career as an elevator mechanic and electrician and worked his way up to the position of minister of the Electrotechnical Industry (1980–1985) before he switched ministries. He served under B. E. Shcherbina as a member of the government commission investigating the Chernobyl accident. He received a strict reprimand and retired in 1989.

Malyshev, Viacheslav Aleksandrovich (1902–1957). The first minister of Medium Machine Building (Sredmash) from 1953 to 1955. Trained as a locomotive engineer and mechanic, he worked at the Kuibyshev locomotive plant from 1934 to 1939 before beginning his Party career. In 1952–1953, he was a member of the Presidium of the Party's Central Committee. In 1953, in addition to serving as minister of Medium Machine Building, he was concurrently appointed deputy chairman of the Council of Ministers. In 1955, Malyshev became chairman of the State Committee for Science and Technology (GKNT), and a year later, first vice chairman of Gosplan.

Margulova, Tereza Khristoforovna (1912–1994). Professor, founder, and chair of the Department of Nuclear Power Plants at the Moscow Power Engineering Institute (MEI). Trained as an engineer at the Industrial Institute in Baku, Azerbaidzhan, and later MEI, she taught at MEI her entire career and developed the first Soviet university level program to train nuclear engineers through the doctorate level. All the major engineering universities throughout the Soviet Union subsequently copied her program. She is the author of over 300 publications, and her textbook—*Atomnye elektricheskie stantsii* ("Nuclear Power Plants")—remains the core textbook for all Russian and former Eastern Bloc countries' graduate nuclear engineering programs.

Mar'in, Vladimir Vasil'evich (no dates). Worked in the Central Committee's nuclear energy sector since 1969; in 1986 in the Department for Machine Building; after 1988 in the Department for Heavy Machine Building and Power Engineering.

Meshkov, Aleksandr Grigor'evich (1927–1994). First deputy minister of Medium Machine Building (Sredmash) from 1982 to 1986. Trained as a chemical engineer, he worked on the first industrial uranium-graphite reactor in Cheliabinsk. He began working for Sredmash in 1979. Dismissed from his position following the Chernobyl accident, he worked as director of an engineering plant in Elektrostal from 1986 to 1990. He was promoted to deputy minister of Minatomenergoprom in 1990 and retired a year later.

Neporozhnii, Petr Stepanovich (1910–1999). Minister of Energy and Electrification (Minenergo) from 1962 to 1985. Neporozhnii became first deputy minister of the Construction of Electrical Power Plants in 1959. He advanced to chairman of the Soviet State Production Committee for Energy and Electrification, Minenergo's predecessor, and as head of Minenergo accomplished a massive power plant construction program. Internationally, he was widely known for his innovations in large-scale hydroelectric power plants.

Pavlenko, Aleksei Sergeevich (1904–1984). Head of Gosplan's Department of Energy and Electrification from 1959 to 1974, when he retired. Trained as an electrical engineer, Pavlenko worked as a civil servant in various ministries throughout his career, notably serving as minister of power plants in 1954–1955 and 1957–1958.

Pervukhin, Mikhail Georgievich (1904–1978). Minister of Medium Machine Building (Sredmash) between April and June 1957. Trained as an electrical engineer, his early career in the electrical industry culminated in his appointment to the People's Commissar for Electric Power Stations in 1939. His short tenure as head of Sredmash was due to his involvement with the Antiparty Group's failed attempt to remove N. S. Khrushchev from office. Pervukhin was demoted to ambassador to the German Democratic Republic from 1958 to 1963. There, he was Khrushchev's personal representative during construction of the Berlin Wall. He was called back in 1963 and served in Gosplan's collegium, first as head of the Department for Energy and Electrification and then from 1965 to 1978 as head of the Department for Territorial Planning, where he oversaw site selection for new power plants.

Petros'iants, Andranik Melkonovich (1906–2005). Director of the Chief Administration for the Utilization of Atomic Energy from 1962 to 1986, replacing V. S. Emel'ianov. Trained as a mechanical engineer, he held a number of positions on heavy industry committees before joining the Ministry of Medium Machine Building (Sredmash) in 1953. He represented Sredmash internationally and became a key public figure in international nuclear cooperation, especially through his role in the Soviet Union's Council for Mutual Economic Assistance (CMEA). He retired in 1987 following the Chernobyl accident, of which he infamously said, "Science requires sacrifices."

Polushkin, Konstantin Konstantinovich (no dates). One of the RBMK-1000 designers at the Scientific Research and Design Institute of Energy Technologies (NIKIET). He was also a member of the coordinating group, under G. A. Veretennikov, that investigated the Chernobyl accident for Minenergo. Polushkin served as an expert witness for the state at the trial of the Chernobyl accident defendants.

Prushinskii, Boris Iakovlevich (b. 1938). Soiuzatomenergo's chief engineer in 1986; one of the first nuclear experts from Minenergo to arrive at the disaster site. Graduated from MEI in 1962, as a specialist in the planning and operation of nuclear power plants. Between 1962 and 1974 worked at the Beloiarsk nuclear power plant, and later at other Minenergo enterprises.

Riabev, Lev Dmitrievich (b. 1933). Deputy minister of Sredmash from 1984 to 1986, then succeeded Slavskii as minister of Medium Machine Building.

From 1989 to 1991, he served as deputy chairman of the Council of Ministers, and simultaneously chaired the Council's influential Bureau for the Fuel and Energy Complex. From 1993 to 2002 he served as first deputy minister of Atomic Energy (Minatom), then began compiling many volumes of primary sources on the Soviet weapons program. Riabev graduated from MIFI as an engineer-physicist, and from 1957 to 1978 worked at the All-Union Institute of Experimental Physics in the closed city of Arzamas-16, where he worked his way up from rank-and-file engineer to the institute's director. From 1978 to 1984, he directed the Central Committee's Sector for Medium Machine Building.

Rumiantsev, Alexander Iur'evich (b. 1945). Appointed minister of Atomic Energy of the Russian Federation in 2001. Trained as a nuclear physicist, he began working at the Kurchatov Institute in 1969 and became director in 1994. In 2004, when the ministry was reorganized into the Federal Agency on Atomic Energy, Rumiantsev became chief executive officer. In 2005, he signed the nuclear fuel agreement with Iran. Later that year he stepped down from his post in the wake of the international scandal involving his predecessor, Iu. O. Adamov, and subsequently served as Russian ambassador to Finland.

Ryzhkov, Nikolai Ivanovich (b. 1929). Chairman of the Council of Ministers from 1985 to 1990. As leader of the Strategic Group reporting directly to M. S. Gorbachev, Ryzhkov personally toured the Chernobyl accident site on May 2–4, 1986, and arbitrarily (he later admitted) established the 30-km exclusion zone that still exists. A graduate of the Urals Polytechnic Institute, he worked his way up in industry and in 1975 was appointed first deputy minister of Heavy and Transport Engineering. In 1979 he transferred to Gosplan as first deputy chairman. He became a member of the Central Committee in 1981 and the following year was elected secretary.

Semenov, Aleksandr Nikolaevich (b. 1926). Deputy minister of Energy and Electrification (Minenergo) from 1977 to 1992. A hydropower engineer by training, he worked in the hydroelectric industry in Turkmenistan in his early career. In 1982, he was assigned responsibility for all nuclear power plant construction. Semenov served under B. E. Shcherbina as a member of the government commission investigating the Chernobyl accident, and following the accident he was responsible for shutting down unit 4 at Chernobyl. Since 1993, Semenov has managed several national energy trade associations.

Shasharin, Gennadii Aleksandrovich (1934–2004). Deputy minister of Energy and Electrification (Minenergo), responsible for nuclear power, from

1982 to 1986. He was trained as a power engineer and worked in leading positions at the Obninsk, Beloiarsk, and Loviisa nuclear power plants from 1957 to 1977. In 1986, he ran a working group for Minenergo responsible for keeping units 1, 2, and 3 online during the period immediately after the Chernobyl accident. He was dismissed from his position after Chernobyl, but subsequently became general director of Interatomenergo from 1986 to 2004, one of the leading CMEA associations connected to nuclear technology transfer.

Shcherbina, Boris Evdokimovich (1919–1990). Deputy chairman of the Council of Ministers from 1984 to 1989. A railroad transportation engineer by training, he worked his way up through the Party and became minister for the Construction of Oil and Gas Facilities in 1973. He joined the Central Committee in 1976. Shcherbina was appointed head of the government commission on Chernobyl in April 1986. He led the first group of government commission representatives to Chernobyl and ordered the evacuation of Pripyat. His commission reported to the Central Committee's Strategic Group, led by N. I. Ryzhkov.

Shteinberg, Nikolai Aleksandrovich (b. 1947). Appointed chief engineer of the Chernobyl nuclear power plant in May 1986, following the accident. In April 1987 he became deputy chair of Gosatomenergonadzor, and beginning in 1989 he spearheaded efforts to revise the initial Chernobyl investigation report. A graduate of MEI's Department of Nuclear Power Plants, he had worked at the Chernobyl and then the Balakovo nuclear power plant from 1971 to 1986. In August 1991 the Ukrainian State Committee for nuclear and radiological safety appointed him its chair. From 2002 to 2006, he served as Ukraine's deputy minister for fuel and energy. Most recently, he was chair of the Council for Reactor Safety under the Ukrainian regulatory agency.

Sidorenko, Viktor Alekseevich (b. 1929). First deputy chairman of Gosatomenergonadzor in 1986. He was reprimanded for safety failures that led to the Chernobyl accident. Sidorenko graduated from MEI and spent most of his career at the Institute of Atomic Energy. He is a corresponding member of the Academy of Sciences, a former member of the International Nuclear Safety Advisory Group (INSAG) within the International Atomic Energy Agency (IAEA), and a former deputy director at the Kurchatov Institute. Sidorenko also served as deputy minister of the Russian Ministry of Atomic Energy from 1993 to 1996.

Slavskii, Efim Pavlovich (1898–1991). Minister of Medium Machine Building (Sredmash) from 1957 to 1986. Slavskii was trained as a coal miner,

Biographical Notes

but following World War I went to college and became a metallurgical engineer and worked in the aluminum industry until 1945. Due to his long tenure as minister of Sredmash, as well as briefly serving as the first director of the Chief Administration for the Utilization of Atomic Energy under the Council of Ministers in 1956, he is considered one of the founders and leaders of the nuclear industry in the Soviet Union. He retired in 1986, after the completion of the sarcophagus.

Vannikov, Boris L'vovich (1897–1962). From 1945 through 1953 General Vannikov was head of the First Chief Administration of the Council of People's Commissars. In this position he worked under L. P. Beria, overseeing the Soviet atomic bomb project. Although a three-star general and Commissar for Armament, he was briefly arrested in 1941 for "failing to carry out his duties," but was soon released. Following Beria's execution in 1953 he was appointed deputy minister of Medium Machine Building (Sredmash); on A. P. Zaveniagin's death he was promoted to minister, briefly serving in 1956–1957. He retired from government service in 1958.

Vavilov, Sergei Ivanovich (1891–1951). Founder and director of the Lebedev Institute of Physics of the Academy of Sciences (FIAN) in Moscow from 1934 to 1951. Under Vavilov's leadership FIAN grew from a small physics laboratory to the premier scientific institution in Russia that would produce six Nobel laureates and major discoveries, such as the Vavilov-Cherenkov effect. In 1945, Vavilov was elected president of the Academy of Sciences, and he served in this role until his death. During his tenure, he is widely credited with greatly improving the overall international standing of the Soviet scientific community, their access to resources, and their domestic status during Stalin's regime.

Velikhov, Evgenii Pavlovich (b. 1935). Vice president of the Academy of Sciences from 1977 to 1996. Trained as a physicist, he began working at the Institute of Atomic Energy (Kurchatov Institute) in 1961 and spent his entire career there. He was named director in 1988 and president in 1992. Velikhov also served as president (1992) and chairman (2009) of the international council of the ITER Program on the creation of a fusion reactor.

Veretennikov, Gennadii Anatol'evich (b. 1934). Director of Soiuzatomenergo from 1982 to 1986. He briefly served as deputy minister of Energy and Electrification (Minenergo) in 1983–1984. Trained as an engineer-physicist, in 1982 he led a government commission investigating radiation leaks at unit 1 in Chernobyl. In 1986, he ran Minenergo's coordinating emergency response group during the Chernobyl accident.

He was removed from his position after Chernobyl and subsequently worked as a senior researcher for the Academy of Sciences.

Vernadskii, Vladimir Ivanovich (1863–1945). Founder of the State Radium Institute in Leningrad and director from 1922 to 1939. The Radium Institute grew out of Vernadskii's 1910s research, where he predicted the potential of radioactive material to produce energy and surveyed the radium and uranium deposits in Siberia. At Vernadskii's urging in 1940, the government established a Commission on the Uranium Problem to explore nuclear energy's potential to meet the electrical needs of the economy.

Volkov, Vladimir P. (no dates). Scientific researcher at the Institute of Atomic Energy. Volkov warned about the RBMK's design flaws before Chernobyl; reportedly, he had the support of I. F. Zhezherun, a physicist and senior collaborator at the Institute of Atomic Energy. Volkov took his concerns "public"—that is, wrote to Gorbachev directly—after the Chernobyl disaster.

Zaveniagin, Avraamii Pavlovich (1901–1956). Minister of Medium Machine Building (Sredmash) in 1955–1956, replacing V. A. Malyshev. Trained as a mining engineer, he worked in the mining industry until 1941. Zaveniagin worked closely with L. P. Beria in the Commissariat for Internal Affairs from 1941 to 1950. He became deputy minister of Sredmash in 1953–1954 and vice chairman of the Council of Ministers in 1955.

Methodological Appendix

To shed light on the social, political, economic, and technical complexities and contingencies that tend to get obliterated in official narratives, I used three major data sources: archival documents, in-depth interviews with nuclear specialists, and published sources (primary and secondary). All three types of sources, to varying degrees, raise the question of whether they can be trusted. Especially in published Soviet sources, the analyst has to decipher a language in which political rhetoric was intricately woven into the texture of even fairly technical narratives. The classic technique of triangulation—that is, checking whether the stories people tell can be backed up with either published or archival sources—often works too well to be reliable in the Soviet context. This remarkable overlap should instead be interpreted as proof of the pervasiveness of Soviet ideology. I used two strategies to get around this problem. The first was to compare Soviet sources with foreign ones, such as CIA reports, publications by the U.S. Office of Technology Assessment, non-Soviet reports from international conferences related to nuclear energy, as well as reports from foreign delegations visiting Soviet nuclear facilities. The second strategy was to consult dry, matter-of-fact institutional memory, preserved in administrative document collections. Studying these documents over an extended period, as I was able to, helped me get a "feel" for the style of these documents and understand the unmarked "codes" (for example, what a "satisfactory" evaluation meant became clear only when I found an "unsatisfactory" one). The eerie consistency of discursive choices also made clear how Soviet political ideology could become relatively straightforward to "decode," at least for those unwilling to buy into the dream of a communist future.

Archival Sources

During extensive research in Russia during 2003 and on subsequent research trips, I consulted archival collections ranging from administrative documents pertaining to the nuclear power industry in its various stages, to governmental and institutional protocols of different agencies, legal documents, and scientists' personal records. Archival material relating to the civilian nuclear industry is still largely classified. The archives of the Ministry of Atomic Energy (now *Rosatom, Gosudarstvennaia korporatsiia po atomnoi energii*), the archives of the Kurchatov Institute and NIKIET, as well as the archive at the IPPE/FEI at Obninsk are still closed, at least to most foreign researchers, and the documents relating to nuclear power in the Central Committee's Sector for Mechanical Engineering (in the Russian State Archive for Contemporary History, RGANI) have not been declassified either. So far, the only documentation on nuclear power plants is preserved in the Russian State Archive for the Economy (RGAE). This archive holds collections of the Ministry of Energy and Electrification (*Minenergo*), collections of *Gosplan's* Sector for Electrification, and collections of the State Committee for Science and Technology's (GKNT) Council on New Technologies for the Power Industry. All of these organizations were involved with the nuclear power industry to some degree, and although some documents relating to nuclear plants have been removed from the binders (after having been listed in the table of contents), the majority are accessible to researchers.

The document collection of Minenergo at the Russian State Archive for the Economy (RGAE, fond 7964) contains the majority of documents that this research is based on. It holds decrees and orders for long-term planning in the power industry, annual reports on the ministry's activities, transcripts of meetings of the ministry's decision-making council (*kollegiia*) and of meetings convened by the minister or his deputies, decrees issued by the minister, reports to the Council of Ministers, correspondence with Gosplan, Gosstroi, and GKNT, material relating to assignments by the Council of Ministers involving the construction and operation of nuclear power plants, and decisions regarding proposals and complaints by citizens to the Minenergo apparatus.

Additionally, the collection holds annual reports from individual nuclear power plants to *Glavatomenergo*, and from Glavatomenergo to the ministry (reports on financial activities, progress in construction work, etc.). It includes transcripts of technical meetings, orders issued by Glavatomenergo, decisions regarding the financial and project design of nuclear power plants, and decisions by Glavatomenergo's accounting commission (*balansovaia komissiia*). These latter documents are an extraordinary source: they very briefly summarize the annual reports from the individual power plants, outline the main achievements and shortcomings (where the plant's

Methodological Appendix

management met the plan, exceeded it, or failed), formulaically assess the plant's work as "satisfactory" (*udovletvoritel'no*), and make suggestions and give instructions for the following year. These documents offer a comparative view of all nuclear power plants under construction and in operation. The critical comments in these summaries are open and sharp, and sometimes include warnings to the plant's management. Beginning in 1978, *Soiuzatomenergo* takes Glavatomenergo's place; the collection holds orders, transcripts of meetings convened by Soiuzatomenergo's director, and decisions by Soiuzatomenergo's accounting commission affecting the activities of nuclear power plants.[1]

The same archive, RGAE, holds a small collection of documents pertaining to Glavatomenergo (1956–1959) that is separate from the Minenergo collection (RGAE, fond 9599). It contains annual financial plans for the construction of nuclear power plants, transcripts of meetings and decisions made by Glavatomenergo, reports of technical meetings, reports of siting commissions, as well as specific reports on the construction of the Beloiarsk and Novo-Voronezh nuclear power plants.

Several groups of documents from the collection on the State Committee for Planning, Gosplan (RGAE, fond 4372), relate to the nuclear power industry. There are documents pertaining to Gosplan's Sector for Electrification (*Otdel elektrifikatsii*, responsible for planning the construction of new power plants) and the Sector for Electricity Distribution (*Otdel raspredeleniia elektroenergii*). The *opisi* extend from 1945/1955 (op. 54) to 1975 (op. 66) and contain documents on construction management, directives from the government regarding construction, reconstruction, and start-up of industrial facilities (in particular with regard to the development of the power industry), transcripts of meetings on priority construction projects, reports on plan fulfillment, projections of electricity demand, and material to substantiate revisions to plans.

Some documents from the State Committee for Science and Technology (GKNT) collection (RGAE, fond 9480, 1950–1975) also relate to the nuclear power industry. I reviewed correspondence with the Council of Ministers, the Central Committee, the Academy of Sciences, individual ministries, and scientific and technological institutes about introducing innovative technologies in industry, in particular in the power industry; plans and reports about the implementation of new technologies; and reports of meetings held by GKNT's Scientific-Technical Council on questions relating to the power industry and electrification.

The Archive of the Russian Academy of Sciences (ARAN) holds more recent documents than the slightly outdated guidebook (*putevoditel'*) that was available to me had suggested, but I have found relatively few collections that relate directly to the nuclear power industry. In the collection of the Academy's Commission on Nuclear Energy, documentation goes as far as the late 1970s. The information mostly concerns research reactors, schedules for conducting experiments at the available facilities, and the coordination of nuclear research across the various Soviet republics.[2] The documents from the Scientific-Technical Sector within the Scientific Council of the Presidium of the Soviet Academy of Sciences include plans and draft decrees (*proekty postanovlenii*) for the development of nuclear physics research, correspondence with domestic and international organizations involved in the development of nuclear energy applications (among other themes, on the standardization of radiation hazards, and the use of radioactive isotopes), articles and permissions for publication, materials relating to the United Nations Conferences on Peaceful Uses of Atomic Energy in Geneva, and summaries of foreign press reports on the Soviet contributions to these and other conferences.[3] Several collections of academicians' personal documents, which relate to the period of interest to the nuclear power industry, are currently being processed. In 2003, the documents pertaining to Anatolii Aleksandrov's tenure as the Academy's president became available.[4]

The Youth League (*Komsomol*) archive, now a branch of the Russian State Archive for Social and Political History (RGASPI), holds textual and, more fascinatingly, visual materials on nuclear power plant construction sites that had been declared Komsomol "shock-work" sites, that is, construction projects that relied on cohorts of enthusiastic young workers from the Komsomol for their timely completion. The collection contains correspondence between the Komsomol administration in Moscow and these construction sites, newspaper clippings (e.g., from *Pravda* and *Molodaia gvardiia*) about the success of Komsomol brigades,[5] and photo albums of Komsomol brigades on nuclear power plant construction sites.[6] There are also minutes of Komsomol conventions[7] and materials relating to them,[8] as well as transcripts of Komsomol conventions that include parts pertaining to the nuclear industry.[9] In addition, there are reports from Komsomol brigades[10] and materials relating to decrees that the VLKSM bureau and Minenergo issued.[11] Not all of the Komsomol archive's documents relating to nuclear power have been declassified.[12]

Among the few declassified document collections at the Russian State Archive for Contemporary History (RGANI), fond 89 is a collection of documents that became available to the public in the wake of the Communist Party trials under President Yeltsin.[13] This collection also contains

Methodological Appendix

documents on the lawsuit following the Chernobyl accident (*O sudebnom razbiratel'stve ugolovnogo dela, sviazannogo s avariei na ChAES*).[14] The small number of RGANI's declassified documents pertaining to the apparatus of the Central Committee (fond 5, *Apparat TsK KPSS*) contain one subcollection relating to the Sector for Mechanical Engineering (*Otdel mashinostroeniia*, opis' 40). A few of these documents are connected to the nuclear power industry, especially the early period.[15]

The Russian State Archive for Scientific and Technical Documentation (RGANTD) in Samara contains managerial documents from a wide range of scientific and technical institutes and construction bureaus involved with designing and manufacturing equipment for the nuclear industry. Among these institutes are the All-Union Thermal Engineering Institute named after F. E. Dzerzhinskii,[16] the State Power Engineering Institute named after G. M. Krzhizhanovskii,[17] and certain Chief Administrations of the All-Union State Planning Institute "Teploelektroproekt,"[18] all subordinate to the Ministry of Energy and Electrification (Minenergo). The archive also holds documents from the Institute for Nuclear Power Engineering under the Ministry of Power Engineering,[19] and the only documents relating to the former Ministry of Atomic Energy that I was able to review freely: documents from the Institute "Atomenergoproekt" for the years 1986–1992.[20]

Interviews

I conducted twenty-eight interviews with veterans of the Soviet nuclear power program in Moscow, Obninsk, Visaginas, and Vienna between 2001 and 2006, and six more interviews with a slightly different focus in Dresden, Saint Petersburg, Kiev, and Vienna in 2011 and 2012. Although some of these experts had retired by the time I approached them, many were willing to share their insights and considerable experience with me.

I planned these interviews to complement information that was not available in accessible archives, or to provide the kind of stories that would never have ended up in written form in the first place. I started with only a few contacts through private referrals, who subsequently referred me to others.[21] On occasion, I approached potential interviewees at conferences I attended, I contacted a publishing house for a potential interviewee's contact information, or I used the Internet to find someone's work phone number and then made blind calls. My affiliation with the Russian Academy of Sciences' Institute for the History of Science and Technology was often very helpful, but the value of personal networks trumped every other method.

The semistructured interviews followed a list of questions but frequently departed from it, especially when the specific expertise of the individual I was talking to prompted different questions and led in new directions. Often, informal conversation after an interview (on the way to the metro, for example) or during a break provided insights as enlightening as those I was able to record. I sent the list of questions, along with a summary of my research project, to my interviewees in advance, and then recorded the actual interviews with their permission. For the text of the book, I transcribed critical passages and translated them into English.

Published Sources

Few Western publications have focused exclusively on the civilian applications of nuclear energy in the Soviet Union. An exception is Paul R. Josephson's *Red Atom: Russia's Nuclear Power Program from Stalin to Today*, which covers a broad spectrum of applications in the power industry, biology, medicine, and the food industry.[22] Maria Vasilieva explores the history of decision making in and for the nuclear power industry (nuclear power reactors and propulsion reactors) in her comprehensive study *Soleils rouges: L'ambition nucléaire soviétique*.[23] In the former Soviet Union, by contrast, the history of nuclear energy has been the subject of numerous books over the past twenty years. While the military project still attracts more attention, civilian nuclear technologies have moved to center stage either explicitly (as in the five edited volumes by Viktor A. Sidorenko on the history of nuclear power in the Soviet Union and Russia),[24] or as part of memoirs or other books published on the occasion of anniversaries of important scientists, policymakers, institutes, or agencies (for example, many publications were devoted to the centennials of the birth of Efim Slavskii, Anatolii Aleksandrov, Igor Kurchatov, and Aleksandr Leipunskii).[25] Other books on prominent Soviet nuclear scientists and important organizations, and historical accounts presented from the perspective of different institutes, have appeared as well.[26] Many of these publications are celebratory rather than analytical, but since they often include contributions from a range of authors, there are sections that provide alternative perspectives.[27]

The five volumes edited by Sidorenko are particularly useful for students of Soviet nuclear power. The first volume, which appeared in 2001, features an essay by Goncharov on the early period of the Soviet nuclear power industry (*Pervyi period razvitiia atomnoi energetiki v SSSR*), which had been issued as a preprint by the Kurchatov Institute in 1990;[28] a reprint of Kurchatov's 1956 speech at Harwell;[29] a programmatic conference essay by

Anatolii Aleksandrov from 1968;[30] and essays on the history of the Obninsk and the Beloiarsk nuclear power plants as well as on the history of military uranium-graphite reactors, pressurized water reactors, RBMKs, fast breeder reactors, and gas-cooled reactors. The first volume also includes chapters by Sidorenko on the management of nuclear power plants and on nuclear safety.[31]

The second volume (published in 2002) contains essays on the history of the VVER. They focus on the development of this reactor design for power reactors, on the specific design of fuel elements, on computer programs for computing the core's parameters, on the history of the Novo-Voronezh nuclear power plant and further developments, and on safety issues.[32] This volume also has a chapter by Sidorenko on "scientific management" (*nauchnoe rukovodstvo*) in the nuclear power industry.[33]

Volume 3, which came out in 2003, is devoted to the history of the RBMK.[34] It contains essays on the history of the design development in the Kurchatov Institute (Institute of Atomic Energy), on the first RBMK, including specific technical features of this reactor type, and on the creation of a full-scale RBMK simulator.

Volume 4 (published in 2002) is subtitled "Lessons from the Chernobyl Accident" (*Uroki avarii na Chernobyl'skoi AES*). It includes reprints of several important reports published in the years following the accident,[35] as well as Sidorenko's personal report to the Central Committee.[36]

And volume 5, which came out in 2004, concludes the discussion of the nuclear power industry by describing the development of small power reactors. Among others, the chapters depict the mobile nuclear power plant TES-3, the Bilibino nuclear power plant, and current projects involving floating nuclear power plants.[37] These books are extremely useful collections of personal accounts from participants in the Soviet nuclear power program. They are not official accounts, and therefore rarely include archival or other scholarly references.

By contrast, the archives of the former Ministry of Atomic Energy (*Minatom*)[38] and the Russian Research Center "Kurchatov Institute" (previously the Institute of Atomic Energy)[39] have been publishing selected archival documents and essays on the atomic project. Former employees of top nuclear policymaking bodies have put together useful compilations of facts and figures—for example, those produced by former Minatom associate Arkadii Kruglov.[40]

Historical journals like *Voprosy istorii estestvoznanii i tekhniki* (*Issues in the History of Science and Technology*, published by the Russian Academy of Sciences' Institute for the History of Science and Technology), *Istoriia nauki i tekhniki* (*History of Science and Technology*), and even specialized technical periodicals like *Atomnaia energiia* (*Atomic Energy*), have also been publishing material related to the nuclear power industry. Historian of physics Vladimir Vizgin (from the Academy's Institute for the History of Science and Technology) edited two volumes on the history of the Soviet atomic project.[41] Conference proceedings provide valuable overviews of contemporary assessments of the nuclear history of the Soviet Union,[42] and published "strategies" for the country's future energy policy provide updates on the still-changing plans.[43]

The privilege of conducting research in the post-Soviet era was brought home to me in working with publications that couldn't have been published under Soviet rule, in particular, fairly outspoken memoirs and critical assessments. As participants in the nuclear program, both military and civilian, are reaching retirement age, personal memoirs have been appearing, some of them self-published.[44] These accounts rely on the private memories of participants. One former reactor operator, Mikhail Grabovskii, has turned to a new literary form, "documentary novels" (*dokumental'nye povesti*), as he calls them, to describe the history of the Soviet nuclear industry.[45] Vladimir Gubarev, former chief science editor of *Pravda*, has also written on the history of the Soviet nuclear industry. His books are fascinating because they're based on archival material only he was able to gain access to, and easy to read due to their journalistic style.[46]

A vast body of literature has been published on the Chernobyl disaster, apart from the reports appearing in official Soviet journals and through the International Atomic Energy Agency.[47] Publications on Chernobyl include technical assessments,[48] publications related to consequences of the accident for public health and the environment,[49] publications that address specific consequences for former Soviet regions (in particular, Belorus[50] and Ukraine[51]), and a range of Russian and international publications on general issues related to the accident.[52] In addition, dramatized treatments of the accident were published; among the well-known ones are Iurii Shcherbak's *Chernobyl: A Documentary Story* and Vladimir Gubarev's *Sarcophagus: A Tragedy*.[53] The Internet has become an indispensable resource for researchers, as well as a way for authors to publish material they could not otherwise find an outlet for. In addition, archival material and interview transcripts are often available online.[54]

Some post-Soviet publications on the Russian and Soviet economy reference the power industry in particular.[55] On the history of electrification, for example, I have used contemporary Soviet sources, which best convey the spirit of ambitious growth.[56] Several books have come out on Aleksei

Kosygin, and some of his speeches have been published separately.[57] In 1996, Alla Iaroshinskaia, former advisor to President Boris Yeltsin, edited a *Nuclear Encyclopedia*, which was evenly criticized by nuclear power promoters and opponents but contains a great deal of helpful information.[58] Another useful reference work is *Who Is Who in Nuclear Power Engineering and Industry of Russia*.[59] Recent industry publications sometimes include historical sections—for example, a publication by the Sverdlovsk (Ekaterinburg) branch of NIKIET.[60] Other publications can be expected as key documents are declassified.

List of Interviews

To protect the anonymity of my interviewees, I identify the interviews only by number, date, and location, along with a general description of the scope of their work. All interviews but one were recorded; I often had additional conversations with my interviewees that were not recorded.

#	Date	Location	About the Interviewee
1	3/2002	Vienna	Engineer; worked as government representative at the IAEA. (No recording.)
2	1/16/2001	Moscow	Professor, Russian Academy of Sciences.
3	2/16/2003	Moscow	Nuclear engineer; worked at almost all types of reactors from the earliest days of the Soviet program, from basic technical positions to management functions, always for Minenergo.
4	3/12/2003	Moscow	Engineer; worked on plutonium-producing reactors at military sites, for Sredmash.
5	3/13/2003	Obninsk	Nuclear engineer; involved with the start-up of several early nuclear power reactors; worked in research.
6	3/13/2003	Obninsk	Nuclear physicist; worked in the nuclear weapons program and later in research and development for the civilian nuclear industry.

#	Date	Location	About the Interviewee
7	3/26/2003	Moscow	Physicist-engineer; worked at military sites before transferring to Minenergo. Also held management positions in government agencies.
8	3/26/2003	Moscow	Nuclear physicist, generalist; worked in top technical positions for Sredmash and in various management positions in other government agencies.
9	3/29/2003	Moscow	Nuclear engineer; worked at almost all types of reactors from the earliest days of the Soviet program, from basic technical positions to management functions, always for Minenergo.
10	3/30/2003	Moscow	Engineer; specialist in graphite-water reactors; worked with RBMKs from their earliest days.
11	4/3/2003	Moscow	Power engineer turned nuclear specialist; worked at various nuclear power plants since the 1960s, and later held management positions in government agencies.
12	4/7/2003	Obninsk	Nuclear physicist; worked in the nuclear weapons program and later in research and development for the civilian nuclear industry.
13	4/8/2003	Obninsk	Two engineers who worked for Sredmash at military sites on graphite-water reactors.
14	5/28/2003	Moscow	Engineer; worked at some of the first nuclear power plants; also served in management positions for Minenergo.
15	9/8/2003	Moscow	Physicist-engineer who worked at Obninsk and served at the IAEA for some time.
16	10/8/2003	Visaginas	Engineer and nuclear safety expert; specialist in RBMKs; worked for Sredmash.

List of Interviews

#	Date	Location	About the Interviewee
17	10/8/2003	Visaginas	Engineer; RBMK operator.
18	10/8/2003	Visaginas	Engineer; RBMK specialist; worked for Sredmash at several nuclear power plants from the very beginning.
19	12/5/2003	Obninsk	Engineer; worked for Sredmash at military sites.
20	12/5/2003	Obninsk	Engineer, worked for Sredmash at military sites and later transferred to Obninsk.
21	12/10/2003	Moscow	Engineer; worked for Minenergo and its subsidiaries, both in the Soviet Union and abroad, in the nuclear industry and the general power industry.
22	12/15/2003	Moscow	Physicist and economist; worked for Sredmash.
23	7/5/2004	Moscow	Nuclear physicist who worked in research and development under Sredmash; specialist in RBMKs.
24	7/5/2004	Moscow	Science journalist.
25	6/6/2005	Moscow	Physicist-engineer; worked at military sites before transferring to Minenergo. Also held management positions in government agencies.
26	9/26/2006	Moscow	Physicist-engineer; worked at military sites; held management positions in Sredmash and other government agencies.
27	10/2/2006	Moscow	Nuclear physicist and nuclear safety expert; worked in research.
28	10/3/2006	Moscow	Engineer; held management positions in the government, where his responsibilities included oversight of the nuclear industry.
29	10/15/2011–10/16/2011	Dresden	Nuclear physicist-engineer, Ukrainian Academy of Sciences.

#	Date	Location	About the Interviewee
30	10/18/2011	Saint Petersburg	Engineer; worked for Sredmash and managed important nuclear construction projects.
31	10/21/2011	Kiev	Geologist, academician; worked in research.
32	10/21/2011	Kiev	Nuclear engineer; worked for Minenergo and held management positions in other government agencies.
33	10/23/2011	Kiev	Engineer; worked for the nuclear navy before coming to work in the nuclear industry for Minenergo.
34	Summer 2012	Vienna	Engineer; worked for the military in NBC defense and later for Sredmash in disaster response.

Notes

Introduction

1. "In all, 67 employees have been sacked or demoted, amongst them 20 specialists who were present in the control room above the no. 4 reactor during the experiment. ... It appears that the trial proceedings will go beyond considerations of the operators' culpability and focus on the responsibility of the specialists who designed the experiment and of the nuclear power station's management, supervisory staff and safety inspectors" ("Chernobyl Trial Set for July," *Financial Times Business Limited, FT Energy Newsletters—European Energy*, June 26, 1987, 15). 27 of those 67 were also expelled from the Communist Party (John Greenwald and Ken Olsen, "Disasters Judgment at Chernobyl: Six Defendants Go on Trial for Causing a Nuclear Catastrophe," *Time* 130, no. 3 (July 20, 1987): 44–45; "Chernobyl Trial Begins in Soviet [Union]," *New York Times*, late city final ed., July 8, 1987, section A, p. 5). All media sources cited in this chapter were retrieved from LexisNexis Academic.

2. Robert Paine, "'Chernobyl Reaches Norway: The Accident, Science, and the Threat to Cultural Knowledge," *Public Understanding of Science* 1 (1992): 261–280; Vasilii Borisovich Nesterenko, *Masshtaby i posledstviia katastrofy na Chernobyl'skoi AES dlia Belorusi, Ukrainy i Rossii* (Minsk: Pravo i ekonomika, 1996); Vasil' Gigevich and Oleg Chernov, *Stali vody gor'kimi: Khronika Chernobyl'skoi bedy* (Minsk: Belorus', 1991).

3. International Nuclear Safety Advisory Group, *Summary Report on the Post-Accident Review Meeting on the Chernobyl Accident*, No. 75-INSAG-1, Safety Series (Vienna: International Atomic Energy Agency, 1986).

4. The Party's Central Committee decree of July 14, 1986 was classified as top secret, but large parts of it were published on the front page of *Pravda* on July 20. For details, see chapter 5; see also "A Soviet Aide Says Chernobyl Officials Will Be Put on Trial" (*New York Times*, late city final ed., March 14, 1987, section 1, p. 6); Anna Christensen, "Trial to Be Held Soon in Chernobyl," *United Press International*, March 13, 1987.

5. "Scapegoats of Chernobyl."

6. David Marples points out that the Soviet authorities initially allowed Western journalists to report directly from the site of the accident, but subsequently opted for a stricter information control strategy (David R. Marples, *The Social Impact of the Chernobyl Disaster* (London: Macmillan, 1988)).

7. Nikolai V. Karpan, *Chernobyl': Mest' mirnogo atoma* (Kiev: Kantri Laif, 2005).

8. Yaron Ezrahi, *The Descent of Icarus: Science and the Transformation of Contemporary Democracy* (Cambridge, MA: Harvard University Press, 1990), especially 67–96.

9. As a reaction to what was perceived as Western propaganda, "The reporting on Chernobyl in the Soviet press has been matched, dispatch for dispatch, by articles on problems in Western nuclear stations and by attacks on the Western press for sensationalizing the accident in the early days when official Soviet information was scarce to nonexistent" (Bill Keller, "The 1986 Disaster at Chernobyl: A Year Later, Lessons Are Drawn; in Soviet [sic], Heroism and Candor Are Hailed, but Questions Linger," *New York Times*, April 26, 1987, late city final ed., section 1, p. 1).

10. "Soviet radiation experts in white coats disclosed that radiation in the area was four times higher than normal, although they told reporters it was safe for humans" (Stephen Handelman, "Chernobyl Facts Covered Up," *Toronto Star*, July 12, 1987, Sunday 2nd ed., p. H3). See also Christopher Walker, "Design Row Opens Chernobyl Trial," *Times* (London), July 8, 1987. Gorbachev reports a radiation level on the safest streets of Chernobyl as reaching 1 milliroentgen per hour (Boris Gorbachev, "Tainy Chernobyl'skogo suda," *Zerkalo nedeli* 6, no. 491 (April 2004): 24–29).

11. Kendall E. Bailes, *Technology and Society under Lenin and Stalin: Origins of the Soviet Technical Intelligentsia, 1917–1941*, Studies of the Russian Institute, Columbia University (Princeton, NJ: Princeton University Press, 1978), 90.

12. On opening day the courtroom was packed with members of the press as well as about 150 relatives and coworkers of the victims and accused (Handelman, "Chernobyl Facts Covered Up"); "Persons Guilty of Chernobyl Accident to Go on Trial Soon," *ITAR-TASS*, March 13, 1987; "Briefing—Chernobyl," *ITAR-TASS*, July 2, 1987; "Trial of Culprits of Chernobyl Accident," *Russian Information Agency ITAR-TASS*, Moscow, July 15, 1987; Greenwald and Olsen, "Disasters Judgment at Chernobyl." On the choice of location see RGANI, f. 89, op. 4, d. 22. Access to the town of Chernobyl was possible only with a special permit ("Chernobyl Trial Set for July"). And yet TASS called the trial "public" even after it was over, and the discrepancy between "public" and a complete lack of media coverage must have become apparent: "The public trial lasted for more than three weeks. Thirty-eight witnesses and thirteen victims of the disaster were interrogated, thus providing a true picture of why the accident at the atomic power plant had happened on the night of April 25–26, 1986" ("Trial in Chernobyl Ends," *ITAR-TASS*, July 29, 1987).

Notes

13. According to the *Guardian*, only five foreign journalists, from Japanese television, BBC radio, and a French and American news agency, were to be admitted to the trial (Martin Walker, "Three Go on Trial after World's Worst Atomic Disaster," *Guardian* (London), July 7, 1987). The BBC reported that the Soviet Foreign Ministry admitted ten foreign correspondents to the proceedings ("Foreign Ministry briefing: USA's 'new demands' on INF, Afghanistan, Chernobyl trial," *BBC Summary of World Broadcasts*, July 7, 1987). See also "Briefing—Chernobyl" and Christopher Walker, "Anger at Chernobyl Trial Curb on Press," *Times* (London), July 6, 1987. The *London Times* reported that twelve "specially selected reporters from Moscow were permitted to attend yesterday," none from a Western newspaper (Walker, "Design Row"). See also "Chernobyl Trial Closed, Press Told," *Globe and Mail* (Canada), July 9, 1987.

14. "Chernobyl Trial Begins."

15. Patrick Cockburn, "Six Go on Trial in Chernobyl," *Financial Times* (London), July 8, 1987. According to Aleksandr Kovalenko, the chief information officer for the Chernobyl rescue operation, there was "logic in holding the trial at the scene of the crime," which led some to speculate that the move also served to avoid seeking responsibility among high-ranking officials in Moscow (Walker, "Anger"; "Scapegoats of Chernobyl").

16. Just prior to the trial, speculation ran wild on who else would be tried. But neither Ivan Emelyianov, a deputy director of the Institute of Energy Technologies (NIKIET), who the Central Committee had dismissed from his post, nor any of the three deputy directors of the Chernobyl station, one of whom had fled the scene of the accident, were prosecuted ("Chernobyl Trial Set for July"; Richard Levine, Milt Freudenheim, and James F. Carity, "Fixing the Blame at Chernobyl," *New York Times*, June 22, 1986, "The World" section).

17. John-Thor Dahlburg, "Chernobyl Gears Up for Trial of Officials," *Globe and Mail* (Canada), July 7, 1987.

18. "V Politbiuro TsK KPSS," *Pravda*, July 20, 1986, 1, 3; Dahlburg, "Chernobyl Gears Up."

19. "Chernobyl Trial Set for July"; Dahlburg, "Chernobyl Gears Up."

20. Fomin had broken his eyeglasses and slit his wrists with the shards; see Grigori Medvedev, *The Truth about Chernobyl* (New York: Basic Books, 1989), and Richard F. Mould, *Chernobyl Record: The Definitive History of the Chernobyl Catastrophe* (Bristol: Institute of Physics Publishing, 2000). According to Mould, "The trial was apparently postponed once because one of the accused, the chief engineer, Fomin, had not recovered sufficiently" (p. 300). See also Mary Dejevsky, "Chernobyl Chief Faces 10 Years in Labour Camp: Sentences Leave Question of Ministerial Responsibility Unexplained," *Times* (London), July 30, 1987. The trial was now to begin July 7 ("Briefing—Chernobyl").

21. Dahlburg, "Chernobyl Gears Up."

22. "Western Reporters Barred from Trial," United Press International, July 8, 1987; "Chernobyl Trial Closed, Press Told." The prosecutor was Iurii Shadrin (*starshii pomoshchnik general'nogo prokurora SSSR*; see A. V. Illesh and A. E. Pral'nikov, eds., *Reportazh iz Chernobylia: Zapiski ochevidtsev. Kommentarii. Razmyshleniia* (Moscow: Mysl', 1988), 147).

23. Handelman, "Chernobyl Facts Covered Up."

24. "Results of the Chernobyl Trial," *ITAR-TASS*, July 31, 1987.

25. See above, note 4; also Walker, "Three Go on Trial." The Central Committee's top-secret decree had found fault with the nuclear industry's organizational culture, the ministry's supervision of personnel performance, and discipline in all the organizations involved. The decree itself has been declassified in the meantime (Postanovlenie TsK KPSS, "O reszul'tatakh rassledovaniia prichin avarii na ChAES i merakh po likvidatsii ee posledstvii, osobenno bezopasnosti atomnoi energetiki," ss P 21/10, July 14, 1986, RGANI, f. 89, op. 53, d. 12, l. 2).

26. The *London Times* summarized the pretrial common knowledge as follows: "An unauthorized experiment conducted while safety mechanisms were shut off . . . shortcomings in the system of responsibility, design faults in the reactor and the risks in siting nuclear power stations close to populated areas" ("Scapegoats of Chernobyl").

27. "Chernobyl Trial Closed, Press Told," *Globe and Mail* (Canada).

28. Greenwald and Olsen, "Disasters Judgment at Chernobyl." The indictment apparently mentioned that similar unauthorized experiments had been conducted at the same station in 1982 and 1985, leading to a near accident in 1985 ("Western Reporters Barred"; Handelman, "Chernobyl Facts Covered Up").

29. Ugolovnyi kodeks Ukrainskoi SSR, part 2, article 220 (in Illesh and Pral'nikov, *Reportazh iz Chernobylia*, 147). See also Walker, "Design Row"; "Western Reporters Barred"; Dahlburg, "Chernobyl Gears Up"; Milt Freudenheim, Katherine Roberts, and James F. Clarity, "The Trial Begins at Chernobyl," *New York Times*, July 12, 1987, late city final ed., section 4, p. 2; Handelman, "Chernobyl Facts Covered Up." The maximum penalty for these charges was ten years in prison ("Western Reporters Barred"; Cockburn, "Six Go on Trial"; "Chernobyl Trial Closed, Press Told"). See also "Chernobyl Officials Get 10 Years," *Financial Times Energy Newsletters—European Energy*, August 7, 1987, 1.

30. The legal concept "explosion-prone plants (or facilities)" is contested.

31. Dahlburg, "Chernobyl Gears Up."

32. Walker, "Design Row." The trial confirmed rumors that the evacuation of Pripyat did not begin until thirty-six hours after the explosions. This evidence contra-

dicted previous official statements about the evacuation and public health ("Chernobyl Officials Get 10 Years").

33. For example, as late as 2004 the journalist Boris Gorbachev dismissed attempts to exculpate the director or the chief engineers as a propaganda campaign aimed at discrediting scientists and reactor experts (Gorbachev, "Tainy Chernobyl'skogo suda").

34. Walker, "Anger"; Dahlburg, "Chernobyl Gears Up"; Charles Mitchell, "Chernobyl Trial Closed to Public and Media," *United Press International*, July 9, 1987; "Chernobyl Officials Are Sentenced to Labor Camp," *New York Times*, July 30, 1987, late city final ed., section A, p. 5. Details on post-Chernobyl Soviet information management are also available in the declassified documents of RGANI, fond 89.

35. V. Vozniak and S. Troitskii, *Chernobyl: Tak eto bylo* (Moscow: Libris, 1993).

36. "The Soviet press is also expected to cover the prospective trial of officials being blamed for the Chernobyl accident, as it did the recent trial of captains held responsible for a ship collision in the Black Sea last August" (Keller, "The 1986 Disaster at Chernobyl"). Charles Mitchell reported that "diplomats have speculated the trial may have been closed because testimony might reveal the poor state of safety in the Soviet nuclear power industry and other accidents or near-accidents that have not been disclosed" (Mitchell, "Chernobyl Trial Closed to Public and Media"). See also Handelman, "Chernobyl Facts Covered Up"; Dejevsky, "Chernobyl Chief Faces 10 Years in Labour Camp." One source noted that "accounts of the trial itself, which began July 7, were sketchy" ("Chernobyl-Plant Officials Sentenced," *Facts on File World News Digest*, July 31, 1987, section D3, 557). See also Patrick Cockburn, "Chernobyl Nuclear Plant Chiefs Given 10-Year Jail Sentences," *Financial Times* (London), July 30, 1987, 40. The articles that did appear revealed details of the disaster for the first time ("Chernobyl Officials Get 10 Years").

37. See, for example, Handelman, "Chernobyl Facts Covered Up"; "Chernobyl Trial Begins."

38. Freudenheim, Roberts, and Clarity, "The Trial Begins at Chernobyl"; "Trial of Culprits of Chernobyl Accident."

39. "Western Reporters Barred."

40. "Western Reporters Barred"; "Trial of Culprits of Chernobyl Accident"; "Chernobyl Trial Closed, Press Told."

41. Karpan notes that the trial allowed some degree of controversy and a limited, but frank, discussion of factors other than human error as causes of the disaster (Karpan, *Chernobyl': Mest' mirnogo atoma*). In 2004, a group of lay archivists connected loosely to the former satellite town of the Chernobyl plant launched a website, http://pripyat.com. It was intended initially as an "unofficial site of the town of Pripyat," a site that would commemorate the ghost town and enable its former

inhabitants, now spread all over the world, to connect in cyberspace. The expressed goal of the site is to protect the town as a kind of contemporary history museum. In the process, the site's archive of personal photographs, memoirs, documents, and other materials has grown. Today, this unique site features a treasure trove of visual material, current media reports, a library of documents, and much more. It was on this website that I was first able to find notes from the trial proceedings: plant personnel had been taking turns attending and transcribing what went on behind closed doors. Obviously, these notes are a rather problematic, but nevertheless extraordinary source.

42. Karpan, *Chernobyl': Mest' mirnogo atoma*. Diatlov sent his research to international journals while he was in prison; some of it was published only posthumously (Anatolii S. Diatlov, *Chernobyl': Kak eto bylo* (Moscow: Nauchtekhlitizdat, 2003); Anatoly Dyatlov [Anatolii S. Diatlov], "26 April 1986," *Nuclear Engineering International* 41, no. 501 (April 1996): 18–22; Anatoly Dyatlov [Anatolii S. Diatlov], "Why INSAG Has Still Got It Wrong," *Nuclear Engineering International* 40, no. 494 (September 1995): 17–21).

43. The RBMK is a graphite-moderated, water-cooled design. The acronym is Russian for "high-power channel/boiling-water reactor" *(reaktor bol'shoi moshchnosti kanal'nyi/kipiashchii)*.

44. For a selection of news reports see, for example, "Chernobyl Officials Get 10 Years"; "Ten Years in Stir for Chernobyl's Scapegoats," *Newsweek*, August 10, 1987, 47; "Chernobyl Officials Are Sentenced to Labor Camp"; Dejevsky, "Chernobyl Chief Faces 10 Years in Labour Camp"; "Results of the Chernobyl Trial." A brief Russian summary can be found in Illesh and Pral'nikov, *Reportazh iz Chernobylia*, 154.

45. Karpan lists these experts' home institutions and reaches the conclusion that they were all affiliated, in one way or another, with the reactor designer's institute, and concludes that they may not have been completely impartial (Karpan, *Chernobyl': Mest' mirnogo atoma*).

46. *Dostat'* was the word capturing this process: it literally means "to track down, to locate." Soviet managers, from Beria to Briukhanov, obviously also knew when to enforce what kinds of punishment. The resulting arbitrariness in decision making made the system extremely vulnerable to what Vaughan calls the "normalization of deviance" (Diane Vaughan, *The Challenger Launch Decision: Risky Technology, Culture, and Deviance at NASA* (Chicago: University of Chicago Press, 1996)).

47. Vozniak and Troitskii, *Chernobyl: Tak eto bylo*.

48. Chapter 2 goes into great detail about these two ministries. Throughout, I use *Sredmash* as the abbreviation for the Ministry of Medium Machine Building (*Ministerstvo srednego mashinostroeniia*) and *Minenergo* for the Ministry of Energy and Electrification (*Ministerstvo energetiki i elektrifikatsii*). These are not the only abbreviations

Notes

used by Russians, but since they are critically important institutions in this story, I am using labels that will help non-Russian readers to keep these two ministries apart.

49. "Chernobyl Officials Get 10 Years."

50. In addition to the five years, Rogozhkin received a two-year sentence, to run concurrently, for negligence and failure to execute his duties. As one Russian journalist put it in 2004, they were only guilty of following the orders of their superiors, and "de facto they were sentenced for their inadvertent participation in a technological mess" (Gorbachev, "Tainy Chernobyl'skogo suda"). Rogozhkin, Kovalenko, and Laushkin pleaded not guilty; Briukhanov, Fomin, and Diatlov, as mentioned above, accepted professional responsibility for the accident but denied criminal liability ("Chernobyl Officials Are Sentenced to Labor Camp"). See also "Trial in Chernobyl Ends"; "Chernobyl Officials Get 10 Years"; "Chernobyl Director and Aides Get 10 Years Labor Camp," *Xinhua General Overseas News Service*, July 29, 1987; Dejevsky, "Chernobyl Chief Faces 10 Years in Labour Camp."

51. "Chernobyl Officials Are Sentenced to Labor Camp."

52. "Ten Years in Stir for Chernobyl's Scapegoats."

53. Cockburn, "Chernobyl Nuclear Plant Chiefs Given 10-Year Jail Sentences"; "Chernobyl Officials Are Sentenced to Labor Camp." Briukhanov, Fomin, and Diatlov reacted to their sentencing very differently. Briukhanov accepted his sentence without objection, while Fomin apparently experienced severe shock. Diatlov continued to defend himself during his subsequent imprisonment. He wrote countless letters from prison, and with the tireless support of his wife, was pardoned by Gorbachev in the fall of 1990; he died in December 1995 (Diatlov, *Chernobyl': Kak eto bylo*, 167).

54. "Results of the Chernobyl Trial." The journalist Boris Gorbachev considered the three main defendants lucky in that they were not tried according to the all-Union law, where a conviction for violating technical safety regulations at a dangerous nuclear facility, and for losing control over this facility with grave consequences that included the loss of human life, would have allowed a death sentence (Gorbachev, "Tainy Chernobyl'skogo suda").

55. "Results of the Chernobyl Trial." This quote is provided in its original English version.

56. "In reports to his superiors, he [Briukhanov] underestimated these readings by twelve times" ("Chernobyl Officials Get 10 Years"). See also Cockburn, "Chernobyl Nuclear Plant Chiefs Given 10-Year Jail Sentences"; "Chernobyl-Plant Officials Sentenced."

57. "Results of the Chernobyl Trial."

58. "It is still not known whether the experiment was authorized at ministerial level or whether it was conducted at the instigation of the plant's management. The additional sentence on Bryukhanov for abuse of power suggests that he has been blamed" (Dejevsky, "Chernobyl Chief Faces 10 Years in Labour Camp").

59. The press release ends with what can almost be read as a mission statement: "A reliable and safe operation of complex modern equipment can be ensured only given a high level of discipline, organization, competence and responsibility of the personnel" ("Results of the Chernobyl Trial").

60. Briukhanov was released after serving five years of his sentence and granted interviews to international media on various anniversaries of the disaster. For example, see Maksym Asaulyak, "Viktor Bryukhanov: I Could Have Been Sentenced to Death," *Kyiv Weekly*, April 28, 2011, http://kyivweekly.com.ua/pulse/theme/2011/04/28/164825.html; "Neponiatnyi Atom: Interv'iu s Viktorom Briukhanovym," *Profil'*, April 24, 2006, http://www.profile.ru/obshchestvo/item/50192-items_18814; Anton Samarin, "Chernobyl nikogo i nichemy ne nauchil," *Odnako*, 26 April 2010, http://www.odnako.org/almanac/material/chernobil-nikogo-i-nichemu-ne-nauchil-1/. Diatlov and Fomin were also released early, both for medical reasons. Diatlov died in 1995 of heart failure, four years after his release from prison, and after trying to publicize his version of the accident. Fomin spent part of his sentence in a neurological facility and was also released early. He worked at the Kalinin nuclear power plant until he retired. Both Kovalenko and Rogozhkin were released early and returned to work at Chernobyl. Former inspector Laushkin died of stomach cancer shortly after his release (Mould, *Chernobyl Record: The Definitive History of the Chernobyl Catastrophe*, 301). Kovalenko also died soon after his release.

61. On the international level, this strategy tends to emphasize that "this could never happen at any of our nuclear plants."

62. This attitude comes through quite clearly in some of the interviews used for *The Second Russian Revolution*, a documentary produced by Brian Lapping Associates for BBC Television, the Discovery Channel, and NHK, especially episode 2, *The Battle for Glasnost'*.

63. Given the sheer complexity of the technical, political, historical, and economic issues surrounding this accident, but also the abundance of publications on the subject that rarely agree on the accident's causes, I find catchy titles such as those used by Richard Mould disturbing, despite the useful information the books contain: "Chernobyl: The *Real Story*," and "Chernobyl Record: The *Definitive History* of the Chernobyl Catastrophe" (my emphases). (See Mould's *Chernobyl Record: The Definitive History of the Chernobyl Catastrophe*, cited earlier, and his *Chernobyl: The Real Story* (Oxford: Pergamon Press, 1988).)

64. As in English, *operators* in Russian can refer either to the technician in the control room of a nuclear reactor or to the utility running one or more nuclear power

Notes

plants. I have used *reactor operator* and *plant operator* in instances where the terminology would otherwise have been ambiguous. For examples of plant operators mishandling the reactor, see Lev P. Feoktistov, "Uroki Chernobylia," *Priroda* 9 (1986): 123–124; Anatolii P. Aleksandrov, "Izmeniat', chto izmenit' eshche vozmozhno. ...," *Ogonek* 35 (August 1990): 6–10.

65. John Krige, "Atoms for Peace, Scientific Internationalism, and Scientific Intelligence," *Osiris* 21 (2006): 161–181; John Krige, "The Peaceful Atom as Political Weapon: Euratom and American Foreign Policy in the Late 1950s," *Historical Studies in the Natural Sciences* 38, no. 1 (2008): 5–44.

66. Glenys A. Babcock, "The Role of Public Interest Groups in Democratization: Soviet Environmental Groups and Energy Policy-Making, 1985–1991," doctoral dissertation, RAND Graduate School, 1997; Jane I. Dawson, *Eco-Nationalism: Anti-Nuclear Activism and National Identity in Russia, Lithuania, and Ukraine* (Durham: Duke University Press, 1996).

67. I first wrote this introduction before the dramatic events of March 2011 at the Fukushima-1 nuclear plant in Japan's Tohoku province. I have tried to capture some of the connections in the epilogue (see also Sonja D. Schmid, "Both Better and Worse Than Chernobyl," *London Review of Books Blog*, March 17, 2011, http://www.lrb.co.uk/blog/2011/03/17/sonja-schmid/both-better-and-worse-than-chernobyl).

Chapter 1

1. Nikolai A. Dollezhal', *U istokov rukotvornogo mira: Zapiski konstruktora* (Moscow: GUP NIKIET, IzdAt, 2002), 230. In a memorandum to Khrushchev from the Central Committee's Department of Machine Engineering (*dokladnaia zapiska*), titled "On the Universal Electrification of the USSR" (*O sploshnoi elektrifikatsii SSSR*), which was categorized as "secret" (RGANI, f. 5, op. 40, d. 149, l. 2–78), I. Novikov reported that in 1958 there were 41.8 million television sets and 48.5 million radios in the United States, while in the Soviet Union, there were only 2.7 million TV sets and 12.3 million radios (l. 13). The Central Committee and the Council of Ministers subsequently approved a "drastic increase of productivity of labor" in an attempt to create the "material and technical basis of communism" (l. 3).

2. There were some private niches in the agricultural sector that were legal in the Soviet Union; however, they are irrelevant to our topic (Alec Nove, *The Soviet Economy: An Introduction*, 2nd ed. (New York: Praeger, 1969), 61–65).

3. George T. Mazuzan and J. Samuel Walker, *Controlling the Atom: The Beginnings of Nuclear Regulation, 1946–1962* (Berkeley: University of California Press, 1985); Brian Balogh, *Chain Reaction: Expert Debate and Public Participation in American Commercial Nuclear Power, 1945–1975* (Cambridge: Cambridge University Press, 1991); Gabrielle Hecht, *The Radiance of France: Nuclear Power and National Identity after World War II*

(Cambridge, MA: MIT Press, 1998); Gabrielle Hecht, *Being Nuclear: Africans and the Global Uranium Trade* (Cambridge, MA: MIT Press, 2012).

4. This is not to say that the state did not play an important role in nuclear industries around the world, including in liberal democracies—it most certainly did (e.g., Hecht, *The Radiance of France;* J. Samuel Walker, *Containing the Atom: Nuclear Regulation in a Changing Environment, 1963–1971* (Berkeley: University of California Press, 1992); Margaret Gowing, *Britain and Atomic Energy, 1935–1945* (London: Macmillan, 1964); Margaret Gowing and Lorna Arnold, *Independence and Deterrence: Britain and Atomic Energy, 1945–52*, Volume 1: *Policy Making* (London: Macmillan, 1974); Margaret Gowing and Lorna Arnold, *Independence and Deterrence: Britain and Atomic Energy, 1945–52*, Volume 2: *Policy Execution* (London: Macmillan, 1974)).

5. Translated and quoted in Arnold Kramish, *Atomic Energy in the Soviet Union* (Stanford, CA: Stanford University Press, 1959), 6. In 1939, Vernadskii became the director of the newly created Commission for Isotopes (ibid., 23, 117). One of my interviewees came to our conversation prepared with this very quote on a little piece of paper. He read the note to me, and emphasized its prophetic value (Interview #23).

6. An international discussion on siting policies can be found, for example, in International Atomic Energy Agency, ed. *Siting of Reactors and Nuclear Research Centres: Proceedings of the Symposium on Criteria for Guidance in the Selection of Sites for the Construction of Reactor and Nuclear Research Centres, Bombay, 11–15 March 1963* (Vienna: International Atomic Energy Agency, 1963). See also Charles K. Dodd, *Industrial Decision-Making and High-Risk Technology: Siting Nuclear Power Facilities in the USSR* (Lanham, MD: Rowman & Littlefield, 1994).

7. For example, Chernobyl was part of the Kievenergo dispatch system (see chapter 5). At least two of the Ukrainian nuclear power plants were also designed to export electricity to East European CMEA countries: they partly financed their construction in exchange for free electricity delivery (Office of Technology Assessment, *Technology & Soviet Energy Availability* (Washington, DC: Congress of the U.S., Office of Technology Assessment, 1981)).

8. The planning for a nuclear power plant site sometimes included considerations about the imminent availability of workers once a nearby industrial facility was completed (e.g., RGAE, f. 7964, op. 3, f. 2015, vol. 2: "Ob"iasnitel'naia zapiska k godovomu otchetu za 1958 god po kapital'nomu stroitel'stvu direktsii stroiashcheisia Leningradskoi GRES No. 16," l. 38).

9. David Holloway, *Stalin and the Bomb: The Soviet Union and Atomic Energy 1939–1956* (New Haven, CT: Yale University Press, 1994). For the U.S. context see Richard Rhodes, *The Making of the Atomic Bomb* (New York: Touchstone, 1986).

10. V. K. Ulasevich, ed., *Sozdano pod rukovodstvom N. A. Dollezhalia: O iadernykh reaktorakh i ikh tvortsakh (k 100-letiiu N. A. Dollezhalia)*, 2nd ed. (Moscow: GUP NIKIET,

2002); Boris A. Fain, *Aktivnaia zona: Povest' ob atomnom institute* (Moscow: Skripto, 1998); Dollezhal', *U istokov rukotvornogo mira*.

11. Paul R. Josephson, "Rockets, Reactors, and Soviet Culture," in Loren Graham, ed., *Science and the Soviet Social Order*, 168–191 (Cambridge, MA: Harvard University Press, 1990); Holloway, *Stalin and the Bomb*; Kramish, *Atomic Energy in the Soviet Union*.

12. Kurchatov and Aleksandrov did not specify locations for these reactors, but a year later, four sites were under discussion: one near Moscow, one near Leningrad, and two in the region where the Beloiarsk plant was later built. According to Soviet scientists at the First United Nations Conference on Peaceful Uses of Atomic Energy, held in 1955 in Geneva, the plant near Moscow was originally to be built near Podolsk (Fermi 1957), but eventually the site near Voronezh replaced that earlier location. Archival documents suggest that as early as 1956, plans were made for the Novo-Voronezh nuclear power plant (RGAE, f. 9599, op. 1, d. 7, l. 23); in 1957, the deputy head of *Glavatomenergo*, Iu. Ponomarev signed detailed plans on major construction work and capital investments for the Novo-Voronezh site (RGAE, f. 9599, op. 1, d. 1, l. 22). The plant intended for Leningrad was later handed over to Sredmash entirely. See Vladimir V. Goncharov, "Pervyi period razvitiia atomnoi energetiki v SSSR," in Viktor A. Sidorenko, ed., *Istoriia atomnoi energetiki Sovetskogo Soiuza i Rossii*, 16–70 (Moscow: IzdAt, 2001) (especially 32, 19).

13. A planning period of five years was the signature Soviet interval since 1929 (Nove, *The Soviet Economy*). With the exception of World War II, which cut short the third five-year plan, and Khrushchev's decision to abandon the sixth prematurely in favor of a new seven-year plan (1959–1965), the Soviet economy maintained this planning interval until its demise.

14. Goncharov, "Pervyi period," 9, 34.

15. Josephson, "Rockets, Reactors, and Soviet Culture"; Vladimir P. Vizgin, ed., *Istoriia Sovetskogo Atomnogo Proekta: Dokumenty, Vospominaniia, Issledovaniia*, vol. 1 (Moscow: Ianus-K, 1998) and vol. 2 (Saint Petersburg: Izdatel'stvo Russkogo Khristianskogo gumanitarnogo instituta, 2002); Holloway, *Stalin and the Bomb*.

16. Josephson, "Rockets, Reactors, and Soviet Culture," 168–191, 174. In fact, Josephson argues that only "the Chernobyl disaster and the decline of the Soviet Union were to shake the foundations of Soviet nuclear culture" (Paul R. Josephson, "Atomic-Powered Communism: Nuclear Culture in the Postwar USSR," *Slavic Review* 55, no. 2 (1996): 297–324 (quote on 322)). On nuclear power exhibitions at the Exhibition of the Achievements of the People's Economy (VDNKh) in Moscow, see Sonja D. Schmid, "Celebrating Tomorrow Today: The Peaceful Atom on Display in the Soviet Union," *Social Studies of Science* 36, no. 3 (2006): 331–365. On revolutionary and utopian dreams, see Richard Stites, *Revolutionary Dreams: Utopian Vision and Experimental Life in the Russian Revolution* (New York: Oxford University Press, 1989).

17. Josephson, "Rockets, Reactors, and Soviet Culture"; Josephson, "Atomic-Powered Communism." For examples of how scientists popularized this vision see, for example, V. S. Emel'ianov, "Atomnaia nauka i tekhnika i stroitel'stvo kommunizma," *Atomnaia energiia* 11, no. 4 (1961): 301–312; Andranik M. Petros'iants, *Atomnaia energetika* (Moscow: Nauka, 1976); Andranik M. Petros'iants, *Iadernaia energetika: Nauka i tekhnicheskii progress*, 2nd ed. (Moscow: Nauka, 1981); Andranik M. Petros'iants, *Atomnaia nauka i tekhnika SSSR* (Moscow: Energoatomizdat, 1987).

18. Sonja D. Schmid, "Shaping the Soviet Experience of the Atomic Age: Nuclear Topics in Ogonyok, 1945–1965," in Dick van Lente, ed., *The Nuclear Age in Popular Media: A Transnational History, 1945–1965*, 19–52 (New York: Palgrave Macmillan, 2012).

19. In a 1969 letter to Nikolai K. Baibakov, then head of Gosplan, Pavlenko (the head of Gosplan's Department for Energy and Electrification) and two colleagues explained their problems with coordinating work on this scale by pointing out that as an emerging technology, nuclear power presented planners with a series of unknown factors: the equipment was sophisticated and required extraordinary quality control, there were only a few specialized factories, and the economics of nuclear power plants was still poorly understood ("Letter to comrade Baibakov, N. K." from A. Pavlenko, K. Vinogradov, and A. Nekrasov, No. 22–9, of January 10, 1969 (RGAE, f. 4372, op. 66, d. 3215, l. 1–3)). In their letter, Pavlenko and his colleagues asked comrade Baibakov to personally coordinate the development of a nuclear industry sector, or at the very least to assign one of his first deputies to the task. They also requested additional positions for their department, for newly created groups of specialists in other departments, and for the planning and supervision of the emerging nuclear power industry.

20. Interview #28.

21. Nove, *The Soviet Economy*, 18. See also Ian D. Thatcher, "Alec Nove: A Bibliographical Tribute," *Europe-Asia Studies* 47, no. 8 (1995): 1383–1410.

22. Recent work in STS has addressed the history of economics, and in particular the social construction of "the market" and its supposedly abstract principles and autonomous mechanics (e.g., Michel Callon, "What Does It Mean to Say That Economics Is Performative?," in Donald MacKenzie, Fabian Muniesa, and Lucia Siu, eds., *Do Economists Make Markets? On the Performativity of Economics*, 311–357 (Princeton, NJ: Princeton University Press, 2007); Philip Mirowski and Edward Nik-Khah, "Markets Made Flesh: Performativity, and a Problem in Science Studies, Augmented with Consideration of the FCC Auctions," in Donald MacKenzie, Fabian Muniesa, and Lucia Siu, eds., *Do Economists Make Markets? On the Performativity of Economics*, 190–224 (Princeton, NJ: Princeton University Press, 2007); Michel Callon, ed., *The Laws of the Markets* (Oxford: Blackwell, 1998); Donald MacKenzie and Yuval Millo,

"Constructing a Market, Performing Theory: The Historical Sociology of a Financial Derivatives Exchange," *American Journal of Sociology* 109 (2003): 107–145).

23. Alec Nove, *Studies in Economics and Russia* (New York: St. Martin's Press, 1990), 132. See also Alexei Kojevnikov, "The Great War, the Russian Civil War, and the Invention of Big Science," *Science in Context* 15, no. 2 (2002): 239–276.

24. Martha Lampland, "The Technopolitical Lineage of State Planning in Hungary, 1930–1956," in Gabrielle Hecht, ed., *Entangled Geographies: Empire and Technopolitics in the Global Cold War*, 155–184 (Cambridge, MA: MIT Press, 2011).

25. Nove, *Studies in Economics and Russia*, 131.

26. James C. Scott, *Seeing Like a State: How Certain Schemes to Improve the Human Condition Have Failed* (New Haven, CT: Yale University Press, 1998); Loren R. Graham, ed., *Science and the Soviet Social Order* (Cambridge, MA: Harvard University Press, 1990); Ed A. Hewett et al., "Soviet Economy," *Soviet Economy* 1, no. 1 (1985): 5; Ed A. Hewett, *Reforming the Soviet Economy: Equality versus Efficiency* (Washington, DC: Brookings Institution, 1988).

27. Marxists conceptualized history as unfolding in six consecutive stages: primitive communism, slavery, feudalism, capitalism, socialism, and full communism. See Alexander Balinky et al., *Planning and the Market in the U.S.S.R.: The 1960s* (New Brunswick, NJ: Rutgers University Press, 1967), 25; Leon Trotsky, *The Russian Revolution: The Overthrow of Tzarism and the Triumph of the Soviets*, trans. Max Eastman (Garden City, NY: Doubleday, 1959); Martin Malia, *The Soviet Tragedy: A History of Socialism in Russia, 1917–1991* (New York: Macmillan, 1994).

28. See Balinky et al., *Planning and the Market in the U.S.S.R.*, 31; Nove, *Studies in Economics and Russia*, 129.

29. Valerie Bunce, *Subversive Institutions: The Design and the Destruction of Socialism and the State*, Cambridge Studies in Comparative Politics (Cambridge: Cambridge University Press, 1999), 22–23 (emphasis in original).

30. Bunce, *Subversive Institutions*; Nikolai L. Krementsov, *Stalinist Science* (Princeton, NJ: Princeton University Press, 1997); Steven Lee Solnick, *Stealing the State: Control and Collapse in Soviet Institutions* (Cambridge, MA: Harvard University Press, 1998).

31. The chairman of the Council of Ministers was one of the roughly twenty members of the Politburo. The Politburo was called "Presidium of the Central Committee" from 1952 to 1966, then it reverted to its original name. The Presidium had more members than the Politburo (Nove, *The Soviet Economy*, 26).

32. In 1969, Nove wrote that "the Minister and the Deputy-Ministers must be seen essentially as senior business executives or civil servants, not as politicians in the western sense" (ibid., 70).

33. The management of Soviet enterprises was appointed by the state and typically consisted of the director, the chief engineer (who was also the deputy director), and the chief accountant, who together were in charge of operations and legally responsible for them. Enterprise performance was evaluated according to predetermined efficiency plans. If an enterprise managed to reduce its cost by maximizing output or minimizing input, a portion of such "overplan profit" went directly to the enterprise as an incentive (Balinky et al., *Planning and the Market in the U.S.S.R.*, 12–15, 47; Nove, *The Soviet Economy*, 34).

34. Reports from nuclear power plants under construction often contained complaints about poor quality or delayed delivery of construction materials by subcontractors. For example, in their 1972 annual report, the management of the Armenian nuclear power plant complained that the factory assigned to produce reinforced concrete for the plant had delivered parts of extremely poor quality during the first half of the year. Management initiated a technical inspection by a research institute, which determined that the factory had delivered 200,000 rubles worth of *brak*, defective parts. If nothing else, this inspection prompted the factory to produce better concrete during the second half of 1972 (RGAE, f. 7964, op. 15, d. 5693, l. 25).

Starting in the late 1960s, organizations emerged that mediated between individual enterprises and ministries, "associations" (*ob"edineniia*), and trusts (*tresty*). These organizations sometimes functioned like chief administrations, but outside the formal structure of a ministry (Nove, *The Soviet Economy*, 43–44, 68). See also David Shearer, *Industry, State, and Society in Stalin's Russia, 1926–1934* (Ithaca, NY: Cornell University Press, 1996). The big regional construction trusts—for example, *Tsentratomenergostroi, Iuzhatomenergostroi, Donbassatomenergomontazh, Spetsatomenergomontazh,* and *Mosspetsatomenergomontazh*—were the most relevant to the nuclear industry (RGAE, f. 7964, op. 15).

35. RGAE, f. 7964, op. 3 (Narkom elektrostantsii i elektropromyshlennosti SSSR, Ministerstvo elektrostantsii SSSR (1939–1959)), l. 4.

36. RGAE, f. 7964, op. 3, l. 2–3.

37. This is from an early 1960s Soviet textbook (M. G. Kolodnyi and A. P. Stepanov, *Planirovanie narodnogo khoziaistva SSSR* (Kiev: Izd-vo Kievskogo universiteta, 1963), 217–219, quoted in Nove, *The Soviet Economy*, 91).

38. Nove, *Studies in Economics and Russia*, 135. This behavior was exacerbated by past experience, when attempts to amend unrealistic plans by writing to the responsible planning bodies had remained unsuccessful. In the 1972 report to *Glavatomenergo*, the management of the Armenian nuclear power plant wrote: "The failure to fulfill the plan for capital investments can basically be explained by erroneous planning. Glavatomenergo and the leading republican organizations did not pay attention to our frequent written requests regarding an amendment of the plan" (RGAE, f. 7964, op. 15, d. 5693, l. 2, Ministerstvo energetiki i elektrifikatsii, Glavatomenergo, Direktsiia stroiashcheisia Armianskoi AES, godovoi otchet za 1972 god).

Notes

39. RGAE, f. 7964, op. 3, l. 4. These plans determined exact deadlines for the completion of a given task (usually in terms of *kvartaly*, quarter years), the money to be spent on a given aspect of the task (e.g., industrial construction work, construction of apartment buildings, provision of healthcare, and *sotskul'tbyt* or social and cultural infrastructure), the enterprises responsible for providing supplies, and much more (RGAE, f. 7964, op. 3, l. 5).

40. Nove, *The Soviet Economy*, 90–91.

41. Ibid., 42.

42. Ibid., 229. Among the nonpriority sectors that encountered shortages were consumer goods. The refusal to meet consumer satisfaction was justified by Marxist-Leninist theory: on the way to communism, society was expected to experience a period of hardship, where needs could not yet be fully met. In exchange for these sacrifices, the state guaranteed citizens secure employment (often with low expectations in terms of work ethic) and low prices for rents and necessities (Nove, *Studies in Economics and Russia*, 136; Bunce, *Subversive Institutions*, 33). What was "necessary," as opposed to indicative of "bourgeois decadence," was up to the Party, which portrayed citizens as "truly free" only when they desired what was "historically necessary" (Balinky et al., *Planning and the Market in the U.S.S.R.*, 31–32).

43. Many of the economists originally serving on Gosplan were former Mensheviks (the defeated opposition to the Bolsheviks), but when they opposed what they perceived as unrealistic targets of the first five-year plan (1929–1933), they were removed (Nove, *The Soviet Economy*, 71–74).

44. Ibid., 77. In 1932, Gosplan was put in charge of long- and short-term planning, of resource allocation, and of the development of new techniques. Gosplan allocated resources for large investment programs, including the civilian nuclear power industry. Gosplan even absorbed the Central Statistical Office, following the elimination of the Supreme Council of the National Economy (*Vesenkha*) (Nove, *Studies in Economics and Russia*, 133). In 1948–1949, Stalin changed the State Planning *Commission* to State Planning *Committee* and relieved it of the tasks of material resource allocation, statistics, and new technologies. These tasks were instead assigned to individual State Committees directly subordinated to the Council of Ministers (Gossnab, Gosstatistika, Gostekhnika). (The collection of documents relating to Gostekhnika from 1948 to 1951 are at RGAE, f. 9480, op. 1.) After Stalin's death in 1953, the pre-1948 status was largely restored; only statistics remained a separate body under the Council of Ministers. In 1955, the State Economic Commission (Gosekonomkomissiia) was created to relieve Gosplan of short-term planning, but it was abolished two years later. The introduction of new technologies was also singled out under the revived Gostekhnika. (The new Gostekhnika's tasks were identical to those the organization had in 1948 to 1951, except for standards and patents, which were assigned to two separate State Committees (RGAE, f. 9480, preface to op. 2).) Gostekhnika was again reorganized in 1957 (as the State Scientific-Technical Committee, GNTK

SSSR). The only change in tasks was an emphasis on international scientific contacts. This organization lasted until April 1961 (RGAE, f. 9480, preface to op. 3). After that, it became the State Committee for the Coordination of Science and Technology, until October 1965, when it was transformed into the State Committee for Science and Technology (GKNT, under the Council of Ministers; RGAE, f. 9480, preface to op. 7). Apart from facilitating, coordinating, and supervising research on innovative technologies and their implementation, the GKNT was also in charge of popularizing scientific information, of exhibiting the latest achievements, and of other forms of public dissemination of scientific knowledge (see also RGAE, f. 9480, preface to op. 9, vol. 1). From 1960 to 1962, Gosplan was put in charge of short-term planning (up to five years), while long-term planning was assigned to a new agency, the Scientific-Economic Council (*Nauchno-ekonomicheskii sovet, Gosekonomsovet*)—again in an effort to emphasize long-term economic plans. See also RGAE, f. 4372, op. 57, d. 468, l. 57–63, 64, and 117–119.

45. Nove, *The Soviet Economy*, 73. Due to the chronic uncertainties of supplies and interministerial competition for them, each ministry strove to set up its own supply base and make sure its own factories produced the needed components. On the power of individual ministries, especially Sredmash, see Maria N. Vasilieva, "L'évolution des systèmes de prise de décisions dans le nucléaire soviétique (Russe)," *Histoire, Économie et Société* 20, no. 2 (April-June 2001): 257–275; Maria N. Vasilieva, *Soleils rouges: L'ambition nucléaire soviétique [Essai sur l'évolution des systèmes de prise de décision dans le nucléaire soviétique (Russe)]* (Paris: Institut d'Histoire de l'Industrie et Éditions Rive Droite, 1999); Vitalii P. Nasonov, *E. P. Slavskii: Stranitsy zhizni* (Moscow: IzdAT, 1998); Igor' A. Beliaev and German G. Malkin, eds., *E. P. Slavskii: 100 let so dnia rozhdeniia* (Moscow: IzdAt, 1999).

46. Delayed delivery of supplies from subcontractors or their poor quality were some of the most common reasons cited in the annual reports of nuclear power plants for the underfulfillment of the plan. Delays caused by others were considered legitimate reasons for not meeting plan targets, and they had no consequences for the plant's management. The factories accused of delayed delivery of supplies or of faulty manufacturing usually had another subcontractor they could blame for the problems. Once that excuse was exhausted, an enterprise could fall back on the common excuse that they themselves had received plans with significant delays—for example, the plan for the current year had not arrived at the factory until March or April.

47. Minenergo conducted annual inspections of power plants and transmission lines (examples of reports are RGAE, f. 7964, op. 15, d. 802, d. 4222, and d. 5378). Nuclear power plants received a certificate of technical readiness (*pasport tekhnicheskoi gotovnosti*) after a successful inspection (RGAE, f. 7964, op. 15, d. 5378, l. 155–156).

48. Nove, *Studies in Economics and Russia*, 133.

Notes

49. For an insightful critique of the concept of "economic reform," see Ed A. Hewett, *Soviet Central Planning: Probing the Limits of the Traditional Model* (Washington, DC: Kennan Institute for Advanced Russian Studies, 1984).

50. Nove, *The Soviet Economy*, 66.

51. Western analysts predicted that "it would be difficult but not quite impossible to arrive at a 'technically' balanced plan, that is, one where the needed inputs match the intended output, but *quite* impossible to see how one could approach an *economic* optimum" (Nove, *Studies in Economics and Russia*, 133, emphases in original).

52. Bunce, *Subversive Institutions*, 24.

53. Ibid., 37. By contrast, Kotkin has argued that the Soviet Union was essentially stable until the 1980s (Stephen Kotkin, *Armageddon Averted: The Soviet Collapse, 1970–2000* (Oxford: Oxford University Press, 2001)).

54. For a rich biography on Khrushchev, see William Taubman, *Khrushchev: The Man and His Era* (New York: Norton, 2003).

55. There were two notable exceptions: the Ministry of Medium Machine Building (Sredmash), which he left undisturbed, and the Ministry of the Electric Power Industry (later Minenergo), which was renamed but survived the reforms intact (Nove, *The Soviet Economy*, 76). The Ministry of the Electric Power Industry was liquidated in late 1958/early 1959 and replaced by a Ministry of the Construction of Power Plants. As a consequence, a large number of organizations tried to assert claims to individual enterprises that had been associated with the disassembled ministry (RGAE, f. 4372, op. 58, d. 461, l. 1–90). See also Philip Hanson, *The Rise and Fall of the Soviet Economy: An Economic History of the USSR from 1945* (London: Longman, 2003).

56. Balinky et al., *Planning and the Market in the U.S.S.R.*, 81–82.

57. Balinky et al., *Planning and the Market in the U.S.S.R.*, 67–69.

58. Jeremy Smith and Melanie Ilic, eds., *Khrushchev in the Kremlin: Policy and Government in the Soviet Union, 1953–1964* (New York: Routledge, 2011).

59. Goncharov, "Pervyi period," 23.

60. Ibid., 9, 23, 36–37.

61. Kramish, *Atomic Energy in the Soviet Union*, 145.

62. Letter from Igor V. Kurchatov to the deputy chairman of the Council of Ministers, and chairman of Gosplan, Iosif I. Kuzmin, dated March 2, 1959 (Goncharov, "Pervyi period," 47–48).

63. Ibid., 24, 49, 59.

64. Ibid., 9, 49–51. Goncharov provides two of Kurchatov's letters as appendixes to his article: one is from June 21, 1958, and addressed to Leonid Brezhnev, then a member of the Central Committee's Presidium (Letter to comrade L. I. Brezhnev from I. V. Kurchatov, June 21, 1958, No. G/590ss (also in RGANI, f. 5, op. 40, d. 107, rolik 7213, l. 64–66)); the other dates from April 1959 and was sent to Kosygin, as well as to two high Party officials (Goncharov, "Pervyi period," 65–70). In 1964, nuclear power plants were expected to become competitive with other power plants by 1970 (Statement on "The Soviet Fuel-Energy Balance," letter from I. Poliakov dated March 21, 1964, forwarded to P. F. Lomako and V. E. Dymshits (Gosplan) on March 31, 1964 (RGAE, f. 4372, op. 65, d. 771, l. 22–47)). In the copy preserved at RGAE in the Gosplan document collection, the relevant passage is underlined by hand with a big question mark added in the left margin.

65. Criteria for more specific site selections were manifold, as discussed earlier. See also Dodd, *Industrial Decision-Making and High-Risk Technology*.

66. See, for example, the letter from A. Nekrasov to G. Pervukhin (Gosplan), April 20, 1967, suggesting it was unnecessary to build a separate Latvian nuclear power plant, given the planned Leningrad nuclear plant (RGAE, f. 4372, op. 66, d. 1736, l. 53–54); another letter is from the chairman of the Belorus Council of Ministers, T. Kisilev, to the Ukrainian Council of Ministers (March 12, 1968, No. 0212–255), requesting a nuclear power plant in the Belorus SSR (RGAE, f. 4372, op. 66, d. 2495, l. 81–82). Ia. Finogenov (deputy minister of power and electrification) explained to Pervukhin (Gosplan) on April 19, 1968 (No. F-3814), that Minenergo intended to start construction of a Belorus nuclear power plant in 1971–1975 (l. 83). Finally, Pervukhin wrote back to the Belorus Council of Ministers on June 21, 1968 (No. N.22–352), reporting that Minenergo had been given the responsibility of identifying suitable sites for the construction of new nuclear power plants, including one in the Belorus SSR. He indicated that after this work was completed, a decision about further plans would be made (l. 84–85).

67. An interesting case of adjustment occurred in 1966, when after the first quarter of the year, actual electricity use remained way below expectations. So the plan needed to be adjusted *down* to reflect this situation, as well as to avoid financial problems and a destabilizing effect on the economy (Letter No. ES-217 from P. S. Neporozhnii to the Council of Ministers, April 28, 1966; RGAE, f. 4372, op. 66, d. 908, l. 208–210). Despite doubts by the Ministry of Finance (l. 212), Gosplan approved the suggested modifications (l. 213). Again in 1969, Neporozhnii reported problems with anticipated electricity use: this time, he stated that the ministries and departments (that operated within "limits") had not used the anticipated amount of electricity, while "unlimited" consumers, like households or agriculture, had been underrated in that year's plan. As a solution, he in effect suggested that the actual use of electricity up to the preset "limits" should be more strictly enforced, and requested that the Council of Ministers and Gosplan review this issue (RGAE, f. 4372, op. 66, d. 3214, l. 80–84). The practice of "limits" for industry was not new;

see letter from A. Salmin (secretary of the Cheliabinsk Party committee) No. 97s, dated August 29, 1956 (RGANI, f. 5, op. 40, d. 41, l. 38).

68. The Ordzhonikidze factory in Podolsk had failed to set up a required test stand. See RGAE, f. 4372, op. 64, d. 576, l. 238–239 ("Tov. Kosyginu A. N., O polozhenii na stroitel'stve Novo-Voronezhskoi atomnoi elektrostantsii," by F. Maiboroda and A. Cherepnev, January 11, 1962), and 240–252 ("O polozhenii na stroitel'stve Novo-Voronezhskoi atomnoi elektrostantsii," by G. V. Ermakov (Chief Engineer of the Ministry of the Construction of Power Plants), A. V. Nikolaev (State Committee for the Use of Atomic Energy), V. V. Goncharov and S. A. Skvortsov (Institute of Atomic Energy), A. A. Khokhlachev (Ordzhonikidze factory, Podolsk), M. I. Ivanov (Project Manager TEP), N. A. Rogovin (Head of the construction of the Novo-Voronezh nuclear power plant), and I. F. Chepak (Director of the Novo-Voronezh nuclear power plant)).

69. RGAE, f. 4372, op. 64, d. 576, l. 253.

70. On March 27, 1962, Gosplan submitted a revised delivery schedule of equipment for the Novo-Voronezh and Beloiarsk nuclear power plants (RGAE, f. 4372, op. 64, d. 576, l. 254).

71. Balinky et al., *Planning and the Market in the U.S.S.R.*, 72–73, 87.

72. Although originally, Khrushchev and Bulganin had split Malenkov's combined role as general secretary and premier, Khrushchev later combined these two roles in his own person (Balinky et al., *Planning and the Market in the U.S.S.R.*, 71). In the 1970s, long before Kosygin's retreat from politics in October 1980 (he died in December 1980), Brezhnev took on both of these roles (Viktor Andriianov, *Kosygin: Zhizn' zamechatel'nykh liudei* (Moscow: Molodaia gvardiia, 2003)).

73. Balinky et al., *Planning and the Market in the U.S.S.R.*, 44, 67; T. I. Fetistov, ed., *Prem'er izvestnyi i neizvestnyi: Vospominaniia o A. N. Kosygine* (Moscow: Respublika, 1997); Andriianov, *Kosygin: Zhizn' zamechatel'nykh liudei*; Aleksei N. Kosygin, *Ob uluchshenii upravleniia promyshlennost'iu, sovershenstvovanii planirovaniia i usilenii ekonomicheskogo stimulirovaniia promyshlennogo proizvodstva*. Doklad na plenume TsK KPSS, 27 sentiabria 1965 goda (Moscow: Politizdat, 1965).

74. Kosygin had headed various ministries under Stalin but fell from Stalin's favor in 1952, when he was removed from the Politburo. Under Khrushchev, he served as chairman of Gosplan, and later as deputy chairman of the Council of Ministers. After Khrushchev's ouster, Kosygin headed the government as chairman of the Council of Ministers, while Brezhnev became First Secretary of the Party (Andriianov, *Kosygin: Zhizn' zamechatel'nykh liudei*; Fetistov, *Prem'er izvestnyi i neizvestnyi*).

75. Kosygin, *Ob uluchshenii upravleniia promyshlennost'iu*; see also Balinky et al., *Planning and the Market in the U.S.S.R.*, 44, 67; Andriianov, *Kosygin*; Archie Brown, *The Rise and Fall of Communism* (New York: Harper Collins, 2009). Kosygin's reforms

were arguably inspired by Evsei Liberman's new methods of economic planning that he saw based on the principles of a "new democratic centralism." See Michael Kaser, "Kosygin, Liberman, and the Pace of Soviet Industrial Reform," *The World Today* 21, no. 9 (1965): 375–388; Vladimir G. Tremla, "The Politics of 'Libermanism,'" *Soviet Studies* 19, no. 4 (1968): 567–572; Robert Stuart, "Evsei Grigor'evich Liberman," in George W. Simmonds, ed., *Soviet Leaders*, 193–199 (New York: Crowell, 1967); Myron Sharpe, ed., *Planning, Profit, and Incentives in the USSR*, Volume 1: *The Liberman Discussion—a New Phase in Soviet Economic Thought* (White Plains, NY: International Arts and Sciences Press, 1966).

76. In contrast to the pre-Khrushchev pattern, central planners and regional administrators were now supposed to engage in a shared effort to enhance economic efficiency. Also, under Kosygin's reforms enterprise directors were strengthened vis-à-vis trade unions and the Party. The role of the trade unions was stabilized as management watchdogs, supervising the introduction of innovative technologies and the correct functioning of bureaucratic procedures (Balinky et al., *Planning and the Market in the U.S.S.R.*, 79–86).

77. Nove, *The Soviet Economy*, 84, 221.

78. Other important aspects of this reform process included the reinstating of Gosplan as the sole planning agency.

79. Only the State Committee for Construction (*Gosstroi*) and the State Committee for Scientific Research (which was renamed as the "State Committee for Science and Technology") survived these reforms by being placed directly under the patronage of the Council of Ministers (ibid., 82–84).

80. Interview #21. Kosygin actively supported the RBMK design proposed by Sredmash (Ulasevich, *Sozdano pod rukovodstvom N. A. Dollezhalia*, 33–35, 41–53). Slavskii's medals include the Hero of Socialist Labor (three times), ten Orders of Lenin, Order of the October Revolution, two Orders of the Red Banner of Labor, Order of the Patriotic War (first degree), a Medal "For Labor Valor," five anniversary medals, the Lenin prize, and the State Prize (three times) (Nasonov, *E. P. Slavskii*, 226). His ministry had a reputation—that because of the classified nature of the evidence cannot be verified—for always having money and being able to pay its bills, so industry competed for Sredmash contracts (Interview #3).

81. Nove, *The Soviet Economy*, 78; Hewett, *Soviet Central Planning*. Just before the State Committee for Energy and Electrification became a ministry again, on September 8, 1965, Neporozhnii urged Kosygin in a letter (No. ES-725) "to examine one more time and to decide favorably" the question of allocating factories to his committee that had previously been assets of the Ministry of Power Plants (RGAE, f. 4372, f. 66, d. 231, l. 86–87; RGAE, f. 4372, op. 58, d. 461, l. 1–90). Thus, while enterprises in a socialist society did not engage in direct competition (a crucial ingredient of market economies), there was competition for control over enterprises on the level of ministries.

82. In his letter to the Council of Ministers of October 19, 1965 (No. ES-26), quoting order No. 755 of October 12, 1965, Neporozhnii refers to an earlier letter (dated October 9, 1965, No. ES-9) that had supposedly contained a detailed list of enterprises (RGAE, f. 4372, op. 66, d. 231, l. 98).

83. For example, RGAE, f. 4372, op. 65, d. 769.

84. RGAE, f. 4372, op. 65, d. 771, l. 151–152 and 191–192.

85. Ibid., l. 195.

86. Letter No. ES-82 (RGAE, f. 4372, op. 66, d. 907, l. 57–65).

87. Ibid.

88. Letter No. ES-579 of August 17, 1967 (RGAE, f. 4372, op. 66, d. 1723, l. 145–149). For a broader argument on these interinstitutional struggles for power see Jerry F. Hough and Merle Fainsod, *How the Soviet Union Is Governed* (Cambridge, MA: Harvard University Press, 1979).

89. This line of argument continued in 1968 in the context of nuclear power plants: costs continued to rise for reactors, main circulation pumps, steam turbines, computers, and specialized stainless steel equipment (Letter from Neporozhnii to the Council of Ministers, July 9, 1968, No. ES-489 (RGAE, f. 4372, op. 66, d. 2496, l. 188–189)).

90. Neporozhnii wrote to the Central Committee on August 25, 1962, complaining about delays in the delivery of materials and equipment for the Beloiarsk and Novo-Voronezh nuclear power plants, and objecting to the poor quality of the equipment supplied (Letter from P. S. Neporozhnii to the Central Committee, No. 2996-Is (RGANI, f. 5, op. 40, d. 257, l. 64)).

91. Letter to V. M. Riabikov, November 22, 1968, No. 22–693 (RGAE, f. 4372, op. 66, d. 2501, l. 72–74).

92. RGAE, f. 4372, op. 66, d. 3209, l. 116–118.

93. RGAE, f. 4372, op. 66, d. 3209, l. 119.

94. Letter No. 22–680 to Baibakov from M. Pervukhin, A. Pavlenko, and A. Sapozhnikov, July 16, 1976, addressed the need to import stainless steel pipes for power engineering in addition to the domestically produced ones (RGAE, f. 4372, op. 66, d. 6047, l. 116–118). These stainless steel pipes were among the most sought-after parts in the nuclear power industry, but Soviet industry in the early 1970s couldn't manufacture more than a fraction of the quantities needed. The rest had to be imported, until more national factories could start production (Letter No. 22–741 to V. Isaev from A. M. Nekrasov (Department of Energy and Electrification), August 3, 1973 (RGAE, f. 4372, op. 66, d. 6047, l. 154)). Sredmash apparently had accepted orders for enriched nuclear fuel to be delivered to France and Italy between 1973 and 1977.

The Department of Energy and Electrification requested that Gosplan dedicate part of this income to importing special stainless steel pipes for nuclear power plants in 1974 and 1975, and in addition that it ask these countries for the material in advance (RGAE, f. 4372, op. 66, d. 6047, l. 117–118).

95. Sonja D. Schmid, "Nuclear Colonization? Soviet Technopolitics in the Second World," in Gabrielle Hecht, ed., *Entangled Geographies: Empire and Technopolitics in the Global Cold War*, 125–154 (Cambridge, MA: MIT Press, 2011).

96. Letter from the Ministry of Energy and Electrification to the Council of Ministers, March 31, 1969, No. ES-230 (RGAE, f. 4372, op. 66, d. 3210, l. 37).

97. Letter from P. Neporozhnii to A. Kosygin, July 4, 1969, No. ES-553 (RGAE, f. 4372, op. 66, d. 3210, l. 79–84).

98. Iurii I. Koriakin, *Okrestnosti iadernoi energetiki Rossii: Novye vyzovy* (Moscow: GUP NIKIET, 2002), 49.

99. Goncharov, "Pervyi period," 9.

100. Viktor I. Riabko, "Stroiteli energozhilstroia—Chernobyl'skoi AES," in A. N. Semenov, ed., *Chernobyl' desiat' let spustia: Neizbezhnost' ili sluchainost'?*, 325–331 (Moscow: Energoatomizdat, 1995) (especially 325–327).

101. See, for example, RGASPI, f. 1, op. 65, d. 536–537. This production-line vision was never actually accomplished, because nuclear power plant construction chronically lagged behind schedule and managers had to work out unforeseen problems, adjust to manufacturing delays, and so on.

102. An unconfirmed story I heard from one interviewee reinforces the salience of this process: during the initial operation of Leningrad's reactor number 1, the sudden failure of the cooling system threatened the reactor's safe operation, but operators were able switch over to the already-completed cooling system of unit 2 (Interview #18).

103. In 1971, RGAE, f. 4372, op. 66, d. 4387, l. 102.

104. RGAE, f. 4372, op. 66, d. 3210, l. 81–82.

105. "According to comrade E. P. Slavskii's conclusion, this program will be supplied with nuclear fuel, but it will necessitate the expansion of existing production capacities" (RGAE, f. 4372, op. 66, d. 3210, l. 83).

106. This phrase is shorthand for referring to interministerial and interdepartmental collaborations ("sovmestno s osnovnymi zainteresovannymi ministerstvami") (Letter to comrade N. K. Baibakov, signed by M. Pervukhin, A. Nekrasov, and K. Vinogradov, August 25, 1969, No. 22–544 (RGAE, f. 4372, op. 66, d. 3215, l. 38–40)).

107. Letter No. ES-544 to the Council of Ministers, June 10, 1971 (RGAE, f. 4372, op. 66, d. 4701, l. 94).

Notes

108. Letter from V. Ia. Isaev, July 15, 1971 (RGAE, f. 4372, op. 66, d. 4701, l. 97).

109. Letter No. ES-156 to V. E. Dymshits, March 7, 1972 (RGAE, f. 4372, op. 66, d. 5416, l. 22–23).

110. Letter No. 583-P from V. Isaev (Gosplan) and F. Manoilo (Construction Bank of the USSR), March 31, 1972 (RGAE, f. 4372, op. 66, d. 5416, l. 126).

111. Letter to A. M. Lalaiants (deputy chairman of Gosplan) from A. Pavlenko, September 5, 1973 (RGAE, f. 4372, op. 66, d. 6259, l. 4–5). Imports of stainless steel pipes with no welded seams were anticipated to be as high as 40 percent until 1978 (RGAE, f. 4372, op. 66, d. 6259, l. 12).

112. In other regions of the Soviet Union, where natural resources were nearby and easy to develop, nuclear power was not the top choice. But in the European part, nuclear power looked comparatively cheap.

113. Letter No. 50–356 to the chairman of Gosplan, N. K. Baibakov, from G. Krasnikovskii (head of the state expert commission), September 26, 1973 (RGAE, f. 4372, op. 66, d. 6259, l. 8). The commission's full report, dated September 20, 1973, is attached to this document (RGAE, f. 4372, op. 66, d. 6259, l. 9–16), with the signatures of fourteen members (not including the chairman) on l. 14.

114. RGAE, f. 4372, op. 66, d. 6259, l. 12. At that point, a second production line was not scheduled for completion until the early 1980s.

115. Gas deliveries to Eastern Europe had started in 1974; in contrast to oil deliveries that had started earlier, gas prices were not subsidized (Office of Technology Assessment, *Technology & Soviet Energy Availability*).

116. GKNT Report to the Council of Ministers, No. 356-p, signed by V. Kirillin, N. Baibakov, and P. Neporozhnii, December 31, 1974 (RGAE, f. 9480, op. 9, d. 2403, l. 34–38).

117. The difference between peak and base demands was 26 million kW in 1970–1971, and the capacity to cover peak demand was 30 million kW. For 1975 the difference was anticipated to rise to 47 million kW (Letter from A. Nekrasov to N. K. Baibakov, "On measures to cover peak demands in electrical power systems," December 22, 1970 (RGAE, f. 4372, op. 66, d. 3976, l. 161–163); see also the letter from M. Pervukhin and A. Pavlenko to N. Baibakov, December 29, 1970, "regarding the question of locating energy production and covering peak demands in electrical power systems of the European part of the USSR" (RGAE, f. 4372, op. 66, d. 3976, l. 173–175)).

118. This report was approved by Gosplan and was intended for discussion in the session on May 26, 1975, at 10:00 a.m. (RGAE, f. 9480, op. 9, d. 2403, l. 71b; the actual report is on l. 72–88).

119. RGAE, f. 9480, op. 9, d. 2403, l. 72–73.

120. Ibid., l. 74.

121. "Electrification is the backbone of the construction of an economy of a communist society; it plays an important role in all branches of the national economy in the realization of modern technological progress" (from the program of the Communist Party of the Soviet Union, in A. S. Pavlenko and A. M. Nekrasov, eds., *Energetika SSSR v 1971–1975 godakh* (Moscow: Energiia, 1972), 7).

122. Josephson, "Atomic-Powered Communism."

123. Nove makes the argument that as early as in the late 1960s, palpable political influence on economic decisions decreased (Nove, *The Soviet Economy*, 160). As Bunce puts it, there "was an implicit deal struck in the 1960s between the regime and the society, wherein publics agreed to comply with the regime and tolerate declining opportunities for social mobility in exchange for a well-developed social security net, price stability, steady if unspectacular improvements in the standard of living, increased access to consumer goods, and a relatively depoliticized environment" (Bunce, *Subversive Institutions*, 33; see also Nove, *The Soviet Economy*, 17).

124. Political science scholars have emphasized this active role of the state (e.g., Theda Skocpol and Dietrich Rueschemeyer, eds., *States, Social Knowledge, and the Origins of Modern Social Policies* (Princeton, NJ: Princeton University Press, 1996); Dietrich Rueschemeyer, *Power and the Division of Labour* (Stanford, CA: Stanford University Press, 1986); Theda Skocpol, *Protecting Soldiers and Mothers: The Political Origin of Social Policy in the United States* (Cambridge, MA: Harvard University Press, 1995)). For analyses of the relationship between science, technology, and the state see, for example, Benedict Anderson, *Imagined Communities: Reflections on the Origins and Spread of Nationalism* (London: Verso, 1983); Yaron Ezrahi, *The Descent of Icarus: Science and the Transformation of Contemporary Democracy* (Cambridge, MA: Harvard University Press, 1990); Yaron Ezrahi, "Technology and the Illusion of the Escape from Politics," in Yaron Ezrahi, Everett Mendelsohn, and Howard M. Segal, eds., *Technology, Pessimism, and Postmodernism*, 29–37 (Dordrecht: Kluwer Academic Publishers, 1994); Scott, *Seeing Like a State*; Scott Lash, Bronislaw Szerszynski, and Brian Wynne, eds., *Risk, Environment and Modernity: Toward a New Ecology* (Thousand Oaks, CA: Sage, 1996); Sheila Jasanoff, ed., *States of Knowledge: The Co-Production of Science and Social Order* (London: Routledge, 2004).

125. The rhetoric of international cooperation, subtly present since the first Geneva Conference in 1955, also changed registers over time. This language evolved from vague declarations of "nuclear assistance" and ambivalent promises of technology transfer, into slowly emerging cooperative agreements with partners in the Council for Mutual Economic Assistance (for references see Schmid, "Nuclear Colonization?").

Chapter 2

1. Many global nuclear histories start with the atomic bomb and end with nuclear power programs, as if the latter were "trickle-down" effects of harnessing nuclear

Notes

energy for the bomb. In the discussion that follows, I reverse this order, in part to honor chronology and in part to demonstrate how nonmilitary bureaucracies came to govern nuclear power.

2. On the idea of "social technologies" see, for example, Michel Foucault, *Discipline and Punish: The Birth of the Prison* (New York: Vintage Books, 1979); Wiebe E. Bijker and John Law, eds., *Shaping Technology/Building Society: Studies in Sociotechnical Change* (Cambridge, MA: MIT Press, 1992).

3. Cf. Gareth Morgan, *Images of Organization* (Newbury Park, CA: Sage, 1986), 278.

4. Weber defined bureaucracy as "a form of organization that emphasizes precision, speed, clarity, regularity, reliability, and efficiency achieved through the creation of a fixed division of tasks, hierarchical supervision, and detailed rules and regulations" (ibid., 24–25). See also Richard Swedberg, ed., *Essays in Economic Sociology: Max Weber* (Princeton, NJ: Princeton University Press, 1999); Max Weber, *Economy and Society: An Outline of Interpretive Sociology* (New York: Bedminster, 1968); Sam Whimster, ed., *The Essential Weber: A Reader* (London: Routledge, 2004); Robert K. Merton, Ailsa P. Gray, Barbara Hockey, and Hanan C. Selvin, eds., *Reader in Bureaucracy* (Glencoe: Free Press, 1952).

5. Thomas Hughes identifies the part of a large technological system that lags behind the rest as "reverse salient"—that is, a part that can impair the functioning of the entire system (Thomas P. Hughes, "The Evolution of Large Technological Systems," in Wiebe E. Bijker, Thomas P. Hughes, and Trevor Pinch, eds., *The Social Construction of Technological Systems*, 51–82 (Cambridge, MA: MIT Press, 1987) (especially 73–74)).

6. Langdon Winner has argued that a technology like nuclear power suggests certain forms of politics, institutional structures, and practices surrounding it (Langdon Winner, *The Whale and the Reactor: A Search for Limits in an Age of High Technology* (Chicago: University of Chicago Press, 1986)). Contrary to Winner's argument, the history of the Soviet nuclear industry shows that nuclear power can be and in fact is administered quite differently in different national contexts, and depending on the institutional culture.

7. Secondary sources include Loren R. Graham, *The Ghost of the Executed Engineer: Technology and the Fall of the Soviet Union* (Cambridge, MA: Harvard University Press, 1993); David Holloway, *Stalin and the Bomb: The Soviet Union and Atomic Energy 1939–1956* (New Haven, CT: Yale University Press, 1994); Paul R. Josephson, *Red Atom: Russia's Nuclear Power Program from Stalin to Today* (New York: Freeman, 1999); Arkadii K. Kruglov, *Kak sozdavalas' atomnaia promyshlennost' v SSSR* (Moscow: TSNIIatominform, 1995); Arkadii K. Kruglov, *Shtab Atomproma* (Moscow: TSNIIatominform, 1998); Vladimir M. Kuznetsov, *Rossiiskaia atomnaia energetika vchera, segodnia, zavtra: Vzgliad nezavisimogo eksperta* (Moscow: Natsional'nyi Institut Pressy, 2000); David R. Marples, "The Post-Soviet Nuclear Power Program," *Post-Soviet Geography* 34, no. 3 (1993): 172–184; Viktor A. Sidorenko, ed., *Istoriia atomnoi energetiki Sovetskogo Soiuza i Rossii*, vol. 1 (Moscow: IzdAt, 2001); Viktor A. Sidorenko, ed., *Istoriia*

atomnoi energetiki Sovetskogo Soiuza i Rossii: Istoriia VVER, vol. 2 (Moscow: IzdAt, 2002); Viktor A. Sidorenko, ed., *Istoriia atomnoi energetiki Sovetskogo Soiuza i Rossii: Istoriia RBMK*, vol. 3 (Moscow: IzdAt, 2003); Viktor A. Sidorenko, ed., *Istoriia atomnoi energetiki Sovetskogo Soiuza i Rossii: Uroki avarii na Chernobyl'skoi AES*, vol. 4 (Moscow: IzdAt, 2002); Viktor A. Sidorenko, ed., *Istoriia atomnoi energetiki Sovetskogo Soiuza i Rossii: Istoriia maloi atomnoi energetiki*, vol. 5 (Moscow: IzdAt, 2004).

8. Martha Lampland, "The Technopolitical Lineage of State Planning in Hungary, 1930–1956," in Gabrielle Hecht, ed., *Entangled Geographies: Empire and Technopolitics in the Global Cold War*, 155–184 (Cambridge, MA: MIT Press, 2011); Charles S. Maier, "Between Taylorism and Technocracy: European Ideologies and the Vision of Industrial Productivity in the 1920s," *Contemporary History* 5, no. 2 (1970): 27–61.

9. On March 15, 1956, a government decree set the goal of constructing nuclear power plants with a combined power output of 2175 MW within the next five years, and assigned 775 MW to Sredmash, and 1400 MW to the ministry of power plants (Viktor A. Sidorenko, "Upravlenie atomnoi energetikoi," in Viktor A. Sidorenko, ed., *Istoriia atomnoi energetiki Sovetskogo Soiuza i Rossii*, vol. 1 (Moscow: IzdAt, 2001), 218). This division of labor appears in archival references as well, albeit less explicitly. In 1971, for example, Gosplan anticipated an increase in power capacities of 154.3–164.3 million kW, of which 146.5–156.5 would be produced at power plants managed by Minenergo (RGAE, f. 4372, op. 66, d. 4387, l. 114–115).

10. These included the ministries of petrochemical engineering *(Minneftemash)*, of the instrumentation industry *(Minpriborprom)*, of ferrous and nonferrous metals *(Minchermet* and *Mintsvetmet)*, and of the chemical industry *(Minkhimprom)* (see "Letter to comrade Baibakov, N. K." from A. Pavlenko, K. Vinogradov, and A. Nekrasov, No. 22–9, of January 10, 1969 (RGAE, f. 4372, op. 66, d. 3215, l. 1–3)). In the mid-1950s, Sredmash was responsible for designing and building reactors, Minenergo for managing the overall plant construction and assembly, and the Ministry of Heavy Machine Building *(Mintiazhmash)* for manufacturing parts for the two ministries (Vladimir V. Goncharov, "Pervyi period razvitiia atomnoi energetiki v SSSR," in Viktor A. Sidorenko, ed., *Istoriia atomnoi energetiki Sovetskogo Soiuza i Rossii*, vol. 1, 16–70 (Moscow: IzdAt, 2001) (especially 33)).

11. On "crisis," see Ann Swidler, "Culture in Action: Symbols and Strategies," *American Sociological Review* 51 (April 1986): 273–286; Nikolai L. Krementsov, *Stalinist Science* (Princeton, NJ: Princeton University Press, 1997).

12. A good summary of how top-tier cadres were recruited in the Soviet era occurs in Nikolai I. Ryzhkov's preface to a volume on Vitalii F. Konovalov, minister of nuclear energy from 1989 to 1991: "The vast majority [of promoted cadres] consisted of professionally trained, talented organizers. And all good things in the country were accomplished with their active and positive participation. . . . Back then, loyalty to the Homeland, to the people, formed the basis [of personnel manage-

ment]" (V. V. Chernyshev, ed., *Vitalii Fedorovich Konovalov: Stranitsy zhizni. Tvortsy iadernogo veka* (Moscow: IzdAt, 2003), 3).

13. Historian of technology Paul Josephson sharply criticizes these early Soviet attempts to mass-produce equipment for the nuclear industry. According to him, this "premature standardization" was the main reason the Soviet nuclear power industry failed in terms of safety and economic efficiency (Josephson, *Red Atom*). But who determines when a standard is set "prematurely"?

14. Even the reactor designs that the Soviets labeled "standardized" (*seriinyi proekt*) continued to be modified and improved.

15. Sonja D. Schmid, "Organizational Culture and Professional Identities in the Soviet Nuclear Power Industry," *Osiris* 23 (2008): 82–111 (especially 83).

16. GOELRO is the acronym for the state commission appointed to create the plan, *Gosudarstvennaia komissiia po elektrifikatsii Rossii*. (See Iurii I. Koriakin, *Okrestnosti iadernoi energetiki Rossii: Novye vyzovy* (Moscow: GUP NIKIET, 2002); Petr S. Neporozhnii, *Energetika strany glazami ministra: Dnevniki 1935–1985 gg.* (Moscow: Energoatomizdat, 2000); Dimitrii G. Zhimerin, ed., *Sovremennye problemy energetiki* (Moscow: Energoatomizdat, 1984); Jonathan Coopersmith, *The Electrification of Russia, 1880–1926* (Ithaca, NY: Cornell University Press, 1992); see also RGAE, f. 7964, op. 3, p. 1 (Narkom elektrostantsii i elektropromyshlennosti SSSR, Ministerstvo elektrostantsii SSSR, 1939–1959).)

17. Coopersmith, *The Electrification of Russia*, 169–170. In fact, some critics argue that the revolution actually hampered an already-ongoing process of electrification and that the GOELRO plan was too often fetishized (Koriakin, *Okrestnosti*).

18. Coopersmith, *The Electrification of Russia*, 189.

19. Petr S. Neporozhnii and Vladimir Iu. Steklov, eds., *50 let Leninskogo plana GOELRO [1920–1970]: Sbornik materialov* (Moscow: Energiia, 1970); Vladimir Iu. Steklov, *V. I. Lenin i elektrifikatsiia*, 3rd ed. (Moscow: Nauka, 1982); *Energetika narodnogo khoziaistva v plane GOELRO* (Moscow: Ekonomika, 1966).

20. Coopersmith, *The Electrification of Russia*, 190.

21. Holloway, *Stalin and the Bomb*, 10.

22. The construction efforts initially relied heavily on prison labor, until the Council of Ministers shut down the GULag system in 1960 (see, e.g., Memorial, http://www.memo.ru/history/NKVD/GULAG/r1/r1-4.htm). Memorial links the official end of the GULag system to order No. 020 by the Ministry of Internal Affairs (MVD), dated January 25, 1960, which followed decree No. 44–16 of January 13, 1960, by the Council of Ministers. See also http://russiapedia.rt.com/of-russian-origin/the-gulag/. Koriakin dates the end of the prison labor system earlier, around 1956, which reflects the transfer of labor camps supporting the construction of military projects

in 1955 from the central GULag administration to industrial and "special" construction administrations (*Glavpromstroi* and *Glavspetsstroi*) (Koriakin, *Okrestnosti*, 31). In 1939, the "People's Commissariat of Power Plants and the Electrical Industry" was created as an offspring of the People's Commissariat of Machine Building. Its subsequent reorganizations were in part due to the involvement of the Secret Police (People's Commissariat of Internal Affairs, NKVD) in the construction of power plants until 1956.

23. Arnold Kramish, *Atomic Energy in the Soviet Union* (Stanford, CA: Stanford University Press, 1959), 23.

24. Holloway, *Stalin and the Bomb*, 75.

25. David Holloway, *Stalin and the Bomb*, especially 76–79; Thomas B. Cochran, Robert S. Norris, and Oleg A. Bukharin, *Making the Russian Bomb: From Stalin to Yeltsin* (Boulder, CO: Westview Press, 1995).

26. Holloway, *Stalin and the Bomb*, 116.

27. Beria's Special Committee came into existence following a top-secret decree on August 20, 1945 (Postanovlenie gosudarstvennogo komiteta oborony No. 9887, ss/op ("top secret/special folder"—the highest level of security)); its members were Georgii Malenkov, one of the Central Committee secretaries; Nikolai Voznesenskii, head of Gosplan; three industrial managers (Vannikov, Zaveniagin, and Pervukhin); the scientists Kurchatov and Kapitsa; and General Makhnev from the People's Commissariat of Internal Affairs (NKVD) (Holloway, *Stalin and the Bomb*, 135). On Beria, see Amy Knight, *Beria: Stalin's First Lieutenant* (Princeton, NJ: Princeton University Press, 1993).

28. Kramish, *Atomic Energy in the Soviet Union*, 117; Knight, *Beria*; Peter DeLeon, *Development and Diffusion of the Nuclear Power Reactor: A Comparative Analysis* (Cambridge, MA: Ballinger, 1979), 74–75; Kruglov, *Shtab atomproma*.

29. Kramish, *Atomic Energy in the Soviet Union*, 323; Sidorenko, "Upravlenie atomnoi energetikoi," 218. Beria was arrested on June 26, 1953, and executed after his trial in December 1953. Kramish asserts that this arrest marked "a general lessening of tensions within the Soviet atomic energy program" (Kramish, *Atomic Energy in the Soviet Union*, 177). The new Ministry of Medium Machine Building was created on the basis of the First Chief Administration (PGU), and the Third Chief Administration, an organization involved with rockets, aircraft, missiles, and missile defense (Pavel L. Podvig, "Protivoraketnaia oborona kak faktor strategicheskikh vzaimootnoshenii SSSR/Rossii i SShA v 1945–2003 gg.," doctoral dissertation, Rossiiskaia Akademiia Nauk, 2004; David Holloway, "Physics, the State, and Civil Society in the Soviet Union," *Historical Studies in the Physical and Biological Sciences* 30, no. 1 (1999): 173–193).

30. The Soviet nuclear weapons project no doubt benefited from espionage, but it still involved tremendous ingenuity, coordination, and expenditures domestically, as Holloway has convincingly documented in *Stalin and the Bomb*. See also Vladimir P. Vizgin, ed., *Istoriia Sovetskogo atomnogo proekta: Dokumenty, vospominaniia, issledovaniia.*, vol. 1 (Moscow: Ianus-K, 1998); Vladimir P. Vizgin, ed., *Istoriia Sovetskogo atomnogo proekta: Dokumenty, vospominaniia, issledovaniia*, vol. 2 (Saint Petersburg: Izdatel'stvo Russkogo Khristianskogo gumanitarnogo instituta, 2002).

31. Morris Janowitz, *The Professional Soldier* (Glencoe, IL: Free Press, 1960); Boris A. Fain, *Aktivnaia zona: Povest' ob atomnom institute* (Moscow: Skripto, 1998); Mikhail P. Grabovskii, *Atomnyi avral* (Moscow: Nauchnaia kniga, 2001).

32. Cf. Holloway, *Stalin and the Bomb*; V. K. Ulasevich, ed., *Sozdano pod rukovodstvom N. A. Dollezhalia: O iadernykh reaktorakh i ikh tvortsakh (K 100-letiiu N. A. Dollezhalia)*, 2nd ed. (Moscow: GUP NIKIET, 2002); V. K. Ulasevich, ed., *O iadernykh reaktorakh i ikh tvortsakh: Prodolzhenie traditsii (K 50-letiiu NIKIET im. N. A. Dollezhalia)* (Moscow: GUP NIKIET, 2002); Lev D. Riabev, ed., *Atomnyi proekt SSSR: Dokumenty i materialy, 1938–1945*, vol. 1, chast' 2 (Moscow: Ministerstvo Rossiiskoi Federatsii po atomnoi energii, Rossiiskaia akademiia nauk, 2002); Lev. D. Riabev, ed. *Atomnyi proekt SSSR: Dokumenty i materialy, 1945–1954*, vol. 2, kn. 1 (Sarov: Ministerstvo Rossiiskoi Federatsii po atomnoi energii, Rossiiskaia akademiia nauk, 1999); Lev D. Riabev, ed. *Atomnyi proekt SSSR: Dokumenty i materialy, 1945–1954*, vol. 2, kn. 2 (Sarov: Ministerstvo Rossiiskoi Federatsii po atomnoi energii, Rossiiskaia akademiia nauk, 2000); Lev D. Riabev, ed. *Atomnyi proekt SSSR: Dokumenty i materialy, 1945–1954*, vol. 2, kn. 3 (Sarov: Ministerstvo Rossiiskoi Federatsii po atomnoi energii, Rossiiskaia akademiia nauk, 2002); Lev D. Riabev, ed. *Atomnyi proekt SSSR: Dokumenty i materialy: Atomnaia bomba, 1945–1954*, vol. 2, kn. 4 (Moscow and Sarov: Nauka and Fizmatlit, Ministerstvo Rossiiskoi Federatsii po atomnoi energii, 2003); Lev D. Riabev, ed. *Atomnyi proekt SSSR: Dokumenty i materialy: Atomnaia bomba, 1945–1954*, vol. 2, kn. 5 (Moscow and Sarov: Nauka and Fizmatlit, Federal'noe agentstvo po atomnoi energii, 2005). As we will see throughout this book, the two programs cannot be clearly separated from an organizational viewpoint (see also DeLeon, *Development and Diffusion of the Nuclear Power Reactor*, 101).

33. Holloway, *Stalin and the Bomb*; Raisa V. Kuznetsova, ed., *Kurchatov v zhizni: Pis'ma, dokumenty, vospominaniia (iz lichnogo arkhiva)* (Moscow: Mosgorarkhiv, 2002); Sidorenko, *Istoriia atomnoi energetiki Sovetskogo Soiuza i Rossii*, vol. 1. For example, Kurchatov gave a passionate speech about the peaceful future of nuclear energy at the twentieth congress of the CPSU in 1956 (Igor' V. Kurchatov, "Rech' tovarishcha I. V. Kurchatova," *Pravda* 53, no. 22 (February 1956): 7); on June 21, 1958, he wrote a letter to Leonid Brezhnev about delays on the Novo-Voronezh nuclear power plant construction site (Letter No. G-590 ss; RGANI, f. 5, op. 40, d. 107, rolik 7213, l. 64–66) (reproduced in Goncharov, "Pervyi period," 65–66); in the spring of 1959, he wrote to the secretaries of the Party's Central Committee, F. R. Kozlov (April 16) and

A. I. Kirichenko (April 6), as well as to the Council of Ministers (Aleksei Kosygin, April 24), again promoting the Novo-Voronezh nuclear power plant (ibid., 67–70).

34. This is the first official reference to peaceful applications of nuclear energy. See, for example, Viktor A. Sidorenko, "Vvedenie k 1-mu vypusku," in Viktor A. Sidorenko, ed., *Istoriia atomnoi energetiki Sovetskogo Soiuza i Rossii*, vol. 1 (Moscow: IzdAt, 2001), 5; Vladimir G. Asmolov et al., *Atomnaia energetika: Otsenki proshlogo, realii nastoiashchego, ozhidaniia budushchego* (Moscow: IzdAt, 2004), 8.

35. Lev A. Kochetkov, "K istorii sozdaniia Obninskoi AES," in V. A. Sidorenko, ed., *Istoriia atomnoi energetiki Sovetskogo Soiuza i Rossii*, vol. 1, 96–101 (Moscow: IzdAt, 2001); Lev A. Kochetkov, ed., *Ot Pervoi v mire AES k atomnoi energetike XXI veka. Sbornik tezisov, dokladov i soobshchenii* (Proceedings of the 10th Annual Conference, Obninsk, June 28–July 2, 1999) (Obninsk: Iadernoe obshchestvo Rossii, 1999).

36. Interview #12.

37. The pressurized water and liquid metal reactors eventually proved more suitable for naval propulsion (Maria Nicolaevna Vasilieva, *Soleils rouges: L'ambition nucléaire soviétique [Essai sur l'évolution des systèmes de prise de décision dans le nucléaire soviétique (Russe)]* (Paris: Institut d'Histoire de l'Industrie et Éditions Rive Droite, 1999); Ulasevich, *Sozdano pod rukovodstvom: O iadernykh reaktorakh*). Also see Interviews #4, #5, and #7.

38. "People's Commissariat" was the label Soviet political leaders preferred for what eventually became "ministries" after Stalin's death. The "People's Commissariat for Power Plants and the Power Industry" was created on January 24, 1939 (RGAE, f. 7964, op. 15, t. 1, l. 5, Moscow). See also "Elektroenergetika: Nekotorye vazhneishie sobytiia," prepared by Vanguard Ltd. as part of the project Elektromysl' in March and April 2001, which contains a summary of the history of this industry from the nineteenth century to the early 1990s (http://www.sapov.ru/consul/reports/electro/el-sense_06.htm).

39. In its post-1962 form, it came to life through order No. 985 from the Communist Party's Central Committee and the Council of Ministers dated September 21, 1962, "On the organization of a union-republican ministry of power and electrification" (Ob organizatsii soiuzno-republikanskogo Ministerstva energetiki i elektrifikatsii SSSR) (mentioned in RGAE, f. 4372, f. 66, d. 231). The Russian word *energetika* encompasses both the engineering, and the industrial, operational, and commercial aspects of the power industry. For the sake of consistency, I have translated *energetika* as "energy."

40. Schattenberg was able to locate an unedited manuscript of Lavrenenko's memoirs (RGAE, f. 9592, op. 1, d. 404) (Susanne Schattenberg, *Stalins Ingenieure: Lebenswelten Zwischen Technik und Terror in den 1930er Jahren* (Munich: Oldenbourg, 2002)).

Notes

41. "Glavnoe upravlenie po kapital'nomu stroitel'stvu atomnykh elektrostantsii (Glavatomenergo). Godovoi finansovyi plan Glavka po kapital'nomu stroitel'stvu i izmeneniia k nemu na 1957 god. Plan finansirovaniia kapital'nogo stroitel'stva po Glavatomenergo na 1957, i svedeniia ob ego izmeneniia" (RGAE, f. 9599, op.1, d. 2). The official document of acceptance *(Akt priemki)* is in RGAE, f. 9599, op.1, d. 10, l. 17–32. Teploelektroproekt's Leningrad branch (LOTEP) was in charge of constructing the Beloiarsk plant. See also the minutes of the technical meeting in Glavatomenergo on February 19, 1959 (RGAE, f. 9599, op. 1, d. 15, l. 6–7, "On the question of confirming a container wagon for the Beloiarsk GRES (state regional power station)" and "On the question of designing and manufacturing a container-wagon for the transport of fuel assemblies [for] V-1 at the Novo-Voronezh GRES").

42. The original plans had been for a conventional power plant at the Beloiarsk site, according to Glavatomenergo's annual capital investment report for 1957 (RGAE, f. 7964, op. 3, d. 1881, l. 2). When the Novo-Voronezh and Beloiarsk plants started operation in 1964, they were still perceived as experimental stations, not as powerful industrial power plants (RGAE, f. 4372, op. 66, d. 233, l. 245–250). Even in late March 1965, neither plant was considered an industrial energy production facility (RGAE, f. 4372, op. 66, d. 233, l. 245–250; Sidorenko, "Upravlenie atomnoi energetikoi," 217; Neporozhnii, *Energetika strany glazami ministra*).

43. The Ministry of Power Plants and their project managing organization Teploelektroproekt (with its suborganization LOTEP in Leningrad) in May 1957 were still designing and planning the VVER plant near Leningrad, on the assumption that they would be able to use plans developed for the Novo-Voronezh nuclear power plant, since the basic equipment was expected to be analogous at the Leningrad site (RGAE, f. 9599, op. 1, d. 8, l. 20).

44. In the early 1960s, as a consequence of Khrushchev's reforms, the ministry was called the State Production Committee for Power and Electrification (*Gosudarstvennyi proizvodstvennyi komitet po energetike i elektrifikatsii SSSR*), with Neporozhnii as its chairman. The committee was responsible for supervising the construction of huge hydroelectric and nuclear power plants, as well as fossil fuel plants and high-voltage power supply lines (RGAE, f. 4372, op. 65, d. 765, l. 79–88).

45. Sidorenko, "Upravlenie atomnoi energetikoi," 217; Neporozhnii, *Energetika strany glazami ministra*. See also "Ministerstvo energetiki i elektrifikatsii SSSR, Glavnoe proizvodstvenno-tekhnicheskoe upravlenie po stroitel'stvu, Vsesoiuznyi institut po proektirovaniiu organizatsii energeticheskogo stroitel'stva 'Orgenergostroi': Organizatsiia opytnogo stroitel'stva Zaporozhskoi, Krymskoi i Chigirinskoi AES metodom nepreryvnogo dolgovremennogo potoka: Rukovoditel' raboty professor F. V. Sapozhnikov," Moscow, 1981 (RGASPI (Komsomol), f. 1, op. 65, d. 536, str. 1–34). Neporozhnii reportedly opposed the graphite-water reactor (RBMK) and its promoters, primarily on economic grounds (Sidorenko, *Istoriia atomnoi energetiki*

Sovetskogo Soiuza i Rossii: Istoriia RBMK, vol. 3, 217–218; Viktor P. Tatarnikov, "Atomnaia elektroenergetika (s VVER i drugimi reaktorami)," in Viktor A. Sidorenko, ed., *Istoriia atomnoi energetiki Sovetskogo Soiuza i Rossi. Istoriia VVER*, vol. 2, 303–399 (Moscow: IzdAt, 2002) (especially 340–342); see also Interviews #8 and #25).

46. RGAE, f. 7964, op. 15, t. 1, l. 8.

47. RGAE, f. 4372, op. 65, d. 769, l. 60–63.

48. Draft plan for the development of the nuclear power industry in 1966–1970, generated by A. Pavlenko (from Gosplan's Department of Energy and Electrification), sent to N. Baibakov, July 8, 1967 (Otdel energetiki i elektrifikatsii: Proekt plana razvitiia energetiki na 1966–1970 gg., razrabotannyi otdelom (RGAE, f. 4372, op. 66, d. 1737, l. 1–11)).

49. Aleksandr Emel'ianenkov, *Ostrova Sredmasha* (Moscow: Rossiiskaia gazeta & Izd. Parad, 2005); Vladimir Gubarev, *Agoniia Sredmasha: Ot Chernobylia do Chubaisa* (Moscow: Akademkniga, 2006); Alexander Yemelyanenkov, *The Sredmash Archipelago* (Moscow: IPPNW-Russia, 2000); Fain, *Aktivnaia zona*.

50. Mikhail P. Grabovskii, *Nakanune avrala* (Moscow: Nauchnaia kniga, 2000); see also Vitalii P. Nasonov, *B. L. Vannikov: Memuary, vospominaniia, stat'i* (Moscow: TSNIIatominform, 1997).

51. As chairman of Gostekhnika, Malyshev exercised technical control on a higher level, but he died on February 20, 1957, of leukemia (Kramish, *Atomic Energy in the Soviet Union*, 178). On the history of Gostekhnika and its later incarnations, see Stephen Fortescue, *Science Policy in the Soviet Union* (London: Routledge, 1990). For Zaveniagin's tenure at the Magnitogorsk Metallurgical Complex from 1933 to 1936, see M. Ia. Vazhnov and I. S. Aristov, eds., *A. P. Zaveniagin: Stranitsy zhizni* (Moscow: PoliMediia, 2002); Stephen Kotkin, *Magnetic Mountain: Stalinism as a Civilization* (Berkeley: University of California Press, 1995).

52. Sidorenko, "Upravlenie atomnoi energetikoi," 218. Kramish notes that Zaveniagin's death "marked the beginning of several organizational crises within the Soviet atomic energy program" (Kramish, *Atomic Energy in the Soviet Union*, 178).

53. Pervukhin was sent to the GDR as ambassador, to return only in the late 1960s, when he took on a position as a member of Gosplan's board (also see Interview #7).

54. Sidorenko, "Upravlenie atomnoi energetikoi," 218. On Slavskii, see also Igor' A. Beliaev and German G. Malkin, eds., *E. P. Slavskii: 100 let so dnia rozhdeniia* (Moscow: IzdAT, 1999); Vitalii P. Nasonov, *E. P. Slavskii: Stranitsy zhizni* (Moscow: IzdAT, 1998).

55. Sredmash was apparently able to keep the high level of government support alive, which in turn reinforced its reputation as powerful "state within the state" (Fain, *Aktivnaia zona*).

Notes

56. DeLeon, *Development and Diffusion of the Nuclear Power Reactor*, 98.

57. Sidorenko, "Upravlenie atomnoi energetikoi," 217.

58. While part of Sredmash, Glavatom directly answered to the Council of Ministers. Kramish dates the creation of this agency to April 18, 1956 (Kramish, *Atomic Energy in the Soviet Union*, 178), while Sidorenko gives the earlier date of March 20, 1956 (Sidorenko, "Upravlenie atomnoi energetikoi," 218).

59. Josephson, *Red Atom*.

60. Emelyianov had been chairman of the Committee on Standards during the Second World War (Kramish, *Atomic Energy in the Soviet Union*, 179); this previous qualification could have backed up, if not inspired, the drive toward standardization of nuclear reactors, plant details, and construction processes.

61. Sidorenko, "Upravlenie atomnoi energetikoi," 218. Sidorenko describes this as "detachment" from Sredmash, but the exact administrative subordination of ministries, *glavki* (Chief Administrations), and committees was shuffled frequently, without substantially altering their functions. Glavatom shared its fate with other State Committees. See also RGAE, f. 4372–62–571, l. 220–222.

62. Andranik M. Petros'iants, *Dorogi zhizni, kotorye vybirali nas* (Moscow: Energoatomizdat, 1993); Sidorenko, "Upravlenie atomnoi energetikoi," 220.

63. No wonder international observers kept puzzling over its exact institutional scope. As one asked, "Did it encompass both peaceful and military nuclear applications, R&D, regulation, and safety standards?" (DeLeon, *Development and Diffusion of the Nuclear Power Reactor*, 75). One of the nine Administrations was in charge of nuclear power plants; its director was Nikolai Nikolaev, a power engineer who had led operations of one of the plutonium production reactors at Chelyabinsk-40, and later became director of the Obninsk nuclear power plant (Sidorenko, "Upravlenie atomnoi energetikoi," 218).

64. This agency's mandate and its level of autonomy fluctuated between ministerial and Union-wide for decades, and its designation reflects that; its name changed back to Chief Administration in 1965 and to State Committee in 1978. In everyday operations, the difference between State Committee and Chief Administration may not have mattered, and authors certainly conflate the two frequently.

65. Kramish, *Atomic Energy in the Soviet Union*, 181.

66. The IAE was one of the scientific research institutes that reported to the GU-16, which I discuss later in this chapter.

67. Holloway, *Stalin and the Bomb*, 355–363. Holloway's account also refutes DeLeon's earlier conclusion that "the complete domination by the Soviet state of its nuclear research during the early stages makes it difficult to imagine that Russian nuclear scientists could have voiced an independent policy about nuclear energy

research beyond describing the theoretical knowledge and technical applications" (DeLeon, *Development and Diffusion of the Nuclear Power Reactor*, 93). Also see Igor' V. Kurchatov, "Nekotorye voprosy razvitiia atomnoi energetiki v SSSR," *Pravda* 141, no. 20 (May 1956): 2; "Nekotorye voprosy razvitiia atomnoi energetiki v SSSR (Doklad, sdelannyi I. V. Kurchatovym v Kharuelle (Angliia) v aprele 1956g.)," in Viktor A. Sidorenko, ed., *Istoriia atomnoi energetiki Sovetskogo Soiuza i Rossii*, vol. 1, 71–82 (Moscow: IzdAt, 2001).

68. Grabovskii, *Nakanune avrala;* Mikhail P. Grabovskii, *Atomnyi avral* (Moscow: Nauchnaia kniga, 2001); Vizgin, *Istoriia Sovetskogo atomnogo proekta*, vols. 1 and 2. Kurchatov even "saved" Soviet genetics by providing an umbrella institute for them (see also Mark B. Adams, ed., *The Wellborn Science: Eugenics in Germany, France, Brazil, and Russia* (New York: Oxford University Press, 1990)). Vizgin has described the nuclear physics community as a small cell of "civil society" in the Soviet Union (see also Holloway, "Physics, the State, and Civil Society").

69. "Ia schastliv, chto rodilsia v Rossii i posviatil svoiu zhizn' atomnoi nauke velikoi Strany Sovetov" (Kurchatov, "Rech'," 7).

70. Iurii N. Rudenko and Vladimir A. Semenov, eds., *Avtomatizatsiia dispetcherskogo upravleniia v elektroenergetike* (Moscow: Izdatel'stvo MEI, 2000).

71. Sonja D. Schmid, "Envisioning a Technological State: Reactor Design Choices and Political Legitimacy in the Soviet Union and Russia," doctoral dissertation, Cornell University, 2005; Sonja D. Schmid, "Organizational Culture and Professional Identities in the Soviet Nuclear Power Industry."

72. This question continued to be debated even after the creation of Soiuzatomenergo, the All-Union operating organization set up in 1978 (Sidorenko, "Upravlenie atomnoi energetikoi," 223).

73. On the tension between the opposing views of nuclear materials and facilities as trivial or special, see also Gabrielle Hecht, *Being Nuclear: Africans and the Global Uranium Trade* (Cambridge, MA: MIT Press, 2012).

74. This transfer did not come as a surprise: it was anticipated by the ministries and committees involved. On April 30, 1964, Neporozhnii, chairman of the State Committee for Power and Electrification, wrote to the chairman of Gosplan (P. F. Lomako at that point) about the development of the power industry during the eighth five-year plan (No. N-4958, a reaction to order No. 1082 of the Council of Ministers and the Central Committee from October 19, 1963, "On the order and schedule of creating a draft of the five-year plan of developing the Soviet economy for 1966–1970" (RGAE, f. 4372, op. 65, d. 769, l. 55–98)).

75. In addition, the Ministry of Heavy Machine Building (*Mintiazhmash*) would manufacture heat-exchange equipment, steam turbines, steam conductors, and transportation equipment for all types of reactors; the Ministry of the Defense

Industry (*Minoboronprom*) would manufacture circulation pumps and specialized optical devices; and the Ministry of the Electrotechnical Industry (*Minelektrotekhprom*) would produce all electrical equipment, as well as the control and safety systems for all reactor types. Additional ministries were responsible for even more specialized items.

76. In July 1967, the Department for Energy and Electrification in Gosplan credited nuclear power plants as an increasingly important source of energy, with an estimated 10 percent of electricity to be generated at these plants by 1975 (Draft plan for the development of the power industry in 1966–1970, generated by A. Pavlenko, sent to N. Baibakov, July 8, 1967 (Otdel energetiki i elektrifikatsii. Proekt plana razvitiia energetiki na 1966–1970 gg., razrabotannyi otdelom; RGAE, f. 4372, op. 66, d. 1737, l. 1–11)).

77. For example, the construction bureau OKB Gidropress, originally a classified Sredmash enterprise, was transferred to the authority of the Ordzhonikidze Machine Building Factory of Podolsk, a factory working for a civilian ministry (the Ministry of Heavy, Power, and Transport Engineering), in 1966 (RGAE, f. 4372, op. 66, d. 911, l. 20).

78. For example, in 1978 it would start operating a state-of-the-art training center for VVER control room operators at the Novo-Voronezh plant, replacing earlier temporary training simulators (Sidorenko, "Upravlenie atomnoi energetikoi," 222). Much later, a similar center for RBMK operators was established at Smolensk.

79. In 1978, the former director of the Novo-Voronezh nuclear power plant, Fedor Ovchinnikov, was appointed deputy minister of nuclear power, and from 1982 to 1986, Gennadii Shasharin filled the position. Shasharin had worked as chief engineer at the Beloiarsk plant, supervised construction of the Loviisa plant in Finland, and later served in the Central Committee's Department of Mechanical Engineering (Sidorenko, "Upravlenie atomnoi energetikoi," 221). According to one interviewee, the team at the Beloiarsk plant (where the first two reactors were a graphite-water design) had been recruited mostly from Minenergo cadres, while most of the cadres for the Novo-Voronezh (the first VVER) and the Leningrad (the first RBMK) plants came from Sredmash (Interview #25).

80. Sidorenko writes that Glavatomenergo was "created" in 1966, but since this organization had existed before, it could only have been recreated, reorganized, or updated to the new organizational management structures. Georgii Ermakov served as chief engineer under Grigoriants. In late 1969, Leonid Voronin replaced Ermakov, and he remained in this position until May 1978, when Glavatomenergo was liquidated. The chief engineer was the highest scientific-technical position, and it was the highest management position involving the least amount of administrative work (see Kendall E. Bailes, *Technology and Society under Lenin and Stalin: Origins of the Soviet Technical Intelligentsia, 1917–1941* (Princeton, NJ: Princeton University Press, 1978)).

81. Sidorenko, "Upravlenie atomnoi energetikoi," 219. I have been unable to locate the decree, but the majority of Soviet nuclear power plants trace their existence back to decree No. 800–252, issued by the Central Committee and the Council of Ministers in September 1966.

82. *Vsesoiuznoe promyshlennoe ob"edinenie "Soiuzatomenergo"* (Sidorenko, "Upravlenie atomnoi energetikoi," 221). Order No. 190 *Minenergo USSR*, June 2, 1978, implementing decree No. 1044r of the Council of Ministers from May 23, 1978 (RGAE, f. 7964, op. 16, t. 2, foreword p. 1).

83. Vladimir Nevskii was appointed director of the new organization. Nevskii came to Soiuzatomenergo from the Beloiarsk nuclear power plant, where he had served as director. Iurii Markov became his first deputy (Sidorenko, "Upravlenie atomnoi energetikoi," 221). Markov was transferred from Sredmash's GU-16, and returned to Sredmash in 1982. In 1982, Nevskii died and Gennadii Veretennikov stepped in as director of Soiuzatomenergo. Like several other top Minenergo managers, he was released from this position after the Chernobyl disaster in 1986 (Sidorenko, "Upravlenie atomnoi energetikoi," 222).

84. Sidorenko, "Upravlenie atomnoi energetikoi," 222. To facilitate nuclear power development in CMEA countries, two joint enterprises had been established in 1972 and 1973, respectively. *Interatominstrument* was set up to oversee the manufacture of high-technology equipment for nuclear power plants (Office of Technology Assessment, *Technology & Soviet Energy Availability* (Washington, DC: Congress of the U.S., Office of Technology Assessment, 1981), 295). *Interatomenergo* was established to coordinate supplies, to supervise the start-up of plants, and to train nuclear power managers (Vladimir Sobell, *The Red Market: Industrial Co-Operation and Specialisation in Comecon* (Aldershot: Gower, 1984), 155; Office of Technology Assessment, *Technology and Soviet Energy Availability*, 295).

85. Sidorenko, "Upravlenie atomnoi energetikoi," 219.

86. NIKIET provided this quality control to plants where RBMKs were assembled. Apparently, there were significant differences in how well this service worked, depending on which ministry managed a given plant (Fain, *Aktivnaia zona*, 114–123).

87. Sidorenko, "Upravlenie atomnoi energetikoi," 219–220.

88. December 1958 report from Lavrenenko (Glavatomenergo) to the Central Committee (RGANI, f. 5, op. 40, d. 107, rolik 7213, l. 80–88). See also the correspondence between the secretary of the Leningrad Regional Party Committee (Obkom KPSS), comrade Rodionov, the Central Committee's Department of Mechanical Engineering, and the Ministry of Power Plants in November 1957, about the initial plans of the Ministry of Power Plants to build a nuclear power plant with VVERs (RGANI, f. 5, op. 40, d. 69, rolik 7205, l. 39–48).

Notes

89. In March 1958, Lavrenenko (Glavatomenergo) reported to the Central Committee on construction work at the Leningrad nuclear power plant (RGANI, f. 5, op. 40, d. 107, rolik 7213, l. 43–51).

90. December 1958 report from Lavrenenko (Glavatomenergo) to the Central Committee (RGANI, f. 5, op. 40, d. 107, rolik 7213, l. 80–88).

91. Ulasevich, *Sozdano pod rukovodstvom*, 34.

92. The site changed to Sosnovyi Bor (Interview #8 and personal communication). Aleksandrov and his deputy Savelii Feinberg from the Institute of Atomic Energy served as scientific directors, NII-8 (Dollezhal's institute, the later NIKIET) as the chief design engineer, and the Leningrad enterprise GSPI-11 (the later NIPIET) as the general project manager, with the participation of a series of other factories (Ulasevich, *Sozdano pod rukovodstvom*, 42). Apparently, Minenergo or some of its enterprises were still involved in the process until the start-up of the first unit in 1973: as late as January 1974, Pervukhin from Gosplan stated in a letter to the deputy chairman of the Council of Ministers, Veniamin Dymshits, that Minenergo had turned over all responsibilities for the Leningrad nuclear power plant to Sredmash (l. 51 in letter No. PP-17277 to V. E. Dymshits from M. Pervukhin, January 11, 1974 (RGAE, f. 4372, op. 66, d. 6042, l. 50–57)).

93. Leonid A. Belianin, ed. *Leningradskaia AES: Gody, sobytiia, liudi* (Moscow: Energoatomizdat, 1998). Additionally, the plant "survived" all subsequent reorganizations of the nuclear power industry as an independent entity under the aegis of Sredmash. When Sredmash was liquidated in 1989, and even when the Soviet Union disintegrated in 1991, the Leningrad plant's directors managed to keep some of its special status within the new administrative framework for the civilian nuclear sector and under the new nuclear authorities. The plant blocked Rosenergoatom, the newly created operating agency that was to coordinate the overall technological policy, to generalize operating experience, and to provide and develop the scientific, technological, and production support for nuclear power plant operation, from taking over the Leningrad plant's agendas (Sidorenko, "Upravlenie atomnoi energetikoi," 234). Sidorenko credits the direction of Anatolii Eperin with efforts to modernize and upgrade their reactor units, which resulted in performance parameters that surpassed those of other RBMK-equipped nuclear plants administered by Rosenergoatom (Sidorenko, "Upravlenie atomnoi energetikoi," 235). For the past and continuing problems of the Leningrad nuclear power plant, see Judith Perera, *The Nuclear Industry in the Former Soviet Union: Transition from Crisis to Opportunity*, 2 vols. (London: Financial Times Energy Publishing, 1997).

94. All of these reactors were prototypes of new designs: the first RBMK-1000 at Leningrad, the first RBMK-1500 at Ignalina, and the first fast neutron reactor at Shevchenko.

95. Ministerstvo Rossiiskoi Federatsii po atomnoi energii and Departament po atomnoi energetike, eds., *Shestnadtsatoe glavnoe: Istoriia i sovremennost'* (Moscow: Ministerstvo Rossiiskoi Federatsii po atomnoi energii, 2003). When Petrosyiants was appointed First Deputy Minister of Sredmash in 1967, the Chief Administration (GU IAE) was split into two Chief Administrations, GU-16 and GU-17. GU-17 was in charge of instruments for the nuclear industry (Glavatompribor) (Sidorenko, "Upravlenie atomnoi energetikoi," 220).

96. Among its powerful leaders were Nikolai Nikolaev (GU-16's first director) and Nikolai Ermakov. Little information is available on Ermakov, other than that he graduated from Moscow's Power Engineering Institute (MEI) and worked for Sredmash and later Minatom as a reactor specialist. Between the fall of 1986 and 2000, he served as head of GU-16, which by then had been reorganized from a Chief Administration into a Department. Other leaders include Boris Baturov (1968–1969), Aleksandr Meshkov (10/1969–3/1979, when he became deputy minister, and later first deputy minister), Evgenii Kulov (4/1979–3/1982, when he was appointed deputy minister), and Evgenii Kulikov (4/1982–6/1986) (Sidorenko, "Upravlenie atomnoi energetikoi," 220).

97. Sidorenko, "Upravlenie atomnoi energetikoi," 220–221.

98. Kapitsa's outspoken conflict with Beria, and Stalin's surprising tolerance of it, has been the subject of many historical analyses (Alexei B. Kojevnikov, "Piotr Kapitza and Stalin's Government: A Study in Moral Choice," *Historical Studies in the Physical and Biological Sciences* 22, no. 1 (1991): 131–164; Alexei B. Kojevnikov, *Stalin's Great Science: The Times and Adventures of Soviet Physicists* (London: Imperial College Press, 2004); Loren R. Graham, *Moscow Stories* (Bloomington: Indiana University Press, 2006)). Although Kapitsa lost his position as director, Stalin and Beria knew only too well that they needed Kapitsa's team of outstanding scientists for the success of the weapons program (see, e.g., Boris Gorobetz, "V treugol'nike Kapitsa-Beria-Stalin," *Mirovaia energiia/World Energy*, 2008, http://www.worldenergy.ru/doc_20_53_2819.html).

99. Movies were made about the first launch of the icebreaker *Lenin*, featuring Aleksandrov at the reactor control panel. Some are available in the motion picture collection of the National Archives and Records Administration (NARA) in College Park, MD (e.g., *The Atomic Flagship*, Record #326.036, and *Atomic Icebreaker*, Record #326.063). Submarine propulsion was a classified subject and therefore not discussed in public sources; in recent years, however, more information on the Soviet nuclear navy has been forthcoming—for example, in Ulasevich, *Sozdano pod rukovodstvom*; Ulasevich, *O iadernykh reaktorakh*; Mikhail P. Grabovskii, *Pervaia Sovetskaia atomnaia podvodnaia lodka K-3* (Moscow: Samizdat, 2005); and Vasilieva, *Soleils Rouges*. Together with Kurchatov, Aleksandrov is credited with the development of the Soviet pressurized water reactor (Kramish, *Atomic Energy in the Soviet Union*, 182).

Notes

100. His secret projects started during the Second World War (A. P. Aleksandrov, ed., *Vospominaniia ob Igore Vasil'eviche Kurchatove* (Moscow: Nauka, 1988); P. A. Aleksandrov, *Akademik Anatolii Petrovich Aleksandrov, priamaia rech'*, 2nd ed. (Moscow: Nauka, 2002); Nikolai S. Khlopkin, ed., *A. P. Aleksandrov: Dokumenty i vospominaniia. K 100-letiiu so dnia rozhdeniia* (Moscow: IzdAt, 2003)). Aleksandrov's personal record in the Archive of the Russian Academy of Sciences was released in 2003 (ARAN, f. 1916).

101. Decree No. 684–200, issued by the Council of Ministers on September 16, 1971, established the MVTS, the *Mezhvedomstvennyi Tekhnicheskii Sovet po atomnym elektrostantsiiam pri Ministerstve srednego mashinostroeniia SSSR* (Sidorenko, "Upravlenie atomnoi energetikoi," 237).

102. Among these ministries were Sredmash, Minenergo, the Ministry of Heavy Machine Building (Mintiazhmash), the Ministry of Power Engineering (Minenergomash), the Ministry of Chemical Machine Building (Minkhimmash), the Ministry of Electrotechnical Industry (Minelektrotekhprom), and the Ministry of Health (Minzdrav). Research organizations included, for example, IAE, FEI, NIIAR, VNII for Inorganic Materials, TsNII "Prometei," VTI im. F. E. Dzerzhinskogo, TsKTEI im. Polzunova, TsNIITMASh, and the Institute of Biophysics. Construction bureaus included, among others, OKB Mashinostroeniia, OKB Gidropress, and NIKIET. Industrial organizations included the Institute Teploelektroproekt, Atomenergoproekt, the Izhora works, the Podol'skii mashinostroitel'nyi zavod, the Khar'kovskii turbinnyi zavod, as well as others.

103. Sidorenko, "Upravlenie atomnoi energetikoi," 250. See also Interviews #8 and #21. At the apex of his power, Aleksandrov sometimes took the liberty of advising his colleagues in the MVTS—for example, minister Neporozhnii—on what to present when to which board (see for example ARAN, f. 1916, op. 1, d. 212, dated "not earlier than March 1981": Zamechaniia k proektu doklada Ministra energetiki i elektrifikatsii Neporozhnego P. S. O merakh po uluchsheniiu tekhniko-ekonomicheskikh pokazatelei, povysheniiu effektivnosti i snizheniiu stoimosti stroitel'stva atomnykh elektrostantsii.").

104. Sidorenko, "Upravlenie atomnoi energetikoi," 240–246. According to one interviewee, open discussion was possible in this assembly, although Aleksandrov tightly controlled the actual decision-making process (Interview #7).

105. Interview #4.

106. Sredmash's Scientific-Technical Council had begun reviewing the first version of the "General regulations to ensure the safety of nuclear power plants during design, construction, and operation" (*Obshchie polozheniia obespecheniia bezopasnosti atomnykh elektrostantsii pri proektirovanii, stroitel'stve i ekspluatatsii, OKB-73*) on February 20, 1971 (Sidorenko, "Upravlenie atomnoi energetikoi," 238).

107. This discussion had been referred to as the "V-230/V-213 problem": the V-230 design did not feature a steel containment structure but the V-213 did.

108. One important actor, who I do not discuss in detail, was Veniamin Dymshits, deputy chairman of the Council of Ministers from 1962 until his retirement in 1985, and chair of the State Committee for Supplies (Gossnab) from 1965 to 1976. In these positions, Dymshits coordinated the allocation of resources to enterprises, and oversaw the country's energy policy. He played an important role, though often behind the scenes, in the development of the Soviet nuclear industry (see, e.g., M. P. Alekseev, "Ob organizatsii nadzora za bezopasnost'iu v atomnoi energetike," in B. G. Gordon, ed., *Gosatomnadzoru Rossii—20 let*, 38–50 (Moscow: NTTs IaRB, 2003) (especially 43–44); Viktor A. Sidorenko, "Kak eto bylo," in B. G. Gordon, ed., *Gosatomnadzoru Rossii—20 let*, 51–61 (Moscow: NTTs IaRB, 2003) (especially 55); Alec Nove, *The Soviet Economy: An Introduction*, 2nd ed. (New York: Praeger, 1969) (especially 84, 221)).

109. Grigorii Medvedev, "Chernobyl'skaia Tetrad'," *Novyi Mir* 6 (1989): 3–108 (especially 36).

110. From 1989 until 1991, Kopchinskii directed the Department of Nuclear Energy in the Council of Ministers' Bureau of the Fuel and Energy Complex—yet another duplicate administrative unit, which provided some nuclear expertise directly to the Council of Ministers (see Georgii A. Kopchinskii and Nikolai A. Shteinberg, *Chernobyl: Kak eto bylo. Preduprezhdenie* (Moscow: Litterra, 2011)).

111. Vladimir V. Mar'in, "O deiatel'nosti operativnoi gruppy Politburo TsK KPSS na Chernobyl'skoi AES," in A. N. Semenov, ed., *Chernobyl' desiat' let spustia: Neizbezhnost' ili sluchainost'?*, 263–282 (Moscow: Energoatomizdat, 1995) (especially 264).

112. The tasks of Gosplan's Department of Energy and Electrification were updated on October 15, 1969 (RGAE, f. 4372, op. 66, d. 2900, l. 72–77).

113. Letter No. 22–828, "On the construction of nuclear power plants," to V. Isaev (chairman of Gosplan), from A. Nekrasov (Department of Energy and Electrification), August 28, 1974 (RGAE, f. 4372, op. 66, d. 6648, l. 108–109).

114. This thirty-page draft document of "Temporary occupational health and safety requirements for the design of nuclear power plants" ("Vremennye sanitarnye trebovaniia k proektirovaniiu atomnykh elektrostantsii: Proekt"; RGAE, f. 9599, op. 1, d. 9, l. 42–72) was apparently sent to Pozdniakov, a representative of the Chief Administration for the Use of Atomic Energy (under the Council of Ministers) by Glavatomenergo's chief engineer Ermakov (RGAE, f. 9599, op. 1, d. 9, l. 78) and commented on by Teploelektroproekt (RGAE, f. 9599, op. 1, d. 9, l. 73–77; RGAE, f. 9599, op. 1, d. 9, l. 73–77), together with a three-page letter written with knowledge of this commentary from Glavatomenergo (RGAE, f. 9599, op. 1, d. 9, l. 79–81; RGAE, f. 9599, op. 1, d. 9, l. 79–81).

115. Letter No. ES-579, September 28, 1966 (RGAE, f. 4372, op. 66, d. 910, l. 280–282).

116. Viktor A. Sidorenko, "Nuclear Power in the Soviet Union and in Russia," *Nuclear Engineering and Design* 173 (1997): 3–20 (especially 7).

117. Department of Physical and Technical Problems of Power Engineering, Soviet Academy of Sciences (RGAE, f. 4372, op. 66, d. 4704, l. 164–165). Harmonization with international nuclear regulation was further accelerated by the Soviet-led construction of the Finnish nuclear plant at Loviisa, where the Finnish government held Soviet contractors accountable to Western safety standards (Sidorenko, "Kak eto bylo," 52–53).

118. N. I. Kozlov et al., *Pravila iadernoi bezopasnosti atomnykh elektrostantsii PBIa-04-74*, 2nd ed. (Moscow: Atomizdat 1977); Viktor A. Sidorenko, "Problemy bezopasnosti atomnoi energetiki," in Viktor A. Sidorenko, ed., *Istoriia atomnoi energetiki Sovetskogo Soiuza i Rossii*, vol. 1, 194–216 (Moscow: IzdAt, 2001) (especially 196); Sidorenko, "Kak eto bylo," 53. The original document, OPB-71, was restricted to internal use (see, e.g., A. M. Bukrinskii, "Neizvestnye stranitsy iz istorii sozdaniia Gosatomnadzora Rossii," in B. G. Gordon, ed., *Gosatomnadzoru Rossii—20 let*, 102–110 (Moscow: NTTs IaRB, 2003) (especially 103)).

119. Alekseev, "Ob organizatsii nadzora," 38.

120. Viktor A. Sidorenko, "Ob"iasnitel'naia zapiska Sidorenko V. A. v komitet partiinogo kontrolia pri TsK KPSS," in Viktor A. Sidorenko, ed., *Istoriia atomnoi energetiki Sovetskogo Soiuza i Rossii: Uroki avarii na Chernobyl'skoi AES*, vol. 4, 44–47 (Moscow: IzdAt, 2002) (especially 46). See also Viktor A. Sidorenko, "Nauchnoe rukovodstvo v atomnoi energetike," in Viktor A. Sidorenko, ed., *Istoriia atomnoi energetiki Sovetskogo Soiuza i Rossii: Istoriia VVER*, vol. 2, 5–28 (Moscow: IzdAt, 2002) (especially 11); Sidorenko, "Kak eto bylo," 54.

121. Bukrinskii, "Neizvestnye stranitsy iz istorii sozdaniia Gosatomnadzora Rossii," 105.

122. This new committee, which initially received 185 approved positions (and had great difficulty filling them), merged Gosgortekhnadzor's nuclear safety division with two nuclear safety divisions formerly under Sredmash. According to Alekseev, deputy chairman of Gosatomenergonadzor from 1983 to 1987, decree No. 653-207, "On the creation of an All-Union Soviet State Committee for Oversight of the safe conduct of work in the nuclear power industry," was the direct outcome of a Central Committee meeting on the country's future energy policy, especially nuclear energy, which involved a number of high-ranking political functionaries (Alekseev, "Ob organizatsii nadzora," 43–44, 46).

123. V. M. Malyshev, "Istoriia stanovleniia gosudarstvennogo nadzora za bezopasnost'iu atomnoi energetiki SSSR (1983–1991 gg.)," in B. G. Gordon, ed., *Gosatomnadzoru Rossii—20 let*, 26–37 (Moscow: NTTs IaRB, 2003) (especially 26).

124. Ibid., 27.

125. O. M. Kovalevich, "Ob obrazovanii Gosatomenergonadzora SSSR," in B. G. Gordon, ed., *Gosatomnadzoru Rossii—20 let*, 69–78 (Moscow: NTTs IaRB, 2003) (especially 70).

126. A. V. Ageev, "Vospominaniia," in B. G. Gordon, ed., *Gosatomnadzoru Rossii—20 let*, 89–101 (Moscow: NTTs IaRB, 2003) (especially 93–94). Ageev also notes that the centralized, "total" oversight was lost in this process. Instead, "we understood that with the transition to regulatory principles we had to . . . transition to periodic, selective inspections" (ibid., 94). Also see Kovalevich, "Ob obrazovanii Gosatomenergonadzora SSSR," 69; Bukrinskii, "Neizvestnye stranitsy iz istorii sozdaniia Gosatomnadzora Rossii," 129.

127. Sidorenko, "Upravlenie atomnoi energetikoi," 228–229. This division was realized to different degrees in Western countries (France, Canada, Britain, and the United States). See, for example, Dorothy Nelkin and Michael Pollak, *The Atom Besieged: Extraparliamentary Dissent in France and Germany* (Cambridge, MA: MIT Press, 1981); Ferdinand Henry Kim Krenz, *Deep Waters: The Ottawa River and Canada's Nuclear Adventure* (Montreal: McGill–Queen's University Press, 2004); Rebecca S. Lowen, "Entering the Atomic Power Race: Science, Industry, and Government," *Political Science Quarterly* 102, no. 3 (1987): 459–479; J. Samuel Walker, *A Short History of Nuclear Regulation, 1946–1990* (Washington, DC: U.S. Nuclear Regulatory Commission, 1993). There was some state involvement in all these nuclear programs, but private industry took on an independent role and not always a very supportive one (see Lowen, "Entering the Atomic Power Race: Science, Industry, and Government").

128. Sidorenko, "Problemy bezopasnosti atomnoi energetiki," 196.

129. It is important to note, however, that 1966 marks only the official date of this transfer. Preparations for Minenergo to take over the operation of nuclear plants had been going on since the mid-1950s, both in terms of preparing personnel and in terms of siting and significant construction activity.

130. The Beloiarsk nuclear plant, where two prototypical reactors operated, as well as all sites operating new VVERs, were not subject to Sredmash's direct oversight. As we will see in chapter 4, proliferation concerns may have played a role in determining which reactor stayed under Sredmash's aegis, but there was no consistent rationale behind which reactor types or generations needed "extra" attention and which ones didn't.

131. For example, Interviews #3, #4, #8, #27. This assessment echoes some of the discussion surrounding "Normal Accidents" and "High Reliability Organizations" (Charles Perrow, *Normal Accidents: Living with High-Risk Technologies*, 2nd ed. (Princeton, NJ: Princeton University Press, 1999); Todd R. LaPorte and Paula M. Consolini, "Working in Practice but Not in Theory: Theoretical Challenges of 'High-Reliability Organizations,'" *Journal of Public Administration Research and Theory* 1, no. 1 (1991):

19–48; Karlene H. Roberts, "Some Characteristics of One Type of High Reliability Organization," *Organization Science* 1, no. 2 (1990): 160–176; Karl E. Weick, "Organizational Culture as a Source of High Reliability," *California Management Review* 29, no. 2 (1987): 112–127).

132. Sidorenko, "Nuclear Power in the Soviet Union and in Russia," 7.

133. Sidorenko, "Upravlenie atomnoi energetikoi," 224–225.

134. The concept of "safety culture" gained currency after the Chernobyl accident. The notion encompasses the design and operation of a plant, and also its management (Sidorenko, *Istoriia atomnoi energetiki Sovetskogo Soiuza i Rossii: Uroki avarii na Chernobyl'skoi AES*, vol. 4, 11).

135. Sidorenko, "Upravlenie atomnoi energetikoi," 225.

136. Dubovskii's quote is from Vladimir Anisinov, "AES: Stepen' riska (beseda s B. G. Dubovskim)," *Smena* 10 (1994): 55–61, on 58. The second quote ("Za kazhdim operatorom soldat s avtomatom ne postavish'") is from Interview #27.

137. Sidorenko, "Upravlenie atomnoi energetikoi," 225.

138. Most prominently, economic efficiency clashed with safety considerations (Ulasevich, *Sozdano pod rukovodstvom*; Fain, *Aktivnaia zona*, 108–130). Unfortunately, this kind of specific information does not appear in accessible managerial documents (but was likely discussed at the meetings of the MVTS, for example). Diane Vaughan talks about these competing imperatives guiding the American space program. The dilemma between tight schedules and how-safe-is-safe-enough can probably be considered a fundamental problem in engineering in general (Diane Vaughan, *The Challenger Launch Decision: Risky Technology, Culture, and Deviance at NASA* (Chicago: University of Chicago Press, 1996)).

139. In a way, the Soviet nuclear power industry was therefore an "experiment" that used society as a "laboratory" for identifying acceptable risk (W. Krohn and J. Weyer, "Society as a Laboratory: The Social Risks of Experimental Research," *Science & Public Policy* 21, no. 3 (1994): 173–183).

140. Bailes, *Technology and Society under Lenin and Stalin*; Jeffrey Brooks, *Thank You, Comrade Stalin! Soviet Public Culture from Revolution to Cold War* (Princeton, NJ: Princeton University Press, 2000); Vaughan, *The Challenger Launch Decision*. See also Joseph R. Gusfield, *The Culture of Public Problems: Drinking-Driving and the Symbolic Order* (Chicago: University of Chicago Press, 1981); Thomas F. Gieryn and Anne E. Figert, "Ingredients for a Theory of Science in Society: O-Rings, Ice Water, C-Clamp, Richard Feynman, and the Press," in Susan E. Cozzens and Thomas F. Gieryn, eds., *Theories of Science in Society*, 67-97 (Bloomington: Indiana University Press, 1990); Sheila Jasanoff, ed., *Learning from Disaster: Risk Management after Bhopal* (Philadelphia: University of Pennsylvania Press, 1994); Asa Boholm, "The Cultural Nature of Risk: Can There Be an Anthropology of Uncertainty?," *Ethnos* 68, no. 2 (2003): 159–

178; Brian Wynne, *Rationality and Ritual: Participation and Exclusion in Nuclear Decision-Making* (New York: Earthscan, 2011).

141. In Balzer's words, they were "leaders with special traits—political acumen, blue-collar credentials, and superb networks" (Harley D. Balzer, "Engineers: The Rise and Decline of a Social Myth," in Loren R. Graham, ed., *Science and the Soviet Social Order*, 141–167 (Cambridge, MA: Harvard University Press, 1990) (quote on 153)).

142. Nove, *The Soviet Economy*.

143. James C. Scott, *Seeing Like a State: How Certain Schemes to Improve the Human Conditio Have Failed* (New Haven, CT: Yale University Press, 1998); Theodore M. Porter, *Trust in Numbers: The Pursuit of Objectivity in Science and Public Life*, 2nd ed. (Princeton, NJ: Princeton University Press, 1995).

144. Gosplan, Upravlenie delami (Administrative Department), "Doklad o general'noi scheme energeticheskikh system SSSR na period do 1980 goda," 1971 (RGAE, f. 4372, op. 66, d. 4387, l. 124). Also see Interview #25.

145. Their public representation stressed the peacefulness of nuclear power (in contrast to the American aggressors), and its contribution to the general electrification of the country (which was marketed as the basis for the developing national economy). See Sonja D. Schmid, "Shaping the Soviet Experience of the Atomic Age: Nuclear Topics in Ogonyok, 1945–1965," in Dick van Lente, ed., *The Nuclear Age in Popular Media: A Transnational History, 1945–1965*, 19–52 (New York: Palgrave Macmillan, 2012); Paul R. Josephson, "Rockets, Reactors and Soviet Culture," in Loren Graham, ed., *Science and the Soviet Social Order*, 168–191 (Cambridge, MA: Harvard University Press, 1990); Paul R. Josephson, "Atomic-Powered Communism: Nuclear Culture in the Postwar USSR," *Slavic Review* 55, no. 2 (1996): 297–324; K. Polushkin, "Atomnyi bogatyr'," *Nauka i zhizn'* 11 (1980): 44–52; V. S. Emel'ianov, "Atomnaia nauka i tekhnika i stroitel'stvo kommunizma," *Atomnaia energiia* 11, no. 4 (1961): 301–312; Neporozhnii, *Energetika strany glazami ministra*.

Chapter 3

1. The power plants not transferred to Minenergo were all prototypes of new designs: the first RBMK-1000 at Leningrad (start-up in 1973), the first RBMK-1500 at Ignalina (Lithuania, start-up in 1983), and the first fast breeder reactor at Shevchenko (Kazakhstan, start-up in 1973). I was not able to see the actual document authorizing the transfer.

2. The vast literature on "human factors," informed primarily by psychology, tries to capture and formalize the elements of this tacit expertise, and to find ways to convey that which cannot be formalized in sophisticated types of peer-to-peer training. See, for example, Jyuji Misumi, Bernhard Wilpert, and Rainer Miller, *Nuclear Safety: A Human Factors Perspective* (London: Taylor & Francis, 1999); Kim J. Vicente,

The Human Factor: Revolutionizing the Way People Live with Technology (New York: Routledge, 2004).

3. Nikolai Krementsov has characterized this emphasis on institutional structures, rather than on individual biographies, as a consequence of the Second World War, which profoundly affected "the structural and functional dynamics of the Stalinist science system" (Nikolai L. Krementsov, *Stalinist Science* (Princeton, NJ: Princeton University Press, 1997), 288–289; see also Ethan Pollock, *Stalin and the Soviet Science Wars* (Princeton, NJ: Princeton University Press, 2006)). At the core of these changes was the emergence of interest groups within the Soviet scientific community (and, by extension, within the technical intelligentsia) that knew how to work the system and that knew how to use shifts in political authority and industrial policy to their advantage. These changes were retained throughout, and reinforced by, the Cold War.

4. See the following works by Thomas P. Hughes: *Networks of Power: Electrification in Western Society, 1880–1930* (Baltimore: Johns Hopkins University Press, 1983); *American Genesis: A Century of Invention and Technological Enthusiasm, 1870–1970* (New York: Viking, 1989); *Rescuing Prometheus: Four Monumental Projects That Changed the Modern World* (New York: Pantheon Books, 1998).

5. International Nuclear Safety Advisory Group, *Summary Report on the Post-Accident Review Meeting on the Chernobyl Accident*, No. 75-INSAG-1, Safety Series (Vienna: International Atomic Energy Agency, 1986).

6. Several of my interviewees proudly emphasized that Soviet nuclear specialists in general were highly qualified, and that the percentage of nuclear industry cadres with higher education degrees was higher in the Soviet Union than in the United States (e.g., Interviews #1 and #16; see also Sonja D. Schmid, "When Safe Enough Is Not Good Enough: Organizing Safety at Chernobyl," *Bulletin of the Atomic Scientists* 67, no. 2 l (2011): 19–29).

7. Examples include K. E. Baskin, L. P. Drach, and A. I. Glushchenko, *Eshche mozhno spasti! Edinaia elektroenergeticheskaia sistema—bazis ekonomiki Rossii: Uroki Chernobylia. Opasnost' iadernogo terrorizma* (Moscow: Fizmatlit, 2006); Anatolii S. Diatlov, *Chernobyl': Kak eto bylo* (Moscow: Nauchtekhlitizdat, 2003). For documentation of cynicism in the Soviet Youth League (Komsomol), see Steven Lee Solnick, *Stealing the State: Control and Collapse in Soviet Institutions* (Cambridge, MA: Harvard University Press, 1998). The moral problem of taking part in the industry that developed nuclear weapons was countered by the necessity of creating a "shield" for the fatherland and of ensuring nuclear parity.

8. David Holloway, *Stalin and the Bomb: The Soviet Union and Atomic Energy 1939–1956* (New Haven, CT: Yale University Press, 1994).

9. For example, Raisa V. Kuznetsova, ed., *Kurchatov v zhizni: Pis'ma, dokumenty, vospominaniia (iz lichnogo arkhiva)* (Moscow: Mosgorarkhiv, 2002); Nikolai A. Dolle-

zhal', *U istokov rukotvornogo mira: Zapiski konstruktora* (Moscow: GUP NIKIET, IzdAt, 2002); Boris A. Fain, *Aktivnaia zona: Povest' ob atomnom institute* (Moscow: Skripto, 1998); V. K. Ulasevich, ed., *Sozdano pod rukovodstvom N. A. Dollezhalia: O iadernykh reaktorakh i ikh tvortsakh (k 100-letiiu N. A. Dollezhalia)*, 2nd ed. (Moscow: GUP NIKIET, 2002); V. K. Ulasevich, ed., *O iadernykh reaktorakh i ikh tvortsakh: Prodolzhenie traditsii (k 50-letiiu NIKIET im. N. A. Dollzhalia* (Moscow: GUP NIKIET, 2002); Vitalii P. Nasonov, *E. P. Slavskii: Stranitsy zhizni* (Moscow: IzdAT, 1998); Igor' A. Beliaev and German G. Malkin, eds., *E. P. Slavskii: 100 let so dnia rozhdeniia* (Moscow: IzdAt, 1999); A. P. Aleksandrov, ed., *Vospominaniia ob Igore Vasil'eviche Kurchatove* (Moscow: Nauka, 1988); P. A. Aleksandrov, *Akademik Anatolii Petrovich Aleksandrov, priamaia rech'*, 2nd ed. (Moscow: Nauka, 2002); Nikolai S. Khlopkin, *Stranitsy zhizni* (Moscow: IzdAt, 2003); Nikolai S. Khlopkin, ed., *A. P. Aleksandrov: Dokumenty i vospominaniia: K 100-letiiu so dnia rozhdeniia* (Moscow: IzdAt, 2003).

10. Harley D. Balzer, ed., *Russia's Missing Middle Class: The Professions in Russian History* (Armonk, NY: Sharpe, 1996); Harley D. Balzer, "Engineers: The Rise and Decline of a Social Myth," in Loren R. Graham, ed., *Science and the Soviet Social Order*, 141–167 (Cambridge, MA: Harvard University Press, 1990) (especially 141); Sheila Fitzpatrick, *Education and Social Mobility in the Soviet Union, 1921–1934* (Cambridge: Cambridge University Press, 1979). Engineers became one of the most influential political groups in the Soviet Union (Loren R. Graham, *Science in Russia and the Soviet Union: A Short History* (Cambridge: Cambridge University Press, 1993), 73). In the 1960s, physicists were another group with an extremely positive self-image, who enjoyed correspondingly high social prestige (Petr Wail' and Aleksandr Genis, *60-e: Mir Sovetskogo cheloveka* (Moscow: Novoe literaturnoe obozrenie, 1996)). In an interview with A. I. Mikoian, Victor Perlo notes "the extremely rapid rise in the number and quality of trained scientific-technical personnel, and the lead which the USSR has established over all other countries in the extent of scientific-engineering education" (Victor Perlo, *How the Soviet Economy Works: An Interview with A. I. Mikoyan, First Deputy Minister of the U.S.S.R.* (New York: International Publishers, 1961), 28).

11. Arkadii K. Kruglov, *Kak sozdavalas' atomnaia promyshlennost' v SSSR* (Moscow: TSNIIatominform, 1995); *Shtab atomproma* (Moscow: TSNIIatominform, 1998).

12. Dollezhal was drawn into the atomic bomb project by Kurchatov in 1946 (Holloway, *Stalin and the Bomb*, 183). In 1952, Dollezhal's construction bureau was expanded to form a new institute, NII-8 (later NIKIET), with him as the director.

13. One major influence was the NKVD, which stands for Narodnyi komissariat vnutrennikh del, "People's Commissariat for Internal Affairs."

14. Jokes about radiation's preservative effects abounded among my Sredmash interviewees, mostly men, who without exception were well above the average age of their compatriots.

Notes

15. Sredmash employees who led "regular" lives typically lived in big cities, where they followed the standard model of commuting between separate places for work and residence. Life in closed Soviet cities, by contrast, merged professional and residential life in a way similar to what Janowitz describes for U.S. army bases (Morris Janowitz, *The Professional Soldier* (Glencoe, IL: Free Press, 1960), 175–176; see also Sharon K. Weiner, *Our Own Worst Enemy? Institutional Interests and the Proliferation of Nuclear Weapons Expertise* (Cambridge, MA: MIT Press, 2011)).

16. Fitzpatrick, *Education and Social Mobility*, 183–184; Michael David-Fox, "What Is Cultural Revolution?," *Russian Review* 58 (April 1999): 181–201.

17. Balzer, "Engineers," 141.

18. Graham, *Short History*, 164; see also Viktor A. Sidorenko, *Ob atomnoi energetike, atomnykh stantsiiakh, uchiteliakh, kollegakh i o sebe* (Moscow: IzdAt, 2003).

19. Sidorenko, *Ob atomnoi energetike*, especially 232–256.

20. Among those who received training at the Obninsk plant were military nuclear submarine crews. When the framework of this training was first discussed late in 1954, the director of the Obninsk plant, Nikolai Nikolaev, suggested a one-year placement for mastering the operation of a nuclear reactor. The military officers settled for a three-month training program, after which the officers had to pass an exam that would certify them to operate a nuclear reactor on their own (Fain, *Aktivnaia zona*, 39–40).

21. Interview #5.

22. Interview #7.

23. On the vicious cycle of ineffectiveness in the system of raspredelenie see Solnick, *Stealing the State*, 125–174.

24. By the time the first industrial-scale nuclear power plants were started up in 1964, the first generation of nuclear engineers had been trained successfully (Aleksandr N. Semenov and A. B. Chubais, eds., *Elektroenergetika. Stroiteli Rossii: XX vek* (Moscow: Master, 2003), 760–768). Also see Interviews #3 and #9. And yet as late as 1968, there were still not enough engineers who also had expertise in industrial planning. The first graduates of such training programs were not expected until 1972 (RGAE, f. 7964, op. 15, d. 64, l. 89).

25. For an elaboration of "honor" as the basis of the belief system in the U.S. Army, see Janowitz, *The Professional Soldier*, 215. Janowitz also notes that political ideology (in the sense of strong political alliances) was common only in higher tiers.

26. For a succinct explanation of the system of nomenklatura see Krementsov, *Stalinist Science*. Initially "devised for the personnel of party organs and agencies, the

system was expanded in the early 1930s into the scientific community" (Krementsov, *Stalinist Science*, 40). See also Interview #25.

27. Alec Nove, *The Soviet Economy: An Introduction*, 2nd ed. (New York: Praeger, 1969), 108–109.

28. The record in the weapons program and Sredmash is mixed: while some specialists were "deselected" based on political criteria, at other times ideological loyalty could take a backseat if the technical expertise in question was critical enough (Paul R. Josephson, *Physics and Politics in Revolutionary Russia*, California Studies in the History of Science (Berkeley: University of California Press, 1991); Karl Hall, "The Schooling of Lev Landau: The European Context of Postrevolutionary Soviet Theoretical Physics," *Osiris* 23 (2008): 230–259; Loren R. Graham, *Science and Philosophy in the Soviet Union* (New York: Knopf, 1972); Loren R. Graham, *Between Science and Values* (New York: Columbia University Press, 1981); Loren R. Graham, *The Ghost of the Executed Engineer: Technology and the Fall of the Soviet Union* (Cambridge, MA: Harvard University Press, 1993); Kate Brown, *Plutopia: Nuclear Families, Atomic Cities, and the Great Soviet and American Plutonium Disasters* (New York: Oxford University Press, 2013)).

29. Valerie Bunce, *Subversive Institutions: The Design and the Destruction of Socialism and the State* (Cambridge: Cambridge University Press, 1999), 23.

30. The nomenklatura system kicked into high gear, for example, when Minenergo's operating organization, Soiuzatomenergo, nominated Vladimir Bronnikov as chief engineer at the Chernobyl nuclear power plant. The Ukrainian Party committee blocked Bronnikov's promotion "for their own reasons" (*po svoim kriteriiam*) (Gennadii A. Shasharin, "Chernobyl'skaia tragediia," in Aleksandr N. Semenov, ed., *Chernobyl' desiat' let spustia: Neizbezhnost' ili sluchainost'?*, 75–132 (Moscow: Energoatomizdat, 1995)). See also chapter 5.

31. Viktor A. Sidorenko, "Upravlenie atomnoi energetikoi," in Viktor A. Sidorenko, ed., *Istoriia atomnoi energetiki Sovetskogo Soiuza i Rossii*, vol. 1, 217–253 (Moscow: IzdAt, 2001) (especially 219).

32. One often used example is learning how to ride a bicycle, but tacit knowledge has also proven highly relevant in scientific experiments: the replication of a particular research experiment may depend not only on the correct setup and procedure, but on the tacit skills of one of the lab workers (Harry Collins, "What Is Tacit Knowledge?," in Theodore R. Schatzki, Karin Knorr-Cetina, and Eike von Savigny, eds., *The Practice Turn in Contemporary Theory*, 107–119 (New York: Routledge, 2001); Michael Polanyi, *Personal Knowledge: Toward a Post-Critical Philosophy* (Chicago: University of Chicago Press, 1958); Michael Polanyi, *The Tacit Dimension* (Gloucester, MA: P. Smith, [1966] 1983); Jeremy Howells, "Tacit Knowledge, Innovation, and Technology Transfer," *Technology Analysis & Strategic Management* 8, no. 2 (1996): 91–106; Alice Lam, "Tacit Knowledge, Organizational Learning and Societal Institutions: An

Integrated Framework," *Organization Studies* 21, no. 3 (2000): 487–513; Joy Parr, *Sensing Changes: Technologies, Environments, and the Everyday* (Vancouver, BC: UBC Press, 2010); Joy Parr, "A Working Knowledge of the Insensible? Radiation Protection in Nuclear Generating Stations, 1962–1992," *Comparative Studies in Society and History* 48, no. 4 (2006): 820–851; Harry Collins and Robert Evans, "The Third Wave of Science Studies: Studies of Expertise and Experience," *Social Studies of Science* 32, no. 2 (2002): 235–296; Harry Collins, *Tacit and Explicit Knowledge* (Chicago: University of Chicago Press, 2010)).

33. At least since Chernobyl, the international nuclear community has recognized the training of nuclear cadres as a major issue, and also that an aging workforce poses serious problems in terms of knowledge transfer (e.g., C. R. Clark et al., "Achieving Excellence in Human Performance in the Nuclear Industry through Leadership, Education, and Training (IAEA-CN-114/F-8)," in IAEA, ed., *Fifty Years of Nuclear Power—the Next Fifty Years*, Proceedings of an international conference held in Moscow and Obninsk, June 27–July 2, 2004, Conference Material IAEA-CN-114 (Vienna: International Atomic Energy Agency, 2004); see also the IAEA's emphasis on "safety culture" and the development of related training modules).

34. "Godovoi otchet Glavatomenergo po kapvlozheniiam za 1957 god," RGAE, f. 7964, op. 3, d. 1881, l. 11.

35. The final, fifth edition, appeared in 1994, months after the author passed away. Margulova had tried to revise the textbook in light of the Chernobyl experience (Tereza Khristoforovna Margulova, *Atomnye elektricheskie stantsii*, 5th ed. (Moscow: IzdAT, 1994)).

36. "Godovoi otchet Glavatomenergo po kapvlozheniiam za 1957 god," RGAE, f. 7964, op. 3, d. 1881, l. 12.

37. As of January 1, 1958, there were ninety-four students enrolled ("Godovoi otchet Glavatomenergo," 1957 (RGAE, f. 7964, op. 3, d. 1881)).

38. RGAE, f. 7964, op. 3, d. 1881, l. 12.

39. Interview #9. However, one interviewee recalled that what such a "praktikum" often meant was that the student would be led into the main control room, and then told to sit down and not touch anything (Interview #25).

40. RGAE, f. 7964, op. 3, d. 1881, l. 13. This corresponds to what other nuclear specialists have described: they went through several positions, getting to know the nuts and bolts of a given reactor, and gradually worked their way up the professional hierarchy (Mikhail P. Grabovskii, *Vtoroi Ivan: Sovershenno sekretno* (Moscow: Nauchnaia kniga, 1998); Sidorenko, *Ob atomnoi energetike*).

41. Interviews #3 and #9.

42. Sredmash specialists and recently discharged navy personnel from nuclear submarines brought experience with reactor operation and maintenance, whereas Minenergo specialists contributed the experience of operating complex industrial facilities (Interview #7). The Soviet nuclear navy's influence in the nuclear industry came up rarely in written sources or interviews; while there clearly was some connection, the Soviet Navy's ties to the nuclear industry were not nearly as significant as those in the United States.

43. Interview #7.

44. Tereza Margulova was instrumental in developing curricula and setting up nuclear power engineering departments at established technical universities all over the country—for example, at the Urals Polytechnic Institute in Sverdlovsk (today Ural Federal University), at the Tomsk Polytechnic Institute (today Tomsk National Research Polytechnic University), and in Obninsk (a branch of MEI).

45. This mutual distrust between ministries or people's commissariats has a long tradition; see, for example, Balzer, "Engineers," 152.

46. Viktor A. Sidorenko, "Vvedenie k 1-mu vypusku," in Viktor A. Sidorenko, ed., *Istoriia atomnoi energetiki Sovetskogo Soiuza i Rossii*, vol. 1, 5–15 (Moscow: IzdAt, 2001) (especially 6); Viktor A. Sidorenko, "Nuclear Power in the Soviet Union and in Russia," *Nuclear Engineering and Design* 173 (1997): 3–20 (especially 5).

47. Full-scale, sophisticated simulators for the Soviet nuclear navy (*Voenno-morskoi flot*) were designed and built as early as 1967, according to S. D. Malkin, one of the country's leading developers of reactor simulators. By contrast, the authorities did not acknowledge the need for similarly sophisticated and expensive simulators for nuclear power reactors until Chernobyl (S. D. Malkin, "O polnomasshtabnom trenazhere dlia Leningradskoi AES," in Viktor A. Sidorenko, ed., *Istoriia atomnoi energetiki Sovetskogo Soiuza i Rossii: Istoriia RBMK*, vol. 3, 147–155 (Moscow: IzdAt, 2003)). Apparently there were smaller-scale simulators that started operating in the late 1970s at the Novo-Voronezh plant (for VVERs), and just before Chernobyl for RBMKs (Interview #7).

A Central Scientific Research Institute (TsNII) had been set up at the Novo-Voronezh nuclear power plant that was specifically involved with starting up VVERs. Glavatomenergo acknowledged this institute's contribution to the training of operating personnel, assistance with the launch preparation, and the actual start-up (order No. 12 issued by Glavatomenergo on July 23, 1973 (RGAE, f. 7964, op. 15, d. 6792, l. 23–24): five employees of the Novo-Voronezh nuclear power plant were presented with financial awards (100–250 rubles)). Similarly, although apparently less formally, staff at the Beloiarsk nuclear plant helped train operating personnel for RBMKs (RGAE, f. 7964, op. 15, d. 7918, l. 9), until much later, especially after Chernobyl, when RBMK operators received training at the Smolensk nuclear plant.

48. For a fascinating account of such a "collegial model of workplace relations" see Joy Parr, "A Working Knowledge of the Insensible?" Perin's *Shouldering Risks* provides an anthropology of the U.S. nuclear power industry, and stresses the importance of protocols encouraging "doubt, discovery, and interpretation" rather than "command and control" for work in nuclear power plants (Constance Perin, *Shouldering Risks: The Culture of Control in the Nuclear Power Industry* (Princeton, NJ: Princeton University Press, 2005)).

49. This was not unusual in the Soviet economy as a whole: as Nove put it, "There exists an informal network of personal links and contacts, which plays an essential role in overcoming a variety of obstacles" (Nove, *The Soviet Economy*, 227).

50. This stands in stark contrast to the findings of studies on risk taking in contemporary organizations, where shirking attribution and liability sometimes produces a spiraling avoidance of any kind of risk, which in turn produces risk of risk avoidance (see, e.g., Henry Rothstein, Michael Huber, and George Gaskell, "A Theory of Risk Colonization: The Spiralling Regulatory Logics of Societal and Institutional Risk," *Economy and Society* 35, no. 1 (2006): 91–112).

51. Institution of Mechanical Engineers, *Symposium on the Education and Training of Engineers in the Nuclear Industry: A Symposium Arranged by the Nuclear Energy and the Education and Training Groups, 5th December 1968, London* (London: Institution of Mechanical Engineers, 1969); John Krige, "The Peaceful Atom as Political Weapon: Euratom and American Foreign Policy in the Late 1950s," *Historical Studies in the Natural Sciences* 38, no. 1 (2008): 5–44.

52. Perepiska s Gosplanom SSSR o perspektivnom i tekushchem planirovanii v energetike, 3.I.1968–27.XII.1968 (RGAE, f. 7964, op. 15, d. 64, l. 78).

53. RGAE, f. 7964, op. 15, d. 64, l. 80.

54. RGAE, f. 9480, op. 9, d. 2403, l. 74.

55. Letter from Petr S. Neporozhnii to deputy chairman of the Council of Ministers, M. T. Efremov, July 16, 1970, No. ES-671 (RGAE, f. 7964, op. 15, d. 3924, l. 12).

56. RGAE, f. 7964, op. 15, d. 6803, l. 26–27. Sites under Sredmash's tutelage seem to have suffered less from these limitations; the ministry clearly had more discretionary funds on hand.

57. Discrimination, both positive and negative, toward certain groups was common, openly as well as covertly. On the Soviet system of higher education see, for example, Harley D. Balzer, *Russian Higher Education* (Washington, DC: National Council for Soviet and East European Research, 1993); Michael David-Fox, *Revolution of the Mind: Higher Learning among the Bolsheviks, 1918–1929* (Ithaca, NY: Cornell University Press, 1997); Michael David-Fox and György Péteri, eds., *Academia in Upheaval: Origins, Transfers, and Transformations of the Communist Academic Regime in Russia and East Central Europe* (Westport, CT: Bergin & Garvey, 2000); Boris N. Onykiy and

Eduard F. Kryuchkov, "Nuclear Education in Russia: Status, Peculiarities, Problems and Perspectives," *International Journal of Nuclear Knowledge Management* 1, no. 4 (2005): 308–316; Lewis H. Siegelbaum and Ronald G. Suny, eds., *Making Workers Soviet: Power, Class, and Identity* (Ithaca, NY: Cornell University Press, 1994).

58. See Sonja D. Schmid, "Shaping the Soviet Experience of the Atomic Age: Nuclear Topics in Ogonyok, 1945–1965," in Dick van Lente, ed., *The Nuclear Age in Popular Media: A Transnational History, 1945–1965*, 19–52 (New York: Palgrave Macmillan, 2012).

59. This corresponds to Nikolai Krementsov's argument that ideology played a subordinate role in concrete science-policy decision making even in the 1930s and the 1940s (Krementsov, *Stalinist Science*, 288–289). All of my interviewees were reluctant to relate their career choices and their interest in nuclear power to what they perceived as "political" ideas, as most popular-scientific literature on the subject might make us believe. This reaction may have been an artifact of my asking directly for this connection, and therefore an example of what Gilbert and Mulkay have called "discursive repertoires," and more specifically, the "empirical repertoire" (G. Nigel Gilbert and Michael Mulkay, *Opening Pandora's Box: A Sociological Analysis of Scientists' Discourse* (Cambridge: Cambridge University Press, 1984)). This device, according to Gilbert and Mulkay, is used to organize rational reconstructions of a scientist's own (correct) position, while the "contingent repertoire" is used to account for error—in my case, this would most likely be a belief that nuclear power would bring about communism. More or less utopian visions about the communist future were part of the official discourse, and without doubt attractive and seemingly within reach for a great number of Soviet citizens (Andranik M. Petros'iants, *Atomnaia energetika* (Moscow: Nauka, 1976); Andranik M. Petros'iants, *Iadernaia energetika: Nauka i tekhnicheskii progress*, 2nd ed. (Moscow: Nauka, 1981); Andranik M. Petros'iants, *Atomnaia nauka i tekhnika SSSR* (Moscow: Energoatomizdat, 1987); V. S. Emel'ianov, "Atomnaia nauka i tekhnika i stroitel'stvo kommunizma," *Atomnaia energiia* 11, no. 4 (1961): 301–312; P. T. Astashenkov, *Atomnaia promyshlennost'* (Moscow: Gosudarstvennoe izdatel'stvo literatury v oblasti atomnoi nauki i tekhniki, 1962); Andrei P. Ermakov and Anatolii G. Syrmai, *Atomnaia energiia i transport* (Moscow: Izd-vo Akademii nauk SSSR, 1963); I. D. Morokhov et al., *Atomnoi energetike XX let* (Moscow: Atomizdat, 1974)). The fact that relatively unrestricted research and experimenting could be justified with reference to its usefulness for the state was not lost on promoters of the civilian nuclear industry (Sonja Schmid, "Envisioning a Technological State: Reactor Design Choices and Political Legitimacy in the Soviet Union and Russia," doctoral dissertation, Cornell University, 2005; Holloway, *Stalin and the Bomb*; Krementsov, *Stalinist Science*, 287–288).

60. Several recent Russian publications celebrate this older generation of designers as heroic spirits, who altruistically devoted their lives and talents to their fatherland. See note 9 in this chapter.

61. In *The Ghost of the Executed Engineer*, Loren Graham has famously written about the exceedingly narrow training of Soviet engineers, as opposed to the generalists of the pre-Soviet generation. But many young technical specialists joined the nuclear industry with very specialized training and broadened their skills as the industry, and the tasks for its workforce, developed and professionalized (Sean F. Johnston, *The Neutron's Children: Nuclear Engineers and the Shaping of Identity* (Oxford: Oxford University Press, 2012)).

62. Balzer, "Engineers," 159. See also Moshe Lewin, *The Gorbachev Phenomenon: A Historical Interpretation* (Berkeley: University of California Press, 1988).

63. Solnick, *Stealing the State*, 218–219.

64. Ibid., 58–59.

65. Stephen Kotkin, *Armageddon Averted: The Soviet Collapse, 1970–2000* (Oxford: Oxford University Press, 2001), 178.

66. "The scientific rather than the technical intelligentsia has been the more vocal force in dissident activity" (Balzer, "Engineers," 167). See also Martin Malia, "What Is the Intelligentsia?," in Richard Pipes, ed., *The Russian Intelligentsia*, 1–18 (New York: Columbia University Press, 1961); Albert Parry, "Science and Technology versus Communism," *Russian Review* 25, no. 3 (1966): 227–241; James H. Billington, "The Renaissance of the Russian Intelligentsia," *Foreign Affairs* 35 (1957): 525–530.

67. See, for example, the famous article by Dollezhal and Koriakin (Nikolai A. Dollezhal' and Iurii F. Koriakin, "Iadernaia elektroenergetika: Dostizheniia i problemy," *Kommunist* 14 (1979): 19–28): intended as a proposal to further increase the economic efficiency of the nuclear industry by suggesting remotely located "nuclear energy complexes," it was perceived as a criticism of current practice. See also Interview #22.

Loren Graham showed that the centrally planned economy that took shape in the 1920s was extraordinarily compatible with the technocratic tendencies of the time (Graham, *Short History*, 159–160).

68. One of my interviewees told me that he had "fallen in love" with nuclear power early in his career (Interview #11).

69. Sonja D. Schmid, "Organizational Culture and Professional Identities in the Soviet Nuclear Power Industry," *Osiris* 23 (2008): 82–111; also Interviews #3 and #9.

70. Very few managed to separate the "political" from the "rational" as Andrei Sakharov did. His boundary drawing allowed him to criticize the Soviet "political" regime (the lack of intellectual freedom) while remaining faithful to its "rational" values (modernization, progress, scientific rationality).

71. In particular Interview #16.

72. "In political terms, the intelligentsia leadership [of the late 1920s and early 1930s] came from the Academy of Sciences and the high-salaried specialists and consultants associated with the government commissariats; and for these men the issue of intellectual freedom was secondary to the issue of political influence and specialist input in government policy-making" (Fitzpatrick, *Education and Social Mobility*, 84–85). According to Loren Graham, engineers stood by the implicit agreement struck with the party in the late 1920s, that they "would not raise basic political questions, but instead carry out the party's orders" in exchange for promotions in industry, agriculture, and the military (Graham, *Short History*, 164). See also Bunce, *Subversive Institutions*, 33.

73. Yuri Orlov, *Dangerous Thoughts: Memoirs of a Russian Life* (New York: Morrow, 1991); Andrei Sakharov, *Memoirs*, trans. Richard Lourie (New York: Knopf, 1990).

74. The Interdepartmental Technical Council on Nuclear Power Plants (MVTS) is a good example: the most powerful decision-making body for the Soviet Union's nuclear energy policy, it was intended to serve as a forum for open expert discussion. (On the creation of this council in 1971, and its demolition after the Chernobyl disaster, see Sidorenko, "Upravlenie atomnoi energetikoi," 237.) Another example involves publication patterns, in which instead of publishing controversial replies to a provocative argument, follow-up articles were published that provided the "correct interpretation" of the original thesis (see, e.g., Dollezhal' and Koriakin, "Iadernaia elektroenergetika"). On censorship and self-control in the Soviet mass media, see, for instance, Gayle D. Hollander, *Soviet Political Indoctrination: Developments in Mass Media and Propaganda since Stalin* (New York: Praeger, 1972), and Ellen Mickiewicz, *Split Signals: Television and Politics in the Soviet Union* (New York: Oxford University Press, 1988).

75. Holloway, *Stalin and the Bomb*, 5. For a more detailed discussion of the Russian and Soviet technical intelligentsia see Kendall E. Bailes, *Technology and Society under Lenin and Stalin: Origins of the Soviet Technical Intelligentsia, 1917–1941* (Princeton, NJ: Princeton University Press, 1978), 6–7, 15.

76. When the system failed, when responsibility was to be assigned, the first charge was usually "wrecking" or "sabotage," and when this proved unfounded, "personnel error" (Bailes, *Technology and Society*).

77. Johnston argues that these three countries, the first to devote significant resources to nuclear research and development, "created templates that influenced the creation of subsequent national programmes" (Johnston, *The Neutron's Children*, 12).

78. Johnston, *The Neutron's Children*, 2.

79. Ibid., 6.

80. Ibid., 10.

Notes

81. Ibid., 13.

82. Ibid., 14. Johnston counters the idea that "the Soviet context simultaneously vaunted and eviscerated engineering identities, allying them to socialist progress and centralized governance" (ibid., 13). See also Schmid, "Organizational Culture and Professional Identities."

83. These concepts are fundamentally actors' categories that involve a variety of associations; it is therefore important to note that as analytical categories, I use them only to refer to the institutional affiliations of these specialists.

84. Interview with the minister of Atomic Energy, Aleksandr Iu. Rumiantsev, on *Ekho Moskvy*, May 29, 2003, 16:08–16:30, emphasis added, www.echo.msk.ru/interview/22335. (Topics: Minatom's international programs; cooperation with Iran on nuclear power technology; shutdown of Russian plutonium-producing reactors. Moderators: Matvei Ganapol'skii and Aleksei Venediktov.)

85. This tension is not limited to cadres for the nuclear power industry; it is characteristic of all applications of nuclear energy and fuels nonproliferation debates to this day.

86. Discussions of the "human factor" were not new in Soviet industry. Fitzpatrick has identified the idea of operators being "cogs in a machine" as part of a long-standing institutional conflict between the People's Commissariat of Enlightenment (Narkompros) and the Supreme Council of the People's Economy (Vesenkha) that culminated in 1928, when Narkompros argued that "workers were simply conditioned (*trenirovany*) to become efficient cogs in the industrial machine" and concluded: "Certainly the Soviet Union must adopt modern industrial methods, including the conveyer belt and the assembly line. But this did not mean that workers could be treated as automata" (Fitzpatrick, *Education and Social Mobility*, 127).

87. Grabovskii, *Vtoroi Ivan*. Grabovskii was not able to use archival material, and therefore labeled his story fictional. However, the story is clearly autobiographical. He had been one of the young operators.

88. Theodore Porter, "Quantification and the Accounting Ideal in Science," *Social Studies of Science* 22 (1992): 633–652; Theodore M. Porter, *Trust in Numbers: The Pursuit of Objectivity in Science and Public Life*, 2nd ed. (Princeton, NJ: Princeton University Press, 1995).

89. Interview #4 and personal communication.

90. I chose these translations to make the division of tasks, and the scope of the respective assignments, as clear as possible.

91. The Institute of Atomic Energy was scientific director of nuclear reactors—that is, not just nuclear power plant reactors but also reactors for submarines, icebreakers, space vehicles, and so on (Sidorenko, *Ob atomnoi energetike*). See also Viktor

A. Sidorenko, "Nauchnoe rukovodstvo v atomnoi energetike," in Viktor A. Sidorenko, ed., *Istoriia atomnoi energetiki Sovetskogo Soiuza i Rossii: Istoriia VVER*, vol. 2, 5–28 (Moscow: IzdAt, 2002). On Aleksandrov's role in the development of Soviet power reactor designs, see Arnold Kramish, *Atomic Energy in the Soviet Union* (Stanford, CA: Stanford University Press, 1959); Ulasevich, *Sozdano pod rukovodstvom*, 42.

92. Kramish, *Atomic Energy*, 182; Ulasevich, *Sozdano pod rukovodstvom*, 42.

93. Sidorenko, "Upravlenie atomnoi energetikoi," 237.

94. Interview #3.

95. Khlopkin, *Stranitsy zhizni*.

96. For a description of this process by Nikolai Vladimirovich Zhukov, head of NIKIET's *avtorskii nadzor*, see, for example, Fain, *Aktivnaia zona*, 114–120..

97. Apparently, this happened at the Kursk nuclear power plant: NIKIET's inspectors blocked work from proceeding, and their objections were found valid by the scientific director (Fain, *Aktivnaia zona*, 114–117).

98. On NIKIET (Nauchno-issledovatel'skii i konstruktorskii institut energotekhniki) and Dollezhal, see Nikolai A. Dollezhal', *U istokov rukotvornogo mira*; Ulasevich, *O iadernykh reaktorakh*; *Sozdano pod rukovodstvom*; Fain, *Aktivnaia zona*.

99. V. P. Denisov and Iu. G. Dragunov, *Reaktornye ustanovki VVER dlia atomnykh elektrostantsii* (Moscow: IzdAt, 2002). The largest factory for manufacturing VVER reactor vessels, *Atommash* in Volgodonsk, was designed to produce several reactor vessels per year, essentially guaranteeing the conveyer-belt-like production of pressurized water reactors. However, construction proceeded slowly (Paul R. Josephson, *Red Atom: Russia's Nuclear Power Program from Stalin to Today* (New York: Freeman, 1999), 97–108). Once the Soviets started exporting VVERs to CMEA countries in the 1960s, engineering cooperation began to develop, especially with Czechoslovakia and Yugoslavia (Sonja D. Schmid, "Nuclear Colonization? Soviet Technopolitics in the Second World," in Gabrielle Hecht, ed., *Entangled Geographies: Empire and Technopolitics in the Global Cold War*, 125–154 (Cambridge, MA: MIT Press, 2011)).

100. Interview #7. These organizations were typically regional branches of Minenergo's own construction trust, *Teploelektroproekt* (*TEP*).

101. For example, so-called science cities included Obninsk, Dubna, and Melekess (Dimitrovgrad), to mention but a few (e.g., Judith Perera, *The Nuclear Industry in the Former Soviet Union: Transition from Crisis to Opportunity*, vol. 2 (London: Financial Times Energy Publishing, 1997), 21–22).

102. Gidropress had also been producing parts for the RBMK and had repeatedly reported problems with the RBMK equipment (Viktor P. Tatarnikov, "Atomnaia elektroenergetika (s VVER i drugimi reaktorami)," in Viktor A. Sidorenko, ed., *Istoriia atomnoi energetiki Sovetskogo Soiuza i Rossii: Istoriia VVER*, vol. 2, 303–399 (Moscow:

IzdAt, 2002); Ulasevich, *Sozdano pod rukovodstvom;* Ulasevich, *O iadernykh reaktorakh;* Fain, *Aktivnaia zona;* Dollezhal', *U istokov rukotvornogo mira;* Iurii I. Koriakin, *Okrestnosti iadernoi energetiki Rossii: Novye vyzovy* (Moscow: GUP NIKIET, 2002); Evgenii O. Adamov, ed., *Belaia kniga iadernoi energetiki* (Moscow: GUP NIKIET, 2001)).

103. For a rather skeptical view of shifting personnel, see Balzer, "Engineers," 198–201.

104. Notable exceptions were, as previously mentioned, the Leningrad, Ignalina, and Shevchenko nuclear power plants.

105. Minister Petr Neporozhnii maintained friendships with the long-term chairman of the Council of Ministers, Aleksei Kosygin, and with the State Planning Commission (Gosplan) functionary in charge of the country's energy complex, Veniamin Dymshits (Petr S. Neporozhnii, *Energetika strany glazami ministra: Dnevniki 1935–1985 gg.* (Moscow: Energoatomizdat, 2000)).

106. International Nuclear Safety Advisory Group, *Summary Report on the Post-Accident Review Meeting on the Chernobyl Accident* (INSAG-1).

107. Anthropologist Constance Perin has pointed out for the U.S. context that there is a persistent ambivalence between rule following and situated expert judgment: "Safety may depend on the exercise of individual and/or collective judgment. Nevertheless, the dominant risk-handling strategy remains strict adherence to rules and procedures. The industry frames this dilemma as one of a choice between the proceduralization of global, algorithmic knowledge and the localism of professional experience and knowledge, or between routinization and latitude for 'disciplined improvisation'" (Constance Perin, "Operating as Experimenting: Synthesizing Engineering and Scientific Values in Nuclear Power Production," *Science, Technology & Human Values* 23, no. 1 (1998): 98–128 (quote on 105); see also Perin, *Shouldering Risks*).

108. In the archival documents, I found a maximum of 29 percent of the salary consisting of rewards, and according to one interviewee, at times this percentage rose to 60 percent. Administrators criticized a 29 percent bonus (*premiia*) as too low (RGAE, f. 7964, op. 15, d. 7267, l. 73–74; Interview #17, and personal communication).

109. Sidorenko, "Upravlenie atomnoi energetikoi," 224–225; Perera, *The Nuclear Industry in the Former Soviet Union*. Without exception, the atomshchiki I interviewed also professed that they were only too aware of the risks involved.

110. Evidence includes, for example, the chapters in Aleksandr N. Semenov, ed., *Chernobyl' desiat' let spustia: Neizbezhnost' ili sluchainost'?* (Moscow: Energoatomizdat, 1995).

111. The first report on the results of such a state inspection conducted at power plants and power lines that I was able to locate was from 1971. See "Gosudarstvennaia

inspektsiia po ekspluatatsii elektrostantsii i setei: Svodnye otchety inspektsii po avariiam za 1971g." (State inspection of the operation of power plants and grids: Summary inspection reports on accidents during 1971) (RGAE, f. 7964, op. 15, d. 4222).

112. RGAE, f. 7964, op. 15, d. 5378.

113. Accidents involving problems with the nuclear reactor itself were reported to Sredmash; these reports are not accessible at this point.

114. RGAE, f. 7964, op. 15, d. 64, l. 85. In other words, Minenergo saw nuclear plant personnel as "special" and as in need of "special training."

115. Commemorative Seminar at the World's First Nuclear Power Plant, May 16, 2003, Obninsk; also Interview #21.

116. Glavatomenergo, rukovodstvo, RGAE, f. 7964, op. 15, d. 802.

117. Glavatomenergo, Ekspluatatsionno-proizvodstvennyi otdel. Protokoly tekhnicheskikh soveshchanii po tekhnicheskim voprosam za 1968 g., "Protokol po voprosu kontrolia energovydeleniia rabochikh kanalov Beloiarskoi AES," March 18, 1968 (RGAE, f. 7964, op. 15, d. 821, l. 8).

118. "Protokol po voprosu kontrolia energovydeleniia rabochikh kanalov Beloiarskoi AES," March 18, 1968 (RGAE, f. 7964, op. 15, d. 821, l. 9).

119. "Protokol opredeleniia maksimal'noi pogreshnosti pri raschete potoka teplovykh neitronov v rezul'tate vygoraniia sterzhnei RR reaktora I bloka na Beloiarskoi atomnoi eektrostantsii," signed by the chief engineer of the Beloiarsk nuclear power plant, Gennadii A. Shasharin (RGAE, f. 7964, op. 15, d. 802; RGAE, f. 7964, op. 15, d. 821, l. 33–38).

120. This episode is also characteristic of the technological optimism of both designers and operators: their behavior reflected a deep confidence that mistakes were lessons to be learned on the way to perfection. See, for example, Susanne Schattenberg, *Stalins Ingenieure: Lebenswelten zwischen Technik und Terror in den 1930er Jahren* (Munich: Oldenbourg, 2002).

121. Letter No. ES-881, September 16, 1971, to the Council of Ministers ("O sroke vvoda v deistvie III energobloka Novovoronezhskoi AES," signed by P. Falaleev (Minenergo)) (RGAE, f. 7964, op. 15, d. 3924, l. 56).

122. Karl E. Weick, "Organizational Culture as a Source of High Reliability," *California Management Review* 29, no. 2 (1987): 112–127.

123. Vladimir Anisinov, "AES: Stepen' riska (beseda s B. G. Dubovskim)," *Smena* 10 (1994): 55–61; Nadezhda Nadezhdina, "Zalozhniki reaktora," *Trud* 3 (April 1996): n.p.

Notes

124. Another strategy was to transfer trusted individuals to key positions in the nuclear industry, when Sredmash felt there was not enough in-house expertise.

125. Schmid, "Organizational Culture and Professional Identities."

126. Viktor A. Sidorenko, "Vvodnye zamechaniia k urokam Chernobyl'skoi avarii," in Viktor A. Sidorenko, ed., *Istoriia atomnoi energetiki Sovetskogo Soiuza i Rossii: Uroki avarii na Chernobyl'skoi AES*, vol. 4, 4–16 (Moscow: IzdAt, 2002). See also J. Samuel Walker, *Three Mile Island: A Nuclear Crisis in Historical Perspective* (Berkeley: University of California Press, 2004).

127. Several Minenergo employees I interviewed claimed that Sredmash had concealed the potentially catastrophic scale of accidents at nuclear power plants (e.g., Interviews #7 and #11).

128. This report, INSAG-1 (International Nuclear Safety Advisory Group, *Summary Report on the Post-Accident Review Meeting on the Chernobyl Accident*), was published in September, immediately after the meeting, and was based on working documents prepared by the USSR State Committee on the Utilization of Atomic Energy for the IAEA Meeting of Experts, Vienna, August 25–29, 1986, and on additional material presented by the Soviet experts during the meeting. The Chernobyl trial a year later confirmed this verdict one more time (see introduction; also Boris Gorbachev, "Tainy Chernobyl'skogo suda," *Zerkalo nedeli* 6, no. 491 (April 2004): 24–29; A. V. Illesh and A. E. Pral'nikov, eds., *Reportazh iz Chernobylia: Zapiski ochevidtsev. Kommentarii. Razmyshleniia* (Moscow: Mysl', 1988); Nikolai V. Karpan, *Chernobyl': Mest' mirnogo atoma* (Kiev: Kantri Laif, 2005); V. Vozniak and S. Troitskii, *Chernobyl: Tak eto bylo* (Moscow: Libris, 1993)).

129. On the functionality of ignorance see M. Michael, "Ignoring Science: Discourses of Ignorance in the Public Understanding of Science," in Alan Irwin and Brian Wynne, eds., *Misunderstanding Science? The Public Reconstruction of Science and Technology*, 107–125 (Cambridge: Cambridge University Press, 1996).

130. Sidorenko, "Upravlenie atomnoi energetikoi," 226. See also Sidorenko, "Nuclear Power," 7; Sidorenko, "Vvedenie," 10–11.

131. Alexander Shlyakhter and Richard Wilson, "Chernobyl: The Inevitable Results of Secrecy," *Public Understanding of Science* 1 (1992): 251–259; Sidorenko, "Nuclear Power"; Kruglov, *Shtab atomproma*; Kruglov, *Kak sozdavalas'*. But this assessment is still problematic because it does not take into account that nuclear power plants went from total secrecy to quite comprehensive civilian control and back, in tight interconnection with organizational responsibilities, overall economic reforms, and the adoption of specific technical choices. See Schmid, "Envisioning a Technological State."

132. Sidorenko, "Upravlenie atomnoi energetikoi," 223.

133. See Holloway's argument about the nuclear physicists' freedom amid the Stalinist terror (Holloway, "Physics, the State, and Civil Society"). See also Asif A. Siddiqi, "Within the First Circle: Science and Engineering in the Gulag," paper presented at the Annual Convention of the American Association for the Advancement of Slavic Studies, Washington, DC, November 16–19, 2006; Michael A. Dennis, "Secrecy and Science Revisited: From Politics to Historical Practice and Back," in Ronald E. Doel and Thomas Söderqvist, eds., *The Historiography of Contemporary Science, Technology, and Medicine*, 172–184 (London: Routledge, 2006).

Chapter 4

1. Viktor A. Sidorenko, "Vvedenie k 1-mu vypusku," in Viktor A. Sidorenko, ed., *Istoriia atomnoi energetiki Sovetskogo Soiuza i Rossii*, vol. 1, 5–15 (Moscow: IzdAt, 2001) (especially 5); Lev A. Kochetkov, ed., *Ot Pervoi v mire AES k atomnoi energetike XXI veka: Sbornik tezisov, dokladov i soobshchenii* (Proceedings of the Tenth Annual Conference, June 28–July 2, 1999, Obninsk) (Obninsk: Iadernoe obshchestvo Rossii, 1999).

2. Sidorenko, "Vvedenie," 5; Vladimir G. Asmolov et al., *Atomnaia energetika: Otsenki proshlogo, realii nastoiashchego, ozhidaniia budushchego* (Moscow: IzdAt, 2004), 8, 12; Kochetkov, *Ot pervoi v mire*.

3. V. P. Denisov, "Evoliutsiia vodo-vodianykh energeticheskikh reaktorov dlia AES," in Viktor A. Sidorenko, ed., *Istoriia atomnoi energetiki Sovetskogo Soiuza i Rossii: Istoriia VVER*, vol. 2, 218–302 (Moscow: IzdAt, 2002).

4. Sidorenko, "Vvedenie," 5; Asmolov et al., *Atomnaia energetika*, 8.

5. I owe this observation to Jonathan Coopersmith. At Rosenergoatom annual conference in June 2004, Aleksandr Rumiantsev, then Russian minister of Atomic Energy, deplored the diversity of reactor designs developed in the USSR (see Rossiiskii gosudarstvennyi kontsern po proizvodstvu elektricheskoi i teplovoi energii na atomnykh stantiiakh (Rosenergoatom), ed. *50 let atomnoi energetike*, Proceedings of the Fourth International Scientific and Technical conference on Nuclear Power Safety, Efficiency and Economics held in Moscow, June 16–17 (Moscow: Mashmir, 2004). By contrast, he praised the early standardization in France. Other countries' nuclear power programs may not *actually* be as straightforward and clear (cf., e.g., Gabrielle Hecht, *The Radiance of France: Nuclear Power and National Identity after World War II* (Cambridge, MA: MIT Press, 1998)), and, conversely, the Soviet program might look fairly "logical" to an outsider in retrospect.

6. Peter DeLeon, *Development and Diffusion of the Nuclear Power Reactor: A Comparative Analysis* (Cambridge, MA: Ballinger, 1979), 99.

7. Vladimir V. Goncharov, "Pervyi period razvitiia atomnoi energetiki v SSSR," in Viktor A. Sidorenko, ed., *Istoriia atomnoi energetiki Sovetskogo Soiuza i Rossii*, vol. 1,

Notes

16–70 (Moscow: IzdAt, 2001); Igor' V. Kurchatov, "Rech' tovarishcha I. V. Kurchatova (Akademiia Nauk SSSR)," *Pravda* 53, no. 22 (February 1956): 7.

8. Viktor A. Sidorenko, "Nuclear Power in the Soviet Union and in Russia," *Nuclear Engineering and Design* 173 (1997): 3–20 (especially 5); Sidorenko, "Vvedenie," 6.

9. Interview #4.

10. Had Kurchatov's group failed, instead of receiving prestigious awards, they would have been shot or imprisoned (David Holloway, *Stalin and the Bomb: The Soviet Union and Atomic Energy 1939–1956* (New Haven, CT: Yale University Press, 1994), 215).

11. "Stabilization," "closure," and the preceding chaos or "interpretative flexibility" are stages in the "Social Construction of Technology" program that Trevor Pinch, Harry Collins, Thomas Hughes, and others developed in the 1980s (Wiebe E. Bijker, Thomas P. Hughes, and Trevor Pinch, eds., *The Social Construction of Technological Systems: New Directions in the Sociology and History of Technology* (Cambridge, MA: MIT Press, 1987)). I use "stabilization" here because "closure" has since been shown to be a thoroughly leaky process (Paul Rosen, "The Social Construction of Mountain Bikes: Technology and Postmodernity in the Cycle Industry," *Social Studies of Science* 23 (1993): 479–513) that is hardly ever permanent, and rarely even approaches the definition of "stable state characterized by consensus" (Thomas J. Misa, "Controversy and Closure in Technological Change: Constructing 'Steel,'" in W. E. Bijker and J. Law, eds., *Shaping Technology/Building Society: Studies in Sociotechnical Change*, 109–139 (Cambridge, MA: MIT Press, 1992) (especially 109)).

12. In 1956, Kurchatov accompanied Nikita Khrushchev to Britain, where he gave two talks at the leading nuclear research center at Harwell.

13. Many nuclear research centers, design institutes, and construction bureaus were secret *"iashchiki,"* identified only by their post office box numbers.

14. Postanovlenie SNK SSSR No. 3117–937ss; see www.ippe.ru/ist/date.php.

15. Paul R. Josephson, *Red Atom: Russia's Nuclear Power Program from Stalin to Today* (New York: Freeman, 1999); Alexei Kojevnikov, "Piotr Kapitza and Stalin's Government: A Study in Moral Choice," *Historical Studies in the Physical and Biological Sciences* 22, no. 1 (1991): 131–164.

16. An excellent, detailed biography can be found at a local Obninsk site: http://iobninsk.ru/aleksandr-ilyich-leypunskiy/; see also the short biographical note provided by the Russian Academy of Sciences' Institute for the History of Science and Technology, http://www.ihst.ru/projects/sohist/repress/kharkov/leipunsky.htm.

17. A year later, in 1950, Leipunskii started his own program to develop fast neutron reactors.

18. Kochetkov, *Ot pervoi v mire*, 15; Sidorenko, "Vvedenie," 5; Asmolov et al., *Atomnaia energetika*, 12.

19. Sidorenko, "Vvedenie," 5.

20. Kurchatov and Zaveniagin also justified the choice of the graphite-moderated, water-cooled design as follows: "The installation AM (with water coolant) has the advantage that experience with regular boilers could be applied more directly than with the other designs ...; the relative simplicity of the installation makes its construction easier and cheaper" (quoted in Asmolov et al., *Atomnaia energetika*, 13).

21. Holloway, *Stalin and the Bomb*; Arkadii K. Kruglov, *Kak sozdavalas' atomnaia promyshlennost' v SSSR* (Moscow: TSNIIatominform, 1995); DeLeon, *Development and Diffusion*, 59; Helen Knorre, "Frontiers of Technology: U.S.S.R.," *Nuclear Engineering* 9, no. 100 (1964): 317–318.

22. Natural uranium contains mostly uranium 238 and only traces of uranium 235. Through complex, time-consuming, and costly processes, the percentage of uranium 235 can be increased (this is called "enrichment"); the result is called "enriched uranium," and the percentage of enrichment refers to the portion of uranium 235. The availability of enriched uranium allowed the use of light water as a coolant. Uranium separation and enrichment are tightly controlled technologies; facilities are very complex and expensive, and for some time, only the United States and the USSR could manufacture enriched uranium. The United States initially refused to supply even its allies (France, Britain) with enriched uranium, and so these countries at first had little choice other than to develop reactors operating on natural uranium. Only after their own separation plants provided them with the ability to enrich uranium did they gradually (and at great cost) switch to reactors operating on enriched uranium (DeLeon, *Development and Diffusion*, 57–60).

23. Goncharov, "Pervyi period," 17.

24. Most prominently, Kurchatov spoke at the twentieth Party congress (Kurchatov, "Rech' tovarishcha I. V. Kurchatova"). Feinberg's book, *Theory of Nuclear Reactors*, seems to have been a standard textbook for nuclear physics students (S. M. Feinberg, S. B. Shikhov, and B. V. Troianskii, *Teoriia iadernykh reaktorov*, 2 vols. (Moscow: Energoatomizdat, 1983)).

25. SM stands for *sverkh-moshchnyi*, "high power," but also—according to informal evidence—for Savelii Moiseevich, Feinberg's first name and father's name (Viktor A. Sidorenko, *Ob atomnoi energetike, atomnykh stantsiiakh, uchiteliakh, kollegakh i o sebe* (Moscow: IzdAt, 2003); Boris A. Fain, *Aktivnaia zona: Povest' ob atomnom institute* (Moscow: Skripto, 1998); Nikolai A. Dollezhal', *U istokov rukotvornogo mira: zapiski konstruktora* (Moscow: GUP NIKIET, IzdAt, 2002).

26. On March 15, 1956, the Soviet Council of Ministers issued a decree that, among other things, officially ordered the construction of the Beloiarsk nuclear power plant (Goncharov, "Pervyi period," 33–34).

27. Sidorenko, "Nuclear Power," 6. Usually, steam produced in nuclear reactors is more saturated than in conventional power plants, and thus less efficient with conventional turbines. In the ensuing decades, efforts were made to facilitate the production of turbines specifically engineered for nuclear power plants, with a reduced rotation speed.

28. Interview #8.

29. Asmolov et al., *Atomnaia energetika*, 17.

30. Brian Wynne, "Unruly Technology," *Social Studies of Science* 18, no. 1 (1988): 147–167; Bijker, Hughes, and Pinch, *The Social Construction of Technological Systems*.

31. L. A. Alekhin and G. V. Kiselev, "Istoriia sozdaniia pervogo v SSSR i v mire dvukhtselevogo uran-grafitovogo reaktora EI-2 dlia odnovremennogo proizvodstva oruzheinogo plutoniia i elektroenergii," *Istoriia nauki i tekhniki* 12 (2003): 2–35.

32. Goncharov, "Pervyi period," 60.

33. Named after the Moscow scientist Bilibin, who in the 1930s conjectured that the far north was rich in gold, the plant owes its existence to the Soviet government, which decreed on January 12, 1966, that a nuclear plant would be the most suitable energy provider for this remote region: it would provide heat and electricity and require minimal maintenance. The plant was declared an All-Union shock-work construction site in 1967. The first two Bilibino 12 MW reactors went operational in 1974, the third in 1975, and the fourth on December 28, 1976; they remain in operation today.

34. Goncharov, "Pervyi period," 31; Sidorenko, "Nuclear Power," 6.

35. In 1994, FEI started cooperating with NIKIET on the technical design for a second series of reactors at the Bilibino site.

36. In 1964, at the Third United Nations Conference on Peaceful Uses of Atomic Energy in Geneva, Andranik Petrosyiants reported dissent regarding the immediate future prospects of breeder reactors. Petrosyiants reported that Great Britain, France, Germany, and the Soviet Union proposed a fast transition to breeder reactors, while Canada and the United States considered them a relatively distant option. The argument did not seem to center on financial or safety issues; breeders were simply considered the logical, "rational" next step (Andranik M. Petros'iants, "Tret'ia mezhdunarodnaia Zhenevskaia konferentsiia atomnikov," *Atomnaia Energiia* 17, no. 5 (1964): 323–328). Breeder development took very different paths—it was abandoned in France and Germany, mostly because of safety concerns, energetically pursued in Japan, and hesitantly pursued in the USSR.

37. Goncharov, "Pervyi period," 28; Sidorenko, "Nuclear Power," 15–16.

38. The 1959 reactor at Obninsk was an experimental breeder reactor with 5 MW thermal capacity and sodium coolant. It was the prototype of the first Soviet commercial breeder reactor, which was built on the Caspian Sea (in what today is Kazakhstan) with the purpose of desalinating water and producing electricity for a new city, Shevchenko. Today, the nuclear power plant is referred to as the Mangistau nuclear complex and the city is called Aqtau, which means "white mountain" in Kazakh. The Shevchenko reactor (BN-350) had a capacity of 350 MW. It started operation in 1973, but due to operational difficulties, it never consistently operated at full power. The experimental fast neutron reactor BOR-60 (with 12 MW capacity) was considered the prototype for a breeder reactor designed for power generation, even though it was launched in the territory of a then classified research institute (Sidorenko, "Nuclear Power," 16). The BN-600 reactor went operational at the Beloiarsk site in 1980, and in 2010 it received a license extension until 2020. A larger reactor based on the same design, the BN-800, has been under construction at the Beloiarsk site since 1984. The Russian government continued to include the BN-800 in its target programs, in part because fast reactors are seen by some as a way to deal with the problem of spent nuclear fuel (http://www.belnpp.rosenergoatom.ru/wps/wcm/connect/rosenergoatom/belnpp/about/prospects).

39. See, for example, Josephson, *Red Atom*.

40. Sidorenko, "Vvedenie," 8; Sidorenko, "Nuclear Power," 3; Asmolov et al., *Atomnaia energetika*, 17.

41. The exact location was not revealed at the time, but it is now known that this reactor was built in the territory of the Siberian Chemical Combine (Combine 816, or Tomsk-7, later renamed Seversk), about 12 kilometers northwest of the city of Tomsk (Alekhin and Kiselev, "Istoriia sozdaniia"; see also Global Security's site on the Tomsk-7/Seversk Siberian Chemical Combine (Combine 816), at http://www.globalsecurity.org/wmd/world/russia/tomsk-7_nuc.htm).

42. Mikhail P. Grabovskii, *Vtoroi Ivan: Sovershenno sekretno* (Moscow: Nauchnaia kniga, 1998).

43. Its initial power output was 100 MWe, which was increased to 600 in subsequent years (Sidorenko, "Vvedenie").

44. Interview #5.

45. Michele Stenehjem Gerber, *On the Home Front: The Cold War Legacy of the Hanford Nuclear Site* (Lincoln: University of Nebraska Press, 1992).

46. The last dual-use reactor in Zheleznogorsk was shut down only in 2010, because the nearby towns relied on them for heat and hot water (Stephen Bunnell, "Russian Plutonium-Producing Reactors Closed," *Arms Control Today* July/August (2008), http://www.armscontrol.org/act/2008_07-08/RussianPlutonium; Frank N. von

Hippel and Matthew Bunn, "Saga of the Siberian Plutonium-Production Reactors," *Journal of the Federation of American Scientists* 53, no. 6 (2000), http://www.fas.org/faspir/v53n6.htm).

47. The abbreviation "ADE" most likely stands for "atomic dual-use power reactor" (*atomnyi reaktor dvukhtselevoi energeticheskii*). Dual-use reactors were built at Tomsk-7 (today Seversk), Cheliabinsk-40 (today Ozersk), and Krasnoiarsk (today Zheleznogorsk). ADE-3 was started up in 1961, and construction of ADE-4 and ADE-5 began in 1963 and 1965, respectively. The decision to build these dual-use reactors was made in 1957, even before the "Second Ivan" had started up.

48. Letter to A. N. Kosygin, chairman of the SM, "On the construction of a complex of heat-supply facilities in the city of Tomsk" (RGAE f. 4372, op. 66, d. 3973, l. 170–172).

49. Information on the construction of a complex of heat-supply facilities in the city of Tomsk ("Spravka o stroitel'stve kompleksa sooruzhenii po teplosnabzheniiu goroda Tomska"), November 2, 1970 (RGAE, f. 4372, op. 66, d. 3973, l. 173–174); letter from Gosplan's N. Baibakov to the Tomsk regional party committee (E. K. Ligachev), January 14, 1971 (RGAE, f. 4372, op. 66, d. 3973, l. 175).

50. The planning of a nuclear power plant site sometimes included considerations about the imminent availability of workers once a nearby industrial facility was completed (e.g., RGAE, f. 7964, op. 3, f. 2015, vol. 2: "Ob"iasnitel'naia zapiska k godovomu otchetu za 1958 god po kapital'nomu stroitel'stvu direktsii stroiashcheisia Leningradskoi GRES No. 16," l. 38).

51. "Atomnuiu energiiu—na sluzhbu mirnomu stroitel'stvu: Beseda korrespondenta 'Izvestii' s nachal'nikom Glavnogo upravleniia po ispol'zovaniiu atomnoi energii pri Sovete Ministrov SSSR E. P. Slavskim," *Izvestiia*, no. 23 (May 1956): 2–3.

52. Goncharov, "Pervyi period," 21–22; "Atomnuiu energiiu—na sluzhbu mirnomu stroitel'stvu."

53. Goncharov, "Pervyi period," 54; Sidorenko, "Nuclear Power," 8.

54. This "TETs-3" was planned to be sited in Khovrino, with two VVER reactors and a total power output of 400 MW (Asmolov et al., *Atomnaia energiia*, 17).

55. Goncharov, "Pervyi period," 22–23.

56. Ibid., 59; see also some of the letters Kurchatov wrote, which are included as appendixes to Goncharov's chapter (Letters to Leonid I. Brezhnev, June 21, 1958; to secretary of the Party's Central Committee Frol R. Kozlov, April 16, 1959; to secretary of the Party's Central Committee A. I. Kirichenko, April 6, 1959; to the chairman of the Council of Ministers Aleksei N. Kosygin, April 24, 1959) (ibid., 65–70)).

57. Sidorenko, "Nuclear Power," 6.

58. Ibid., 9; Viktor P. Tatarnikov, "Atomnaia elektroenergetika (s VVER i drugimi reaktorami)," in Viktor A. Sidorenko, ed., *Istoriia atomnoi energetiki Sovetskogo Soiuza i Rossii: Istoriia VVER*, vol. 2, 303–399 (Moscow: IzdAt, 2002); Interview #11.

59. Sidorenko, "Nuclear Power," 9.

60. In 1956, an intergovernment agreement was signed between the USSR and the GDR, and in 1957 construction work on the first East German nuclear power plant at Rheinsberg, with a capacity of 70 MW, began. It was commissioned in 1966. From 1971 to 1975, six VVER-440 units went critical in the Soviet Union (at Novo-Voronezh, Kola, and the Armenian nuclear power plant), and from 1974 to 1982, ten such reactors were commissioned in Bulgaria, Czechoslovakia, and the GDR under CMEA agreements (Sidorenko, "Nuclear Power," 8–10).

61. Maria Nicolaevna Vasilieva, *Soleils rouges: L'ambition nucléaire soviétique [Essai sur l'évolution des systèmes de prise de décision dans le nucléaire soviétique (Russe)]* (Paris: Institut d'Histoire de l'Industrie et Éditions Rive Droite, 1999); V. K. Ulasevich, ed., *Sozdano pod rukovodstvom N. A. Dollezhalia: O iadernykh reaktorakh i ikh tvortsakh (k 100-letiiu N. A. Dollezhalia)* (Moscow: GUP NIKIET, 2002); V. K. Ulasevich, ed., *O iadernykh reaktorakh i ikh tvortsakh: Prodolzhenie traditsii (k 50-letiiu NIKIET im. N. A. Dollzhalia* (Moscow: GUP NIKIET, 2002).

62. Sidorenko, "Nuclear Power," 8; DeLeon, *Development and Diffusion*, 113. In addition to the pressurized water reactors, Soviet engineers also built prototype submarine reactors cooled with liquid metal. Only one of them was produced for a series of submarines in the late 1970s: seven Alfa class submarines were equipped with liquid metal cooled reactors, but the design did not catch on. See Goncharov, "Pervyi period," 54; "Atomnuiu energiiu—na sluzhbu mirnomu stroitel'stvu."

63. See George T. Mazuzan and J. Samuel Walker, *Controlling the Atom: The Beginnings of Nuclear Regulation, 1946–1962* (Berkeley: University of California Press, 1985), 1–31.

64. Propulsion reactors use uranium with a much higher fuel enrichment (20 to 90 percent) than power reactors, which usually operate with a maximum enrichment of 3 to 4 percent.

65. Goncharov lists the following scientists as involved in the development of these reactors: A. P. Aleksandrov, S. M. Feinberg, I. I. Afrikantov, N. S. Khlopkin, and G. A. Gladkov (Goncharov, "Pervyi period," 61). The Russian icebreaker fleet currently encompasses six icebreakers (*Rossiia, Taimyr, Sovetskii Soiuz, Vaygach, Yamal,* and *50 let Pobedy*), a container ship (*Sevmorput*), and two service ships (*Imandra and Lotta*), as well as a special tanker for liquid radioactive waste (*Serebrianka*) and a vessel for personnel cleanup and dose measurement (*Rosta-1*) ("Nuclear Icebreakers," http://www.rosatom.ru/en/about/activities/nuclear_icebreakers). In 1964, Germany produced a nuclear freighter (*Otto Hahn*), and Japan was working on its first nuclear ship. The United States had launched the *NS Savannah* around the same time as the *Lenin*.

Notes

Soviet analysts concluded that the *NS Savannah* failed due to "a lack of trust from trade companies and passengers" (Petros'iants, "Tret'ia mezhdunarodnaia Zhenevskaia konferentsiia atomnikov," 327; see also David Kuechle, *The Story of the Savannah: An Episode in Maritime Labor-Management Relations* (Cambridge, MA: Harvard University Press, 1971)).

66. Sidorenko, "Nuclear Power," 12. When Western nuclear experts assessed the safety of Eastern European VVERs in the 1990s, they concluded that the horizontal steam generators made these reactors more forgiving than Western pressurized water reactors with vertical steam generators (http://insp.pnnl.gov/-profiles-reactors-vver230.htm; see also Thomas R. Wellock, "The Children of Chernobyl: Engineers and the Campaign for Safety in Soviet-Designed Reactors in Central and Eastern Europe," *History and Technology* 29, no. 1 (2013): 3–32).

67. Convenience thus contrasted with quality: parts assembled on site could not be guaranteed to meet the same consistent quality standards that factory-manufactured parts for nuclear reactors did (Interview #8).

68. Sidorenko, "Nuclear Power," 8–10; Goncharov, "Pervyi period," 55.

69. Neutron shielding can be achieved by creating a thick protective layer of water and steel between the core and the vessel, but this "increases the non-productive part of the vessel" (Sidorenko, "Nuclear Power," 10). Engineers therefore created types of special nickel-plated steel that would retain their strength despite irradiation for the reactor's lifetime (then projected at twenty to forty years).

70. Goncharov, "Pervyi period," 55.

71. The Atommash factory—under construction and behind schedule for most of this story—was intentionally built on a large river system, so these limitations could eventually be overcome by loading nuclear equipment on barges and shipping it to its ultimate destination.

72. Sidorenko, "Nuclear Power," 8; DeLeon, *Development and Diffusion*, 113.

73. Sidorenko, "Nuclear Power," 9. At least the first VVER-440 units (of the 440/230 variety) had isolation valves that allowed "plant operators to take one or more of the six coolant loops out of service for repair while continuing to operate the plant" (http://insp.pnnl.gov/-profiles-reactors-vver230.htm).

74. Sidorenko, "Nuclear Power," 9.

75. The earlier design version of the VVER-440 is also referred to as "Model 230" or "V-230," whereas the later one, which contains several modernized design features (including a containment structure), is referred to as "Model 213" or "V-213." After 1991, and a lengthy process of safety evaluation, the V-230 reactors in Eastern Europe were shut down for good (Wellock, "Children of Chernobyl").

76. Sidorenko, "Nuclear Power," 17.

77. AST/ATETs reactors were essentially versions of the VVER; they were equipped with so-called inherent and passive safety features, including natural circulation, low power densities in the core, slow-proceeding normal and accident processes, great reserves of coolant in the primary circuit, and passive emergency heat-removal systems, to name but a few (Sidorenko, "Nuclear Power," 16–17).

78. Several of my interviewees were very disgruntled by the fact that a very successful politician, Boris Nemtsov, started his political career "riding the green wave"—that is, by opposing the Gorky nuclear heating plant. Nemtsov followed Sergei Kirienko (one of Boris Yeltsin's luckless premiers) from Gorky to Moscow, where he eventually became leader of the *Soiuz pravykh sil* party ("Union of Right Forces"). The Gorky plant (at least temporarily) housed a vodka production facility. This halt in the construction of new nuclear power plants after Chernobyl is usually attributed to "public pressure," but the concurrent economic decline should not be neglected (Stephen Kotkin, *Armageddon Averted: The Soviet Collapse, 1970–2000* (Oxford: Oxford University Press, 2001); Glenys A. Babcock, "The Role of Public Interest Groups in Democratization: Soviet Environmental Groups and Energy Policy-Making, 1985–1991," doctoral dissertation, RAND Graduate School, 1997; Valerie Bunce, *Subversive Institutions: The Design and the Destruction of Socialism and the State* (Cambridge: Cambridge University Press, 1999); Sonja D. Schmid, "Transformation Discourse: Nuclear Risk as a Strategic Tool in Late Soviet Politics of Expertise," *Science, Technology & Human Values* 29, no. 3 (2004): 353–376; Jeremy J. Richardson, ed., *Pressure Groups* (Oxford: Oxford University Press, 1993); David R. Marples, "The Post-Soviet Nuclear Power Program," *Post-Soviet Geography* 34, no. 3 (1993): 172–184; Donna Bahry and Brian D. Silver, "Soviet Citizen Participation on the Eve of Democratization," *American Political Science Review* 84, no. 3 (1990): 821–847; James H. Oliver, "Citizen Demand and the Soviet Political System," *American Political Science Review* 63, no. 2 (1969): 465–475; Jerry F. Hough, "Political Participation in the Soviet Union," *Soviet Studies* 28, no. 1 (1976): 3–20).

79. Sidorenko, "Nuclear Power," 17–18. These designs would also allow a reduction in the operating personnel by a factor of 2.5–3, a measure not so much aimed at cost-cutting as at reducing the potential for human error (ibid., 18).

80. Around the same time, the staff at the Beloiarsk nuclear power plant, then the only industrial-scale graphite-water reactor in operation, received a design draft for review: it was a graphite-water reactor different from the one they were managing (Interviews #3 and #9). The Beloiarsk specialists were asked to evaluate, it turned out, an early version of the RBMK: a graphite-water design that would soon be adopted as the second standardized reactor for mass implementation in the Soviet territory. After several weeks of studying these blueprints, the experts at Beloiarsk concluded that this design retained the negative features of early power reactors, and in their final report recommended that the design needed significant improvements. As one of my interviewees predicted, I was not able to locate this report in an archive.

81. Ulasevich, *Sozdano pod rukovodstvom*, 42. According to veterans of the Leningrad nuclear power plant, these goals of physical and thermal efficiency, along with reliability and safety, were guiding principles in the design process (Leonid A. Belianin, ed., *Leningradskaia AES: Gody, sobytiia, liudi* (Moscow: Energoatomizdat, 1998)). This stood in marked contrast to production reactors, where the primary goal was to maximize the output of weapons-grade plutonium.

82. The State Specialized Design Institute (GSPI-11) was appointed chief project manager, the Kharkov Turbine Factory was selected as chief engineer of the nonnuclear part of the plant, and several factories were tasked with manufacturing equipment (Ulasevich, *Sozdano pod rukovodstvom*, 41–42).

83. These reactors had an electrical power of 1000 MW, and a thermal power of 3200 MW (ibid., 33). On November 11, 1966, the minister of Medium Machine Building, Efim Slavskii, issued an order that held the following individuals personally responsible for the design of the first two blocks of the Leningrad nuclear power plant: A. P. Aleksandrov as scientific director, S. M. Feinberg as his deputy, N. A. Dollezhal as the chief design engineer, Iu. M. Bulkin as his deputy, and A. A. Bochvar as the chief designer of the fuel assemblies. Additionally, NII-8 was put in charge of addressing the comments of the experts and of updating and improving the design (ibid., 48).

84. Ulasevich, *Sozdano pod rukovodstvom*, 34, 42. One difference between the Beloiarsk reactor and the RBMK design was that the fuel elements at Obninsk, as well as at the Beloiarsk reactors and Bilibino, were ring-shaped and steel-clad, while the RBMK's fuel elements are pellet-shaped and zirconium-clad.

85. The government decree (Postanovlenie Soveta Ministrov No. 500–252, September 29, 1966) that identified the RBMK as the reactor type to be implemented at Leningrad, and several other locations, was issued several months *before* Dollezhal's institute was appointed chief design engineer. On the Internet, including Rosatom's official website, there seems to be some confusion about the date of this government decree (September or November) and so far I have not been able to verify the date; however, several authoritative sources use the September date (V. P. Vasilevskii et al., "Razrabotka proekta i sozdanie pervogo energobloka s reaktorom RBMK-1000," in Viktor A. Sidorenko, ed., *Istoriia atomnoi energetiki Sovetskogo Soiuza i Rossii: Istoriia RBMK*, vol. 3, 61–101 (Moscow: IzdAt, 2003) (especially 63); A. N. Kuz'min, "Sorok let s RBMK," in Viktor A. Sidorenko, ed., *Istoriia atomnoi energetiki Sovetskogo Soiuza i Rossii: Istoriia RBMK*, vol. 3, 156–170 (Moscow: IzdAt, 2003) (especially 157); Ulasevich, *Sozdano pod rukovodstvom*; Ulasevich, *O iadernykh reaktorakh*).

86. The original fuel enrichment was 1.8 percent, which was subsequently recognized as a design flaw, facilitating a very high positive steam coefficient of reactivity. In the late 1970s the designers increased the enrichment to 2 percent; at the Lithuanian RBMKs, the enrichment was further raised to 2.4 percent, then to 2.6 percent, and later to 2.8 percent (Interview #16).

87. Sidorenko, "Nuclear Power," 13.

88. Ibid., 13.

89. World Nuclear Association, "RBMK Reactors," http://www.world-nuclear.org/info/Nuclear-Fuel-Cycle/Power-Reactors/Appendices/RBMK-Reactors.

90. The remotely controlled refueling machine, essentially a tall crane that moves atop the reactor's upper biological shield, is brought in position over the desired channel, seals the head, and (after equalizing the pressure and feeding water into the channel) draws up the spent fuel assembly. It then automatically inserts a fresh fuel assembly, seals the channel, and transports the spent fuel to a pool for cooling. The Russian acronym for this machine is PRM, *Pogruzochno-razgruzochnaia mashina* (Sidorenko, "Nuclear Power," 13).

91. Variations in the fuel cycles can be used to increase or decrease the amount of plutonium, or electricity, produced. The longer the fuel rods are left in the reactor core (i.e., the better the fuel is burned up), the more electricity can be generated; the less time they are left in the core, the more plutonium is produced (Interview #4).

92. At an international conference in Moscow in June 2004 (Rosenergoatom, VNIIAES), a physicist from the Kurchatov Institute who talked about fuel burn-up in RBMKs mentioned that "now that we don't need to produce extra plutonium anymore, this doesn't matter" (quoted from memory), indicating that there had been some options as to how to utilize the fuel in order to get (or not) a maximum of plutonium out of it. So the RBMKs *could* be used to produce additional plutonium (a fact noticed by Western observers and analysts), just in case the Siberian installations broke down or were incapacitated for other reasons. But RBMKs were not intended as primary plutonium producers—for that purpose the Soviets had their military reactors in Siberia (also Interview #11).

93. Despite the fact that Western sources have claimed that RBMKs were used for plutonium production, I haven't found evidence to support these claims. The plutonium production capacity of military and dual-use reactors in Siberia was so great that the use of the RBMK—a design optimized for power generation—for weapons-grade plutonium production seems unlikely, at least under normal circumstances.

94. DeLeon, *Development and Diffusion*, 112.

95. Ibid., 113, and Interview #22.

96. The "void coefficient," also called "steam (or bubble) coefficient of reactivity," was one of the physical causes for the reactor accident in Chernobyl (www.euronuclear.org/info/encyclopedia/s/steam-bubble-coefficient.htm). I return to this design feature in more detail in chapter 5.

97. Ulasevich, *Sozdano pod rukovodstvom*, 51. The physical launch in Russian is *fizicheskii pusk*, or *fizpusk*.

98. This period of work, leading up to the launch of the reactor, is called *puskonaladochnye raboty* (start-up and adjustment work) (Ulasevich, *Sozdano pod rukovodstvom*, 50).

99. This is referred to as *energeticheskii pusk*.

100. The "Den' energetika" is still celebrated in Russia on December 22 (the day of the "atomshchik" is September 28).

101. This mode of operation (*opytno-promyshlennaia operatsiia* (Ulasevich, *Sozdano pod rukovodstvom*, 51)) is distinct from the actual industrial operation.

102. Ibid., 51.

103. Ibid., 52.

104. Sidorenko, "Nuclear Power," 13.

105. Goncharov, "Pervyi period," 56. The zirconium-niobium alloy used in the cladding provided more economical use of neutrons in the chain reaction, and more easily managed coolant temperatures (Sidorenko 1997, 11–12).

106. Gennadii A. Shasharin, "Chernobyl'skaia tragediia," in Aleksandr N. Semenov, ed., *Chernobyl' desiat' let spustia: Neizbezhnost' ili sluchainost'?*, 75–132 (Moscow: Energoatomizdat, 1995) (especially 126–127). Nuclear safety expert Viktor Sidorenko distinguished seven different "modes" or "modifications" of the RBMK that somewhat overlap with Shasharin's "generations." Sidorenko divides up the first generation RBMKs into two, and the second generation into four modes (Sidorenko, "Nuclear Power," 13–15).

107. Sidorenko, "Nuclear Power," 14.

108. The first edition of safety regulations for nuclear power plant design went into effect in 1968 (ibid., 7). The first edition of the "General Regulations for Nuclear Power Plant Safety" was approved in 1971 (ibid., 9).

109. "Accident localization system" essentially means measures to contain an accident and to prevent the release of radioactive materials.

110. Sidorenko, "Nuclear Power," 13.

111. MKR is short for *metallurgicheskii kol'tsevoi reaktor* ("metallurgical ring reactor") (Ministerstvo Rossiiskoi Federatsii po atomnoi energii, *Strategiia razvitiia atomnoi energetiki Rossii v pervoi polovine XXI veka* (Moscow: FGUP "TsNIIatominform," 2001); Sidorenko, "Nuclear Power," 15). This reactor was supposed to replace some of the first-generation RBMKs—for example, at the Leningrad nuclear power plant. However, by 2006, not a single graphite-water design was part of the country's nuclear energy strategy (Natsional'nyi issledovatel'skii tsentr "Kurchatovskii institut," *O strategii iadernoi energetiki Rossii do 2050 goda* (Moscow: NITs "Kurchatovskii institut," 2012)).

112. Viktor A. Sidorenko, "Upravlenie atomnoi energetikoi," in Viktor A. Sidorenko, ed., *Istoriia atomnoi energetiki Sovetskogo Soiuza i Rossii*, vol. 1, 217–253 (Moscow: IzdAt, 2001) (especially 227); Sidorenko, "Nuclear Power," 13.

113. Sidorenko, "Nuclear Power," 13. For the decision to develop the RBMK, see Ulasevich, *Sozdano pod rukovodstvom*, 41–53.

114. Josephson, *Red Atom*, 25. Aleksandrov had succeeded the IFP's previous director, Petr Kapitsa, who was reinstated after Stalin's death. Peter Holquist has suggested translating *sharik* as "balloon," referring to the helium used in this design. I am not sure whether Aleksandrov's proposal already featured spherical fuel elements (as later designs did; cf. Goncharov, "Pervyi period," 30), but if it did, *sharik* may also have referred to the spherical shape of the fuel elements. Helium is an excellent coolant and can produce heat and steam very efficiently.

115. The first series of fuel elements for the "EG" reactor (*energeticheskii-gazovyi*), produced by the All-Union Scientific and Technical Institute for Aviation Materials (VIAM), had already been produced and was being tested in research reactors (Goncharov, "Pervyi period," 30; Asmolov et al., *Atomnaia energetika*, 65).

116. Sidorenko, "Vvedenie," 8–9; Vasilieva, *Soleils rouges*.

117. This reactor, the ABTU-Ts (VGR-50), was never constructed either, and in June 1987 (after Chernobyl!), another decree ordered the construction of the VG-400 instead of the VGR-50 (Goncharov, "Pervyi period," 30). As far as I could determine, the VG-400, which was supposed to produce electrical power and energy for applications in the chemical and metallurgical industry, was never built (cf. also Sidorenko, "Nuclear Power," 4). The main ideologue behind this design, Nikolai Ponomarev-Stepnoi, in the early 2000s promoted the related idea of a "hydrogen economy," where nuclear power plants produce electricity during the day, and hydrogen fuel cells during the night, when demand for electricity is low (Rosenergoatom's Fourth International Scientific and Technical Conference, "Nuclear Power Safety, Efficiency, and Economics," held June 16–17, 2004, in Moscow). Gabrielle Hecht has described the development and demise of the gas-graphite design in France (Hecht, *The Radiance of France*, especially 271–323), and Maria Vasilieva investigated why the Soviets did not adopt gas-cooled designs like the British and French in the first place (Vasilieva, *Soleils rouges*).

118. Kruglov, *Kak sozdavalas'*.

119. B. L. Ioffe and O. V. Shvedov, "Heavy Water Reactors and Nuclear Power Plants in the USSR and Russia: Past, Present, and Future," *Atomic Energy* 86, no. 4 (1999): 295–304. In October 1945, the Technical Council of the Special Committee on the Atomic Bomb charged Abram Alikhanov with leading the newly established Laboratory No. 3 of the Academy of Sciences. Alikhanov led efforts to construct a reactor using heavy water as a moderator (Abram I. Ioirysh et al., *Gosudarstvennyi nadzor za obespecheniem bezopasnosti atomnoi energetiki: pravovye problemy* (Moskva: Nauka,

Notes

1991); Kruglov, *Kak sozdavalas'*). The same institute also spearheaded efforts to construct a homogeneous reactor (cf. Asmolov et al., *Atomnaia energetika*, 17). The 500 kW reactor had been engineered by the construction bureau OKB Gidropress in the city of Podolsk. In 1957, it was reconstructed and its output raised five times to reach 2500 kW (Goncharov, "Pervyi period," 29).

120. Ioffe and Shvedov, "Heavy Water Reactors."

121. The construction of the fuel rods proved particularly challenging: these consisted of metallic uranium in a cladding made of a magnesium and beryllium alloy and designed to withstand temperatures of up to 500°C (Goncharov, "Pervyi period," 29–30).

122. Asmolov et al., *Atomnaia energetika*, 66; Andranik M. Petros'iants, *Dorogi zhizni, kotorye vybirali nas* (Moscow: Energoatomizdat, 1993). Goncharov suggests that several heavy-water reactors were planned for military sites in the Soviet Union, but they were abandoned after the mishaps with the operation of the Czechoslovakian reactor, which also revealed design and construction flaws (Goncharov, "Pervyi period," 33, 58). Canada, by contrast, developed its national nuclear power program based on a heavy-water design, the CANDU. According to a nuclear physicist I interviewed, the Canadians also encountered severe problems with their fuel rods and received assistance from the Soviets with the technology the latter had mastered by then. He recalled that "the Canadians said 'Thank you,' and that was it" (Interview #23).

123. I use "momentum" or "technological momentum" in Thomas Hughes's sense, as "a mass of technical and organizational components" that technological systems acquire over a prolonged period of growth and consolidation. At some point, these technological systems "possess direction, or goals; and they display a rate of growth suggesting velocity" (Thomas P. Hughes, "The Evolution of Large Technological Systems," in Wiebe E. Bijker, Thomas P. Hughes, and Trevor Pinch, eds., *The Social Construction of Technological Systems*, 51–82 (Cambridge, MA: MIT Press, 1987) (quotes on 76)).

124. These numbers include all units that started up by the end of 1986. They include the unique Bilibino (four 12 MW units) and Beloiarsk reactors (100, 200, and 600 MW, respectively), and the breeder reactor at Shevchenko (350 MW). I did not include military dual-use reactors in this count.

125. The restarted civilian nuclear program included four designs: in addition to the AMB, under construction at Beloiarsk, and the VVER, under construction at Novo-Voronezh, these were a gas-graphite design and a heavy-water reactor with an organic coolant (see chapter one). According to Sidorenko, the heavy-water design was later replaced with light-water reactors, and the gas-graphite design with an emphasis on breeders, which were seen as a solution to the problem of fuel availability—at least until fusion would become operational (Sidorenko, "Vvedenie," 9).

126. Interview #4; Holloway, *Stalin and the Bomb*.

127. Ulasevich, *Sozdano pod rukovodstvom*, 53. A version of it was also provided in an interview (Interview #16). My English translation.

128. Tatarnikov, "Atomnaia elektroenergetika."

129. Interviews #3 and #9. See also Ulasevich, *Sozdano pod rukovodstvom*; Leonid A. Belianin, ed., *Leningradskaia AES: Gody, sobytiia, liudi* (Moscow: Energoatomizdat, 1998); Nikolai A. Dollezhal', *U istokov rukotvornogo mira: Zapiski konstruktora* (Moscow: GUP NIKIET, IzdAt, 2002). This production bottleneck would be cleared once the Volga-Don *Atommash* factory was completed, which was intended to release several reactor vessels for VVERs each year. But this factory was not to be completed until the early 1980s, and then only partially (Josephson, *Red Atom*, 97–108; Marsha Freeman, "Atommash: Assembly Line Nuclear Plants," *Executive Intelligence Review* 6, no. 28 (1979): 20–21; V. A. Il'ichev and A. A. Prigoryan, "Structure Settlements at the Atommash Plant as a Result of Prolonged Soil Wetting," *Soil Mechanics and Foundation Engineering* 25, no. 4 (1988): 150–157).

130. Sidorenko, "Nuclear Power," 13. See also Ulasevich, *Sozdano pod rukovodstvom*, 41–53.

131. In 1975, the Institute of Atomic Energy issued an expert summary titled "Nuclear Power: Fundamental Problems and Perspectives of its Development." In this report, the choice of the RBMK in addition to the VVER was justified in terms of the relief it would bring to the machine-building industry, and also in terms of the potential to build reactors with very high power outputs (Asmolov et al., *Atomnaia energetika*, 21–23).

132. Interview #8.

133. Presumably, the RBMK could also be assembled using fewer skilled workers than the VVER; however, this argument was never made publicly.

134. Sidorenko, "Nuclear Power."

135. With the curious exception of the heavy-water reactor at Bohunice (in what today is Slovakia), the only design approved for export was the VVER (for details see Sonja D. Schmid, "Nuclear Colonization? Soviet Technopolitics in the Second World," in Gabrielle Hecht, ed., *Entangled Geographies: Empire and Technopolitics in the Global Cold War*, 125–154 (Cambridge, MA: MIT Press, 2011)).

136. Lev A. Kochetkov, "K istorii pervoi ocheredi Beloiarskoi AES," in Viktor A. Sidorenko, ed., *Istoriia atmnoi energetiki Sovetskogo Soiuza i Rossii*, vol. 1, 117–133 (Moscow: IzdAt, 2001).

137. The siting of the VVER vessel factory Atommash does, in fact, suggest that barging the heavy, oversized vessels was being planned. But this factory failed, and the argument was dropped from official history.

138. Among the specialists who spent a formative period of their careers at the young Beloiarsk station were Gennadii Veretennikov, Boris Prushinski, and Artem Grigoryiants.

139. DeLeon, *Development and Diffusion*, 56; *Reactors of the World* (New York: Simmons-Boardman, 1958); U.S. Energy Research and Development Administration, Division of Reactor Research and Development, *Soviet Power Reactors 1974. Report of the United States of America Nuclear Power Reactor Delegation Visit to the Union of Soviet Socialist Republics, September 19–October 1, 1974* (ERDA-2, UC-79). (Washington, DC: U.S. Energy Research and Development Administration, 1975).

140. Andranik M. Petros'iants, "Tret'ia mezhdunarodnaia Zhenevskaia konferentsiia atomnikov," *Atomnaia energiia* 17, no. 5 (1964): 323–328.

141. In 1970, Sidorenko reported to an audience of almost 200 on a trip to the United States (Ministerstvo energetiki i elektrifikatsii SSSR. Vsesoiuznyi teplotekhnicheskii nauchno-issledovatel'skii institut im. F. E. Dzerzhinskogo. NTS. Protokol i stenogramma zasedaniia NTS instituta ot 16.II.1970 po voprosu "Atomanaia energiia SShA." Dokladchiki: V. V. Stekol'nikov, V. A. Sidorenko (RGANTD, f. R-277, op. 2–6, d. 1117). See also Viktor A. Sidorenko, "Nauchnoe rukovodstvo v atomnoi energetike," in Viktor A. Sidorenko, ed., *Istoriia atomnoi energetiki Sovetskogo Soiuza i Rossii: Istoriia VVER*, vol. 2, 5–28 (Moscow: IzdAt, 2002); Tatarnikov, "Atomnaia elektroenergetika." But see Mazuzan and Walker for a counterargument to the likely profitability of this reactor: they report that the United States initially considered its economic prospects worse than those of other designs (George T. Mazuzan and J. Samuel Walker, *Controlling the Atom: The Beginnings of Nuclear Regulation, 1946–1962* (Berkeley: University of California Press, 1985), 1–31).

142. Sidorenko, "Nuclear Power," 13. For a depiction in this spirit see, for example, K. Polushkin, "Atomnyi bogatyr' [Atomic Giant]," *Nauka i zhizn'* 11 (1980): 44–52; Dollezhal', *U istokov rukotvornogo mira*; Belianin, *Leningradskaia AES*.

143. See Hecht, *The Radiance of France*, 3–4.

144. Ibid., 1998.

145. Sonja D. Schmid, "Transformation Discourse: Nuclear Risk as a Strategic Tool in Late Soviet Politics of Expertise," *Science, Technology & Human Values* 29, no. 3 (2004): 353–376.

146. Alekhin and Kiselev, "Istoriia sozdaniia."

Chapter 5

1. This procedure has often been referred to as an "experiment," implying an inadmissible process at a civilian installation. However, tests are conducted at any

industrial installation, nuclear or nonnuclear; they're part of the normal operation of a plant. For this reason I'll use the term *test* rather than *experiment*.

2. Gennadii A. Shasharin, "Chernobyl'skaia tragediia," in Aleksandr N. Semenov, ed., *Chernobyl' desiat' let spustia: Neizbezhnost' ili sluchainost'?*, 75–132 (Moscow: Energoatomizdat, 1995) (especially 110).

3. The test also included measurements of the turbogenerator's vibrations, a problem caused by manufacturing defects that dated back to the start-up of unit 4 (Razim I. Davletbaev, "Posledniaia smena," in Aleksandr N. Semenov, ed., *Chernobyl' desiat' let spustia: Neizbezhnost' ili sluchainost'?*, 366–383 (Moscow: Energoatomizdat, 1995) (especially 368)).

4. Shasharin, "Chernobyl'skaia tragediia," 111.

5. Davletbaev, "Posledniaia smena," 381.

6. Lenina S. Kaibysheva, "Posle Chernobylia," in A. N. Semenov, ed., *Chernobyl' desiat' let spustia: Neizbezhnost' ili sluchainost'?*, 384–396 (Moscow: Energoatomizdat, 1995) (especially 385); Constance Perin, "Operating as Experimenting: Synthesizing Engineering and Scientific Values in Nuclear Power Production," *Science, Technology & Human Values* 23, no. 1 (1998): 98–128.

7. Davletbaev, "Posledniaia smena," 369. A prominent science journalist I interviewed suggested that the accident happened because of soccer: the Kiev regional transmission system operator needed more electricity than anticipated because the soccer team Dinamo Kiev was playing, and everyone was watching TV (Interview #24). However, according to Robert Edelman, Dinamo Kiev actually played Spartak Moscow in Kiev two nights later, on April 27, in an open stadium, and won 2–1 (personal communication, October 2007).

8. Shasharin, "Chernobyl'skaia tragediia," 111.

9. Xenon 135 is an element that comes into being when iodine 135 decays—a routine process in nuclear reactors. Xenon 135 is an extremely good neutron absorber and its half-life is 9.2 hours (Anatolii S. Diatlov, *Chernobyl': Kak eto bylo* (Moscow: Nauchtekhlitizdat, 2003), 22). When the reactivity of a reactor is decreased (such as in the shutdown test described here), the reactor cannot be restarted until the xenon 135 that forms in the core has decayed. The maximum xenon 135 concentration is reached after about 12 hours. Several of my interviewees referred to this period of roughly 24 hours as *ksenovaia iama*, literally "xenon pit." The United States encountered this phenomenon at its Hanford reactors; in the Soviet Union, it was well known at military reactors, but apparently this knowledge was not transferred to civilian graphite-water reactor operators (European Nuclear Society, www.euronuclear.org/info/encyclopedia/x/xenon-poisoning.htm).

10. I followed the very clear description in Shasharin, "Chernobyl'skaia tragediia," 116–117, and the timeline, based on INSAG-7, at http://www.world-nuclear.org/

info/Safety-and-Security/Safety-of-Plants/Appendices/Chernobyl-Accident---Appendix-1--Sequence-of-Events. For more technical specifics on the RBMK see chapter 4.

11. After shutdown, even with the control rods completely inserted and no nuclear chain reaction occurring, however, the reactor continues to emit residual (decay) heat and needs to be continuously cooled. Without cooling, the decay of fission products in the reactor produces additional heat, which can drive the core's temperature up even with all control rods inserted.

12. The exact positioning of the control rods varies depending, among other things, on the fuel burn-up in the core. Since the RBMK can be refueled online (see chapter 4), refueling, or regrouping of fuel assemblies that are burned up to different degrees, occurs on a daily basis to optimize power output (Shasharin, "Chernobyl'skaia tragediia," 115–116).

13. Shasharin, "Chernobyl'skaia tragediia," 115.

14. Ibid.; International Nuclear Safety Advisory Group, ed., *Summary Report on the Post-Accident Review Meeting on the Chernobyl Accident*, No. 75-INSAG-1, Safety Series (Vienna: International Atomic Energy Agency, 1986). Anatolii Diatlov, deputy chief engineer on duty at unit 4 that night, describes the situation as calm and routine right up until that time (Diatlov, *Chernobyl'*, 29–61). The RBMK's scram button is sometimes referred to as AZ-5 or EPS-5.

15. As described earlier, the operators had pulled out the control rods in an effort to raise the reactor's power level, while the reactor was already entering the phase of "xenon poisoning." After 1986, the operating instructions were changed to require a minimum of forty control rods permanently inserted into the core (Shasharin, "Chernobyl'skaia tragediia," 125–126).

16. Minenergo's experts kept puzzling over where this additional reactivity came from—initially, they seriously considered the possibility of sabotage (Shasharin, "Chernobyl'skaia tragediia," 93; Boris Ia. Prushinskii, "Etogo ne mozhet byt'—no eto sluchilos' (pervye dni posle katastrofy)," in A. N. Semenov, ed., *Chernobyl' desiat' let spustia: Neizbezhnost' ili sluchainost'?*, 308–324 (Moscow: Energoatomizdat, 1995) (especially 316)).

17. Shasharin, "Chernobyl'skaia tragediia," 93. The question of whether the explosion was thermal or nuclear is still contested.

18. This exponential rise in power is the same process that takes place in an atomic bomb, except that a weapon is built to exploit this process, whereas a power reactor is designed to avoid it under any circumstances (Interview #23).

19. The warning system that in fact had been switched off was the reactor emergency cooling system (*sistema avariinogo okhlazhdeniia reaktora*, SAOR), which gets activated automatically during the maximum design accident (*maksimal'naia*

proektnaia avariia, MPA). The instructions for the test required switching off this system. In addition, Shasharin argues that the operators were confident about switching it off because they knew that six RBMK units (the two older reactors at Leningrad, Kursk, and Chernobyl) did not have this system at all. Besides, even if the system had been in operation, it was notoriously slow and would not have been able to alter the course of events (Shasharin, "Chernobyl'skaia tragediia," 112–113).

20. Davletbaev, "Posledniaia smena," 371.

21. "Proizoshlo prakticheski mgnovennoe (vzryvnoe) narastanie moshchnosti" (Shasharin, "Chernobyl'skaia tragediia," 93). See also Diatlov, *Chernobyl'*, 9.

22. Aleksandr A. Iadrikhinskii, *Iadernaia avariia na 4-om bloke Chernobyl'skoi AES i iadernaia bezopasnost' reaktorov RBMK* (Kurchatov: [n.p.], 1989) (quote on 10). This report is available online (e.g., http://ilya-sirius.ucoz.com/load/1-1-0-1). Others have speculated that what sounded like a second explosion could have been the reactor's upper biological shield, a disk-shaped concrete structure weighing a thousand tons (two million pounds), crashing back down on the reactor shaft after the first explosion lifted it off its base (Interview #34 and personal communication).

23. It is still disputed just how much radioactive material was released into the atmosphere and how much of the core ended up underground, solidified as an "elephant's foot" (e.g., Boris E. Burakov et al., "The Behavior of Nuclear Fuel in the First Days of the Chernobyl Accident," *Materials Research Society Symposium Proceedings* 465 (1996): 1297–1308). Official reports on the percentage of nuclear fuel that reached the environment often quote figures in the range of 3–5 percent (Shasharin, "Chernobyl'skaia tragediia," 108). Alternative accounts maintain that the original discharge was 25–30 percent, and that eventually the entire fuel mass was outside of the reactor (e.g., Shasharin, "Chernobyl'skaia tragediia," 109; Prushinskii, "Etogo ne mozhet byt'," 313). Iadrikhinskii writes that at least 80 percent of the nuclear fuel was ejected (Iadrikhinskii, *Iadernaia avariia*, 6).

24. During the first 48 hours, 203 people had to seek medical treatment; 129 were sent to Moscow (Shasharin, "Chernobyl'skaia tragediia," 83–84).

25. See, for example, "Moscow News Disputes Official Chornobyl Toll," *Ukrainian Weekly* 57, no. 47 (November 19, 1989): 1, 5.

26. Davletbaev, "Posledniaia smena," 377.

27. These tablets are used to prevent the thyroid gland from taking up radioactive iodine, and apparently there would have been sufficient quantities available in the area (A. N. Semenov, "K 10-letiiu katastrofy na Chernobyl'skoi AES," in A. N. Semenov, ed., *Chernobyl desiat' let spustia: Neizbezhnost' ili sluchainost'?*, 7–74 (Moscow: Energoatomizdat, 1995) (especially 18)). It is beyond the scope of this study to go into detail on the radiological, medical, or demographic consequences of the Chernobyl accident. The literature on the health consequences of the Chernobyl

accident is extensive; see, for example, Vasilii B. Nesterenko, *Masshtaby i posledstviia katastrofy na Chernobyl'skoi AES dlia Belorusi, Ukrainy i Rossii* (Minsk: Pravo i ekonomika, 1996); Mezhdunarodnyi Chernobyl'skii Proekt, *Mezhdunarodnyi Chernobyl'skii Proekt: Otsenka radiologicheskikh posledstvii i zashchitnykh mer* (Moscow: IzdAT, 1991); International Atomic Energy Agency, *The International Chernobyl Project: An Overview. Assessment of Radiological Consequences and Evaluation of Protective Measures* (Vienna: International Atomic Energy Agency, 1991); International Atomic Energy Agency, *The International Chernobyl Project: Technical Report—Assessment of Radiological Consequences and Evaluation of Protective Measures* (Vienna: International Atomic Energy Agency, 1991); Rudol'f M. Aleksakhin et al., *Problemy smiagcheniia posledstvii Chernobyl'skoi katastrofy: materialy mezhdunarodnogo seminara* (Briansk: Rossiia, 1993); Zbigniew Jaworowski, "All Chernobyl's Victims: A Realistic Assessment of Chernobyl's Health Effects," *21st Century Science and Technology* 11, no. 1 (1998): 14–25; E. B. Burlakova, ed., *Consequences of the Chernobyl Catastrophe: Human Health* (Moscow: Center for Russian Environmental Policy; Scientific Council on Radiobiology, Russian Academy of Sciences, 1996); V. M. Zakharov and E. Yu. Krysanov, eds., *Consequences of the Chernobyl Catastrophe: Environmental Health* (Moscow: Center for Russian Environmental Policy; Moscow Affiliate of the International "Biotest" Foundation, 1996); Alexey V. Yablokov et al., "Chernobyl: Consequences of the Catastrophe for People and the Environment," *Annals of the New York Academy of Sciences* 1181 (2009).

28. Lenina S. Kaibysheva, *Posle Chernobylia*, 2 vols. (Moscow: IzdAt, 1996–2001).

29. Prushinskii, "Etogo ne mozhet byt'," 321.

30. Vladimir V. Mar'in, "O deiatel'nosti operativnoi gruppy Politbiuro TsK KPSS na Chernobyl'skoi AES," in A. N. Semenov, ed., *Chernobyl' desiat' let spustia: Neizbezhnost' ili sluchainost'?*, 263–282 (Moscow: Energoatomizdat, 1995) (especially 267–269). At the time of Briukhanov's initial report to the Central Committee, the available information was still very vague (Shasharin, "Chernobyl'skaia tragediia," 80). Briukhanov has often been criticized for having been overwhelmed by the situation after the accident, an assessment several eyewitnesses refute (Shasharin, "Chernobyl'skaia tragediia," 97; Grigorii Medvedev, *Chernobyl Notebook*, JPRS-UEA-034-89 (Washington, DC: Joint Publications Research Service, October 23, 1989)). Shasharin, for example, attributes Briukhanov's reluctance to provide more than sketchy information to the common habit of not talking in excessive detail over a regular phone line, and also to a fear of being asked questions he couldn't yet answer. Prushinskii, Soiuzatomenergo's chief engineer and one of the first specialists to travel from Moscow to Chernobyl, is also sympathetic to Briukhanov. He suggests that Briukhanov didn't provide deliberate misinformation, but that he was struggling to believe what he saw with his own eyes, like many other experts when they first arrived on site. Also, Prushinskii implies that Briukhanov was deliberately trying to prevent a mass panic (Prushinskii, "Etogo ne mozhet byt'," 314). But see Clarke

(Lee Clarke, "Panic: Myth or Reality?," *Contexts* 1, no. 3 (2002): 21–26) on how the authorities' fear of a mass panic might itself be something of a myth.

31. Council of Ministers, decree No. 830, April 26, 1986 (Semenov, "K 10-letiiu katastrofy," 13).

32. The members of Shcherbina's government commission were Evgenii I. Vorob'ev (first deputy minister of Health), Vasilii I. Drugov (deputy minister of Internal Affairs), Valerii A. Legasov (academician, first deputy director of the IAE), Aleksandr G. Meshkov (first deputy minister of Sredmash), Anatolii I. Maiorets (minister of Minenergo), Nikolai F. Nikolaev (deputy chairman of the Ukrainian Council of Ministers), Ivan S. Pliush (chairman of the executive committee (*ispolkom*) of the regional Kiev Council of People's Delegates), Viktor A. Sidorenko (first deputy chairman of Gosatomenergonadzor), Nikolai P. Simochatov (chairman of the Central Committee of the Union of Power Plant Workers and Workers in the Electrotechnical Industry), Oleg V. Soroka (deputy procurator-general), and Fedor A. Shcherbak (head of the Sixth Administration of the KGB) (Viktor A. Sidorenko, "Nauchnoe rukovodstvo v atomnoi energetike," in Viktor A. Sidorenko, ed., *Istoriia atomnoi energetiki Sovetskogo Soiuza i Rossii: Uroki avarii na Chernobyl'skoi AES*, vol. 4 (Moscow: IzdAt, 2002) (especially 18)). See also Prushinskii, "Etogo ne mozhet byt'," 316.

33. Semenov, "K 10-letiiu katastrofy," 18–20.

34. Prushinskii reports that the second team arrived as early as May 2 (Prushinskii, "Etogo ne mozhet byt'," 323). He left Chernobyl on May 4, together with A. N. Semenov and M. S. Tsvirko (ibid., 323).

35. Kaibysheva, "Posle Chernobylia," 391.

36. This group of experts for emergency situations under Soiuzatomenergo was called OPAS, *gruppa okazaniia pomoshchi atomnym stantsiiam pri avariiakh* (Shasharin, "Chernobyl'skaia tragediia," 79–80; Prushinskii, "Etogo ne mozhet byt'," 309–311).

37. The formation of this group was suggested by Mikhail S. Gorbachev (*Operativnaia gruppa Politbuto TsK KPSS*) (Semenov, "K 10-letiiu katastrofy," 23; Mar'in, "O deiatel'nosti operativnoi gruppy," 271).

38. Semenov, *Chernobyl' desiat' let spustia*. Among the Strategic Group's members were the chairman of the Russian FSSR's Council of Ministers V. I. Vorotnikov, the Central Committee's secretary E. K. Ligachev, the head of the KGB V. M. Chebrikov (all of whom were also members of the Politburo), another secretary of the Central Committee, V. I. Dolgikh, defense minister S. L. Sokolov, and the minister of internal affairs A. V. Vlasov (Mar'in, "O deiatel'nosti operativnoi gruppy," 271).

39. Fond 89 is available at RGANI and the Hoover Institution. Also, Semenov reproduced several archival documents in his article (Semenov, "K 10-letiiu katastrofy," 25–58); see also RGANI, f. 89, op. 51, d. 20–22, 24. This collection of documents in

Fond 89 is a small selection of the historical record and, more than anything, provides an idea of the actual quantity of documents that remain unavailable.

40. Shasharin argued that the possibility of a renewed chain reaction was eliminated in the early morning of April 27, but this conclusion was not yet shared by everyone. The question of whether the reactor could "start" again worried the agencies until May 5; they argued that the regrouping of the fuel could create a critical mass (Shasharin, "Chernobyl'skaia tragediia," 86).

41. Ibid., 87.

42. Semenov lists 14,506 as the exact number of children registered in Pripyat at the time of the accident (Semenov, "K 10-letiiu katastrofy," 14).

43. Prushinskii, "Etogo ne mozhet byt'"; Medvedev, *Chernobyl Notebook*.

44. Vladimir Gubarev, *Pravda's* science editor, could barely control his outrage when he reported to the Central Committee on May 16 on his visit to Pripyat and what he had learned about the course of the evacuation (RGANI, f. 89, op. 53, d. 6, l. 1–5, k P 13/III from May 22, 1986, secret, No. 14757).

45. Estimates of the scale of the actual danger were ambivalent, and top authorities were reluctant to listen to experts who advocated immediate evacuation (Shasharin, "Chernobyl'skaia tragediia," 89, 96; Prushinskii, "Etogo ne mozhet byt'," Medvedev, *Chernobyl Notebook*).

46. See, for example, Semenov, "K 10-letiiu katastrofy," 14; Prushinskii, "Etogo ne mozhet byt'," 317.

47. Postanovlenie TsK KPSS "O reszul'tatakh rassledovaniia prichin avarii na ChAES i merakh po likvidatsii ee posledstvii, osobenno bezopasnosti atomnoi energetiki," ss P 21/10, July 14, 1986 (RGANI, f. 89, op. 53, d. 12, l. 2–13).

48. Shasharin, "Chernobyl'skaia tragediia," 91–92. It's not entirely clear what medical support these centers could provide, but given how high the radiation level was, and that there were no reliable instruments to measure it, people likely continued to get sick. The medical centers could at least provide temporary relief from symptoms and help decide whether the affected could resume work after a period of rest, or whether they would need to leave the "zone."

49. Igor' A. Beliaev, *Beton marki "Sredmash": Proshlo 15 let* (Moscow: IzdAt, 2001), 65. These 30,000 people subsequently became known as the "liquidators." This neologism is derived from Russian *likvidatsiia* for cleanup, or accident mitigation.

50. Semenov, "K 10-letiiu katastrofy," 53.

51. Shasharin, "Chernobyl'skaia tragediia," 91–92.

52. Ibid., 96–97.

53. Ibid., 85–86.

54. Semenov, "K 10-letiiu katastrofy," 22.

55. Their poetic/profane motto was: *Esli khochesh' byt' ottsom—zakryvai iaitsa svintsom* ("If you want to be a father, cover your balls with lead") (ibid.).

56. Kaibysheva, "Posle Chernobylia," 392.

57. Shasharin, "Chernobyl'skaia tragediia," 99, 106.

58. In other words, 75 percent of the releases occurred during the nine days following the explosion (Shasharin, "Chernobyl'skaia tragediia,"105).

59. Semenov, "K 10-letiiu katastrofy," 21.

60. Letter from B. Shcherbina to the Strategic Group of the Politburo, July 29, 1986 (reprinted in Semenov, "K 10-letiiu katastrofy," 45); Interview #27.

61. According to Viktor Briukhanov, in an interview he gave a newspaper in 2006, then Minenergo head Maiorets called for "repair work" at unit 4 to be completed by the November holidays—the celebration of the Great Socialist Revolution in 1917 ("Neponiatnyi atom: Interv'iu s Viktorom Briukhanovym," *Profil'*, April 24, 2006, http://www.profile.ru/obshchestvo/item/50192-items_18814). By mid-May, Minenergo was ordered to bring reactors 1 and 2 back to normal operation (Mar'in, "O deiatel'nosti operativnoi gruppy," 272).

62. B. Korolev, "Radiatsiia i kapusta," *Ogonek* 22 (May/June 1986): 7; Sonja D. Schmid, "Transformation Discourse: Nuclear Risk as a Strategic Tool in Late Soviet Politics of Expertise," *Science, Technology & Human Values* 29, no. 3 (2004): 353–376.

63. Martin C. Mahoney et al., "Thyroid Cancer Incidence Trends in Belarus: Examining the Impact of Chernobyl," *International Journal of Epidemiology* 33, no. 5 (2004): 1025–1033; Wilmar M. Wiersinga, "Differentiated Thyroid Carcinoma in Pediatric Age," in G. E. Krassas, S. A. Rivkees, and W. Kiess, eds., *Diseases of the Thyroid in Childhood and Adolescence*, 210–224 (Basel: Karger, 2007); V. K. Ivanov et al., "Dynamics of Thyroid Cancer Incidence in Russia Following the Chernobyl Accident," *Journal of Radiological Protection* 19 (1999): 305–318; V. K. Ivanov et al., "Cancer Risks in the Kaluga Oblast of the Russian Federation 10 Years after the Chernobyl Accident," *Radiation and Environmental Biophysics* 36 (1997): 161–167; A. Prisyazhniuk et al., "The Time Trends of Cancer Incidence in the Most Contaminated Regions of the Ukraine before and after the Chernobyl Accident," *Radiation and Environmental Biophysics* 34 (1995): 3–6; K. Baverstock et al., "Thyroid Cancer after Chernobyl," *Nature* 359 (1992): 21–22; K. B. Moysich, R. J. Menezes, and A. M. Michalek, "Chernobyl-Related Ionizing Radiation Exposure and Cancer Risk: An Epidemiological Review," *Lancet Oncology* 3 (2002): 269–279; Nuclear Energy Agency, *Chernobyl: Assessment of Radiological and Health Impacts*, 2002 update of *Chernobyl: Ten Years On* (Paris: Nuclear Energy Agency, OECD, 2002); Nuclear Energy Agency,

Notes

Committee on Radiation Protection and Public Health, *Chernobyl Ten Years On: Radiological and Health Impact—An Assessment* (Paris: Nuclear Energy Agency, OECD, 1995).

64. Velikhov voiced concerns that if enough nuclear fuel pieces fell into the cement mix, once that mix hardened, it might explode like an atomic bomb (Semenov, "K 10-letiiu katastrofy," 41, 44).

65. Ibid., 44.

66. This was in stark contrast to Minenergo's resources (Kaibysheva, "Posle Chernobylia," 394–395).

67. Semenov, "K 10-letiiu katastrofy," 55; Interview #30.

68. Semenov, "K 10-letiiu katastrofy," 62; see also Beliaev, *Beton*.

69. David R. Marples, *Chernobyl and Nuclear Power in the USSR* (New York: St. Martin's Press, 1986), 174.

70. Mar'in, "O deiatel'nosti operativnoi gruppy," 272–273. This work eventually resulted in the construction of the town of Slavutich. The city maintains a website that contains copies of the original documents on the construction of the sarcophagus; see www.slavutichcity.net.

71. Diane Vaughan, *The Challenger Launch Decision: Risky Technology, Culture, and Deviance at NASA* (Chicago: University of Chicago Press, 1996).

72. Diatlov, *Chernobyl'*, 109.

73. Shasharin, "Chernobyl'skaia tragediia," 105.

74. The first eight sections of the report are reproduced in Sidorenko's forth volume (Boris E. Shcherbina et al., "Doklad pravitel'stvennoi komissii po rassledovaniiu prichin avarii na Chernobyl'skoi AES 26 aprelia 1986 g. (iiun' 1986)," in Viktor A. Sidorenko, ed., *Istoriia atomnoi energetiki Sovetskogo Soiuza i Rossii: Uroki avarii na Chernobyl'skoi AES*, vol. 4, 17–47 (Moscow: IzdAt, 2002)).

75. Meeting No. 119, June 12, 1986, "Results of the accident analysis on unit 4 at the Chernobyl NPP [nuclear power plant] on April 26, 1986"; and meeting No. 120, June 17, 1986, "Questions on determining reasons for the development of the accident on April 26, 1986, at the 4th unit of the Chernobyl NPP [nuclear power plant] and elaboration of measures to improve the safety of the RBMK type reactor" (Viktor A. Sidorenko, ed., *Istoriia atomnoi energetiki Sovetskogo Soiuza i Rossii*, vol. 1 (Moscow: IzdAt, 2001), 246). Diatlov argues that this version did not do justice to the design flaws in the reactor, but in fact, the report does give a description of the design details (Shcherbina et al., "Doklad pravitel'stvennoi komissii"; Diatlov, *Chernobyl'*, 159).

76. Shasharin, "Chernobyl'skaia tragediia," 77.

77. Shasharin notes that when they died, they were still puzzling over why the explosion had occurred (ibid., 88).

78. Ibid., 93. The president of the Academy of Sciences, Aleksandrov, sent a damaged tape from the Chernobyl reactor number 4 to the KGB, with a request to recover whatever they could, using their special secret service techniques (Letter from Anatolii Aleksandrov to the first deputy minister of Interior Affairs, Iu. Churbanov, request to restore the lost recording on the *samopistsa* of the Chernobyl nuclear power plant in connection with the accident at the plant, early May 1986 (ARAN, f. 1916, op. 1, d. 227)).

79. Shasharin, "Chernobyl'skaia tragediia," 88–89.

80. Ibid., 76.

81. Ibid., 76. The deputy chief engineer of unit 4 at Chernobyl, Anatolii Diatlov, in his account of the accident noted that the report produced by Shasharin's group was the only one acknowledging that the reactor did not conform to the required safety norms (Diatlov, *Chernobyl'*, 80).

82. This report did not, in fact, represent Minenergo's "official" position, but Shasharin made his point consistently ("Dopolnenie k aktu rassledovaniia prichin avarii na energobloke No. 4 Chernobyl'skoi AES, proisshedshei 26 aprelia 1986 g.," *Minenergo SSSR, Soizatomenergo* inv. No. 4/611, 1986 (http://accidont.ru/refer.html).

83. Shasharin, "Chernobyl'skaia tragediia," 78.

84. According to Shasharin, Mikhail Gorbachev had personally initiated the insertion of this additional information into the Politburo's final report, which acknowledged not only mistakes made by the personnel but also design flaws (ibid., 78).

85. This decree has been declassified in the meantime: Postanovlenie TsK KPSS, "O reszul'tatakh rassledovaniia prichin avarii na ChAES i merakh po likvidatsii ee posledstvii, osobenno bezopasnosti atomnoi energetiki," ss P 21/10, July 14, 1986 (RGANI, f. 89, op. 53, d. 12, l. 2).

86. "V Politbiuro TsK KPSS," *Pravda* 20 July 1986, 1, 3.

87. Postanovlenie TsK KPSS, "O reszul'tatakh rassledovaniia prichin avarii na ChAES i merakh po likvidatsii ee posledstvii, osobenno bezopasnosti atomnoi energetiki," ss P 21/10, July 14, 1986 (RGANI, f. 89, op. 53, d. 12, l. 4–5).

88. "Utverzhedenie rukovoditelei Minsredmasha i AN SSSR ob absoliutnoi bezopasnosti deistvuiushchikh reaktorov na AES priveli k nedootsenke vazhnosti sovremennoi vyrabotki mer na sluchai avariinykh situatsii" (Ibid., l. 6)).

89. Ibid., l. 9).

90. The idiom *s zaneseniem v uchetnuiu kartochku* ("entered on his record") refers to a permanent entry in one's Party registration card, which in the Soviet system was analogous to a criminal record.

91. Postanovlenie TsK KPSS, "O reszul'tatakh rassledovaniia prichin avarii na ChAES i merakh po likvidatsii ee posledstvii, osobenno bezopasnosti atomnoi energetiki," ss P 21/10, July 14, 1986 (RGANI, f. 89, op. 53, d. 12, l. 7–8).

92. Ibid., l. 7. Dollezhal—officially the chief designer of this reactor type—delegated responsibility to his deputy, who in fact had been the chief designer of the control rods (Nadezhda Nadezhdina, "Zalozhniki reaktora," *Trud* 3 (April 1996): n.p.).

93. Postanovlenie TsK KPSS, "O reszul'tatakh rassledovaniia prichin avarii na ChAES i merakh po likvidatsii ee posledstvii, osobenno bezopasnosti atomnoi energetiki," ss P 21/10, July 14, 1986 (RGANI, f. 89, op. 53, d. 12, l. 8).

94. However, this did not prompt Slavskii to abandon "his" Sredmash. According to leading "liquidators," he came to the Chernobyl disaster site regularly, to boost morale among the exhausted builders of the sarcophagus (Interview #30). See also E. P. Slavskii, "Uvol'nenie (Semeinye istorii; vospominaet byvshii nachal'nik operativnogo shtaba Goskomiteta po inspol'zovaniiu atomnoi energii, chlen Pravitel'svennoi komissii Igor' Arkad'evich Beliaev)" (http://www.famhist.ru/famhist/ap/001d4ba4.htm).

95. Mar'in, "O deiatel'nosti operativnoi gruppy," 275–276; see also Semenov, *Chernobyl' desiat' let spustia*. It's difficult to assess actual public impact, but almost three weeks after the accident, Gorbachev's public appearance may no longer have had the effect it might have had three days after the disaster.

96. Mar'in, "O deiatel'nosti operativnoi gruppy," 270. See also Kaibysheva, *Posle Chernobylia*, vols. 1 and 2.

97. Mar'in, "O deiatel'nosti operativnoi gruppy," 277; Diatlov, *Chernobyl'*; "Informatsiia ob avarii na Chernobyl'skoi AES i ee posledstviiakh, podgotovlennaia dlia MAGATE," *Atomnaia energiia* 61 (1986): 301–320. The official report is reprinted in Sidorenko's fourth volume (Gosudarstvennyi komitet po ispol'zovaniiu atomnoi energii SSSR, "Avariia na Chernobyl'skoi AES i ee posledstviia: Informatsiia, podgotovlennaia dlia soveshchaniia ekspertov MAGATE (25–29 avgusta 1986 g., Vena," in Viktor A. Sidorenko, ed., *Istoriia atomnoi energetiki Sovetskogo Soiuza i Rossii: Uroki avarii na Chernobyl'skoi AES*, vol. 4, 49–84(Moscow: IzdAt, 2002)).

98. N. S. Babaev et al., "Problemy bezopasnosti na atomnykh elektrostantsiiakh," *Priroda* 6 (1980): 30–43. Legasov committed suicide on the second anniversary of the Chernobyl accident. His suicide fed speculation about the truthfulness of his testimony at the IAEA conference in 1986, but cannot clearly be linked to the report or the accident. The transcript of five audiotapes, where Legasov talks "About the

accident at the Chernobyl nuclear power plant," is online at lib.web-malina.com/getbook.php?bid=2755.

99. Shasharin, "Chernobyl'skaia tragediia," 106.

100. "Informatsiia ob avarii na Chernobyl'skoi AES."

101. Letter from the Central Committee's Department of Heavy Industry and Energy to the Central Committee, February 26, 1987 (ss, No. St-42/18 gs) (RGANI, f. 89, op. 11, d. 137, l. 2).

102. April 13, 1987, Postanovlenie TsK KPSS ss P61/88, "O plane osnovnykh meropriiatii v sviazi s godovshchinoi avarii na Chernobyl'skoi AES" (RGANI, f. 89, op. 12, d. 4, esp. l. 6, 10, 16–21). Some of these movies were *Preduprezhdenie, Kolokol Chernobylia, Trudnye nedeli Chernobylia, Chernobyl—dva tsveta vremeni*. On one of the most prominent exhibitions—in the Pavilion for Atomic Energy at the "Exhibition of the Achievements of the People's Economy" (VDNKh)—see Sonja D. Schmid, "Celebrating Tomorrow Today: The Peaceful Atom on Display in the Soviet Union," *Social Studies of Science* 36, no. 3 (2006): 331–365.

103. Sidorenko, "Nauchnoe rukovodstvo," 12; B. G. Gordon, ed., *Gosatomnadzoru Rossii—20 let* (Moscow: NTTs IaRB, 2003); Soraya Boudia, "Global Regulation: Controlling and Accepting Radioactivity Risks," *History and Technology* 23, no. 4 (2007): 389–406; L. Malone, "The Chernobyl Accident: A Case Study in International Law Regulating State Responsibility for Transboundary Nuclear Pollution," *Journal of Environmental Law* 12 (1987): 203–241; Interview #22. The Ukrainian Security Service (*Sluzhba bezpeki Ukraïni*) has made a series of declassified documents relating to Chernobyl accessible on the web; see http://www.ssu.gov.ua/sbu/control/uk/publish/article?art_id=49046&cat_id=53036.

104. The Soviet censorship agency, *Glavlit* (*Glavnoe upravlenie po delam literatury i izdatel'stv*), ceased to exist in 1991 (see Arlen V. Blium, *Zakat Glavlita: Kak razrushalas' sistema Sovetskoi tsenzury: Dokumental'naia khronika 1985–1991* (Moscow: Terra, 1995); Arlen V. Blium, "Kak bylo razrusheno 'Ministerstvo pravdy': Sovetskaia tsenzura epokhi glasnosti i perestroiki (1985–1991)," *Zvezda* 6 (1996): 212–221; Gennadii V. Zhirkov, *Istoriia tsenzury v Rossii XIX–XX vv.: Uchebnoe posobie* (Moscow: Aspect Press, 2001)). Also see, for example, Glenys A. Babcock, "The Role of Public Interest Groups in Democratization: Soviet Environmental Groups and Energy Policy-Making, 1985–1991," doctoral dissertation, RAND Graduate School, 1997; Schmid, "Transformation Discourse."

105. The evidence includes references to these internal reports in the open press—for instance, in Diatlov, *Chernobyl'*.

106. Diatlov, *Chernobyl'*; Alla Yaroshinskaya, *Chernobyl: The Forbidden Truth* (Lincoln: University of Nebraska Press, 1995); and many popular publications too numerous to list here.

Notes

107. Alexei Yurchak, *Everything Was Forever, until It Was No More: The Last Soviet Generation* (Princeton, NJ: Princeton University Press, 2006).

108. His writings were eventually published in English and Russian (Diatlov, *Chernobyl'*, 1995).

109. As explained in more detail in chapter 4, a loss of cooling water in this graphite-water reactor still allows the chain reaction to proceed, since the moderator (graphite) is not affected. Soviet physicists knew about this design feature, and they attempted to lower the positive steam coefficient starting in the early 1970s, when they experienced problems at the Leningrad nuclear power plant (Interview #16). The entire RBMK project was kept under a layer of secrecy, in part because of the reactor's potential to switch to plutonium production (Diatlov, *Chernobyl'*, 184).

110. See chapter four; Interviews #3 and #9.

111. Shasharin, "Chernobyl'skaia tragediia," 123–124; see also Diatlov, *Chernobyl'*, 11; Polivanov, "Chernobyl'skaia katastrofa," http://treeofknowledge.narod.ru/chernob.htm.

112. Diatlov, *Chernobyl'*, 51. One of my interviewees, a designer, dismissed that accident as insignificant: "Oh well, they fused a channel, so what?" (*Nu i chto, kanal zazhgli, nichego!*) (Interview #23).

113. Quoting a report by Aleksandr Iadrikhinskii from the Kursk nuclear power plant, Diatlov argues that skeptical voices were not heard at all (Diatlov, *Chernobyl'*, 118–119). Ulasevich, however, lists some delays in implementing the RBMK due to a series of concerns and suggestions that had to be considered (V. K. Ulasevich, ed., *Sozdano pod rukovodstvom N. A. Dollezhalia: O iadernykh reaktorakh i ikh tvortsakh (k 100-letiiu N. A. Dollezhalia)*, 2nd ed. (Moscow: GUP NIKIET, 2002), 41–42).

114. Diatlov, *Chernobyl'*, 51.

115. Ibid., 188.

116. Ibid., 105. Only in 1983–1984 did the oversight committee, Gosatomnadzor, become independent from Sredmash (B. G. Gordon, ed., *Gosatomnadzoru Rossii—20 let* (Moscow: NTTs IaRB, 2003)).

117. Diatlov, *Chernobyl'*, 80–81, 184.

118. I was not able to obtain any of Volkov's reports. The direct quotes from Volkov's report are quoted by I. F. Polivanov, a nuclear safety specialist, physicist and engineer, and consultant, who published a summary of Volkov's critique in Russian (Polivanov, "Chernobyl'skaia katastrofa," http://treeofknowledge.narod.ru/chernob.htm). According to Polivanov, Volkov even listed the names of those he considered culpable for the Chernobyl catastrophe: "Guilty for what has happened are: the scientific director (IAE), the chief design engineer (NIKIET), and also Minen-

ergo, which began operating a reactor without any protection against acceleration even from delayed neutrons" (ibid.).

119. Report by Vladimir P. Volkov, cited in Diatlov, *Chernobyl'*, 83.

120. Iadrikhinskii, *Iadernaia avariia*. This report is now available online (e.g., http://ilya-sirius.ucoz.com/load/1-1-0-1).

121. Prikaz predsedatelia Gosatomenergonadzora No. 11, February 27, 1990, cited in Diatlov, *Chernobyl'*, 178. The delay between Volkov's letter to Gorbachev and the creation of the commission can be explained by the ongoing conflict between Party officials who wanted to save face vis-à-vis the international community and technical specialists who argued that Western specialists had already figured out for themselves what had happened at Chernobyl and might as well be told the plain truth (Viktor A. Sidorenko, *Ob atomnoi energetike, atomnykh stantsiiakh, uchiteliakh, kollegakh i o sebe* (Moscow: IzdAt, 2003), 249).

122. Prikaz predsedatelia Gosatomenergonadzora No. 11, February 27, 1990, cited in Diatlov, *Chernobyl'*, 178. See also Georgii A. Kopchinskii and Nikolai A. Shteinberg, *Chernobyl: Kak eto bylo. Preduprezhdenie* (Moscow: Litterra, 2011).

123. Gosudarstvennyi komitet SSSR po nadzoru za bezopasnym vedeniem rabot v promyshlennosti i atomnoi energetike, "O prichinakh i obstoiatel'stvakh avarii na 4 bloke Chernobyl'skoi AES 26 aprelia 1986 g. Doklad komissii Gospromatomnadzora SSSR," in V. A. Sidorenko, ed., *Istoriia atomnoi energetiki Sovetskogo Soiuza i Rossii: Uroki avarii na Chernobyl'skoi AES*, vol. 4, 333–409 (Moscow: IzdAt, [1991] 2002). See also Diatlov, *Chernobyl'*, 178–183.

124. Diatlov, *Chernobyl'*, 118; Polivanov, "Chernobylskaia katastrofa." Sidorenko also reports that "suggestions from the IAE meant to increase safety were usually obstructed or slowed down [by NIKIET representatives], irrespective of decisions made by scientific-technical councils etc." (Viktor A. Sidorenko, "Ob"iasnitel'naia zapiska Sidorenko V. A. v komitet partiinogo kontrolia pri TsK KPSS," in Viktor A. Sidorenko, ed., *Istoriia atomnoi energetiki Sovetskogo Soiuza i Rossii: Uroki avarii na Chernobyl'skoi AES*, vol. 4, 44–47 (Moscow: IzdAt, 2002) (quote on 46)). While Aleksandrov was quick to attribute responsibility for the accident to the RBMK's chief engineer, Nikolai Dollezhal, Diatlov claims that Aleksandrov had received the monetary benefit for inventing the RBMK (Anatolii P. Aleksandrov, "Izmeniat', chto izmenit' eshche vozmozhno ...," *Ogonek* 35 (August 1990): 6–10). Apparently, the application for the invention had been declined twice by the Soviet patent office. It justified the rejection by stating that this was not a new design, and that an increase in economic efficiency was not considered worth a patent. After that, Aleksandrov filed the patent for the RBMK through Sredmash as a "classified" invention (Diatlov, *Chernobyl'*, 120; Igor' B. Beliaev, "Po tomu li puti? Dialog-rassledovanie (beseda s Viktorom Aleksandrovichem Bobrovym)," *Literaturnaia gazeta* 20 (5242), no. 17 (May 1989): 13).

125. International Nuclear Safety Advisory Group, *The Chernobyl Accident—Updating of INSAG-1 (INSAG-7)* (Vienna: International Atomic Energy Agency, 1992), especially the appended report by Abagian et al.

126. Michael Gordin, Karl Hall, and Alexei Kojevnikov, eds., *Intelligentsia Science: The Russian Century, 1860–1960, Osiris*, vol. 23 (special issue) (Chicago: University of Chicago Press, 2008).

127. As an employee of the FEI in Obninsk, Dubovskii inspected nuclear safety for the Institute of Atomic Energy (IAE) in Moscow; the IAE's safety inspector in turn assessed nuclear safety at Obninsk (Vladimir Anisinov, "AES: Stepen' riska (beseda s B. G. Dubovskim)," *Smena* 10 (1994): 55–61 (especially 58–59)).

128. Ibid., 56; see also Sidorenko, "Ob"iasnitel'naia zapiska," 44.

129. Anisinov, "AES: Stepen' riska." See also Gordon, *Gosatomnadzoru Rossii—20 let*; Polivanov, "Chernobyl'skaia katastrofa," http://treeofknowledge.narod.ru/chernob.htm.

130. Nadezhdina, "Zalozhniki reaktora."

131. This design flaw was not eliminated until 1992.

132. Anisinov, "AES: Stepen' riska," 57. On the *polikritichnost'* (multiple criticality) of the RBMK's core see, for example, Beliaev, "Po tomu li puti?"; Nikolai V. Karpan, *Chernobyl': Mest' mirnogo atoma* (Kiev: Kantri Laif, 2005); Interview #27. One interviewee put it bluntly: in the RBMK, there was not one core, but multiple cores (Interview #9).

133. Interviews #6 and #12; Anisinov, "AES: Stepen' riska," 56. See also Sidorenko, "Ob"iasnitel'naia zapiska," 44; Nadezhdina, "Zalozhniki reaktora"; Boris G. Dubovskii, "O faktorakh neustoichivosti iadernykh reaktorov na primere reaktora RBMK" (Obninsk: [n.p.], 1989).

134. Diatlov, *Chernobyl'*, 120, citing an essay (*referat*) by B. G. Dubovskii. See also Polivanov, "Chernobyl'skaia katastrofa," http://treeofknowledge.narod.ru/chernob.htm.

135. Letter from B. G. Dubovskii to M. S. Gorbachev, November 27, 1989, cited in Diatlov, *Chernobyl'*, 172–173.

136. In particular, the physicists noted an initially positive surge of reactivity in the reactor's emergency shutdown system.

137. Viktor A. Sidorenko, "Vvodnye zamechaniia k urokam Chernobyl'skoi avarii," in Viktor A. Sidorenko, ed., *Istoriia atomnoi energetiki Sovetskogo Soiuza i Rossii: Uroki avarii na Chernobyl'skoi AES*, vol. 4, 4–16 (Moscow: IzdAt, 2002) (especially 8).

138. "Sluchilos' to samoe" (Sidorenko, *Ob atomnoi energetike*, 249).

139. The fourth volume on the history of nuclear energy in the Soviet Union that Sidorenko edited contains his July 1986 testimony (*ob"iasnitel'naia zapiska*) to the Party's Accident Investigation Committee. In this short essay, Sidorenko admits to "moral guilt," acknowledges shortcomings in the regulatory organization's recruitment policies, and agrees with the government commission's conclusion that he had often been too accommodating when cooperating with ministries and other agencies, which undermined overall discipline (Sidorenko, "Ob"iasnitel'naia zapiska").

140. Apparently, this was the situation at most of the military reactors (Mar'in, "O deiatel'nosti operativnoi gruppy," 264).

141. Interviews #23 and #28.

142. Interview #32.

143. Diatlov assumes that Dollezhal and Emelyianov had positions where they did not feel threatened, even when their actions (or lack thereof) contradicted the decisions of the MVTS (Diatlov, *Chernobyl'*, 202).

144. Mar'in, "O deiatel'nosti operativnoi gruppy," 265–266.

145. This was the title of the June 13, 1983 MVTS session ("O nedostatkakh v rabote AES s RBMK-1000 I povyshenii nadezhnosti etikh AES.") These concerns were also put forward in a letter from the Central Committee's Vladimir Dolgikh. A note from the deputy director of the Department of Mechanical Engineering in the Central Committee, Arkadii Volskii, would be considered as well (MVTS session No. 88; Sidorenko, *Istoriia atomnoi energetiki Sovetskogo Soiuza i Rossii*, vol. 1, 244). These questions were also discussed in several later sessions in 1983, on June 27 (No. 89, "Doklad komissii MVTS po resul'tatam rassmotreniia proektnykh materialov po osnovnym tekhnicheskim i komponovochnym resheniiam unifitsirovannykh proektov energobloka RBMK-1000 (poruchenie MVTS ot 21.03.81)"), July 18 (No. 95, "O tselesoobraznosti prodolzheniia stroitel'stva Kostromskoi AES s reaktorom RBMK-1500 na vybrannoi ploshchadke po usloviiam seismichnosti," and No. 96, "O khode rabot po UVS RBMK-1000 2-i ocheredi Smolenskoi i 3-i ocheredi Kurskoi AES"), and December 19 (No. 97, "O khode vypolneniia resheniia MVTS ot 13.06.83 po voprosam povysheniia nadezhnosti raboty AES s reaktorami RBMK-1000") (ibid., 244–245).

146. Mar'in, "O deiatel'nosti operativnoi gruppy," 266–267. See also Diatlov, *Chernobyl'*, 202.

147. Sidorenko, *Istoriia atomnoi energetiki Sovetskogo Soiuza i Rossii*, vol. 1, 238.

148. Ibid., 202.

149. Viktor A. Sidorenko, "Kak eto bylo," in B. G. Gordon, ed., *Gosatomnadzoru Rossii—20 let*, 51–61 (Moscow: NTTs IaRB, 2003) (especially 60–61).

Notes

150. J. Samuel Walker, *Three Mile Island: A Nuclear Crisis in Historical Perspective* (Berkeley: University of California Press, 2004).

151. Babcock, "The Role of Public Interest Groups"; Jane I. Dawson, *Eco-Nationalism: Anti-Nuclear Activism and National Identity in Russia, Lithuania, and Ukraine* (Durham, NC: Duke University Press, 1996). See also Schmid, "Transformation Discourse."

152. But even within the Russian Federation, construction of several reactor units was halted (see, e.g., the movie *Vse atomnye elektrostantsii Rossii*, "All Russian Nuclear Power Plants," produced on CD-ROM by Rosenergoatom, Moscow, and released in 2003).

153. "Pri proektirovanii novykh AES schitat' netselesoobraznym ispol'zovanie reaktorov etogo tipa" ("It is not advisable to consider reactors of this type for the planning of new nuclear power plants") (Postanovlenie TsK KPSS, "O rezul'tatakh rassledovaniia prichin avarii na ChAES i merakh po likvidatsii ee posledstvii, osobenno bezopasnosti atomnoi energetiki," ss P 21/10, July 14, 1986 (RGANI, f. 89, op. 53, d. 12, l. 10)). Later, the MKR, a reactor type based on the RBMK design, became the cornerstone of the country's new "energy strategy," for more or less the same reasons that the RBMK had been chosen for mass implementation in the late 1960s: the industrial capacities for graphite-water reactors were available; also, the personnel had accumulated construction and operating experience with graphite-water reactors and when the RBMKs were phased out, they would not have to be retrained on pressurized water reactors (see also chapter 4).

154. Shasharin, "Chernobyl'skaia tragediia," 129.

155. "Ustanovit', chto proekty i mesta raspolozheniia AES utverzhdaiutsia SM SSSR." Responsibility for the truthful implementation of this decree was assigned to the secretary of the Central Committee, Dolgikh, and to several departments serving the Central Committee (Postanovlenie TsK KPSS, "O rezul'tatakh rassledovaniia prichin avarii na ChAES i merakh po likvidatsii ee posledstvii, osobenno bezopasnosti atomnoi energetiki," ss P 21/10, July 14, 1986 (RGANI, f. 89, op. 53, d. 12, l. 11)).

156. The death toll from this 1988 earthquake (6.9 on the Richter scale) was over 45,000; it also caused extensive damage in the area around the city of Spitak.

157. Lilly Torosyan, "Revisiting the Metsamor Nuclear Power Plant," *Armenian Weekly*, December 7, 2012, http://www.armenianweekly.com/2012/12/07/revisiting-the-metsamor-nuclear-power-plant.

158. Ukraine, Kazakhstan, and Belorus also inherited other nuclear artifacts—the subject of other work (e.g., Joseph Cirincione, Jon B. Wolfsthal, and Miriam Rajkumar, *Deadly Arsenals: Nuclear, Biological, and Chemical Threats* (Washington, DC: Carnegie Endowment for International Peace, 2005)).

159. On December 30, 1991, the new independent Russian government passed a resolution approving the resumption of construction on the Balakovo, Bilibino, Kola, Smolensk, and South Urals nuclear power plants (Babcock, "The Role of Public Interest Groups," 178).

160. S. D. Malkin, "O polnomasshtabnom trenazhere dlia Leningradskoi AES," in Viktor A. Sidorenko, ed., *Istoriia atomnoi energetiki Sovetskogo Soiuza i Rossii: Istoriia RBMK*, vol. 3, 147–155 (Moscow: IzdAt, 2003). Accident simulations, as helpful as they no doubt can be, still can't provide nuclear plant staff with guidelines for how to handle "beyond design-basis accidents," that is, accidents that the plant's designers had not anticipated.

161. Bronnikov had just been reassigned and had returned to Pripyat to pick up his family on the day of the accident. He volunteered to stay and left only after having received a hefty dose of radiation (Shasharin, "Chernobyl'skaia tragediia," 98).

162. The position of director of a plant (nuclear or conventional) involved a large number of administrative duties and public functions—for example, speeches at regional conventions and meetings, appearances at schools and factories, frequent trips to Moscow, and so on (Interview #25).

163. This story exemplifies the pitfalls of the *nomenklatura* system (see chapter 3), where candidates nominated for high-level industry positions had to be approved by the Communist Party.

164. Shasharin, "Chernobyl'skaia tragediia," 98.

165. The United States had built this type of reactor for plutonium production, but abandoned the design for commercial reactors.

166. Sidorenko, "Nauchnoe rukovodstvo," 14. Some British analysts, in their assessment of the accident, interpreted the tilted biological shield as a "safety valve" and argued that, had the Chernobyl reactor had a containment structure, the consequences might have been even more severe (Don Arnott and Robert Green, "Unique Safety Valve for a Reactor Nuclear Explosion?," paper presented at the national conference "The Legacy of Chernobyl—Lessons for the UK," Council House, Bristol, March 11, 1992 (organized by the National Steering Committee of Nuclear Free Local Authorities)).

167. One of the compromises worked out with the newly empowered oversight committee was a general reduction of power levels in all operating RBMKs. According to Vadim Malyshev, who was appointed head of Gosatomenergonadzor in September 1986, a power level reduced to 70 percent improved the physics of RBMK-type reactors and made them operate in a more stable manner (V. M. Malyshev, "Istoriia stanovleniia gosudarstvennogo nadzora za bezopasnost'iu atomnoi energetiki SSSR (1983–1991 gg.)," in B. G. Gordon, ed., *Gosatomnadzoru Rossii—20 let*, 26–37 (Moscow: NTTs IaRB, 2003)).

168. Aleksandr N. Semenov, ed., *Chernobyl' desiat' let spustia: Neizbezhnost' ili sluchainost'?* (Moscow: Energoatomizdat, 1995); Viktor A. Sidorenko, ed. *Istoriia atomnoi energetiki Sovetskogo Soiuza i Rossii: Istoriia RBMK*, vol. 3 (Moscow: IzdAt, 2003); Aleksandrov, "Izmeniat', chto izmenit' eshche vozmozhno ..."; I. A. Bashmakov and S. Ia. Chernavskii, eds., *Zakliuchenie na rabotu: Kontseptsiia razvitiia atomnoi energetiki v Rossiiskoi Federatsii* (Moscow: n.p., 1993); N. A. Dollezhal', *U istokov rukotvornogo mira: Zapiski konstruktora* (Moscow: GUP NIKIET, IzdAt, 2002). Nikolai A. Dollezhal declared that in the mid-1960s, the RBMK's fuel had been enriched at 1.8 percent with uranium 235—that is, as low a percentage as possible, to keep costs down. For references to Aleksandrov's efforts to promote the RBMK with regard to its economic efficiency, see Beliaev, "Po tomu li puti?" See also a report by A. N. Dollezhal (NIKIET), "Iadernaia bezopasnost' reaktora RBMK vtorykh ocheredei: Neitronno-fizicheskie parametry," quoted in Diatlov, *Chernobyl'*, 44.

169. These additional absorber rods are referred to as "DP," *dopolnitel'nye poglotiteli* (Diatlov, *Chernobyl'*, 44; Interview #16). Some of these modifications, however, negatively affected the reactors' economics and were later modified again (e.g., a uranium-erbium mix replaced the original fuel in some RBMKs (Interview # 16)). According to deputy chief engineer Anatolii S. Diatlov, the fuel enrichment at Chernobyl's unit 4 prior to the accident had been 2 percent, and there had been no additional absorber rods (Diatlov, *Chernobyl'*, 44). Boris Dubovskii seems to assume the existence of these additional absorber rods in the lower part of the reactor (a design modification he had initiated in the mid-1970s), but charges that they were not connected to the emergency shutdown system (*avariinaia zashchita, AZ*) (Diatlov, *Chernobyl'*, 171, citing Dubovskii, "O faktorakh neustoichivosti").

170. Sidorenko, "Ob"iasnitel'naia zapiska," 45; Postanovlenie TsK KPSS "O reszul'tatakh rassledovaniia prichin avarii na ChAES i merakh po likvidatsii ee posledstvii, osobenno bezopasnosti atomnoi energetiki," ss P 21/10, July 14, 1986 (RGANI, f. 89, op. 53, d. 12, l. 2–13).

171. Outsourcing nuclear plants to regional electricity networks, a question debated since the beginning of the nuclear industry, was now moot.

172. Viktor A. Sidorenko, "Upravlenie atomnoi energetikoi," in Viktor A. Sidorenko, ed., *Istoriia atomnoi energetiki Sovetskogo Soiuza i Rossii*, vol. 1, 217–253 (Moscow: IzdAt, 2001) (especially 222).

173. Ibid., 227; also Interview #23. Despite the fact that Sredmash officially ceased to exist in 1989, the new ministry was a direct successor organization of Sredmash, and many nuclear experts still frequently referred to it as Sredmash.

174. V. V. Chernyshev, ed., *Vitalii Fedorovich Konovalov: Stranitsy zhizni* (Moscow: IzdAt, 2003).

175. Sidorenko, *Ob atomnoi energetike*, 92–94.

176. Sidorenko, "Upravlenie," 230.

177. Ibid., 230. Sidorenko was involved in planning this corporation after 1991.

178. The idea of creating a corporation, this time under the label *Atomprom*, was revived only when Evgenii Adamov, former director of NIKIET, was appointed minister of atomic energy in 1998. The proposal was slightly modified, but the main goal remained the preservation of the nuclear industry's infrastructure, now in the interest of profitability and competitiveness (ibid., 236).

179. Several options for how to organize the nuclear energy complex were discussed. One alternative was to create an executive corporation for the nonmilitary sector, and combine this with a state committee for nuclear energy, which would regulate the entire nuclear industry and directly manage all military nuclear enterprises (ibid., 231–232).

180. Ibid., 235–236; Viktor N. Mikhailov, *Ia—"iastreb"* (Moscow: Kron-Press, 1993).

181. Sidorenko, "Upravlenie," 236. Two more deputy ministers, A. G. Meshkov, and E. A. Reshetnikov, served on this commission, together with the leaders of several other departments, administrations, commissions, and organizations.

182. A good, personal biography of Riabev can be found at "Ministry Sovetskoi epokhi," http://www.minister.su/article/1263.html.

183. For example, "Strategiia razvitiia atomnoi energetiki v ramkakh dolgosrochnoi kompleksnoi gosudarstvennoi toplivno-energeticheskoi programmy Rossiiskoi Federatsii na period do 2010 goda, 'Energeticheskaia strategiia Rossii'" (Strategy for the development of nuclear power in the framework of the long-term, complex state fuel and power program of the Russian Federation for the period until 2010, "Energy Policy of Russia"), passed by the Minatom Council in 1992 and endorsed by Minatom's Scientific-Technical Council in 1994; and "Programma razvitiia atomnoi energetiki Rossiiskoi Federatsii na 1998–2005 gody i na period do 2010 goda" (Program for nuclear power development in the Russian Federation for 1998–2005, and the period until 2010), passed by a government decree of the Russian Federation on June 21, 1998, No. 815 (Sidorenko, "Upravlenie," 236).

184. Decree issued by the president of the Russian Federation on September 7, 1992, "On the organization that operates nuclear power plants of the Russian Federation," No. 1055 (ibid., 233). The driving force behind the organization of Rosenergoatom was Evgenii Ignatenko, who later became the organization's director. Erik Pozdyshev was elected president of Rosenergoatom, and the manager responsible for the operation of nuclear power plants was Boris Antonov.

185. These organizations included the scientific production association "Energiia" (which encompassed VNIIAES), the production association "Soiuzatomtekhenergo," the production association "Atomenergoremont," the repair companies "Balakovo-turboatomenergoremont" and "Kursktuurbatomenergoremont," the factory "Atom-

remmash," the production association "Atomenergozapchast'" (spare parts), and a factory for experimental and power engineering equipment (Sidorenko, "Upravlenie," 234).

186. Sidorenko, "Upravlenie," 235.

187. Ibid., 235.

188. Ibid., 234.

189. Specifically, these were unit 6 at the Zaporozhye nuclear plant, unit 4 at the Rovno nuclear plant, and unit 2 at the Khmelnitskii nuclear plant. All Ukrainian plants now also received Ukrainian names: the Zaporizka, Rivenska, Khmelnitska, and Iuzhno-Ukrainska nuclear power plants.

190. This excludes the Chernobyl reactors. According to Ukraine's Energoatom, unit 6 at Zaporozhye was completed and commissioned in October 1995, making it the largest nuclear power plant (at 6 GW) in Europe.

191. http://energoatom.kiev.ua/en.

192. Ibid. Until 2005, Energoatom's website featured a statement on personnel policy that included features such as "enhancement of [the] personnel's self-esteem for involvement in nuclear-power engineering, awareness of the prestige associated with being a worker in this field of activity," and "the creation of positive public opinion regarding the activity of nuclear-power engineering, its priority with regard to the provision of cheap, environmentally clean energy for the population and national economy of Ukraine."

193. For SSE Chernobyl NPP, see http://www.chnpp.gov.ua/index.php?lang=en ; also Interview #33.

194. In 1997, the European Union, the United States, and Ukraine set up a fund to finance a massive project to secure the Chernobyl site; its most visible component is the "New Safe Confinement," a giant archlike steel structure that workers are assembling off site and then plan to slide over the old entombment on train tracks—essentially a "second sarcophagus." Construction began in 2010 and as of this writing is scheduled to be completed by 2015 (http://www.ebrd.com/pages/sector/nuclearsafety/chernobyl-sip.shtml).

Chapter 6

1. Sonja D. Schmid, "Shaping the Soviet Experience of the Atomic Age: Nuclear Topics in Ogonyok, 1945–1965," in Dick van Lente, ed., *The Nuclear Age in Popular Media: A Transnational History, 1945–1965*, 19–52 (New York: Palgrave Macmillan, 2012); Paul R. Josephson, "Rockets, Reactors and Soviet Culture," in Loren Graham, ed., *Science and the Soviet Social Order*, 168–191 (Cambridge, MA: Harvard University

Press, 1990); Paul R. Josephson, "Atomic-Powered Communism: Nuclear Culture in the Postwar USSR," *Slavic Review* 55, no. 2 (1996): 297–324; K. Polushkin, "Atomnyi bogatyr'," *Nauka i zhizn'* 11 (1980): 44–52; V. S. Emel'ianov, "Atomnaia nauka i tekhnika i stroitel'stvo kommunizma," *Atomnaia energiia* 11, no. 4 (1961): 301–312.

2. Sonja D. Schmid, "Organizational Culture and Professional Identities in the Soviet Nuclear Power Industry," *Osiris* 23 (2008): 82–111 (especially 83).

3. On the rhetoric of international cooperation, in the context of the United Nations Conferences on Peaceful Uses of Atomic Energy and of CMEA cooperation, see chapter 1.

4. One example for this claim of a logical development is Viktor A. Sidorenko, "Nuclear Power in the Soviet Union and in Russia," *Nuclear Engineering and Design* 173 (1997): 3–20.

5. Cf. Sheila Jasanoff, ed., *States of Knowledge: The Co-Production of Science and Social Order* (London: Routledge, 2004); Walter W. Powell and Paul J. DiMaggio, eds., *The New Institutionalism in Organizational Analysis* (Chicago: University of Chicago Press, 1991); Sven Steinmo, Kathleen Thelen, and Frank Longstreth, eds., *Structuring Politics: Historical Institutionalism in Comparative Analysis*, Cambridge Studies in Comparative Politics (Cambridge: Cambridge University Press, 1992).

6. "My vse mozhem i umeem" (Anatolii V. Kocherga, "Pervyi mesiats posle avarii," in A. N. Semenov, ed., *Chernobyl' desiat' let spustia: Neizbezhnost' ili sluchainost'?*, 170–181 (Moscow: Energoatomizdat, 1995) (especially 171)). I am grateful to Asif Siddiqi for suggesting this elegant translation.

7. Viktor A. Sidorenko, "Nauchnoe rukovodstvo v atomnoi energetike," in Viktor A. Sidorenko, ed., *Istoriia atomnoi energetiki Sovetskogo Soiuza i Rossii: Istoriia VVER*, vol. 2, 5–28 (Moscow: IzdAt, 2002) (especially 11).

8. Ibid., 10. "During the mitigation work after the [Chernobyl] accident it became clear that all the fundamental capabilities in terms of technologies, qualification of personnel, . . . and other attributes necessary during this critical period, were found in Sredmash, whereas the ministry in charge of operating nuclear plants [Minenergo] held them only in very limited ways" (Viktor A. Sidorenko, "Upravlenie atomnoi energetikoi," in Viktor A. Sidorenko, ed., *Istoriia atomnoi energetiki Sovetskogo Soiuza i Rossii*, vol. 1, 217–253 (Moscow: IzdAt, 2001) (quote on 227)).

9. "[Efim P. Slavskii and Nikolai A. Dollezhal] considered the demands for new safety rules superfluous and detrimental. The Ministry of Energy [Minenergo] opposed the diffusion and implementation of the RBMK within their field of activity, motivated by [the RBMK's] high cost and its difficult assembly and operation" (Viktor A. Sidorenko, "Ob"iasnitel'naia zapiska Sidorenko V. A. v komitet partiinogo kontrolia pri TsK KPSS," in Viktor A. Sidorenko, ed., *Istoriia atomnoi energetiki Sovetskogo Soiuza i Rossii: Uroki avarii na Chernobyl'skoi AES*, vol. 4, 44–47 (Moscow: IzdAt,

2002) (quote on 46)). Also see Sidorenko, "Nauchnoe rukovodstvo v atomnoi energetike," 11.

10. Gennadii A. Shasharin, "Chernobyl'skaia tragediia," in Aleksandr N. Semenov, ed., *Chernobyl' desiat' let spustia: Neizbezhnost' ili sluchainost'?*, 75–132 (Moscow: Energoatomizdat, 1995) (especially 124).

11. Sonja D. Schmid, "Transformation Discourse: Nuclear Risk as a Strategic Tool in Late Soviet Politics of Expertise," *Science, Technology & Human Values* 29, no. 3 (2004): 353–376.

12. "Gor'kii urok," *Atomnaia Energiia* 6, no. 60 (1986): 370–371.

13. The nuclear establishment remained divided over the advantages or disadvantages of a strictly centralized, hierarchically organized management structure, versus a privatized operating agency modeled on the idea of a corporation. In some ways, the situation in the nuclear industry reflects the political status quo of the Russian Federation as a whole: while the state is allegedly no longer authoritarian, it is clearly not (yet) democratic, but definitely capitalist. To this day, there is no unequivocal solution to the dilemma of the Russian nuclear industry (see Gaukhar Mukhatzhanova, "Russian Nuclear Industry Reforms: Consolidation and Expansion," *CNS Research Story*, May 22, 2007, http://cns.miis.edu/stories/070522.htm).

14. James Scott has characterized this "high modernist" approach as "social engineering" (James C. Scott, *Seeing Like a State: How Certain Schemes to Improve the Human Condition Have Failed* (New Haven, CT: Yale University Press, 1998)). See also Michel Callon, "Society in the Making: The Study of Technology as a Tool for Sociological Analysis," in Wiebe E. Bijker, Thomas P. Hughes, and Trevor Pinch, eds., *The Social Construction of Technological Systems*, 83–103 (Cambridge, MA: MIT Press, 1987). On the proposed corporation "Atom," see Sidorenko, "Upravlenie atomnoi energetikoi," 230. Sidorenko was involved in planning this corporation after 1991. See also Arkadii K. Kruglov, *Shtab atomproma* (Moscow: TSNIIatominform, 1998).

15. Sidorenko, "Upravlenie atomnoi energetikoi," 231.

16. Wiebe E. Bijker and John Law, eds., *Shaping Technology/Building Society: Studies in Sociotechnical Change* (Cambridge, MA: MIT Press, 1992).

17. Stephen Kotkin, *Armageddon Averted: The Soviet Collapse, 1970–2000* (Oxford: Oxford University Press, 2001).

18. I would not go as far as Babcock, who argues that "the authoritarian rulers of the Soviet Union did act against their own and the state's best interests" (Glenys A. Babcock, "The Role of Public Interest Groups in Democratization: Soviet Environmental Groups and Energy Policy-Making, 1985–1991," doctoral dissertation, RAND Graduate School, 1997, 15)—that "best interest" would have to be defined in the first place.

19. According to Rosatom's website, as of 2014, the company is the world leader in the number of nuclear reactors under construction simultaneously (currently nine in Russia and nineteen abroad); it is also among the major uranium producers and generates about 18 percent of Russia's total electricity. Furthermore, Rosatom controls 40 percent of the global uranium enrichment market, and 17 percent of the global nuclear fuel market (http://www.rosatom.ru/en/about).

20. "Akademik Lomonosov" is scheduled to start operation in 2016 (OKBM Afrikantov, FNPP "Academician Lomonosov," http://www.okbm.nnov.ru/english/lomonosov).

21. See www.lnpp2.ru.

22. World Nuclear Association, Nuclear Power in Russia (updated Dec 2013), http://www.world-nuclear.org/info/Country-Profiles/Countries-O-S/Russia—Nuclear-Power.

23. As of November 13, 2013, the "Russian state nuclear enterprise Rosatom reported an increase of almost 31% in export orders in 2012. The corporation's long-term strategy aims to significantly increase foreign orders by 2030" (http://www.world-nuclear-news.org/C-Rosatom-sees-exports-jump-in-2012-1311134.html).

24. On MIFI's history, see, for example, http://mephi.ru/about/index.php?sphrase_id=314856.

Epilogue

1. International Federation of Red Cross and Red Crescent Societies, *Learning Lessons from Fukushima: Red Cross Red Crescent Moves to Step Up Nuclear Preparedness*, May 17, 2012, http://www.ifrc.org/en/news-and-media/press-releases/asia-pacific/japan/learning-lessons-from-fukushima-red-cross-red-crescent-moves-to-step-up-nuclear-preparedness.

2. This scale, known as INES, is a tool that experts from the International Atomic Energy Agency and the OECD's Nuclear Energy Agency developed in 1989.

3. That's when the U.S. Army moved in. See Kyle Cleveland, "Mobilizing Nuclear Bias: The Fukushima Nuclear Crisis and the Politics of Uncertainty," paper presented at the Inaugural Meeting of the STS Forum on the 2011 Fukushima/East Japan Disaster, University of California at Berkeley, May 11–14, 2013.

4. Institute of Nuclear Power Operations, *Special Report on the Nuclear Accident at the Fukushima Daiichi Nuclear Power Station, INPO 11–005* (Atlanta: INPO, November 2011); Institute of Nuclear Power Operations, *Special Report INPO 11–005 Addendum: Lessons Learned from the Nuclear Accident at the Fukushima Daiichi Nuclear Power Station* (Atlanta: INPO, August 2012).

Notes

5. Questions remain why plant operators did not vent the containment earlier than they did, which may have averted further damage (Institute of Nuclear Power Operations, *Special Report, INPO 11–005*, November 2011). But Fukushima's unit 1 manager, Masao Yoshida, explicitly disobeyed orders from TEPCO to discontinue seawater cooling ("Disregard Tepco Order, Boss Told Plant Workers," *Japan Times*, December 1, 2011).

6. For example, see "GE Engineers and American Government Officials Warned of Dangerous Nuclear Design," *Washington's Blog*, December 11, 2013, http://www.washingtonsblog.com/2013/12/general-electric-knew-reactor-design-unsafe-isnt-ge-getting-heat-fukushima.html; Bill Dedman, "General Electric-Designed Reactors in Fukushima Have 23 Sisters in U.S.," NBC News Investigations, http://investigations.nbcnews.com/_news/2011/03/13/6256121-general-electric-designed-reactors-in-fukushima-have-23-sisters-in-us?lite.

7. Kohta Juraku, "'Made in Japan' Fukushima Nuclear Accident: A Critical Review for Accident Investigation Activities in Japan," paper presented at the Inaugural Meeting of the STS Forum on the 2011 Fukushima/East Japan Disaster, University of California at Berkeley, May 11–14, 2013; National Diet of Japan Fukushima Nuclear Accident Independent Investigation Commission (NAIIC), "Executive Summary of the Official Report of Fukushima Nuclear Accident Independent Investigation Commission, 5 July 2012," 2012, http://warp.da.ndl.go.jp/info:ndljp/pid/3856371/naiic.go.jp/wp-content/uploads/2012/09/NAIIC_report_lo_res10.pdf.

8. U.S. Nuclear Regulatory Commission, *Recommendations for Enhancing Reactor Safety in the 21st Century: The Near-Term Task Force Review of Insights from the Fukushima Dai-Ichi Accident* (Washington, DC: U.S. Nuclear Regulatory Commission, 2011); International Atomic Energy Agency, *Mission Report: IAEA International Peer Review Mission on Mid- and Long-Term Roadmap towards the Decommissioning of TEPCO's Fukushima Daiichi Nuclear Power Stations Units 1–4, Tokyo and Fukushima Prefecture, Japan, 15–22 April 2013* (Vienna: International Atomic Energy Agency, 2013).

9. European Nuclear Safety Regulators Group, "Peer Review Report: Stress Tests Performed on European Nuclear Power Plants," 2012, http://www.ensreg.eu/EU-Stress-Tests.

10. Nikolai Spasskii, deputy chief of Russia's Rosatom, suggested that international law should force countries operating nuclear plants to abide by international safety standards ("EurActiv G8 Summit Urges Stringent Nuclear Safety Rules," May 27, 2011, http://www.euractiv.com/energy/g8-summit-urges-stringent-nuclear-safety-rules-news-505185).

Methodological Appendix Notes

1. Among the parts of this vast collection (most *opisi* have several volumes) that I examined in detail are RGAE, f. 7964, op. 3 and op. 8 (on the years 1939–1959), op. 15 (1968–1974), and op. 16 (1976–1981).

2. ARAN, fond 1745, op. 1, *Komissiia po atomnoi energii*. I reviewed documents from 1964 to 1978.

3. ARAN, fond 1522, op. 1, *Uchenyi sovet pri prezidiume AN SSSR, Nauchno-tekhnicheskii otdel uchenogo soveta: Otdel rabot po atomnoi energii AN SSSR*. I reviewed documents from 1949 to 1963.

4. ARAN, fond 1916, *Lichnyi fond A. P. Aleksandrova*. Other collections of potential interest for nuclear energy are f. 447 (*Institut fizicheskikh problem im. S. I. Vavilova AN SSSR*); f. 495 (*Tekhnicheskii sovet AN SSSR*, 1935–); f. 532 (*Fizicheskii institut im. P. N. Lebedeva AN SSSR*); f. 1728 (*Otdelenie iadernoi fiziki AN SSSR*, 1963–); f. 1747 (*Komissiia po iadernoi fizike pri prezidiume AN SSSR*, 1967–); f. 1827 (*Otdelenie fiziko-tekhnicheskikh problem energetiki AN SSSR*, 1963–); f. 1989 (*Nauchnyi sovet po toplivnym elementam*).

5. RGSAPI (Komsomol), f. 1, op. 35, d. 564.

6. One such album from 1979, for example, included sections on the Rovno (l. 1–7), Chernobyl (l. 8–11), Smolensk (l. 12–13), Kalinin (l. 23–26), and Kursk nuclear power plants (l. 27–30), the *Atommash* factory (l. 31–34), and the Balakovo nuclear power plant (RGASPI (Komsomol), f. 1, op. 1, d. 647, Otdel rabochei molodezhi). A brochure *"Atomnaia energetika Ukrainskoi SSR"* was published in 1980 by Ministerstvo energetiki i elektrifkatsii USSR, Kiev, Reklama 1980, and is preserved in the Komsomol archive (RGASPI (Komsomol), f. 1, op. 88, d. 332, l. 1–9).

7. For example, minutes of the 1978 All-Union Convention of the secretaries of the Komsomol committees of industrial enterprises and planning institutes that worked for Komsomol "shock-construction sites" (*Protokol vsesoiuznogo soveshchaniia sekretarei komitetov VLKSM promyshlennykh predpriiatii i proektnykh organizatsii, vypolniaiushchikh zakazy udarnykh komsomol'skikh stroek atomnoi energetiki*, Kurskaia obl., p. Kurchatov 1978 g. RGASPI (Komsomol), f. 1 op. 65, d. 258). See also *Protokol No. 9 zasedaniia biuro TsK VLKSM, 29.XII.1970–19.I.1971* (RGASPI (Komsomol), f. 1, op. 67, d. 316s (*rassekrecheno*), which includes a decree from 1970 about the work done by the Komsomol organization at the Institute of Atomic Energy (l. 13–17); and *Protokol No. 45 zasedaniia biuro TsK VLKSM, 12.V.1981 g*. (RGASPI (Komsomol), f. 1, op. 88, d. 329s (*rassekrecheno*)).

8. For example, *Materialy k protokolu No. 9 zasedaniia biuro TsK VLKSM (§§20–29, 1a–4a), nachato 29.XII.1970, okoncheno 19.I.1971 g.* (RGASPI (Komsomol), f. 1, op. 67, d. 318); *Materialy k protokolu No. 45 zasedaniia biuro TsK VLKSM §§1–22," 12.V.1981 g.* (RGASPI (Komsomol), f. 1, op. 88, d. 331); *Materialy k protokolu N. 8 zasedaniia biuro TsK VLKSM, nachato 19.XI.1970, okoncheno 22.XII.1970 g.* (RGASPI (Komsomol), f. 1, op. 67, delo 310s).

9. For instance, *Stenogramma soveshchaniia, protokol zasedaniia shtaba TsK VLKSM po shefstvu nad "Atommashem," dogovor i obrashchenie uchastnikov soveshchaniia k komsomol'tsam i molodezhi strany*. G. Volgodonsk, Rostovskaia obl. 23.9.1978–

(RGASPI (Komsomol), f. 1, op. 65, d. 261); *Stenogramma zasedaniia Biuro TsK VLKSM po obsuzhdeniiu voprosa "O rabote komsomol'skoi organizatsii instituta atomnoi energii imeni I.V. Kurchatova"* No. 8/8 zhd. 1. Nachato 22. XII 1970 (RGASPI (Komsomol), f. 1, op. 67, d. 311).

10. For example, *Otchet shtaba TsK VLKSM Vsesoiuznoi udarnoi komsomol'skoi stroiki IV energobloka s reaktorom BN-800 Beloiarskoi AES im. I. V. Kurchatova Sverdlovskoi oblasti* (RGASPI (Komsomol), f. 1, op. 65, d. 916).

11. For instance, *Materialy i postanovleniia biuro VLKSM i kollegii Ministerstva energetiki i elektrifikatsii SSSR "O shefstve komsomol'skikh organizatsii Ukrainy pod sooruzheniem ob"ektov atomnoi energetiki"* (1981) (RGASPI (Komsomol), f. 1, op. 65, d. 537); *Materialy k postanovleniiu biuro TsK VKLSM i kollegii Ministerstva energetiki i elektrifikatsii SSSR "O shefstve komsomol'skikh organizatsii Ukrainy nad sooruzheniem ob"ektov atomnoi energetiki,"* dekabr 1980–avgust 1981g. (RGASPI (Komsomol), f. 1, op. 65, d. 536); *Protokol sektora obshchego otdela: Prilozhenie k postanovleniiu § 13 protokla No. 45 zasedaniia Biuro TsK VLKSM (materialy k otchetu TsK LKSM Ukrainy: Illustrativnyi material, gazety, metodicheskie rekomendatsii, broshiura), nachato, okoncheno 12 maia 1981 g.* (RGASPI (Komsomol), f. 1, op. 88, d. 332), which includes a promotional pamphlet on nuclear power in Ukraine from 1980.

12. I reviewed documents covering the period 1973–1981.

13. This collection is also available (at least in part) at the Hoover Institution at Stanford, which has published a detailed English language guide to the collection: "This finding aid describes the records of Fond 89, consisting of documents submitted to the Constitutional Court of the Russian Federation for the trial of the Communist Party of the Soviet Union. This unique collection of documents came into being as a result of President Yeltsin's decision on November 6, 1992, to outlaw the Communist Party. This decision was challenged in the Constitutional Court. For the trial, government prosecutors drew on a wide range of documents emanating from the highest organs of the Soviet Communist Party and State. Covering the period 1919–1992, the documents were selected to prove that the Communist Party showed a complete disregard for human rights and international law. They constitute the most revealing collection of documents of the Soviet Union to have emerged since its collapse" (http://www.oac.cdlib.org/findaid/ark:/13030/kt767nf11z/entire_text/?query=fond%2089#hitNum7).

14. For example, RGANI, f. 89, op. 4, d. 22, pertains to the trial in the city of Chernobyl. On information policies regarding the accident, see RGANI, f. 89, op. 9, d. 24; RGANI, f. 89, op. 11, d. 137; RGANI, f. 89, op. 12, d. 4; RGANI, f. 89, op. 23, d. 21; and RGANI, f. 89, op. 53, d. 27. RGANI, f. 89, op. 23, d. 26, and RGANI, f. 89, op. 42, d. 58, relate to the energy supply situation in the country after the accident. See RGANI, f. 89, op. 46, d. 1, on Emelyianov's nomination for the "Atoms for Peace" award. RGANI, f. 89, op. 51, d. 20; RGANI, f. 89, op. 51, d. 22; and RGANI, f. 89, op. 51, d. 24, are transcripts of the meetings of the Central Committee's *Operativnaia*

gruppa set up after the Chernobyl accident. RGANI, f. 89, op. 53, d. 6, is a letter from science journalist Vladimir Gubarev about the situation at the Chernobyl nuclear power plant in May 1986. RGANI, f. 89, op. 53, d. 12, is a decree by the Central Committee on the Chernobyl accident.

15. For example, delo 69 (rolik 7250) on the construction of the Leningrad nuclear power plant and other nuclear power plants; delo 107 (rolik 7213) on various design proposals and Kurchatov's interventions; delo 147 on the construction of the Beloiarsk and Novo-Voronezh nuclear power plants; and delo 149 on the development of the nuclear power industry from 1960 to 1980.

16. *Ministerstvo energetiki i elektrifikatsii SSSR. Vsesoiuznyi ordena Trudovogo Krasnogo Znameni teplotekhnicheskii nauchno-issledovatel'skii institut im. F. E. Dzherzhinskogo (Ural'skii filial), g. Cheliabinsk. Op. 2–6: dela upravlencheskoi dokumetantsii postoiannogo khraneniia za 1956–1970 gody* (RGANTD (Samara), f. R-184, op. 2–6, t. 1); and *Ministerstvo energetiki i elektrifikatsii SSSR, Soiuzglavenergo, Vsesoiuznyi ordena Trudovogo Krasnogo Znameni teplotekhnicheskii nauchno-issledovatel'skii institut im. F. E. Dzherzhinskogo (VTI im. F. E. Dzerzhinskogo), 1931–1970* (RGANTD (Samara), f. R-277, op. 2–6).

17. *Ministerstvo energetiki i elektrifikatsii, Glavnoe upravlenie nauchno-issledovatel'skikh i proektnykh organizatsii, GlavNIIproekt, Gosudarstvennyi nauchno-issledovatel'skii energeticheskii institut im. G. M. Krzhizhanovskogo (ENIN). Dela postoiannogo khraneniia upravlencheskoi dokumentatsii za 1961–1980 gg.* (RGANTD (Samara), f. R-249, op. 2–6).

18. *Vsesoiuznyi gosudarstvennyi ordena Lenina proektnyi institut "Teploelektroproekt," Glavnogo tekhnicheskogo upravleniia po stroitel'stvu i proektirovaniiu elektrostantsii, podstantsii i setei "Glavtekhstroiproekt" Ministerstva energetiki i elektrifikatsii SSSR, 1934–1935, 1938–1970* (RGANTD (Samara), f. R-272, op. 9–6), and *Vsesoiuznyi gosudarstvennyi ordena Lenina i ordena Oktiabr'skoi revoliutsii proektnyi institut "Teploelektroproekt," Gor'kovskoe otdelenie (GOTEP), 1969–1975* (RGANTD (Samara), f. R-289, op. 1–6).

19. *Ministerstvo energeticheskogo mashinostroeniia SSSR, Tekhnicheskoe upravlenie, Vsesoiuznyi nauchno-issledovatel'skii i proektno-konstruktorskii institut atomnogo energeticheskogo mashinostroeniia, Dela postoiannogo khraneniia 1944–1981* (RGANTD (Samara), R-268, op. 1–6).

20. "Atomenergoproekt," short for State Scientific Research, Design, Construction, and Prospecting Institute (*Gosudarstvennyi nauchno-issledovatel'skii, proektno-konstruktorskii i izyskatel'skii institute*) was originally part of the Minenergo apparatus, but after Chernobyl had been repeatedly reassigned to various ministries (e.g., the Ministry of Atomic Energy, the Ministry of Atomic Energy and Industry, and the Ministry of Atomic Energy). By the time I was able to see this collection of documents, it belonged to Minatom (RGANTD (Samara), R-811, op. 1–6, 1986–1991 gg.).

21. This method of identifying research subjects through the personal networks of an initially small group of people is known as "snowball sampling."

22. Paul R. Josephson, *Red Atom: Russia's Nuclear Power Program from Stalin to Today* (New York: Freeman, 1999).

23. Maria N. Vasilieva, *Soleils rouges: L'ambition nucléaire soviétique* [Essai sur l'évolution des systèmes de prise de décision dans le nucléaire soviétique (Russe)], Histoire industrielle (Paris: Institut d'Histoire de l'Industrie et Éditions Rive Droite, 1999); Maria N. Vasilieva, "L'évolution des systèmes de prise de décisions dans le nucléaire soviétique (Russe)," *Histoire, Économie et Société*, no. 2 (April-June 2001): 257–275.

24. Viktor A. Sidorenko, ed., *Istoriia atomnoi energetiki Sovetskogo Soiuza i Rossii*, vol. 1 (Moscow: IzdAt, 2001); Viktor A. Sidorenko, ed., *Istoriia atomnoi energetiki Sovetskogo Soiuza i Rossii: Istoriia VVER*, vol. 2 (Moscow: IzdAt, 2002); Viktor A. Sidorenko, ed., *Istoriia atomnoi energetiki Sovetskogo Soiuza i Rossii: Istoriia RBMK*, vol. 3 (Moscow: IzdAt, 2003); Viktor A. Sidorenko, ed., *Istoriia atomnoi energetiki Sovetskogo Soiuza i Rossii: Uroki avarii na Chernobyl'skoi AES*, vol. 4 (Moscow: IzdAt, 2002); Viktor A. Sidorenko, ed., *Istoriia atomnoi energetiki Sovetskogo Soiuza i Rossii: Istoriia maloi atomnoi energetiki*, vol. 5 (Moscow: IzdAt, 2004).

25. A. P. Aleksandrov, ed., *Vospominaniia ob Igore Vasil'eviche Kurchatove* (Moscow: Nauka, 1988); P. A. Aleksandrov, *Akademik Anatolii Petrovich Aleksandrov, Priamaia rech'*, 2nd ed. (Moscow: Nauka, 2002); Raisa V. Kuznetsova, ed., *Kurchatov v zhizni: Pis'ma, dokumenty, vospominaniia (iz lichnogo arkhiva)* (Moscow: Mosgorarkhiv, 2002); Vitalii P. Nasonov, *E. P. Slavskii: Stranitsy zhizni* (Moscow: IzdAT, 1998); V. K. Ulasevich, ed., *Sozdano pod rukovodstvom N. A. Dollezhalia: O iadernykh reaktorakh i ikh tvortsakh (k 100-letiiu N. A. Dollezhalia)*, 2nd ed. (Moscow: GUP NIKIET, 2002); V. K. Ulasevich, ed., *O iadernykh reaktorakh i ikh tvortsakh: Prodolzhenie traditsii (k 50-letiiu NIKIET im. N.A. Dollzhalia* (Moscow: GUP NIKIET, 2002); Nikolai A. Dollezhal', *U istokov rukotvornogo mira: Zapiski konstruktora* (Moscow: GUP NIKIET, IzdAt, 2002); Boris A. Fain, *Aktivanaia zona: Povest' ob atomnom institute* (Moscow: Skripto, 1998); Iu. A. Kazanskii, ed., *Iadernaia energetika: K 100-letiiu A. I. Leipunskogo, Izvestiia vysshikh uchebnykh zavedenii* (Obninsk: Ministerstvo obrazovaniia RF, 2003); Nikolai S. Khlopkin, *Stranitsy zhizni* (Moscow: IzdAt, 2003); Leonid A. Belianin, ed., *Leningradskaia AES: Gody, sobytiia, liudi* (Moscow: Energoatomizdat, 1998).

26. Ivan I. Larin, *Tiazheloe bremia podviga* (Moscow: IzdAt, 1996); Vitalii P. Nasonov, B. L. Vannikov: *Memuary, vospominaniia, stat'i* (Moscow: TSNIIatominform, 1997); E. P. Velikhov et al., ed., *Nauka i obshchestvo: Istoriia sovetskogo atomnogo proekta (40–50 gody), Trudy mezhdunarodnogo simpoziuma ISAP-06*. Vol. 1 (Moscow: IzdAt, 1997); E. P. Velikhov et al., ed., *Nauka i obshchestvo: Istoriia sovetskogo atomnogo proekta (40–50 gody), Trudy mezhdunarodnogo simpoziuma ISAP-06*. Vol. 2 (Moscow: IzdAt, 1999); E. P. Velikhov et al., ed., *Nauka i obshchestvo: Istoriia sovetskogo atomnogo proekta (40–50*

gody), Trudy mezhdunarodnogo simpoziuma ISAP-06. Vol. 3 (Moscow: IzdAt, 2003); P. Astashenkov, *Kurchatov: Zhizn' zamechatel'nykh liudei* (Moscow: Molodaia gvardiia, 1967); Ministerstvo Rossiiskoi Federatsii po atomnoi energii and Departament po atomnoi energetike, eds., *Shestnadtsatoe glavnoe: Istoriia i sovremennost'* (Moscow: Ministerstvo Rossiiskoi Federatsii po atomnoi energii, 2003); M. Ia. Vazhnov and I. S. Aristov, eds., *A. P. Zaveniagin: Stranitsy zhizni* (Moscow: PoliMediia, 2002); Vladimir G. Asmolov et al., *Atomnaia energetika: Otsenki proshlogo, realii nastoiashchego, ozhidaniia budushchego* (Moscow: IzdAt, 2004); V. P. Denisov and Iu. G. Dragunov, *Reaktornye ustanovki VVER dlia atomnykh elektrostantsii* (Moscow: IzdAt, 2002); V. M. Kulygin, Iu. N. Smirnov, and M. E. Khalizeva, eds., *Golovin, Igor' Nikolaevich: Stranitsy zhizni. Tvortsy iadernogo veka* (Moscow: IzdAt, 2004); Vera N. Tiushevskaia, *I. K. Kikoin: Stranitsy zhizni* (Moscow: IzdAt, 1995); E. A. Negin et al., *Sovetskii atomnyi proekt: Konets atomnoi monopolii: Kak eto bylo* . . . (Sarov: RFIaTs-VNIIEF, 2003).

27. For example, Sidorenko's contribution to the volume dedicated to Anatolii P. Aleksandrov on the centennial of his birth is written in a distanced way that is very distinct from other contributions (Viktor A. Sidorenko, "A.P. Aleksandrov i atomnaia energetika," in Nikolai S. Khlopkin, ed., *A. P. Aleksandrov: Dokumenty i vospominaniia, k 100-letiiu so dnia rozhdeniia*, 212–219 (Moscow: IzdAt, 2003)). Boris Fain's *Aktivnaia zona* includes excerpts from personal accounts, conversations, and interviews with nuclear engineers at the design institute NIKIET that would otherwise be inaccessible (Fain, *Aktivnaia zona*).

28. V. V. Goncharov, "Pervyi period razvitiia atomnoi energetiki v SSSR," in Viktor A. Sidorenko, ed., *Istoriia atomnoi energetiki Sovetskogo Soiuza i Rossii*, vol. 1, 16–70 (Moscow: IzdAt, 2001).

29. Igor V. Kurchatov, "Nekotorye voprosy razvitiia atomnoi energetiki v SSSR. Doklad, sdelannyi I. V. Kurchatovym v Kharuelle (Angliia) v aprele 1956g.," in Viktor A. Sidorenko, ed., *Istoriia atomnoi energetiki Sovetskogo Soiuza i Rossii*, vol. 1, 71–82 (Moscow: IzdAt, 2001).

30. Anatolii P. Aleksandrov, "Iadernaia energetika i ee rol' v tekhnicheskom progresse (General'nyi adres, zachitannyi A. P. Aleksandrovym na konferentsii VI mirovogo energeticheskogo kongressa, Moskva 1968g.," in V. A. Sidorenko, ed., *Istoriia atomnoi energetiki Sovetskogo Soiuza i Rossii*, vol. 1, 83–95 (Moscow: IzdAt, 2001).

31. Lev A. Kochetkov, "K istorii sozdaniia Obninskoi AES," in V. A. Sidorenko, ed., *Istoriia atomnoi energetiki Sovetskogo Soiuza i Rossii*, vol. 1, 96–101 (Moscow: IzdAt, 2001); Lev A. Kochetkov, "K istorii pervoi ocheredi Beloiarskoi AES," in V. A. Sidorenko, ed., *Istoriia atomnoi energetiki Sovetskogo Soiuza i Rossii*, vol. 1, 117–133 (Moscow: IzdAt, 2001); Lev A. Kochetkov and M. F. Troianov, "Reaktory na bystrykh neitronakh," in V. A. Sidorenko, ed., *Istoriia atomnoi energetiki Sovetskogo Soiuza i Rossii*, vol. 1, 164–187 (Moscow: IzdAt, 2001); A. Ia. Kramerov, "Kanal'nye vodookhlazhdaemye uran-grafitovye reaktory (UGR) tipa RBMK," in V. A. Sidorenko, ed., *Istoriia atomnoi energetiki Sovetskogo Soiuza i Rossii*, vol. 1, 154–163

(Moscow: IzdAt, 2001); R. G. Bogoiavlenskii, "Razrabotka gazookhlazhdaemykh iadernykh reaktorov," in V. A. Sidorenko, ed., *Istoriia atomnoi energetiki Sovetskogo Soiuza i Rossii*, vol. 1, 188–193 (Moscow: IzdAt, 2001); Viktor A. Sidorenko, "Upravlenie atomnoi energetikoi," in Viktor A. Sidorenko, ed., *Istoriia atomnoi energetiki Sovetskogo Soiuza i Rossii*, vol. 1, 217–253 (Moscow: IzdAt, 2001); Viktor A. Sidorenko, "Problemy bezopasnosti atomnoi energetiki," in Viktor A. Sidorenko, ed., *Istoriia atomnoi energetiki Sovetskogo Soiuza i Rossii*, vol. 1, 194–216 (Moscow: IzdAt, 2001).

32. For example, Viktor P. Tatarnikov, "Atomnaia elektroenergetika (s VVER i drugimi reaktorami)," in Viktor A. Sidorenko, ed., *Istoriia atomnoi energetiki Sovetskogo Soiuza i Rossii: Istoriia VVER*, vol. 2, 303–399 (Moscow: IzdAt, 2002); V. S. Osmachkin, "Problemy nadezhnogo teploobmena v aktivnoi zone reaktora VVER 1-go bloka NVAES pri ego proektirovanii," in Viktor A. Sidorenko, ed., *Istoriia atomnoi energetiki Sovetskogo Soiuza i Rossii: Istoriia VVER*, vol. 2, 113–125 (Moscow: IzdAt, 2002); A. N. Kamyshan, "Sobytiia i liudi (Vospominaniia uchastnika)," in Viktor A. Sidorenko, ed., *Istoriia atomnoi energetiki Sovetskogo Soiuza i Rossii: Istoriia VVER*, vol. 2, 145–193 (Moscow: IzdAt, 2002).

33. Viktor A. Sidorenko, "Nauchnoe rukovodstvo v atomnoi energetike," in Viktor A. Sidorenko, ed., *Istoriia atomnoi energetiki Sovetskogo Soiuza i Rossii: Istoriia VVER*, vol. 2, 5–28 (Moscow: IzdAt, 2002).

34. Sidorenko, *Istoriia atomnoi energetiki*, vol. 3.

35. Among others, Gosudarstvennyi komitet SSSR po nadzoru za bezopasnym vedeniem rabot v promyshlennosti i atomnoi energetike, "O prichinakh i obstoiatel'stvakh avarii na 4 bloke Chernobyl'skoi AES 26 aprelia 1986 g., Doklad Komissii Gospromatomnadzora SSSR," in V. A. Sidorenko, ed., *Istoriia atomnoi energetiki Sovetskogo Soiuza i Rossii: Uroki avarii na Chernobyl'skoi AES*, vol. 4, 333–409 (Moscow: IzdAt, [1991] 2002); Boris E. Shcherbina et al., "Doklad Pravitel'stvennoi Komissii po rassledovaniiu prichin avarii na Chernobyl'skoi AES 26 aprelia 1986 g. (iiun' 1986)," in Viktor A. Sidorenko, ed., *Istoriia atomnoi energetiki Sovetskogo Soiuza i Rossii: Uroki avarii na Chernobyl'skoi AES*, vol. 4, 17–47 (Moscow: IzdAt, 2002).

36. Viktor A. Sidorenko, "Ob"iasnitel'naia zapiska Sidorenko V. A. v Komitet Partiinogo Kontrolia pri TsK KPSS," in Viktor A. Sidorenko, ed., *Istoriia atomnoi energetiki Sovetskogo Soiuza i Rossii: Uroki avarii na Chernobyl'skoi AES*, vol. 4, 44–47 (Moscow: IzdAt, 2002).

37. Sidorenko, *Istoriia atomnoi energetiki*, vol. 5.

38. Lev D. Riabev, ed., *Atomnyi proekt SSSR: Dokumenty i materialy*; see the bibliography for the various volumes.

39. O. V. Bazanova, ed., *Istoriia atomnogo proekta*, vols. 1–4 (Moscow: Rossiiskii Nauchnyi Tsentr "Kurchatovskii Institut," 1995); O. V. Bazanova, ed., *Istoriia atomnogo proekta*, vol. 5 (Moscow: Rossiiskii Nauchnyi Tsentr "Kurchatovskii Institut,"

1996); O. V. Bazanova and G. Ia. Karmadonova, eds., *Istoriia atomnogo proekta*, vol. 14 (Moscow: Rossiiskii Nauchnyi Tsentr "Kurchatovskii Institut," 1998); G. Ia. Karmadonova, ed., *Istoriia atomnogo proekta*, vols. 6, 8–13 (Moscow: Rossiiskii Nauchnyi Tsentr "Kurchatovskii Institut," 1996–1998); G. Ia. Karmadonova and O. V. Bazanova, eds., *Istoriia atomnogo proekta*, vol. 7 (Moscow: Rossiiskii Nauchnyi Tsentr "Kurchatovskii Institut," 1996); Rossiiskii Nauchnyi Tsentr "Kurchatovskii Institut," ed., *Istoriia atomnogo proekta*, vols. 15–16 (Moscow: Rossiiskii Nauchnyi Tsentr "Kurchatovskii Institut," 1998).

40. Arkadii K. Kruglov, *Kak sozdavalas' atomnaia promyshlennost' v SSSR* (Moscow: TSNIIatominform, 1995); Arkadii K. Kruglov, *Shtab atomproma* (Moscow: TSNIIatominform, 1998).

41. Vladimir P. Vizgin, ed., *Istoriia sovetskogo atomnogo proekta: Dokumenty, vospominaniia, issledovaniia*, vol. 1 (Moscow: Ianus-K, 1998); V. P. Vizgin, ed. *Istoriia sovetskogo atomnogo proekta. Dokumenty, vospominaniia, issledovaniia*, vol. 2 (Saint Petersburg: Izdatel'stvo russkogo khristianskogo gumanitarnogo instituta, 2002).

42. E. P. Velikhov et al., ed., *Nauka i obshchestvo: Istoriia sovetskogo atomnogo proekta (40–50 gody). Trudy mezhdunarodnogo simpoziuma ISAP-06*, vol. 1 (Moscow: IzdAt, 1997); E. P. Velikhov et al., ed., *Nauka i obshchestvo: Istoriia sovetskogo atomnogo proekta (40–50 gody). Trudy mezhdunarodnogo simpoziuma ISAP-06*, vol. 2 (Moscow: IzdAt, 1999); E. P. Velikhov et al., eds. Nauka i obshchestvo: Istoriia sovetskogo atomnogo proekta (40–50 gody). Trudy ISAP, vol. 3 (Moscow: IzdAt, 2003).

43. Ministerstvo Rossiiskoi Federatsii po atomnoi energii, *Strategiia razvitiia atomnoi energetiki Rossii v pervoi polovine XXI veka* (Moscow: FGUP "TsNIIatominform," 2001); Natsional'nyi issledovatel'skii tsentr "Kurchatovskii institut," *O strategii iadernoi energetiki Rossii do 2050 g.* (Moscow: Kurchatovskii institut, 2012).

44. These include memoirs of nuclear physicists (Oleg D. Kazachkovskii, *Fizik na sluzhbe atoma* (Moscow: Energoatomizdat, 2002); Pavel A. Zhuravlev, *Moi atomnyi vek: O vremeni, ob atomshchikakh i o sebe* (Moscow: Khronos-press, 2003)), accounts by engineers (Viacheslav V. Girnis, *Zapiski atomshchika* (Moscow: Energoatomizdat, 2000)), the memoirs of the former minister of Atomic Energy (Viktor N. Mikhailov, *Ia—"iastreb"* (Moscow: Kron-Press, 1993) and the former deputy minister of Atomic Energy (Viktor A. Sidorenko, *Ob atomnoi energetike, atomnykh stantsiiakh, uchiteliakh, kollegakh i o sebe* (Moscow: IzdAt, 2003)), as well as the diaries of the former minister of Energy and Electrification (Petr S. Neporozhnii, *Energetika strany glazami ministra: Dnevniki 1935–1985 gg.* (Moscow: Energoatomizdat, 2000)).

45. See the following works by Mikhail P. Grabovskii: *Vtoroi Ivan: Sovershenno sekretno* (Moscow: Nauchnaia kniga, 1998); *Puskovoi ob"ekt* (Moscow: Nauchnaia kniga, 1999); *Nakanune avrala* (Moscow: Nauchnaia kniga, 2000); *Atomnyi avral* (Moscow: Nauchnaia kniga, 2001); *Plutonievaia zona* (Moscow: Nauchnaia kniga,

2002); *Pervaia sovetskaia atomnaia podvodnaia lodka K-3* (Moscow: Samizdat, 2005). Other creative formats include collections of poetry and "folklore" from the nuclear energy community (A. I. Veretennikov, ed., *Fol'klor na sluzhbe atoma: Sbornik pesen, stikhov, tostov, baek, sochinennykh atomshchikami na poligonakh* (Moscow: TsNI-IAtominform, 1996)).

46. For Vladimir S. Gubarev's books, see *Iadernyi vek: Bomba* (Moscow: IzdAt, 1995); *Iadernyi vek: Chernobyl'* (Moscow: Nekos, 1996); *XX vek: Ispovedi. Sud'ba nauki i uchenykh v Rossii* (Moscow: Nauka/Interperiodika, 2000); *Agoniia Sredmasha: Ot Chernobylia do Chubaisa* (Moscow: Akademkniga, 2006).

47. The official report was published in large part in the journal *Atomnaia energiia* in 1986 ("Informatsiia ob avarii na Chernobyl'skoi AES i ee posledstviiakh, podgotovlennaia dlia MAGATE," *Atomnaia Energiia* 61 (1986): 301–320). See also International Nuclear Safety Advisory Group, *The Chernobyl Accident—Updating of INSAG-1 (INSAG-7)* (Vienna: International Atomic Energy Agency, 1992). The IAEA maintained a project called "The International Chernobyl Project" for several years, but it no longer has permanent status (International Atomic Energy Agency, *The International Chernobyl Project: An Overview. Assessment of Radiological Consequences and Evaluation of Protective Measures* (Vienna: International Atomic Energy Agency, 1991); International Atomic Energy Agency, *The International Chernobyl Project: Technical Report. Assessment of Radiological Consequences and Evaluation of Protective Measures* (Vienna: International Atomic Energy Agency, 1991); International Atomic Energy Agency, "Strengthening Radiation and Nuclear Safety Infrastructures in Countries of the Former USSR," paper presented at the conference on "Strengthening Radiation and Nuclear Safety Infrastructures in Countries of the Former USSR," Vienna, May 4–7, 1993; International Atomic Energy Agency, *Nuclear Power Reactors in the World* (Vienna: International Atomic Energy Agency, 1996); Mezhdunarodnyi Chernobyl'skii Proekt, "Mezhdunarodnyi Chernobyl'skii Proekt: Otsenka radiologicheskikh posledstvii i zashchitnykh mer" (Moscow: IzdAT, 1991)).

48. For example, Don Arnott and Robert Green, "Unique Safety Valve for a Reactor Nuclear Explosion?," paper presented at the national conference "The Legacy of Chernobyl—Lessons for the UK," Council House, Bristol, March 11, 1992 (organized by the National Steering Committee of Nuclear Free Local Authorities); Anatolii S. Diatlov, *Chernobyl': Kak eto bylo* (Moscow: Nauchtekhlitizdat, 2003); Nikolai A. Shteinberg, "O prichinakh i obstoiatel'stvakh avarii na 4-m bloke Chernobyl'skoi AES 26 aprelia 1986 g. Doklad" (Moscow: Komissiia Gospromatomnadzora SSSR, 1991); A. A. Iadrikhinskii, *Iadernaia avariia na 4-om bloke Chernobyl'skoi AES i iadernaia bezopasnost' reaktorov RBMK* (Kurchatov: [n.p.], 1989).

49. For example, E. B. Burlakova, ed., *Consequences of the Chernobyl Catastrophe: Human Health* (Moscow: Center for Russian Environmental Policy; Scientific Council on Radiobiology, Russian Academy of Sciences, 1996); Iu. A. Izrael' et al., *Chernobyl':*

Radioaktivnoe zagriaznenie prirodnykh sred (Leningrad: Gidrometeoizdat, 1990); Vladimir K. Savchenko, *The Ecology of the Chernobyl Catastrophe: Scientific Outlines of an International Program of Collaborative Research*, Volume 16: *Man and the Biosphere*, ed. J. N. R. Jeffers (Paris: UNESCO, 1995); V. M. Zakharov and E. Yu. Krysanov, eds., *Consequences of the Chernobyl Catastrophe: Environmental Health* (Moscow: Center for Russian Environmental Policy; Moscow Affiliate of the International "Biotest" Foundation, 1996); with a focus on radioactive waste, see Vladimir M. Kuznetsov, *Rossiiskaia atomnaia energetika vchera, segodnia, zavtra: Vzgliad nezavisimogo eksperta* (Moscow: Natsional'nyi Institut Pressy, 2000).

50. For instance, Vasil' Gigevich and Oleg Chernov, *Stali vody gor'kimi: Khronika Chernobyl'skoi bedy* (Minsk: Belorus', 1991); N. A. Kartel, ed., *Chernobyl Digest 1994–95*, vol. 4 (Minsk: Center for Russian Environmental Policy et al., 1996); Vasilii B. Nesterenko, *Masshtaby i posledstviia katastrofy na Chernobyl'skoi AES dlia Belorusi, Ukrainy i Rossii* (Minsk: Pravo i ekonomika, 1996).

51. For example, V. G. Bar'iakhtar, ed., *Chernobyl'skaia katastrofa* (Kiev: Naukova dumka, 1995); Liubov' Kovalevskaia, *Chernobyl' "DSP"; Posledstviia Chernobylia, Chornobyl', Ukraine, 1986* (Kiev: Abris, 1995); Adriana Petryna, *Life Exposed: Biological Citizens after Chernobyl* (Princeton, NJ: Princeton University Press, 2013).

52. Among the Russian sources, see for example, Grigorii Medvedev, "Chernobyl'skaia tetrad'," *Novyi Mir* 6 (1989): 3–108; E. I. Ignatenko et al., eds., *Chernobyl': Sobytiia i uroki. Voprosy i otvety* (Moscow: Izdatel'stvo politicheskoi literatury, 1989); Nikolai D. Tarakanov, *Chernobyl'skie zapiski, ili Razdum'ia o nravstvennosti* (Moscow: Voenizdat, 1989); Alla Yaroshinskaya, *Chernobyl: The Forbidden Truth* (Lincoln: University of Nebraska Press, 1995); Grigorii Medvedev, *The Truth about Chernobyl* (New York: Basic Books, 1989); Rudol'f M. Aleksakhin et al. *Problemy smiagcheniia posledstviii Chernobyl'skoi katastrofy: materialy mezhdunarodnogo seminara* (Briansk: Rossiia, 1993); *K 10-letiiu avarii na Chernobyl'skoi AES. Sotsial'naia i psikhologicheskaia reabilitatsiia postradavshikh ot Chernobyl'skoi katastrofy: Opyt i perspektivy* (Moscow: MChS Rossii, 1996); Iurii V. Sivintsev and V. A. Kachalov, eds., *Chernobyl': Piat' trudnykh let. Sbornik materialov o rabotakh po likvidatsii posledstvii avarii na Chernobyl'skoi AES v 1986–1990 gg.* (Moscow: IzdAT, 1992); Helen Knorre, "The Star Called Wormwood: The Cause and Effect of the Chernobyl Catastrophe," *Public Understanding of Science* 1 (1992): 241–249; Aleksandr N. Semenov, ed., *Chernobyl' desiat' let spustia: Neizbezhnost' ili sluchainost'?* (Moscow: Energoatomizdat, 1995); Igor' A. Beliaev, *Beton marki "Sredmash": Proshlo 15 let* (Moscow: IzdAT, 2001); Gubarev, *Iadernyi vek: Chernobyl'*; Lenina S. Kaibysheva, *Posle Chernobylia*, 2 vols. (Moscow: IzdAT, 1996–2001); A. A. Karasiuk and A. I. Sidorenko, *Vokrug Chernobylia: Dialogi s uchenymi* (Moscow: IzdAT, 1991); M. I. Kostenetskii and G. T. Gribinenko, *Ekho Chernobylia v Zaporozh'e: Nauchno-populiarnyj ocherk* (Zaporozh'e: MP Bereginia, 1992). International publications include Ed A. Hewett, "Introductory Comment on the Consequences of Chernobyl'," *Soviet Economy* 2, no. 2 (1986): 95–96; Ed A.

Hewett et al., "Panel on the Economic and Political Consequences of Chernobyl'," *Soviet Economy* 2, no. 2 (1986): 97–130; Paul R. Josephson, "The Historical Roots of the Chernobyl Disaster," *Soviet Union/Union Soviétique* 13, no. 3 (1986): 275–299; Paul R. Josephson, "Atomic Energy and 'Atomic Culture' in the USSR: The Ideological Roots of Economic and Safety Problems Facing the Nuclear Power Industry after Chernobyl," in T. Anthony Jones, David Powell, and Walter Connor, eds., *Soviet Social Problems*, 55–77 (Boulder, CO: Westview Press, 1991); Michael K. Lindell and Ronald W. Perry, "Effects of the Chernobyl Accident on Public Perceptions of Nuclear Plant Accident Risks," *Risk Analysis* 10, no. 3 (1990): 393–399; David R. Marples, *Chernobyl and Nuclear Power in the USSR* (New York: St. Martin's Press, 1986); David R. Marples, *The Social Impact of the Chernobyl Disaster* (London: Macmillan, 1988); Judith Thornton, "Soviet Electric Power after Chernobyl': Economic Consequences and Options," *Soviet Economy* 2, no. 2 (1986): 131–179. There has even been an attempt to compile bibliographical information on scientific literature on the accident (Evgenii F. Konoplia, I. V. Rolevich, and Institut radiobiologii (Akademiia nauk Belarusi), *Chernobyl'skaia katastrofa: Bibliografiia nauchnoi literatury* (Minsk: Pravo i ekonomika, 1996)).

53. Iurii Shcherbak, *Chernobyl: A Documentary Story*, trans. Ian Press (from the Ukrainian) and foreword by David R. Marples (New York: St. Martin's Press, 1989); Vladimir Gubarev, *Sarcophagus: A Tragedy*, trans. Michael Glenny, with a preface by Robert Gale (New York: Vintage Books, 1987).

54. The Legasov transcripts are online at lib.web-malina.com/getbook.php?bid=2755; the city of Slavutich maintains a very informative website at www.slavutichcity.net; and the declassified documents relating to the Chernobyl nuclear power plant are at http://www.sbu.gov.ua/sbu/control/uk/publish/article?art_id=49046&cat_id=5303. Also, books published in small numbers have been made available online—for example, Diatlov's testimony on the Chernobyl accident has appeared online at multiple sites, including rrc2.narod.ru.

55. For example, I. G. Belousov, "Bez vedomestvennogo patriotizma: K probleme bezopasnosti iadernoi energetiki," *Energiia: Ekonomika, tekhnika, ekologiia* 9 (1989): 6–8. Also see the following works by Rem A. Belousov: *Ekonomicheskaia istoriia Rossii: XX vek. Kniga I: Na rubezhe dvukh stoletii* (Moscow: IzdAt, 1999); *Ekonomicheskaia istoriia Rossii: XX vek. Kniga II: Cherez revoliutsiiu k NEPu* (Moscow: IzdAt, 2000); *Ekonomicheskaia istoriia Rossii: XX vek. Kniga III: Tiazhelye gody rosta i obnovleniia* (Moscow: IzdAt, 2002); *Ekonomicheskaia istoriia Rossii: XX vek. Kniga IV: Ekonomika Rossii v usloviiakh "goriachei" i "kholodnoi" voin* (Moscow: IzdAt, 2004). In addition, see Iurii I. Koriakin, *Okrestnosti iadernoi energetiki Rossii: Novye vyzovy* (Moscow: GUP NIKIET, 2002).

56. Dimitrii G. Zhimerin, ed., *Sovremennye problemy energetiki* (Moscow: Energoatomizdat, 1984); A. S. Pavlenko and A. M. Nekrasov, eds., *Energetika SSSR v 1971–1975*

godakh (Moscow: Energiia, 1972); A. M. Nekrasov and M. G. Pervukhin, eds., *Energetika SSSR v 1976–1980 godakh* (Moscow: Energiia, 1977); A. M. Nekrasov and A. A. Troitskii, eds., *Energetika SSSR v 1981–1985 godakh* (Moscow: Energoizdat, 1981); A. A. Troitskii, ed., *Energetika SSSR v 1986–1990 godakh* (Moscow: Energoatomizdat, 1987).

57. Viktor Andriianov, *Kosygin: Zhizn' zamechatel'nykh liudei* (Moscow: Molodaia gvardiia, 2003); Frank Church, *Interview with Kosygin: Report to the Committee on Foreign Relations, United States Senate* (Washington, DC: U.S. Government Printing Office, 1971); T. I. Fetistov, ed., *Prem'er izvestnyi i neizvestnyi: Vospominaniia o A. N. Kosygine* (Moscow: Respublika, 1997); Aleksei N. Kosygin, *Ob uluchshenii upravleniia promyshlennost'iu, sovershenstvovanii planirovaniia i usilenii ekonomicheskogo stimulirovaniia promyshlennogo proizvodstva. Doklad na Plenume TsK KPSS, 27 sentiabria 1965 goda* (Moscow: Politizdat, 1965); Aleksei N. Kosygin, *Rech' na vneocherednom XXI s"ezde KPSS* (Moscow: Gospolitizdat, 1959); Aleksei N. Kosygin, *O gosudarstevennom piatiletnem plane razvitiia narodnogo khoziaistva SSSR na 1971–1975 gody i o gosudarstvennom plane razvitiia narodnogo khoziaistva SSSR na 1972 god* (Moscow: Politizdat, 1971).

58. Alla Iaroshinskaia, ed., *Iadernaia entsiklopediia* (Moscow: Fond Iaroshinskoi, 1996).

59. V. G. Terent'ev, ed., *Kto est' kto v atomnoi energetike i promyshlennosti Rossii/Who Is Who in Nuclear Power Engineering and Industry of Russia* (Obninsk: Titul, 1995).

60. B. P. Shevelin, ed., *Put' k priznaniiu* (Ekaterinburg: UrO RAN, Ministerstvo Rossiiskoi Federatsii po atomnoi energii, and Sverdlovskii nauchno-issledovatel'skii institut khimicheskogo mashinostroeniia, 2002).

Bibliography

Adamov, Evgenii O., ed. *Belaia kniga iadernoi energetiki*. Moscow: GUP NIKIET, 2001.

Adams, Mark B., ed. *The Wellborn Science: Eugenics in Germany, France, Brazil, and Russia*. New York: Oxford University Press, 1990.

Ageev, A. V. Vospominaniia. In B. G. Gordon, ed., *Gosatomnadzoru Rossii—20 let*, 89–101. Moscow: NTTs IaRB, 2003.

Alekhin, L. A., and G. V. Kiselev. Istoriia sozdaniia pervogo v SSSR i v mire dvukhtselevogo uran-grafitovogo reaktora EI-2 dlia odnovremennogo proizvodstva oruzheinogo plutoniia i elektroenergii. *Istoriia nauki i tekhniki* 12 (2003): 2–35.

Aleksakhin, Rudol'f M., et al. *Problemy smiagcheniia posledstvii Chernobyl'skoi katastrofy: materialy mezhdunarodnogo seminara*. Briansk: Rossiia, 1993.

Aleksandrov, Anatolii P., ed. *Vospominaniia ob Igore Vasil'eviche Kurchatove*. Moscow: Nauka, 1988.

Aleksandrov, Anatolii P. Iadernaia energetika i ee rol' v tekhnicheskom progresse (General'nyi adres, zachitannyi A. P. Aleksandrovym na konferentsii VI mirovogo energeticheskogo kongressa, Moskva 1968g.). In V. A. Sidorenko, ed., *Istoriia atomnoi energetiki Sovetskogo Soiuza i Rossii*, vol. 1, 83–95. Moscow: IzdAt, 2001.

Aleksandrov, Anatolii P. Izmeniat', chto izmenit' eshche vozmozhno . . . *Ogonek* 35 (August 1990): 6–10.

Aleksandrov, P. A. *Akademik Anatolii Petrovich Aleksandrov, priamaia rech'*. 2nd ed. Moscow: Nauka, 2002.

Alekseev, M. P. Ob organizatsii nadzora za bezopasnost'iu v atomnoi energetike. In B. G. Gordon, ed., *Gosatomnadzoru Rossii—20 let*, 38–50. Moscow: NTTs IaRB, 2003.

Anderson, Benedict. *Imagined Communities: Reflections on the Origins and Spread of Nationalism*. London: Verso, 1983.

Andriianov, Viktor. *Kosygin: Zhizn' zamechatel'nykh liudei*. Moscow: Molodaia gvardiia, 2003.

Anisinov, Vladimir. AES: Stepen' riska (beseda s B. G. Dubovskim). *Smena* 10 (1994): 55–61.

Arnott, Don, and Robert Green. Unique safety valve for a reactor nuclear explosion? Paper presented at the national conference "The Legacy of Chernobyl—Lessons for the UK," Council House, Bristol, March 11, 1992 (organized by the National Steering Committee of Nuclear Free Local Authorities).

Asaulyak, Maksym. Viktor Bryukhanov: I could have been sentenced to death. *Kyiv Weekly*, April 28, 2011. http://kyivweekly.com.ua/pulse/theme/2011/04/28/164825.html.

Asmolov, Vladimir G., Andrei Iu. Gagarinskii, Viktor A. Sidorenko, and Iurii F. Chernilin. *Atomnaia energetika: Otsenki proshlogo, realii nastoiashchego, ozhidaniia budushchego*. Moscow: IzdAt, 2004.

Astashenkov, P. *Kurchatov: Zhizn' zamechatel'nykh liudei*. Moscow: Molodaia gvardiia, 1967.

Astashenkov, P. T. *Atomnaia promyshlennost'*. Moscow: Gosudarstvennoe izdatel'stvo literatury v oblasti atomnoi nauki i tekhniki, 1962.

Atomnuiu energiiu—na sluzhbu mirnomu stroitel'stvu: Beseda korrespondenta "Izvestii" s nachal'nikom Glavnogo upravleniia po ispol'zovaniiu atomnoi energii pri Sovete Ministrov SSSR E. P. Slavskim. *Izvestiia* 23 (May 1956): 2–3.

Azrael, Jeremy R. *Managerial Power and Soviet Politics*. Russian Research Center Studies, 52. Cambridge, MA: Harvard University Press, 1966.

Babaev, N. S., et al. Problemy bezopasnosti na atomnykh elektrostantsiiakh. *Priroda* 6 (1980): 30–43.

Babcock, Glenys A. The role of public interest groups in democratization: Soviet environmental groups and energy policy-making, 1985–1991. Doctoral dissertation, RAND Graduate School, 1997.

Bahry, Donna, and Brian D. Silver. Soviet citizen participation on the eve of democratization. *American Political Science Review* 84, no. 3 (1990): 821–847.

Bailes, Kendall E. *Technology and Society under Lenin and Stalin: Origins of the Soviet Technical Intelligentsia, 1917–1941*. Studies of the Russian Institute, Columbia University. Princeton, NJ: Princeton University Press, 1978.

Balinky, Alexander, Abram Bergson, John N. Hazard, and Peter Wiles. *Planning and the Market in the U.S.S.R.: The 1960's*. New Brunswick, NJ: Rutgers University Press, 1967.

Balogh, Brian. *Chain Reaction: Expert Debate and Public Participation in American Commercial Nuclear Power, 1945–1975*. Cambridge: Cambridge University Press, 1991.

Bibliography

Balzer, Harley D. Engineers: The rise and decline of a social myth. In Loren R. Graham, ed., *Science and the Soviet Social Order*, 141–167. Cambridge, MA: Harvard University Press, 1990.

Balzer, Harley D. *Russian Higher Education*. Washington, DC: National Council for Soviet and East European Research, 1993.

Balzer, Harley D., ed. *Russia's Missing Middle Class: The Professions in Russian History*. Armonk, NY: Sharpe, 1996.

Bar'iakhtar, V. G., ed. *Chernobyl'skaia katastrofa*. Kiev: Naukova dumka, 1995.

Bashmakov, I. A., and S. Ia. Chernavskii, eds. *Zakliuchenie na rabotu: Kontseptsiia razvitiia atomnoi energetiki v Rossiiskoi Federatsii*. Moscow, 1993.

Baskin, K. E., L. P. Drach, and A. I. Glushchenko. *Eshche mozhno spasti! Edinaia elektroenergeticheskaia sistema—bazis ekonomiki Rossii: Uroki Chernobylia. Opasnost' iadernogo terrorizma*. Moscow: Fizmatlit, 2006.

Baverstock, K., et al. Thyroid cancer after Chernobyl. *Nature* 359 (1992): 21–22.

Bazanova, O. V., ed. *Istoriia atomnogo proekta*. Vol. 1. Moscow: Rossiiskii Nauchnyi Tsentr "Kurchatovskii Institut," 1995.

Bazanova, O. V., ed. *Istoriia atomnogo proekta*. Vol. 2. Moscow: Rossiiskii Nauchnyi Tsentr "Kurchatovskii Institut," 1995.

Bazanova, O. V., ed. *Istoriia atomnogo proekta*. Vol. 3. Moscow: Rossiiskii Nauchnyi Tsentr "Kurchatovskii Institut," 1995.

Bazanova, O. V., ed. *Istoriia atomnogo proekta*. Vol. 4. Moscow: Rossiiskii Nauchnyi Tsentr "Kurchatovskii Institut," 1995.

Bazanova, O. V., ed. *Istoriia atomnogo proekta*. Vol. 5. Moscow: Rossiiskii Nauchnyi Tsentr "Kurchatovskii Institut," 1996.

Bazanova, O. V., and G. Ia. Karmadonova, eds. *Istoriia atomnogo proekta*. Vol. 14. Moscow: Rossiiskii Nauchnyi Tsentr "Kurchatovskii Institut," 1998.

Beliaev, Igor'. Po tomu li puti? Dialog-rassledovanie (beseda s Viktorom Aleksandrovichem Bobrovym). *Literaturnaia gazeta* 20 (5242), no. 17 (May 1989): 13.

Beliaev, Igor' A. *Beton marki "Sredmash": Proshlo 15 let*. 2001. Moscow: IzdAt.

Beliaev, Igor' A., and German G. Malkin, eds. *E. P. Slavskii: 100 let so dnia rozhdeniia*. Moscow: IzdAt, 1999.

Belianin, Leonid A., ed. *Leningradskaia AES: Gody, sobytiia, liudi*. Moscow: Energoatomizdat, 1998.

Belousov, I. G. Bez vedomestvennogo patriotizma: K probleme bezopasnosti iadernoi energetiki. *Energiia: Ekonomika, tekhnika, ekologiia* 9 (1989): 6–8.

Belousov, Rem A. *Ekonomicheskaia istoriia Rossii: XX Vek. Kniga I: Na rubezhe dvukh stoletii*. Moscow: IzdAt, 1999.

Belousov, Rem A. *Ekonomicheskaia istoriia Rossii: XX Vek. Kniga II: Cherez revoliutsiiu k NEPu*. Moscow: IzdAt, 2000.

Belousov, Rem A. *Ekonomicheskaia istoriia Rossii: XX Vek. Kniga III: Tiazhelye gody rosta i obnovleniia*. Moscow: IzdAt, 2002.

Belousov, Rem A. *Ekonomicheskaia istoriia Rossii: XX Vek. Kniga IV: Ekonomika Rossii v usloviiakh "goriachei" i "kholodnoi" voin*. Moscow: IzdAt, 2004.

Bijker, Wiebe E., Thomas P. Hughes, and Trevor Pinch, eds. *The Social Construction of Technological Systems: New Directions in the Sociology and History of Technology*. Cambridge, MA: MIT Press, 1987.

Bijker, Wiebe E., and John Law, eds. *Shaping Technology/Building Society: Studies in Sociotechnical Change*. Cambridge, MA: MIT Press, 1992.

Billington, James H. The Renaissance of the Russian Intelligentsia. *Foreign Affairs* 35 (1957): 525–530.

Blium, Arlen V. Kak bylo razrusheno "Ministerstvo pravdy": Sovetskaia tsenzura epokhi glasnosti i perestroiki (1985-1991). *Zvezda* 6 (1996): 212–221.

Blium, Arlen V. *Zakat Glavlita: Kak razrushalas' sistema Sovetskoi tsenzury: Dokumental'naia khronika 1985–1991*. Moscow: Terra, 1995.

Bogoiavlenskii, R. G. Razrabotka gazookhlazhdaemykh iadernykh reaktorov. In V. A. Sidorenko, ed., *Istoriia atomnoi energetiki Sovetskogo Soiuza i Rossii*, vol. 1, 188–193. Moscow: IzdAt, 2001.

Boholm, Asa. The cultural nature of risk: Can there be an anthropology of uncertainty? *Ethnos* 68, no. 2 (2003): 159–178.

Boudia, Soraya. Global regulation: Controlling and accepting radioactivity risks. *History and Technology* 23, no. 4 (2007): 389–406.

Briefing—Chernobyl. *ITAR-TASS*, July 2, 1987.

Brooks, Jeffrey. *Thank You, Comrade Stalin! Soviet Public Culture from Revolution to Cold War*. Princeton, NJ: Princeton University Press, 2000.

Brown, Archie. *The Rise and Fall of Communism*. New York: HarperCollins, 2009.

Brown, Kate. *Plutopia: Nuclear Families, Atomic Cities, and the Great Soviet and American Plutonium Disasters*. New York: Oxford University Press, 2013.

Bukrinskii, A. M. Neizvestnye stranitsy iz istorii sozdaniia Gosatomnadzora Rossii. In B. G. Gordon, ed., *Gosatomnadzoru Rossii—20 let*, 102–110. Moscow: NTTs IaRB, 2003.

Bibliography

Bunce, Valerie. *Subversive Institutions: The Design and the Destruction of Socialism and the State*. Cambridge Studies in Comparative Politics. Cambridge: Cambridge University Press, 1999.

Bunnell, Stephen. Russian plutonium-producing reactors closed. *Arms Control Today*, July/August 2008. http://www.armscontrol.org/act/2008_07-08/RussianPlutonium.

Burakov, Boris E., et al., The Behavior of Nuclear Fuel in the First Days of the Chernobyl Accident, *Materials Research Society Symposium Proceedings* 465 (1996): 1297-1308.

Burlakova, E. B., ed. *Consequences of the Chernobyl Catastrophe: Human Health*. Moscow: Center for Russian Environmental Policy; Scientific Council on Radiobiology, Russian Academy of Sciences, 1996.

Callon, Michel, ed. *The Laws of the Markets*. Oxford: Blackwell, 1998.

Callon, Michel. Society in the making: The study of technology as a tool for sociological analysis. In Wiebe E. Bijker, Thomas P. Hughes, and Trevor Pinch, eds., *The Social Construction of Technological Systems*, 83–103. Cambridge, MA: MIT Press, 1987.

Callon, Michel. What does it mean to say that economics is performative? In Donald MacKenzie, Fabian Muniesa, and Lucia Siu, eds., *Do Economists Make Markets? On the Performativity of Economics*, 311–357. Princeton, NJ: Princeton University Press, 2007.

Chernobyl director and aides get 10 years labor camp. *Xinhua General Overseas News Service*, July 29, 1987.

Chernobyl officials are sentenced to labor camp. *New York Times*, July 30, 1987, late city final ed., section A, p. 5.

Chernobyl officials get 10 years. *Financial Times Energy Newsletters—European Energy*, August 7, 1987, 1.

Chernobyl plant officials sentenced. *Facts on File World News Digest*, July 31, 1987, section D3, 557.

Chernobyl trial begins in Soviet [Union]. *New York Times*, July 8, 1987, late city final ed., section A, p. 5.

Chernobyl trial closed, press told. *Globe and Mail* (Canada), July 9, 1987.

Chernobyl trial set for July. *Financial Times Business Limited, FT Energy Newsletters—European Energy*, June 26, 1987, 15.

Chernyshev, V. V., ed. *Vitalii Fedorovich Konovalov: Stranitsy zhizni. Tvortsy iadnernogo veka*. Moscow: IzdAt, 2003.

Christensen, Anna. Trial to be held soon in Chernobyl. *United Press International*, March 13, 1987.

Church, Frank. *Interview with Kosygin: Report to the Committee on Foreign Relations, United States Senate.* Washington, DC: U.S. Government Printing Office, 1971.

Cirincione, Joseph, Jon B. Wolfsthal, and Miriam Rajkumar. *Deadly Arsenals: Nuclear, Biological, and Chemical Threats.* Washington, DC: Carnegie Endowment for International Peace, 2005.

Clark, C. R., et al. Achieving excellence in human performance in the nuclear industry through leadership, education, and training (IAEA-CN-114/F-8). In IAEA, ed., *Fifty Years of Nuclear Power—the Next Fifty Years.* Proceedings of an international conference held in Moscow and Obninsk, June 27–July 2, 2004. Conference Material IAEA-CN-114. Vienna: International Atomic Energy Agency, 2004.

Clarke, Lee. Panic: Myth or reality? *Contexts* 1, no. 3 (2002): 21–26.

Cleveland, Kyle. Mobilizing nuclear bias: The Fukushima nuclear crisis and the politics of uncertainty. Paper presented at the Inaugural Meeting of the STS Forum on the 2011 Fukushima/East Japan Disaster, University of California Berkeley, May 11–14, 2013.

Cochran, Thomas B., Robert S. Norris, and Oleg A. Bukharin. *Making the Russian Bomb: From Stalin to Yeltsin.* Boulder, CO: Westview Press, 1995.

Cockburn, Patrick. Chernobyl nuclear plant chiefs given 10-year jail sentences. *Financial Times* (London), July 30, 1987.

Cockburn, Patrick. Six go on trial in Chernobyl. *Financial Times* (London), July 8, 1987.

Collins, Harry. *Tacit and Explicit Knowledge.* Chicago: University of Chicago Press, 2010.

Collins, Harry. What is tacit knowledge? In Theodore R. Schatzki, Karin Knorr-Cetina, and Eike von Savigny, eds., *The Practice Turn in Contemporary Theory,* 107–119. New York: Routledge, 2001.

Collins, Harry, and Robert Evans. The third wave of science studies: Studies of expertise and experience. *Social Studies of Science* 32, no. 2 (2002): 235–296.

Coopersmith, Jonathan. *The Electrification of Russia, 1880–1926.* Ithaca, NY: Cornell University Press, 1992.

Dahlburg, John-Thor. Chernobyl gears up for trial of officials. *Globe and Mail* (Canada), July 7, 1987.

David-Fox, Michael. *Revolution of the Mind: Higher Learning among the Bolsheviks, 1918–1929.* Ithaca, NY: Cornell University Press, 1997.

David-Fox, Michael. What is cultural revolution? *Russian Review* 58 (April 1999): 181–201.

Bibliography

David-Fox, Michael, and György Péteri, eds. *Academia in Upheaval: Origins, Transfers, and Transformations of the Communist Academic Regime in Russia and East Central Europe.* Westport, CT: Bergin & Garvey, 2000.

Davletbaev, Razim I. Posledniaia smena. In A. N. Semenov, ed., *Chernobyl' desiat' let spustia: Neizbezhnost' ili sluchainost'?*, 366–383. Moscow: Energoatomizdat, 1995.

Dawson, Jane I. *Eco-Nationalism: Anti-Nuclear Activism and National Identity in Russia, Lithuania, and Ukraine.* Durham, NC: Duke University Press, 1996.

Dedman, Bill. General Electric–designed reactors in Fukushima have 23 sisters in U.S. NBC News Investigations, March 13, 2011. http://investigations.nbcnews.com/_news/2011/03/13/6256121-general-electric-designed-reactors-in-fukushima-have-23-sisters-in-us?lite.

Dejevsky, Mary. Chernobyl chief faces 10 years in labour camp: Sentences leave question of ministerial responsibility unexplained. *Times* (London), July 30, 1987.

DeLeon, Peter. *Development and Diffusion of the Nuclear Power Reactor: A Comparative Analysis.* Cambridge, MA: Ballinger, 1979.

Denisov, V. P. Evoliutsiia vodo-vodianykh energeticheskikh reaktorov dlia AES. In Viktor A. Sidorenko, ed., *Istoriia atomnoi energetiki Sovetskogo Soiuza i Rossii: Istoriia VVER*, vol. 2, 218–302. Moscow: IzdAt, 2002.

Denisov, V. P., and Iu. G. Dragunov. *Reaktornye ustanovki VVER dlia atomnykh elektrostantsii.* Moscow: IzdAt, 2002.

Dennis, Michael A. Secrecy and science revisited: From politics to historical practice and back. In Ronald E. Doel and Thomas Söderqvist, eds., *The Historiography of Contemporary Science, Technology, and Medicine*, 172–184. London: Routledge, 2006.

Diatlov, Anatolii S. *Chernobyl': Kak eto bylo.* Moscow: Nauchtekhlitizdat, 2003.

Disregard Tepco order, boss told plant workers. *Japan Times,* December 1, 2011.

Dodd, Charles K. *Industrial Decision-Making and High-Risk Technology: Siting Nuclear Power Facilities in the USSR.* Lanham, MD: Rowman & Littlefield, 1994.

Dollezhal', Nikolai A. *U istokov rukotvornogo mira: Zapiski konstruktora.* Moscow: GUP NIKIET, IzdAt, 2002.

Dollezhal', Nikolai A., and Iurii F. Koriakin. Iadernaia elektroenergetika: Dostizheniia i problemy. *Kommunist* 14 (1979): 19–28.

Dubovskii, Boris G. *O faktorakh neustoichivosti iadernykh reaktorov na primere reaktora RBMK.* Obninsk: [n.p.], 1989.

Dyatlov, Anatoly [Diatlov, Anatolii S.]. 26 April 1986. *Nuclear Engineering International* (April 1996): 18–22.

Dyatlov, Anatoly [Diatlov, Anatolii S.]. Why INSAG has still got it wrong. *Nuclear Engineering International* 40, no. 494 (1995): 17–21.

Emel'ianenkov, Aleksandr. *Ostrova Sredmasha*. Moscow: Rossiiskaia gazeta & Izd. Parad, 2005.

Emel'ianov, V. S. Atomnaia nauka i tekhnika i stroitel'stvo kommunizma. *Atomnaia energiia* 11, no. 4 (1961): 301–312.

Energetika narodnogo khoziaistva v plane GOELRO. 1966. Moscow: Ekonomika.

Ermakov, Andrei P., and Anatolii G. Syrmai. *Atomnaia energiia i transport*. Moscow: Izd-vo Akademii nauk SSSR, 1963.

EurActiv G8 Summit urges stringent nuclear safety rules. May 27, 2011. http://www.euractiv.com/energy/g8-summit-urges-stringent-nuclear-safety-rules-news-505185.

European Nuclear Safety Regulators Group. Peer review report: Stress tests performed on European nuclear power plants. 2012. http://www.ensreg.eu/EU-Stress-Tests.

Ezrahi, Yaron. *The Descent of Icarus: Science and the Transformation of Contemporary Democracy*. Cambridge, MA: Harvard University Press, 1990.

Ezrahi, Yaron. Technology and the illusion of the escape from politics. In Yaron Ezrahi, Everett Mendelsohn, and Howard M. Segal, eds., *Technology, Pessimism, and Postmodernism*, 29–37. Dordrecht: Kluwer Academic Publishers, 1994.

Fain, Boris A. *Aktivnaia zona: Povest' ob atomnom institute*. Moscow: Skripto, 1998.

Feinberg, S. M., S. B. Shikhov, and B. V. Troianskii. *Teoriia iadernykh reaktorov*. 2 vols. Moscow: Energoatomizdat, 1983.

Feoktistov, Lev P. Uroki Chernobylia. *Priroda* 9 (1986): 123–124.

Fetistov, T. I., ed. *Prem'er izvestnyi i neizvestnyi: Vospominaniia o A. N. Kosygine*. Moscow: Respublika, 1997.

Fitzpatrick, Sheila. *Education and Social Mobility in the Soviet Union, 1921–1934*. Cambridge: Cambridge University Press, 1979.

Foreign Ministry briefing: USA's "new demands" on INF, Afghanistan, Chernobyl trial. *BBC Summary of World Broadcasts*, July 7, 1987.

Fortescue, Stephen. *Science Policy in the Soviet Union*. London: Routledge, 1990.

Foucault, Michel. *Discipline and Punish: The Birth of the Prison*. New York: Vintage Books, 1979.

Freeman, Marsha. Atommash: Assembly line nuclear plants. *Executive Intelligence Review* 6, no. 28 (1979): 20–21.

Freudenheim, Milt, Katherine Roberts, and James F. Clarity. The trial begins at Chernobyl. *New York Times*, July 12, 1987, late city final ed., section 4, p. 2.

GE engineers and American government officials warned of dangerous nuclear design. *Washington's Blog*, December 11, 2013. http://www.washingtonsblog.com/2013/12/general-electric-knew-reactor-design-unsafe-isnt-ge-getting-heat-fukushima.html.

Gerber, Michele Stenehjem. *On the Home Front: The Cold War Legacy of the Hanford Nuclear Site*. Lincoln: University of Nebraska Press, 1992.

Gieryn, Thomas F., and Anne E. Figert. Ingredients for a theory of science in society: O-rings, ice water, C-clamp, Richard Feynman, and the press. In Susan E. Cozzens and Thomas F. Gieryn, eds., *Theories of Science in Society*, 67–86. Bloomington: Indiana University Press, 1990.

Gigevich, Vasil', and Oleg Chernov. *Stali vody gor'kimi: Khronika Chernobyl'skoi bedy*. 1991. Minsk: Belorus.

Gilbert, G. Nigel, and Michael Mulkay. *Opening Pandora's Box: A Sociological Analysis of Scientists' Discourse*. Cambridge: Cambridge University Press, 1984.

Girnis, Viacheslav V. *Zapiski atomshchika*. Moscow: Energoatomizdat, 2000.

Goncharov, Vladimir V. Pervyi period razvitiia atomnoi energetiki v SSSR. In Viktor A. Sidorenko, ed., *Istoriia atomnoi energetiki Sovetskogo Soiuza i Rossii*, vol. 1, 16–70. Moscow: IzdAt, 2001.

Gorbachev, Boris. Tainy Chernobyl'skogo suda. *Zerkalo nedeli* 6, no. 491 (April 2004): 24–29.

Gordin, Michael, Karl Hall, and Alexei Kojevnikov, eds. *Intelligentsia Science: The Russian Century, 1860–1960*. Osiris, vol. 23. Chicago: University of Chicago Press, 2008.

Gordon, B. G., ed. *Gosatomnadzoru Rossii—20 let*. Moscow: NTTs IaRB, 2003.

Gor'kii urok. *Atomnaia energiia* 6, no. 60 (1986): 370–371.

Gorobetz, Boris. V treugol'nike Kapitsa-Beria-Stalin. *Mirovaia energiia/World Energy*, 2008. http://www.worldenergy.ru/doc_20_53_2819.html.

Gosudarstvennyi komitet po ispol'zovaniiu atomnoi energii SSSR. Avariia na Chernobyl'skoi AES i ee posledstviia: Informatsiia, podgotovlennaia dlia soveshchaniia ekspertov MAGATE (25–29 avgusta 1986 g., Vena). In Viktor A. Sidorenko, ed., *Istoriia atomnoi energetiki Sovetskogo Soiuza i Rossii: Uroki avarii na Chernobyl'skoi AES*, vol. 4, 49–84. Moscow: IzdAt, 2002.

Gosudarstvennyi komitet SSSR po nadzoru za bezopasnym vedeniem rabot v promyshlennosti i atomnoi energetike. O prichinakh i obstoiatel'stvakh avarii na 4 bloke Chernobyl'skoi AES 26 Aprelia 1986 g. Doklad komissii Gospromatomnadzora

SSSR. In Viktor A. Sidorenko, ed., *Istoriia atomnoi energetiki Sovetskogo Soiuza i Rossii: Uroki avarii na Chernobyl'skoi AES*, vol. 4, 333–409. Moscow: IzdAt, [1991] 2002.

Gowing, Margaret. *Britain and Atomic Energy, 1935–1945*. London: Macmillan, 1964.

Gowing, Margaret, and Lorna Arnold. *Independence and Deterrence: Britain and Atomic Energy, 1945–52*, Volume 1: *Policy Making*. London: Macmillan, 1974.

Gowing, Margaret, and Lorna Arnold. *Independence and Deterrence: Britain and Atomic Energy, 1945–52*, Volume 2: *Policy Execution*. London: Macmillan, 1974.

Grabovskii, Mikhail P. *Atomnyi avral*. Moscow: Nauchnaia kniga, 2001.

Grabovskii, Mikhail P. *Nakanune avrala*. Moscow: Nauchnaia kniga, 2000.

Grabovskii, Mikhail P. *Pervaia Sovetskaia atomnaia podvodnaia lodka K-3*. Moscow: Samizdat, 2005.

Grabovskii, Mikhail P. *Plutonievaia zona*. Moscow: Nauchnaia kniga, 2002.

Grabovskii, Mikhail P. *Puskovoi ob"ekt*. Moscow: Nauchnaia kniga, 1999.

Grabovskii, Mikhail P. *Vtoroi Ivan: Sovershenno sekretno*. Moscow: Nauchnaia kniga, 1998.

Graham, Loren R. *The Ghost of the Executed Engineer: Technology and the Fall of the Soviet Union*. Cambridge, MA: Harvard University Press, 1993.

Graham, Loren R. *Moscow Stories*. Bloomington: Indiana University Press, 2006.

Graham, Loren R. *Science and Philosophy in the Soviet Union*. New York: Knopf, 1972.

Graham, Loren R. *Science in Russia and the Soviet Union: A Short History*. Cambridge: Cambridge University Press, 1993.

Graham, Loren R., ed. *Science and the Soviet Social Order*. Cambridge, MA: Harvard University Press, 1990.

Graham, Loren R. *Between Science and Values*. New York: Columbia University Press, 1981.

Greenwald, John, and Ken Olsen. Disasters judgment at Chernobyl: Six defendants go on trial for causing a nuclear catastrophe. *Time* 130, no. 3 (July 20, 1987): 44-45.

Gubarev, Vladimir. *Agoniia Sredmasha: Ot Chernobylia do Chubaisa*. Moscow: Akademkniga, 2006.

Gubarev, Vladimir. *Iadernyi vek: Bomba*. Moscow: IzdAt, 1995.

Gubarev, Vladimir. *Iadernyi vek: Chernobyl'*. Moscow: Agentstvo "Nekos," 1996.

Gubarev, Vladimir. *Sarcophagus: A Tragedy*. Trans. Michael Glenny, with a preface by Robert Gale. New York: Vintage Books, 1987.

Bibliography

Gubarev, Vladimir. *XX vek: Ispovedi. Sud'ba nauki i uchenykh v Rossii.* Moscow: Nauka/Interperiodika, 2000.

Gusfield, Joseph R. *The Culture of Public Problems: Drinking-Driving and the Symbolic Order.* Chicago: University of Chicago Press, 1981.

Hall, Karl. The schooling of Lev Landau: The European context of postrevolutionary Soviet theoretical physics. *Osiris* 23 (2008): 230–259.

Handelman, Stephen. Chernobyl facts covered up. *Toronto Star*, July 12, 1987, Sunday 2nd ed., p. H3.

Hanson, Philip. *The Rise and Fall of the Soviet Economy: An Economic History of the USSR from 1945.* London: Longman, 2003.

Hecht, Gabrielle. *Being Nuclear: Africans and the Global Uranium Trade.* Cambridge, MA: MIT Press, 2012.

Hecht, Gabrielle. *The Radiance of France: Nuclear Power and National Identity after World War II.* Cambridge, MA: MIT Press, 1998.

Hewett, Ed A. Introductory comment on the consequences of Chernobyl'. *Soviet Economy (Silver Spring, Md.)* 2, no. 2 (1986): 95–96.

Hewett, Ed A. *Reforming the Soviet Economy: Equality versus Efficiency.* Washington, DC: Brookings Institution, 1988.

Hewett, Ed A. *Soviet Central Planning: Probing the Limits of the Traditional Model.* Prepared for presentation at the conference "The Soviet Union and Eastern Europe in the World Economy" at the Kennan Institute for Advanced Russian Studies, Washington, DC, October 18–19, 1984. Washington, DC: Kennan Institute for Advanced Russian Studies, 1984.

Hewett, Ed A., et al. Panel on the economic and political consequences of Chernobyl'. *Soviet Economy (Silver Spring, Md.)* 2, no. 2 (1986): 97–130.

Hewett, Ed A., et al. Soviet economy. *Soviet Economy (Silver Spring, Md.)* 1, no. 1 (1985): 5.

Hippel, Frank N. von, and Matthew Bunn. Saga of the Siberian plutonium-production reactors. *Journal of the Federation of American Scientists* 53, no. 6 (2000). http://www.fas.org/faspir/v53n6.htm.

Hollander, Gayle D. *Soviet Political Indoctrination: Developments in Mass Media and Propaganda since Stalin.* New York: Praeger, 1972.

Holloway, David. Physics, the state, and civil society in the Soviet Union. *Historical Studies in the Physical and Biological Sciences* 30, no. 1 (1999): 173–193.

Holloway, David. *Stalin and the Bomb: The Soviet Union and Atomic Energy 1939–1956.* New Haven, CT: Yale University Press, 1994.

Hough, Jerry F. Political participation in the Soviet Union. *Soviet Studies* 28, no. 1 (1976): 3–20.

Hough, Jerry F., and Merle Fainsod. *How the Soviet Union Is Governed*. Cambridge, MA: Harvard University Press, 1979.

Howells, Jeremy. Tacit knowledge, innovation, and technology transfer. *Technology Analysis and Strategic Management* 8, no. 2 (1996): 91–106.

Hughes, Thomas P. *American Genesis: A Century of Invention and Technological Enthusiasm, 1870–1970*. New York: Viking, 1989.

Hughes, Thomas P. The evolution of large technological systems. In Wiebe E. Bijker, Thomas P. Hughes, and Trevor Pinch, eds., *The Social Construction of Technological Systems*, 51–82. Cambridge, MA: MIT Press, 1987.

Hughes, Thomas P. *Networks of Power: Electrification in Western Society, 1880–1930*. Baltimore: Johns Hopkins University Press, 1983.

Hughes, Thomas P. *Rescuing Prometheus: Four Monumental Projects That Changed the Modern World*. New York: Pantheon Books, 1998.

Iadrikhinskii, Aleksandr A. *Iadernaia avariia na 4-om bloke Chernobyl'skoi AES i iadernaia bezopasnost' reaktorov RBMK*. Kurchatov: [n.p.], 1989.

Iaroshinskaia, Alla, ed. *Iadernaia entsiklopediia*. Moscow: Fond Iaroshinskoi, 1996.

Ignatenko, E. I., and V. Ia. Vozniak, A. P. Kovalenko, and S. N. Trotskii, eds. *Chernobyl': Sobytiia i uroki. Voprosy i otvety*. Moscow: Izdatel'stvo politicheskoi literatury, 1989.

Il'ichev, V. A., and A. A. Prigoryan. Structure settlements at the Atommash plant as a result of prolonged soil wetting. *Soil Mechanics and Foundation Engineering* 25, no. 4 (1988): 150–157.

Illesh, A. V., and A. E. Pral'nikov, eds. *Reportazh iz Chernobylia: Zapiski ochevidtsev. Kommentarii. Razmyshleniia*. Moscow: Mysl', 1988.

Informatsiia ob avarii na Chernobyl'skoi AES i ee posledstviiakh, podgotovlennaia dlia MAGATE. *Atomnaia energiia* 61 (1986): 301–320.

Institute of Electrical and Electronics Engineers. *Proceedings of the 2002 IEEE 7th Conference on Human Factors and Power Plants*. New York: Institute of Electrical and Electronics Engineers, 2002.

Institute of Nuclear Power Operations. *Special Report on the Nuclear Accident at the Fukushima Daiichi Nuclear Power Station*. INPO 11–005. Atlanta, GA: INPO, November 2011.

Bibliography

Institute of Nuclear Power Operations. *Special Report INPO 11–005 Addendum: Lessons Learned from the Nuclear Accident at the Fukushima Daiichi Nuclear Power Station.* Atlanta, GA: INPO, August 2012.

Institution of Mechanical Engineers. *Symposium on the Education and Training of Engineers in the Nuclear Industry: A Symposium Arranged by the Nuclear Energy and the Education and Training Groups, 5th December 1968, London.* London: Institution of Mechanical Engineers, 1969.

International Atomic Energy Agency. *The International Chernobyl Project: An Overview. Assessment of Radiological Consequences and Evaluation of Protective Measures.* Vienna: International Atomic Energy Agency, 1991.

International Atomic Energy Agency. *The International Chernobyl Project: Technical Report. Assessment of Radiological Consequences and Evaluation of Protective Measures.* Vienna: International Atomic Energy Agency, 1991.

International Atomic Energy Agency. *Mission Report: IAEA International Peer Review Mission on Mid- and Long-Term Roadmap towards the Decommissioning of TEPCO's Fukushima Daiichi Nuclear Power Stations Units 1–4, Tokyo and Fukushima Prefecture, Japan, 15–22 April 2013.* Vienna: International Atomic Energy Agency, 2013.

International Atomic Energy Agency. *Nuclear Power Reactors in the World.* Vienna: International Atomic Energy Agency, 1996.

International Atomic Energy Agency. *Siting of Reactors and Nuclear Research Centres: Proceedings of the Symposium on Criteria for Guidance in the Selection of Sites for the Construction of Reactor and Nuclear Research Centres, Bombay, 11–15 March 1963.* Vienna: International Atomic Energy Agency, 1963.

International Atomic Energy Agency. Strengthening radiation and nuclear safety infrastructures in countries of the former USSR. Paper presented at the conference "Strengthening Radiation and Nuclear Safety Infrastructures in Countries of the Former USSR," Vienna, May 4–7, 1993.

International Federation of Red Cross and Red Crescent Societies. *Learning Lessons from Fukushima: Red Cross Red Crescent Moves to Step Up Nuclear Preparedness.* May 17, 2012. http://www.ifrc.org/en/news-and-media/press-releases/asia-pacific/japan/learning-lessons-from-fukushima-red-cross-red-crescent-moves-to-step-up-nuclear-preparedness/.

International Nuclear Safety Advisory Group. *The Chernobyl Accident—Updating of INSAG-1 (INSAG-7).* Vienna: International Atomic Energy Agency, 1992.

International Nuclear Safety Advisory Group. *Summary Report on the Post-Accident Review Meeting on the Chernobyl Accident.* No. 75-INSAG-1, Safety Series. Vienna: International Atomic Energy Agency, 1986.

Ioffe, B. L., and O. V. Shvedov. Heavy water reactors and nuclear power plants in the USSR and Russia: Past, present, and future. *Atomic Energy* 86, no. 4 (1999): 295–304.

Ioirysh, Abram I., et al. *Gosudarstvennyi nadzor za obespecheniem bezopasnosti atomnoi energetiki: Pravovye problemy*. Moscow: Nauka, 1991.

Ivanov, V. K., et al. Cancer risks in the Kaluga Oblast of the Russian Federation 10 years after the Chernobyl accident. *Radiation and Environmental Biophysics* 36 (1997): 161–167.

Ivanov, V. K., et al. Dynamics of thyroid cancer incidence in Russia following the Chernobyl accident. *Journal of Radiological Protection* 19 (1999): 305–318.

Izrael', Iu. A., S. M. Vakulovskii, V. A. Vetrov, V. N. Petrov, F. Ia. Rovinskii, and E. D. Stukin. *Chernobyl': Radioaktivnoe zagriaznenie prirodnykh sred*. Leningrad: Gidrometeoizdat, 1990.

Janowitz, Morris. *The Professional Soldier*. Glencoe, IL: Free Press, 1960.

Jasanoff, Sheila, ed. *Learning from Disaster: Risk Management after Bhopal*. Philadelphia: University of Pennsylvania Press, 1994.

Jasanoff, Sheila, ed. *States of Knowledge: The Co-Production of Science and Social Order*. London: Routledge, 2004.

Jaworowski, Zbigniew. All Chernobyl's victims: A realistic assessment of Chernobyl's health effects. *21st Century Science and Technology* 11, no. 1 (1998): 14–25.

Johnston, Sean F. *The Neutron's Children: Nuclear Engineers and the Shaping of Identity*. Oxford: Oxford University Press, 2012.

Josephson, Paul R. Atomic energy and "atomic culture" in the USSR: The ideological roots of economic and safety problems facing the nuclear power industry after Chernobyl. In T. Anthony Jones, David Powell, and Walter Connor, eds., *Soviet Social Problems*, 55–77. Boulder, CO: Westview Press, 1991.

Josephson, Paul R. Atomic-powered communism: Nuclear culture in the postwar USSR. *Slavic Review* 55, no. 2 (1996): 297–324.

Josephson, Paul R. The historical roots of the Chernobyl disaster. *Soviet Union / Union Soviétique* 13, no. 3 (1986): 275–299.

Josephson, Paul R. *Physics and Politics in Revolutionary Russia*. California Studies in the History of Science. Berkeley: University of California Press, 1991.

Josephson, Paul R. *Red Atom: Russia's Nuclear Power Program from Stalin to Today*. New York: Freeman, 1999.

Josephson, Paul R. Rockets, reactors, and Soviet culture. In Loren Graham, ed., *Science and the Soviet Social Order*, 168–191. Cambridge, MA: Harvard University Press, 1990.

Juraku, Kohta. "Made in Japan" Fukushima nuclear accident: A critical review for accident investigation activities in Japan. Paper presented at the Inaugural Meeting of the STS Forum on the 2011 Fukushima/East Japan Disaster, University of California at Berkeley, May 11–14, 2013.

K 10-letiiu avarii na Chernobyl'skoi AES. Sotsial'naia i psikhologicheskaia reabilitatsiia postradavshikh ot Chernobyl'skoi katastrofy: Opyt i perspektivy. Moscow: MChS Rossii, 1996.

Kaibysheva, Lenina S. *Posle Chernobylia.* Vol. 1. Moscow: IzdAt, 1996.

Kaibysheva, Lenina S. *Posle Chernobylia.* Vol. 2. Moscow: IzdAt, 2001.

Kaibysheva, Lenina S. Posle Chernobylia. In A. N. Semenov, ed., *Chernobyl' desiat' let spustia: Neizbezhnost' ili sluchainost'?*, 384–396. Moscow: Energoatomizdat, 1995.

Kamyshan, A. N. Sobytiia i liudi (Vospominaniia uchastnika). In Viktor A. Sidorenko, ed., *Istoriia atomnoi energetiki Sovetskogo Soiuza i Rossii: Istoriia VVER*, vol. 2, 145–193. Moscow: IzdAt, 2002.

Karasiuk, A. A., and A. I. Sidorenko. *Vokrug Chernobylia: Dialogi s uchenymi.* Moscow: IzdAT, 1991.

Karmadonova, G. Ia., ed. *Istoriia atomnogo proekta.* Vol. 6. Moscow: Rossiiskii Nauchnyi Tsentr "Kurchatovskii Institut," 1996.

Karmadonova, G. Ia., ed. *Istoriia atomnogo proekta.* Vol. 8. Moscow: Rossiiskii Nauchnyi Tsentr "Kurchatovskii Institut," 1996.

Karmadonova, G. Ia., ed. *Istoriia atomnogo proekta.* Vols. 9–10. Moscow: Rossiiskii Nauchnyi Tsentr "Kurchatovskii Institut," 1997.

Karmadonova, G. Ia., ed. *Istoriia atomnogo proekta.* Vol. 11. Moscow: Rossiiskii Nauchnyi Tsentr "Kurchatovskii Institut," 1997.

Karmadonova, G. Ia., ed. *Istoriia atomnogo proekta.* Vol. 12. Moscow: Rossiiskii Nauchnyi Tsentr "Kurchatovskii Institut," 1997.

Karmadonova, G. Ia., ed. *Istoriia atomnogo proekta.* Vol. 13. Moscow: Rossiiskii Nauchnyi Tsentr "Kurchatovskii Institut," 1998.

Karmadonova, G. Ia., and O. V. Bazanova, eds. *Istoriia atomnogo proekta.* Vol. 7. Moscow: Rossiiskii Nauchnyi Tsentr "Kurchatovskii Institut," 1996.

Karpan, Nikolai V. *Chernobyl': Mest' mirnogo atoma.* Kiev: Kantri Laif, 2005.

Kartel, N. A., ed. *Chernobyl Digest 1994–95.* Vol. 4. Minsk: Center for Russian Environmental Policy et al., 1996.

Kaser, Michael. Kosygin, Liberman, and the pace of Soviet industrial reform. *World Today* 21, no. 9 (1965): 375–388.

Kazachkovskii, Oleg D. *Fizik na sluzhbe atoma*. Moscow: Energoatomizdat, 2002.

Kazanskii, Iu. A., ed. *Iadernaia energetika: K 100-letiiu A. I. Leipunskogo, Izvestiia vysshikh uchebnykh zavedenii*. Obninsk: Ministerstvo obrazovaniia RF, 2003.

Keller, Bill. The 1986 disaster at Chernobyl: A year later, lessons are drawn; in Soviet [Union], heroism and candor are hailed, but questions linger. *New York Times*, April 26, 1987, late city final ed., section 1, p. 1.

Khlopkin, Nikolai S., ed. *A. P. Aleksandrov: Dokumenty i vospominaniia, k 100-letiiu so dnia rozhdeniia*. Moscow: IzdAt, 2003.

Khlopkin, Nikolai S. *Stranitsy zhizni*. Moscow: IzdAt, 2003.

Knight, Amy. *Beria: Stalin's First Lieutenant*. Princeton, NJ: Princeton University Press, 1993.

Knorre, Helen. Frontiers of technology: U.S.S.R. *Nuclear Engineering* 9, no. 100 (1964): 317–318.

Knorre, Helen. "The Star Called Wormwood": The cause and effect of the Chernobyl catastrophe. *Public Understanding of Science (Bristol, England)* 1 (1992): 241–249.

Kocherga, Anatolii V. Pervyi mesiats posle avarii. In A. N. Semenov, ed., *Chernobyl' desiat' let spustia: Neizbezhnost' ili sluchainost'?*, 170–181. Moscow: Energoatomizdat, 1995.

Kochetkov, Lev A. K istorii pervoi ocheredi Beloiarskoi AES. In V. A. Sidorenko, ed., *Istoriia atomnoi energetiki Sovetskogo Soiuza i Rossii*, vol. 1, 117–133. Moscow: IzdAt, 2001.

Kochetkov, Lev A. K istorii sozdaniia Obninskoi AES. In V. A. Sidorenko, ed., *Istoriia atomnoi energetiki Sovetskogo Soiuza i Rossii*, vol. 1, 96–101. Moscow: IzdAt, 2001.

Kochetkov, Lev A., ed. *Ot Pervoi v mire AES k atomnoi energetike XXI veka: Sbornik tezisov, dokladov i soobshchenii* (Proceedings of the 10th Annual Conference, Obninsk, June 28–July 2, 1999). Obninsk: Iadernoe obshchestvo Rossii, 1999.

Kochetkov, Lev A., and M. F. Troianov. Reaktory na bystrykh neitronakh. In V. A. Sidorenko, ed., *Istoriia atomnoi energetiki Sovetskogo Soiuza i Rossii*, vol. 1, 164–187. Moscow: IzdAt, 2001.

Kojevnikov, Alexei B. The Great War, the Russian Civil War, and the invention of Big Science. *Science in Context* 15, no. 2 (2002): 239–276.

Kojevnikov, Alexei B. Piotr Kapitza and Stalin's government: A study in moral choice. *Historical Studies in the Physical and Biological Sciences* 22, no. 1 (1991): 131–164.

Kojevnikov, Alexei B. *Stalin's Great Science: The Times and Adventures of Soviet Physicists*. London: Imperial College Press, 2004.

Bibliography

Kommunisticheskaia partiia Sovetskogo Soiuza, Tsentral'nyi Komitet, Plenum. *Ob uluchshenii upravleniia promyshlennost'iu, sovershenstvovanii planirovaniia i usilenii ekonomicheskogo stimulirovaniia promyshlennogo proizvodstva.* Postanovleniia Plenuma TsK KPSS, priniatye 29 sentiabria 1965 g. Moscow: Politizdat, 1965.

Konoplia, Evgenii F., I. V. Rolevich, and Institut radiobiologii (Akademiia nauk Belarusi). *Chernobyl'skaia katastrofa: Bibliografiia nauchnoi literatury.* Minsk: Pravo i ekonomika, 1996.

Kopchinskii, Georgii A., and Nikolai A. Shteinberg. *Chernobyl: Kak eto bylo. Preduprezhdenie.* Moscow: Litterra, 2011.

Koriakin, Iurii I. *Okrestnosti iadernoi energetiki Rossii: Novye vyzovy.* Moscow: GUP NIKIET, 2002.

Korolev, B. Radiatsiia i kapusta. *Ogonek* 22 (May/June 1986): 7.

Kostenetskii, M. I., and G. T. Gribinenko. *Ekho Chernobylia v Zaporozh'e: Nauchno-populiarnyi ocherk.* Zaporozh'e: MP Bereginia, 1992.

Kosygin, Aleksei N. *Ob uluchshenii upravleniia promyshlennost'iu, sovershenstvovanii planirovaniia i usilenii ekonomicheskogo stimulirovaniia promyshlennogo proizvodstva.* Doklad na plenume TsK KPSS, 27 sentiabria 1965 goda. Moscow: Politizdat, 1965.

Kosygin, Aleksei N. *O gosudarstevennom piatiletnem plane razvitiia narodnogo khoziaistva SSSR na 1971–1975 gody i o gosudarstvennom plane razvitiia narodnogo khoziaistva SSSR na 1972 god.* Moscow: Politizdat, 1971.

Kosygin, Aleksei N. *Rech' na vneocherednom XXI s"ezde KPSS.* Moscow: Gospolitizdat, 1959.

Kotkin, Stephen. *Armageddon Averted: The Soviet Collapse, 1970–2000.* Oxford: Oxford University Press, 2001.

Kotkin, Stephen. *Magnetic Mountain: Stalinism as a Civilization.* Berkeley: University of California Press, 1995.

Kovalevich, O. M. Ob obrazovanii Gosatomenergonadzora SSSR. In B. G. Gordon, ed., *Gosatomnadzoru Rossii—20 let,* 69–78. Moscow: NTTs IaRB, 2003.

Kovalevskaia, Liubov'. *Chernobyl' "DSP"; Posledstviia Chernobylia, Chornobyl', Ukraine, 1986.* Kiev: Abris, 1995.

Kozlov, N. I., et al. *Pravila iadernoi bezopasnosti atomnykh elektrostantsii PBIa-04-74.* 2nd ed. Moscow: Atomizdat, 1977.

Kramerov, A. Ia. Kanal'nye vodookhlazhdaemye uran-grafitovye reaktory (UGR) tipa RBMK. In V. A. Sidorenko, ed., *Istoriia atomnoi energetiki Sovetskogo Soiuza i Rossii,* vol. 1, 154–163. Moscow: IzdAt, 2001.

Kramish, Arnold. *Atomic Energy in the Soviet Union.* Stanford, CA: Stanford University Press, 1959.

Krementsov, Nikolai L. *Stalinist Science.* Princeton, NJ: Princeton University Press, 1997.

Krenz, Ferdinand, and Henry Kim. *Deep Waters: The Ottawa River and Canada's Nuclear Adventure.* Montreal: McGill–Queen's University Press, 2004.

Krige, John. Atoms for peace, scientific internationalism, and scientific intelligence. *Osiris* 21 (2006): 161–181.

Krige, John. The peaceful atom as political weapon: Euratom and American foreign policy in the late 1950s. *Historical Studies in the Natural Sciences* 38, no. 1 (2008): 5–44.

Krohn, Wolfgang, and Johannes Weyer. Society as a laboratory: The social risks of experimental research. *Science & Public Policy* 21, no. 3 (1994): 173–183.

Kruglov, Arkadii K. *Kak sozdavalas' atomnaia promyshlennost' v SSSR.* Moscow: TSNIIatominform, 1995.

Kruglov, Arkadii K. *Shtab atomproma.* Moscow: TSNIIatominform, 1998.

Kuchinskaya, Olga. *The Politics of Invisibility Public Knowledge about Radiation Health Effects after Chernobyl.* Cambridge, MA: MIT Press, 2014.

Kuechle, David. *The Story of the Savannah: An Episode in Maritime Labor-Management Relations.* Cambridge, MA: Harvard University Press, 1971.

Kulygin, V. M., Iu. N. Smirnov, and M. E. Khalizeva, eds. *Golovin, Igor' Nikolaevich: Stranitsy zhizni. Tvortsy iadernogo veka.* Moscow: IzdAt, 2004.

Kurchatov, Igor' V. Nekotorye voprosy razvitiia atomnoi energetiki v SSSR. *Pravda* 141, no. 20 (1956): 2.

Kurchatov, Igor' V. Nekotorye voprosy razvitiia atomnoi energetiki v SSSR (Doklad, sdelannyi I. V. Kurchatovym v Kharuelle (Angliia) v aprele 1956g.). In Viktor A. Sidorenko, ed., *Istoriia atomnoi energetiki Sovetskogo Soiuza i Rossii*, vol. 1, 71–82. Moscow: IzdAt, 2001.

Kurchatov, Igor' V. *Nekotorye voprosy razvitiia atomnoi energetiki v SSSR/Some Aspects of Atomic Power Development in the USSR* (Russian and English). Moscow: [IAE], 1956.

Kurchatov, Igor' V. Rech' tovarishcha I. V. Kurchatova *Pravda* 53, no. 22 (1956): 7.

Kuz'min, A. N. Sorok let s RBMK. In Viktor A. Sidorenko, ed., *Istoriia atomnoi energetiki Sovetskogo Soiuza i Rossii: Istoriia RBMK*, vol. 3, 156–170. Moscow: IzdAt, 2003.

Kuznetsov, Vladimir M. *Rossiiskaia atomnaia energetika vchera, segodnia, zavtra: Vzgliad nezavisimogo eksperta.* Moscow: Natsional'nyi Institut Pressy, 2000.

Kuznetsova, Raisa V., ed. *Kurchatov v zhizni: Pis'ma, dokumenty, vospominaniia (iz lichnogo arkhiva)*. Moscow: Mosgorarkhiv, 2002.

Lam, Alice. Tacit knowledge, organizational learning and societal institutions: An integrated framework. *Organization Studies* 21, no. 3 (2000): 487–513.

Lampland, Martha. The technopolitical lineage of state planning in Hungary, 1930–1956. In Gabrielle Hecht, ed., *Entangled Geographies: Empire and Technopolitics in the Global Cold War*, 155–184. Cambridge, MA: MIT Press, 2011.

LaPorte, Todd R., and Paula M. Consolini. Working in practice but not in theory: Theoretical challenges of "high-reliability organizations." *Journal of Public Administration: Research and Theory* 1, no. 1 (1991): 19–48.

Larin, Ivan I. *Tiazheloe bremia podviga*. Moscow: IzdAt, 1996.

Lash, Scott, Bronislaw Szerszynski, and Brian Wynne, eds. *Risk, Environment, and Modernity: Towards a New Ecology*. Thousand Oaks, CA: Sage, 1996.

Levine, Richard, Milt Freudenheim, and James F. Carity. Fixing the blame at Chernobyl. *New York Times*, June 22, 1986, "The World" section.

Lewin, Moshe. *The Gorbachev Phenomenon: A Historical Interpretation*. Berkeley: University of California Press, 1988.

Lindell, Michael K., and Ronald W. Perry. Effects of the Chernobyl accident on public perceptions of nuclear plant accident risks. *Risk Analysis* 10, no. 3 (1990): 393–399.

Lowen, Rebecca S. Entering the atomic power race: Science, industry, and government. *Political Science Quarterly* 102, no. 3 (1987): 459–479.

MacKenzie, Donald, and Yuval Millo. Constructing a market, performing theory: The historical sociology of a financial derivatives exchange. *American Journal of Sociology* 109 (2003): 107–145.

Mahoney, Martin C., et al. Thyroid cancer incidence trends in Belarus: Examining the impact of Chernobyl. *International Journal of Epidemiology* 33, no. 5 (2004): 1025–1033.

Maier, Charles S. Between Taylorism and technocracy: European ideologies and the vision of industrial productivity in the 1920s. *Contemporary History* 5, no. 2 (1970): 27–61.

Malia, Martin. *The Soviet Tragedy: A History of Socialism in Russia, 1917–1991*. New York: Macmillan, 1994.

Malia, Martin. What is the intelligentsia? In Richard Pipes, ed., *The Russian Intelligentsia*, 1–18. New York: Columbia University Press, 1961.

Malkin, S. D. O polnomasshtabnom trenazhere dlia Leningradskoi AES. In Viktor A. Sidorenko, ed., *Istoriia atomnoi energetiki Sovetskogo Soiuza i Rossii: Istoriia RBMK*, vol. 3, 147–155. Moscow: IzdAt, 2003.

Malone, L. The Chernobyl accident: A case study in international law regulating state responsibility for transboundary nuclear pollution. *Journal of Environmental Law* 12 (1987): 203–241.

Malyshev, V. M. Istoriia stanovleniia gosudarstvennogo nadzora za bezopasnost'iu atomnoi energetiki SSSR (1983–1991 gg.). In B. G. Gordon, ed., *Gosatomnadzoru Rossii—20 let*, 26–37. Moscow: NTTs IaRB, 2003.

Margulova, Tereza Kh. *Atomnye elektricheskie stantsii*. 5th ed. Moscow: IzdAT, 1994.

Mar'in, Vladimir V. O deiatel'nosti operativnoi gruppy Politburo TsK KPSS na Chernobyl'skoi AES. In A. N. Semenov, ed., *Chernobyl' desiat' let spustia: Neizbezhnost' ili sluchainost'?*, 263–282. Moscow: Energoatomizdat, 1995.

Marples, David R. *Chernobyl and Nuclear Power in the USSR*. New York: St. Martin's Press, 1986.

Marples, David R. The post-Soviet nuclear power program. *Post-Soviet Geography* 34, no. 3 (1993): 172–184.

Marples, David R. *The Social Impact of the Chernobyl Disaster*. London: Macmillan, 1988.

Mazuzan, George T., and J. Samuel Walker. *Controlling the Atom: The Beginnings of Nuclear Regulation, 1946–1962*. Berkeley: University of California Press, 1985.

Medvedev, Grigorii. *Chernobyl Notebook*. JPRS-UEA-034-89. Washington, DC: Joint Publications Research Service, October 23, 1989.

Medvedev, Grigorii. Chernobyl'skaia tetrad'. *Novyi Mir* 6 (1989): 3–108.

Medvedev, Grigorii. *The Truth about Chernobyl*. New York: Basic Books, 1989.

Merton, Robert K., Ailsa P. Gray, Barbara Hockey, and Hanan C. Selvin, eds. *Reader in Bureaucracy*. Glencoe, IL: Free Press, 1952.

Mezhdunarodnyi Chernobyl'skii Proekt. *Mezhdunarodnyi Chernobyl'skii Proekt: Otsenka radiologicheskikh posledstvii i zashchitnykh mer*. Moscow: IzdAT, 1991.

Michael, M. Ignoring science: Discourses of ignorance in the public understanding of science. In Alan Irwin and Brian Wynne, eds., *Misunderstanding Science? The Public Reconstruction of Science and Technology*, 107–125. Cambridge: Cambridge University Press, 1996.

Mickiewicz, Ellen. *Split Signals: Television and Politics in the Soviet Union*. New York: Oxford University Press, 1988.

Bibliography

Mikhailov, Viktor N. *Ia—"iastreb."* Moscow: Kron-Press, 1993.

Ministerstvo Rossiiskoi Federatsii po atomnoi energii. *Strategiia razvitiia atomnoi energetiki Rossii v pervoi polovine XXI veka*. Moscow: FGUP TsNIIatominform, 2001.

Ministerstvo Rossiiskoi Federatsii po atomnoi energii and Departament po atomnoi energetike, eds. *Shestnadtsatoe glavnoe: Istoriia i sovremennost'*. Moscow: Ministerstvo Rossiiskoi Federatsii po atomnoi energii, 2003.

Mirowski, Philip, and Edward Nik-Khah. Markets made flesh: Performativity, and a problem in science studies, augmented with consideration of the FCC auctions. In Donald MacKenzie, Fabian Muniesa, and Lucia Siu, eds., *Do Economists Make Markets? On the Performativity of Economics*, 190–224. Princeton, NJ: Princeton University Press, 2007.

Misa, Thomas J. Controversy and closure in technological change: Constructing "steel." In W. E. Bijker and J. Law, eds., *Shaping Technology/Building Society: Studies in Sociotechnical Change*, 109–139. Cambridge, MA: MIT Press, 1992.

Misumi, Jyuji, Bernhard Wilpert, and Rainer Miller. *Nuclear Safety: A Human Factors Perspective*. London: Taylor & Francis, 1999.

Mitchell, Charles. Chernobyl trial closed to public and media. *United Press International*, July 9, 1987.

Morgan, Gareth. *Images of Organization*. Newbury Park, CA: Sage, 1986.

Morokhov, I. D., et al. *Atomnoi energetike XX let*. Moscow: Atomizdat, 1974.

Moscow News disputes official Chornobyl toll. *Ukrainian Weekly* 57, no. 47 (November 19, 1989): 1, 5.

Mould, Richard F. *Chernobyl: The Real Story*. Oxford: Pergamon Press, 1988.

Mould, Richard F. *Chernobyl Record: The Definitive History of the Chernobyl Catastrophe*. Bristol: Institute of Physics Publishing, 2000.

Moysich, K. B., R. J. Menezes, and A. M. Michalek. Chernobyl-related ionizing radiation exposure and cancer risk: An epidemiological review. *Lancet Oncology* 3 (2002): 269–279.

Mukhatzhanova, Gaukhar. Russian nuclear industry reforms: Consolidation and expansion. *CNS Research Story*, May 22, 2007.

Nadezhdina, Nadezhda. Zalozhniki reaktora. *Trud* 3 (April 1996): n.p.

Nasonov, Vitalii P. *B. L. Vannikov: Memuary, vospominaniia, stat'i*. Moscow: TSNIIatominform, 1997.

Nasonov, Vitalii P. *E. P. Slavskii: Stranitsy zhizni*. Moscow: IzdAT, 1998.

National Diet of Japan Fukushima Nuclear Accident Independent Investigation Commission (NAIIC). Executive summary of the official report of Fukushima Nuclear Accident Independent Investigation Commission. July 5, 2012. http://warp.da.ndl.go.jp/info:ndljp/pid/3856371/naiic.go.jp/wp-content/uploads/2012/09/NAIIC_report_lo_res10.pdf.

Natsional'nyi issledovatel'skii tsentr "Kurchatovskii institut." *O strategii iadernoi energetiki Rossii do 2050 goda*. Moscow: NITs "Kurchatovskii institut," 2012.

Negin, E. A. et al. *Sovetskii atomnyi proekt: Konets atomnoi monopolii: Kak eto bylo . . .* Sarov: RFIaTs-VNIIEF, 2003.

Nekrasov, A. M., and M. G. Pervukhin, eds. *Energetika SSSR v 1976–1980 Godakh*. Moscow: Energiia, 1977.

Nekrasov, A. M., and A. A. Troitskii, eds. *Energetika SSSR v 1981–1985 Godakh*. Moscow: Energiia, 1981.

Nelkin, Dorothy, and Michael Pollak. *The Atom Besieged: Extraparliamentary Dissent in France and Germany*. Cambridge, MA: MIT Press, 1981.

Neponiatnyi atom: Interv'iu s Viktorom Briukhanovym. *Profil'*, April 24, 2006. http://www.profile.ru/obshchestvo/item/50192-items_18814.

Neporozhnii, Petr S. *Energetika strany glazami ministra: Dnevniki 1935–1985 gg.* Moscow: Energoatomizdat, 2000.

Neporozhnii, Petr S., and Vladimir Iu. Steklov, eds. *50 let Leninskogo plana GOELRO [1920–1970]: Sbornik materialov*. Moscow: Energiia, 1970.

Nesterenko, Vasilii B. *Masshtaby i posledstviia katastrofy na Chernobyl'skoi AES dlia Belorusi, Ukrainy i Rossii*. Minsk: Pravo i ekonomika, 1996.

Nove, Alec. *The Soviet Economy: An Introduction*. 2nd ed. New York: Praeger, 1969.

Nove, Alec. *Studies in Economics and Russia*. New York: St. Martin's Press, 1990.

Nuclear Energy Agency. *Chernobyl: Assessment of Radiological and Health Impacts*. 2002 update of *Chernobyl: Ten Years On*. Paris: Nuclear Energy Agency, OECD, 2002.

Nuclear Energy Agency, Committee on Radiation Protection and Public Health. *Chernobyl Ten Years On: Radiological and Health Impact—An Assessment*. Paris: Nuclear Energy Agency, OECD, 1995.

Office of Technology Assessment. *Technology & Soviet Energy Availability*. Washington, DC: Congress of the U.S., Office of Technology Assessment, 1981.

Oliver, James H. Citizen demand and the Soviet political system. *American Political Science Review* 63, no. 2 (1969): 465–475.

Bibliography

Onykiy, Boris N., and Eduard F. Kryuchkov. Nuclear education in Russia: Status, peculiarities, problems and perspectives. *International Journal of Nuclear Knowledge Management* 1, no. 4 (2005): 308–316.

Orlov, Yuri. *Dangerous Thoughts: Memoirs of a Russian Life*. New York: Morrow, 1991.

Osmachkin, V. S. Problemy nadezhnogo teploobmena v aktivnoi zone reaktora VVER 1-go bloka NVAES pri ego proektirovanii. In Viktor A. Sidorenko, ed., *Istoriia atomnoi energetiki Sovetskogo Soiuza i Rossii: Istoriia VVER*, vol. 2, 113–125. Moscow: IzdAt, 2002.

Paine, Robert. "Chernobyl" reaches Norway: The accident, science, and the threat to cultural knowledge. *Public Understanding of Science (Bristol, England)* 1 (1992): 261–280.

Parr, Joy. *Sensing Changes: Technologies, Environments, and the Everyday*. Vancouver, BC: UBC Press, 2010.

Parr, Joy. A working knowledge of the insensible? Radiation protection in nuclear generating stations, 1962–1992. *Comparative Studies in Society and History* 48, no. 4 (2006): 820–851.

Parry, Albert. Science and technology versus communism. *Russian Review* 25, no. 3 (1966): 227–241.

Pavlenko, A. S., and A. M. Nekrasov, eds. *Energetika SSSR v 1971–1975 godakh*. Moscow: Energiia, 1972.

Perera, Judith. *The Nuclear Industry in the Former Soviet Union: Transition from Crisis to Opportunity*. 2 vols. London: Financial Times Energy Publishing, 1997.

Perin, Constance. Operating as experimenting: Synthesizing engineering and scientific values in nuclear power production. *Science, Technology & Human Values* 23, no. 1 (1998): 98–128.

Perin, Constance. *Shouldering Risks: The Culture of Control in the Nuclear Power Industry*. Princeton, NJ: Princeton University Press, 2005.

Perlo, Victor. *How the Soviet Economy Works: An Interview with A. I. Mikoyan, First Deputy Minister of the U.S.S.R.* New York: International Publishers, 1961.

Perrow, Charles. *Normal Accidents: Living with High-Risk Technologies*. 2nd ed. Princeton, NJ: Princeton University Press, 1999.

Persons guilty of Chernobyl accident to go on trial soon. *ITAR-TASS*, March 13, 1987.

Petros'iants, Andranik M. Tret'ia mezhdunarodnaia Zhenevskaia konferentsiia atomnikov. *Atomnaia energiia* 17, no. 5 (1964): 323–328.

Petros'iants, Andranik M. *Atomnaia energetika*. Moscow: Nauka, 1976.

Petros'iants, Andranik M., ed. *Atomnaia nauka i tekhnika SSSR*. Moscow: Energoatomizdat, 1987.

Petros'iants, Andranik M. *Dorogi zhizni, kotorye vybirali nas*. Moscow: Energoatomizdat, 1993.

Petros'iants, Andranik M. *Iadernaia energetika: Nauka i tekhnicheskii progress*. 2nd ed. Moscow: Nauka, 1981.

Petryna, Adriana. *Life Exposed: Biological Citizens after Chernobyl*. Princeton, NJ: Princeton University Press, 2013.

Podvig, Pavel L. Protivoraketnaia oborona kak faktor strategicheskikh vzaimootnoshenii SSSR/Rossii i SShA v 1945–2003 gg. Doctoral dissertation, Rossiiskaia Akademiia Nauk, 2004.

Polanyi, Michael. *Personal Knowledge: Towards a Post-Critical Philosophy*. Chicago: University of Chicago Press, 1958.

Polanyi, Michael. *The Tacit Dimension*. Gloucester, MA: P. Smith [1966] 1983.

Polivanov, I. F., Chernobyl'skaia katastrofa. [no date] http://treeofknowledge.narod.ru/chernob.htm.

Pollock, Ethan. *Stalin and the Soviet Science Wars*. Princeton, NJ: Princeton University Press, 2006.

Polushkin, K. Atomnyi bogatyr'. *Nauka i zhizn'* 11 (1980): 44–52.

Porter, Theodore M. Quantification and the accounting ideal in science. *Social Studies of Science* 22 (1992): 633–652.

Porter, Theodore M. *Trust in Numbers: The Pursuit of Objectivity in Science and Public Life*. 2nd ed. Princeton, NJ: Princeton University Press, 1995.

Powell, Walter W., and Paul J. DiMaggio, eds. *The New Institutionalism in Organizational Analysis*. Chicago: University of Chicago Press, 1991.

Prisyazhniuk, A., et al. The time trends of cancer incidence in the most contaminated regions of the Ukraine before and after the Chernobyl accident. *Radiation and Environmental Biophysics* 34 (1995): 3–6.

Prushinskii, Boris Ia. Etogo ne mozhet byt'—no eto sluchilos' (pervye dni posle katastrofy). In A. N. Semenov, ed., *Chernobyl' desiat' let spustia: Neizbezhnost' ili sluchainost'?*, 308–324. Moscow: Energoatomizdat, 1995.

Reactors of the World. New York: Simmons-Boardman, 1958.

Results of the Chernobyl trial. *ITAR-TASS*, July 31, 1987.

Rhodes, Richard. *The Making of the Atomic Bomb*. New York: Touchstone, 1986.

Riabev, Lev D., ed. *Atomnyi proekt SSSR: Dokumenty i materialy, 1938–1945*, vol. 1, chast' 1. Moscow: Nauka—Fizmatlit, Ministerstvo Rossiiskoi Federatsii po atomnoi energii, Rossiiskaia akademiia nauk, 1998.

Riabev, Lev D., ed. *Atomnyi proekt SSSR: Dokumenty i materialy, 1938–1945*, vol. 1, chast' 2. Moscow: Ministerstvo Rossiiskoi Federatsii po atomnoi energii, Rossiiskaia akademiia nauk, 2002.

Riabev, Lev D., ed. *Atomnyi proekt SSSR: Dokumenty i materialy, 1945–1954*, vol. 2, kn. 1. Sarov: Ministerstvo Rossiiskoi Federatsii po atomnoi energii, Rossiiskaia akademiia nauk, 1999.

Riabev, Lev D., ed. *Atomnyi proekt SSSR: Dokumenty i materialy, 1945–1954*, vol. 2, kn. 2. Sarov: Ministerstvo Rossiiskoi Federatsii po atomnoi energii, Rossiiskaia akademiia nauk, 2000.

Riabev, Lev D., ed. *Atomnyi proekt SSSR: Dokumenty i materialy, 1945–1954*, vol. 2, kn. 3. Sarov: Ministerstvo Rossiiskoi Federatsii po atomnoi energii, Rossiiskaia akademiia nauk, 2002.

Riabev, Lev D., ed. *Atomnyi proekt SSSR: Dokumenty i materialy: Atomnaia bomba, 1945–1954*, vol. 2, kn. 4. Moscow and Sarov: Nauka and Fizmatlit, Ministerstvo Rossiiskoi Federatsii po atomnoi energii, 2003.

Riabev, Lev D., ed. *Atomnyi proekt SSSR: Dokumenty i materialy: Atomnaia bomba, 1945–1954*, vol. 2, kn. 5. Moscow and Sarov: Nauka and Fizmatlit, Federal'noe agentstvo po atomnoi energii, 2005.

Riabko, Viktor I. Stroiteli energozhilstroia—Chernobyl'skoi AES. In A. N. Semenov, ed., *Chernobyl' desiat' let spustia: Neizbezhnost' ili sluchainost'?*, 325–331. Moscow: Energoatomizdat, 1995.

Richardson, Jeremy J., ed. *Pressure Groups*. Oxford: Oxford University Press, 1993.

Roberts, Karlene H. Some characteristics of one type of high reliability organization. *Organization Science* 1, no. 2 (1990): 160–176.

Rosen, Paul. The social construction of mountain bikes: Technology and postmodernity in the cycle industry. *Social Studies of Science* 23 (1993): 479–513.

Rossiiskii gosudarstvennyi kontsern po proizvodstvu elektricheskoi i teplovoi energii na atomnykh stantiiakh (Rosenergoatom), ed. *50 let atomnoi energetike*. Proceedings of the Fourth International Scientific and Technical conference on Nuclear Power Safety, Efficiency and Economics held in Moscow, June 16–17, 2004. Moscow: Mashmir, 2004.

Rossiiskii Nauchnyi Tsentr "Kurchatovskii Institut," ed. *Istoriia atomnogo proekta*. Vol. 15. Moscow: Rossiiskii Nauchnyi Tsentr "Kurchatovskii Institut," 1998.

Rothstein, Henry, Michael Huber, and George Gaskell. A theory of risk colonization: The spiralling regulatory logics of societal and institutional risk. *Economy and Society* 35, no. 1 (2006): 91–112.

Rudenko, Iurii N., and Vladimir A. Semenov, eds. *Avtomatizatsiia dispetcherskogo upravleniia v elektroenergetike*. Moscow: Izdatel'stvo MEI, 2000.

Rueschemeyer, Dietrich. *Power and the Division of Labour*. Stanford, CA: Stanford University Press, 1986.

Sakharov, Andrei. *Memoirs*. Trans. Richard Lourie. New York: Knopf, 1990.

Samarin, Anton. Chernobyl' nikogo i nichemy ne nauchil. *Odnako*, [2009–2010]. http://www.odnako.org/almanac/material/show_8453.

Savchenko, Vladimir K. *The Ecology of the Chernobyl Catastrophe: Scientific Outlines of an International Program of Collaborative Research*, Volume 16: *Man and the Biosphere*. Ed. J. N. R. Jeffers. Paris: UNESCO, 1995.

Scapegoats of Chernobyl. *Times* (London), July 7, 1987.

Schattenberg, Susanne. *Stalins Ingenieure: Lebenswelten zwischen Technik und Terror in den 1930er Jahren*. Munich: Oldenbourg, 2002.

Schmid, Sonja D. Both better and worse than Chernobyl. *London Review of Books Blog*, March 17, 2011. http://www.lrb.co.uk/blog/2011/03/17/sonja-schmid/both-better-and-worse-than-chernobyl/.

Schmid, Sonja D. Celebrating tomorrow today: The peaceful atom on display in the Soviet Union. *Social Studies of Science* 36, no. 3 (2006): 331–365.

Schmid, Sonja D. Envisioning a technological state: Reactor design choices and political legitimacy in the Soviet Union and Russia. Doctoral dissertation, Cornell University, 2005.

Schmid, Sonja D. Nuclear colonization? Soviet technopolitics in the Second World. In Gabrielle Hecht, ed., *Entangled Geographies: Empire and Technopolitics in the Global Cold War*, 125–154. Cambridge, MA: MIT Press, 2011.

Schmid, Sonja D. Organizational culture and professional identities in the Soviet nuclear power industry. *Osiris* 23 (2008): 82–111.

Schmid, Sonja D. Shaping the Soviet experience of the atomic age: Nuclear topics in Ogonyok, 1945–1965. In Dick van Lente, ed., *The Nuclear Age in Popular Media: A Transnational History, 1945–1965*, 19–52. New York: Palgrave Macmillan, 2012.

Bibliography

Schmid, Sonja D. Transformation discourse: Nuclear risk as a strategic tool in late Soviet politics of expertise. *Science, Technology & Human Values* 29, no. 3 (2004): 353–376.

Schmid, Sonja D. When safe enough is not good enough: Organizing safety at Chernobyl. *Bulletin of the Atomic Scientists* 67, no. 2 I (2011): 19–29.

Scott, James C. *Seeing Like a State: How Certain Schemes to Improve the Human Condition Have Failed*. New Haven, CT: Yale University Press, 1998.

Semenov, Aleksandr N., ed. *Chernobyl' desiat' let spustia: Neizbezhnost' ili sluchainost'?*. Moscow: Energoatomizdat, 1995.

Semenov, Aleksandr N. K 10-letiiu katastrofy na Chernobyl'skoi AES. In A. N. Semenov, ed., *Chernobyl' desiat' let spustia: Neizbezhnost' ili sluchainost'?*, 7–74. Moscow: Energoatomizdat, 1995.

Sharpe, Myron, ed. *Planning, Profit, and Incentives in the USSR*, Volume 1: *The Liberman Discussion—a New Phase in Soviet Economic Thought*. White Plains, NY: International Arts and Sciences Press, 1966.

Shasharin, Gennadii A. Chernobyl'skaia tragediia. In Aleksandr N. Semenov, ed., *Chernobyl' desiat' let spustia: Neizbezhnost' ili sluchainost'?*, 75–132. Moscow: Energoatomizdat, 1995.

Shcherbak, Iurii. *Chernobyl: A Documentary Story*. Trans. Ian Press (from the Ukrainian) and foreword by David R. Marples. New York: St. Martin's Press, 1989.

Shcherbina, Boris E., et al. Doklad pravitel'stvennoi komissii po rassledovaniiu prichin avarii na Chernobyl'skoi AES 26 aprelia 1986 g. (iiun' 1986). In Viktor A. Sidorenko, ed., *Istoriia atomnoi energetiki Sovetskogo Soiuza i Rossii: Uroki avarii na Chernobyl'skoi AES*, vol. 4, 17–47. Moscow: IzdAt, 2002.

Shearer, David. *Industry, State, and Society in Stalin's Russia, 1926–1934*. Ithaca, NY: Cornell University Press, 1996.

Shevelin, B. P., ed. *Put' k priznaniiu*. Ekaterinburg: UrO RAN, Ministerstvo Rossiiskoi Federatsii po atomnoi energii, and Sverdlovskii nauchno-issledovatel'skii institut khimicheskogo mashinostroeniia, 2002.

Shlyakhter, Alexander, and Richard Wilson. Chernobyl: The inevitable results of secrecy. *Public Understanding of Science (Bristol, England)* 1 (1992): 251–259.

Shteinberg, Nikolai A. *O prichinakh i obstoiatel'stvakh avarii na 4-m bloke Chernobyl'skoi AES 26 aprelia 1986 g. Doklad*. Moscow: Komissiia Gospromatomnadzora SSSR, 1991.

Siddiqi, Asif A. Within the first circle: Science and engineering in the gulag. Paper presented at the Annual Convention of the American Association for the Advancement of Slavic Studies, Washington, DC, November 16–19, 2006.

Sidorenko, Viktor A., ed. *Istoriia atomnoi energetiki Sovetskogo Soiuza i Rossii.* Vol. 1. Moscow: IzdAt, 2001.

Sidorenko, Viktor A., ed. *Istoriia atomnoi energetiki Sovetskogo Soiuza i Rossii: Istoriia VVER.* Vol. 2. Moscow: IzdAt, 2002.

Sidorenko, Viktor A., ed. *Istoriia atomnoi energetiki Sovetskogo Soiuza i Rossii: Istoriia RBMK.* Vol. 3. Moscow: IzdAt, 2003.

Sidorenko, Viktor A., ed. *Istoriia atomnoi energetiki Sovetskogo Soiuza i Rossii: Uroki avarii na Chernobyl'skoi AES.* Vol. 4. Moscow: IzdAt, 2002.

Sidorenko, Viktor A., ed. *Istoriia atomnoi energetiki Sovetskogo Soiuza i Rossii: Istoriia maloi atomnoi energetiki.* Vol. 5. Moscow: IzdAt, 2004.

Sidorenko, Viktor A. A. P. Aleksandrov i atomnaia energetika. In N. S. Khlopkin, ed. *A. P. Aleksandrov: Dokumenty i vospominaniia, k 100-letiiu so dnia rozhdeniia,* 212–219. Moscow: IzdAt, 2003.

Sidorenko, Viktor A. Kak eto bylo. In B. G. Gordon, ed., *Gosatomnadzoru Rossii—20 let,* 51–61. Moscow: NTTs IaRB, 2003.

Sidorenko, Viktor A. Nauchnoe rukovodstvo v atomnoi energetike. In Viktor A. Sidorenko, ed., *Istoriia atomnoi energetiki Sovetskogo Soiuza i Rossii: Istoriia VVER,* vol. 2, 5–28. Moscow: IzdAt, 2002.

Sidorenko, Viktor A. Nuclear power in the Soviet Union and in Russia. *Nuclear Engineering and Design* 173 (1997): 3–20.

Sidorenko, Viktor A. *Ob atomnoi energetike, atomnykh stantsiiakh, uchiteliakh, kollegakh i o sebe.* Moscow: IzdAt, 2003.

Sidorenko, Viktor A. Ob"iasnitel'naia zapiska Sidorenko V. A. v komitet partiinogo kontrolia pri TsK KPSS. In Viktor A. Sidorenko, ed., *Istoriia atomnoi energetiki Sovetskogo Soiuza i Rossii: Uroki avarii na Chernobyl'skoi AES,* vol. 4, 44–47. Moscow: IzdAt, 2002.

Sidorenko, Viktor A. Problemy bezopasnosti atomnoi energetiki. In Viktor A. Sidorenko, ed., *Istoriia atomnoi energetiki Sovetskogo Soiuza i Rossii,* vol. 1, 194–216. Moscow: IzdAt, 2001.

Sidorenko, Viktor A. Upravlenie atomnoi energetikoi. In Viktor A. Sidorenko, ed., *Istoriia atomnoi energetiki Sovetskogo Soiuza i Rossii,* vol. 1, 217–253. Moscow: IzdAt, 2001.

Sidorenko, Viktor A. Vvedenie k 1-mu vypusku. In Viktor A. Sidorenko, ed., *Istoriia atomnoi energetiki Sovetskogo Soiuza i Rossii,* vol. 1, 5–15. Moscow: IzdAt, 2001.

Sidorenko, Viktor A. Vvodnye zamechaniia k urokam Chernobyl'skoi avarii. In Viktor A. Sidorenko, ed., *Istoriia atomnoi energetiki Sovetskogo Soiuza i Rossii: Uroki avarii na Chernobyl'skoi AES,* vol. 4, 4–16. Moscow: IzdAt, 2002.

Siegelbaum, Lewis H., and Ronald G. Suny, eds. *Making Workers Soviet: Power, Class, and Identity*. Ithaca, NY: Cornell University Press, 1994.

Sivintsev, Iurii V., and V. A. Kachalov, eds. Chernobyl': Piat' trudnykh let. Sbornik materialov o rabotakh po likvidatsii posledstvii avarii na Chernobyl'skoi AES v 1986–1990 gg. Moscow: IzdAT, 1992.

Skocpol, Theda. *Protecting Soldiers and Mothers: The Political Origin of Social Policy in the United States*. Cambridge, MA: Harvard University Press, 1995.

Skocpol, Theda, and Dietrich Rueschemeyer, eds. *States, Social Knowledge, and the Origins of Modern Social Policies*. Princeton, NJ: Princeton University Press, 1996.

Smith, Jeremy, and Melanie Ilic, eds. *Khrushchev in the Kremlin: Policy and Government in the Soviet Union, 1953–1964*. New York: Routledge, 2011.

Sobell, Vladimir. *The Red Market: Industrial Co-Operation and Specialisation in Comecon*. Aldershot: Gower, 1984.

Solnick, Steven Lee. *Stealing the State: Control and Collapse in Soviet Institutions*. Cambridge, MA: Harvard University Press, 1998.

A Soviet aide says Chernobyl officials will be put on trial. *New York Times*, March 14, 1987, late city final ed., section 1, p. 6.

Steinmo, Sven, Kathleen Thelen, and Frank Longstreth, eds. *Structuring Politics: Historical Institutionalism in Comparative Analysis*. Cambridge Studies in Comparative Politics. New York: Cambridge University Press, 1992.

Steklov, Vladimir Iu. *V. I. Lenin i elektrifikatsiia*. 3rd ed. Moscow: Nauka, 1982.

Stites, Richard. *Revolutionary Dreams: Utopian Vision and Experimental Life in the Russian Revolution*. New York: Oxford University Press, 1989.

Stuart, Robert. Evsei Grigor'evich Liberman. In George W. Simmonds, ed., *Soviet Leaders*, 193–199. New York: Crowell, 1967.

Swedberg, Richard, ed. *Essays in Economic Sociology: Max Weber*. Princeton, NJ: Princeton University Press, 1999.

Swidler, Ann. Culture in action: Symbols and strategies. *American Sociological Review* 51 (April 1986): 273–286.

Tarakanov, Nikolai D. *Chernobyl'skie zapiski, ili Razdum'ia o nravstvennosti*. Moscow: Voenizdat, 1989.

Tatarnikov, Viktor P. Atomnaia elektroenergetika (s VVER i drugimi reaktorami). In Viktor A. Sidorenko, ed., *Istoriia atomnoi energetiki Sovetskogo Soiuza i Rossii: Istoriia VVER*, vol. 2, 303–399. Moscow: IzdAt, 2002.

Taubman, William. *Khrushchev: The Man and His Era*. New York: Norton, 2003.

Ten years in stir for Chernobyl's scapegoats. *Newsweek*, August 10, 1987, 47.

Terent'ev, V. G., ed., *Kto est' kto v atomnoi energetike i promyshlennosti Rossii/Who Is Who in Nuclear Power Engineering and Industry of Russia*. Obninsk: Titul, 1995.

Thatcher, Ian D. Alec Nove: A bibliographical tribute. *Europe-Asia Studies* 47, no. 8 (1995): 1383–1410.

Thornton, Judith. Soviet electric power after Chernobyl: Economic consequences and options. *Soviet Economy (Silver Spring, MD)* 2, no. 2 (1986): 131–179.

Three go on trial after world's worst atomic disaster. *Guardian* (London), July 7, 1987.

Tiushevskaia, Vera N. *I. K. Kikoin: Stranitsy zhizni. Tvortsy iadernogo veka*. Moscow: IzdAt, 1995.

Torosyan, Lilly. Revisiting the Metsamor nuclear power plant. *Armenian Weekly*, December 7, 2012. http://www.armenianweekly.com/2012/12/07/revisiting-the-metsamor-nuclear-power-plant/.

Tremla, Vladimir G. The politics of "Libermanism." *Soviet Studies* 19, no. 4 (1968): 567–572.

Trial of culprits of Chernobyl accident. *Russian Information Agency ITAR-TASS*, Moscow, July 15, 1987.

Trial in Chernobyl ends. *ITAR-TASS*, July 29, 1987.

Troitskii, A. A., ed. *Energetika SSSR v 1986–1990 godakh*. Moscow: Energoatomizdat, 1987.

Trotsky, Leon. *The Russian Revolution: The Overthrow of Tzarism and the Triumph of the Soviets*. Trans. Max Eastman. Garden City, NY: Doubleday, 1959.

Ulasevich, V. K., ed. *O iadernykh reaktorakh i ikh tvortsakh: Prodolzhenie traditsii (k 50-letiiu NIKIET im. N. A. Dollzhalia)*. Moscow: GUP NIKIET, 2002.

Ulasevich, V. K., ed. *Sozdano pod rukovodstvom N. A. Dollezhalia: O iadernykh reaktorakh i ikh tvortsakh (k 100-letiiu N. A. Dollezhalia)*. 2nd ed. Moscow: GUP NIKIET, 2002.

U.S. Energy Research and Development Administration, Division of Reactor Research and Development. *Soviet Power Reactors 1974*. Report of the United States of America Nuclear Power Reactor Delegation Visit to the Union of Soviet Socialist Republics, September 19–October 1, 1974 (ERDA-2, UC-79). Washington, DC: U.S. Energy Research and Development Administration, 1975.

U.S. Nuclear Regulatory Commission. *Recommendations for Enhancing Reactor Safety in the 21st Century: The Near-Term Task Force Review of Insights from the Fukushima Dai-Ichi Accident*. Washington, DC: U.S. Nuclear Regulatory Commission, 2011.

Bibliography

Vasilevskii, V. P., et al. Razrabotka proekta i sozdanie pervogo energobloka s reaktorom RBMK-1000. In Viktor A. Sidorenko, ed., *Istoriia atomnoi energetiki Sovetskogo Soiuza i Rossii: Istoriia RBMK*, vol. 3, 61–101. Moscow: IzdAt, 2003.

Vasilieva, Maria N. L'évolution des systèmes de prise de décisions dans le nucléaire soviétique (Russe). *Histoire, Economie et Société*, no. 2 (April-June 2001): 257–275.

Vasilieva, Maria N. *Soleils rouges: L'ambition nucléaire soviétique [Essai sur l'évolution des systèmes de prise de décision dans le nucléaire soviétique (Russe)]*. Paris: Institut d'Histoire de l'Industrie et Éditions Rive Droite, 1999.

Vaughan, Diane. *The Challenger Launch Decision: Risky Technology, Culture, and Deviance at NASA*. Chicago: University of Chicago Press, 1996.

Vazhnov, M. Ia., and I. S. Aristov, eds. *A. P. Zaveniagin: Stranitsy zhizni*. Moscow: PoliMediia, 2002.

Velikhov, E. P., et al. eds. *Nauka i obshchestvo: Istoriia sovetskogo atomnogo proekta (40–50 gody). Trudy mezhdunarodnogo simpoziuma ISAP-06*. Vol. 1. Moscow: IzdAt, 1997.

Velikhov, E. P., et al. eds. *Nauka i obshchestvo: Istoriia sovetskogo atomnogo proekta (40–50 gody). Trudy mezhdunarodnogo simpoziuma ISAP-06*. Vol. 2. Moscow: IzdAt, 1999.

Velikhov, E. P., et al. eds. *Nauka i obshchestvo: Istoriia sovetskogo atomnogo proekta (40–50 gody). Trudy ISAP*. Vol. 3. Moscow: IzdAt, 2003.

Veretennikov, A. I., ed. *Fol'klor na sluzhbe atoma: Sbornik pesen, stikhov, tostov, baek, sochinennykh atomshchikami na poligonakh*. Moscow: TsNIIAtominform, 1996.

Vicente, Kim J. *The Human Factor: Revolutionizing the Way People Live with Technology*. New York: Routledge, 2004.

Vizgin, Vladimir P., ed. *Istoriia sovetskogo atomnogo proekta: Dokumenty, vospominaniia, issledovaniia*. Vol. 1. Moscow: Ianus-K, 1998.

Vizgin, Vladimir P., ed. *Istoriia sovetskogo atomnogo proekta: Dokumenty, vospominaniia, issledovaniia*. Vol. 2. Saint Petersburg: Izdatel'stvo Russkogo Khristianskogo gumanitarnogo instituta, 2002.

Vol'skii, A. I., and A. B. Chubais, eds. *Elektroenergetika: Stroiteli Rossii: XX vek*. Moscow: Master, 2003.

Vozniak, V., and S. Troitskii. *Chernobyl: Tak eto bylo*. Moscow: Libris, 1993.

V Politbiuro TsK KPSS. *Pravda*, July 20, 1986, 1, 3.

Wail', Petr, and Aleksandr Genis. *60-e: Mir Sovetskogo cheloveka*. Moscow: Novoe literaturnoe obozrenie, 1996.

Walker, Christopher. Anger at Chernobyl trial curb on press. *Times* (London), July 6, 1987.

Walker, Christopher. Design row opens Chernobyl trial. *Times* (London), July 8, 1987.

Walker, J. Samuel. *Containing the Atom: Nuclear Regulation in a Changing Environment, 1963–1971*. Berkeley: University of California Press, 1992.

Walker, J. Samuel. *A Short History of Nuclear Regulation, 1946–1990*. Washington, DC: U.S. Nuclear Regulatory Commission, 1993.

Walker, J. Samuel. *Three Mile Island: A Nuclear Crisis in Historical Perspective*. Berkeley: University of California Press, 2004.

Walker, Martin. Three go on trial after world's worst atomic disaster. *Guardian* (London), July 7, 1987.

Weber, Max. *Economy and Society: An Outline of Interpretive Sociology*. New York: Bedminster, 1968.

Weick, Karl E. Organizational culture as a source of high reliability. *California Management Review* 29, no. 2 (1987): 112–127.

Weiner, Sharon K. *Our Own Worst Enemy? Institutional Interests and the Proliferation of Nuclear Weapons Expertise*. Cambridge, MA: MIT Press, 2011.

Wellock, Thomas R. The children of Chernobyl: Engineers and the campaign for safety in Soviet-designed reactors in Central and Eastern Europe. *History and Technology* 29, no. 1 (2013): 3–32.

Western reporters barred from trial. United Press International, July 8, 1987.

Whimster, Sam, ed. *The Essential Weber: A Reader*. London: Routledge, 2004.

Wiersinga, Wilmar M. Differentiated thyroid carcinoma in pediatric age. In G. E. Krassas, S. A. Rivkees, and W. Kiess, eds., *Diseases of the Thyroid in Childhood and Adolescence*, 210–224. Basel: Karger, 2007.

Winner, Langdon. *The Whale and the Reactor: A Search for Limits in an Age of High Technology*. Chicago: University of Chicago Press, 1986.

Wynne, Brian. *Rationality and Ritual: Participation and Exclusion in Nuclear Decision-Making*. 2nd ed. New York: Earthscan, 2011.

Wynne, Brian. Unruly technology. *Social Studies of Science* 18, no. 1 (1988): 147–167.

Yablokov, Alexey V., Vassily B. Nesterenko, and Alexey V. Nesterenko. Chernobyl: Consequences of the catastrophe for people and the environment. *Annals of the New York Academy of Sciences* 1181 (2009).

Bibliography

Yaroshinskaya [Iaroshinskaia], Alla. *Chernobyl: The Forbidden Truth*. Lincoln: University of Nebraska Press, 1995.

Yemelyanenkov [Emel'ianenkov], Alexander. *The Sredmash Archipelago*. Moscow: IPPNW-Russia, 2000.

Yurchak, Alexei. *Everything Was Forever, until It Was No More: The Last Soviet Generation*. Princeton, NJ: Princeton University Press, 2006.

Zakharov, V. M., and E. Yu. Krysanov, eds. *Consequences of the Chernobyl Catastrophe: Environmental Health*. Moscow: Center for Russian Environmental Policy; Moscow Affiliate of the International "Biotest" Foundation, 1996.

Zhimerin, Dimitrii G., ed. *Sovremennye problemy energetiki*. Moscow: Energoatomizdat, 1984.

Zhirkov, Gennadii V. *Istoriia tsenzury v Rossii XIX–XX vv.: Uchebnoe posobie*. Moscow: Aspect Press, 2001.

Zhuravlev, Pavel A. *Moi atomnyi vek: O vremeni, ob atomshchikakh i o sebe*. Moscow: Khronos-press, 2003.

Index

Note: Page numbers in italics refer to figures.

Abagian, Armen, 133, 139, 177
ABTU-Ts (VGR-50) reactor, 116, 274n117
"Academician Lomonosov" floating nuclear power plant, 169
Accident analysis, RBMK reactors and, 91–92, 125, 273n109
Adamov, Egenii, 296n178
Afrikantov Experimental Design Bureau for Mechanical Engineering, 170
Ageev, A. V., 244n126
Akimov, Aleksandr, 128, 140
Aleksandrov, Anatolii
 biographical note on, 177
 Chernobyl disaster and, 136–137, 142–143, 146–147, 149, 167, 286n78, 290n124
 evolution of Soviet nuclear industry and, 12, 20–21, 28–29, 213n12
 gas-cooled reactor design and, 116
 in motion pictures, 240n99
 organization of nuclear industry and, 55–56, *57*, 229n92
 RBMK reactor design and, 110, 114, 274n114
 reactor design collaboration and, 107–108, 123
 as scientific director, 85, 271n83

All-Union Exhibition of the Achievements of the People's Economy (VDNKh), 144
All-Union Ministry for the Construction of Power Plants, 47–49, 243n122
All-Union Research Institute for the Operation of Nuclear Power Plants (VNIIAES), 53–55, 133–134, 147, 243n122, 296n185
All-Union Scientific and Technical Institute for Aviation Materials (VIAM), 274n115
All-Union Scientific Research and Design Institute of Energy Technologies (VNIPIET), 137
"AM" (*atom mirnyi*, "peaceful atom") reactors, 46
"Annushka" nuclear reactor, 45
Antinuclear movement in Soviet Union, 150–151, 167–168
Archival sources, overview of, 189–192, 303n13
Armenia, nuclear power in, 151
Atomenergonaladka (industrial enterprise), 53
Atomenergoremont, 53
Atomic Energy of the Russian Federation, 83–84
Atomic project (*atomnyi proekt*), 45

Atommash reactor vessel plant, 38, *121*, 269n71, 276n129
Atomnaia energiia, 143
Atomprom (state corporation), 156, 168–169, 296nn178–179
Atomremontservis (Ukraine), 158
Atomshchiki
  celebration of, 273n100
  classification of, 67–68
  community building and knowledge transfer among, 83–85
  differences and commonalities with energetiki, 88–92, 163–168
  duties and work culture of, 87–88, 94–95

Baibakov, Nikolai, 214n19
Baturov, Boris, 240n96
Beloiarsk power plant
  BN-600 reactor at, 266n38
  BN-800 reactor development at, 266n38
  development of, 29–30, 34–35, 47, 244n130, 265n26
  documentation on construction of, 304n15
  expertise of personnel at, 122–123
  failures and problems at, 90–91
  graphite-water reactor at, 103–104, 122
  reactor design at, 270n80, 271n84
  staffing issues for, 74–75
  training program at, 252n47
Beria, Lavrentii, 45, 55, 177, 230n27
Bilibino Station (BATETs), 104–105, 265n33, 271n84, 275n124
BN-600 reactor, 170, 266n38
BN-800 reactor, 170, 266n38
BN-1200 reactor, 170
Bochvar, A. A., 271n83
Boiling-water reactors, 171–175
Breeder reactors, 105, 265n36, 266n38
Brezhnev, Leonid, 31, 221n72

Briukhanov, Viktor
  autobiographical note on, 178
  Chernobyl disaster trial and, 2–3, *3*, 5–6, 8–9, 209n50, 209n53
  report on Chernobyl authored by, 133, 152, 281n30, 284n61
  sentencing of, 8–9, 210n60
Brize, Raimond, 4, 8–9
Bronnikov, Vladimir, 152, 250n30, 294n161
Bulgaria, Soviet nuclear industry and, 121–122
Bureaucracy
  Chernobyl disaster and role of, 8
  evolution of Soviet nuclear industry and, 24–26, 42–65, 228n10
  governance of nuclear power industry and, 57–61
  workforce transfer and normalization and, 76–77

Canada
  nuclear power industry in, 265n36, 275n122
  wartime nuclear research in, 81, 83
Career development in Soviet nuclear industry, 70–72, 78–82
Central Committee. *See* Communist Party Central Committee
Centralized planning, evoution of Soviet nuclear industry and, 26–27
Central Scientific Research Institute (TsNII), 252n47
Challenger shuttle disaster, 137–138
Chernobyl nuclear power plant
  accident sequence at, 128–135, *129*, *131*, 279n19
  Central Committee report on disaster at, 141–143
  conflicting information on responsibility for, 137–139

Index

divided responsibilities for nuclear power and, 61–65, 87, 261n128, 261n131
Fukushima Daiichi nuclear disaster and, 16, 171–175
Government Commission report on disaster at, 139–140
health consequences of disaster at, 280n27
initial disaster response, 135–136
international consequences of, 143–144
investigation of disaster at, 1–16
legacy of disaster at, 150–151, 158–159, 163–168
long-term mitigation of disaster at, 136–137
Minergo disaster assessment, 140–141
nuclear industry restructuring following disaster at, 9–16, *154*, 154–157
pre-disaster Soviet nuclear history and, 162–168
RBMK reactor design in, 114–115, 125, 144–149, 153, 289n109
research sources on, 189–197
testing at, 128, 277n1, 278n3
training and workforce at, 67, 69
Ukrainian nuclear industry and, 157–158
warning signs of trouble at, 127–128
Chief design engineer (*glavnyi konstruktor*), role in Soviet nuclear industry of, 86
Churin, Aleksandr, 110–111
Civilian nuclear program. *See also* Military nuclear technology; Soviet nuclear industry
current and future projects in, 169–170
evolution of, 45–46, 47–49
nomenklatura system in, 72, 249n26, 250n30
politics and economic pressures in, 164–168
pressurized water reactors and, 109–110
professionalization of workforce and, 73–75
reactor design and, 99–101, 275n125
technical training and engineering programs and, 67–70
workforce reliability and, *89*, 89–90
Cold War politics. *See also* Politics
Chernobyl disaster and, 161
international nuclear industry and, 81, 83
reactor design problems and, 92
Soviet nuclear power industry and, 21–24
Commission for Nuclear Power Engineering, 156
Communist Party
nuclear industry career development and, 71–72, 79–81
Yeltsin's outlawing of, 303n13
Communist Party Central Committee
Chernobyl disaster decree, 141–143
Department of Heavy Industry and Energy, 58, 143–144
evolution of Soviet nuclear industry and, 23–24, 31–40
Sector for Nuclear Energy, 149–150
Strategic Group, Chernobyl disaster report and, 139–143
trial on Chernobyl disaster and, 1, 206n25
Control and Safety System (*SUZ—sistema upravleniia i zashchity*), 153
Control rods in RBMK reactors, 130–133, *131*, 279n15, 279nn11–12, 295n169
Council of Mutual Economic Assistance (CMEA), 34, 51, 117, 212n7, 238n84
Czechoslovakia, Soviet nuclear industry and, 121–122, 275n122

Decentralization, Soviet nuclear industry and impact of, 27–30
Derzhkomatom, 157–158
Diatlov, Anatolii
  autobiographical note on, 178
  Chernobyl disaster and, 144–145, 147, 279n13, 286n81, 289n113, 290n124, 292n143, 295n169
  Chernobyl trial and, 3, 4, 6, 8–9, 209n50, 209n53, 210n60
Discursive repertoires, politics of science and, 254n59
Dolgikh, Vladimir, 143, 149, 178
Dollezhal, Nikolai
  autobiographical note on, 178
  Chernobyl disaster and, 147, 290n124, 292n143
  reactor design and, 102, 111, 114, 123, 271n83
  Soviet nuclear industry and, 55, 70, 86
Dostat', Chernobyl disaster trial and role of, 208n46
Driver-error analogy, Chernobyl disaster analysis and, 9–16
Dual-use reactor design, 106–107, 266n46, 267n47
Dubovskii, Boris, 62, 147–148, 167, 178–179, 291n127, 295n169
Dymshits, Veniamin, 37, 179, 242n108, 259n105

Earthquakes
  in Armenia, 151, 293n156
  Fukushima Daiichi disaster and, 171–175
Eastern Europe, Soviet nuclear industry and, 121–122, 269n66
Economic policy
  Chernobyl disaster and, 7, 14–15, 18
  evolution Soviet nuclear industry and, 22–40, 162–168, 217n44, 218n45, 223n123

  impact on nuclear industry of, 270n78
  reactor design and, 117–122
  technocratic ideology and, 255n67
Efremov, Mikhail, 78
"EG" (energeticheskii-gazovyi) reactor, 274n115
EI-2 project, 106–107
Eisenhower, Dwight D., 121
Ekho Moskvy (Echo of Moscow) radio station, 83–84
Emelyianov, Ivan, 91, 142, 179, 205n16, 235n60
Emelyianov, Vasilii, 50–51, 179, 235n60, 292n143
Energetiki
  celebration of, 273n100
  classification of, 67–68
  community building and knowledge transfer among, 83–85
  differences and commonalities with atomshchiki, 88–92, 163–168
  duties and work culture of, 88, 94–95, 255n61
Engineering education
  cynicism and politics concerning, 70–72, 78–82, 256n72
  professionalization of workforce and, 73–75, 249n24
  Soviet development of, 69–70
Enriched uranium. *See* Uranium, reactor design and
Eperin, Anatolii, 239n93
Equipment production and quality, Soviet nuclear industry and, 77–78, 82, 229n13
Ermakov, Georgii, 237n80
Ermakov, Nikolai, 240n96
Espionage, Soviet nuclear weapons project and, 231n30
Europe, Chernobyl disaster and contamination in, 136
European Union, Ukrainian nuclear institutions and, 157–158

Index

Experimental Design Bureau for
  Machine Building (OKBM), 87

Fast neutron reactors, 266n38
  development of, 105
Federal Agency for Atomic Energy, 169
Feinberg, Savelii, 102–105, 111, 114,
  179, 239n92, 264n24, 271n83
Finland, nuclear power in, 151
First Chief Administration (*Pervoe
  Glavnoe Upravlenie*, PGU), 45, 50
Flerov, Georgii, 44, 179–180
"Floating nuclear power plant," 169
Fomin, Nikolai
  autobiographical note, 180
  Chernobyl disaster and, 152–153
  trial and sentencing of, 3, 3–4, 6,
    8–9, 205n20, 209n50, 209n53,
    210n60
France, nuclear power industry in, 77–
  78, 123–124, 265n36
Fukushima Daiichi nuclear disaster
  (Japan), 16, 171–175, 301n5

Gas-cooled reactors, 116, 274n117,
  275n125
General Electric, Fukushima Daiichi
  disaster and, 173–175
General project manager (*generalnyi
  proektirovshchik*), 85–87
"General Regulations for Nuclear Power
  Plant Safety," 114–115
German Democratic Republic, Soviet
  nuclear industry and, 121–122,
  268n60
Germany
  nuclear freighters in, 268n65
  nuclear power industry in, 265n36
Glasnost policy
  antinuclear movement in Soviet
    Union and, 150–151
  Chernobyl disaster and, 2, 13–16,
    166–168

Glavatom (Sredmash subdivision), 50–
  51, 235n58
Glavatomenergo (Chief Administration
  for the Construction of Atomic
  Power Plants, Minenergo)
  organizational structure of nuclear
    industry and, 47–49, 53, 55–57,
    237n80
  power plant failures and accidents
    and, 91
  reactor design and, 252n47
  workforce training and, 74
Glavotomenergo (GU-16, Sredmash), 55
GOELRO. *See* State Plan for the
  Electrification of Russia (GOELRO)
Goncharov, Vladimir, 104, 116,
  275n122
Gorbachev, Mikhail, 2, 5, 13–16,
  80, 143, 146–147, 150–151, 167,
  286n84, 287n95
Gosplan
  Department of Energy and
    Electrification and, 58, 237n76
  evoution of Soviet nuclear industry
    and, 26–40, 217n44, 220n67
  nuclear oversight authority and, 59–61
  nuclear power administration and,
    52–57
  "Second Ivan" reactor and, 107
  technical and engineering education
    and, 71–72
Gospromatomnadzor, 150. *See also*
  Oversight authorities, Soviet nuclear
  industry and
Gostekhnika, 49–51, 234n51
Government Commission Report on
  Chernobyl disaster, 139–140
Grabovskii, Mikhail, 49, 84–85
Graphite-water reactors
  at Chernobyl, 144–149, 171
  early designs, 99–105, 264n20
  production and assembly of, 121–123
Grigoryiants, Artem, 180, 277n138

Health consequences of nuclear disasters
  at Chernobyl, 280n27
  at Fukushima, 171–175
Heavy-water reactors, 116–117, 275nn121–122, 275n125
Human error
  in Chernobyl disaster, 137–139, 144
  in Fukushima disaster, 301n5
Human expertise
  Chernobyl disaster response and, 135–136
  Soviet nuclear industry reliance on, 67–70, 122–123, 163–168, 165, 246n2, 257n86
Hungary, Soviet nuclear industry and, 121–122
Hydrogen bomb, Soviet detonation of, 18, 45, 51
"Hydrogen economy" policy, 274n117
Hydropower, Soviet nuclear industry and, 22–23

Iadrikhinskii, Aleksandr, 132, 146, 180
Icebreaker fleet, nuclear power for, 46, 240n99, 268n65
Ideology
  cynicism of workforce concerning, 79–80, 249n25, 254n59
  evolution of Soviet nuclear industry and, 34–40, 226n123
Ignalina power plant, 114–115, 151, 155, 239n94, 246n1, 259n104
Improvisation, tacit knowledge and, in nuclear industry, 81–85
INSAG-1 report on Chernobyl, 147, 261n128
INSAG-7 report on Chernobyl, 147
Institute of Atomic Energy, 20, 28
  Chernobyl disaster and, 141–143, 145, 149
  evolution of Soviet nuclear industry and, 51, 55–57
  management structure of nuclear industry and, 85, 257n91
  RBMK reactor design and, 110, 114
  reactor design and, 104, 106–107
  safety issues and, 92
Institute of Physical Problems, 55, 102
Institute of Physics and Power Engineering (FEI), 59–61, 86
  Chernobyl disaster and, 147–148
  reactor design and, 101–105
Institute of Theoretical and Experimental Physics (ITEF), 116–117
Institutional culture
  nuclear oversight and safety issues and, 63–65, 227n6
  training and workforce transfer and, 67–70
Interatomenergo, 238n84
Interatominstrument enterprise, 238n84
Interdepartmental Scientific-Technical Council (MVNTS), 149–150
Interdepartmental Technical Council (MVTS), 85, 140–143, 149–150, 155, 256n74
International Atomic Energy Agency (IAEA), 51
  Chernobyl disaster and, 1, 9, 12, 143, 147
  Ukrainian nuclear institutions and, 157–158
International Nuclear and Radiological Events Scale (INES), 171, 300n2
International nuclear industry. *See also* Cold War politics
  Chernobyl disaster reaction by, 143–144
  Cold War politics and, 81, 83
  problems and accidents in, 166–168
  reactor design and, 123–124, 163–168, 265n36
  Russian reactor exports and, 170
  Soviet comparisons with, 77–78
  training programs and, 251n33

Index

Interviews, as research source, 193–194, 199–202
Iran, nuclear power industry in, 83–84
Isaev, Vasilii, 37, 180
ITAR-TASS (Soviet news agency), Chernobyl disaster trial coverage, 9
Ivan II: Top Secret (Grabovski), 84–85
Ivanov, V., 145
Izhora factory, pressurized water reactor production, 109–110, 120

Japan
 Fukushima Daiichi disaster in, 171–175
 nuclear freighters in, 268n65
 nuclear power industry in, 16, 265n36

Kapitsa, Petr, 55, 180–181, 240n98, 274n114
Karpan, Nikolai, Chernobyl disaster trial and, 2, 207n41, 208n45
KGB, Chernobyl disaster and, 133, 286n78
Kharkov Turbine Factory, 271n82
Khruschev, Nikita, 263n12
 ouster of, 31
 Soviet nuclear industry and, 27–30, 51, 221n72, 233n44
Kievenergo, 7, 128, 212n7
Kirienko, Sergei, 169–170, 270n78
Kirov power plant, 29
"Kombinat No. 817" (secret reprocessing facility), 50–51
Konovalov, Vitalii, 155, 228n12
Kopchinskii, Georgii, 58, 149, 181, 242n110
Kosygin, Aleksei, 29–32, 34, 107, 221n74, 222n76, 259n105
Kovalenko, Aleksandr P., 4, 9–10, 205n15, 210n60
Kozlov, Frol, 29, 181
KS-150 heavy-water reactor, 116–117
Kulikov, Evgenii, 60, 141–142, 181, 240n96

Kurchatov, Igor
 autobiographical note on, 181
 evolution of Soviet nuclear power industry and, 20–21, 28–29, 45–46, 54, 213n12
 gas-cooled reactor design and, 116
 Institute of Atomic Energy and, 55
 Laboratory No. 2 research institute and, 105–117
 nuclear weapons development and, 44–45, 51
 reactor design and, 99–105, 107–108
 as scientific director, 85
Kurchatov Institute of Atomic Energy, 12, 51, 57, 60
 RBMK reactor development and, 111–115, 123, 263n10
 reactor design and, 106, 263n12, 264n20, 264n24
Kursk nuclear plant, 114–115, 146
Kuzmin, Iosif, 28–29, 181–182

Laboratory for Measuring Instruments of the Soviet Academy of Sciences (LIPAN SSSR), 51, 106
Laboratory No. 2 research institute, 44–45, 59, 101, 105–117
Laboratory V (Obninsk), 86, 97–98, 101–105
Laushkin, Yurii, 4, 9, 210n60
Lavrenenko, Konstantin, 47–49, 74, 182
Legasov, Valerii, 139–140, 143, 182, 287n98
Leipunskii, Aleksandr, 101–102, 105, 182, 263n17
Lenin (icebreaker), 240n99, 268n65
Lenin, Vladimir, 41, 44
Leningrad power plant, *113*
 Chernobyl disaster and, 145, 155, 271n81, 271n83, 289n109
 documentation on construction of, 304n15

Leningrad power plant (cont.)
  history of, 114–115, 119–120, 239n93
  management of, 271n81
  reactor design at, 271n83, 289n109
Lithuania, nuclear power in, 54–55, 81, 112, 114–115, 151
Lukonin, Nikolai, 155

Magnitogorsk (steel town), 4
Maiorets, Anatolii, 141–142, 182
Malkin, S. D., 252n47
Malyshev, Vadim, 294n167
Malyshev, Viacheslav, 49, 182–183, 234n51
Management issues, Chernobly disaster and role of, 13–16
Mangistau nuclear complex, 266n38
Margulova, Tereza, 74, 183, 251n35, 252n44
Mark-1 containment design, Fukushima Daiichi disaster and, 173–175
Market-economic model
  Fukushima Daiichi disaster and, 172–175
  post-Soviet nuclear industry and, 169–170, 299n13
Marxist doctrine
  Chernobyl trial and role of, 5
  Soviet nuclear industry and, 217n42
Maryin, Vladimir, 58, 149, 183
Media coverage
  Chernobyl disaster coverage, 136, 143–144
  Chernobyl trial proceedings, 1–16, 204n6, 204n9, 204n12, 205n13
  of Soviet nuclear power, 21–22, 166–168
  Three Mile Island accident in U.S. and, 150
Medvedev, Grigorii, 58
Meshkov, Aleksandr, 141–142, 183, 240n96

Mikhailov, Viktor, 156
Military nuclear technology. *See also* Soviet navy, nuclear industry and; Submarine reactor designs
  early nuclear research and, 97–101, 275n122
  nuclear industry independence from, 70
  reactor design and, 109–110, 163–168
Ministry of Atomic Energy (*Minatomenergo*), establishment of, *154*, 155
Ministry of Atomic Energy and Industry (*Minatomenergoprom*), 155–156, 168–169
Ministry of Atomic Energy of the Russian Federation (*Ministerstvo atomnoi energii Rossiiskoi Federatsii, Minatom*), 156
Ministry of Energy and Electrification (*Minenergo*)
  atomshchiki and, 88
  Chernobyl disaster and role of, 8, 15, 92, 133–134, 139–143, 146, 208n48, 279n16
  Communist party politics and, 72
  divided responsibilities for nuclear power and, 52–57, 61–65, 234n55, 244n.129
  energetiki at, 88
  information service (*Informenergo*), 143
  institutional culture at, 76–77, 249n15, 252n42
  international comparisons of nuclear industry and, 77–78
  nuclear oversight authority and, 59–61
  organizational structure of nuclear industry and, 41–65, 236n74, 239n92
  origins of, 46–49
  secrecy policies of, 93–94
  Soiuzatomenergo and, 53–57

Index

Soviet nuclear power organization and, 41–42
training and workforce transfer and, 67–95, 152–153
Ministry of Health, nuclear oversight and, 59–61
Ministry of Heavy Machine Building (*Mintiazhmash*), 236n75
Ministry of Medium Machine Building (*Sredmash*)
atomshchiki and, 88
career opportunities in, 70–72
Chernobyl disaster and role of, 8, 15, 20, 92, 133–134, 208n48
construction of Chernobyl sarcophagus, 137
divided responsibilities for nuclear power and, 52–57, 61–65
EI-2 reactor design and, 106–107
evolution of Soviet nuclear industry and, 28, 31–32, 219n55
Glavotomenergo (GU-16), 55
independence from military of, 70
institutional culture at, 76–77, 252n42
nuclear weapons program and, 49–51, 250n28
organizational structure of nuclear industry and, 41–65, 234n55, 236n74, 239nn92–93
outsource to Minenergo, 61–65, 239n93
oversight authority and, 59–61
post-Chernobyl restructuring of, *154*, 154–157, 295n173
RBMK reactor design and, 110–115, 120–124
secrecy policies of, 93–94
training and workforce transfer following restructuring of, 67–95
Ministry of the Defense Industry (*Minoboronprom*), 236n75
MKR (*metallurgicheskii kol'tsevoi reaktor*) multiloop reactor, 115, 273n111, 293n153

Moscow Engineering and Physics Institute (*MIFI*), 75, 101, 170
Moscow Power Engineering Institute (*Moskovskii Energeticheskii Institut, MEI*), 74, 148
Multidirectional reactor design approach, 99–101, 163–168

National Atomic Energy Generating Company of Ukraine (*Energoatom*), 157–158, 297n192
National Nuclear Research University, 170. *See also* Moscow Engineering and Physics Institute (*MIFI*)
Natural resources, Soviet nuclear industry and asymmetry of, 22–23
"Naval atom" (*atom morskoi*), 46
Nemtsov, Boris, 270n78
Neporozhnii, Petr
autobiographical note, 183
evolution of Soviet nuclear industry and, 32–37, 220n67, 223n90
organizational structure of nuclear industry and, 47–49, *49*, 51, 56, 65, 233n44, 236n74
political friendships of, 259n105
safety issues and policies of, 90–92
transfer of nuclear workforce and, 76–78, 88
Neutron shielding, 269n69
Nevskii, Vladimir, 238n83
NIIKhimmash institute. *See* Scientific Research and Design Institute of Energy Technologies
NIKIET. *See also* Scientific Research and Design Institute of Energy Technologies (NIKIET)
Nikolaev, Nikolai, 235n63, 240n95
NIPIET design institute. *See* State Specialized Design Institute (GSPI)
Nomenklatura system, 294n163
Soviet nuclear industry and, 72, 249n26, 250n30

Novo-Voronezh nuclear power plant,
    29–30, 33–35, 47, 54, 213n12,
    233n43
  documentation on construction of,
    304n15
  expertise of personnel at, 122–123
  problems and accidents at, 91
  reactor design at, 108–110, 252n47
  staffing issues for, 74–75
Nuclear heating plants, development
    of, 110
Nuclear weapons program
  career development and, 70–72, 79–80
  hydrogen bomb, 18, 45, 51
  reactor design and, 99–101
  scientists and engineers in
    development of, 69–70
  secrecy and, 93–94
  Soviet nuclear industry and, 41–65,
    226n1
  Sredmash role in, 49–51, 250n28

Obninsk nuclear power plant, 19–20,
    46. *See also* Laboratory V
  control room in, *103*
  early nuclear research and, 97–101
  reactor design at, 102–105, 122,
    266n38, 271n84
  technical training programs at, 71–72,
    74–75, 249n20
*Obshchie polozheniia obespecheniia
    bezopasnosti pri proektirovanii,
    stroitel'stve i ekspluatatsii AES*, (OPB-
    73), 59
Occupational health and safety zone, 87
OKB Gidropress, 86–87, 237n77,
    258n102
  reactor design and, 102, 108
OPAS group, 282n36
Organizational structure of Soviet
    nuclear industry
  oversight and safety issues and, 15,
    41–65, 216n38

plant organization, 68–70
post-Chernobyl restructuring and,
    154, 154–157, 162–168, 299n13
tripartite management structure,
    85–87
Ovchinnikov, Fedor, 237n79
Oversight authorities, Soviet nuclear
    industry and, 59–61. *See also* State
    Oversight Committee for Nuclear
    Safety (*Gosatomnadazor*)

Pavlenko, Aleksei
  autobiographical note, 183–184
  evolution of nuclear industry and,
    26–28, 33, 37–40, 214n19
  organizational structure of nuclear
    industry and, 58, 237n76
People's Commissariat of
    Enlightenment (Narkompros),
    257n86
People's Commissariat of Power Plants
    and Electrical Industry. *See* Ministry
    of Energy and Electrification
    (*Minenergo*)
People's Commissariats, 232n38
Pervukhin, Mikhail, 28, 33, 49–50, 184,
    239n92
Petrosyiants, Andranik, 51, 184,
    265n36
Physics Institute of the Soviet Academy
    of Sciences (FIAN), 44
Plutonium
  fuel cycles and, 272nn91–93
  heavy-water reactors and, 116–117
  nuclear weapons development and,
    45, 235n63
  "Second Ivan" reactor design and,
    106–107
  technical problems with, 123–124
Politburo, 215n31
Politics. *See also* Cold War politics
  Chernobyl disaster and role of, 161,
    166–169

Index

Fukushima Daiichi disaster and, 172–175
nuclear workforce training and transfer and, 67–70, 79–81, 162–168, 253n57, 254n59, 255n70, 256n72
reactor design selection and, 119–120, 122–123, 270n78
Polushkin, Konstantin, 133–134, 184
Ponomarev-Stepnoi, Nikolai, 274n117
Power Industry Workers' Union, 133
Power plant operators, role in Soviet nuclear industry, 15, 210n64
Pressurized water reactors (VVERs), 45, 232n37, 233n43
  competition and standardization of, 117–119
  development of, 34–35, 38–40, 240n99, 244n130
  early designs, 98–99, 107–110, 269n75, 275n125
  in Eastern Europe, 121–122, 269n66
  limitations of, 120–122, 269n73, 270n77
  manufacture of, 258n99
  post-Soviet era designs for, 169–170
  training programs, 252n47
Priamotochnye reactors, 106–107
Prison labor, nuclear power construction and, 229n22
Professional communities in nuclear industry
  politics and economics and, 162–168
  tacit knowledge and improvisation and, 81–85
Professionalization of nuclear industry workforce, 73–75
Prushinskii, Boris, 133, 139, 281n30
Public opposition
  Fukushima Daiichi disaster and, 174–175
  post-Chernobyl emergence of, 150–151, 161, 167–169

Published sources on Soviet nuclear industry, 194–197
Putin, Vladimir, 170

Quality control service (*avtorskii nadsor*), 54, 238n86
  chief design engineer and, 86

Radioactive emissions
  from Chernobyl disaster, 132–133, 280n23
  from Fukushima Daiichi disaster, 171–175
Raspredelenie program, 71–72
RBMK reactor design
  basic specifications, 111–112
  Central Committee debate over, 58
  Chernobyl disaster and, 6–8, 12–16, 128–133, *131*, 141–142, 149–150, 150–151, 279nn11–12, 279n19
  competition and standardization of, 117–119
  early designs, 98–99, 104–105, 110–115, *113*
  evolution of, 34–36, 38–40
  fuel enrichment in, 271n86, 272n92
  government decree concerning, 271n85
  international nuclear community and, 123–124
  justification for selection of, 119–120, 163–168
  modifications and generations of, 114, 273n106
  plutonium production and, 272nn91–93
  post-Chernobyl assessment of, 153, 158–159, 166–168, 289n109, 294n167
  problems and accidents with, 91–92, 125
  production and assembly of, 120–122
  training programs, 252n47

RBMK reactor design (cont.)
  unreliable instrumentation and, *82*
  whistleblowers and controversy over, 144–149
Reactor design *See also* specific reactors
  atomshchiki, 87–88
  boiling-water reactors, 171–175
  breeder reactors, 105, 265n36, 266n38
  Chernobyl disaster and role of, 12, 15–16, 137–139, 206n26, 206n32
  civilian design programs, 101–105
  competition and standardization, 117–119
  dual-use reactors, 106–107, 266n46, 267n47
  evolution of, 59–65, 97–125, 163–168, 239n94
  fast neutron reactors, 105, 266n38
  fuel cycles and, 272n91
  Fukushima Daiichi disaster and, 173–175
  gas-cooled reactors, 116, 274n117, 275n125
  graphite-water reactors, 99–105, 121–123, 144–149, 171, 264n20
  heavy-water reactors, 116–117, 275n125, 275nn121–122
  Laboratory 2 projects in, 106–117
  military reactors, 97–101
  Minergo oversight of, 246n1
  multidirectional approach to, 99–101
  post-Chernobyl assessment of, 153
  pressurized water reactors, 34–35, 38–40, 45, 98–99, 107–110, 117–119, 120–122, 169–170, 232n37, 233n43, 240n99, 244n130, 252n47, 269n33, 269n73, 269n75, 270n77, 275n125
  RBMK, 98–99, 104–105, 110–115, 117–119
  refueling machine, 272n90
  simulators and, 252n47
  submarine reactors, 109–110, 268n62

Recruitment of nuclear industry workforce, 73–75, 152–153
Regulation, nuclear industry. *See* Oversight authorities, Soviet nuclear industry and
Rekunkov, A., 146
Research methodology, overview of, 189–197, 305n21
Retention of Soviet nuclear workforce, 73–75
"Reverse salient" in organizational structure, 227n5
Riabev, Lev, 156, 184–185
Riabko, Viktor, 36
Riazantsev, Evgenii, 149
Risk avoidance behavior, Soviet nuclear industry and, 253n50
Robots, Chernobyl disaster response and, 135–136
Rogozhkin, Boris, 4, 209n50, 210n60
Rosatom
  in post-Soviet era, 169–170, 300n19, 301n10
  RBMK reactor design and, 271n85
Rosenergoatom, 53, 156, 157, 239n93, 262n5, 296n184
  Ukrainian nuclear institutions and, 157–158
Rumiantsev, Aleksandr, 83–84, 185, 262n5
Russian Federal SSR, nuclear industry restructuring and, 156, 168–170, 299n13
Ryzhkov, Nikolai, 136–137, 140, 146, 185, 228n12

Safety issues
  atomshchiki and energetiki attitudes concerning, 90–92, 163–168
  Central Committee decree concerning, 141–143
  international concern over, 301n10

Index

post-Chernobyl concern over, 152–153, 166–168, 245n134, 294n166
recruitment and importance of, 152–153
Sakharov, Andrei, 255n70
Sarcophagus at Chernobyl, construction of, 136–137, *138*
Scientific community, Soviet nuclear industry and, 20–22, 69–70, 254n59, 256n72
Scientific director (*nauchnyi rukovoditel*), role in in Soviet nuclear industry of, 85–86
Scientific Research and Design Institute of Energy Technologies (NIKIET), 54–55, 70, 86–87, 91, 102, 238n86, 239n92, 258n97
  Chernobyl disaster and, 141–143, 145, 148
  reactor design and, 106
Scientific Research Institute No. 8 (NII-8), 111, 271n83
Scientific-Technical Council (NTS) (Sredmash), 56, 101, 110
"Second Ivan" (EI-2) reactor design, 106–107, 124, 266n41
Secrecy, culture of
  Chernobyl disaster and role of, 137–139
  nuclear industry and role of, 92–94
  nuclear workforce training and retention and, 70–72, 76–77
  reactor design and, 101, 263n13
Semenov, Aleksandr, 133, 136–137, 185
Sharik reactor design, 116, 274n114
Shasharin, Gennadii
  autobiographical note on, 185–186
  Chernobyl disaster and, 152–153, 167, 279n19, 281n30, 283n40, 286nn81–82
  Soviet nuclear industry and, 58, 114, 139–143, 237n79

Shcherbina, Boris, 133, 139–141, 186, 282n32
Shevchenko reactor (BN-350), 266n38
Shteinberg, Nikolai, 146–147, 186
Siberian nuclear power plants. *See* "Second Ivan" (EI-2) reactor design
Sidorenko, Viktor, 62, 92, 237n80, 239n93, 273n106
  autobiographical note, 186
  Chernobyl disaster and, 139–141, 148–149, 290n124
  post-Chernobyl nuclear industry restructuring and, 155–156, 292n139
  writings of, 306n27
Slavskii, Efim, 28, 32
  autobiographical note, 186–187
  Chernobyl disaster and, 141–143, 287n94
  collaboration with Aleksandrov, 85–86
  Leningrad nuclear power plant and, 271n83
  reactor design and, 107–110, 123–124
  Sredmash restructuring and, 50–52, *57*, 64
  transfer of nuclear workforce and, 76–77
Slavutich (city), construction of, 285n70
SM-2 reactor design, 103
Smolensk nuclear power plant, 78, 114–115, *165*
"Social Construction of Technology" program, 263n11
Sociotechnical systems, Soviet nuclear industry reliance on, 67–70
Soiuzatomenergo (All-Union Industrial Association for Nuclear Power), 53–57, 133–134, 141, 152, 250n30, 282n36
Sosnovyi Bor
  nuclear power plant at, 112–114, 239n92
  RBMK reactor at, 120–122

Soviet Academy of Sciences, 44, 59, 85, 142–143, 256n72
Soviet national identity, reactor design linked to, 123–124
Soviet navy, nuclear industry and, 252n42, 252n47
Soviet nuclear industry. *See also* Civilian nuclear program
 career path in, 70–72
 divided responsibilities in, 52–57, 162–168
 economic pressures on, 14–16
 equipment mass production and, 229n13
 future challenges in, 169–170
 governance issues for, 57–61
 historical evolution of, 17–40
 iconography of, 21–22
 international comparisons with, 77–78
 legacy of Chernobyl disaster for, 150–151
 map of Soviet nuclear power plants, 35
 nuclear policymaking bodies and, 56
 organizational structure of, 15, 41–65, 216n38
 oversight authorities, 59–61
 plant locations, 213n12
 post-Chernobyl restructuring, *154*, 154–157
 post-Soviet restructuring of, 167–169
 professionalization, recruitment, and retention in, 73–75
 quality issues in, 216n34, 218n46, 223n90
 relevance of Chernobyl disaster for, 9–16
 research sources on, 189–197
 revision to historiography of, 124–125
 shortage of materials in, 223n94
 training and workforce development, 67–95

tripartite management structure, 85
Ukrainian nuclear institutions and, 157–158
Soviet state, Chernobyl trial and role of, 5–16
Soviet State Defense Committee (GKO), 44
Soviet Union dissolution
 Chernobyl disaster and, 167–169
 nuclear industry and, 151
Soviet Youth League (Komsomol), 79–80
Spasskii, Nikolai, 301n10
Special Committee for the Problem of Uranium, 44
Special Committee on the Atomic Bomb, 45
Stabilization in reactor design, 100–101, 263n11
Stalin, Iosif, 27–28, 41
 white-collar technocrats under, 69
Start-up commissions (*puskovye komissii*), 54
State asset ownership, nuclear oversight and, 60–61
State Committee for Science and Technology (GKNT), 38
State electrification plan, Soviet nuclear industry and, 41–43, 228n9
State Oversight Committee for Nuclear Safety (*Gosatomnadzor*), 59–61, 145–146
State Oversight Committee for the Safe Conduct of Work in the Nuclear Power Industry (Gosatomenergonadzor), 60, 93, 139, 141–143, 146, 147–148, 243n122
State-owned enterprises. *See also Atomprom* (state corporation)
 evolution of Soviet nuclear industry and, 24–26, 216n33
State Plan for the Electrification of Russia (GOELRO), 43–65

Index

State planning, evolution of Soviet nuclear industry and role of, 23–24, 226n124
State Radium Institute, 18, 44
"State Service for Radiation Safety Control," 59
State Specialized Design Institute (GSPI), 102, 239n92, 271n82
State Technical and Mining Inspectorate (*Gosgortekhnadzor*), 59, 243n122
State Technical and Mining Oversight Committee for the Power Industry (*Gosgorenergotekhnadzor*), 59
Submarine reactor designs, 109–110, 268n62
Supreme Council of the People's Economy (Vesenkha), 257n86
Sweden, nuclear power in, 151

Tacit knowledge in nuclear industry
  improvisation and, 81–85
  scientific research and, 250n32
  secrecy culture and, 92–94
  transfer of workforce and, 70–72, 76–77
Technical training programs
  cynicism and politics concerning, 78–82
  elements of, 251nn39–40
  limitations in Soviet nuclear industry of, 124, 163–168, 275n123
  post-Chernobyl recruitment and, 152–153
  professionalization of, 73–75
  reliability and proficiency of, 89–92
  Soviet development of, 68–70
  Three Mile Island accident, 60–61, 92, 150
Tokyo Electric (TEPCO), 172–175
Toptunov, Leonid, 140
Tripartite management structure, in Soviet nuclear industry, 85–87
Tsunami, Fukushima Daiichi disaster and, 171–175

Turbine production, nuclear reactors and, 265n27

Ukrainian Criminal Code, article 220 of, 4–5
Ukrainian Ministry of Fuel and Energy, 157–158
Ukrainian nuclear industry, 157–158
Ukrainian Physical-Technical Institute, 101
Ukratomenergoprom, 157–158
Unified Power System (*Edinaia energeticheskaia sistema*), 19
United Kingdom
  gas-cooled reactors in, 116
  reactor design in, 123–124, 265n36
  Ukrainian nuclear institutions and, 157–158
  wartime nuclear research in, 81, 83
United Nations Conferences on Peaceful Uses of Atomic Energy, 13, 50–51, 77–78, 97
  reactor design and, 106–107, 265n36
United States
  automation of nuclear power in, 68
  Fukushima Daiichi disaster and reactors from, 172–175
  nuclear freighters in, 268n65
  nuclear industry workforce in, 77–78, 253n48
  nuclear oversight in, 60, 245n138, 259n107
  pressurized water reactors and, 109–110
  reactor design in, 123–124, 265n36
  Ukrainian nuclear institutions and, 157–158
  wartime nuclear research in, 81, 83
  xenon reactions in Hanford reactors, 278n9
Uranium, reactor design and, 102, 105–106, 109, 111, 115–117, 264n22

V-10 (*ustanovka V-10*) reactor design, 97–99
"V-230/V-213 problem," 241n107
Vannikov, Boris, 45, 49–50, 187
Vavilov, Sergei, 44, 187
Velikhov, Evgenii, 136–137, 187, 285n64
Veretennikov, Gennadii, 133–134, 141, 152, 187–188
Vernadskii, Vladimir, 18, 44, 188
VG-400 reactor, 274n117
Void coefficient, 272n96
  RBMK reactor design, 112
Volgodonsk reactor vessel plant. *See* Atommash reactor vessel plant
Volkov, Vladimir, 145–147, 167, 188, 289n118, 290n121
Volskii, Arkadii, 149–150
VTUZy (*Vysshchie tekhnicheskie uchebnye zavedeniia*) (technical colleges), 75
VVER reactors. *See* Pressurized water reactors (VVERs)

Water contamination
  Chernobyl disaster and, 136
  from Fukushima Daiichi disaster, 171–175
Whistleblowers, RBMK design controversy and, 144–149
Workforce training and transfer
  cynicism and politics in, 78–82
  expertise factor in, 67–70, 122–123
  post-Chernobly recruitment and, 152–153
  professionalization, recruitment and retention issues, 73–75
  Soviet nuclear industry and, 67–95
  tacit knowledge and improvisation and, 81–85
World Association of Nuclear Operators (WANO), 157–158

Xenon 135, Chernobyl disaster and, 128, 278n9, 279n15
"Xenon pit" (*xenovaia iama*), 278n9

Yeltsin, Boris, 151, 156, 270n78, 303n13
Yoshida, Masao, 301n5

Zaveniagin, Avraamii, 20, 49, 102, 188, 264n20
Zelenyi Mys (Green Cape) (town), post-Chernobyl construction of, 137
Zhezherun, Ivan, 145
Zirconium, RBMK reactor and, 114, 273n105

www.ingramcontent.com/pod-product-compliance
Lightning Source LLC
Chambersburg PA
CBHW071358300426
44114CB00016B/2094